GREAT CHRISTIAN CLASSICS

GREAT CHRISTIAN CLASSICS

Four Essential Works of the Faith

EDITED BY

Kevin Swanson & Joshua Schwisow

ISBN: 978-1-7350719-1-6

Published by Generations
19039 Plaza Dr. Ste. 210
Parker, Colorado 80134
www.generations.org

For more information on this and other titles from Generations,
visit *www.generations.org* or call *888-389-9080*.

Contents

The Pilgrim's Progress

Book 1

Book 2

❧ Introduction

There is little question in the minds of Christians living in the Western world that they are facing the post-Christian zeitgeist. K-12 schools are mostly post-Christian or anti-Christian, as are most universities and colleges. Most institutions have abandoned almost everything of the Christian heritage in the West. Education has been hijacked by the secularists, and Christian families are paying dearly for it. Education has largely become the Trojan Horse by which the Christian faith has been undermined. By the corruption of knowledge in the schools and universities, the secularists have systematically eroded the foundations of Western civilization, destroying much of what was a Christian heritage—the integrity of the family, sexuality, political freedom, economies, and education itself.

Now, as much as at any time in church history, God is calling Christian parents to disciple their children in the nurture and admonition of the Lord. This can only be accomplished if Christians will employ a serious discipleship model for both the family and the church. As we enter the third millennium of our Lord's commission to disciple families and nations, the time has come to replace godless education with a Christian discipleship model. This model of Christian discipleship could be summarized briefly as follows:

1. A Christian education must be formed on a Christian worldview. Christian parents and educators must never concede neutrality in education. They must stand guard to ensure that their children are not robbed of the truth in Christ by "philosophy and empty deceit, according to the tradition of men, according to the basic principles of the world" (Col. 2:8). This philosophy rooted in the traditions of men of which Paul spoke represented the presuppositional framework taught by Aristotle, Plato, and others which served as a basis upon which men would live their lives. These ideas are extremely dangerous for Christian families and children—especially when they are exposed to them day in and day out. We cannot allow a sacred-secular division to exist in education. We must never concede that a "secular" education is neutral while asserting that a Christian education is biased. Every education has a worldview (religious) foundation, and there is only one right worldview—a Christian, Trinitarian worldview.

All knowledge is formed on a certain worldview, a basic understanding of reality, origins, ethics, and truth. When children are discipled in schools representing the wrong worldview, they will usually fail to carry on the faith of their parents and grandparents. Christian parents who hand their children over to Muslim madrassa schools would probably lose the next generation to Islam. Likewise, those Christian families who turn their children over to schools that hold to an anti-supernaturalistic, materialistic, humanist worldview will generally lose their children to that worldview.

2. Jesus Christ must be presented throughout the pedagogy as the source of all wisdom and knowledge (Col. 2:3). Christ must be preeminent in all things—in science and history, as well as in mathematics and geography (Col. 1:18). We cannot allow for two distinct forms of knowledge—secular and sacred—within the Christian mind. Though God has given us two revelations of knowledge (natural revelation and special revelation), there is only one knowledge. These two revelations produce one and the same knowledge concerning God, man, and the world. To ignore Christ in discussions on epistemology (the theory of knowledge) or metaphysics (the theory of reality) is to ignore the ultimate Truth and Reality. This would amount to the ultimate apostasy for Christians who purport to teach knowledge in their schools or textbooks.

3. *The fear of God and humility must serve as the foundation of knowledge and learning for the Christian.* The world finds pride and prestige to be the primary motivator and value in education. Worldly education rejects the fear of God, the significance of God, the glory of God, and even any recognition of the existence of God. However, for Christians, academic pride is the destruction of knowledge. The atheist who refuses to acknowledge God in the schools is the real fool, according to Psalm 14. If Proverbs 1:7 is not foremost in the perspective of those Christian leaders who claim to be involved in education, Christian families would do well to avoid their conferences, schools, and curriculum offerings.

4. *The Word of God must be integrated into every aspect of a Christian education* because the secular-sacred divide can never be countenanced by true Christian educators. Deuteronomy 6:7 presents the Word of God as a "frontlet" before our eyes, to be placed on the posts and gates of our houses. This obliterates the idea of a "secular" education as a separate kind of knowledge. There is nothing to which the Word of God does not speak, apply, and tie in.

5. *The purpose of Christian education is not to glorify man but to glorify God.* Thus, competitions and awards will not be as important for Christians as for non-Christians. The worship and praise of God should not appear strange in the history textbook and the science classroom. Teachers and speakers in our conferences and classrooms should break out in praise and worship to the Father and to His Son the Lord Jesus Christ, who must be preeminent in all things. The integration of the worship of Christ into a classroom seems odd to the modern

mind only because Christian education has been replaced by secular man-centered worldview in public and private schools and homeschools over the last 150 years.

6. Faith and prayer are essential for the success of a Christian education. We do not encourage self-confidence but instead God-confidence in a Christian education and training. While the disciples were busy rowing all night (and making little progress at that), Jesus was in the mountains praying. Then He walked over the water, climbed into the boat, and "immediately they were on the shore." Very different from the modern setting, Jesus' seminary occurred in a boat, and His approach to solving problems involved faith and prayer. He wanted His disciples to exercise faith in all of their experiences. We should do the same in the education of our children. Prayer and faith should mark every step of the educational process.

7. Christ-like discipleship and education takes place in the context of life and always requires some degree of life-integration. The one who hears the Word but does not do the Word is like the man who sees himself in a mirror and quickly forgets what he looks like (Jas. 1:23-24). Christian teachers and disciplers will insist upon life application as an essential element of learning itself. Education cannot be reduced to stuffing facts into the minds of students. If the theory does not produce a life application, it is a waste and will serve only to produce a knowledge that puffs up (1 Cor. 8:1). If the knowledge learned does not produce love and works that edify and build up, the knowledge is worthless.

Studying Literature in the Discipleship Model

In this second volume of *Great Christian Classics*, the Christian approach to literature is presented as follows:

1. Christian. We focus on the Bible and Christian authors through the centuries, featuring the kingdom of Christ rather than what is produced by pre-Christian pagans or post-Christian and anti-Christian writers.

2. Discernment. We first want to equip young people with truth before introducing the faulty worldviews of unbelieving thinkers, philosophers, and writers. Thus, until a child has mastered the Bible and Christian thinking, it is manifestly unwise to submerge them in antithetical worldviews. To mix Christian and anti-Christian worldviews into the reading content of an 8-12-year-old child introduces confusion and conflicts with a discipleship method of raising that child in the nurture of the Lord.

As in the case of bank tellers who must tell the difference between good money and counterfeits, our children should gain a mastery of what is right and true before being exposed to what is false. They must be rooted and grounded in certain truth before they are given the false worldviews of uncertainty, doubt, humanism, materialism, polytheism, and the rest. Before tackling non-Christian or post-Christian authors, they must be able to detect the wrong worldviews and cast down "arguments and every high thing that exalts itself against the knowledge of God, bringing every thought into captivity to the obedience of Christ" (2 Cor. 10:5).

On the one hand, young people must understand that a war of ideas is fully operational in the world around them. We must encourage them to be watchful and full of faith, not paranoid or fearful. When the student begins to read the writings of non-Christians or post-Christians, we would encourage them to identify any truth that might still be seeping through the cracks. These writers and thinkers may be working off of some degree of Christian heritage or common grace. This is baseline. But the heart trajectory of the post-Christian thinker or writer usually moves in an anti-Christian, unbiblical, wrong direction. This is the trajectory of thought which must be discerned and rejected by the careful reader.

3. Balance. Literature is often used as a means of mere entertainment and escape for young readers. This turns out to be an unhealthy use of this human art of communication, yet a balance in reading is necessary for young children. Thus, for Christian families, a careful balance of fiction and non-fiction as well as reading aloud together and reading to oneself is recommended. Fantasy and science fiction are some of the most addictive and unproductive forms of literature, especially as they yield no immediate application to life and disconnect the child from God's reality. The metaphors in fictional literature should teach us to better engage our minds and lives in God's reality instead of disconnecting us from it.

4. Discipleship. In a Christ-oriented view of discipleship (or education), the teacher should not be described as a "lecturer," "educator," or "professor in literature." The Christian teacher considers himself or herself to be like Jesus—one who disciples his students in faith and character. We are not seeking mere head knowledge. Such a goal would be dangerous and counter-productive to this form of learning. He who reads the Scriptures and all the Christian classics and yet had not done his Master's will would be "beaten with many stripes," in the words of Christ (Luke 12:47). Of course, none of us wants this to happen. Thus, the teacher is one who disciples in faith and looks for an application of the material in the life of the student. Whether the teacher be a parent or not, the end goal is the same. We are discipling our students in faith and life and are using the Christian classics to assist us in this process.

5. Cross-cultural and Kingdom of God Oriented. In an age of pessimism in which the kingdoms of men are cracking and crumbling on every side, there has never been a better time for a Christ-centered curriculum. The Christian church has gained a tremendous heritage after 2,000 years of Jesus' influence around the world. The present age of pessimism, decline, and Christian apostasy in the West is not the time for a Western-centric or Ameri-centric curriculum. This is the time to give our children a 2,000-year, hope-filled, worldwide view of the kingdom of God in history. There is nothing more cross-cultural than the Kingdom of Christ, the Scriptures, and Christian authors. More than at any other time in history, this has become the age of the international church. Therefore, the curriculum to be used for our children's education should be rooted in the ageless, boundary-less kingdom of God, including the best literature produced from every corner of this kingdom.

6. Core. The Bible must be the core reading curriculum— not a separate course of study. This helps to dispense with the sacred-secular distinction that has relegated the Christian worldview to irrelevance in education. Biblical vocabulary becomes the preeminent basis for this pedagogy. Although children will still learn common words used in their various cultural contexts, a Christian worldview must form the vocabulary and the thought categories of every Christian student.

7. Whole Books. Best Books. Some books survive the test of time. The world calls them great books. But there are better books than these. There are the *best books,* of which the best is *the Bible.* Then come the Christian books that have survived the test of time, republished a thousand times over a thousand years. These are far and above the top priority selections when it comes to our children's reading program. When studying such works, we recommend that students read all of these books, not just snippets from "classic" stories. It is much better for the student to follow the entire story through so that they will comprehend a cohesive worldview as laid out by these great thinkers and writers from Christian history. This is the most effective form of education. If these are truly the best books, they are worth reading through multiple times. That is why we are not hesitant to tell the stories five times over. If possible, it is best for parents to read the classics aloud before their children are old enough to read them through by themselves.

This text covers four of the greatest classics of all time, each of which was selected for the enduring quality of its literature, the edifying nature of its content, and the powerful influence of the ideas contained within it.

A Church Father - Athanasius   *On the Incarnation of the Word*
A Pre-Reformer - Thomas à Kempis   *The Imitation of Christ*
A Reformer   - John Calvin   *Institutes of the Christian Religion*
A Baptist Writer - John Bunyan   *The Pilgrim's Progress*

Other notable books written in 2,000 years of Christian history include Augustine's *Confessions* and *The City of God*, Martin Luther's *Bondage of the Will*, Anselm's *Cur Deus Homo*, John Foxe's *Book of Martyrs*, Bede's *Ecclesiastical History of the English Church*, Jonathan Edwards' *Treatise Concerning Religious Affections*, and Eusebius' *Ecclesiastical History*. The poetry of John Donne, John Milton, and Anne Bradstreet could also be added to this list.

These four classics were chosen to represent different periods in church history as well as different ecclesiastical communions. A thorough study of these great books will help the Christian high school or college student understand the life, theology, and worldview reflected in the works of the greatest Christian thinkers in the history of the church. Throughout this study, the student will witness the development of Christian thought over time, the range and diversity of thought, and the incarnation of that thought in Christian culture and life. Taken seriously, read with faith and with an eye towards Scripture, these writings will be life transforming and will help to root and ground the Christian student in the truth.

In this edition, annotations are provided to help the reader with summaries, contextualization of unfamiliar names and places, and interpretation of concepts. This is especially helpful for first-time readers, whether teacher or student.

May the Lord bless these works once more to the conversion of souls, the strengthening of the worldwide Church, and the sustaining of generational faith among Christian families in the third millennium of His Kingdom!

Kevin Swanson
Pastor - May 2020

ON THE INCARNATION

Athanasius of Alexandria
AD 318

Explanatory Notes by
Kevin Swanson

Introduction to
On the Incarnation

Athanasius was born around AD 293 in the Egyptian city of Alexandria. This early church Father is most well known for his courageous stand against the Arian heresy that afflicted the Christian church in the third and fourth centuries. The Arian controversy was provoked by Arius, a presbyter in Alexandria who taught that Jesus Christ, the Son of God, had a beginning and had been created by God the Father. It was said by Arius and others about the Son that "there was a time when he was not." This phrase made clear the commitment of Arius and his followers to a Unitarian conception of God that excluded Jesus Christ the Son from the Godhead.

Athanasius understood the grave danger of this teaching far better than many of his contemporaries. His opposition to the Arian cause led to repeated exiles and persecution; even leading to an extended period of time living in the deserts of Egypt. His last exile before his death was by order of Emperor Valens, who was a supporter of the Arian cause. Yet this last exile was short lived, and he was returned to his post by order of the Emperor. After his last exile in 366, he returned as Bishop for the last seven years of his life. Athanasius died peacefully in Alexandria surrounded by other ministers and faithful friends.

It was rumored to have once been said to Athanasius: "The whole world is against you," referring to the fact that Arianism was at that time becoming the dominant perspective of certain sectors within the church. Athanasius replied, "If the world is against Athanasius, then Athanasius is against the world!" This gave rise to the phrase: "Athanasius Contra Mundum" (Athanasius against the world); a phrase that has defined Athanasius' place in church history for hundreds of years.

Athanasius wrote many works that remain influential today. His most popular and important work (covered in this textbook) is *On the Incarnation of the Word*, written when he was in his twenties. His *Letter to Serapion* on the Holy Spirit was translated into many languages and remains an influential work in Christian theology. His *Life of St. Antony* was one of the earliest Christian biographies written. This book covers the life of St. Antony, an Egyptian ascetic monk who was influential in laying the foundations for monasticism in the East and West. He also wrote several commentaries, primarily on the Old Testament books. Several excerpts from these works are preserved today covering Genesis, Song of Solomon, and the Psalms. His *39th Festal Letter* written to Pope Damasus is an important historical witness to the development of the New Testament canon. In that letter, Athanasius listed the 27 books of the New Testament that the church holds as canonical today.

Other works have still been highly influenced by Athanasius' teaching. In particular, the so-called *Athanasian Creed* reflects a commitment to Athanasius' strong Trinitarianism. While few today hold that Athanasius actually penned this creed, it nevertheless reflects indebtedness to the theology of Athanasius and upholds the orthodox Trinitarian view of God. This creed remains influential in the Western Church and is often recited by Roman Catholics, Lutherans, Anglicans, Presbyterians, and others.

Athanasius' short work, *On the Incarnation of the Word* is one of the greatest theological works left behind for us by the early Church Fathers. While this book was probably written before the Arian controversy, it defends with great simplicity and clarity the orthodox teaching of the deity of Christ with a particular focus upon His incarnation, death, and resurrection. In this short book, Athanasius sets out to answer the question, "Why did God become man in Jesus Christ?" Athanasius recognized the necessity of the incarnation for God to defeat sin and death and to destroy the devil. Athanasius then defends this teaching against the objections of both Jew and Gentile in his day.

The value of Athanasius' work lies in its simplicity, brevity, clarity, and truthfulness. As C.S. Lewis said in his introduction to this work, "When I first opened his [Athanasius'] *De Incarnatione* I soon discovered I was reading a masterpiece… for only a master mind could have written so deeply on a subject with such classical simplicity."[1] The foundations of the Christian faith rest upon the existence of the Triune God as revealed in Scripture. Christian students can do no better than to sit at the feet of this Church Father and not only learn of the glory of our Lord in His incarnation, death, and resurrection, but also learn how to defend this precious truth against the assaults of unbelievers in our generation.

1. C.S. Lewis, "Introduction to On The Incarnation," *On the Incarnation*, trans. John Behr (Yonkers: SVS Press, 2011), 14.

Chapter 1
Creation and the Fall

In our former book we dealt fully enough with a few of the chief points about the heathen worship of idols, and how those false fears originally arose. We also, by God's grace, briefly indicated that the Word of the Father is Himself divine, that all things that are owe their being to His will and power, and that it is through Him that the Father gives order to creation, by Him that all things are moved, and through Him that they receive their being.[1] Now, Macarius,[2] true lover of Christ, we must take a step further in the faith of our holy religion, and consider also the Word's becoming Man and His divine Appearing in our midst. That mystery the Jews traduce,[3] the Greeks deride, but we adore; and your own love and devotion to the Word also will be the greater, because in His Manhood He seems so little worth.[4] For it is a fact that the more unbelievers pour scorn on Him, so much the more does He make His Godhead evident. The things which they, as men, rule out as impossible, He plainly shows to be possible; that which they deride as unfitting, His goodness makes most fit; and things which these wiseacres laugh at as "human" He by His inherent might declares divine. Thus by what seems His utter poverty and weakness on the cross He overturns the

1. Athanasius is referring to a previous book he wrote. The book was called *Against the Heathen*, written around AD 318. In that work, he addressed the problem of idolatry, and the absolute sovereignty of God over everything that happens in the universe. God is Creator and God is Sovereign. This makes up the foundation of the Christian faith today as it did then.
2. The book is written for Macarius, a recent convert to the Christian faith. In this way, this work may be seen as a basic introduction to the faith.

3. Traduce - To tell lies (about Christians) in order to ruin their reputation.
4. If Jesus was just human, He would not be worthy of our worship. It is His deity and His human nature that demand our praise.

5. Jesus is more impressive for two reasons. First, He has proven His power by overcoming the false gods by His cross. Secondly, He has made even the mockers to realize His deity through the centuries.

6. The Son of God took on a human body for one reason—for the salvation of men.

7. The same Person (the Son of God) who created the world brings about a renewal of the fallen creation in His incarnation.

8. The Epicureans followed the teaching of the Greek philosopher Epicurus (writing around 307 BC). He believed in materialism and denied the supernatural entirely. He also taught that man ought to live his life on earth to achieve maximum pleasure. According to his teaching, the universe self-originates.

9. Athanasius argues that if the Universe was self-originating there would be no distinction between material objects in the Universe.

pomp and parade of idols, and quietly and hiddenly wins over the mockers and unbelievers to recognize Him as God.[5]

Now in dealing with these matters it is necessary first to recall what has already been said. You must understand why it is that the Word of the Father, so great and so high, has been made manifest in bodily form. He has not assumed a body as proper to His own nature, far from it, for as the Word He is without body. He has been manifested in a human body for this reason only, out of the love and goodness of His Father, for the salvation of us men.[6] We will begin, then, with the creation of the world and with God its Maker, for the first fact that you must grasp is this: the renewal of creation has been wrought by the Self-same Word Who made it in the beginning.[7] There is thus no inconsistency between creation and salvation for the One Father has employed the same Agent for both works, effecting the salvation of the world through the same Word Who made it in the beginning.

In regard to the making of the universe and the creation of all things there have been various opinions, and each person has propounded the theory that suited his own taste. For instance, some say that all things are self-originated and, so to speak, haphazard. The Epicureans are among these; they deny that there is any Mind behind the universe at all.[8] This view is contrary to all the facts of experience, their own existence included. For if all things had come into being in this automatic fashion, instead of being the outcome of Mind, though they existed, they would all be uniform and without distinction. In the universe everything would be sun or moon or whatever it was, and in the human body the whole would be hand or eye or foot. But in point of fact the sun and the moon and the earth are all different things, and even within the human body there are different members, such as foot and hand and head. This distinctness of things argues not a spontaneous generation but a prevenient Cause; and from that Cause we can apprehend God, the Designer and Maker of all.[9]

Others take the view expressed by Plato, that giant among the Greeks. He said that God had made all things out of pre-existent and uncreated matter, just as the carpenter makes things only out of wood that already exists. But those who hold this view do not realize that to deny that God is Himself the Cause of matter is to impute limitation to Him, just as it is undoubtedly a limitation on the part of the carpenter that he can make nothing unless he has the wood.[10] How could God be called Maker and Artificer if His ability to make depended on some other cause, namely on matter itself? If He only worked up existing matter and did not Himself bring matter into being, He would be not the Creator but only a craftsman.

Then, again, there is the theory of the Gnostics, who have invented for themselves an Artificer of all things other than the Father of our Lord Jesus Christ.[11] These simply shut their eyes to the obvious meaning of Scripture. For instance, the Lord, having reminded the Jews of the statement in Genesis, "He Who created them in the beginning made them male and female . . . ," and having shown that for that reason a man should leave his parents and cleave to his wife, goes on to say with reference to the Creator, "What therefore God has joined together, let no man put asunder" (Matt. 19:4-6). How can they get a creation independent of the Father out of that? And, again, St. John, speaking all inclusively, says, "All things became by Him and without Him came nothing into being" (John 1:3). How then could the Artificer be someone different, other than the Father of Christ?

Such are the notions which men put forward. But the impiety of their foolish talk is plainly declared by the divine teaching of the Christian faith. From it we know that, because there is Mind behind the universe, it did not originate itself; because God is infinite, not finite, it was not made from pre-existent matter, but out of nothing and out of non-existence absolute and utter God brought it into being through the Word. He says as much in Genesis: "In the beginning God created the heavens and the earth (Gen. 1:1); and again

10. Plato, considered one of the greatest of the Greek philosophers, wrote down his philosophies around 400 BC. He thought a god made the world out of pre-existent materials. Alas, his god was too small. The Christian God is the ultimate source of all reality, and Plato's god is limited to pre-existence of some sort. Christians like Athanasius affirm that God is the Creator (not a craftsman who makes things out of pre-existent matter).

11. The Gnostics are a group of people that could be classified as apostate Jews and apostate Christians in the 1st and 2nd centuries. They considered the material world as something to be despised. Thus, they saw that the Father and the Son (who created the material world) as smaller gods. They thought there must have been another god over the Father and the Son. This contradicts John 1:3 however. All things were made by Him (the Son of God).

through that most helpful book The Shepherd,[12] "Believe thou first and foremost that there is One God Who created and arranged all things and brought them out of non-existence into being." Paul also indicates the same thing when he says, "By faith we understand that the worlds were framed by the Word of God, so that the things which we see now did not come into being out of things which had previously appeared" (Heb. 11:3). For God is good—or rather, of all goodness He is Fountainhead, and it is impossible for one who is good to be mean or grudging about anything. Grudging existence to none therefore, He made all things out of nothing through His own Word, our Lord Jesus Christ and of all these His earthly creatures He reserved especial mercy for the race of men. Upon them, therefore, upon men who, as animals, were essentially impermanent, He bestowed a grace which other creatures lacked—namely the impress of His own Image, a share in the reasonable being of the very Word Himself, so that, reflecting Him and themselves becoming reasonable and expressing the Mind of God even as He does, though in limited degree they might continue for ever in the blessed and only true life of the saints in paradise. But since the will of man could turn either way,[13] God secured this grace that He had given by making it conditional from the first upon two things—namely, a law and a place. He set them in His own paradise, and laid upon them a single prohibition. If they guarded the grace and retained the loveliness of their original innocence, then the life of paradise should be theirs, without sorrow, pain or care, and after it the assurance of immortality in heaven. But if they went astray and became vile, throwing away their birthright of beauty, then they would come under the natural law of death and live no longer in paradise, but, dying outside of it, continue in death and in corruption. This is what Holy Scripture tells us, proclaiming the command of God, "Of every tree that is in the garden thou shalt surely eat, but of the tree of the knowledge of good and evil ye shall not eat, but in the day that ye do eat, ye shall surely die" (Gen.

12. A reference to a key book called The *Shepherd of Hermas* written somewhere around AD 140—very popular among Christian churches. Although not received as Scripture, the book would be as popular as *Pilgrim's Progress* has been for the last 500 years.

13. God created man with a will that could choose to obey or not to obey. Man's nature was not bent towards evil, and his will was free to choose.

2:16-17). "Ye shall surely die"—not just die only, but remain in the state of death and of corruption.

You may be wondering why we are discussing the origin of men when we set out to talk about the Word's becoming Man. The former subject is relevant to the latter for this reason: it was our sorry case that caused the Word to come down, our transgression that called out His love for us, so that He made haste to help us and to appear among us. It is we who were the cause of His taking human form, and for our salvation that in His great love He was both born and manifested in a human body. For God had made man thus (that is, as an embodied spirit), and had willed that he should remain in incorruption. But men, having turned from the contemplation of God to evil of their own devising, had come inevitably under the law of death. Instead of remaining in the state in which God had created them, they were in process of becoming corrupted entirely, and death had them completely under its dominion. For the transgression of the commandment was making them turn back again according to their nature; and as they had at the beginning come into being out of non-existence, so were they now on the way to returning, through corruption, to non-existence again. The presence and love of the Word had called them into being; inevitably, therefore when they lost the knowledge of God, they lost existence with it; for it is God alone Who exists, evil is non-being, the negation and antithesis of good.[14] By nature, of course, man is mortal, since he was made from nothing; but he bears also the Likeness of Him Who is, and if he preserves that Likeness through constant contemplation, then his nature is deprived of its power and he remains incorrupt. So is it affirmed in Wisdom: "The keeping of His laws is the assurance of incorruption" (Wisd. 6:18).[15] And being incorrupt, he would be henceforth as God, as Holy Scripture says, "I have said, Ye are gods and sons of the Highest all of you: but ye die as men and fall as one of the princes" (Ps. 82:6).

14. When Adam fell into sin, man lost the knowledge of God. He also lost existence. Athanasius defines evil as non-being. He also sees this death as a "process of becoming corrupted." Whether this process of corruption is eternal (in hell fire), Athanasius does not clarify here.

15. The Book of Wisdom was part of the Septuagint (Greek Old Testament), translated around 100-200 BC. Athanasius did not believe this to be part of the canon of Scripture. However he said it was "appointed to the fathers to read."

This, then, was the plight of men. God had not only made them out of nothing, but had also graciously bestowed on them His own life by the grace of the Word. Then, turning from eternal things to things corruptible, by counsel of the devil, they had become the cause of their own corruption in death; for, as I said before, though they were by nature subject to corruption, the grace of their union with the Word made them capable of escaping from the natural law, provided that they retained the beauty of innocence with which they were created. That is to say, the presence of the Word with them shielded them even from natural corruption, as also Wisdom says: "God created man for incorruption and as an image of His own eternity; but by envy of the devil death entered into the world" (Wisd. 2:23). When this happened, men began to die, and corruption ran riot among them and held sway over them to an even more than natural degree, because it was the penalty of which God had forewarned them for transgressing the commandment. Indeed, they had in their sinning surpassed all limits; for, having invented wickedness in the beginning and so involved themselves in death and corruption, they had gone on gradually from bad to worse, not stopping at any one kind of evil, but continually, as with insatiable appetite, devising new kinds of sins. Adulteries and thefts were everywhere, murder and raping filled the earth, law was disregarded in corruption and injustice, all kinds of iniquities were perpetrated by all, both singly and in common. Cities were warring with cities, nations were rising against nations, and the whole earth was rent with factions and battles, while each strove to outdo the other in wickedness. Even crimes contrary to nature were not unknown, but as the martyr-apostle of Christ says: "Their women changed the natural use into that which is against nature; and the men also, leaving the natural use of the woman, flamed out in lust towards each other, perpetrating shameless acts with their own sex, and receiving in their own persons the due recompense of their pervertedness" (Rom. 1:26ff).[16]

16. Adam's sin opened man up to a nightmare of many evil sins, the worst of which Athanasius calls "crimes contrary to nature" (or homosexuality).

Chapter 2
The Divine Dilemma and its Solution in the Incarnation
Part 1

We saw in the last chapter that, because death and corruption were gaining ever firmer hold on them, the human race was in process of destruction. Man, who was created in God's image and in his possession of reason reflected the very Word Himself, was disappearing, and the work of God was being undone.[1] The law of death, which followed from the Transgression, prevailed upon us, and from it there was no escape. The thing that was happening was in truth both monstrous and unfitting. It would, of course, have been unthinkable that God should go back upon His word and that man, having transgressed, should not die; but it was equally monstrous that beings which once had shared the nature of the Word should perish and turn back again into non-existence through corruption.[2] It was unworthy of the goodness of God that creatures made by Him should be brought to nothing through the deceit wrought upon man by the devil; and it was supremely unfitting that the work of God in mankind should disappear, either through their own negligence or through the deceit of evil spirits. As, then, the creatures whom He had created reasonable, like the Word,

1. The Word is a reference to the Son of God before His incarnation. Before his fall, man could reason because he reflected the image and the knowing of the Son of God. After the fall, Athanasius sees human cultures slipping into increasing levels of darkness.

2. Athanasius suggests that God would have failed in His creation of man and His goodness if he left all mankind to corrupt and die.

were in fact perishing, and such noble works were on the road to ruin, what then was God, being Good, to do? Was He to let corruption and death have their way with them? In that case, what was the use of having made them in the beginning? Surely it would have been better never to have been created at all than, having been created, to be neglected and perish; and, besides that, such indifference to the ruin of His own work before His very eyes would argue not goodness in God but limitation, and that far more than if He had never created men at all. It was impossible, therefore, that God should leave man to be carried off by corruption, because it would be unfitting and unworthy of Himself.

3. Athanasius explores other solutions to man's problems. What if man just repented? Would this be sufficient to reverse the curse of death? If man changed his ways, this would not have taken care of the sins he already sinned. It was man's sin against God in the garden that merited him death.

Yet, true though this is, it is not the whole matter. As we have already noted, it was unthinkable that God, the Father of Truth, should go back upon His word regarding death in order to ensure our continued existence. He could not falsify Himself; what, then, was God to do? Was He to demand repentance from men for their transgression? You might say that that was worthy of God, and argue further that, as through the Transgression they became subject to corruption, so through repentance they might return to incorruption again.[3] But repentance would not guard the Divine consistency, for, if death did not hold dominion over men, God would still remain untrue. Nor does repentance recall men from what is according to their nature; all that it does is to make them cease from sinning. Had it been a case of a trespass only, and not of a subsequent corruption, repentance would have been well enough;

4. Moreover, man was incapable of changing himself. Sin brought a corruption to his nature, such that he could not but sin.

but when once transgression had begun men came under the power of the corruption proper to their nature and were bereft of the grace which belonged to them as creatures in the Image of God.[4] No, repentance could not meet the case. What—or rather Who was it that was needed for such grace and such recall as we required? Who, save the Word of God Himself, Who also in the beginning had made all things out of nothing? His part it was, and His alone, both to bring again the corruptible to incorruption and to maintain for the Father His consistency of character with all. For He alone, being Word of the Father and above all, was in consequence both able to recreate all, and worthy to suffer on behalf of all and to be an ambassador for all with the Father.[5]

For this purpose, then, the incorporeal and incorruptible and immaterial Word of God entered our world. In one sense, indeed, He was not far from it before, for no part of creation had ever been without Him Who, while ever abiding in union with the Father, yet fills all things that are. But now He entered the world in a new way, stooping to our level in His love and Self-revealing to us. He saw the reasonable race, the race of men that, like Himself, expressed the Father's Mind, wasting out of existence, and death reigning over all in corruption. He saw that corruption held us all the closer, because it was the penalty for the Transgression; He saw, too, how unthinkable it would be for the law to be repealed before it was fulfilled. He saw how unseemly it was that the very things of which He Himself was the Artificer should be disappearing. He saw how the surpassing wickedness of men was mounting up against them; He saw also their universal liability to death. All this He saw and, pitying our race, moved with compassion for our limitation,[6] unable to endure that death should have the mastery, rather than that His creatures should perish and the work of His Father for us men come to nought, He took to Himself a body, a human body even as our own. Nor did He will merely to become embodied or merely to appear; had that been so, He could have revealed His divine majesty in some other and better way. No, He took our body, and not only so, but He took it directly from a spotless, stainless virgin, without the agency of human father—a pure body, untainted by intercourse with man. He, the Mighty One, the Artificer of all, Himself prepared this body in the virgin as a temple for Himself, and took it for His very own, as the instrument through which He was known and in which He dwelt.[7] Thus, taking a body like our own, because all our bodies were liable to the corruption of death, He surrendered His body to death

5. Only the Word, the Son of God could reverse the curse, make a new creation, and provide a proper sacrifice for sin.

6. The primary motive for the Son to take on human flesh like us was pity and compassion for us.

7. This is an awesome consideration, that the Creator of the Universe entered into the womb of the Virgin Mary as a tiny microscopic embryo. The contrast is overwhelming to the mind. Glorify our Christ for this!

8. The primary goal for Christ was to take on human flesh so he could die, and then conquer death for us.

instead of all, and offered it to the Father. This He did out of sheer love for us, so that in His death all might die, and the law of death thereby be abolished because, having fulfilled in His body that for which it was appointed, it was thereafter voided of its power for men.[8] This He did that He might turn again to incorruption men who had turned back to corruption, and make them alive through death by the appropriation of His body and by the grace of His resurrection. Thus He would make death to disappear from them as utterly as straw from fire.

The Word perceived that corruption could not be got rid of otherwise than through death; yet He Himself, as the Word, being immortal and the Father's Son, was such as could not die. For this reason, therefore, He assumed a body capable of death, in order that it, through belonging to the Word Who is above all, might become in dying a sufficient exchange for all, and, itself remaining incorruptible through His indwelling, might thereafter put an end to corruption for all others as well, by the grace of the resurrection. It was by surrendering to death the body which He had taken, as an offering and sacrifice free from every stain, that He forthwith abolished death for His human brethren by the offering of the equivalent. For naturally, since the Word of God was above all, when He offered His own temple and bodily instrument as a substitute for the life of all, He fulfilled in death all that was required. Naturally also, through this union of the immortal Son of God with our human nature, all men were clothed with incorruption in the promise of the resurrection. For the solidarity of mankind is such that, by virtue of the Word's indwelling in a single human body, the corruption which goes with death has lost its power over all.[9] You know how it is when some great king enters a large city and dwells in one of its houses; because of his dwelling in that single house, the whole city is honored, and enemies and robbers cease to molest it. Even so is it with the King of all; He has come into our country and dwelt in one body amidst the many, and in consequence the designs

9. Athanasius appears to be suggesting a "universalism" here—that all will be raised to life and none will go to hell. He roots this in the assumption of the "solidarity" of all men. In his other writings however, Athanasius rejects the doctrine of universalism.

of the enemy against mankind have been foiled and the corruption of death, which formerly held them in its power, has simply ceased to be. For the human race would have perished utterly had not the Lord and Savior of all, the Son of God, come among us to put an end to death.

This great work was, indeed, supremely worthy of the goodness of God. A king who has founded a city, so far from neglecting it when through the carelessness of the inhabitants it is attacked by robbers, avenges it and saves it from destruction, having regard rather to his own honor than to the people's neglect. Much more, then, the Word of the All-good Father was not unmindful of the human race that He had called to be; but rather, by the offering of His own body He abolished the death which they had incurred, and corrected their neglect by His own teaching. Thus by His own power He restored the whole nature of man. The Savior's own inspired disciples assure us of this. We read in one place: "For the love of Christ constraineth us, because we thus judge that, if One died on behalf of all, then all died, and He died for all that we should no longer live unto ourselves, but unto Him who died and rose again from the dead, even our Lord Jesus Christ" (2 Cor. 5:14-15). And again another says: "But we behold Him Who hath been made a little lower than the angels, even Jesus, because of the suffering of death crowned with glory and honor, that by the grace of God He should taste of death on behalf of every man" (Heb. 2:9ff). The same writer goes on to point out why it was necessary for God the Word and none other to become Man: "For it became Him, for Whom are all things and through Whom are all things, in bringing many sons unto glory, to make the Author of their salvation perfect through suffering." He means that the rescue of mankind from corruption was the proper part only of Him Who made them in the beginning. He points out also that the Word assumed a human body, expressly in order that He might offer it in sacrifice for other like bodies: "Since then the children are sharers in flesh and blood, He also Himself assumed the same, in order that through death He might bring to nought Him that hath the power of death, that is to say, the Devil, and might rescue those who all their lives were enslaved by the fear of death." For by the sacrifice of His own body He did two things: He put an end to the law of death which barred our way; and He made a new beginning of life for us, by giving us the hope of resurrection. By man death has gained its power over men; by the Word made Man death has been destroyed and life raised up anew. That is what Paul says, that true servant of Christ: "For since by man came death, by man came also the resurrection of the dead. Just as in Adam all die, even so in Christ shall all be made alive" (1 Cor. 15:21-22), and so forth. Now, therefore, when we die we no longer do so as men condemned to death, but as those who are even now in process of rising we await the general resurrection of all, "which in its own times He shall show," even God Who wrought it and bestowed it on us.

This, then, is the first cause of the Savior's becoming Man. There are, however, other things which show how wholly fitting is His blessed presence in our midst; and these we must now go on to consider.

Chapter 3

The Divine Dilemma and its Solution in the Incarnation

Part 2

When God the Almighty was making mankind through His own Word, He perceived that they, owing to the limitation of their nature, could not of themselves have any knowledge of their Artificer, the Incorporeal and Uncreated. He took pity on them, therefore, and did not leave them destitute of the knowledge of Himself, lest their very existence should prove purposeless. For of what use is existence to the creature if it cannot know its Maker? How could men be reasonable beings if they had no knowledge of the Word and Reason of the Father, through Whom they had received their being? They would be no better than the beasts, had they no knowledge save of earthly things; and why should God have made them at all, if He had not intended them to know Him? But, in fact, the good God has given them a share in His own Image, that is, in our Lord Jesus Christ, and has made even themselves after the same Image and Likeness.[1] Why? Simply in order that through this gift of Godlikeness in themselves they may be able to perceive the Image Absolute, that is the Word Himself, and through Him to apprehend the

1. Another benefit we receive from the incarnation of Christ is that we come to know God through Him. Knowing God is the highest form of knowledge. This was not achievable in man's fallen estate.

2. Idolatry extends to humanism, where man is encouraged to worship himself. This is the primary false religion active in Western countries today.
3. The demons pressed the primitive, pagan tribes to sacrificing beasts and humans to themselves.
4. In astrology, causation on the earth is attributed to the position of the stars. This contradicts clear biblical teaching, that all things are under God's sovereign control. Fallen man was always looking to demons or to the stars to understand the future. It was a lie.

5. God gave three forms of revelation to man. The first was natural revelation. We see His power and glory through the mountains, the oceans, and the galaxies about us (Psalm 19:1). Athanasius distinguishes between the prophets and the law, as two separate forms of revelation.

Father; which knowledge of their Maker is for men the only really happy and blessed life.

But, as we have already seen, men, foolish as they are, thought little of the grace they had received, and turned away from God. They defiled their own soul so completely that they not only lost their apprehension of God, but invented for themselves other gods of various kinds. They fashioned idols for themselves in place of the truth and reverenced things that are not, rather than God Who is, as St. Paul says, "worshipping the creature rather than the Creator" (Rom. 1:25). Moreover, and much worse, they transferred the honor which is due to God to material objects such as wood and stone, and also to man;[2] and further even than that they went, as we said in our former book. Indeed, so impious were they that they worshipped evil spirits as gods in satisfaction of their lusts. They sacrificed brute beasts and immolated men, as the just due of these deities, thereby bringing themselves more and more under their insane control.[3] Magic arts also were taught among them, oracles in sundry places led men astray, and the cause of everything in human life was traced to the stars as though nothing existed but that which could be seen.[4] In a word, impiety and lawlessness were everywhere, and neither God nor His Word was known. Yet He had not hidden Himself from the sight of men nor given the knowledge of Himself in one way only; but rather He had unfolded it in many forms and by many ways.

God knew the limitation of mankind, you see; and though the grace of being made in His Image was sufficient to give them knowledge of the Word and through Him of the Father, as a safeguard against their neglect of this grace, He provided the works of creation also as means by which the Maker might be known.[5] Nor was this all. Man's neglect of the indwelling grace tends ever to increase; and against this further frailty also God made provision by giving them a law, and by sending prophets, men whom they knew. Thus, if they were tardy in looking up to heaven, they might still gain knowledge of their Maker from those close at hand; for men can learn directly about higher things from other men. Three ways thus lay open to them, by which they might obtain the knowledge of God. They could look up into the immensity of heaven, and by pondering the harmony of creation come to know its Ruler, the Word of the Father, Whose all-ruling providence makes known the Father to all. Or, if this was beyond them, they could converse with holy men, and through them learn to know God, the Artificer of all things, the Father of Christ, and to recognize the worship of idols as the negation of the truth and full of all impiety. Or else, in the third place, they could cease from lukewarmness and lead a good life merely by knowing the law. For the law was not given only for the Jews, nor was it solely for their sake that God sent the prophets, though it was to the Jews that they were sent and by the Jews that they were persecuted. The law and the prophets were a sacred school of the knowledge of God and the conduct of the spiritual life for the whole world.[6]

So great, indeed, were the goodness and the love of God. Yet men, bowed down by the pleasures of the moment and by the frauds and illusions of the evil spirits, did not lift up their heads towards the truth. So burdened were they with their wickednesses that they seemed rather to be brute beasts than reasonable men, reflecting the very Likeness of the Word.[7]

What was God to do in face of this dehumanising of mankind, this universal hiding of the knowledge of Himself by the wiles of evil spirits? Was He to keep silence before so great a wrong and let men go on being thus deceived and kept in ignorance of Himself? If so, what was the use of having made them in His own Image originally? It would surely have been better for them always to have been brutes, rather than to revert to that condition when once they had shared the nature of the Word. Again, things being as they were, what was the use of their ever having had the knowledge of God? Surely it would have been better for God never to have bestowed it, than that men should subsequently be found unworthy to

6. Athanasius considered the law a rule by which men could live. Yet, it should be noted that men fall far short of living to the standard of the law because of their sinful nature.

7. Athanasius speaks of the inglorious condition of man in his fallen state. He interacts with the purposes of God in creating a creature of high estate that would sin and fall into a low estate. He makes a logical argument based on the goodness and the glory of God that He more or less had to bring about a Savior in His Son.

receive it. Similarly, what possible profit could it be to God Himself, Who made men, if when made they did not worship Him, but regarded others as their makers? This would be tantamount to His having made them for others and not for Himself. Even an earthly king, though he is only a man, does not allow lands that he has colonized to pass into other hands or to desert to other rulers, but sends letters and friends and even visits them himself to recall them to their allegiance, rather than allow His work to be undone. How much more, then, will God be patient and painstaking with His creatures, that they be not led astray from Him to the service of those that are not, and that all the more because such error means for them sheer ruin, and because it is not right that those who had once shared His Image should be destroyed.

8. How could the image of God be renewed in man? Man alone could not do it for he had already perverted the image of God, and they are made after the image of God. Angels could not because they did not bear the image of God. Only Jesus could do this, because He is the very Image of God (Col. 1:15).

What, then, was God to do? What else could He possibly do, being God, but renew His Image in mankind, so that through it men might once more come to know Him? And how could this be done save by the coming of the very Image Himself, our Savior Jesus Christ? Men could not have done it, for they are only made after the Image; nor could angels have done it, for they are not the images of God.[8] The Word of God came in His own Person, because it was He alone, the Image of the Father Who could recreate man made after the Image.

In order to effect this re-creation, however, He had first to do away with death and corruption. Therefore He assumed a human body, in order that in it death might once for all be destroyed, and that men might be renewed according to the Image. The Image of the Father only was sufficient for this need. Here is an illustration to prove it.

9. Athanasius likens the recreation of the New Man in Christ as the re-painting of the original image on the same canvas (after the original painting had been stained and marred).

You know what happens when a portrait that has been painted on a panel becomes obliterated through external stains. The artist does not throw away the panel, but the subject of the portrait has to come and sit for it again, and then the likeness is re-drawn on the same material.[9] Even so was it with the All-holy Son of God. He, the Image of the Father, came and dwelt in our midst, in order that He might renew mankind made after Himself, and seek out His lost sheep, even as He says in the Gospel: "I came to seek and to save that which was lost" (Luke 19:10). This also explains His saying to the Jews: "Except a man be born anew..." (John 3:3) He was not referring to a man's natural birth from his mother, as they thought, but to the re-birth and re-creation of the soul in the Image of God.

Nor was this the only thing which only the Word could do. When the madness of idolatry and irreligion filled the world and the knowledge of God was hidden, whose part was it to teach the world about the Father? Man's, would you say? But men cannot run everywhere over the world, nor would their words carry sufficient weight if they did, nor would they be, unaided, a match for the evil spirits. Moreover, since even the best of men were confused and blinded by evil, how could they convert the souls and minds of others? You cannot put straight in others what is warped in yourself. Perhaps you will say, then, that creation was enough to teach men about the Father. But if that had been so, such great evils would never have occurred. Creation was there all the time, but it did not prevent men from wallowing in error.[10] Once more, then, it was the Word of God, Who sees all that is in man and moves all things in creation, Who alone could meet the needs of the situation. It was His part and His alone, Whose ordering of the universe reveals the Father, to renew the same teaching. But how was He to do it? By the same means as before, perhaps you will say, that is, through the works of creation. But this was proven insufficient. Men had neglected to consider the heavens before, and now they were looking in the opposite direction. Wherefore, in all naturalness and fitness, desiring to do good to men, as Man He dwells, taking to Himself a body like the rest; and through His actions done in that body, as it were on their own level, He teaches those who would not learn by other means to know Himself, the Word of God, and through Him the Father.[11]

10. Natural revelation is just not sufficient to help nations who are so overcome by error. An over-optimistic view of natural law and natural revelation continued through the post-Christian era of the 1700s and 1800s. When men forsake the written Word and living Word, they are left to confusion.

11. Jesus Christ gave the final revelation of God to man. It was far and away better than any previous revelation, especially that which came by natural revelation.

12. As Jesus came to earth, he did not come as a great philosopher whose teaching is hard to follow. He came with a fairly simple message, and He shared a knowledge of God by His day-to-day life—a truly Remarkable Revelation of God!

13. Even to those who were looking to men or to evil spirits or to the elements, Jesus Christ presented a sensible message to them. He communicated the power of God and the wisdom of God as far and away above the demons and the men to whom they were looking. He smashed their idolatries and their low conception of God.

14. For those pagans involved in ancestor worship, Jesus conquered death and proved that He is the greatest Hero of all.

15. The incarnated Word, the Son of God must convince men by His works. As we teach the Gospel (the works of Christ), we call them from the paths of error to know the true and living God.

He deals with them as a good teacher with his pupils, coming down to their level and using simple means. St. Paul says as much: "Because in the wisdom of God the world in its wisdom knew not God, God thought fit through the simplicity of the News proclaimed to save those who believe" (1 Cor. 1:21). Men had turned from the contemplation of God above, and were looking for Him in the opposite direction, down among created things and things of sense. The Savior of us all, the Word of God, in His great love took to Himself a body and moved as Man among men, meeting their senses, so to speak, half way. He became Himself an object for the senses, so that those who were seeking God in sensible things might apprehend the Father through the works which He, the Word of God, did in the body.[12] Human and human minded as men were, therefore, to whichever side they looked in the sensible world they found themselves taught the truth. Were they awe-stricken by creation? They beheld it confessing Christ as Lord. Did their minds tend to regard men as Gods? The uniqueness of the Savior's works marked Him, alone of men, as Son of God. Were they drawn to evil spirits? They saw them driven out by the Lord and learned that the Word of God alone was God and that the evil spirits were not gods at all.[13] Were they inclined to hero-worship and the cult of the dead? Then the fact that the Savior had risen from the dead showed them how false these other deities were, and that the Word of the Father is the one true Lord, the Lord even of death.[14] For this reason was He both born and manifested as Man, for this He died and rose, in order that, eclipsing by His works all other human deeds, He might recall men from all the paths of error to know the Father.[15] As He says Himself, "I came to seek and to save that which was lost" (Luke 19:10).

When, then, the minds of men had fallen finally to the level of sensible things, the Word submitted to appear in a body, in order that He, as Man, might center their senses on Himself, and convince them through His human acts that He Himself is not man only but also God, the Word and Wisdom of the true God.[16] This is what Paul wants to tell us when he says: "That ye, being rooted and grounded in love, may be strong to apprehend with all the saints what is the length and breadth and height and depth, and to know the love of God that surpasses knowledge, so that ye may be filled unto all the fullness of God" (Eph. 3:17ff). The Self-revealing of the Word is in every dimension—above, in creation; below, in the Incarnation; in the depth, in Hades; in the breadth, throughout the world. All things have been filled with the knowledge of God.

For this reason He did not offer the sacrifice on behalf of all immediately after when He came, for if He had surrendered His body to death and then raised it again at once He would have ceased to be an object of our senses. Instead of that, He stayed in His body and let Himself be seen in it, doing acts and giving signs which showed Him to be not only man, but also God the Word. There were thus two things which the Savior did for us by becoming Man. He banished death from us and made us anew; and, invisible and imperceptible as in Himself He is, He became visible through His works and revealed Himself as the Word of the Father, the Ruler and King of the whole creation.[17]

There is a paradox in this last statement which we must now examine. The Word was not hedged in by His body, nor did His presence in the body prevent His being present elsewhere as well. When He moved His body He did not cease also to direct the universe by His Mind and might. No. The marvelous truth is, that being the Word, so far from being Himself contained by anything, He actually contained all things Himself.[18] In creation He is present everywhere, yet is distinct in being from it; ordering, directing, giving life to all, containing all, yet is He Himself the Uncontained, existing solely in His Father. As with the whole, so also is it with the part. Existing in a human body, to which He Himself gives life, He is still Source of life to all the universe, present in every part of it, yet outside the whole; and He is revealed both through the works of His body and through His activity in

16. Now, Athanasius will defend the deity of Christ (as well as His humanity).

17. It was important that Christ come to reveal God in Himself to us. He came to banish death and make us a new creation, but He also wanted us to come to know God by His own life and teaching.

18. Athanasius takes up the mystery of how Christ could be contained in a small body walking around on the earth, and yet still be controlling the whole universe (as God) at the same time. How can He be inside the universe and outside of it at the same time?

19. Some Gnostics considered the material creation as an evil. Athanasius dispels this myth, pointing out that Jesus was holy and undefiled, and He had not given in to sin.

20. The incarnate Savior had both a Divine nature and a human nature. The natures are unified and not separate in one person. The Athanasian Creed would put the relationship in these words: "One altogether, not by confusion of substance, but by unity of person."

the world. It is, indeed, the function of soul to behold things that are outside the body, but it cannot energize or move them. A man cannot transport things from one place to another, for instance, merely by thinking about them; nor can you or I move the sun and the stars just by sitting at home and looking at them. With the Word of God in His human nature, however, it was otherwise. His body was for Him not a limitation, but an instrument, so that He was both in it and in all things, and outside all things, resting in the Father alone. At one and the same time—this is the wonder—as Man He was living a human life, and as Word He was sustaining the life of the universe, and as Son He was in constant union with the Father. Not even His birth from a virgin, therefore, changed Him in any way, nor was He defiled by being in the body.[19] Rather, He sanctified the body by being in it. For His being in everything does not mean that He shares the nature of everything, only that He gives all things their being and sustains them in it. Just as the sun is not defiled by the contact of its rays with earthly objects, but rather enlightens and purifies them, so He Who made the sun is not defiled by being made known in a body, but rather the body is cleansed and quickened by His indwelling, "Who did no sin, neither was guile found in His mouth" (1 Pet. 2:22).

You must understand, therefore, that when writers on this sacred theme speak of Him as eating and drinking and being born, they mean that the body, as a body, was born and sustained with the food proper to its nature; while God the Word, Who was united with it, was at the same time ordering the universe and revealing Himself through His bodily acts as not man only but God.[20] Those acts are rightly said to be His acts, because the body which did them did indeed belong to Him and none other; moreover, it was right that they should be thus attributed to Him as Man, in order to show that His body was a real one and not merely an appearance. From such ordinary acts as being born and taking food, He was recognized as being actually present in the body; but by the extraordinary acts which He did through the body He proved Himself to be the Son of God. That is the meaning of His words to the unbelieving Jews: "If I do not the works of My Father, believe Me not; but if I do, even if ye believe not Me, believe My works, that ye may know that the Father is in Me and I in the Father" (John 10:37-38).

Invisible in Himself, He is known from the works of creation; so also, when His Godhead is veiled in human nature, His bodily acts still declare Him to be not man only, but the Power and Word of God. To speak authoritatively to evil spirits, for instance, and to drive them out, is not human but divine; and who could see-Him curing all the diseases to which mankind is prone, and still deem Him mere man and not also God? He cleansed lepers, He made the lame to walk, He opened the ears of the deaf and the eyes of the blind, there was no sickness or weakness that He did not drive away. Even the most casual observer can see that these were acts of God.[21]

The healing of the man born blind, for instance, who but the Father and Artificer of man, the Controller of his whole being, could thus have restored the faculty denied at birth? He Who did thus must surely be Himself the Lord of birth. This is proved also at the outset of His becoming Man. He formed His own body from the virgin; and that is no small proof of His Godhead, since He Who made that was the Maker of all else.[22] And would not anyone infer from the fact of that body being begotten of a virgin only, without human father, that He Who appeared in it was also the Maker and Lord of all beside?

Again, consider the miracle at Cana. Would not anyone who saw the substance of water transmuted into wine understand that He Who did it was the Lord and Maker of the water that He changed? It was for the same reason that He walked on the sea as on dry land—to prove to the onlookers that He had mastery over all. And the feeding of the multitude, when He made little into much, so that from five loaves

21. Still, as we watch Him in His human nature, walking around in His human body, we see the divine nature of the Lord Jesus Christ in his amazing power over demons and nature.

22. Wondrous consideration here, that the Son of God created His mother's egg and His own body in which He lived and moved.

five thousand mouths were filled—did not that prove Him none other than the very Lord Whose Mind is over all?

Chapter 4
The Death of Christ

All these things the Savior thought fit to do, so that, recognizing His bodily acts as works of God, men who were blind to His presence in creation might regain knowledge of the Father. For, as I said before, who that saw His authority over evil spirits and their response to it could doubt that He was, indeed, the Son, the Wisdom and the Power of God? Even the very creation broke silence at His behest and, marvelous to relate, confessed with one voice before the cross, that monument of victory, that He Who suffered thereon in the body was not man only, but Son of God and Savior of all. The sun veiled his face, the earth quaked, the mountains were rent asunder, all men were stricken with awe. These things showed that Christ on the cross was God, and that all creation was His slave and was bearing witness by its fear to the presence of its Master.

Thus, then, God the Word revealed Himself to men through His works. We must next consider the end of His earthly life and the nature of His bodily death. This is, indeed, the very center of our faith,[1] and everywhere you hear men speak of it; by it, too, no less than by His other acts, Christ is revealed as God and Son of God.

We have dealt as far as circumstances and our own understanding permit with the reason for His bodily manifestation. We have seen that to change the corruptible to incorruption

1. The death of Christ is the center of the Christian faith, according to Athanasius.

was proper to none other than the Savior Himself, Who in the beginning made all things out of nothing; that only the Image of the Father could re-create the likeness of the Image in men, that none save our Lord Jesus Christ could give to mortals immortality, and that only the Word Who orders all things and is alone the Father's true and sole-begotten Son could teach men about Him and abolish the worship of idols. But beyond all this, there was a debt owed which must needs be paid; for, as I said before, all men were due to die. Here, then, is the second reason why the Word dwelt among us, namely that having proved His Godhead by His works, He might offer the sacrifice on behalf of all, surrendering His own temple to death in place of all, to settle man's account with death and free him from the primal transgression.[2] In the same act also He showed Himself mightier than death, displaying His own body incorruptible as the first-fruits of the resurrection.

You must not be surprised if we repeat ourselves in dealing with this subject. We are speaking of the good pleasure of God and of the things which He in His loving wisdom thought fit to do, and it is better to put the same thing in several ways than to run the risk of leaving something out. The body of the Word, then, being a real human body, in spite of its having been uniquely formed from a virgin, was of itself mortal and, like other bodies, liable to death. But the indwelling of the Word loosed it from this natural liability, so that corruption could not touch it. Thus it happened that two opposite marvels took place at once: the death of all was consummated in the Lord's body; yet, because the Word was in it, death and corruption were in the same act utterly abolished.[3] Death there had to be, and death for all, so that the due of all might be paid. Wherefore, the Word, as I said, being Himself incapable of death, assumed a mortal body, that He might offer it as His own in place of all, and suffering for the sake of all through His union with it, "might bring to nought Him that had the power of death, that is, the devil, and might deliver

2. The "primal transgression" refers to Adam's sin in the garden. Christ set us free from this sin, because we all inherited this same sin (and the corruption of it).

3. The two marvels Athanasius presents are these: (1) We all died with Christ in His death, referring to the death of the old nature and the old man. (2) Death and corruption were destroyed by Christ's death.

them who all their lifetime were enslaved by the fear of death" (Heb. 2:14).

Have no fears then. Now that the common Savior of all has died on our behalf, we who believe in Christ no longer die, as men died aforetime, in fulfillment of the threat of the law.[4] That condemnation has come to an end; and now that, by the grace of the resurrection, corruption has been banished and done away, we are loosed from our mortal bodies in God's good time for each, so that we may obtain thereby a better resurrection.[5] Like seeds cast into the earth, we do not perish in our dissolution, but like them shall rise again, death having been brought to nought by the grace of the Savior. That is why blessed Paul, through whom we all have surety of the resurrection, says: "This corruptible must put on incorruption and this mortal must put on immortality; but when this corruptible shall have put on incorruption and this mortal shall have put on immortality, then shall be brought to pass the saying that is written, 'Death is swallowed up in victory. O Death, where is thy sting? O Grave, where is thy victory?'" (1 Cor. 15:53ff)

"Well then," some people may say, "if the essential thing was that He should surrender His body to death in place of all, why did He not do so as Man privately, without going to the length of public crucifixion? Surely it would have been more suitable for Him to have laid aside His body with honor than to endure so shameful a death." But look at this argument closely, and see how merely human it is, whereas what the Savior did was truly divine and worthy of His Godhead for several reasons.[6] The first is this. The death of men under ordinary circumstances is the result of their natural weakness. They are essentially impermanent, so after a time they fall ill and when worn out they die. But the Lord is not like that. He is not weak, He is the Power of God and Word of God and Very Life Itself. If He had died quietly in His bed like other men it would have looked as if He did so in accordance with His nature, and as though He was indeed no more than other men. But because He was Himself Word and Life and Power

4. Numerous times, Athanasius reminds us that the death of Christ was for all. He does not distinguish the sense in which the death was for all. However, He notes that it is only those who believe in Christ who no longer die.

5. We look forward to our own final resurrection, by the grace of Christ's resurrection.

6. Now, Athanasius takes up the question of why Christ had to be crucified. He does not answer the question absolutely, because these are the purposes of God. This death of crucifixion had been ordained by God as the perfect sacrifice for sins.

7. Athanasius rightly points out that the crucifixion was a "perfecting of the sacrifice."

His body was made strong, and because the death had to be accomplished, He took the occasion of perfecting His sacrifice not from Himself, but from others.[7] How could He fall sick, Who had healed others? Or how could that body weaken and fail by means of which others are made strong? Here, again, you may say, "Why did He not prevent death, as He did sickness?" Because it was precisely in order to be able to die that He had taken a body, and to prevent the death would have been to impede the resurrection. And as to the unsuitability of sickness for His body, as arguing weakness, you may say, "Did He then not hunger?" Yes, He hungered, because that was the property of His body, but He did not die of hunger because He Whose body hungered was the Lord. Similarly, though He died to ransom all, He did not see corruption. His body rose in perfect soundness, for it was the body of none other than the Life Himself.

Someone else might say, perhaps, that it would have been better for the Lord to have avoided the designs of the Jews against Him, and so to have guarded His body from death altogether. But see how unfitting this also would have been for Him. Just as it would not have been fitting for Him to give His body to death by His own hand, being Word and being Life, so also it was not consonant with Himself that He should avoid the death inflicted by others.[8] Rather, He pursued it to the uttermost, and in pursuance of His nature neither laid aside His body of His own accord nor escaped the plotting Jews. And this action showed no limitation or weakness in the Word; for He both waited for death in order to make an end of it, and hastened to accomplish it as an offering on behalf of all. Moreover, as it was the death of all mankind that the Savior came to accomplish, not His own, He did not lay aside His body by an individual act of dying, for to Him, as Life, this simply did not belong; but He accepted death at the hands of men, thereby completely to destroy it in His own body.

There are some further considerations which enable one to understand why the Lord's body had such an end. The su-

8. Our Lord Jesus Christ would never have committed suicide. But, on the other hand, He did not avoid the evil hands of men who brought about His death.

preme object of His coming was to bring about the resurrection of the body.[9] This was to be the monument to His victory over death, the assurance to all that He had Himself conquered corruption and that their own bodies also would eventually be incorrupt; and it was in token of that and as a pledge of the future resurrection that He kept His body incorrupt. But there again, if His body had fallen sick and the Word had left it in that condition, how unfitting it would have been! Should He Who healed the bodies of others neglect to keep His own in health? How would His miracles of healing be believed, if this were so? Surely people would either laugh at Him as unable to dispel disease or else consider Him lacking in proper human feeling because He could do so, but did not.[10]

Then, again, suppose without any illness He had just concealed His body somewhere, and then suddenly reappeared and said that He had risen from the dead. He would have been regarded merely as a teller of tales, and because there was no witness of His death, nobody would believe His resurrection.[11] Death had to precede resurrection, for there could be no resurrection without it. A secret and unwitnessed death would have left the resurrection without any proof or evidence to support it. Again, why should He die a secret death, when He proclaimed the fact of His rising openly? Why should He drive out evil spirits and heal the man blind from birth and change water into wine, all publicly, in order to convince men that He was the Word, and not also declare publicly that incorruptibility of His mortal body, so that He might Himself be believed to be the Life? And how could His disciples have had boldness in speaking of the resurrection unless they could state it as a fact that He had first died? Or how could their hearers be expected to believe their assertion, unless they themselves also had witnessed His death? For if the Pharisees at the time refused to believe and forced others to deny also, though the things had happened before their very eyes, how many excuses for unbelief would they have contrived, if it had taken place secretly? Or how could the end of death and

9. This is a key element of the theology of Athanasius. The resurrection was the end goal, and the supreme object of the Son of God coming to earth.

10. Athanasius continues to interact with the reasons why Jesus did not die of old age or illness. If he had healed others, he could have healed himself.

11. The public nature of His crucifixion was important that all could witness His death, and thereby not question His later resurrection.

14. An interesting argument presented here, that Christ's body was kept intact, so as to symbolize the unity of the Body of the Church through the ages.

12. Christ was subjected to the greatest powers on earth, as well as to the demonic powers who (in the providence of God) assigned Him to the death on the cross. His resurrection would prove His victory over them. He proved His superior strength by taking on these tremendous forces.

13. The ultimate victory and exaltation follow the ultimate humiliation.

the victory over it have been declared, had not the Lord thus challenged it before the sight of all, and by the incorruption of His body proved that henceforward it was annulled and void?

There are some other possible objections that must be answered. Some might urge that, even granting the necessity of a public death for subsequent belief in the resurrection, it would surely have been better for Him to have arranged an honorable death for Himself, and so to have avoided the ignominy of the cross. But even this would have given ground for suspicion that His power over death was limited to the particular kind of death which He chose for Himself; and that again would furnish excuse for disbelieving the resurrection. Death came to His body, therefore, not from Himself but from enemy action, in order that the Savior might utterly abolish death in whatever form they offered it to Him. A generous wrestler, virile and strong, does not himself choose his antagonists, lest it should be thought that of some of them he is afraid. Rather, he lets the spectators choose them, and that all the more if these are hostile, so that he may overthrow whomsoever they match against him and thus vindicate his superior strength.[12] Even so was it with Christ. He, the Life of all, our Lord and Savior, did not arrange the manner of his own death lest He should seem to be afraid of some other kind. No. He accepted and bore upon the cross a death inflicted by others, and those others His special enemies, a death which to them was supremely terrible and by no means to be faced; and He did this in order that, by destroying even this death, He might Himself be believed to be the Life, and the power of death be recognized as finally annulled. A marvelous and mighty paradox has thus occurred, for the death which they thought to inflict on Him as dishonor and disgrace has become the glorious monument to death's defeat.[13] Therefore it is also, that He neither endured the death of John, who was beheaded, nor was He sawn asunder, like Isaiah: even in death He preserved His body whole and undivided, so that there should be no excuse hereafter for those who would divide the Church.[14]

So much for the objections of those outside the Church. But if any honest Christian wants to know why He suffered death on the cross and not in some other way, we answer thus: in no other way was it expedient for us, indeed the Lord offered for our sakes the one death that was supremely good. He had come to bear the curse that lay on us; and how could He "become a curse" otherwise than by accepting the accursed death?[15] And that death is the cross, for it is written "Cursed is every one that hangeth on tree" (Gal. 3:13). Again, the death of the Lord is the ransom of all, and by it "the middle wall of partition" (Eph. 2:14) is broken down and the call of the Gentiles comes about. How could He have called us if He had not been crucified, for it is only on the cross that a man dies with arms outstretched?[16] Here, again, we see the fitness of His death and of those outstretched arms: it was that He might draw His ancient people with the one and the Gentiles with the other, and join both together in Himself. Even so, He foretold the manner of His redeeming death, "I, if I be lifted up, will draw all men unto Myself" (John 12:32). Again, the air is the sphere of the devil, the enemy of our race who, having fallen from heaven, endeavors with the other evil spirits who shared in his disobedience both to keep souls from the truth and to hinder the progress of those who are trying to follow it. The apostle refers to this when he says, "According to the prince of the power of the air, of the spirit that now worketh in the sons of disobedience" (Eph. 2:2). But the Lord came to overthrow the devil and to purify the air and to make "a way" for us up to heaven, as the apostle says, "through the veil, that is to say, His flesh" (Heb. 10:20). This had to be done through death, and by what other kind of death could it be done, save by a death in the air, that is, on the cross? Here, again, you see how right and natural it was that the Lord should suffer thus; for being thus "lifted up," He cleansed the air from all the evil influences of the enemy.[17] "I beheld Satan as lightning falling" (Luke 10:18), He says; and thus He re-opened the road to heaven, saying again, "Lift up your gates, O ye princes, and be

15. Now, Athanasius takes up the more scriptural argument. Christ was made a curse for us, and this is the fulfillment of Deuteronomy 21:23. **16.** There does appear to be an invitation to us, by the outstretching of Christ's arms on the cross. This is a powerful symbolic image.

17. Athanasius suggests that Christ's death cleanses the air, as He is lifted up on the cross— the devil being the prince of the power of the air.

ye lift up, ye everlasting doors" (Psalm 24:7). For it was not the Word Himself Who needed an opening of the gates, He being Lord of all, nor was any of His works closed to their Maker. No, it was we who needed it, we whom He Himself upbore in His own body—that body which He first offered to death on behalf of all, and then made through it a path to heaven.

Chapter 5
The Resurrection

Fitting indeed, then, and wholly consonant was the death on the cross for us; and we can see how reasonable it was, and why it is that the salvation of the world could be accomplished in no other way. Even on the cross He did not hide Himself from sight; rather, He made all creation witness to the presence of its Maker. Then, having once let it be seen that it was truly dead, He did not allow that temple of His body to linger long, but forthwith on the third day raised it up, impassable and incorruptible,[1] the pledge and token of His victory.

1. "Impassible" meaning "the inability to suffer pain."

It was, of course, within His power thus to have raised His body and displayed it as alive directly after death. But the all-wise Savior did not do this, lest some should deny that it had really or completely died. Besides this, had the interval between His death and resurrection been but two days, the glory of His incorruption might not have appeared. He waited one whole day to show that His body was really dead, and then on the third day showed it incorruptible to all. The interval was no longer, lest people should have forgotten about it and grown doubtful whether it were in truth the same body. No, while the affair was still ringing in their ears and their eyes were still straining and their minds in turmoil, and while those who had put Him to death were still on the spot and themselves witnessing to the fact of it, the Son of God after three days showed His once dead body immortal and incorruptible; and it was evident to all that it was from no natural weakness that the body which the Word indwelt had died, but in order that in it by the Savior's power death might be done away.

A very strong proof of this destruction of death and its conquest by the cross is supplied by a present fact, namely this.[2] All the disciples of Christ despise death; they take the offensive against it and, instead of fearing it, by the sign of the cross and by faith in Christ trample on it as on something dead. Before the divine sojourn of the Savior, even the holiest of men were afraid of death, and mourned the dead as those who perish. But now that the Savior has raised His body, death is no longer terrible, but all those who believe in Christ tread it underfoot as nothing, and prefer to die rather than to deny their faith in Christ, knowing full well that when they die they do not perish, but live indeed, and become incorruptible through the resurrection. But that devil who of old wickedly exulted in death, now that the pains of death are loosed, he alone it is who remains truly dead. There is proof of this too; for men who, before they believe in Christ, think death horrible and are afraid of it, once they are converted despise it so completely that they go eagerly to meet it, and themselves become witnesses of the Savior's resurrection from it. Even children hasten thus to die, and not men only, but women train themselves by bodily discipline to meet it.[3] So weak has death become that even women, who used to be taken in by it, mock at it now as a dead thing robbed of all its strength. Death has become like a tyrant who has been completely conquered by the legitimate monarch; bound hand and foot the passers-by sneer at him, hitting him and abusing him, no longer afraid of his cruelty and rage, because of the king who has conquered him. So has death been conquered and branded for what it is by the Savior on the cross. It is bound hand and foot, all who are in Christ trample it as they pass and as witnesses to Him deride it, scoffing and saying, "O Death, where is thy victory? O Grave, where is thy sting?" (1 Cor. 15:55)

2. Christ's followers do not fear death. In fact, they trample on death as evidenced in the martyrs (which Athanasius would have had full knowledge of). This is another proof of the certainty of the resurrection.

3. This testifies to the amazing faith of these early Christians. Even women and children did not blink in the face of death.

Is this a slender proof of the impotence of death, do you think? Or is it a slight indication of the Savior's victory over it, when boys and young girls who are in Christ look beyond this present life and train themselves to die? Every one is by nature afraid of death and of bodily dissolution; the marvel of marvels is that he who is enfolded in the faith of the cross despises this natural fear and for the sake of the cross is no longer cowardly in face of it. The natural property of fire is to burn. Suppose, then, that there was a substance such as the Indian asbestos is said to be, which had no fear of being burnt, but rather displayed the impotence of the fire by proving itself unburnable. If anyone doubted the truth of this, all he need do would be to wrap himself up in the substance in question and then touch the fire.[4] Or, again, to revert to our former figure, if anyone wanted to see the tyrant bound and helpless, who used to be such a terror to others, he could do so simply by going into the country of the tyrant's conqueror. Even so, if anyone still doubts the conquest of death, after so many proofs and so many martyrdoms in Christ and such daily scorn of death by His truest servants, he certainly does well to marvel at so great a thing, but he must not be obstinate in unbelief and disregard of plain facts. No, he must be like the man who wants to prove the property of the asbestos, and like him who enters the conqueror's dominions to see the tyrant bound. He must embrace the faith of Christ, this disbeliever in the conquest of death, and come to His teaching.[5] Then he will see how impotent death is and how completely conquered. Indeed, there have been many former unbelievers and deriders who, after they became believers, so scorned death as even themselves to become martyrs for Christ's sake.

If, then, it is by the sign of the cross and by faith in Christ that death is trampled underfoot, it is clear that it is Christ Himself and none other Who is the Archvictor[6] over death and has robbed it of its power. Death used to be strong and terrible, but now, since the sojourn of the Savior and the death and resurrection of His body, it is despised; and obviously it is

4. Athanasius compares the Christian's lack of fear of death with the man who covers himself in asbestos and walks into a fire (not fearing that he would be burnt).

5. For somebody to prove the strength of this faith, one would have to come to the faith (and as it were, try on the asbestos suit for himself).

6. Here is a word coined for the purposes of Christ our Lord Himself. He is the ultimate Conqueror of all conquerors, because He has conquered the enemy of all enemies.

by the very Christ Who mounted on the cross that it has been destroyed and vanquished finally. When the sun rises after the night and the whole world is lit up by it, nobody doubts that it is the sun which has thus shed its light everywhere and driven away the dark. Equally clear is it, since this utter scorning and trampling down of death has ensued upon the Savior's manifestation in the body and His death on the cross, that it is He Himself Who brought death to nought and daily raises monuments to His victory in His own disciples.[7] How can you think otherwise, when you see men naturally weak hastening to death, unafraid at the prospect of corruption, fearless of the descent into Hades, even indeed with eager soul provoking it, not shrinking from tortures, but preferring thus to rush on death for Christ's sake, rather than to remain in this present life? If you see with your own eyes men and women and children, even, thus welcoming death for the sake of Christ's religion, how can you be so utterly silly and incredulous and maimed in your mind as not to realize that Christ, to Whom these all bear witness, Himself gives the victory to each, making death completely powerless for those who hold His faith and bear the sign of the cross? No one in his senses doubts that a snake is dead when he sees it trampled underfoot, especially when he knows how savage it used to be; nor, if he sees boys making fun of a lion, does he doubt that the brute is either dead or completely bereft of strength.[8] These things can be seen with our own eyes, and it is the same with the conquest of death. Doubt no longer, then, when you see death mocked and scorned by those who believe in Christ, that by Christ death was destroyed, and the corruption that goes with it resolved and brought to end.

What we have said is, indeed, no small proof of the destruction of death and of the fact that the cross of the Lord is the monument to His victory. But the resurrection of the body to immortality, which results henceforward from the work of Christ, the common Savior and true Life of all, is more effectively proved by facts than by words to those whose mental

7. Athanasius sees the resurrection as clearly as he sees the sun rise in the morning. Only a blind man would argue the point. The hope that shines in Christ's own disciples are clear monuments of this great truth.

8. Two examples are used to describe the enfeeblement of the enemy of death in the eyes of believers. It is like a dead and mangled snake or a dead lion.

vision is sound. For, if, as we have shown, death was destroyed and everybody tramples on it because of Christ, how much more did He Himself first trample and destroy it in His own body! Death having been slain by Him, then, what other issue could there be than the resurrection of His body and its open demonstration as the monument of His victory? How could the destruction of death have been manifested at all, had not the Lord's body been raised? But if anyone finds even this insufficient, let him find proof of what has been said in present facts. Dead men cannot take effective action; their power of influence on others lasts only till the grave.[9] Deeds and actions that energize others belong only to the living. Well, then, look at the facts in this case. The Savior is working mightily among men; every day He is invisibly persuading numbers of people all over the world, both within and beyond the Greek-speaking world,[10] to accept His faith and be obedient to His teaching.[11] Can anyone, in face of this, still doubt that He has risen and lives, or rather that He is Himself the Life? Does a dead man prick the consciences of men, so that they throw all the traditions of their fathers to the winds and bow down before the teaching of Christ? If He is no longer active in the world, as He must needs be if He is dead, how is it that He makes the living to cease from their activities, the adulterer from his adultery, the murderer from murdering, the unjust from avarice, while the profane and godless man becomes religious?[12] If He did not rise, but is still dead, how is it that He routs and persecutes and overthrows the false gods, whom unbelievers think to be alive, and the evil spirits whom they worship? For where Christ is named, idolatry is destroyed and the fraud of evil spirits is exposed; indeed, no such spirit can endure that Name, but takes to flight on sound of it.[13] This is the work of One Who lives, not of one dead; and, more than that, it is the work of God. It would be absurd to say that the evil spirits whom He drives out and the idols which He destroys are alive, but that He Who drives out and destroys, and Whom they themselves acknowledge to be Son of God, is dead.

9. Now Athanasius argues that the entire spread of Christianity around the world must be a result of a living Savior's work.

10. The Greek-speaking world would have included Egypt, Palestine, Syria, and Asia Minor (Turkey). Jesus Christ worked mightily in these areas as He built His church.

11. People's lives are really changed when they believe in Christ and submit themselves to obey His teachings. This sort of thing could not have happened unless Jesus Christ is alive and Lord of all.

12. This is the most powerful argument for the Christian faith. Jesus Christ overcomes sin in people's lives. He sets the captives free from sin, and He enables spiritually dead men to live.

13. Idolatry and demon influence are fairly easily overwhelmed by the Gospel in pagan nation after pagan nation, wherever the Gospel goes. This is the story of the missions over the last 2,000 years.

In a word, then, those who disbelieve in the resurrection have no support in facts, if their gods and evil spirits do not drive away the supposedly dead Christ. Rather, it is He Who convicts them of being dead. We are agreed that a dead person can do nothing: yet the Savior works mightily every day, drawing men to religion, persuading them to virtue, teaching them about immortality, quickening their thirst for heavenly things, revealing the knowledge of the Father, inspiring strength in face of death, manifesting Himself to each, and displacing the irreligion of idols; while the gods and evil spirits of the unbelievers can do none of these things, but rather become dead at Christ's presence, all their ostentation barren and void. By the sign of the cross, on the contrary, all magic is stayed, all sorcery confounded, all the idols are abandoned and deserted, and all senseless pleasure ceases, as the eye of faith looks up from earth to heaven.[14] Whom, then, are we to call dead? Shall we call Christ dead, Who effects all this? But the dead have not the faculty to effect anything. Or shall we call death dead, which effects nothing whatever, but lies as lifeless and ineffective as are the evil spirits and the idols? The Son of God, "living and effective" (Heb. 4:12), is active every day and effects the salvation of all; but death is daily proved to be stripped of all its strength, and it is the idols and the evil spirits who are dead, not He. No room for doubt remains, therefore, concerning the resurrection of His body.

Indeed, it would seem that he who disbelieves this bodily rising of the Lord is ignorant of the power of the Word and Wisdom of God. If He took a body to Himself at all, and made it His own in pursuance of His purpose, as we have shown that He did, what was the Lord to do with it, and what was ultimately to become of that body upon which the Word had descended? Mortal and offered to death on behalf of all as it was, it could not but die; indeed, it was for that very purpose that the Savior had prepared it for Himself. But on the other hand it could not remain dead, because it had become the very temple of Life. It therefore died, as mortal, but lived again be-

14. This is a key element. Without faith, there is no victory over this evil. But with faith simply looking up to Christ, sorcery is confounded, idols become powerless over people, all idolatry is abandoned, and senseless pleasure-seeking is abandoned.

cause of the Life within it; and its resurrection is made known through its works.

It is, indeed, in accordance with the nature of the invisible God that He should be thus known through His works; and those who doubt the Lord's resurrection because they do not now behold Him with their eyes, might as well deny the very laws of nature. They have ground for disbelief when works are lacking; but when the works cry out and prove the fact so clearly, why do they deliberately deny the risen life so manifestly shown? Even if their mental faculties are defective, surely their eyes can give them irrefragable[15] proof of the power and Godhead of Christ. A blind man cannot see the sun, but he knows that it is above the earth from the warmth which it affords; similarly, let those who are still in the blindness of unbelief recognize the Godhead of Christ and the resurrection which He has brought about through His manifested power in others.[16] Obviously He would not be expelling evil spirits and despoiling idols, if He were dead, for the evil spirits would not obey one who was dead.[17] If, on the other hand, the very naming of Him drives them forth, He clearly is not dead; and the more so that the spirits, who perceive things unseen by men, would know if He were so and would refuse to obey Him. But, as a matter of fact, what profane persons doubt, the evil spirits know—namely that He is God; and for that reason they flee from Him and fall at His feet, crying out even as they cried when He was in the body, "We know Thee Who Thou art, the Holy One of God," and, "Ah, what have I in common with Thee, Thou Son of God? I implore Thee, torment me not."

Both from the confession of the evil spirits and from the daily witness of His works, it is manifest, then, and let none presume to doubt it, that the Savior has raised His own body, and that He is very Son of God, having His being from God as from a Father, Whose Word and Wisdom and Whose Power He is. He it is Who in these latter days assumed a body for the salvation of us all, and taught the world concerning the

15. "irrefragable" meaning "cannot be refuted or disproved."

16. Athanasius points out that even unbelievers may have a vague sense of the resurrection by the evidences all around them, similar to blind men who can feel the warmth of the sun (although they cannot see it).

17. Where there is true Christian faith, there will be powerful manifestations of exorcisms or the casting out of demons. This has been proven time and time again in culture after culture around the world, by Christian missionaries with true faith. Athanasius' point is that the demons are very much aware that Christ is alive and they submit to His authority. Demons would not respond to a dead Jesus.

Father. He it is Who has destroyed death and freely graced us all with incorruption through the promise of the resurrection, having raised His own body as its first-fruits, and displayed it by the sign of the cross as the monument to His victory over death and its corruption.

Chapter 6
✣ Refutation of the Jews

We have dealt thus far with the Incarnation of our Savior, and have found clear proof of the resurrection of His Body and His victory over death. Let us now go further and investigate the unbelief and the ridicule with which Jews and Gentiles respectively regard these same facts.[1] It seems that in both cases the points at issue are the same, namely the unfittingness or incongruity (as it seems to them) alike of the cross and of the Word's becoming man at all. But we have no hesitation in taking up the argument against these objectors, for the proofs on our side are extremely clear.

First, then, we will consider the Jews. Their unbelief has its refutation in the Scriptures which even themselves read; for from cover to cover the inspired Book clearly teaches these things both in its entirety and in its actual words.[2] Prophets foretold the marvel of the Virgin and of the Birth from her, saying, "Behold, a virgin shall conceive and bear a son, and they shall call his name 'Emmanuel,' which means 'God is with us'" (Isa. 7:14). And Moses, that truly great one in whose word the Jews trust so implicitly, he also recognized the importance and truth of the matter. He puts it thus: "There shall arise a star from Jacob and a man from Israel, and he shall break in pieces the rulers of Moab" (Num. 24:17). And, again, "How lovely are thy dwellings, O Jacob, thy tents, O Israel! Like

1. Athanasius offers arguments to those Jews and Gentiles who would attempt to argue against the incarnation. Christians have always attempted to bring forward reasoned arguments to those who would doubt the Christian faith. This field of study is typically called "apologetics."

2. Since the Jews accept the Old Testament as authoritative, Athanasius will argue from Old Testament prophecies to attempt to convince his Jewish readers.

woodland valleys they give shade, and like parks by rivers, like tents which the Lord has pitched, like cedar-trees by streams. There shall come forth a Man from among his seed, and he shall rule over many peoples" (Num 24:5-7). And, again, Isaiah says, "Before the Babe shall be old enough to call father or mother, he shall take the power of Damascus and the spoils of Samaria from under the eyes of the king of Assyria" (Isa. 8:4). These words, then, foretell that a Man shall appear.[3] And Scripture proclaims further that He that is to come is Lord of all. These are the words, "Behold, the Lord sitteth on an airy cloud and shall come into Egypt, and the man-made images of Egypt shall be shaken" (Isa. 19:1). And it is from Egypt also that the Father calls him back, saying, "Out of Egypt have I called My Son" (Hos. 11:1).[4]

Moreover, the Scriptures are not silent even about His death. On the contrary, they refer to it with the utmost clearness. They have not feared to speak also of the cause of it. He endures it, they say, not for His own sake, but for the sake of bringing immortality and salvation to all, and they record also the plotting of the Jews against Him and all the indignities which He suffered at their hands. Certainly nobody who reads the Scriptures can plead ignorance of the facts as an excuse for error! There is this passage, for instance: "A man that is afflicted and knows how to bear weakness, for His face is turned away. He was dishonored and not considered, He bears our sins and suffers for our sakes. And we for our part thought Him distressed and afflicted and ill-used; but it was for our sins that He was wounded and for our lawlessness that He was made weak. Chastisement for our peace was upon Him, and by His bruising we are healed" (Isa. 53:3-5). O marvel at the love of the Word for men, for it is on our account that He is dishonored, so that we may be brought to honor. "For all we," it goes on, "have strayed like sheep, man has strayed from his path, and the Lord has given Him up for our sins; and He Himself did not open His mouth at the ill-treatment. Like a sheep He was led to slaughter, and as a lamb is dumb before its

3. First Athanasius proves that the coming Messiah would be a human being.

4. Then Athanasius proves from Old Testament Scripture that the coming Messiah would be Lord.

shearer, so He opened not His mouth; in His humiliation His judgment was taken away" (Isa. 53:6-8). And then Scripture anticipates the surmises of any who might think from His suffering thus that He was just an ordinary man, and shows what power worked in His behalf. "Who shall declare of what lineage He comes?"[5] it says, "for His life is exalted from the earth. By the lawlessnesses of the people was He brought to death, and I will give the wicked in return for His burial and the rich in return for His death. For He did no lawlessness, neither was deceit found in His mouth. And the Lord wills to heal Him of His affliction" (Isa. 53:8-10).[6]

5. Isaiah 53:8

6. Athanasius proves from Isaiah 53 that the Messiah came to suffer for the sins (not His own sins but the sins of others).

You have heard the prophecy of His death, and now, perhaps, you want to know what indications there are about the cross. Even this is not passed over in silence: on the contrary, the sacred writers proclaim it with the utmost plainness. Moses foretells it first, and that right loudly, when he says, "You shall see your Life hanging before your eyes, and shall not believe" (Deut. 28:66). After him the prophets also give their witness, saying, "But I as an innocent lamb brought to be offered was yet ignorant of it. They plotted evil against Me, saying, 'Come, let us cast wood into His bread, and wipe Him out from the land of the living" (Jer. 11:19). And, again, "They pierced My hands and My feet, they counted all My bones, they divided My garments for themselves and cast lots for My clothing" (Ps. 22:16-18).[7] Now a death lifted up and that takes place on wood can be none other than the death of the cross; moreover, it is only in that death that the hands and feet are pierced. Besides this, since the Savior dwelt among men, all nations everywhere have begun to know God; and this too Holy Writ expressly mentions. "There shall be the Root of Jesse," it says, "and he who rises up to rule the nations, on Him nations shall set their hope" (Isa. 11:10).

7. Athanasius uses Psalm 22 to prove that Christ's feet and hands would be nailed to a cross.

These are just a few things in proof of what has taken place; but indeed all Scripture teems with disproof of Jewish unbelief. For example, which of the righteous men and holy prophets and patriarchs of whom the Divine Scriptures tell ever had his bodily birth from a virgin only? Was not Abel born of Adam, Enoch of Jared, Noah of Lamech, Abraham of Terah, Isaac of Abraham, and Jacob of Isaac? Was not Judah begotten by Jacob and Moses and Aaron by Ameram? Was not Samuel the son of Elkanah, David of Jesse, Solomon of David, Hezekiah of Ahaz, Josiah of Amon, Isaiah of Amos, Jeremiah of Hilkiah and Ezekiel of Buzi? Had not each of these a father as author of his being? So who is He that is born of a virgin only, that sign of which the prophet makes so much? Again, which of all those people had his birth announced to the world by a star in the heavens? When Moses was born his parents hid him. David was unknown even in his own neighborhood, so that mighty Samuel himself was ignorant of his existence and asked whether Jesse had yet another son. Abraham again became known to his neighbors as a great man only after his birth. But with Christ it was otherwise. The witness to His birth was not man, but a star shining in the heavens whence He was coming down.

Then, again, what king that ever was reigned and took trophies from his enemies before he had strength to call father or mother?[8] Was not David thirty years old when he came to the throne and Solomon a grown young man? Did not Joash enter on his reign at the age of seven, and Josiah, some time after him, at about the same age, both of them fully able by that time to call father or mother? Who is there, then, that was reigning and despoiling his enemies almost before he was born? Let the Jews, who have investigated the matter, tell us if there was ever such a king in Israel or Judah—a king upon whom all the nations set their hopes and had peace, instead of being at enmity with him on every side! As long as Jerusalem stood there was constant war between them, and they all fought against Israel. The Assyrians oppressed Israel, the Egyptians persecuted them, the Babylonians fell upon them, and, strange to relate, even the Syrians their neighbors were at war with them. And did not David fight with Moab and smite the Syrians, and Hezekiah quail at the boasting of Sen-

8. This is a reference to Isaiah 8:4, which speaks of the Messiah's powerful overcoming of enemies before He is able to speak.

nacherib? Did not Amalek make war on Moses and the Amorites oppose him, and did not the inhabitants of Jericho array themselves against Joshua the son of Nun? Did not the nations always regard Israel with implacable hostility? Then it is worth inquiring who it is, on whom the nations are to set their hopes.[9] Obviously there must be someone, for the prophet could not have told a lie. But did any of the holy prophets or of the early patriarchs die on the cross for the salvation of all? Were any of them wounded and killed for the healing of all? Did the idols of Egypt fall down before any righteous man or king that came there? Abraham came there certainly, but idolatry prevailed just the same; and Moses was born there, but the mistaken worship was unchanged.[10]

Again, does Scripture tell of anyone who was pierced in hands and feet or hung upon a tree at all, and by means of a cross perfected his sacrifice for the salvation of all? It was not Abraham, for he died in his bed, as did also Isaac and Jacob. Moses and Aaron died in the mountain, and David ended his days in his house, without anybody having plotted against him. Certainly he had been sought by Saul, but he was preserved unharmed. Again Isaiah was sawn asunder, but he was not hung on a tree. Jeremiah was shamefully used, but he did not die under condemnation. Ezekiel suffered, but he did so, not on behalf of the people, but only to signify to them what was going to happen.[11] Moreover, all these even when they suffered were but men, like other men; but He Whom the Scriptures declare to suffer on behalf of all is called not merely man but Life of all, although in point of fact He did share our human nature. "You shall see your Life hanging before your eyes," they say, and "Who shall declare of what lineage He comes?" With all the saints we can trace their descent from the beginning, and see exactly how each came to be; but the Divine Word maintains that we cannot declare the lineage of Him Who is the Life. Who is it, then, of Whom Holy Writ thus speaks? Who is there so great that even the prophets foretell of Him such mighty things? There is indeed no

9. Athanasius reviews the many enemies of Israel and presents the Messiah as One who is far and away more glorious and mightier than the Old Testament leaders in Israel.

10. Athanasius makes the point that Abraham was unable to make any positive change on Egypt, especially in terms of their commitment to idolatry. Only the Messiah could address such horrible oppositions to the true and living God.

11. Athanasius argues from the fact that no other figure in history was crucified (as required by Psalm 22), that Jesus Christ is the only reasonable Person that would fit this prophecy.

12. Since Christ was born of a virgin, Athanasius argues His origins then must be shrouded in mystery (as indicated by Isaiah 53:8).

13. This is a reference to the star that pointed out His birth. Only a birth like this one could have been heralded in such a way.

14. Athanasius may be overstating the case a little, but his enthusiasm for Christ's accomplishments is to be commended.

15. Athanasius testifies to the reign of Christ, by the influence He has had on Egypt. Athanasius was a bishop (pastor) in Alexandria from AD 328 to AD 373. Egypt had been steeped in idolatry for 2,000 years, but now with the coming of Christ, this idolatry was very much crushed. This serves as strong evidence to Athanasius that Christ is reigning and conquering.

one in the Scriptures at all, save the common Savior of all, the Word of God, our Lord Jesus Christ. He it is that proceeded from a virgin, and appeared as man on earth, He it is Whose earthly lineage cannot be declared, because He alone derives His body from no human father, but from a virgin alone.[12] We can trace the paternal descent of David and Moses and of all the patriarchs. But with the Savior we cannot do so, for it was He Himself Who caused the star to announce His bodily birth, and it was fitting that the Word, when He came down from heaven, should have His sign in heaven too, and fitting that the King of creation on His coming forth should be visibly recognized by all the world.[13] He was actually born in Judea, yet men from Persia came to worship Him. He it is Who won victory from His demon foes and trophies from the idolaters even before His bodily appearing—namely, all the heathen who from every region have abjured the tradition of their fathers and the false worship of idols and are now placing their hope in Christ and transferring their allegiance to Him. The thing is happening before our very eyes, here in Egypt; and thereby another prophecy is fulfilled, for at no other time have the Egyptians ceased from their false worship save when the Lord of all, riding as on a cloud, came down here in the body and brought the error of idols to nothing and won over everybody[14] to Himself and through Himself to the Father.[15] He it is Who was crucified with the sun and moon as witnesses; and by His death salvation has come to all men, and all creation has been redeemed. He is the Life of all, and He it is Who like a sheep gave up His own body to death, His life for ours and our salvation.

Yet the Jews disbelieve this. This argument does not satisfy them. Well, then, let them be persuaded by other things in their own oracles. Of whom, for instance, do the prophets say, "I was made manifest to those who did not seek Me, I was found by those who had not asked for Me? I said, 'See, here am I,' to the nation that had not called upon My Name. I stretched out My hands to a disobedient and gainsaying people" (Isa. 65:1-2).

Who is this person that was made manifest, one might ask the Jews? If the prophet is speaking of himself, then they must tell us how he was first hidden, in order to be manifested afterwards. And, again, what kind of man is this prophet, who was not only revealed after being hidden, but also stretched out his hands upon the cross?[16] Those things happened to none of those righteous men: they happened only to the Word of God Who, being by nature without body, on our account appeared in a body and suffered for us all. And if even this is not enough for them, there is other overwhelming evidence by which they may be silenced. The Scripture says, "Be strong, hands that hang down and feeble knees, take courage, you of little faith, be strong and do not fear. See, our God will recompense judgment, He Himself will come and save us. Then the eyes of blind men shall be opened and the ears of deaf men shall hear, and stammerers shall speak distinctly" (Isa. 35:3-6). What can they say to this, or how can they look it in the face at all? For the prophecy does not only declare that God will dwell here, it also makes known the signs and the time of His coming.[17] When God comes, it says, the blind will see, the lame will walk, the deaf will hear and the stammerers will speak distinctly. Can the Jews tell us when such signs occurred in Israel, or when anything of the kind took place at all in Jewry? The leper Naaman was cleansed, it is true, but no deaf man heard nor did any lame man walk. Elijah raised a dead person and so did Elisha; but no one blind from birth received his sight. To raise a dead person is a great thing indeed, but it is not such as the Savior did. And surely, since the Scriptures have not kept silence about the leper and the dead son of the widow, if a lame man had walked and a blind man had received his sight, they would have mentioned these as well. Their silence on these points proves that the events never took place. When therefore did these things happen, unless when the Word of God Himself came in the body? Was it not when He came that lame men walked and stammerers spoke clearly and men blind from birth were given sight? And the Jews who saw it

16. From Isaiah 65, Athanasius attempts to prove that Jesus's identity was veiled to the Jews. This explains why He was not recognized in a widespread manner as a Prophet of God and the Son of God.

17. Using Isaiah 35:3-6, Athanasius points out that the salvation of God's people would have to come by God Himself. The Savior could not be a mere man.

18. Athanasius argues for the uniqueness of Christ in that no Old Testament prophet or miracle worker had accomplished the variety of healings that our Lord did. Examples include the healing of the lame and the blind. These are unique to Christ.

themselves testified to the fact that such things had never before occurred. "Since the world began," they said, "it has never been heard of that anyone should open the eyes of a man born blind. If this Man were not from God, He could do nothing" (John 9:32-33).[18]

But surely they cannot fight against plain facts. So it may be that, without denying what is written, they will maintain that they are still waiting for these things to happen, and that the Word of God is yet to come, for that is a theme on which they are always harping most brazenly, in spite of all the evidence against them. But they shall be refuted on this supreme point more clearly than on any, and that not by ourselves but by the most wise Daniel, for he signifies the actual date of the Savior's coming as well as His Divine sojourn in our midst. "Seventy weeks," he says, "are cut short upon thy people and upon the holy city, to make a complete end of sin and for sins to be sealed up and iniquities blotted out, and to make reconciliation for iniquity and to seal vision and prophet, and to anoint a Holy One of holies. And thou shalt know and understand from the going forth of the Word to answer, and to build Jerusalem, until Christ the Prince" (Dan. 9:24-25). In regard to the other prophecies, they may possibly be able to find excuses for deferring their reference to a future time, but what can they say to this one? How can they face it at all? Not only does it expressly mention the Anointed One, that is the Christ, it even declares that He Who is to be anointed is not man only, but the Holy One of holies! And it says that Jerusalem is to stand till His coming, and that after it prophet and vision shall cease in Israel! David was anointed of old, and Solomon, and Hezekiah; but then Jerusalem and the place stood, and prophets were prophesying, Gad and Asaph and Nathan, and later Isaiah and Hosea and Amos and others. Moreover, those men who were anointed were called holy certainly, but none of them was called the Holy of holies.[19] Nor is it any use for the Jews to take refuge in the Captivity, and say that Jerusalem did not exist then, for what about the

19. Here Athanasius points out that none of the Old Testament prophets could be called "the Holy of holies." Only God would be fit for such a title.

prophets? It is a fact that at the outset of the Exile Daniel and Jeremiah were there, and Ezekiel and Haggai and Zechariah also prophesied.

So the Jews are indulging in fiction, and transferring present time to future. When did prophet and vision cease from Israel? Was it not when Christ came, the Holy One of holies? It is, in fact, a sign and notable proof of the coming of the Word that Jerusalem no longer stands, neither is prophet raised up nor vision revealed among them.[20] And it is natural that it should be so, for when He that was signified had come, what need was there any longer of any to signify Him? And when the Truth had come, what further need was there of the shadow? On His account only they prophesied continually, until such time as Essential Righteousness has come, Who was made the Ransom for the sins of all. For the same reason Jerusalem stood until the same time, in order that there men might premeditate the types before the Truth was known. So, of course, once the Holy One of holies had come, both vision and prophecy were sealed. And the kingdom of Jerusalem ceased at the same time, because kings were to be anointed among them only until the Holy of holies had been anointed. Moses also prophesies that the kingdom of the Jews shall stand until His time, saying, "A ruler shall not fail from Judah nor a prince from his loins, until the things laid up for him shall come and the Expectation of the nations Himself" (Gen. 49:10). And that is why the Savior Himself was always proclaiming, "The law and the prophets prophesied until John" (Matt. 11:13). So if there is still king or prophet or vision among the Jews, they do well to deny that Christ is come; but if there is neither king nor vision, and since that time all prophecy has been sealed and city and temple taken, how can they be so irreligious, how can they so flaunt the facts, as to deny Christ Who has brought it all about?[21] Again, they see the heathen forsaking idols and setting their hopes through Christ on the God of Israel; why do they yet deny Christ Who after the flesh was born of the root of Jesse and reigns hence-

20. Athanasius points out that Jerusalem was destroyed (in AD 70). He adds that there is no more prophecy accepted by the Jews after that date.

21. The destruction of Jerusalem meant the end of prophecy and the end of the kingdom. There would be no more kings in Israel, because Christ had come.

22. Athanasius seems to be struck by the hardness of the hearts among the Jews. The Gentiles themselves have come to worship the God of Abraham, Isaac, and Jacob by the influence of Christ. This is an amazing transformation, and he wishes the Jews could see it.

23. o Habakkuk 2:14. Athanasius sees these optimistic kingdom prophecies coming to pass in the present age (not in some future millennium).

forward? Of course, if the heathen were worshipping some other god, and not confessing the God of Abraham and Isaac and Jacob and Moses, then they would do well to argue that God had not come. But if the heathen are honoring the same God Who gave the law to Moses and the promises to Abraham—the God Whose word too the Jews dishonored, why do they not recognize or rather why do they deliberately refuse to see that the Lord of Whom the Scriptures prophesied has shone forth to the world and appeared to it in a bodily form?[22] Scripture declares it repeatedly. "The Lord God has appeared to us" (Ps. 118:27), and again, "He sent forth His Word and healed them" (Ps. 107:20). And again, "It was no ambassador, no angel who saved us, but the Lord Himself" (Isa. 63:9). The Jews are afflicted like some demented person who sees the earth lit up by the sun, but denies the sun that lights it up! What more is there for their Expected One to do when he comes? To call the heathen? But they are called already. To put an end to prophet and king and vision? But this too has already happened. To expose the God-denying-ness of idols? It is already exposed and condemned. Or to destroy death? It is already destroyed. What then has not come to pass that the Christ must do? What is there left out or unfulfilled that the Jews should disbelieve so light-heartedly? The plain fact is, as I say, that there is no longer any king or prophet nor Jerusalem nor sacrifice nor vision among them; yet the whole earth is filled with the knowledge of God,[23] and the Gentiles, forsaking atheism, are now taking refuge with the God of Abraham through the Word, our Lord Jesus Christ.

Surely, then, it must be plain even to the most shameless that the Christ has come, and that He has enlightened all men everywhere, and given them the true and divine teaching about His Father.

Thus the Jews may be refuted by these and other arguments from the Divine teaching.

Chapter 7
Refutation of the Gentiles
Part 1

Ｗe come now to the unbelief of the Gentiles; and
this is indeed a matter for complete astonishment, for they laugh at that which is no fit subject for mockery, yet fail to see the shame and ridiculousness
of their own idols.[1] But the arguments on our side do not lack
weight, so we will confute them too on reasonable grounds,
chiefly from what we ourselves also see.

First of all, what is there in our belief that is unfitting
or ridiculous? Is it only that we say that the Word has been
manifested in a body?[2] Well, if they themselves really love the
truth, they will agree with us that this involved no unfittingness at all. If they deny that there is a Word of God at all, that
will be extraordinary, for then they will be ridiculing what they
do not know. But suppose they confess that there is a Word
of God, that He is the Governor of all things, that in Him
the Father wrought the creation, that by His providence the
whole receives light and life and being, and that He is King
over all, so that He is known by means of the works of His
providence, and through Him the Father. Suppose they confess all this, what then? Are they not unknowingly turning the
ridicule against themselves? The Greek philosophers say that
the universe is a great body, and they say truly, for we perceive
the universe and its parts with our senses. But if the Word of
God is in the universe, which is a body, and has entered into

1. Athanasius challenges the fool in his folly,
"Lest he be wise in his
own eyes." This is a clear
application of Proverbs
26:5. Comparing the
gods (and the authorities)
of the ungodly with the
true and living God—there
really is no comparison.

2. Athanasius is probably
addressing the Neo-Pla-
tonic thinking that finds
matter itself as evil.

3. If the Gentiles would accept the possibility that the Creator of the Universe (the Word) might enter into the universe, they should accept the incarnation as reasonable as well.

it in its every part, what is there surprising or unfitting in our saying that He has entered also into human nature?[3] If it were unfitting for Him to have embodied Himself at all, then it would be unfitting for Him to have entered into the universe, and to be giving light and movement by His providence to all things in it, because the universe, as we have seen, is itself a body. But if it is right and fitting for Him to enter into the universe and to reveal Himself through it, then, because humanity is part of the universe along with the rest, it is no less fitting for Him to appear in a human body, and to enlighten and to work through that. And surely if it were wrong for a part of the universe to have been used to reveal His Divinity to men, it would be much more wrong that He should be so revealed by the whole!

Take a parallel case. A man's personality actuates and quickens his whole body. If anyone said it was unsuitable for the man's power to be in the toe, he would be thought silly, because, while granting that a man penetrates and actuates the whole of his body, he denied his presence in the part. Similarly, no one who admits the presence of the Word of God in the universe as a whole should think it unsuitable for a single human body to be by Him actuated and enlightened.

But is it, perhaps, because humanity is a thing created and brought into being out of non-existence that they regard as unfitting the manifestation of the Savior in our nature? If so, it is high time that they spurned Him from creation too; for it, too, has been brought out of non-being into being by the Word.[4] But if, on the other hand, although creation is a thing that has been made, it is not unsuitable for the Word to be present in it, then neither is it unsuitable for Him to be in man. Man is a part of the creation, as I said before; and the reasoning which applies to one applies to the other. All things derive from the Word their light and movement and life, as the Gentile authors themselves say, "In Him we live and move and have our being" (Acts 17:28). Very well then. That being so, it is by no means unbecoming that the Word should dwell

4. The argument is that the man was created out of nothing, and it would therefore be unbecoming for the Son of God to take on human flesh. But Athanasius argues that nobody thinks it would be unbecoming for the Creator to enter into other parts of the universe, if He would so desire.

in man. So if, as we say, the Word has used that in which He is as the means of His self-manifestation, what is there ridiculous in that? He could not have used it had He not been present in it; but we have already admitted that He is present both in the whole and in the parts. What, then, is there incredible in His manifesting Himself through that in which He is? By His own power He enters completely into each and all, and orders them throughout ungrudgingly; and, had He so willed, He could have revealed Himself and His Father by means of sun or moon or sky or earth or fire or water. Had He done so, no one could rightly have accused Him of acting unbecomingly, for He sustains in one whole all things at once, being present and invisibly revealed not only in the whole, but also in each particular part. This being so, and since, moreover, He has willed to reveal Himself through men, who are part of the whole, there can be nothing ridiculous in His using a human body to manifest the truth and knowledge of the Father. Does not the mind of man pervade his entire being, and yet find expression through one part only, namely the tongue? Does anybody say on that account that Mind has degraded itself? Of course not. Very well, then, no more is it degrading for the Word, Who pervades all things, to have appeared in a human body. For, as I said before, if it were unfitting for Him thus to indwell the part, it would be equally so for Him to exist within the whole.

Some may then ask, why did He not manifest Himself by means of other and nobler parts of creation, and use some nobler instrument, such as sun or moon or stars or fire or air, instead of mere man? The answer is this. The Lord did not come to make a display. He came to heal and to teach suffering men. For one who wanted to make a display the thing would have been just to appear and dazzle the beholders.[5] But for Him Who came to heal and to teach the way was not merely to dwell here, but to put Himself at the disposal of those who needed Him, and to be manifested according as they could

5. Unbelievers forget that the reason Christ entered our world (and human flesh), was not to dazzle us, but to come down on our level and heal us, teach us, and save us from our predicament.

6. This is key to the Christian doctrine of the incarnation. God reveals Himself to us in the incarnation of the Son of God in our language, at our level, so we would be able to receive the message.

7. The problem with the world is man's sin. Only man erred from God's design. It was man who needed to be fixed.

8. Man invented "vanities" and "lies" to replace the truth of God.

9. Athanasius argues that Christ presents His divine works as a human, so that this revelation would be more accessible to men.

10. We can see the attributes of God expressed in the powerful works of Nature (the galaxies, the mighty oceans, and His creative genius). But this does not mean that He takes on the nature of these things. It is quite a different thing when God takes on human nature—the nature of that which He has created.

bear it, not vitiating the value of the Divine appearing by exceeding their capacity to receive it.[6]

Moreover, nothing in creation had erred from the path of God's purpose for it, save only man.[7] Sun, moon, heaven, stars, water, air, none of these had swerved from their order, but, knowing the Word as their Maker and their King, remained as they were made. Men alone having rejected what is good, have invented nothings instead of the truth,[8] and have ascribed the honor due to God and the knowledge concerning Him to demons and men in the form of stones. Obviously the Divine goodness could not overlook so grave a matter as this. But men could not recognize Him as ordering and ruling creation as a whole. So what does He do? He takes to Himself for instrument a part of the whole, namely a human body, and enters into that. Thus He ensured that men should recognize Him in the part who could not do so in the whole, and that those who could not lift their eyes to His unseen power might recognize and behold Him in the likeness of themselves. For, being men, they would naturally learn to know His Father more quickly and directly by means of a body that corresponded to their own and by the Divine works done through it; for by comparing His works with their own they would judge His to be not human but Divine.[9] And if, as they say, it were unsuitable for the Word to reveal Himself through bodily acts, it would be equally so for Him to do so through the works of the universe. His being in creation does not mean that He shares its nature; on the contrary, all created things partake of His power.[10] Similarly, though He used the body as His instrument, He shared nothing of its defect, but rather sanctified it by His indwelling.[11] Does not even Plato, of whom the Greeks think so much, say that the Author of the Universe, seeing it storm-tossed and in danger of sinking into the state of dissolution, takes his seat at the helm of the Life-force of the universe, and comes to the rescue and puts everything right?[12] What, then, is there incredible in our saying that, mankind having gone astray, the Word descended upon it and was manifest as man, so that by His intrinsic goodness and His steersmanship He might save it from the storm?

It may be, however, that, though shamed into agreeing that this objection is void, the Greeks will want to raise another. They will say that, if God wanted to instruct and save mankind, He might have done so, not by His Word's assumption of a body, but, even as He at first created them, by the mere signification of His will.[13] The reasonable reply to that is that the circumstances in the two cases are quite different. In the beginning, nothing as yet existed at all; all that was needed, therefore, in order to bring all things into being, was that His will to do so should be signified. But once man was in existence, and things that were, not things that were not, demanded to be healed, it followed as a matter of course that the Healer and Savior should align Himself with those things that existed already, in order to heal the existing evil.[14] For that reason, therefore, He was made man, and used the body as His human instrument. If this were not the fitting way, and He willed to use an instrument at all, how otherwise was the Word to come? And whence could He take His instrument, save from among those already in existence and needing His Godhead through One like themselves? It was not things non-existent that needed salvation, for which a bare creative word might have sufficed, but man—man already in existence and already in process of corruption and ruin. It was natural and right, therefore, for the Word to use a human instrument and by that means unfold Himself to all.

11. Athanasius reminds his readers that Jesus did not receive the flaws (or the sinfulness) of human nature when He became a man.

12. Athanasius refers to Plato (as the most respected of the Greek philosophers), in order to demonstrate that this idea of God coming to fix that which is broken in the world is not altogether unacceptable to the pagan mind.

13. The next argument to address is the suggestion that God could have just by fiat, by an act of His will re-created man without the trouble of sending His Son into human flesh.

14. Athanasius points out that there is a difference in the case of the original creation. There was no evil and no sin at that time. But now God must deal with the problem of sin in His existing creation.

15. The unbeliever tends to underestimate the problem with the world. The problem was as deep as the human soul, and the life had to be restored within the soul of man. Thus, God the Son was united to the very core of the human existence—the human soul.

16. The problem was not merely death, but the loss of life within the spiritual nature of man. Jesus did not come to conquer death for Himself. He came to conquer our death and give us eternal life.

17. Stubble is always afraid of fire because it is highly combustible. We are easily given to death. What we needed was not a delay of death or an escape from death. We needed to become impervious to the threat of death. Like a firefighter dressed in an asbestos suit, we can walk into fire and not fear it anymore. This is what Jesus Christ did for us. We will no longer need to fear death, upon our final resurrection.

You must know, moreover, that the corruption which had set in was not external to the body but established within it.[15] The need, therefore, was that life should cleave to it in corruption's place, so that, just as death was brought into being in the body, life also might be engendered in it. If death had been exterior to the body, life might fittingly have been the same. But if death was within the body, woven into its very substance and dominating it as though completely one with it, the need was for Life to be woven into it instead, so that the body by thus enduing itself with life might cast corruption off. Suppose the Word had come outside the body instead of in it, He would, of course, have defeated death, because death is powerless against the Life. But the corruption inherent in the body would have remained in it none the less.[16] Naturally, therefore, the Savior assumed a body for Himself, in order that the body, being interwoven as it were with life, should no longer remain a mortal thing, in thrall to death, but as endued with immortality and risen from death, should thenceforth remain immortal. For once having put on corruption, it could not rise, unless it put on life instead; and besides this, death of its very nature could not appear otherwise than in a body. Therefore He put on a body, so that in the body He might find death and blot it out. And, indeed, how could the Lord have been proved to be the Life at all, had He not endued with life that which was subject to death? Take an illustration. Stubble is a substance naturally destructible by fire; and it still remains stubble, fearing the menace of fire which has the natural property of consuming it, even if fire is kept away from it, so that it is not actually burnt. But suppose that, instead of merely keeping the fire from it somebody soaks the stubble with a quantity of asbestos, the substance which is said to be the antidote to fire. Then the stubble no longer fears the fire, because it has put on that which fire cannot touch, and therefore it is safe.[17] It is just the same with regard to the body and death. Had death been kept from it by a mere command, it would still have remained mortal and corruptible, according to its nature.[18] To prevent this, it put on the incorporeal Word of God, and therefore fears neither death nor corruption any more, for it is clad with Life as with a garment and in it corruption is clean done away.

The Word of God thus acted consistently in assuming a body and using a human instrument to vitalize the body. He was consistent in working through man to reveal Himself everywhere, as well as through the other parts of His creation, so that nothing was left void of His Divinity and knowledge. For I take up now the point I made before, namely that the Savior did this in order that He might fill all things everywhere with the knowledge of Himself, just as they are already filled with His presence, even as the Divine Scripture says, "The whole universe was filled with the knowledge of the Lord" (Isa. 11:9). If a man looks up to heaven he sees there His ordering; but if he cannot look so high as heaven, but only so far as men, through His works he sees His power, incomparable with human might, and learns from them that He alone among men is God the Word.[19] Or, if a man has gone astray among demons and is in fear of them, he may see this Man drive them out and judge therefrom that He is indeed their Master. Again, if a man has been immersed in the element of water and thinks that it is God—as indeed the Egyptians do worship water—he may see its very nature changed by Him and learn that the Lord is Creator of all.[20] And if a man has gone down even to Hades, and stands awestruck before the heroes who have descended thither, regarding them as gods, still he may see the fact of Christ's resurrection and His victory over death, and reason from it that, of all these, He alone is very Lord and God.[21]

For the Lord touched all parts of creation, and freed and undeceived them all from every deceit. As St. Paul says, "Having put off from Himself the principalities and the powers, He triumphed on the cross" (Col. 2:15), so that no one could possibly be any longer deceived, but everywhere might find the very Word of God. For thus man, enclosed on every side by

18. Jesus did not merely chase death away for us. He gave us a new life and a new nature that would be unaffected by death's threats.

19. Even more powerful than the creation of the galaxies, is the amazing and powerful redemptive work Christ has done in people when He gives them new life. He fills the whole world with this amazing testimony, that we should all give praise to God.

20. Jesus demonstrated He is more powerful than water when He turned the water into wine (John 2:1-11).

21. Even the greatest heroes of men are dead, and they did not resurrect themselves. Jesus Christ is the greatest obviously, because He is risen from the dead.

22. Christ has defeated all false religions and demonstrates to the world the truth for everybody to see. Athanasius believes the revelation of Christ should be persuasive to the whole world now.

the works of creation and everywhere—in heaven, in Hades, in men and on the earth, beholding the unfolded Godhead of the Word, is no longer deceived concerning God, but worships Christ alone, and through Him rightly knows the Father.[22]

On these grounds, then, of reason and of principle, we will fairly silence the Gentiles in their turn. But if they think these arguments insufficient to confute them, we will go on in the next chapter to prove our point from facts.

Chapter 8

Refutation of the Gentiles

Part 2

When did people begin to abandon the worship of idols, unless it were since the very Word of God came among men?[1] When have oracles ceased and become void of meaning, among the Greeks and everywhere, except since the Savior has revealed Himself on earth? When did those whom the poets call gods and heroes begin to be adjudged as mere mortals, except when the Lord took the spoils of death and preserved incorruptible the body He had taken, raising it from among the dead? Or when did the deceitfulness and madness of demons fall under contempt, save when the Word, the Power of God, the Master of all these as well, condescended on account of the weakness of mankind and appeared on earth? When did the practice and theory of magic begin to be spurned under foot, if not at the manifestation of the Divine Word to men?[2] In a word, when did the wisdom of the Greeks become foolish, save when the true Wisdom of God revealed Himself on earth? In old times the whole world and every place in it was led astray by the worship of idols, and men thought the idols were the only gods that were. But now all over the world men are forsaking the fear of idols and taking refuge with Christ; and by worshipping Him as God they come through Him to know the Father also, Whom formerly they did not know.[3] The amazing thing, moreover, is this. The objects of worship formerly were varied

1. Athanasius points out the success of the Gospel against pagan religions as an argument for its truth. Idolatry was ceasing in the Empire. He was watching it come apart. Indeed, much of the world's idolatrous systems have fallen through the centuries as the Gospel of Christ was received. Then men began to realize how degraded and deceived their minds had been (under Satan's influence before Jesus came).

2. Even the Greek prophets (oracles), the idols, the witchcraft, and the false ideas began to look ridiculous after the Gospel came in.

3. The amazing penetration of the Gospel has crushed idolatry "all over the world."

4. Formerly, religions could not cross cultural and family boundaries. But, the faith of the true and living God (through Jesus Christ) has the most cross-cultural impact of any of the gods of the heathen. In the modern day, Christian spin-offs like monotheistic "Islam" has some limited ability to cross boundaries as well.

5. Boeotia is located in central Greece (known for the city of Thebes). The Kabiri is probably referring to the gods of those who lived on the Island of Lemnos in the Aegean Sea. The Pythoness was a priestess or prophetess at the Temple of Delphi in Central Greece. Athanasius is referring to all the prophets who spoke for demons (and deceived the people for centuries).

6. People often become very impressed with the super heroes and gods of make believe stories (including films and comic books today). But these are all just made-up stories. People increasingly realized the fakery of it, and the truth that came with the Word of God.

and countless; each place had its own idol and the so-called god of one place could not pass over to another in order to persuade the people there to worship him, but was barely reverenced even by his own. Indeed no! Nobody worshipped his neighbor's god, but every man had his own idol and thought that it was lord of all. But now Christ alone is worshipped, as One and the Same among all peoples everywhere; and what the feebleness of idols could not do, namely, convince even those dwelling close at hand, He has effected. He has persuaded not only those close at hand, but literally the entire world to worship one and the same Lord and through Him the Father.[4]

Again, in former times every place was full of the fraud of the oracles, and the utterances of those at Delphi and Dordona and in Boeotia and Lycia and Libya and Egypt and those of the Kabiri and the Pythoness were considered marvelous by the minds of men.[5] But now, since Christ has been proclaimed everywhere, their madness too has ceased, and there is no one left among them to give oracles at all. Then, too, demons used to deceive men's minds by taking up their abode in springs or rivers or trees or stones and imposing upon simple people by their frauds. But now, since the Divine appearing of the Word, all this fantasy has ceased, for by the sign of the cross, if a man will but use it, he drives out their deceits. Again, people used to regard as gods those who are mentioned in the poets—Zeus and Kronos and Apollo and the heroes, and in worshipping them they went astray.[6] But now that the Savior has appeared among men, those others have been exposed as mortal men, and Christ alone is recognized as true God, Word of God, God Himself. And what is one to say about the magic that they think so marvelous? Before the sojourn of the Word, it was strong and active among Egyptians and Chaldeans and Indians and filled all who saw it with terror and astonishment.[7] But by the coming of the Truth and the manifestation of the Word it too has been confuted and entirely destroyed. As to Greek wisdom, however, and the philosophers' noisy talk, I really think no one requires argument from us; for the amazing fact is patent to all that, for all that they had written so much, the Greeks failed to convince even a few from their own neighborhood in regard to immortality and the virtuous ordering of life.[8] Christ alone, using common speech and through the agency of men not clever with their tongues, has convinced whole assemblies of people all the world over to despise death, and to take heed to the things that do not die, to look past the things of time and gaze on things eternal, to think nothing of earthly glory and to aspire only to immortality.[9]

These things which we have said are no mere words: they are attested by actual experience. Anyone who likes may see the proof of glory in the virgins of Christ, and in the young men who practice chastity as part of their religion, and in the assurance of immortality in so great and glad a company of martyrs.[10] Anyone, too, may put what we have said to the proof of experience in another way. In the very presence of the fraud of demons and the imposture of the oracles and the wonders of magic, let him use the sign of the cross which they all mock at, and but speak the Name of Christ, and he shall

7. The peoples of the nations were often terrorized by magicians, witch doctors, and others who were manipulated by demons (and sometimes were able to do a few supernatural things to impress the masses).

8. Athanasius summarizes the Greek philosophies as "noisy talk." The fruits of all of their "great wisdom" turned out to be nothing. They could not get people to overcome the fear of death and live truly moral lives. Greek philosophy was a total moral failure.

9. The best that the humanist Greeks and Romans did was to get people to seek after "earthly glory." This was their highest ethic. But Christ was able to convince His people that earthly glory was meaningless in comparison to heavenly immortality.

10. The commitment required for Christians under severe persecution often called for celibacy for young men and women, because they were headed towards martyrdom. This commitment to Christ was truly remarkable and gave a tremendous testimony to the world (unlike anything their religions produced).

11. Athanasius points out how just speaking the Name of Christ, easily confounded the demons and crushed witchcraft and magic in areas of the world where Satan had dominated for many centuries.

12. The opponents to the faith tried to call Christ just another magician. But Athanasius points out that everywhere the Gospel goes, He puts an end to magic and demonic influence. This brings to mind our Lord's argument in Matthew 12:27-28.

see how through Him demons are routed, oracles cease, and all magic and witchcraft is confounded.[11]

Who, then, is this Christ and how great is He, Who by His Name and presence overshadows and confounds all things on every side, Who alone is strong against all and has filled the whole world with His teaching? Let the Greeks tell us, who mock at Him without stint or shame. If He is a man, how is it that one man has proved stronger than all those whom they themselves regard as gods, and by His own power has shown them to be nothing? If they call Him a magician, how is it that by a magician all magic is destroyed, instead of being rendered strong?[12] Had He conquered certain magicians or proved Himself superior to one of them only, they might reasonably think that He excelled the rest only by His greater skill. But the fact is that His cross has vanquished all magic entirely and has conquered the very name of it. Obviously, therefore, the Savior is no magician, for the very demons whom the magicians invoke flee from Him as from their Master. Who is He, then? Let the Greeks tell us, whose only serious pursuit is mockery! Perhaps they will say that He, too, is a demon, and that is why He prevailed. But even so the laugh is still on our side, for we can confute them by the same proofs as before. How could He be a demon, Who drives demons out? If it were only certain ones that He drove out, then they might reasonably think that He prevailed against them through the power of their Chief, as the Jews, wishing to insult Him, actually said. But since the fact is, here again, that at the mere naming of His Name all madness of the demons is rooted out and put to flight, obviously the Greeks are wrong here, too, and our Lord and Savior Christ is not, as they maintain, some demonic power.

If, then, the Savior is neither a mere man nor a magician, nor one of the demons, but has by His Godhead confounded and overshadowed the opinions of the poets and the delusion of the demons and the wisdom of the Greeks, it must be manifest and will be owned by all that He is in truth Son of God,

Existent Word and Wisdom and Power of the Father. This is the reason why His works are no mere human works, but, both intrinsically and by comparison with those of men, are recognized as being superhuman and truly the works of God.[13]

What man that ever was, for instance, formed a body for himself from a virgin only? Or what man ever healed so many diseases as the common Lord of all? Who restored that which was lacking in man's nature or made one blind from birth to see? Aesculapius was deified by the Greeks because he practiced the art of healing and discovered herbs as remedies for bodily diseases, not, of course, forming them himself out of the earth, but finding them out by the study of nature.[14] But what is that in comparison with what the Savior did when, instead of just healing a wound, He both fashioned essential being and restored to health the thing that He had formed? Hercules, too, is worshipped as a god by the Greeks because he fought against other men and destroyed wild animals by craft. But what is that to what the Word did, in driving away from men diseases and demons and even death itself? Dionysus is worshipped among them, because he taught men drunkenness; yet they ridicule the true Savior and Lord of all, Who taught men temperance.[15]

That, however, is enough on this point. What will they say to the other marvels of His Godhead? At what man's death was the sun darkened and the earth shaken? Why, even to this day men are dying, and they did so also before that time. When did any such marvels happen in their case? Now shall we pass over the deeds done in His earthly body and mention those after His resurrection? Has any man's teaching, in any place or at any time, ever prevailed everywhere as one and the same, from one end of the earth to the other, so that his worship has fairly flown through every land?[16] Again, if, as they say, Christ is man only and not God the Word, why do not the

13. Athanasius concludes that Jesus Christ must be in a league of His own. His works are not merely the works of men. They must be the works of God.

14. People turned Aesculapius into a god only because he discovered the use of herbs in God's created order. Some still idolize science and medicine, instead of the God who created the material world. In Greek mythology, Aesculapius was the son of Apollo who received secret knowledge from a snake concerning medicine and healing.

15. Hercules and Dionysus, the Greek gods of strength and partying. But all these gods could do was kill men and teach them to get drunk. That's not very impressive. Jesus came to bring eternal life and righteousness.

16. Again, Athanasius is impressed at the rapidity by which Christ's message has captured the hearts of nations all around the world. No other faith competes with this.

17. The enemy is especially frightened of Christ's Gospel entering in, because they know that this is the truth and it will easily counter their lies. This is why false religions want to persecute those bringing the Christian Gospel.

18. Athanasius points out that the influence of the Greek philosophers wane quickly after they die. Moreover, they hold radically different opinions about truth and reality, and whatever unity they had quickly dissolves into contentions and arguments. This should not happen in the true church of the Lord Jesus Christ.

19. A biblical view of knowledge is well summarized here. It is simple and can be conveyed in simple language for anybody to understand. It holds some apparent paradox, but Christians can live with this (because they trust in God who is the source of all knowledge and can resolve these apparent paradoxes).

20. One of the strongest arguments for Christianity is the radical transformation seen in those who participate in the New Life.

gods of the Greeks prevent His entering their domains?[17] Or why, on the other hand, does the Word Himself dwelling in our midst make an end of their worship by His teaching and put their fraud to shame?

Many before Him have been kings and tyrants of the earth, history tells also of many among the Chaldeans and Egyptians and Indians who were wise men and magicians. But which of those, I do not say after his death, but while yet in this life, was ever able so far to prevail as to fill the whole world with his teaching and retrieve so great a multitude from the craven fear of idols, as our Savior has won over from idols to Himself? The Greek philosophers have compiled many works with persuasiveness and much skill in words; but what fruit have they to show for this such as has the cross of Christ? Their wise thoughts were persuasive enough until they died; yet even in their lifetime their seeming influence was counterbalanced by their rivalry with one another, for they were a jealous company and declaimed against each other.[18] But the Word of God, by strangest paradox, teaching in meaner language, has put the choicest sophists in the shade, and by confounding their teachings and drawing all men to Himself He has filled His own assemblies.[19] Moreover, and this is the marvelous thing by going down as Man to death He has confounded all the sounding utterances of the wise men about the idols. For whose death ever drove out demons, or whose death did ever demons fear, save that of Christ? For where the Savior is named, there every demon is driven out. Again, who has ever so rid men of their natural passions that fornicators become chaste and murderers no longer wield the sword and those who formerly were craven cowards boldly play the man?[20] In a word, what persuaded the barbarians and heathen folk in every place to drop their madness and give heed to peace, save the faith of Christ and the sign of the cross? What other things have given men such certain faith in immortality as have the cross of Christ and the resurrection of His body? The Greeks told all sorts of false tales, but they could never pretend that their idols rose again from death: indeed it never entered their heads that a body could exist again after death at all.[21] And one would be particularly ready to listen to them on this point, because by these opinions they have exposed the weakness of their own idolatry, at the same time yielding to Christ the possibility of bodily resurrection, so that by that means He might be recognized by all as Son of God.

Again, who among men, either after his death or while yet living, taught about virginity and did not account this virtue impossible for human beings? But Christ our Savior and King of all has so prevailed with His teaching on this subject that even children not yet of lawful age promise that virginity which transcends the law.[22] And who among men has ever been able to penetrate even to Scythians and Ethiopians, or Parthians or Armenians or those who are said to live beyond Hyrcania, or even the Egyptians and Chaldeans, people who give heed to magic and are more than naturally enslaved by the fear of demons and savage in their habits, and to preach at all about virtue and self-control and against the worshipping of idols, as has the Lord of all, the Power of God, our Lord Jesus Christ?[23] Yet He not only preached through His own disciples, but also wrought so persuasively on men's understanding that, laying aside their savage habits and forsaking the worship of their ancestral gods, they learnt to know Him and through Him to worship the Father. While they were yet idolaters, the Greeks and Barbarians were always at war with each other, and were even cruel to their own kith and kin. Nobody could travel by land or sea at all unless he was armed with swords, because of their irreconcilable quarrels with each other. Indeed, the whole course of their life was carried on with the weapons, and the sword with them replaced the staff and was the mainstay of all aid.[24] All this time, as I said before, they were serving idols and offering sacrifices to demons, and for all the superstitious awe that accompanied this idol worship, nothing could wean them from that warlike spirit. But, strange to relate, since they came over to the school of

21. The Christian faith is also the most hopeful, the most optimistic, the most powerful message of all. No other faith, certainly not the Greek gods, could even imagine the resurrection and the eternal life promised by Christ.

22. During this time of persecution, Christians would commit themselves to a celibate life forgoing all possibility of marriage. This is an indication of strong faith (though not the only one).

23. Parthians are those of Persia or modern-day Iran. Armenians are those who live in Armenia - considered far off tribes by the "civilized world." While other faiths were powerless to deal with more savage tribes, the Christian missionaries thought nothing of taking the Gospel to every nation, even the most primitive and savage.

24. Until Christ came, travel in the ancient world was dangerous. The tribes were almost constantly at war with each other.

Christ, as men moved with real compunction they have laid aside their murderous cruelty and are war-minded no more. On the contrary, all is peace among them and nothing remains save desire for friendship.

Who, then, is He Who has done these things and has united in peace those who hated each other, save the beloved Son of the Father, the common Savior of all, Jesus Christ, Who by His own love underwent all things for our salvation?[25] Even from the beginning, moreover, this peace that He was to administer was foretold, for Scripture says, "They shall beat their swords into ploughshares and their spears into sickles, and nation shall not take sword against nation, neither shall they learn any more to wage war" (Isa. 2:4). Nor is this by any means incredible.[26]

The barbarians of the present day are naturally savage in their habits, and as long as they sacrifice to their idols they rage furiously against each other and cannot bear to be a single hour without weapons. But when they hear the teaching of Christ, forthwith they turn from fighting to farming, and instead of arming themselves with swords extend their hands in prayer.[27] In a word, instead of fighting each other, they take up arms against the devil and the demons, and overcome them by their self command and integrity of soul.[28] These facts are proof of the Godhead of the Savior, for He has taught men what they could never learn among the idols. It is also no small exposure of the weakness and nothingness of demons and idols, for it was because they knew their own weakness that the demons were always setting men to fight each other, fearing lest, if they ceased from mutual strife, they would turn to attack the demons themselves. For in truth the disciples of Christ, instead of fighting each other, stand arrayed against demons by their habits and virtuous actions, and chase them away and mock at their captain the devil. Even in youth they are chaste, they endure in times of testing and persevere in toils. When they are insulted, they are patient, when robbed

25. Athanasius almost constantly mentions Christ's work on the cross—the basic Gospel message. He is utterly enthralled by the power and beauty and grace of the Gospel.

26. These passages that are sometimes attributed to the millennium or to heaven, Athanasius applies these to the present day. Indeed, modern Christians tend to forget the vast differences of nations before receiving the Gospel and afterwards.

27. Although largely missing today, the typical position of those who pray is to extend hands towards heaven (1 Tim. 2:8).

28. When we begin to engage in spiritual warfare (Eph. 6:10ff), we will find ourselves less and less fighting with those in our workplace, community, church, and family.

they make light of it, and, marvelous to relate, they make light even of death itself, and become martyrs of Christ.

And here is another proof of the Godhead of the Savior, which is indeed utterly amazing. What mere man or magician or tyrant or king was ever able by himself to do so much? Did anyone ever fight against the whole system of idol-worship and the whole host of demons and all magic and all the wisdom of the Greeks, at a time when all of these were strong and flourishing and taking everybody in, as did our Lord, the very Word of God? Yet He is even now invisibly exposing every man's error, and single-handedly carries off all men from them all, so that those who used to worship idols now tread them under foot, reputed magicians burn their books and the wise prefer to all studies the interpretation of the gospels. They are deserting those whom formerly they worshipped, they worship and confess as Christ and God Him Whom they used to ridicule as crucified. Their so-called gods are routed by the sign of the cross, and the crucified Savior is proclaimed in all the world as God and Son of God.[29] Moreover, the gods worshipped among the Greeks are now falling into disrepute among them on account of the disgraceful things they did, for those who receive the teaching of Christ are more chaste in life than they. If these, and the like of them, are human works, let anyone who will show us similar ones done by men in former time, and so convince us. But if they are shown to be, and are the works not of men but of God, why are the unbelievers so irreligious as not to recognize the Master Who did them?[30] They are afflicted as a man would be who failed to recognize God the Artificer through the works of creation. For surely if they had recognized His Godhead through His power over the universe, they would recognize also that the bodily works of Christ are not human, but are those of the Savior of all, the Word of God. And had they recognized this, as Paul says, "They would not have crucified the Lord of glory" (1 Cor. 2:8).

As, then, he who desires to see God Who by nature is invisible and not to be beheld, may yet perceive and know Him

29. Athanasius is strong on the deity of Christ, even before the Arian controversy broke out (and the Council of Nicaea worked out the doctrine of the Trinity in 325). This book was written around 315.

30. The problem with unbelievers at the very root is that they refuse to recognize the works of God. The transformation that Jesus Christ brings to people's lives is a work of God.

31. It would be better to render this "that we would be restored in the image of God." The Scriptures do not claim that we will be "made God," by our association with Christ. He goes on to show the ways in which we are restored in knowledge and immortality (as those who have been remade in God's image).

32. Athanasius rightly presents this "mystery of godliness," the incarnation of the Son of God as an object of tremendous wonder and awe.

through His works, so too let him who does not see Christ with his understanding at least consider Him in His bodily works and test whether they be of man or God. If they be of man, then let him scoff; but if they be of God, let him not mock at things which are no fit subject for scorn, but rather let him recognize the fact and marvel that things divine have been revealed to us by such humble means, that through death deathlessness has been made known to us, and through the Incarnation of the Word the Mind whence all things proceed has been declared, and its Agent and Ordainer, the Word of God Himself. He, indeed, assumed humanity that we might become God.[31] He manifested Himself by means of a body in order that we might perceive the Mind of the unseen Father. He endured shame from men that we might inherit immortality. He Himself was unhurt by this, for He is impassable and incorruptible; but by His own impassability He kept and healed the suffering men on whose account He thus endured. In short, such and so many are the Savior's achievements that follow from His Incarnation, that to try to number them is like gazing at the open sea and trying to count the waves. One cannot see all the waves with one's eyes, for when one tries to do so those that are following on baffle one's senses. Even so, when one wants to take in all the achievements of Christ in the body, one cannot do so, even by reckoning them up, for the things that transcend one's thought are always more than those one thinks that one has grasped.

As we cannot speak adequately about even a part of His work, therefore, it will be better for us not to speak about it as a whole. So we will mention but one thing more, and then leave the whole for you to marvel at. For, indeed, everything about it is marvelous, and wherever a man turns his gaze he sees the Godhead of the Word and is smitten with awe.[32]

The substance of what we have said so far may be summarized as follows. Since the Savior came to dwell among us, not only does idolatry no longer increase, but it is getting less and gradually ceasing to be. Similarly, not only does the wisdom of the Greeks no longer make any progress, but that which used to be is disappearing. And demons, so far from continuing to impose on people by their deceits and oracle-givings and sorceries, are routed by the sign of the cross if they so much as try. On the other hand, while idolatry and everything else that opposes the faith of Christ is daily dwindling and weakening and falling, see, the Savior's teaching is increasing everywhere![33] Worship, then, the Savior "Who is above all" and mighty, even God the Word, and condemn those who are being defeated and made to disappear by Him. When the sun has come, darkness prevails no longer; any of it that may be left anywhere is driven away. So also, now that the Divine epiphany of the Word of God has taken place, the darkness of idols prevails no more, and all parts of the world in every direction are enlightened by His teaching. Similarly, if a king be reigning somewhere, but stays in his own house and does not let himself be seen, it often happens that some insubordinate fellows, taking advantage of his retirement, will have themselves proclaimed in his stead; and each of them, being invested with the semblance of kingship, misleads the simple who, because they cannot enter the palace and see the real king, are led astray by just hearing a king named. When the real king emerges, however, and appears to view, things stand differently. The insubordinate impostors are shown up by his presence, and men, seeing the real king, forsake those who previously misled them.[34] In the same way the demons used formerly to impose on men, investing themselves with the honor due to God. But since the Word of God has been manifested in a body, and has made known to us His own Father, the fraud of the demons is stopped and made to disappear; and men, turning their eyes to the true God, Word of the Father, forsake the idols and come to know the true God.

Now this is proof that Christ is God, the Word and Power of God. For whereas human things cease and the fact of Christ remains, it is clear to all that the things which cease are temporary, but that He Who remains is God and very Son of God, the sole-begotten Word.[35]

33. The major apologetic argument for Athanasius continues to be the progress the Church and the Kingdom of Christ has made up to that point (around 315). The world has been changed by Christ and continues to be changed, century after century. He crushes His enemies. Idolatries are laid waste, again and again.

34. False religions and demon-inspired idolatries are presented as imposter kings. When the real King shows up, they run away quickly. This is what happens when the Gospel of Jesus Christ is proclaimed to the nations.

35. The permanence of Christ's work is still yet another powerful proof that He is from God, He is God, and His work is God's work.

Chapter 9
Conclusion

1. Macarius is the man to whom Athanasius is writing this tract.

2. This is essential for every new believer. When various churches wander away from this (whether it be the Roman Catholic Church or the Eastern Orthodox churches), the faith dies out.

3. We can also learn from other good teachers who have studied the Scriptures, especially those who have proved their faith by martyrdom.

4. Athanasius believes that the second coming of Christ will result in our resurrection to eternal life. This is also the point at which the final judgment occurs. This eschatological outlook could be classified as "amillennial" or "postmillennial."

Here, then, Macarius,[1] is our offering to you who love Christ, a brief statement of the faith of Christ and of the manifestation of His Godhead to us. This will give you a beginning, and you must go on to prove its truth by the study of the Scriptures.[2] They were written and inspired by God; and we, who have learned from inspired teachers who read the Scriptures and became martyrs for the Godhead of Christ, make further contribution to your eagerness to learn.[3] From the Scriptures you will learn also of His second manifestation to us, glorious and divine indeed, when He shall come not in lowliness but in His proper glory, no longer in humiliation but in majesty, no longer to suffer but to bestow on us all the fruit of His cross—the resurrection and incorruptibility.[4] No longer will He then be judged, but rather will Himself be Judge, judging each and all according to their deeds done in the body, whether good or ill. Then for the good is laid up the heavenly kingdom, but for those that practice evil outer darkness and the eternal fire. So also the Lord Himself says, "I say unto you, hereafter ye shall see the Son of Man seated on the right hand of power, coming on the clouds of heaven in the glory of the Father" (Matt. 26:64). For that Day we have one of His own sayings to prepare us, "Get ready and watch, for ye know not the hour in which He cometh" (Matt 24:42). And blessed Paul says, "We must all stand before the judgment seat of Christ, that each one may receive according as he practiced in the body, whether good or ill" (2 Cor. 5:10).

But for the searching and right understanding of the Scriptures there is need of a good life and a pure soul, and for Christian virtue to guide the mind to grasp, so far as human nature can, the truth concerning God the Word. One cannot possibly understand the teaching of the saints unless one has a pure mind and is trying to imitate their life.[5] Anyone who wants to look at sunlight naturally wipes his eye clear first, in order to make, at any rate, some approximation to the purity of that on which he looks; and a person wishing to see a city or country goes to the place in order to do so. Similarly, anyone who wishes to understand the mind of the sacred writers must first cleanse his own life, and approach the saints by copying their deeds.[6] Thus united to them in the fellowship of life, he will both understand the things revealed to them by God and, thenceforth escaping the peril that threatens sinners in the judgment, will receive that which is laid up for the saints in the kingdom of heaven. Of that reward it is written: "Eye hath not seen nor ear heard, neither hath entered into the heart of man the things that God has prepared" (1 Cor. 2:9). For them that live a godly life and love the God and Father in Christ Jesus our Lord, through Whom and with Whom be to the Father Himself, with the Son Himself, in the Holy Spirit, honor and might and glory to ages of ages. Amen.

5. True knowledge requires right living, to some extent. We do not truly understand until we are walking in the light, and doers of the Word

6. Athanasius speaks of the necessity of "cleansing" (1 John 1:9) and copying the deeds of the saints. He does not necessarily speak of justification by works here. The Christian life does involve an ongoing sanctification process, however.

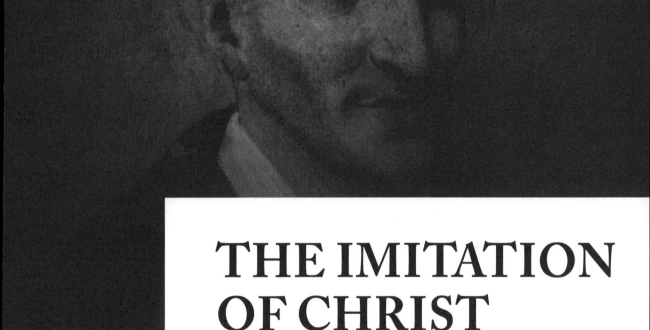

THE IMITATION OF CHRIST

Thomas A'Kempis
AD 1441

Explanatory Notes by
Kevin Swanson and Joshua Schwisow

Introduction to *The Imitation of Christ*

We know of no reading that is more powerfully calculated to shut us up unto the faith, none more fitted to deepen and to strengthen the basis of a sinner's humility and so reconcile him to the doctrine of salvation in all its parts by grace alone, none that by exhibiting the height and perfection of Christian attainments, can better serve the end of prostrating the inquirer into the veriest depths of self abasement, when, on the humbling comparison of what he is, with what he ought to be, he is touched and penetrated by a sense of his manifold deficiencies. It is on this account that the author of such a work may instrumentally speaking, do the office of a schoolmaster to bring us unto Christ: nor do we know at what other time it is, than when eyeing from afar the lofty track of spiritual and seraphic piety which is here delineated, that we more feel our need of the great High Priest, or that His peace speaking blood and His perfect righteousness are more prized by us.

The utter renunciation of self, the surrender of all vanity, the patient endurance of evils and wrongs, the crucifixion of natural and worldly desires, the absorption of all our interests and passions in the enjoyment of God, and the subordination of all we do and of all we feel to His glory, these form the leading virtues of our pilgrimage, and in the very proportion of their rarity and their painfulness are they the more effectual tests of our regeneration. And one

of the main uses of this book is that while it enforces these spiritual graces in all their extent, it lays open the spiritual enjoyment that springs from the cultivation of them revealing the hidden charm which lies in godliness, and demonstrating the sure though secret alliance which obtains between the peace of heaven in the soul, and patience under all the adversities of the path which leads to it.
— Thomas Chalmers (1780-1847),
Introduction to "The Imitation of Christ"

Some believe that the great Reformation of the Christian faith began in June of 1384 in Nemelerberg, Netherlands when Gerard Groote and a few friends formed a discipleship center for young men. Groote was a young preacher who got himself in trouble with the local Roman bishop for preaching against concubinage, simony, and the other sins common in the church at that time. He died two months after forming the Brethren of the Common Life, a religious group dedicated to discipling young men in the faith. Thomas à Kempis was just four years old at the time, but he would later become the most famous member of this pre-reformation movement. A century later, Martin Luther, Martin Bucer, and other reformers would receive early discipleship in these centers.

Between the ages of twelve and nineteen, Thomas à Kempis was discipled by these "Brethren of the Common Life." In his adult years, he continued to live with a community of disciples connected with the Brethren in Zwoll at a place called Mount St. Agnes. Living before the invention of the printing press, his main task was copying manuscripts by hand. Through his lifetime, he made four handwritten copies of the entire Bible. Thomas is best known for his classic devotional writing, *The Imitation of Christ*.

The reader of *The Imitation of Christ* would do well to remember that this work is more descriptive than prescriptive. It describes the Christian as Christ describes His followers in the beatitudes and elsewhere in the Gospels. It paints a picture of what a Christian looks like and what the true Christian wishes to be. A true Christian desires to follow Christ, and within this work à Kempis seeks to mark out the way toward that end.

This is a work that cannot be studied in an academic, detached frame of mind. The reader must be open for self-examination. At first read, these contemplations are unexpected and somewhat jarring because the life of Christ is unnatural to the natural mind and heart. These short lessons require careful meditation and application.

Both Catholic and Protestant readers have claimed benefit from à Kempis' classic work. John Wesley included this book among the influences that brought him to conversion. The Presbyterian Thomas Chalmers warmly endorsed the book, as did Warren Wiersbe. In its list of the most influential works in Christian history, *Christian History* magazine places this as the tenth most influential work, following Augustine's *Confessions* at #1, Calvin's *Institutes of the Christian Religion* at #3, John Bunyan's *Pilgrim's Progress* at #6, and Athanasius' *Of the Incarnation* at #9.

The Imitation of Christ is not a systematic doctrinal treatise. While à Kempis does refer to merit, he still insists that all is of grace. It is a devotional, and it is meant to test our hearts and lives for genuineness of faith and love for Christ.

No Christian author is devoid of faults. The reader is therefore encouraged to read critically, always checking the content against Scripture. When à Kempis' words agree with Scripture, they should be embraced. When they deviate from this bedrock foundation, we must part ways with him. The Voice of Christ appearing in the text may be treated as a preacher directing a word towards the reader, but the Berean spirit still applies. The more noble Bereans "studied the Scriptures to see if these things be true" (Acts 17:11). Let us do the same.

Book 1
Thoughts Helpful in the Life of the Soul

1. Imitating Christ and Despising All Vanities on Earth

He who follows Me, walks not in darkness," says the Lord (John 8:12). By these words of Christ we are advised to imitate His life and habits, if we wish to be truly enlightened and free from all blindness of heart.[1] Let our chief effort, therefore, be to study the life of Jesus Christ.

The teaching of Christ is more excellent than all the advice of the saints, and he who has His spirit will find in it a hidden manna.[2] Now, there are many who hear the Gospel often but care little for it because they have not the spirit of Christ. Yet whoever wishes to understand fully the words of Christ must try to pattern his whole life on that of Christ.

What good does it do to speak learnedly about the Trinity if, lacking humility, you displease the Trinity?[3] Indeed it is not learning that makes a man holy and just, but a virtuous life makes him pleasing to God. I would rather feel contrition than know how to define it. For what would it profit us to know the whole Bible by heart and the principles of all the philosophers if we live without grace and the love of God?

1. This is the basic premise of the book. John 3:21 provides a better scriptural proof text for the premise: "But he who does the truth comes to the light, that his deeds may be clearly seen, that they have been done in God." As we follow the life of Christ and walk in His ways, we will come to the light of truth.

2. A'Kempis encourages the reading of Scripture over all the other writings of the church.

3. Here head knowledge is not enough. Too many students of Scripture are content with this. Mere knowledge makes people proud (1 Cor. 8:1), and this is displeasing to God.

4. The world is filled with vanity. To love God is the highest purpose for life, the first command, and renders the highest value to our lives.

5. When we are told to love the things that are invisible, this does not mean that we are to avoid loving things that are material — for Jesus Christ has a material body. A'Kempis is more referring to setting our affections on "things above" (Col. 3:2). Our first love must be the triune God — the Father, the Son, and the Holy Spirit.

1. This is the most basic lesson for the Christian student. The beginning of all knowledge is the fear of God (Prov. 1:7), and without the fear of God one does not have true knowledge.
2. To really know yourself in the light of God's truth, you will be humble. If you are not humble, you don't know yourself very well.

3. 1 Corinthians 13:2

4. A'Kempis sees the danger of education which does not keep the study of Scripture and the doctrine of salvation at the center. Much of education has corrupted churches and nations.

Vanity of vanities and all is vanity, except to love God and serve Him alone.[4]

This is the greatest wisdom—to seek the kingdom of heaven through contempt of the world. It is vanity, therefore, to seek and trust in riches that perish. It is vanity also to court honor and to be puffed up with pride. It is vanity to follow the lusts of the body and to desire things for which severe punishment later must come. It is vanity to wish for long life and to care little about a well-spent life. It is vanity to be concerned with the present only and not to make provision for things to come. It is vanity to love what passes quickly and not to look ahead where eternal joy abides.

Often recall the proverb: "The eye is not satisfied with seeing nor the ear filled with hearing." Try, moreover, to turn your heart from the love of things visible and bring yourself to things invisible.[5] For they who follow their own evil passions stain their consciences and lose the grace of God.

2. Having a Humble Opinion of Self

Every man naturally desires knowledge; but what good is knowledge without fear of God?[1] Indeed a humble rustic who serves God is better than a proud intellectual who neglects his soul to study the course of the stars. He who knows himself well becomes mean in his own eyes and is not happy when praised by men.[2]

If I knew all things in the world and had not charity, what would it profit me before God Who will judge me by my deeds?[3]

Shun too great a desire for knowledge, for in it there is much fretting and delusion. Intellectuals like to appear learned and to be called wise. Yet there are many things the knowledge of which does little or no good to the soul, and he who concerns himself about other things than those which lead to salvation is very unwise.[4]

Many words do not satisfy the soul; but a good life eases the mind and a clean conscience inspires great trust in God.

The more you know and the better you understand, the more severely will you be judged, unless your life is also the more holy.[5] Do not be proud, therefore, because of your learning or skill. Rather, fear because of the talent given you. If you think you know many things and understand them well enough, realize at the same time that there is much you do not know.[6] Hence, do not affect wisdom, but admit your ignorance. Why prefer yourself to anyone else when many are more learned, more cultured than you?

If you wish to learn and appreciate something worth while, then love to be unknown and considered as nothing. Truly to know and despise self is the best and most perfect counsel. To think of oneself as nothing, and always to think well and highly of others is the best and most perfect wisdom.[7] Wherefore, if you see another sin openly or commit a serious crime, do not consider yourself better, for you do not know how long you can remain in good estate. All men are frail, but you must admit that none is more frail than yourself.

3. The Doctrine of Truth

Happy is he to whom truth manifests itself, not in signs and words that fade, but as it actually is. Our opinions, our senses often deceive us and we discern very little.

What good is much discussion of involved and obscure matters when our ignorance of them will not be held against us on Judgment Day?[1] Neglect of things which are profitable and necessary and undue concern with those which are irrelevant and harmful, are great folly.

We have eyes and do not see.

What, therefore, have we to do with questions of philosophy? He to whom the Eternal Word speaks is free from theorizing.[2] For from this Word are all things and of Him all things speak—the Beginning Who also speaks to us. Without this Word no man understands or judges aright. He to

5. Increasing knowledge makes one more culpable to follow through and do the Word that is studied. This is the principle our Lord brings out in Luke 12:47-48.

6. The more we learn of God, the more we realize how much we do not know. Thus, increased knowledge should result in increased humility.

7. A'Kempis is a highly practical man when it comes to describing the essence of wisdom. He refers here to Phil. 2:3, as Paul instructs his readers: "In lowliness of mind let each esteem others better than himself."

1. A good test for the importance of any matter is whether it will still be important on Judgment Day. What does our Lord speak of as important on Judgment Day? (Reference Matthew 7 and Matthew 25).

2. So much of humanist philosophy taught by the Greeks and modern academics is just theory, mere guesswork, and usually deceitful.

3. This is the most fundamental description of a Christian view of knowledge. All teaching, all knowledge in all subjects must be connected to the Word of God.

4. The cacophony of opinions and ideas has only increased in the modern age. The confusion coming from social media and 1,000 other inputs has only increased. A'Kempis' words are relevant to us.

5. We will be much less frustrated and stressed in life if our number one focus is to do everything to the honor and glory of God.

6. It is the lusts of our hearts for riches and the approval of men that causes us so much distress in our lives.

7. A right and humble view of oneself will be a quicker way to knowledge than the constant pursuance of knowledge through books and college lectures.

8. Doing the Word of God is worth more than all of the knowledge in the world. On the day of judgment, Jesus will have a word of condemnation to those who were against His law (Matt. 7:23).

whom it becomes everything, who traces all things to it[3] and who sees all things in it, may ease his heart and remain at peace with God.

O God, You Who are the truth, make me one with You in love everlasting. I am often wearied by the many things I hear and read, but in You is all that I long for. Let the learned be still, let all creatures be silent before You; You alone speak to me.[4]

The more recollected a man is, and the more simple of heart he becomes, the easier he understands sublime things, for he receives the light of knowledge from above. The pure, simple, and steadfast spirit is not distracted by many labors, for he does them all for the honor of God.[5] And since he enjoys interior peace he seeks no selfish end in anything. What, indeed, gives more trouble and affliction than uncontrolled desires of the heart?[6]

A good and devout man arranges in his mind the things he has to do, not according to the whims of evil inclination but according to the dictates of right reason. Who is forced to struggle more than he who tries to master himself? This ought to be our purpose, then: to conquer self, to become stronger each day, to advance in virtue.

Every perfection in this life has some imperfection mixed with it and no learning of ours is without some darkness. Humble knowledge of self is a surer path to God than the ardent pursuit of learning.[7] Not that learning is to be considered evil, or knowledge, which is good in itself and so ordained by God; but a clean conscience and virtuous life ought always to be preferred. Many often err and accomplish little or nothing because they try to become learned rather than to live well.

If men used as much care in uprooting vices and implanting virtues as they do in discussing problems, there would not be so much evil and scandal in the world, or such laxity in religious organizations. On the day of judgment, surely, we shall not be asked what we have read but what we have done; not how well we have spoken but how well we have lived.[8]

Tell me, where now are all the masters and teachers whom you knew so well in life and who were famous for their learning? Others have already taken their places and I know not whether they ever think of their predecessors. During life they seemed to be something; now they are seldom remembered. How quickly the glory of the world passes away! If only their lives had kept pace with their learning, then their study and reading would have been worth while.

How many there are who perish because of vain worldly knowledge and too little care for serving God. They became vain in their own conceits because they chose to be great rather than humble.[9]

He is truly great who has great charity. He is truly great who is little in his own eyes and makes nothing of the highest honor. He is truly wise who looks upon all earthly things as folly that he may gain Christ. He who does God's will and renounces his own is truly very learned.[10]

9. When a man refuses to be humble and out of pride seeks fame and greatness, then foolishness dominates. This becomes a failure of a life.

10. True wisdom and knowledge is being humble, thinking of yourself as very insignificant, trading in the world's values for Christ and love.

4. Prudence in Action

Do not yield to every impulse and suggestion but consider things carefully and patiently in the light of God's will. For very often, sad to say, we are so weak that we believe and speak evil of others rather than good. Perfect men, however, do not readily believe every talebearer, because they know that human frailty is prone to evil[1] and is likely to appear in speech.

Not to act rashly or to cling obstinately to one's opinion, not to believe everything people say or to spread abroad the gossip one has heard, is great wisdom.[2]

Take counsel with a wise and conscientious man. Seek the advice of your betters in preference to following your own inclinations.

A good life makes a man wise according to God and gives him experience in many things, for the more humble he is and the more subject to God, the wiser and the more at peace he will be in all things.[3]

1. A'Kempis is convinced of the depravity of human nature. Natural man always tends to sin, and he is not to be trusted.

2. Being reticent to believe your own thoughts, as well as the gossip of others is a sign of great wisdom.

3. Here is another recipe for wisdom — be humble and quickly submit to God (in all His instructions and commands) and you will live a peaceful life.

1. A'Kempis does not trust intellectual books. He prefers the simple books that actually yield more humble obedience to God.
2. A wise person will quickly move away from books, blogs, films, or social media that he perceives is a waste of time — and robs him of time in God's Word.

3. A'Kempis' basic method for reading Scripture is to read with humility and simplicity. Take the simple and obvious meaning immediately. Don't get too intellectual about the Bible.

1. A'Kempis speaks of passions, most likely lusts for that which God has not given us. Seeking to satisfy these lusts will always end in frustration or a lack of peace.

2. Vain attractions that usually involve all the novels, movies, sports, or whatever is used as a means of escape. Peace comes when we are drawn to that which is spiritual, especially worship.

5. Reading the Holy Scripture

Truth, not eloquence, is to be sought in reading the Holy Scriptures; and every part must be read in the spirit in which it was written. For in the Scriptures we ought to seek profit rather than polished diction.

Likewise we ought to read simple and devout books as willingly as learned and profound ones. We ought not to be swayed by the authority of the writer, whether he be a great literary light or an insignificant person, but by the love of simple truth.[1] We ought not to ask who is speaking, but mark what is said. Men pass away, but the truth of the Lord remains forever. God speaks to us in many ways without regard for persons.

Our curiosity often impedes our reading of the Scriptures, when we wish to understand and mull over what we ought simply to read and pass by.[2]

If you would profit from it, therefore, read with humility, simplicity, and faith, and never seek a reputation for being learned.[3] Seek willingly and listen attentively to the words of the saints; do not be displeased with the sayings of the ancients, for they were not made without purpose.

6. Unbridled Affections

When a man desires a thing too much, he at once becomes ill at ease. A proud and avaricious man never rests, whereas he who is poor and humble of heart lives in a world of peace. An unmortified man is quickly tempted and overcome in small, trifling evils; his spirit is weak, in a measure carnal and inclined to sensual things; he can hardly abstain from earthly desires. Hence it makes him sad to forego them; he is quick to anger if reproved. Yet if he satisfies his desires, remorse of conscience overwhelms him because he followed his passions and they did not lead to the peace he sought.

True peace of heart, then, is found in resisting passions, not in satisfying them.[1] There is no peace in the carnal man, in the man given to vain attractions, but there is peace in the fervent and spiritual man.[2]

7. Avoiding false hope and pride

Vain is the man who puts his trust in men, in created things.

Do not be ashamed to serve others for the love of Jesus Christ and to seem poor in this world. Do not be self-sufficient but place your trust in God. Do what lies in your power and God will aid your good will. Put no trust in your own learning nor in the cunning of any man, but rather in the grace of God Who helps the humble and humbles the proud.

If you have wealth, do not glory in it, nor in friends because they are powerful, but in God Who gives all things and Who desires above all to give Himself.[1] Do not boast of personal stature or of physical beauty, qualities which are marred and destroyed by a little sickness. Do not take pride in your talent or ability, lest you displease God to Whom belongs all the natural gifts that you have.

Do not think yourself better than others lest, perhaps, you be accounted worse before God Who knows what is in man. Do not take pride in your good deeds, for God's judgments differ from those of men and what pleases them often displeases Him. If there is good in you, see more good in others, so that you may remain humble. It does no harm to esteem yourself less than anyone else, but it is very harmful to think yourself better than even one.[2] The humble live in continuous peace, while in the hearts of the proud are envy and frequent anger.

1. A'Kempis does not condemn wealth, but warns us not to trust in riches or glory in them. Glory rather in God who gives us all things.

2. Always err on the side of devaluing yourself (when comparing yourself with others.) It is always best to esteem yourself less than everybody else.

8. Shunning Over-familiarity

Do not open your heart to every man, but discuss your affairs with one who is wise and who fears God.[1] Do not keep company with young people and strangers. Do not fawn upon the rich, and do not be fond of mingling with the great. Associate with the humble and the simple, with the devout and virtuous, and with them speak of edifying things.[2] Be not intimate with any woman, but generally commend all good women to God. Seek only the intimacy of God and of His angels, and avoid the notice of men.[3]

1. The best counselor is the one who fears God.

2. Romans 12:16

3. A'Kempis discourages spending too much time with others. He rather recommends closeness with God and extended time for prayer.

4. A'Kempis recommends love, but not familiarity. Love is the biblical mandate, and surely closeness is not the priority (which is what people are usually looking for). Closeness introduces risks and may not be wise in some cases. However close relationships are not essentially wrong

We ought to have charity for all men but familiarity with all is not expedient.[4] Sometimes it happens that a person enjoys a good reputation among those who do not know him, but at the same time is held in slight regard by those who do. Frequently we think we are pleasing others by our presence and we begin rather to displease them by the faults they find in us.

9. Obedience and Subjection

1. Subjection to authority is natural in this world. But, we are only happy when we submit to our church leaders or business leaders out of love for God.

It is a very great thing to obey, to live under a superior and not to be one's own master, for it is much safer to be subject than it is to command. Many live in obedience more from necessity than from love. Such become discontented and dejected on the slightest pretext; they will never gain peace of mind unless they subject themselves wholeheartedly for the love of God.[1]

2. People tend to want to move from one church to the next because they find it uncomfortable to submit to church authority. It is easier do this in the present day than it was 600 years ago when this was written.

Go where you may, you will find no rest except in humble obedience to the rule of authority.[2] Dreams of happiness expected from change and different places have deceived many.

Everyone, it is true, wishes to do as he pleases and is attracted to those who agree with him. But if God be among us, we must at times give up our opinions for the blessings of peace.[3]

3. Peace with others is a high priority. It is worthwhile to sacrifice for peace.

Furthermore, who is so wise that he can have full knowledge of everything? Do not trust too much in your own opinions, but be willing to listen to those of others. If, though your own be good, you accept another's opinion for love of God, you will gain much more merit; for I have often heard that it is safer to listen to advice and take it than to give it. It may happen, too, that while one's own opinion may be good, refusal to agree with others when reason and occasion demand it, is a sign of pride and obstinacy.

10. Avoiding Idle Talk

Shun the gossip of men as much as possible, for discussion of worldly affairs, even though sincere, is a great distraction inasmuch as we are quickly ensnared and captivated by vanity.[1]

Many a time I wish that I had held my peace and had not associated with men. Why, indeed, do we converse and gossip among ourselves when we so seldom part without a troubled conscience? We do so because we seek comfort from one another's conversation and wish to ease the mind wearied by diverse thoughts. Hence, we talk and think quite fondly of things we like very much or of things we dislike intensely. But, sad to say, we often talk vainly and to no purpose; for this external pleasure effectively bars inward and divine consolation.[2]

Therefore we must watch and pray lest time pass idly.

When the right and opportune moment comes for speaking, say something that will edify.

Bad habits and indifference to spiritual progress do much to remove the guard from the tongue.[3] Devout conversation on spiritual matters, on the contrary, is a great aid to spiritual progress, especially when persons of the same mind and spirit associate together in God.

1. World news and gossip is seldom that edifying. This can be a great distraction from more important things.

2. Much of day-to-day conversation is unedifying. Are our thoughts and words self-centered or God-centered?

3. Our conversation will be more sanctified when we are concerned about spiritual health first and foremost.

11. Acquiring Peace and Zeal for Perfection

We should enjoy much peace if we did not concern ourselves with what others say and do, for these are no concern of ours. How can a man who meddles in affairs not his own, who seeks strange distractions, and who is little or seldom inwardly recollected, live long in peace?[1]

Blessed are the simple of heart for they shall enjoy peace in abundance.

Why were some of the saints so perfect and so given to contemplation? Because they tried to mortify entirely in themselves all earthly desires, and thus they were able to at-

1. The thing that disturbs us is usually what others say and do. Our major concern should be our inward motives and sins. There is only peace when we know our sins are confessed and we are right with God.

2. The priority for the Christian is to be very watchful so as to avoid ALL distractions to the mind and to put to death sinful lusts and desires.

3. The cure for discouragement is to fight on against the sinful flesh all the while looking to God for help. Also, we need to avoid seeking after human consolation.

4. New converts who have recently come to Christ in faith are often on fire for God. A'Kempis laments that so many lose their fervor and no longer go after their vice.

5. It is always easier to nip our sins in the bud.

tach themselves to God with all their heart and freely to concentrate their innermost thoughts.

We are too occupied with our own whims and fancies, too taken up with passing things. Rarely do we completely conquer even one vice, and we are not inflamed with the desire to improve ourselves day by day; hence, we remain cold and indifferent. If we mortified our bodies perfectly and allowed no distractions to enter our minds, we could appreciate divine things and experience something of heavenly contemplation.[2]

The greatest obstacle, indeed, the only obstacle, is that we are not free from passions and lusts, that we do not try to follow the perfect way of the saints. Thus when we encounter some slight difficulty, we are too easily dejected and turn to human consolations. If we tried, however, to stand as brave men in battle, the help of the Lord from heaven would surely sustain us. For He Who gives us the opportunity of fighting for victory, is ready to help those who carry on and trust in His grace.[3]

If we let our progress in religious life depend on the observance of its externals alone, our devotion will quickly come to an end. Let us, then, lay the ax to the root that we may be freed from our passions and thus have peace of mind.

If we were to uproot only one vice each year, we should soon become perfect. The contrary, however, is often the case—we feel that we were better and purer in the first fervor of our conversion than we are after many years in the practice of our faith. Our fervor and progress ought to increase day by day; yet it is now considered noteworthy if a man can retain even a part of his first fervor.[4]

If we did a little violence to ourselves at the start, we should afterwards be able to do all things with ease and joy. It is hard to break old habits, but harder still to go against our will.

If you do not overcome small, trifling things, how will you overcome the more difficult? Resist temptations in the beginning, and unlearn the evil habit lest perhaps, little by little, it lead to a more evil one.[5]

If you but consider what peace a good life will bring to yourself and what joy it will give to others, I think you will be more concerned about your spiritual progress.

12. The Value of Adversity

It is good for us to have trials and troubles at times, for they often remind us that we are on probation and ought not to hope in any worldly thing. It is good for us sometimes to suffer contradiction, to be misjudged by men even though we do well and mean well. These things help us to be humble and shield us from vainglory.[1] When to all outward appearances men give us no credit, when they do not think well of us, then we are more inclined to seek God Who sees our hearts.[2] Therefore, a man ought to root himself so firmly in God that he will not need the consolations of men.

When a man of good will is afflicted, tempted, and tormented by evil thoughts, he realizes clearly that his greatest need is God, without Whom he can do no good. Saddened by his miseries and sufferings, he laments and prays. He wearies of living longer and wishes for death that he might be dissolved and be with Christ. Then he understands fully that perfect security and complete peace cannot be found on earth.[3]

1. Any criticism we receive from men (whether warranted or not) serves a good purpose. It humbles us, and we can always use that.

2. When men criticize our outward behavior, we ought to be humbled. But the real humility comes when we submit ourselves to God's piercing eye, which evaluates the real problems that lurk deep in our hearts.

3. The sooner we stop looking for complete security and peace on earth, the better. In our afflictions, the sooner we see that God is our greatest need, the better.

13. Resisting Temptation

So long as we live in this world we cannot escape suffering and temptation. Whence it is written in Job: "The life of man upon earth is a warfare."[1] Everyone, therefore, must guard against temptation and must watch in prayer lest the devil, who never sleeps but goes about seeking whom he may devour, find occasion to deceive him.[2] No one is so perfect or so holy but he is sometimes tempted; man cannot be altogether free from temptation.

Yet temptations, though troublesome and severe, are often useful to a man, for in them he is humbled, purified, and

1. Job 7:1

2. 1 Peter 5:8

3. One's response to trials will determine whether his faith was real and substantial or not. A'Kempis refers to the reprobate of Hebrews 12:12-17 and Hebrews 6:4-6.

4. A'Kempis holds to the doctrine of original sin. We were all born sinners.

5. We must develop an inner strength to overcome temptation.

6. We overcome temptation by the help of God and patience, not so much by severe self-discipline or beating on ourselves.

7. The battle against temptation is first fought in the mind.

instructed. The saints all passed through many temptations and trials to profit by them, while those who could not resist became reprobate and fell away.[3] There is no state so holy, no place so secret that temptations and trials will not come. Man is never safe from them as long as he lives, for they come from within us—in sin we were born.[4] When one temptation or trial passes, another comes; we shall always have something to suffer because we have lost the state of original blessedness.

Many people try to escape temptations, only to fall more deeply. We cannot conquer simply by fleeing, but by patience and true humility we become stronger than all our enemies.[5] The man who only shuns temptations outwardly and does not uproot them will make little progress; indeed they will quickly return, more violent than before.

Little by little, in patience and long-suffering you will overcome them, by the help of God rather than by severity and your own rash ways.[6] Often take counsel when tempted; and do not be harsh with others who are tempted, but console them as you yourself would wish to be consoled.

The beginning of all temptation lies in a wavering mind and little trust in God, for as a rudderless ship is driven hither and yon by waves, so a careless and irresolute man is tempted in many ways. Fire tempers iron and temptation steels the just. Often we do not know what we can stand, but temptation shows us what we are.

Above all, we must be especially alert against the beginnings of temptation, for the enemy is more easily conquered if he is refused admittance to the mind and is met beyond the threshold when he knocks.[7]

Someone has said very aptly: "Resist the beginnings; remedies come too late, when by long delay the evil has gained strength." First, a mere thought comes to mind, then strong imagination, followed by pleasure, evil delight, and consent. Thus, because he is not resisted in the beginning, Satan gains full entry. And the longer a man delays in resisting, so much the weaker does he become each day, while the strength of the enemy grows against him.

Some suffer great temptations in the beginning of their conversion, others toward the end, while some are troubled almost constantly throughout their life. Others, again, are tempted but lightly according to the wisdom and justice of Divine Providence Who weighs the status and merit of each and prepares all for the salvation of His elect.[8]

We should not despair, therefore, when we are tempted, but pray to God the more fervently that He may see fit to help us, for according to the word of Paul, He will make issue with temptation that we may be able to bear it.[9] Let us humble our souls under the hand of God in every trial and temptation for He will save and exalt the humble in spirit.

In temptations and trials the progress of a man is measured; in them opportunity for merit and virtue is made more manifest.

When a man is not troubled it is not hard for him to be fervent and devout, but if he bears up patiently in time of adversity, there is hope for great progress.[10]

Some, guarded against great temptations, are frequently overcome by small ones in order that, humbled by their weakness in small trials, they may not presume on their own strength in great ones.

8. A'Kempis testifies to God's absolute sovereign control over all the temptations and trials. God will see that all the elect will be saved, even through these trials He has ordained for them.

9. 1 Corinthians 10:13

10. Devotion in worship is not nearly as important a sign of spiritual maturity as bearing up well under trials.

14. Avoiding Rash Judgment

Turn your attention upon yourself and beware of judging the deeds of other men, for in judging others a man labors vainly, often makes mistakes, and easily sins; whereas, in judging and taking stock of himself he does something that is always profitable.[1]

We frequently judge that things are as we wish them to be, for through personal feeling true perspective is easily lost.[2]

If God were the sole object of our desire, we should not be disturbed so easily by opposition to our opinions. But often

1. Judging others is always a risk. Spend more time judging yourself rather than others.

2. We lose perspective when we fail to judge by God's standard.

something lurks within or happens from without to draw us along with it.

Many, unawares, seek themselves in the things they do. They seem even to enjoy peace of mind when things happen according to their wish and liking, but if otherwise than they desire, they are soon disturbed and saddened.[3] Differences of feeling and opinion often divide friends and acquaintances, even those who are religious and devout.

An old habit is hard to break, and no one is willing to be led farther than he can see.

If you rely more upon your intelligence or industry than upon the virtue of submission to Jesus Christ, you will hardly, and in any case slowly, become an enlightened man. God wants us to be completely subject to Him and, through ardent love, to rise above all human wisdom.[4]

3. When we live our lives in a self-centered way, we are given to ups and downs. Instead, we should be centered on God, His sovereign will, and His revealed law.

4. Ultimate wisdom is found in submitting to Jesus Christ and loving Him.

15. Works Done in Charity

Never do evil for anything in the world, or for the love of any man.[1] For one who is in need, however, a good work may at times be purposely left undone or changed for a better one. This is not the omission of a good deed but rather its improvement.

Without charity external work is of no value, but anything done in charity, be it ever so small and trivial, is entirely fruitful inasmuch as God weighs the love with which a man acts rather than the deed itself.[2]

He does much who loves much. He does much who does a thing well. He does well who serves the common good rather than his own interests.

Now, that which seems to be charity is oftentimes really sensuality, for man's own inclination, his own will, his hope of reward, and his self-interest, are motives seldom absent.[3] On the contrary, he who has true and perfect charity seeks self in nothing, but searches all things for the glory of God. Moreover, he envies no man, because he desires no personal

1. Love can never involve breaking God's commandments (and doing evil).

2. The rightness of an action is measured by the love of God and love for others contained in it.

3. So much of worldly sensual love (including worldly music) is fake love, because self is dominant. This love is not self-sacrificing. It is self-consumed.

pleasure nor does he wish to rejoice in himself; rather he desires the greater glory of God above all things. He ascribes to man nothing that is good but attributes it wholly to God from Whom all things proceed as from a fountain, and in Whom all the blessed shall rest as their last end and fruition.[4]

If man had but a spark of true charity he would surely sense that all the things of earth are full of vanity!

4. Love for God will seek the glory of God, and will note that all goodness flows from God. The result is gratitude.

16. Bearing With the Faults of Others

Until God ordains otherwise, a man ought to bear patiently whatever he cannot correct in himself and in others. Consider it better thus—perhaps to try your patience and to test you, for without such patience and trial your merits are of little account. Nevertheless, under such difficulties you should pray that God will consent to help you bear them calmly.

If, after being admonished once or twice, a person does not amend, do not argue with him but commit the whole matter to God that His will and honor may be furthered in all His servants, for God knows well how to turn evil to good. Try to bear patiently with the defects and infirmities of others, whatever they may be, because you also have many a fault which others must endure.[1]

If you cannot make yourself what you would wish to be, how can you bend others to your will? We want them to be perfect, yet we do not correct our own faults. We wish them to be severely corrected, yet we will not correct ourselves. Their great liberty displeases us, yet we would not be denied what we ask. We would have them bound by laws, yet we will allow ourselves to be restrained in nothing. Hence, it is clear how seldom we think of others as we do of ourselves.

If all were perfect, what should we have to suffer from others for God's sake?[2] But God has so ordained, that we may learn to bear with one another's burdens, for there is no man without fault, no man without burden, no man sufficient to himself nor wise enough. Hence we must support one another,

1. A'Kempis encourages us to be patient with the sins of others. This patience comes by humility when we realize that we struggle with sins of similar seriousness.

2. Much of our suffering is tied into the faults of others, especially when they cause us offenses. These are the trials God has ordained for us. He is testing us to see how well we bear up under them.

console one another, mutually help, counsel, and advise, for the measure of every man's virtue is best revealed in time of adversity—adversity that does not weaken a man but rather shows what he is.

17. Monastic Life

If you wish peace and concord with others, you must learn to break your will in many things. To live in monasteries or religious communities, to remain there without complaint, and to persevere faithfully till death is no small matter. Blessed indeed is he who there lives a good life and there ends his days in happiness.

If you would persevere in seeking perfection, you must consider yourself a pilgrim, an exile on earth. If you would become a religious,[1] you must be content to seem a fool for the sake of Christ. Habit and tonsure[2] change a man but little; it is the change of life, the complete mortification of passions that endow a true religious.[3] He who seeks anything but God alone and the salvation of his soul will find only trouble and grief, and he who does not try to become the least, the servant of all, cannot remain at peace for long.[4]

You have come to serve, not to rule. You must understand, too, that you have been called to suffer and to work, not to idle and gossip away your time. Here men are tried as gold in a furnace. Here no man can remain unless he desires with all his heart to humble himself before God.

18. The Example Set Us by the Holy Fathers

Consider the lively examples set us by the saints, who possessed the light of true perfection and religion, and you will see how little, how nearly nothing, we do. What, alas, is our life, compared with theirs? The saints and friends of Christ served the Lord in hunger and thirst, in cold and nakedness, in work and fatigue, in vigils and fasts, in prayers and holy meditations, in persecutions and many afflictions.[1] How many and severe were the trials they suffered—the Apostles, mar-

---

1. A "religious" is one who has committed himself to a religious order.

2. A habit is the monk's external garb, and a tonsure is the bare spot at the top of his head.

3. Attending church and dressing a certain way is not the test of true piety. It is the mortification of lusts and sins in the life that constitutes true piety.

4. A'Kempis advises that a man seek three things — God, salvation, and humility. This will bring peace.

1. A'Kempis looks back upon the saints who had suffered under the Roman persecutions (AD 33 - AD 325). In some respects, this would be considered the most spiritually mature era of the Western church (in the 15th century).

tyrs, confessors, virgins, and all the rest who willed to follow in the footsteps of Christ! They hated their lives on earth that they might have life in eternity.

How strict and detached were the lives the holy hermits led in the desert![2] What long and grave temptations they suffered! How often were they beset by the enemy! What frequent and ardent prayers they offered to God! What rigorous fasts they observed! How great their zeal and their love for spiritual perfection! How brave the fight they waged to master their evil habits! What pure and straightforward purpose they showed toward God! By day they labored and by night they spent themselves in long prayers. Even at work they did not cease from mental prayer. They used all their time profitably; every hour seemed too short for serving God, and in the great sweetness of contemplation, they forgot even their bodily needs.

They renounced all riches, dignities, honors, friends, and associates. They desired nothing of the world. They scarcely allowed themselves the necessities of life, and the service of the body, even when necessary, was irksome to them. They were poor in earthly things but rich in grace and virtue. Outwardly destitute, inwardly they were full of grace and divine consolation. Strangers to the world, they were close and intimate friends of God. To themselves they seemed as nothing, and they were despised by the world, but in the eyes of God they were precious and beloved. They lived in true humility and simple obedience; they walked in charity and patience, making progress daily on the pathway of spiritual life and obtaining great favor with God.

They were given as an example for all religious, and their power to stimulate us to perfection ought to be greater than that of the lukewarm to tempt us to laxity.

How great was the fervor of all religious in the beginning of their holy institution! How great their devotion in prayer and their rivalry for virtue! What splendid discipline flourished among them! What great reverence and obedience in all

2. This is reference to Anthony the Great, who took to the desert in Egypt around AD 270. Also Paul of Thebes, Arsenius the Great, Macarius of Egypt, and Pachomius. Chrysostom and Athanasius also spend some time as desert monks.

3. A'Kempis may have an overly rosy view of the "good old days" when discipline and piety was strong in the early church. However, his disappointment with the religious orders of his day was probably well-founded. During A'Kempis' lifetime, Pope Urban VI set off the Great Schism, and he was known for murdering his competitors. Pope John XXIII was also deposed on accusations of piracy, rape, sodomy, murder, and incest.

1. The true Christian is interested in sanctification on the inside as well as the outside. All religious hypocrites are skilled at polishing the outside. The genuine Christian seeks a purity on the inside, in thoughts and motives, as well as external actions.

2. This is key. Relying on the grace of God is essential and basic in our sanctification. We cannot overcome sin in our own strength.

things under the rule of a superior! The footsteps they left behind still bear witness that they indeed were holy and perfect men who fought bravely and conquered the world.

Today, he who is not a transgressor and who can bear patiently the duties which he has taken upon himself is considered great. How lukewarm and negligent we are![3] We lose our original fervor very quickly and we even become weary of life from laziness! Do not you, who have seen so many examples of the devout, fall asleep in the pursuit of virtue!

19. The Practices of a Good Religious

The life of a good religious ought to abound in every virtue so that he is interiorly what to others he appears to be. With good reason there ought to be much more within than appears on the outside,[1] for He who sees within is God, Whom we ought to reverence most highly wherever we are and in Whose sight we ought to walk pure as the angels.

Each day we ought to renew our resolutions and arouse ourselves to fervor as though it were the first day of our religious life. We ought to say: "Help me, O Lord God, in my good resolution and in Your holy service. Grant me now, this very day, to begin perfectly, for thus far I have done nothing."

As our intention is, so will be our progress; and he who desires perfection must be very diligent. If the strong-willed man fails frequently, what of the man who makes up his mind seldom or half-heartedly? Many are the ways of failing in our resolutions; even a slight omission of religious practice entails a loss of some kind.

Just men depend on the grace of God rather than on their own wisdom in keeping their resolutions.[2] In Him they confide every undertaking, for man, indeed, proposes but God disposes, and God's way is not man's.[3] If a habitual exercise is sometimes omitted out of piety or in the interests of another, it can easily be resumed later. But if it be abandoned carelessly, through weariness or neglect, then the fault is great and will prove hurtful. Much as we try, we still fail too easily in many things. Yet we must always have some fixed purpose, especially against things which beset us the most. Our outward and inward lives alike must be closely watched and well ordered, for both are important to perfection.

If you cannot recollect yourself continuously, do so once a day at least, in the morning or in the evening. In the morning make a resolution and in the evening examine yourself on what you have said this day, what you have done and thought, for in these things perhaps you have often offended God and those about you.

Arm yourself like a man against the devil's assaults. Curb your appetite and you will more easily curb every inclination of the flesh. Never be completely unoccupied, but read or write or pray or meditate or do something for the common good.[4] Bodily discipline, however, must be undertaken with discretion and is not to be practiced indiscriminately by everyone.

Devotions not common to all are not to be displayed in public, for such personal things are better performed in private. Furthermore, beware of indifference to community prayer through love of your own devotions.[5] If, however, after doing completely and faithfully all you are bound and commanded to do, you then have leisure, use it as personal piety suggests.

Not everyone can have the same devotion. One exactly suits this person, another that. Different exercises, likewise, are suitable for different times, some for feast days and some again for weekdays. In time of temptation we need certain devotions. For days of rest and peace we need others. Some are suitable when we are sad, others when we are joyful in the Lord.

About the time of the principal feasts good devotions ought to be renewed and the intercession of the saints more fervently implored.[6] From one feast day to the next we ought

3. This may be A'Kempis' most famous statement. This acknowledges the sovereignty of God as basic in our salvation, and particularly our sanctification. We may propose to get rid of a sin, but it is God who does the primary work in us "both to will and to do of His good pleasure." (Phil. 2:13)

4. It takes discipline and consistency in prayer and reading the Word to ward off Satanic attack. Too much entertainment and leisure will also tend to get in the way of vigilance.

5. The Christian life must include daily personal devotions and daily family devotions (or corporate devotions with the body of the church).

6. Intercession of the saints has biblical backing if this is a prayer in line with Romans 15:30, living saints interceding for other Christians.

to fix our purpose as though we were then to pass from this world and come to the eternal holyday.

During holy seasons, finally, we ought to prepare ourselves carefully, to live holier lives, and to observe each rule more strictly, as though we were soon to receive from God the reward of our labors. If this end be deferred, let us believe that we are not well prepared and that we are not yet worthy of the great glory that shall in due time be revealed to us. Let us try, meanwhile, to prepare ourselves better for death.

"Blessed is the servant," says Christ, "whom his master, when he cometh, shall find watching. Amen I say to you: he shall make him ruler over all his goods."[7]

7. Matthew 24:47.

20. The Love of Solitude and Silence

Seek a suitable time for leisure and meditate often on the favors of God. Leave curiosities alone. Read such matters as bring sorrow to the heart rather than occupation to the mind. If you withdraw yourself from unnecessary talking and idle running about, from listening to gossip and rumors, you will find enough time that is suitable for holy meditation.

Very many great saints avoided the company of men wherever possible and chose to serve God in retirement. "As often as I have been among men," said one writer, "I have returned less a man."[1] We often find this to be true when we take part in long conversations. It is easier to be silent altogether than not to speak too much. To stay at home is easier than to be sufficiently on guard while away. Anyone, then, who aims to live the inner and spiritual life must go apart, with Jesus, from the crowd.

No man appears in safety before the public eye unless he first relishes obscurity. No man is safe in speaking unless he loves to be silent. No man rules safely unless he is willing to be ruled. No man commands safely unless he has learned well how to obey. No man rejoices safely unless he has within him the testimony of a good conscience.[2]

1. A quotation from Seneca, the Roman historian. The quotation is true as far as the conversations with other men are foolish and unedifying.

2. It is always better to err towards silence, towards avoiding the public eye, and towards submitting to authority. No leader will ever lead well unless he submits first.

More than this, the security of the saints was always enveloped in the fear of God, nor were they less cautious and humble because they were conspicuous for great virtues and graces.[3] The security of the wicked, on the contrary, springs from pride and presumption, and will end in their own deception.

Never promise yourself security in this life, even though you seem to be a good religious, or a devout hermit. It happens very often that those whom men esteem highly are more seriously endangered by their own excessive confidence. Hence, for many it is better not to be too free from temptations, but often to be tried lest they become too secure, too filled with pride, or even too eager to fall back upon external comforts.[4]

If only a man would never seek passing joys or entangle himself with worldly affairs, what a good conscience he would have. What great peace and tranquillity would be his, if he cut himself off from all empty care and thought only of things divine, things helpful to his soul, and put all his trust in God.

No man deserves the consolation of heaven unless he persistently arouses himself to holy contrition. If you desire true sorrow of heart, seek the privacy of your cell and shut out the uproar of the world,[5] as it is written: "In your chamber bewail your sins." There you will find what too often you lose abroad.

Your cell will become dear to you if you remain in it, but if you do not, it will become wearisome. If in the beginning of your religious life, you live within your cell and keep to it, it will soon become a special friend and a very great comfort.

In silence and quiet the devout soul advances in virtue and learns the hidden truths of Scripture. There she finds a flood of tears with which to bathe and cleanse herself nightly, that she may become the more intimate with her Creator the farther she withdraws from all the tumult of the world.[6] For God and His holy angels will draw near to him who withdraws from friends and acquaintances.

It is better for a man to be obscure and to attend to his salvation than to neglect it and work miracles.[7] It is praiseworthy

3. The mature saint will stay on his guard even if he is demonstrating a virtuous life.

4. Some will try to escape the world's influences in hopes they can avoid spiritual battles and live a comfortable life. This is a wrong motive and will lead to complacency and pride (as it does to some sects in our day as well.)

5. The Christian confesses his sins to God in his prayer closet (cell).

6. A'Kempis includes women as well as men in his exhortation to confess sins.

7. A man's relationship with God is of higher priority than working miracles and doing "big things." Reference Matthew 7:22-23.

8. 1 John 2:17.

9. How often do we prefer the trivial or the earthy things to the heavenly things? When we immerse ourselves in worldly gossip, salacious news stories, and things that do not edify, we are usually cast into sorrow and frustration.

for a religious seldom to go abroad, to flee the sight of men and have no wish to see them.

Why wish to see what you are not permitted to have? "The world passes away and the concupiscence thereof."[8] Sensual craving sometimes entices you to wander around, but when the moment is past, what do you bring back with you save a disturbed conscience and heavy heart? A happy going often leads to a sad return, a merry evening to a mournful dawn. Thus, all carnal joy begins sweetly but in the end brings remorse and death.

What can you find elsewhere that you cannot find here in your cell? Behold heaven and earth and all the elements, for of these all things are made. What can you see anywhere under the sun that will remain long? Perhaps you think you will completely satisfy yourself, but you cannot do so, for if you should see all existing things, what would they be but an empty vision?

Raise your eyes to God in heaven and pray because of your sins and shortcomings. Leave vanity to the vain. Set yourself to the things which God has commanded you to do. Close the door upon yourself and call to you Jesus, your Beloved. Remain with Him in your cell, for nowhere else will you find such peace. If you had not left it, and had not listened to idle gossip, you would have remained in greater peace. But since you love, sometimes, to hear news, it is only right that you should suffer sorrow of heart from it.[9]

21. Sorrow of Heart

If you wish to make progress in virtue, live in the fear of the Lord, do not look for too much freedom, discipline your senses, and shun inane silliness. Sorrow opens the door to many a blessing which dissoluteness usually destroys.

It is a wonder that any man who considers and meditates on his exiled state and the many dangers to his soul, can ever be perfectly happy in this life. Lighthearted and heedless of our defects, we do not feel the real sorrows of our souls, but often indulge in empty laughter when we have good reason to weep.[1] No liberty is true and no joy is genuine unless it is founded in the fear of the Lord[2] and a good conscience.

Happy is the man who can throw off the weight of every care and recollect himself in holy contrition. Happy is the man who casts from him all that can stain or burden his conscience.

Fight like a man. Habit is overcome by habit. If you leave men alone, they will leave you alone to do what you have to do. Do not busy yourself about the affairs of others and do not become entangled in the business of your superiors. Keep an eye primarily on yourself and admonish yourself instead of your friends.[3]

If you do not enjoy the favor of men, do not let it sadden you; but consider it a serious matter if you do not conduct yourself as well or as carefully as is becoming for a servant of God and a devout religious.

It is often better and safer for us to have few consolations in this life, especially comforts of the body.[4] Yet if we do not have divine consolation or experience it rarely, it is our own fault because we seek no sorrow of heart and do not forsake vain outward satisfaction.

Consider yourself unworthy of divine solace and deserving rather of much tribulation. When a man is perfectly contrite, the whole world is bitter and wearisome to him.[5]

A good man always finds enough over which to mourn and weep; whether he thinks of himself or of his neighbor he knows that no one lives here without suffering, and the closer he examines himself the more he grieves.[6]

The sins and vices in which we are so entangled that we can rarely apply ourselves to the contemplation of heaven are matters for just sorrow and inner remorse.

I do not doubt that you would correct yourself more earnestly if you would think more of an early death than of a long life. And if you pondered in your heart the future pains of hell or of purgatory,[7] I believe you would willingly endure

1. "Blessed are those who mourn, for they shall be comforted." (Matthew 5:4)

2. Proverbs 1:7, 23:7.

3. Spend more time considering and confessing your own sin, and you will have less time to be thinking about the sins of others.

4. Divine consolation and comfort is better than superficial comforts like food and entertainment (which only serve as band-aids for our spiritual and emotional aches).

5. The world loses its attractiveness, especially as it tempts Christians with lust and pride incessantly — and they witness the almost constant torrent of evil in culture.

6. The believer feels the heart of Jesus in this wicked world. However, he has two reasons to grieve: the sin in the world and the sin in his own heart.

7. A'Kempis maintained the Roman Catholic and unbiblical doctrine of purgatory.

labor and trouble and would fear no hardship. But since these thoughts never pierce the heart and since we are enamored of flattering pleasure, we remain very cold and indifferent. Our wretched body complains so easily because our soul is altogether too lifeless.

Pray humbly to the Lord, therefore, that He may give you the spirit of contrition and say with the Prophet: "Feed me, Lord, with the bread of mourning and give me to drink of tears in full measure."[8]

8. Psalm 80:5.

22. Thoughts on the Misery Of Man

Wherever you are, wherever you go, you are miserable unless you turn to God. So why be dismayed when things do not happen as you wish and desire? Is there anyone who has everything as he wishes? No—neither I, nor you, nor any man on earth. There is no one in the world, be he Pope or king, who does not suffer trial and anguish.

Who is the better off then? Surely, it is the man who will suffer something for God. Many unstable and weak-minded people say: "See how well that man lives, how rich, how great he is, how powerful and mighty." But you must lift up your eyes to the riches of heaven and realize that the material goods of which they speak are nothing. These things are uncertain and very burdensome because they are never possessed without anxiety and fear.[1] Man's happiness does not consist in the possession of abundant goods; a very little is enough.

Living on earth is truly a misery. The more a man desires spiritual life, the more bitter the present becomes to him, because he understands better and sees more clearly the defects, the corruption of human nature. To eat and drink, to watch and sleep, to rest, to labor, and to be bound by other human necessities is certainly a great misery and affliction to the devout man, who would gladly be released from them and be free from all sin. Truly, the inner man is greatly burdened in this world by the necessities of the body, and for this reason the

1. A'Kempis rightly points out that riches actually add more of a burden and are uncertain. Reference 1 Timothy 6:17 and Proverbs 11:28.

Prophet prayed that he might be as free from them as possible, when he said: "From my necessities, O Lord, deliver me."[2]

But woe to those who know not their own misery, and greater woe to those who love this miserable and corruptible life.[3] Some, indeed, can scarcely procure its necessities either by work or by begging; yet they love it so much that, if they could live here always, they would care nothing for the kingdom of God.

How foolish and faithless of heart are those who are so engrossed in earthly things as to relish nothing but what is carnal! Miserable men indeed, for in the end they will see to their sorrow how cheap and worthless was the thing they loved.

The saints of God and all devout friends of Christ did not look to what pleases the body nor to the things that are popular from time to time. Their whole hope and aim centered on the everlasting good. Their whole desire pointed upward to the lasting and invisible realm, lest the love of what is visible drag them down to lower things.

Do not lose heart, then, my brother, in pursuing your spiritual life. There is yet time, and your hour is not past. Why delay your purpose? Arise! Begin at once and say: "Now is the time to act, now is the time to fight, now is the proper time to amend."

When you are troubled and afflicted, that is the time to gain merit. You must pass through water and fire before coming to rest. Unless you do violence to yourself you will not overcome vice.[4]

So long as we live in this fragile body, we can neither be free from sin nor live without weariness and sorrow. Gladly would we rest from all misery, but in losing innocence through sin we also lost true blessedness. Therefore, we must have patience and await the mercy of God until this iniquity passes, until mortality is swallowed up in life.[5]

How great is the frailty of human nature which is ever prone to evil! Today you confess your sins and tomorrow you again commit the sins which you confessed. One moment you

2. The necessities of the body are not evil, and A'Kempis verges into a neo-Platonism here (not unusual, even among some reformers in the 16th century). God created the body with necessities. However, our sinful flesh will often turn necessities into lust.
3. To love this life more than the life which is to come is the problem. Jesus encourages us to hate our life here that we gain the better life (John 12:25).

4. "[...] the kingdom of heaven suffers violence, and the violent take it by force." (Matthew 11:12) The Christian life calls for a violent killing of the flesh — true spiritual effort, true spiritual discipline.

5. There will be no sinless perfection in this life. God's infinite mercy will see to it we are perfected in glory.

resolve to be careful, and yet after an hour you act as though you had made no resolution.

We have cause, therefore, because of our frailty and feebleness, to humble ourselves and never think anything great of ourselves.[6] Through neglect we may quickly lose that which by God's grace we have acquired only through long, hard labor. What, eventually, will become of us who so quickly grow lukewarm? Woe to us if we presume to rest in peace and security when actually there is no true holiness in our lives. It would be beneficial for us, like good novices, to be instructed once more in the principles of a good life, to see if there be hope of amendment and greater spiritual progress in the future.

6. Our sin is a constant reminder of our weakness, and should keep us in a position of humility and crying out to God for His mercy and forgiveness.

23. Thoughts on Death

Very soon your life here will end; consider, then, what may be in store for you elsewhere. Today we live; tomorrow we die and are quickly forgotten. Oh, the dullness and hardness of a heart which looks only to the present instead of preparing for that which is to come!

Therefore, in every deed and every thought, act as though you were to die this very day. If you had a good conscience you would not fear death very much. It is better to avoid sin than to fear death. If you are not prepared today, how will you be prepared tomorrow? Tomorrow is an uncertain day; how do you know you will have a tomorrow?

What good is it to live a long life when we amend that life so little? Indeed, a long life does not always benefit us, but on the contrary, frequently adds to our guilt. Would that in this world we had lived well throughout one single day. Many count up the years they have spent in religion but find their lives made little holier. If it is so terrifying to die, it is nevertheless possible that to live longer is more dangerous. Blessed is he who keeps the moment of death ever before his eyes and prepares for it every day.[1]

1. Wisdom calls us to live with an eye on our eventual death (Ecclesiastes 7:2).

If you have ever seen a man die, remember that you, too, must go the same way. In the morning consider that you may not live till evening, and when evening comes do not dare to promise yourself the dawn. Be always ready, therefore, and so live that death will never take you unprepared. Many die suddenly and unexpectedly, for in the unexpected hour the Son of God will come. When that last moment arrives you will begin to have a quite different opinion of the life that is now entirely past and you will regret very much that you were so careless and remiss.

How happy and prudent is he who tries now in life to be what he wants to be found in death. Perfect contempt of the world, a lively desire to advance in virtue, a love for discipline, the works of penance, readiness to obey, self-denial, and the endurance of every hardship for the love of Christ, these will give a man great expectations of a happy death.[2]

You can do many good works when in good health; what can you do when you are ill? Few are made better by sickness. Likewise they who undertake many pilgrimages seldom become holy.

Do not put your trust in friends and relatives, and do not put off the care of your soul till later, for men will forget you more quickly than you think. It is better to provide now, in time, and send some good account ahead of you than to rely on the help of others. If you do not care for your own welfare now, who will care when you are gone?

The present is very precious; these are the days of salvation; now is the acceptable time. How sad that you do not spend the time in which you might purchase everlasting life in a better way. The time will come when you will want just one day, just one hour in which to make amends, and do you know whether you will obtain it?

See, then, dearly beloved, the great danger from which you can free yourself and the great fear from which you can be saved, if only you will always be wary and mindful of death. Try to live now in such a manner that at the moment of death

2. These are the guidelines that would constitute a good preparedness for the day of death.

you may be glad rather than fearful. Learn to die to the world now, that then you may begin to live with Christ. Learn to spurn all things now, that then you may freely go to Him. Chastise your body in penance now, that then you may have the confidence born of certainty.[3]

Ah, foolish man, why do you plan to live long when you are not sure of living even a day? How many have been deceived and suddenly snatched away! How often have you heard of persons being killed by drownings, by fatal falls from high places, of persons dying at meals, at play, in fires, by the sword, in pestilence, or at the hands of robbers! Death is the end of everyone and the life of man quickly passes away like a shadow.

Who will remember you when you are dead? Who will pray for you? Do now, beloved, what you can, because you do not know when you will die, nor what your fate will be after death. Gather for yourself the riches of immortality while you have time. Think of nothing but your salvation. Care only for the things of God. Make friends for yourself now by honoring the saints of God, by imitating their actions, so that when you depart this life they may receive you into everlasting dwellings.

Keep yourself as a stranger here on earth, a pilgrim whom its affairs do not concern at all. Keep your heart free and raise it up to God, for you have not here a lasting home. To Him direct your daily prayers, your sighs and tears, that your soul may merit after death to pass in happiness to the Lord.

3. Our assurance of salvation comes as we "keep His commandments" (1 John 2:3). The Apostle Paul spoke of bringing his body into "subjection" (1 Cor. 9:27), lest he would be disqualified in the spiritual race.

24. Judgment and the Punishment Of Sin

In all things consider the end; how you shall stand before the strict Judge from Whom nothing is hidden and Who will pronounce judgment in all justice, accepting neither bribes nor excuses. And you, miserable and wretched sinner, who fear even the countenance of an angry man, what answer will you make to the God Who knows all your sins? Why do you not provide for yourself against the day of judgment when no man can be excused or defended by another because each will have enough to do to answer for himself? In this life your work is profitable, your tears acceptable, your sighs audible, your sorrow satisfying and purifying.[1]

The patient man goes through a great and salutary purgatory when he grieves more over the malice of one who harms him than for his own injury; when he prays readily for his enemies and forgives offenses from his heart; when he does not hesitate to ask pardon of others; when he is more easily moved to pity than to anger; when he does frequent violence to himself and tries to bring the body into complete subjection to the spirit.

It is better to atone for sin now and to cut away vices than to keep them for purgation in the hereafter.[2] In truth, we deceive ourselves by our ill-advised love of the flesh. What will that fire feed upon but our sins? The more we spare ourselves now and the more we satisfy the flesh, the harder will the reckoning be and the more we keep for the burning.[3]

For a man will be more grievously punished in the things in which he has sinned. There the lazy will be driven with burning prongs, and gluttons tormented with unspeakable hunger and thirst; the wanton and lust-loving will be bathed in burning pitch and foul brimstone; the envious will howl in their grief like mad dogs.[4]

Every vice will have its own proper punishment. The proud will be faced with every confusion and the avaricious pinched with the most abject want. One hour of suffering there will be more bitter than a hundred years of the most severe penance here. In this life men sometimes rest from work and enjoy the comfort of friends, but the damned have no rest or consolation.

You must, therefore, take care and repent of your sins now so that on the day of judgment you may rest secure with the blessed.[5] For on that day the just will stand firm against those

1. Sorrow for sin is essential, but it is not what purifies us. We are cleansed by the blood of Christ (1 John 1:9).

2. Sin is atoned for by Christ's sacrifice, not by our grieving and cutting away vices here and now.

3. A'Kempis assumes that some of our sinful flesh will be consumed in purgatory—a doctrine that is not found in Scripture.

4. A'Kempis does not seem to be distinguishing between a temporary purgatory and hell in this section.

5. Repentance is essential for the Christian. This is a change of mind concerning sin, a hatred of sin, and a calling to God for mercy, cleansing, and forgiveness.

6. Here A'Kempis rightly divides between the sheep and the goats. There are those who have persecuted Christians, and then there are those who were humble and scorned for the sake of Christ.

who tortured and oppressed them, and he who now submits humbly to the judgment of men will arise to pass judgment upon them. The poor and humble will have great confidence, while the proud will be struck with fear. He who learned to be a fool in this world and to be scorned for Christ will then appear to have been wise.[6]

In that day every trial borne in patience will be pleasing and the voice of iniquity will be stilled; the devout will be glad; the irreligious will mourn; and the mortified body will rejoice far more than if it had been pampered with every pleasure. Then the cheap garment will shine with splendor and the rich one become faded and worn; the poor cottage will be more praised than the gilded palace. In that day persevering patience will count more than all the power in this world; simple obedience will be exalted above all worldly cleverness; a good and clean conscience will gladden the heart of man far more than the philosophy of the learned; and contempt for riches will be of more weight than every treasure on earth.[7]

7. o our Lord's admonition to lay up treasures in heaven rather than on earth (Matthew 6:19-21).

Then you will find more consolation in having prayed devoutly than in having fared daintily; you will be happy that you preferred silence to prolonged gossip.

Then holy works will be of greater value than many fair words; strictness of life and hard penances will be more pleasing than all earthly delights.

Learn, then, to suffer little things now that you may not have to suffer greater ones in eternity. Prove here what you can bear hereafter. If you can suffer only a little now, how will you be able to endure eternal torment? If a little suffering makes you impatient now, what will hell fire do? In truth, you cannot have two joys: you cannot taste the pleasures of this world and afterward reign with Christ.

8. This is the essence of the Christian life. Reference Ecclesiastes 12:10.

If your life to this moment had been full of honors and pleasures, what good would it do if at this instant you should die? All is vanity, therefore, except to love God and to serve Him alone.[8]

He who loves God with all his heart does not fear death or punishment or judgment or hell, because perfect love assures access to God.

It is no wonder that he who still delights in sin fears death and judgment.[9]

It is good, however, that even if love does not as yet restrain you from evil, at least the fear of hell does.[10] The man who casts aside the fear of God cannot continue long in goodness but will quickly fall into the snares of the devil.

9. A'Kempis rightly divides between those who love God and those who love their sin. This truly describes the difference between believers and unbelievers.

10. A'Kempis provides two motives — fear of hell and love for God. While the fear of God is basic for the Christian, it cannot be separated from love (which is a more powerful motive).

25. Zeal in Amending our Lives

Be watchful and diligent in God's service and often think of why you left the world and came here. Was it not that you might live for God and become a spiritual man? Strive earnestly for perfection, then, because in a short time you will receive the reward of your labor, and neither fear nor sorrow shall come upon you at the hour of death.

Labor a little now, and soon you shall find great rest, in truth, eternal joy; for if you continue faithful and diligent in doing, God will undoubtedly be faithful and generous in rewarding.[1] Continue to have reasonable hope of gaining salvation, but do not act as though you were certain of it lest you grow indolent and proud.

1. The Scriptures do speak of eternal rewards (Matthew 5:12, Revelation 22:12).

One day when a certain man who wavered often and anxiously between hope and fear was struck with sadness, he knelt in humble prayer before the altar of a church. While meditating on these things, he said: "Oh if I but knew whether I should persevere to the end!" Instantly he heard within the divine answer: "If you knew this, what would you do? Do now what you would do then and you will be quite secure." Immediately consoled and comforted, he resigned himself to the divine will and the anxious uncertainty ceased. His curiosity

Christians can be encouraged by the promises that God will preserve us and keep us until the day of the Lord Jesus (Philippians 1:6, John 6:39). At the same time, we are called to persevere, and if we would be about keeping God's commandments, we should know that we are the sons of God (1 John 2:4).

3. Psalm 37:3

4. Meriting the most grace is a contradiction in terms. Grace is undeserved favor.

5. When you see faults in others, consider how those faults surface in yourself. This certifies what Jesus instructs us to do in removing the log in our own eye.

no longer sought to know what the future held for him, and he tried instead to find the perfect, the acceptable will of God in the beginning and end of every good work.[2]

"Trust thou in the Lord and do good," says the Prophet; "dwell in the land and thou shalt feed on its riches."[3]

There is one thing that keeps many from zealously improving their lives, that is, dread of the difficulty, the toil of battle. Certainly they who try bravely to overcome the most difficult and unpleasant obstacles far outstrip others in the pursuit of virtue. A man makes the most progress and merits the most grace precisely in those matters wherein he gains the greatest victories over self and most mortifies his will.[4] True, each one has his own difficulties to meet and conquer, but a diligent and sincere man will make greater progress even though he have more passions than one who is more even-tempered but less concerned about virtue.

Two things particularly further improvement—to withdraw oneself forcibly from those vices to which nature is viciously inclined, and to work fervently for those graces which are most needed.

Study also to guard against and to overcome the faults which in others very frequently displease you. Make the best of every opportunity, so that if you see or hear good example you may be moved to imitate it. On the other hand, take care lest you be guilty of those things which you consider reprehensible, or if you have ever been guilty of them, try to correct yourself as soon as possible. As you see others, so they see you.[5]

How pleasant and sweet to behold brethren fervent and devout, well mannered and disciplined! How sad and painful to see them wandering in dissolution, not practicing the things to which they are called! How hurtful it is to neglect the purpose of their vocation and to attend to what is not their business!

Remember the purpose you have undertaken, and keep in mind the image of the Crucified. Even though you may have walked for many years on the pathway to God, you may well be ashamed if, with the image of Christ before you, you do not try to make yourself still more like Him.

The religious who concerns himself intently and devoutly with our Lord's most holy life and passion will find there an abundance of all things useful and necessary for him. He need not seek for anything better than Jesus.[6]

If the Crucified should come to our hearts, how quickly and abundantly we would learn!

A fervent religious accepts all the things that are commanded him and does them well, but a negligent and lukewarm religious has trial upon trial, and suffers anguish from every side because he has no consolation within and is forbidden to seek it from without. The religious who does not live up to his rule exposes himself to dreadful ruin, and he who wishes to be more free and untrammeled will always be in trouble, for something or other will always displease him.

How do so many other religious who are confined in cloistered discipline get along? They seldom go out, they live in contemplation, their food is poor, their clothing coarse, they work hard, they speak but little, keep long vigils, rise early, pray much, read frequently, and subject themselves to all sorts of discipline. Think of the Carthusians[7] and the Cistercians[8], the monks and nuns of different orders, how every night they rise to sing praise to the Lord. It would be a shame if you should grow lazy in such holy service when so many religious have already begun to rejoice in God.

If there were nothing else to do but praise the Lord God with all your heart and voice, if you had never to eat, or drink, or sleep, but could praise God always and occupy yourself solely with spiritual pursuits, how much happier you would be than you are now, a slave to every necessity of the body! Would that there were no such needs, but only the spiritual refreshments of the soul which, sad to say, we taste too seldom![9]

When a man reaches a point where he seeks no solace from any creature, then he begins to relish God perfectly. Then also he will be content no matter what may happen to him.

6. The best instruction for the Christian is to emulate Christ. Reference Romans 8:29.

7. The order of St. Bruno of Cologne founded in 1084.

8. The order of white monks founded by Robert of Molesme in 1098.

9. A'Kempis finds the highest joy to be in the praise and worship of God over eating and drinking.

10. This book ends on a good note. Placing ourselves in the hands of God is a picture of faith — and this is foundational to all of Christian life and endeavor. If there is not faith, then there can be no obedience and no mortification of sin.

He will neither rejoice over great things nor grieve over small ones, but will place himself entirely and confidently in the hands of God, Who for him is all in all, to Whom nothing ever perishes or dies, for Whom all things live, and Whom they serve as He desires.[10]

Always remember your end and do not forget that lost time never returns. Without care and diligence you will never acquire virtue. When you begin to grow lukewarm, you are falling into the beginning of evil; but if you give yourself to fervor, you will find peace and will experience less hardship because of God's grace and the love of virtue.

A fervent and diligent man is ready for all things. It is greater work to resist vices and passions than to sweat in physical toil. He who does not overcome small faults, shall fall little by little into greater ones.

If you have spent the day profitably, you will always be happy at eventide. Watch over yourself, arouse yourself, warn yourself, and regardless of what becomes of others, do not neglect yourself. The more violence you do to yourself, the more progress you will make.

Book 2
The Interior Life

1. Meditation

The kingdom of God is within you," says the Lord.[1]

Turn, then, to God with all your heart. Forsake this wretched world and your soul shall find rest. Learn to despise external things, to devote yourself to those that are within, and you will see the kingdom of God come unto you, that kingdom which is peace and joy in the Holy Spirit, gifts not given to the impious.[2]

Christ will come to you offering His consolation, if you prepare a fit dwelling for Him in your heart, whose beauty and glory, wherein He takes delight, are all from within. His visits with the inward man are frequent, His communion sweet and full of consolation, His peace great, and His intimacy wonderful indeed.

Therefore, faithful soul, prepare your heart for this Bridegroom that He may come and dwell within you; He Himself says: "If any one love Me, he will keep My word, and My Father will love him, and We will come to him, and will make Our abode with him."[3]

1. Luke 17:21

2. Romans 14:17

3. John 14:23

4. Our trust should be in Christ, and not as much in others.

5. Our minds are often concerned with what other people think of us. Man is changeable and unreliable. Christ is not.

6. Hebrews 13:14

7. Colossians 3:2

8. "Stigmata" is defined as a mark of disgrace or reproach.

9. We must be very willing to endure suffering and the scorn of men for Christ, as He was willing to suffer for us. The servant is not greater than his master.

Give place, then, to Christ, but deny entrance to all others, for when you have Christ you are rich and He is sufficient for you. He will provide for you. He will supply your every want, so that you need not trust in frail, changeable men. Christ remains forever, standing firmly with us to the end.[4]

Do not place much confidence in weak and mortal man, helpful and friendly though he be; and do not grieve too much if he sometimes opposes and contradicts you.[5] Those who are with us today may be against us tomorrow, and vice versa, for men change with the wind. Place all your trust in God; let Him be your fear and your love. He will answer for you; He will do what is best for you.

You have here no lasting home.[6] You are a stranger and a pilgrim wherever you may be, and you shall have no rest until you are wholly united with Christ.

Why do you look about here when this is not the place of your repose? Dwell rather upon heaven and give but a passing glance to all earthly things.[7] They all pass away, and you together with them. Take care, then, that you do not cling to them lest you be entrapped and perish. Fix your mind on the Most High, and pray unceasingly to Christ.

If you do not know how to meditate on heavenly things, direct your thoughts to Christ's passion and willingly behold His sacred wounds. If you turn devoutly to the wounds and precious stigmata of Christ,[8] you will find great comfort in suffering, you will mind but little the scorn of men, and you will easily bear their slanderous talk.

When Christ was in the world, He was despised by men; in the hour of need He was forsaken by acquaintances and left by friends to the depths of scorn. He was willing to suffer and to be despised; do you dare to complain of anything?[9] He had enemies and defamers; do you want everyone to be your friend, your benefactor? How can your patience be rewarded if no adversity test it? How can you be a friend of Christ if you are not willing to suffer any hardship? Suffer with Christ and for Christ if you wish to reign with Him.

Had you but once entered into perfect communion with Jesus or tasted a little of His ardent love, you would care nothing at all for your own comfort or discomfort but would rejoice in the reproach you suffer; for love of Him makes a man despise himself.

A man who is a lover of Jesus and of truth, a truly interior man who is free from uncontrolled affections, can turn to God at will and rise above himself to enjoy spiritual peace.

He who tastes life as it really is, not as men say or think it is, is indeed wise with the wisdom of God rather than of men.

He who learns to live the interior life and to take little account of outward things, does not seek special places or times to perform devout exercises. A spiritual man quickly recollects himself because he has never wasted his attention upon externals. No outside work, no business that cannot wait stands in his way. He adjusts himself to things as they happen. He whose disposition is well ordered cares nothing about the strange, perverse behavior of others, for a man is upset and distracted only in proportion as he engrosses himself in externals.[10]

If all were well with you, therefore, and if you were purified from all sin, everything would tend to your good and be to your profit. But because you are as yet neither entirely dead to self nor free from all earthly affection, there is much that often displeases and disturbs you. Nothing so mars and defiles the heart of man as impure attachment to created things. But if you refuse external consolation, you will be able to contemplate heavenly things and often to experience interior joy.

2. Humility

Be not troubled about those who are with you or against you, but take care that God be with you in everything you do.[1] Keep your conscience clear and God will protect you, for the malice of man cannot harm one whom God wishes to help. If you know how to suffer in silence, you will undoubtedly experience God's help. He knows when and how to deliver

10. Christ was grieved by the hardness of hearts in Judea. However, we are not to fret because of evildoers. Rather, our focus should be to delight ourselves in the Lord (Psalm 37:1-5).

1. Our relationship with God is primary.

2. Simply call upon God and He will help you. This is the simplest description of salvation.

3. Humility is winsome with men.

4. Humility is winsome with God.

5. 1 Peter 5:5-6

you; therefore, place yourself in His hands, for it is a divine prerogative to help men and free them from all distress.[2]

It is often good for us to have others know our faults and rebuke them, for it gives us greater humility. When a man humbles himself because of his faults, he easily placates those about him and readily appeases those who are angry with him.[3]

It is the humble man whom God protects and liberates; it is the humble whom He loves and consoles.[4] To the humble He turns and upon them bestows great grace, that after their humiliation He may raise them up to glory.[5] He reveals His secrets to the humble, and with kind invitation bids them come to Him. Thus, the humble man enjoys peace in the midst of many vexations, because his trust is in God, not in the world. Hence, you must not think that you have made any progress until you look upon yourself as inferior to all others.

3. Goodness and Peace in Man

First keep peace with yourself; then you will be able to bring peace to others. A peaceful man does more good than a learned man. Whereas a passionate man turns even good to evil[1] and is quick to believe evil, the peaceful man, being good himself, turns all things to good.

1. The passionate man is referring to the discontented, lustful man. This is a root of much evil.

The man who is at perfect ease is never suspicious, but the disturbed and discontented spirit is upset by many a suspicion. He neither rests himself nor permits others to do so. He often says what ought not to be said and leaves undone what ought to be done. He is concerned with the duties of others but neglects his own.[2]

2. The sins of discontentment, evil thoughts about others, slothfulness, and minding other people's business are all connected — producing a state of restlessness and lack of peace.

Direct your zeal, therefore, first upon yourself; then you may with justice exercise it upon those about you. You are well versed in coloring your own actions with excuses which you will not accept from others, though it would be more just to accuse yourself and excuse your brother. If you wish men to bear with you, you must bear with them. Behold, how far you are from true charity and humility which does not know how to be angry with anyone, or to be indignant save only against self![3]

It is no great thing to associate with the good and gentle, for such association is naturally pleasing. Everyone enjoys a peaceful life and prefers persons of congenial habits. But to be able to live at peace with harsh and perverse men, or with the undisciplined and those who irritate us, is a great grace, a praiseworthy and manly thing.[4]

Some people live at peace with themselves and with their fellow men, but others are never at peace with themselves nor do they bring it to anyone else. These latter are a burden to everyone, but they are more of a burden to themselves. A few, finally, live at peace with themselves and try to restore it to others.

Now, all our peace in this miserable life is found in humbly enduring suffering rather than in being free from it. He who knows best how to suffer will enjoy the greater peace, because he is the conqueror of himself, the master of the world, a friend of Christ, and an heir of heaven.[5]

3. Hold yourself to a much tighter standard than you would hold to others (Matthew 7:1-2).

4. It is a great test of faith to live at peace with difficult people.

5. Humble submission under the fire of trial is where the greatest peace is found.

4. Purity of Mind and Unity of Purpose

A man is raised up from the earth by two wings—simplicity and purity. There must be simplicity in his intention and purity in his desires. Simplicity leads to God, purity embraces and enjoys Him.[1]

If your heart is free from ill-ordered affection,[2] no good deed will be difficult for you. If you aim at and seek after nothing but the pleasure of God and the welfare of your neighbor, you will enjoy freedom within.

If your heart were right, then every created thing would be a mirror of life for you and a book of holy teaching, for there is no creature so small and worthless that it does not show forth the goodness of God.[3] If inwardly you were good and pure, you would see all things clearly and understand them rightly, for a pure heart penetrates to heaven and hell, and as a man is within, so he judges what is without. If there be joy

1. Purity is defined as simplicity and a lack of confusion. The devil is the source of confusion, deceit, and all impurity.

2. Lust and idolatry undermine true love for God and others.

3. Blindness to God's goodness in creation comes from a corrupted heart — where affections are not towards God (preferring idols and self.)

in the world, the pure of heart certainly possess it; and if there be anguish and affliction anywhere, an evil conscience knows it too well.

4. Repentance is first and foremost turning to God. A change of heart comes first however, and it is a work of the Holy Spirit.

As iron cast into fire loses its rust and becomes glowing white, so he who turns completely to God is stripped of his sluggishness and changed into a new man.[4] When a man begins to grow lax, he fears a little toil and welcomes external comfort, but when he begins perfectly to conquer himself and to walk bravely in the ways of God, then he thinks those things less difficult which he thought so hard before.

5. Ourselves

We must not rely too much upon ourselves, for grace and understanding are often lacking in us. We have but little inborn light, and this we quickly lose through negligence. Often we are not aware that we are so blind in heart. Meanwhile we do wrong, and then do worse in excusing it.[1] At times we are moved by passion, and we think it zeal. We take others to task for small mistakes, and overlook greater ones in ourselves. We are quick enough to feel and brood over the things we suffer from others, but we think nothing of how much others suffer from us. If a man would weigh his own deeds fully and rightly, he would find little cause to pass severe judgment on others.[2]

1. Self deception and self-justification comes easily to all of us.

2. If we judged ourselves accurately, we would be far more careful and far less likely to judge others

The interior man puts the care of himself before all other concerns, and he who attends to himself carefully does not find it hard to hold his tongue about others. You will never be devout of heart unless you are thus silent about the affairs of others and pay particular attention to yourself. If you attend wholly to God and yourself, you will be little disturbed by what you see about you.

Where are your thoughts when they are not upon yourself? And after attending to various things, what have you gained if you have neglected self? If you wish to have true peace of mind and unity of purpose, you must cast all else aside and keep only yourself before your eyes.

You will make great progress if you keep yourself free from all temporal cares, for to value anything that is temporal is a great mistake. Consider nothing great, nothing high, nothing pleasing, nothing acceptable, except God Himself or that which is of God.[3] Consider the consolations of creatures as vanity, for the soul that loves God scorns all things that are inferior to Him. God alone, the eternal and infinite, satisfies all, bringing comfort to the soul and true joy to the body.

3. God is the essence of good, and He is the source of all good gifts. All that is perceived as good must be seen in reference to God.

6. The Joy of a Good Conscience

The glory of a good man is the testimony of a good conscience. Therefore, keep your conscience good and you will always enjoy happiness, for a good conscience can bear a great deal and can bring joy even in the midst of adversity. But an evil conscience is ever restive and fearful.

Sweet shall be your rest if your heart does not reproach you.

Do not rejoice unless you have done well. Sinners never experience true interior joy or peace, for "there is no peace to the wicked," says the Lord.[1] Even if they say: "We are at peace, no evil shall befall us and no one dares to hurt us," do not believe them; for the wrath of God will arise quickly, and their deeds will be brought to naught and their thoughts will perish.

To glory in adversity is not hard for the man who loves, for this is to glory in the cross of the Lord.[2] But the glory given or received of men is short lived, and the glory of the world is ever companioned by sorrow.[3] The glory of the good, however, is in their conscience and not in the lips of men, for the joy of the just is from God and in God, and their gladness is founded on truth.

The man who longs for the true, eternal glory does not care for that of time; and he who seeks passing fame or does not in his heart despise it, undoubtedly cares little for the glory of heaven.

1. Isaiah 48:22

2. To love the Lord is to glory in His cross. This is the spirit that is content to bear the cross.

3. Man's glory is temporary and transient. The sooner we leave it the better.

He who minds neither praise nor blame possesses great peace of heart and, if his conscience is good, he will easily be contented and at peace.[4]

4. Too much praise of men and blaming of men indicates a lack of focus on God.

Praise adds nothing to your holiness, nor does blame take anything from it. You are what you are, and you cannot be said to be better than you are in God's sight. If you consider well what you are within, you will not care what men say about you. They look to appearances but God looks to the heart. They consider the deed but God weighs the motive.[5]

5. Reference 1 Samuel 16:7. Man's assessments are not important compared to God's.

It is characteristic of a humble soul always to do good and to think little of itself. It is a mark of great purity and deep faith to look for no consolation in created things. The man who desires no justification from without has clearly entrusted himself to God: "For not he who commendeth himself is approved," says St. Paul, "but he whom God commendeth."

To walk with God interiorly, to be free from any external affection—this is the state of the inward man.

7. Loving Jesus Above All Things

Blessed is he who appreciates what it is to love Jesus and who despises himself for the sake of Jesus. Give up all other love for His, since He wishes to be loved alone above all things.[1]

1. Only God is to be loved with heart, soul, mind, and strength. We are to love Jesus above all else.

Affection for creatures is deceitful and inconstant, but the love of Jesus is true and enduring. He who clings to a creature will fall with its frailty, but he who gives himself to Jesus will ever be strengthened.

Love Him, then; keep Him as a friend. He will not leave you as others do, or let you suffer lasting death.[2] Sometime, whether you will or not, you will have to part with everything. Cling, therefore, to Jesus in life and death; trust yourself to the glory of Him who alone can help you when all others fail.

2. He is the resurrection and life. He will not let you down even in death. His love is perfect and endures all things.

Your Beloved is such that He will not accept what belongs to another—He wants your heart for Himself alone, to be enthroned therein as King in His own right. If you but knew how to free yourself entirely from all creatures, Jesus would gladly dwell within you.[3]

You will find, apart from Him, that nearly all the trust you place in men is a total loss. Therefore, neither confide in nor depend upon a wind-shaken reed, for "all flesh is grass"[4] and all its glory, like the flower of grass, will fade away.

You will quickly be deceived if you look only to the outward appearance of men, and you will often be disappointed if you seek comfort and gain in them. If, however, you seek Jesus in all things, you will surely find Him. Likewise, if you seek yourself, you will find yourself—to your own ruin.[5] For the man who does not seek Jesus does himself much greater harm than the whole world and all his enemies could ever do.

3. A'Kempis seems to be preferring an isolation from all other humans. This finds no support in Scripture. However, there is a dangerous dependency upon relationship with others that can trump our relationship with Christ.

4. Reference 1 Peter 1:24. Trusting in men is disappointing.

5. to seeking the pearl of great price and the treasure in the field. Seeking, asking, and knocking are acts of faith. We seek to know Christ so we might love Him more. To seek yourself is to seek to know yourself, to love yourself, and to glorify yourself first is wrong. It is a trap. Seeking yourself is to isolate yourself from God. Seeking God or Jesus' presence brings true fulfillment and joy.

8. The Intimate Friendship of Jesus

When Jesus is near, all is well and nothing seems difficult. When He is absent, all is hard. When Jesus does not speak within, all other comfort is empty, but if He says only a word, it brings great consolation.

Did not Mary Magdalen rise at once from her weeping when Martha said to her: "The Master is come, and calleth for thee"?[1] Happy is the hour when Jesus calls one from tears to joy of spirit.

1. John 11:28

2. Romans 8:31-39; Hebrews 13:6

3. Matthew 13:44

4. A'Kempis is exploring the abiding in Christ injunction in John 15.

5. 1 John 2:19 sees this leaving as pulling away from the fellowship of the body. John says they were never truly of us.

6. The Lord wants us to love Him above all else.

7. The temptation to seek the love and praise of men is strong. This is a very serious sin because it displaces the praise of God as ultimate.

How dry and hard you are without Jesus! How foolish and vain if you desire anything but Him! Is it not a greater loss than losing the whole world? For what, without Jesus, can the world give you? Life without Him is a relentless hell, but living with Him is a sweet paradise. If Jesus be with you, no enemy can harm you.[2]

He who finds Jesus finds a rare treasure,[3] indeed, a good above every good, whereas he who loses Him loses more than the whole world. The man who lives without Jesus is the poorest of the poor, whereas no one is so rich as the man who lives in His grace.

It is a great art to know how to converse with Jesus, and great wisdom to know how to keep Him.[4] Be humble and peaceful, and Jesus will be with you. Be devout and calm, and He will remain with you. You may quickly drive Him away and lose His grace, if you turn back to the outside world.[5] And, if you drive Him away and lose Him, to whom will you go and whom will you then seek as a friend? You cannot live well without a friend, and if Jesus be not your friend above all else, you will be very sad and desolate.[6] Thus, you are acting foolishly if you trust or rejoice in any other. Choose the opposition of the whole world rather than offend Jesus. Of all those who are dear to you, let Him be your special love. Let all things be loved for the sake of Jesus, but Jesus for His own sake.

Jesus Christ must be loved alone with a special love for He alone, of all friends, is good and faithful. For Him and in Him you must love friends and foes alike, and pray to Him that all may know and love Him.

Never desire special praise or love, for that belongs to God alone Who has no equal.[7] Never wish that anyone's affection be centered in you, nor let yourself be taken up with the love of anyone, but let Jesus be in you and in every good man. Be pure and free within, unentangled with any creature.

You must bring to God a clean and open heart if you wish to attend and see how sweet the Lord is. Truly you will never attain this happiness unless His grace prepares you and draws you on so that you may forsake all things to be united with Him alone.

When the grace of God comes to a man he can do all things, but when it leaves him he becomes poor and weak, abandoned, as it were, to affliction.[8] Yet, in this condition he should not become dejected or despair. On the contrary, he should calmly await the will of God and bear whatever befalls him in praise of Jesus Christ, for after winter comes summer, after night, the day, and after the storm, a great calm.

8. Grace or God's gifts can be withheld for a time in a Christian's life.

9. Wanting No Share in Comfort

It is not hard to spurn human consolation when we have the divine. It is, however, a very great thing indeed to be able to live without either divine or human comforting and for the honor of God willingly to endure this exile of heart, not to seek oneself in anything, and to think nothing of one's own merit.

Does it matter much, if at the coming of grace, you are cheerful and devout? This is an hour desired by all, for he whom the grace of God sustains travels easily enough. What wonder if he feel no burden when borne up by the Almighty and led on by the Supreme Guide! For we are always glad to have something to comfort us, and only with difficulty does a man divest himself of self.

The holy martyr, Lawrence, with his priest, conquered the world because he despised everything in it that seemed pleasing to him, and for love of Christ patiently suffered the great high priest of God, Sixtus, whom he loved dearly, to be taken from him.[1] Thus, by his love for the Creator he overcame the love of man, and chose instead of human consolation the good pleasure of God. So you, too, must learn to part with an intimate and much-needed friend for the love of God.[2] Do not

1. The deacon Lawrence was martyred in AD 258 when Sixtus was pastor/bishop in Rome.

2. Abandonment of friends can be a great test for us. Will we continue to fall back on our love for God and communion with Him?

take it to heart when you are deserted by a friend, knowing that in the end we must all be parted from one another.

A man must fight long and bravely against himself before he learns to master himself fully and to direct all his affections toward God. When he trusts in himself, he easily takes to human consolation. The true lover of Christ, however, who sincerely pursues virtue, does not fall back upon consolations nor seek such pleasures of sense,[3] but prefers severe trials and hard labors for the sake of Christ.

When, therefore, spiritual consolation is given by God, receive it gratefully, but understand that it is His gift and not your meriting. Do not exult, do not be overjoyed, do not be presumptuous, but be the humbler for the gift, more careful and wary in all your actions, for this hour will pass and temptation will come in its wake.[4]

When consolation is taken away, do not at once despair but wait humbly and patiently for the heavenly visit, since God can restore to you more abundant solace.

This is neither new nor strange to one who knows God's ways, for such change of fortune often visited the great saints and prophets of old. Thus there was one who, when grace was with him, declared: "In my prosperity I said: 'I shall never be moved.'"[5] But when grace was taken away, he adds what he experienced in himself: "Thou didst hide Thy face, and I was troubled."[6] Meanwhile he does not despair; rather he prays more earnestly to the Lord, saying: "To Thee, O Lord, will I cry; and I will make supplication to my God."[7] At length, he receives the fruit of his prayer, and testifying that he was heard, says "The Lord hath heard, and hath had mercy on me: the Lord became my helper."[8] And how was he helped? "Thou hast turned," he says, "my mourning into joy, and hast surrounded me with gladness."[9]

If this is the case with great saints, we who are weak and poor ought not to despair because we are fervent at times and at other times cold, for the spirit comes and goes according to

3. People look to food, drink, and human comforts instead of suffering for Christ and seeking spiritual comfort.

4. We often let our guard down when we receive some comfort.

5. Psalm 30:6

6. Psalm 30:7

7. Psalm 30:8

8. Psalm 30:10

9. Psalm 30:11

His will. Of this the blessed Job declared: "Thou visitest him early in the morning, and Thou provest him suddenly."[10]

In what can I hope, then, or in whom ought I trust, save only in the great mercy of God and the hope of heavenly grace? For though I have with me good men, devout brethren, faithful friends, holy books, beautiful treatises, sweet songs and hymns, all these help and please but little when I am abandoned by grace and left to my poverty. At such times there is no better remedy than patience and resignation of self to the will of God.[11]

I have never met a man so religious and devout that he has not experienced at some time a withdrawal of grace and felt a lessening of fervor. No saint was so sublimely rapt and enlightened as not to be tempted before and after. He, indeed, is not worthy of the sublime contemplation of God who has not been tried by some tribulation for the sake of God. For temptation is usually the sign preceding the consolation that is to follow, and heavenly consolation is promised to all those proved by temptation.[12] "To him that overcometh," says Christ, "I will give to eat of the Tree of Life."[13] Divine consolation, then, is given in order to make a man braver in enduring adversity, and temptation follows in order that he may not pride himself on the good he has done.

The devil does not sleep, nor is the flesh yet dead; therefore, you must never cease your preparation for battle, because on the right and on the left are enemies who never rest.[14]

10. Job 7:18

11. When severe trials confront us, emotional uplifts like music or friendship is not enough. Waiting and hoping on God and accepting His purpose as the best is the only way.

12. Severe trial usually goes before the greatest comforts.

13. Revelation 2:7

14. Be watchful, always preparing for battle. The devil and the flesh are mortal enemies.

10. Appreciating God's Grace

Why do you look for rest when you were born to work? Resign yourself to patience rather than to comfort, to carrying your cross rather than to enjoyment.[1]

What man in the world, if he could always have them, would not readily accept consolation and spiritual joy, benefits which excel all earthly delights and pleasures of the body?[2] The latter, indeed, are either vain or base, while spiritual joys, born

1. The Christian life is more cross than a life of leisure.

2. Though not always sinful, there is an emptiness to bodily pleasure.

of virtue and infused by God into pure minds, are alone truly pleasant and noble.

Now, since the moment of temptation is always nigh, since false freedom of mind and overconfidence in self are serious obstacles to these visitations from heaven, a man can never enjoy them just as he wishes.

God does well in giving the grace of consolation, but man does evil in not returning everything gratefully to God. Thus, the gifts of grace cannot flow in us when we are ungrateful to the Giver, when we do not return them to the Fountainhead. Grace is always given to him who is duly grateful, and what is wont to be given the humble will be taken away from the proud.[3]

3. A'Kempis associates gratefulness with humility. God's grace flows to the humble.

I do not desire consolation that robs me of contrition, nor do I care for contemplation that leads to pride, for not all that is high is holy, nor is all that is sweet good, nor every desire pure, nor all that is dear to us pleasing to God. I accept willingly the grace whereby I become more humble and contrite, more willing to renounce self.[4]

4. Recognize the source of all good gifts as God.

The man who has been taught by the gift of grace, and who learns by the lash of its withdrawal, will never dare to attribute any good to himself, but will rather admit his poverty and emptiness. Give to God what is God's and ascribe to yourself what is yours. Give Him thanks, then, for His grace, but place upon yourself alone the blame and the punishment your fault deserves.

Always take the lowest place and the highest will be given you, for the highest cannot exist apart from the lowest. The saints who are greatest before God are those who consider themselves the least, and the more humble they are within themselves, so much the more glorious they are. Since they do not desire vainglory, they are full of truth and heavenly glory. Being established and strengthened in God, they can by no means be proud. They attribute to God whatever good they have received; they seek no glory from one another but only that which comes from God alone. They desire above all things that He be praised in themselves and in all His saints—this is their constant purpose.[5]

Be grateful, therefore, for the least gift and you will be worthy to receive a greater. Consider the least gift as the greatest, the most contemptible as something special. And, if you but look to the dignity of the Giver, no gift will appear too small or worthless.[6] Even though He give punishments and scourges, accept them, because He acts for our welfare in whatever He allows to befall us.

He who desires to keep the grace of God ought to be grateful when it is given and patient when it is withdrawn. Let him pray that it return; let him be cautious and humble lest he lose it.[7]

11. Few Love the Cross of Jesus

Jesus has always many who love His heavenly kingdom, but few who bear His cross. He has many who desire consolation, but few who care for trial. He finds many to share His table, but few to take part in His fasting. All desire to be happy with Him; few wish to suffer anything for Him. Many follow Him to the breaking of bread, but few to the drinking of the chalice of His passion. Many revere His miracles; few approach the shame of the Cross. Many love Him as long as they encounter no hardship; many praise and bless Him as long as they receive some comfort from Him.[1] But if Jesus hides Himself and leaves them for a while, they fall either into complaints or into deep dejection. Those, on the contrary, who love Him for His own sake and not for any comfort of their own, bless Him in all trial and anguish of heart as well as in the bliss of consolation.[2] Even if He should never give them consolation, yet they would continue to praise Him and wish always to give Him thanks. What power there is in pure love for Jesus—love that is free from all self-interest and self-love![3]

Do not those who always seek consolation deserve to be called mercenaries? Do not those who always think of their

5. The cure for pride is always praising God and preferring God's glory over man's glory.

6. The smallest gift from God is to be seen as of inestimable value. We deserve none of His good gifts.

7. A beautiful summary: be humble and grateful. When gifts are taken away, be patient and pray.

1. The life of Christ must include suffering with Him and His people. This isn't always popular.

2. Job was a good example of someone who could bless the Lord in times of severe loss.

3. Love for God and His Son must even trump self-love in the Christian life.

4. To really love someone, it must include some degree of sacrificial love to the point of suffering.

own profit and gain prove that they love themselves rather than Christ?[4] Where can a man be found who desires to serve God for nothing? Rarely indeed is a man so spiritual as to strip himself of all things. And who shall find a man so truly poor in spirit as to be free from every creature? His value is like that of things brought from the most distant lands.

If a man give all his wealth, it is nothing; if he do great penance, it is little; if he gain all knowledge, he is still far afield; if he have great virtue and much ardent devotion, he still lacks a great deal, and especially, the one thing that is most necessary to him. What is this one thing? That leaving all, he forsake himself, completely renounce himself, and give up all private affections.[5] Then, when he has done all that he knows ought to be done, let him consider it as nothing, let him make little of what may be considered great; let him in all honesty call himself an unprofitable servant. For truth itself has said: "When you shall have done all these things that are commanded you, say: 'we are unprofitable servants.'"[6]

5. Self-denial for love of Christ is the most necessary, costly, and rewarding thing for the Christian.

6. Luke 17:10

Then he will be truly poor and stripped in spirit, and with the prophet may say: "I am alone and poor." No one, however, is more wealthy than such a man; no one is more powerful, no one freer than he who knows how to leave all things and think of himself as the least of all.

12. The Royal Road of the Holy Cross

To many the saying, "Deny thyself, take up thy cross and follow Me,"[1] seems hard, but it will be much harder to hear that final word: "Depart from Me, ye cursed, into everlasting fire."[2] Those who hear the word of the cross and follow it willingly now, need not fear that they will hear of eternal damnation on the day of judgment. This sign of the cross will be in the heavens when the Lord comes to judge. Then all the servants of the cross, who during life made themselves one with the Crucified, will draw near with great trust to Christ, the judge.[3]

1. Matthew 16:24

2. Matthew 25:41

3. Those that took up the cross and followed Christ in this life will have no fear on judgment day because they know the Judge.

Why, then, do you fear to take up the cross when through it you can win a kingdom? In the cross is salvation, in the cross is life, in the cross is protection from enemies, in the cross is infusion of heavenly sweetness, in the cross is strength of mind, in the cross is joy of spirit, in the cross is highest virtue, in the cross is perfect holiness. There is no salvation of soul nor hope of everlasting life but in the cross.[4]

Take up your cross, therefore, and follow Jesus, and you shall enter eternal life. He Himself opened the way before you in carrying His cross, and upon it He died for you, that you, too, might take up your cross and long to die upon it. If you die with Him, you shall also live with Him, and if you share His suffering, you shall also share His glory.[5]

Behold, in the cross is everything, and upon your dying on the cross everything depends. There is no other way to life and to true inward peace than the way of the holy cross and daily mortification.[6] Go where you will, seek what you will, you will not find a higher way, nor a less exalted but safer way, than the way of the holy cross. Arrange and order everything to suit your will and judgment, and still you will find that some suffering must always be borne, willingly or unwillingly, and thus you will always find the cross.[7]

Either you will experience bodily pain or you will undergo tribulation of spirit in your soul.[8] At times you will be forsaken by God, at times troubled by those about you and, what is worse, you will often grow weary of yourself. You cannot escape, you cannot be relieved by any remedy or comfort but must bear with it as long as God wills. For He wishes you to learn to bear trial without consolation, to submit yourself wholly to Him that you may become more humble through suffering.[9] No one understands the passion of Christ so thoroughly or heartily as the man whose lot it is to suffer the like himself.

The cross, therefore, is always ready; it awaits you everywhere. No matter where you may go, you cannot escape it, for wherever you go you take yourself with you and shall always

4. Christ's cross in our salvation is distinct from our cross.

5. 2 Timothy 2:11,12

6. The Christian life involves mortifying sinful flesh at the cross.

7. A'Kempis defines the cross as suffering (for Christ and for others).

8. Here A'Kempis describes the suffering a Christian experiences.

9. Humility is the grace received in suffering.

find yourself. Turn where you will—above, below, without, or within—you will find a cross in everything, and everywhere you must have patience if you would have peace within and merit an eternal crown.

If you carry the cross willingly, it will carry and lead you to the desired goal where indeed there shall be no more suffering, but here there shall be. If you carry it unwillingly, you create a burden for yourself and increase the load, though still you have to bear it.[10] If you cast away one cross, you will find another and perhaps a heavier one. Do you expect to escape what no mortal man can ever avoid? Which of the saints was without a cross or trial on this earth? Not even Jesus Christ, our Lord, Whose every hour on earth knew the pain of His passion. "It behooveth Christ to suffer, and to rise again from the dead, . . . and so enter into his glory."[11] How is it that you look for another way than this, the royal way of the holy cross?

The whole life of Christ was a cross and a martyrdom, and do you seek rest and enjoyment for yourself?[12] You deceive yourself, you are mistaken if you seek anything but to suffer, for this mortal life is full of miseries and marked with crosses on all sides. Indeed, the more spiritual progress a person makes, so much heavier will he frequently find the cross, because as his love increases, the pain of his exile also increases.

Yet such a man, though afflicted in many ways, is not without hope of consolation, because he knows that great reward is coming to him for bearing his cross.[13] And when he carries it willingly, every pang of tribulation is changed into hope of solace from God. Besides, the more the flesh is distressed by affliction, so much the more is the spirit strengthened by inward grace. Not infrequently a man is so strengthened by his love of trials and hardship in his desire to conform to the cross of Christ, that he does not wish to be without sorrow or pain, since he believes he will be the more acceptable to God if he is able to endure more and more grievous things for His sake.

It is the grace of Christ, and not the virtue of man, which can and does bring it about that through fervor of spirit

10. This is encouragement to endure suffering willingly.

11. Luke 24:26

12. The servant is not above his Master. Reference Matthew 10:24.

13. The greater the suffering, the greater the hope. Reference Romans 8:18.

frail flesh learns to love and to gain what it naturally hates and shuns.[14]

To carry the cross, to love the cross, to chastise the body and bring it to subjection, to flee honors, to endure contempt gladly, to despise self and wish to be despised, to suffer any adversity and loss, to desire no prosperous days on earth—this is not man's way. If you rely upon yourself, you can do none of these things, but if you trust in the Lord, strength will be given you from heaven and the world and the flesh will be made subject to your word.[15] You will not even fear your enemy, the devil, if you are armed with faith and signed with the cross of Christ.

Set yourself, then, like a good and faithful servant of Christ, to bear bravely the cross of your Lord, Who out of love was crucified for you. Be ready to suffer many adversities and many kinds of trouble in this miserable life, for troublesome and miserable life will always be, no matter where you are; and so you will find it wherever you may hide. Thus it must be; and there is no way to evade the trials and sorrows of life but to bear them.

Drink the chalice of the Lord with affection if you wish to be His friend and to have part with Him.[16] Leave consolation to God; let Him do as most pleases Him.[17] On your part, be ready to bear sufferings and consider them the greatest consolation, for even though you alone were to undergo them all, the sufferings of this life are not worthy to be compared with the glory to come.[18]

When you shall have come to the point where suffering is sweet and acceptable for the sake of Christ, then consider yourself fortunate, for you have found paradise on earth.[19] But as long as suffering irks you and you seek to escape, so long will you be unfortunate, and the tribulation you seek to evade will follow you everywhere. If you put your mind to the things you ought to consider, that is, to suffering and death, you would soon be in a better state and would find peace.

14. This spirit that rejoices in tribulation is a miracle of God's grace.

15. We overcome by faith in the Lord.

16. Suffer for Christ out of a spirit of love for Him.

17. Do not expect consolations. Let them surprise you.

18. Romans 8:18

19. The ultimate achievement for the Christian is to rejoice in suffering (1 Peter 4:13).

20. Paul may have suffered more than all of the Apostles.

21. Acts 9:16

22. Much profit does come to yourself and others in your suffering.

23. Suffering for Christ is how we become like Christ.

24. Luke 9:23

25. Acts 14:22

Although you were taken to the third heaven with Paul, you were not thereby insured against suffering.[20] Jesus said: "I will show him how great things he must suffer for My name's sake."[21] To suffer, then, remains your lot, if you mean to love Jesus and serve Him forever.

If you were but worthy to suffer something for the name of Jesus, what great glory would be in store for you, what great joy to all the saints of God, what great edification to those about you![22] For all men praise patience though there are few who wish to practice it.

With good reason, then, ought you to be willing to suffer a little for Christ since many suffer much more for the world.

Realize that you must lead a dying life; the more a man dies to himself, the more he begins to live unto God.

No man is fit to enjoy heaven unless he has resigned himself to suffer hardship for Christ. Nothing is more acceptable to God, nothing more helpful for you on this earth than to suffer willingly for Christ. If you had to make a choice, you ought to wish rather to suffer for Christ than to enjoy many consolations, for thus you would be more like Christ and more like all the saints.[23] Our merit and progress consist not in many pleasures and comforts but rather in enduring great afflictions and sufferings.

If, indeed, there were anything better or more useful for man's salvation than suffering, Christ would have shown it by word and example. But He clearly exhorts the disciples who follow Him and all who wish to follow Him to carry the cross, saying: "If any man will come after Me, let him deny himself, and take up his cross daily, and follow Me."[24]

When, therefore, we have read and searched all that has been written, let this be the final conclusion—that through much suffering we must enter into the kingdom of God.[25]

❧ Book 3
Internal Consolation

1. The Inward Conversation of Christ with the Faithful Soul

"I will hear what the Lord God will speak in me."

Blessed is the soul who hears the Lord speaking within her, who receives the word of consolation from His lips. Blessed are the ears that catch the accents of divine whispering, and pay no heed to the murmurings of this world.[1] Blessed indeed are the ears that listen, not to the voice which sounds without, but to the truth which teaches within. Blessed are the eyes which are closed to exterior things and are fixed upon those which are interior.[2] Blessed are they who penetrate inwardly, who try daily to prepare themselves more and more to understand mysteries. Blessed are they who long to give their time to God, and who cut themselves off from the hindrances of the world.

Consider these things, my soul, and close the door of your senses, so that you can hear what the Lord your God speaks within you. "I am your salvation," says your Beloved. "I am your peace and your life. Remain with Me and you will find peace.[3] Dismiss all passing things and seek the eternal. What are all temporal things but snares? And what help will all creatures be able to give you if you are deserted by the

1. The world tends to distract from the word of God.

2. There is a discipline involved in blocking out these distractions.

3. John 15:4. Jesus is our salvation, our rest, and life. This is fundamental.

Creator?" Leave all these things, therefore, and make yourself pleasing and faithful to your Creator so that you may attain to true happiness.

2. Truth Speaks Inwardly Without the Sound of Words

The Disciple

1. 1 Samuel 3:9

"Speak, Lord, for Thy servant heareth."[1] "I am Thy servant. Give me understanding that I may know Thine ordinances . . . Incline my heart to Thine ordinances . . . Let Thy speech distil as the dew."[2]

2. Deuteronomy 32:2

The children of Israel once said to Moses: "Speak thou to us and we will hear thee: let not the Lord speak to us, lest we die."

Not so, Lord, not so do I pray. Rather with Samuel the prophet I entreat humbly and earnestly: "Speak, Lord, for Thy servant heareth." Do not let Moses or any of the prophets speak to me; but You speak, O Lord God, Who inspired and enlightened all the prophets; for You alone, without them, can instruct me perfectly, whereas they, without You, can do nothing. They, indeed, utter fine words, but they cannot impart the spirit.[3] They do indeed speak beautifully, but if You remain silent they cannot inflame the heart. They deliver the message; You lay bare the sense. They place before us mysteries, but You unlock their meaning. They proclaim commandments; You help us to keep them. They point out the way; You give strength for the journey. They work only outwardly; You instruct and enlighten our hearts. They water on the outside; You give the increase.

3. A' Kempis explains the work of the Spirit in conjunction with the word.

They cry out words; You give understanding to the hearer.

Let not Moses speak to me, therefore, but You, the Lord my God, everlasting truth, speak lest I die and prove barren if I am merely given outward advice and am not inflamed within; lest the word heard and not kept, known and not loved, believed and not obeyed, rise up in judgment against me.[4]

Speak, therefore, Lord, for Your servant listens. "Thou hast the words of eternal life."[5] Speak to me for the comfort of my soul and for the amendment of my life, for Your praise, Your glory, and Your everlasting honor.

4. Words not kept, loved, obeyed will only serve to condemn.

5. John 6:68

3. Listen Humbly to the Words of God. Many Do Not Heed Them

The Voice of Christ

My child, hear My words, words of greatest sweetness surpassing all the knowledge of the philosophers and wise men of earth.[1] My words are spirit and life,[2] and they are not to be weighed by man's understanding. They are not to be invoked in vanity but are to be heard in silence, and accepted with all humility and with great affection.

1. The wisdom of Christ is wiser than the greatest Greek philosophers.

2. John 6:63

The Disciple

"Happy is the man whom Thou admonishest, O Lord, and teachest out of Thy law, to give him peace from the days of evil,"[3] and that he be not desolate on earth.

3. Psalm 94: 12,13

The Voice of Christ

I taught the prophets from the beginning, and even to this day I continue to speak to all men. But many are hardened. Many are deaf to My voice. Most men listen more willingly to the world than to God. They are more ready to follow the appetite of their flesh than the good pleasure of God. The world, which promises small and passing things, is served with great eagerness: I promise great and eternal things and the hearts of men grow dull. Who is there that serves and obeys Me in all things with as great care as that with which the world and its masters are served?[4]

4. Christ condemns hardness of heart and half-hearted reception of His words.

5. Isaiah 23:4

6. A'Kempis compares the worldly person's zeal for vanity with the often weak commitment to God's truth among professing believers.

7. Christ always delivers on His promises. The world doesn't.

8. Christ teaches us by our trials and His words of comfort.

"Be thou ashamed, O Sidon, for the sea speaketh."[5] And if you ask why, listen to the cause: for a small gain they travel far; for eternal life many will scarcely lift a foot from the ground. They seek a petty reward, and sometimes fight shamefully in law courts for a single piece of money. They are not afraid to work day and night for a trifle or an empty promise. But, for an unchanging good, for a reward beyond estimate, for the greatest honor and for glory everlasting, it must be said to their shame that men begrudge even the least fatigue. Be ashamed, then, lazy and complaining servant, that they should be found more eager for perdition than you are for life, that they rejoice more in vanity than you in truth.[6]

Sometimes indeed their expectations fail them, but My promise never deceives, nor does it send away empty-handed him who trusts in Me. What I have promised I will give. What I have said I will fulfill, if only a man remain faithful in My love to the end. I am the rewarder of all the good, the strong approver of all who are devoted to Me.[7]

Write My words in your heart and meditate on them earnestly, for in time of temptation they will be very necessary. What you do not understand when you read, you will learn in the day of visitation. I am wont to visit My elect in two ways—by temptation and by consolation.[8] To them I read two lessons daily—one reproving their vices, the other exhorting them to progress in virtue. He who has My words and despises them has that which shall condemn him on the last day.

A Prayer for the Grace of Devotion

O Lord my God, You are all my good. And who am I that I should dare to speak to You? I am Your poorest and meanest servant, a vile worm, much more poor and contemptible than I know or dare to say. Yet remember me, Lord, because I am nothing, I have nothing, and I can do nothing. You alone are good, just, and holy. You can do all things, You give all things, You fill all things: only the sinner do You leave empty-handed. Remember Your tender mercies and fill my heart with Your grace, You Who will not allow Your works to be in vain. How can I bear this life of misery unless You comfort me with Your mercy and grace? Do not turn Your face from me. Do not delay Your visitation. Do not withdraw Your consolation, lest in Your sight my soul become as desert land. Teach me, Lord, to do Your will. Teach me to live worthily and humbly in Your sight, for You are my wisdom Who know me truly, and Who knew me even before the world was made and before I was born into it.

4. We Must Walk Before God in Humility and Truth

The Voice of Christ

My child, walk before Me in truth, and seek Me always in the simplicity of your heart. He who walks before Me in truth shall be defended from the attacks of evil, and the truth shall free him from seducers and from the slanders of wicked men. For if the truth has made you free, then you shall be free indeed, and you shall not care for the vain words of men.

The Disciple

O Lord, it is true. I ask that it be with me as You say. Let your truth teach me.[1] Let it guard me, and keep me safe to the end. Let it free me from all evil affection and badly ordered love, and I shall walk with You in great freedom of heart.

The Voice of Christ

I shall teach you those things which are right and pleasing to Me.[2] Consider your sins with great displeasure and sorrow, and never think yourself to be someone because of your good works.[3] You are truly a sinner. You are subject to many passions and entangled in them. Of yourself you always tend to nothing. You fall quickly, are quickly overcome, quickly troubled, and quickly undone. You have nothing in which you can glory, but you have many things for which you should think your-

1. The disciple now humbly expresses his willingness to hear Christ's words, as he was encouraged in previous chapters.

2. A contrite heart God does not despise.

3. The believer cannot take pride in his own works.

4. The believer repents when he abhors his sins.

5. A mere intellectual curiosity or doctrinal knowledge is not enough. Conviction of sin is what is essential.

6. Devotion to mere religious images and rites is not true faith, nor is parroting certain confessions where there is no belief in the heart.

7. The believer values Christ and heavenly things above earthly things, including things like food and wine.

self vile, for you are much weaker than you can comprehend. Hence, let none of the things you do seem great to you. Let nothing seem important or precious or desirable except that which is everlasting. Let the eternal truth please you above all things, and let your extreme unworthiness always displease you. Fear nothing, abhor nothing, and fly nothing as you do your own vices and sins; these should be more unpleasant for you than any material losses.[4]

Some men walk before Me without sincerity. Led on by a certain curiosity and arrogance, they wish to know My secrets and to understand the high things of God, to the neglect of themselves and their own salvation. Through their own pride and curiosity, and because I am against them, such men often fall into great temptations and sins.[5]

Fear the judgments of God! Dread the wrath of the Almighty! Do not discuss the works of the Most High, but examine your sins—in what serious things you have offended and how many good things you have neglected.

Some carry their devotion only in books, some in pictures, some in outward signs and figures. Some have Me on their lips when there is little of Me in their hearts.[6] Others, indeed, with enlightened understanding and purified affections, constantly long for everlasting things; they are unwilling to hear of earthly affairs and only with reluctance do they serve the necessities of nature.[7] These sense what the Spirit of truth speaks within them: for He teaches them to despise earthly things and to love those of heaven, to neglect the world, and each day and night to desire heaven.

5. The Wonderful Effect of Divine Love

The Disciple

I bless You, O heavenly Father, Father of my Lord Jesus Christ, for having condescended to remember me, a poor creature. Thanks to You, O Father of mercies, God of all consolation, Who with Your comfort sometimes refresh me, who am not worthy of it. I bless You always and glorify You with Your only-begotten Son and the Holy Spirit, the Paraclete, forever and ever.

Ah, Lord God, my holy Lover, when You come into my heart, all that is within me will rejoice. You are my glory and the exultation of my heart. You are my hope and refuge in the day of my tribulation. But because my love is as yet weak and my virtue imperfect, I must be strengthened and comforted by You.[1] Visit me often, therefore, and teach me Your holy discipline. Free me from evil passions and cleanse my heart of all disorderly affection so that, healed and purified within, I may be fit to love, strong to suffer, and firm to persevere.

1. Only God's love and work in us can help us to love.

Love is an excellent thing, a very great blessing, indeed.[2] It makes every difficulty easy, and bears all wrongs with equanimity. For it bears a burden without being weighted and renders sweet all that is bitter. The noble love of Jesus spurs to great deeds and excites longing for that which is more perfect.[3] Love tends upward; it will not be held down by anything low. Love wishes to be free and estranged from all worldly affections, lest its inward sight be obstructed, lest it be entangled in any temporal interest and overcome by adversity.[4]

2. A'Kempis enumerates the blessings of love. A'Kempis enumerates the blessings of love.Only God's love and work in us can help us to love.

Nothing is sweeter than love, nothing stronger or higher or wider; nothing is more pleasant, nothing fuller, and nothing better in heaven or on earth, for love is born of God and cannot rest except in God, Who is above all created things.

3. Love is the chief motive for all service to Christ.

4. Nothing must compete with our love for God.

One who is in love flies, runs, and rejoices; he is free, not bound.[5] He gives all for all and possesses all in all, because he rests in the one sovereign Good, Who is above all things, and from Whom every good flows and proceeds.[6] He does not look to the gift but turns himself above all gifts to the Giver.

5. Ultimate freedom is found in loving God, which is the first Law of God.

Love often knows no limits but overflows all bounds. Love feels no burden, thinks nothing of troubles, attempts more than it is able, and does not plead impossibility, because it believes that it may and can do all things. For this reason, it

6. God is Sovereign over all.

is able to do all, performing and effecting much where he who does not love fails and falls.

Love is watchful. Sleeping, it does not slumber. Wearied, it is not tired. Pressed, it is not straitened. Alarmed, it is not confused, but like a living flame, a burning torch, it forces its way upward and passes unharmed through every obstacle.

If a man loves, he will know the sound of this voice. For this warm affection of soul is a loud voice crying in the ears of God, and it says: "My God, my love, You are all mine and I am all Yours. Give me an increase of love, that I may learn to taste with the inward lips of my heart how sweet it is to love, how sweet to be dissolved in love and bathe in it. Let me be rapt in love. Let me rise above self in great fervor and wonder.[7] Let me sing the hymn of love, and let me follow You, my Love, to the heights. Let my soul exhaust itself in praising You, rejoicing out of love.[8] Let me love You more than myself, and let me not love myself except for Your sake. In You let me love all those who truly love You, as the law of love, which shines forth from You, commands."[9]

Love is swift, sincere, kind, pleasant, and delightful. Love is strong, patient and faithful, prudent, long-suffering, and manly. Love is never self-seeking, for in whatever a person seeks himself there he falls from love. Love is circumspect, humble, and upright. It is neither soft nor light, nor intent upon vain things.[10] It is sober and chaste, firm and quiet, guarded in all the senses. Love is subject and obedient to superiors. It is mean and contemptible in its own eyes, devoted and thankful to God; always trusting and hoping in Him even when He is distasteful to it, for there is no living in love without sorrow. He who is not ready to suffer all things and to stand resigned to the will of the Beloved is not worthy to be called a lover.[11] A lover must embrace willingly all that is difficult and bitter for the sake of the Beloved, and he should not turn away from Him because of adversities.

7. Love for God involves a self-denial.

8. Love for God will create in us praise and singing every day.

9. Loving God involves keeping his commands, chief of which is to love one another in the church.

10. Manly love is a tough love that continues despite discouragements and trial.

11. Love for God endures all things for that love.

6. The Proving of a True Lover

The Voice of Christ

My child, you are not yet a brave and wise lover.[1]

The Disciple

Why, Lord?

The Voice of Christ

Because, on account of a slight difficulty you give up what you have undertaken and are too eager to seek consolation.

The brave lover stands firm in temptations and pays no heed to the crafty persuasions of the enemy. As I please him in prosperity, so in adversity I am not displeasing to him. The wise lover regards not so much the gift of Him Who loves as the love of Him Who gives. He regards the affection of the Giver rather than the value of the gift, and sets his Beloved above all gifts.[2] The noble lover does not rest in the gift but in Me Who am above every gift.

All is not lost, then, if you sometimes feel less devout than you wish toward Me or My saints. That good and sweet feeling which you sometimes have is the effect of present grace and a certain foretaste of your heavenly home. You must not lean upon it too much, because it comes and goes. But to fight against evil thoughts which attack you is a sign of virtue and great merit.[3] Do not, therefore, let strange fantasies disturb you, no matter what they concern. Hold strongly to your resolution and keep a right intention toward God.

It is not an illusion that you are sometimes rapt in ecstasy and then quickly returned to the usual follies of your heart.[4] For these are evils which you suffer rather than commit; and so long as they displease you and you struggle against them, it is a matter of merit and not a loss.

You must know that the old enemy tries by all means in his power to hinder your desire for good and to turn you from every devotional practice, especially from the veneration of the saints,[5] from devout meditation on My passion, and from

1. A'Kempis speaks of a tough love that keeps loving Christ through many difficult trials.

2. The secret is not to receive consolation, but to know Christ's love.

3. Fighting the flesh is uncomfortable but of more value than a feeling of piety and peace.

4. Religious feelings don't last long, but the battle with sin is constant.

5. Veneration of saints could descend into idolatry, but this is not necessarily intended by this reference.

6. The devil opposes all holy exercises, confession of sin, prayer, and Bible reading.

your firm purpose of advancing in virtue. He suggests many evil thoughts that he may cause you weariness and horror, and thus draw you away from prayer and holy reading. A humble confession displeases him and, if he could, he would make you omit Holy Communion.[6]

Do not believe him or heed him, even though he often sets traps to deceive you. When he suggests evil, unclean things, accuse him. Say to him: "Away, unclean spirit! Shame, miserable creature! You are but filth to bring such things to my ears. Begone, most wretched seducer! You shall have no part in me, for Jesus will be my strength, and you shall be confounded. I would rather die and suffer all torments than consent to you. Be still! Be silent! Though you bring many troubles upon me I will have none of you. The Lord is my light, my salvation. Whom shall I fear? Though armies unite against me, my heart will not fear, for the Lord is my Helper, my Redeemer."[7]

7. Psalm 27

Fight like a good soldier and if you sometimes fall through weakness, rise again with greater strength than before, trusting in My most abundant grace.[8] But beware of vain complacency and pride. For many are led into error through these faults and sometimes fall into almost perpetual blindness. Let the fall of these, who proudly presume on self, be a warning to you and a constant incentive to humility.

8. Our strength must come from trusting in God's grace in this battle.

7. Grace Must Be Hidden Under the Mantle of Humility

The Voice of Christ

It is better and safer for you to conceal the grace of devotion, not to be elated by it, not to speak or think much of it, and instead to humble yourself and fear lest it is being given to one unworthy of it. Do not cling too closely to this affection, for it may quickly be changed to its opposite. When you are in grace, think how miserable and needy you are without it.[1] Your progress in spiritual life does not consist in having the grace

1. A'Kempis speaks to when things are going well in the Christian life (when consoled and comforted.)

of consolation, but in enduring its withdrawal with humility, resignation, and patience, so that you neither become listless in prayer nor neglect your other duties in the least; but on the contrary do what you can do as well as you know how, and do not neglect yourself completely because of your dryness or anxiety of mind.[2]

There are many, indeed, who immediately become impatient and lazy when things do not go well with them. The way of man, however, does not always lie in his own power. It is God's prerogative to give grace and to console when He wishes, as much as He wishes, and whom He wishes, as it shall please Him and no more.

Some careless persons, misusing the grace of devotion, have destroyed themselves because they wished to do more than they were able. They failed to take account of their own weakness, and followed the desire of their heart rather than the judgment of their reason. Then, because they presumed to greater things than pleased God they quickly lost His grace. They who had built their homes in heaven became helpless, vile outcasts, humbled and impoverished, that they might learn not to fly with their own wings but to trust in Mine.[3]

They who are still new and inexperienced in the way of the Lord may easily be deceived and overthrown unless they guide themselves by the advice of discreet persons. But if they wish to follow their own notions rather than to trust in others who are more experienced, they will be in danger of a sorry end, at least if they are unwilling to be drawn from their vanity. Seldom do they who are wise in their own conceits bear humbly the guidance of others. Yet a little knowledge humbly and meekly pursued is better than great treasures of learning sought in vain complacency. It is better for you to have little than to have much which may become the source of pride.

He who gives himself up entirely to enjoyment acts very unwisely, for he forgets his former helplessness and that chastened fear of the Lord which dreads to lose a proffered grace.[4] Nor is he very brave or wise who becomes too despondent in

2. When life is hard, the mature Christian will be more fervent in prayer and duties.

3. When in this state of comfort, we can fall prey to ambition and self-reliance as well as forget to trust in God.

4. A'Kempis is concerned for a lack of fear of God and watchfulness when enjoying God's gifts.

5. The other trap is to become too depressed and fearful in trials.

6. Humility will provide more self-control over these emotional swings.

7. These are the metrics of mature faith – love, humility, and glorifying God.

times of adversity and difficulty and thinks less confidently of Me than he should.[5] He who wishes to be too secure in time of peace will often become too dejected and fearful in time of trial.

If you were wise enough to remain always humble and small in your own eyes, and to restrain and rule your spirit well, you would not fall so quickly into danger and offense.[6]

When a spirit of fervor is enkindled within you, you may well meditate on how you will feel when the fervor leaves. Then, when this happens, remember that the light which I have withdrawn for a time as a warning to you and for My own glory may again return. Such trials are often more beneficial than if you had things always as you wish. For a man's merits are not measured by many visions or consolations, or by knowledge of the Scriptures, or by his being in a higher position than others, but by the truth of his humility, by his capacity for divine charity, by his constancy in seeking purely and entirely the honor of God, by his disregard and positive contempt of self, and more, by preferring to be despised and humiliated rather than honored by others.[7]

8. Self-Abasement in the Sight of God

The Disciple

1. Self-esteem is worthless next to God's favor of us and our esteem of God.

I will speak to my Lord, I who am but dust and ashes. If I consider myself anything more than this, behold You stand against me, and my sins bear witness to the truth which I cannot contradict. If I abase myself, however, if I humble myself to nothingness, if I shrink from all self-esteem and account myself as the dust which I am, Your grace will favor me, Your light will enshroud my heart, and all self-esteem, no matter how little, will sink in the depths of my nothingness to perish forever.[1]

It is there You show me to myself—what I am, what I have been, and what I am coming to; for I am nothing and I did not know it. Left to myself, I am nothing but total weakness. But if You look upon me for an instant, I am at once made strong and filled with new joy.[2] Great wonder it is that I, who of my own weight always sink to the depths, am so suddenly lifted up, and so graciously embraced by You.

2. God's presence and favor is the source of all joy.

It is Your love that does this, graciously upholding me, supporting me in so many necessities, guarding me from so many grave dangers, and snatching me, as I may truly say, from evils without number. Indeed, by loving myself badly I lost myself; by seeking only You and by truly loving You I have found both myself and You, and by that love I have reduced myself more profoundly to nothing. For You, O sweetest Lord, deal with me above all my merits and above all that I dare to hope or ask.[3]

3. Even one's merits fade when we are recipients of God's grace.

May You be blessed, my God, for although I am unworthy of any benefits, yet Your nobility and infinite goodness never cease to do good even for those who are ungrateful and far from You.[4] Convert us to You, that we may be thankful, humble, and devout, for You are our salvation, our courage, and our strength.

4. God's common grace is shown even to unbelievers and the unthankful.

9. All Things should be Referred to God as their Last End

The Voice of Christ

My child, I must be your supreme and last end, if you truly desire to be blessed. With this intention your affections, which are too often perversely inclined to self and to creatures, will be purified. For if you seek yourself in anything, you immediately fail interiorly and become dry of heart.[1]

1. Seek God as the highest good, and the object most worthy of our affections.

Refer all things principally to Me, therefore, for it is I Who have given them all. Consider each thing as flowing from the

2. Christ is the source of all blessing for us, and therefore worthy of our chief love and glory.

3. Distress comes from another perceived good displacing the Highest good (Christ) in our minds.

4. Our "return" of thanks, our praise and blessing to God

5. Our love for God will conquer all and empower us to mortify sin and overcome the enemy.

highest good, and therefore to Me, as to their highest source, must all things be brought back.[2]

From Me the small and the great, the poor and the rich draw the water of life as from a living fountain, and they who serve Me willingly and freely shall receive grace upon grace. He who wishes to glory in things apart from Me, however, or to delight in some good as his own, shall not be grounded in true joy or gladdened in his heart, but shall be burdened and distressed in many ways.[3] Hence you ought not to attribute any good to yourself or ascribe virtue to any man, but give all to God without Whom man has nothing.

I have given all things. I will that all be returned to Me again, and I exact most strictly a return of thanks.[4] This is the truth by which vainglory is put to flight.

Where heavenly grace and true charity enter in, there neither envy nor narrowness of heart nor self-love will have place. Divine love conquers all and enlarges the powers of the soul.[5]

If you are truly wise, you will rejoice only in Me, because no one is good except God alone, Who is to be praised above all things and above all to be blessed.

10. To Despise the World and Serve God is Sweet

The Disciple

Now again I will speak, Lord, and will not be silent. I will speak to the hearing of my God, my Lord, and my King Who is in heaven. How great, O Lord, is the multitude of Your mercies which You have stored up for those who love You. But what are You to those who love You? What are You to those who serve You with their whole heart?

Truly beyond the power of words is the sweetness of contemplation You give to those who love You. To me You have shown the sweetness of Your charity, especially in having made me when I did not exist, in having brought me back to serve You when I had gone far astray from You, in having commanded me to love You.[1]

O Fountain of unceasing love, what shall I say of You? How can I forget You, Who have been pleased to remember me even after I had wasted away and perished? You have shown mercy to Your servant beyond all hope, and have exhibited grace and friendship beyond his deserving.[2]

What return shall I make to You for this grace? For it is not given every man to forsake all things, to renounce the world, and undertake the religious life. Is it anything great that I should serve You Whom every creature is bound to serve? It should not seem much to me; instead it should appear great and wonderful that You condescend to receive into Your service one who is so poor and unworthy. Behold, all things are Yours, even those which I have and by which I serve You. Behold, heaven and earth which You created for the service of man, stand ready, and each day they do whatever You command. But even this is little, for You have appointed angels also to minister to man—yea more than all this—You Yourself have condescended to serve man and have promised to give him Yourself.[3]

What return shall I make for all these thousands of benefits? Would that I could serve You all the days of my life! Would that for but one day I could serve You worthily! Truly You are worthy of all service, all honor, and everlasting praise. Truly You are my Lord, and I am Your poor servant, bound to serve You with all my powers, praising You without ever becoming weary. I wish to do this—this is my desire. Do You supply whatever is wanting in me.

It is a great honor, a great glory to serve You and to despise all things for Your sake. They who give themselves gladly to Your most holy service will possess great grace. They who cast aside all carnal delights for Your love will find the most sweet consolation of the Holy Ghost. They who enter upon

1. Here is a reference to God's sovereign work in salvation.

2. The humble one who sees his sinful state is the one who best understands grace (unmerited favor).

3. Reference to Christ, the Son of God, descending to earth as a servant.

the narrow way for Your name and cast aside all worldly care will attain great freedom of mind.

O sweet and joyful service of God, which makes man truly free and holy![4] O sacred state of religious bondage which makes man equal to the angels, pleasing to God, terrible to the demons, and worthy of the commendation of all the faithful! O service to be embraced and always desired, in which the highest good is offered and joy is won which shall remain forever!

4. Ultimate freedom is found in servitude to God.

11. The Longings of our Hearts Must Be Examined And Moderated

The Voice of Christ

My child, it is necessary for you to learn many things which you have not yet learned well.

The Disciple

What are they, Lord?

The Voice of Christ

That you conform your desires entirely according to My good pleasure, and be not a lover of self but an earnest doer of My will.[1] Desires very often inflame you and drive you madly on, but consider whether you act for My honor, or for your own advantage. If I am the cause, you will be well content with whatever I ordain. If, on the other hand, any self-seeking lurks in you, it troubles you and weighs you down. Take care, then, that you do not rely too much on a preconceived desire that has no reference to Me, lest you repent later on and be displeased with what at first pleased you and which you desired as being for the best.[2] Not every desire which seems good should be followed immediately, nor, on the other hand, should every contrary affection be at once rejected.

It is sometimes well to use a little restraint even in good desires and inclinations, lest through too much eagerness you

1. The real test of true faith is found in doing the will of God.

2. Our desires are not a reliable test of what is good. Skepticism of desires is recommended.

bring upon yourself distraction of mind; lest through your lack of discipline you create scandal for others; or lest you be suddenly upset and fall because of resistance from others. Sometimes, however, you must use violence and resist your sensual appetite bravely. You must pay no attention to what the flesh does or does not desire, taking pains that it be subjected, even by force, to the spirit.[3] And it should be chastised and forced to remain in subjection until it is prepared for anything and is taught to be satisfied with little, to take pleasure in simple things, and not to murmur against inconveniences.

3. A'Kempis confuses fleshly sin with bodily fleshly appetites.

12. Acquiring Patience in the Fight Against Concupiscence

The Disciple

Patience, O Lord God, is very necessary for me, I see, because there are many adversities in this life. No matter what plans I make for my own peace, my life cannot be free from struggle and sorrow.

The Voice of Christ

My child, you are right, yet My wish is not that you seek that peace which is free from temptations or meets with no opposition, but rather that you consider yourself as having found peace when you have been tormented with many tribulations and tried with many adversities.[1]

If you say that you cannot suffer much, how will you endure the fire of purgatory?[2] Of two evils, the lesser is always to be chosen. Therefore, in order that you may escape the everlasting punishments to come, try to bear present evils patiently for the sake of God.

1. Peace in the storm is a supernatural Spirit-sent gift.

2. The doctrine of purgatory finds no basis in Scripture.

3. Unbelievers suffer in this world.

Do you think that men of the world have no suffering, or perhaps but little? Ask even those who enjoy the most delights and you will learn otherwise.[3] "But," you will say, "they enjoy many pleasures and follow their own wishes; therefore they do not feel their troubles very much." Granted that they do have whatever they wish, how long do you think it will last? Behold, they who prosper in the world shall perish as smoke, and there shall be no memory of their past joys. Even in this life they do not find rest in these pleasures without bitterness, weariness, and fear. For they often receive the penalty of sorrow from the very thing whence they believe their happiness comes. And it is just. Since they seek and follow after pleasures without reason, they should not enjoy them without shame and bitterness.

How brief, how false, how unreasonable and shameful all these pleasures are! Yet in their drunken blindness men do not understand this, but like brute beasts incur death of soul for the miserly enjoyment of a corruptible life.

4. Psalm 37:4

Therefore, My child, do not pursue your lusts, but turn away from your own will. "Seek thy pleasure in the Lord and He will give thee thy heart's desires."[4] If you wish to be truly delighted and more abundantly comforted by Me, behold, in contempt of all worldly things and in the cutting off of all base pleasures shall your blessing be, and great consolation shall be given you.[5] Further, the more you withdraw yourself from any solace of creatures, the sweeter and stronger comfort will you find in Me.

5. Mortify sinful lusts and set affections on things above.

At first you will not gain these blessings without sadness and toil and conflict. Habit already formed will resist you, but it shall be overcome by a better habit.[6] The flesh will murmur against you, but it will be bridled by fervor of spirit. The old serpent will sting and trouble you, but prayer will put him to flight and by steadfast, useful toil the way will be closed to him.

6. The Christian life is strenuous and difficult when we are fighting sin and establishing good habits.

13. The Obedience of One Humbly Subject to the Example of Jesus Christ

The Voice of Christ

My child, he who attempts to escape obeying withdraws himself from grace. Likewise he who seeks private benefits for himself loses those which are common to all. He who does not submit himself freely and willingly to his superior, shows that his flesh is not yet perfectly obedient but that it often rebels and murmurs against him.[1]

Learn quickly, then, to submit yourself to your superior if you wish to conquer your own flesh. For the exterior enemy is more quickly overcome if the inner man is not laid waste. There is no more troublesome, no worse enemy of the soul than you yourself, if you are not in harmony with the spirit. It is absolutely necessary that you conceive a true contempt for yourself if you wish to be victorious over flesh and blood.

Because you still love yourself too inordinately, you are afraid to resign yourself wholly to the will of others.[2] Is it such a great matter if you, who are but dust and nothingness, subject yourself to man for the sake of God, when I, the All-Powerful, the Most High, Who created all things out of nothing, humbly subjected Myself to man for your sake?[3] I became the most humble and the lowest of all men that you might overcome your pride with My humility.

Learn to obey, you who are but dust! Learn to humble yourself, you who are but earth and clay, and bow down under the foot of every man! Learn to break your own will, to submit to all subjection! Be zealous against yourself! Allow no pride to dwell in you, but prove yourself so humble and lowly that all may walk over you and trample upon you as dust in the streets![4]

What have you, vain man, to complain of? What answer can you make, vile sinner, to those who accuse you, you who have so often offended God and so many times deserved hell? But My eye has spared you because your soul was precious

1. A'Kempis enjoins submission to elders (1 Peter 5:5).

2. Lack of submission is tantamount to pride and a failure to deny self.

3. If Christ humbled himself, we should humble ourselves. Reference Phil. 2:4ff.

4. A'Kempis exhorts to a very humble perspective of self.

in My sight, so that you might know My love and always be thankful for My benefits, so that you might give yourself continually to true subjection and humility, and might patiently endure contempt.

14. Consider the Hidden Judgments of God Lest You Become Proud of Your Own Good Deeds

The Disciple

You thunder forth Your judgments over me, Lord. You shake all my bones with fear and trembling, and my soul is very much afraid. I stand in awe as I consider that the heavens are not pure in Your sight.[1] If You found wickedness in the angels and did not spare them, what will become of me? Stars have fallen from heaven, and I—I who am but dust—how can I be presumptuous? They whose deeds seemed worthy of praise have fallen into the depths, and I have seen those who ate the bread of angels delighting themselves with the husks of swine.

There is no holiness, then, if You withdraw Your hand, Lord. There is no wisdom if You cease to guide, no courage if You cease to defend. No chastity is secure if You do not guard it. Our vigilance avails nothing if Your holy watchfulness does not protect us. Left to ourselves we sink and perish, but visited by You we are lifted up and live. We are truly unstable, but You make us strong. We grow lukewarm, but You inflame us.[2]

Oh, how humbly and lowly should I consider myself! How very little should I esteem anything that seems good in me! How profoundly should I submit to Your unfathomable judgments, Lord, where I find myself to be but nothing!

O immeasurable weight! O impassable sea, where I find myself to be nothing but bare nothingness! Where, then, is

1. The fear of God is the basic disposition of mind and heart, for God's judgment and holiness.

2. We are completely and utterly dependent on God for salvation and all good.

glory's hiding place? Where can there be any trust in my own virtue?³ All vainglory is swallowed up in the depths of Your judgments upon me.

What is all flesh in Your sight? Shall the clay glory against Him that formed it? How can he whose heart is truly subject to God be lifted up by vainglory? The whole world will not make him proud whom truth has subjected to itself.⁴ Nor shall he who has placed all his hope in God be moved by the tongues of flatterers. For behold, even they who speak are nothing; they will pass away with the sound of their words, but the truth of the Lord remains forever.

3. Trust in one's own words is condemned.

4. Pride is only possible if one believes falsehood.

15. How One Should Feel and Speak on Every Desirable Thing

The Voice of Christ

My child, this is the way you must speak on every occasion:¹ "Lord, if it be pleasing to You, so be it. If it be to Your honor, Lord, be it done in Your name. Lord, if You see that it is expedient and profitable for me, then grant that I may use it to Your honor. But if You know that it will be harmful to me, and of no good benefit to the welfare of my soul, then take this desire away from me."

Not every desire is from the Holy Spirit, even though it may seem right and good. It is difficult to be certain whether it is a good spirit or a bad one that prompts one to this or that, and even to know whether you are being moved by your own spirit. Many who seemed at first to be led by a good spirit have been deceived in the end.

Whatever the mind sees as good, ask and desire in fear of God and humility of heart. Above all, commit the whole matter to Me with true resignation, and say:² "Lord, You know what is better for me; let this be done or that be done as You

1. A prayer is suggested concerning our desires – to discern whether they would be harmful or beneficial to our souls.

2. A prayer is suggested here wherein we would submit ourselves to the will of God, to pleasing Christ and honoring Him.

please. Grant what You will, as much as You will, when You will. Do with me as You know best, as will most please You, and will be for Your greater honor. Place me where You will and deal with me freely in all things. I am in Your hand; turn me about whichever way You will. Behold, I am Your servant, ready to obey in all things. Not for myself do I desire to live, but for You—would that I could do this worthily and perfectly!"

A Prayer that the Will of God Be Done

3. A prayer which follows Christ's prayer in the Garden, "Not my will, but Thine be done."

Grant me Your grace, O most merciful Jesus, that it may be with me, and work with me, and remain with me to the very end.[3] Grant that I may always desire and will that which is most acceptable and pleasing to You. Let Your will be mine. Let my will always follow Yours and agree perfectly with it. Let my will be one with Yours in willing and in not willing, and let me be unable to will or not will anything but what You will or do not will. Grant that I may die to all things in this world, and for Your sake love to be despised and unknown in this life. Give me above all desires the desire to rest in You, and in You let my heart have peace. You are true peace of heart. You alone are its rest. Without You all things are difficult and troubled. In this peace, the selfsame that is in You, the Most High, the everlasting Good, I will sleep and take my rest. Amen.

16. True Comfort Is to Be Sought in God Alone

The Disciple

1. A'Kempis is concerned with proper desires which prefer the heavenly over the earthly.

Whatever I can desire or imagine for my own comfort I look for not here but hereafter.[1] For if I alone should have all the world's comforts and could enjoy all its delights, it is certain that they could not long endure. Therefore, my soul, you cannot enjoy full consolation or perfect delight except in God, the Consoler of the poor and the Helper of the humble.

Wait a little, my soul, wait for the divine promise and you will have an abundance of all good things in heaven. If you desire these present things too much, you will lose those which are everlasting and heavenly.[2] Use temporal things but desire eternal things. You cannot be satisfied with any temporal goods because you were not created to enjoy them.

Even if you possessed all created things you could not be happy and blessed;[3] for in God, Who created all these things, your whole blessedness and happiness consists—not indeed such happiness as is seen and praised by lovers of the world, but such as that for which the good and faithful servants of Christ wait, and of which the spiritual and pure of heart, whose conversation is in heaven, sometime have a foretaste.[4]

Vain and brief is all human consolation. But that which is received inwardly from the Truth is blessed and true. The devout man carries his Consoler, Jesus, everywhere with him, and he says to Him: "Be with me, Lord Jesus, in every place and at all times. Let this be my consolation, to be willing to forego all human comforting. And if Your consolation be wanting to me, let Your will and just trial of me be my greatest comfort. For You will not always be angry, nor will You threaten forever."[5]

2. The true Christian finds more delight in God and His Christ than the temporal pleasures.

3. Mark 8:36

4. God is our highest delight (Psalm 84:2).

5. Psalm 103:9

17. All Our Care is to Be Placed in God

The Voice of Christ

My child, allow me to do what I will with you. I know what is best for you. You think as a man; you feel in many things as human affection persuades.

The Disciple

Lord, what You say is true.[1] Your care for me is greater than all the care I can take of myself. For he who does not cast all his care upon You stands very unsafely. If only my will remain right and firm toward You, Lord, do with me whatever pleases You. For whatever You shall do with me can only be good.

1. We must be guided by Christ's words, far more so than our own desires.

If You wish me to be in darkness, I shall bless You. And if You wish me to be in light, again I shall bless You. If You stoop down to comfort me, I shall bless You, and if You wish me to be afflicted, I shall bless You forever.

The Voice of Christ

My child, this is the disposition which you should have if you wish to walk with Me. You should be as ready to suffer as to enjoy. You should as willingly be destitute and poor as rich and satisfied.[2]

2. Contentment in all states is encouraged (as Paul testifies in Phil. 4:11).

The Disciple

O Lord, I shall suffer willingly for Your sake whatever You wish to send me. I am ready to accept from Your hand both good and evil alike, the sweet and the bitter together, sorrow with joy; and for all that happens to me I am grateful. Keep me from all sin and I will fear neither death nor hell. Do not cast me out forever nor blot me out of the Book of Life, and whatever tribulation befalls will not harm me.

18. Temporal Sufferings Should Be Borne Patiently, After the Example of Christ

The Voice of Christ

1. Christ teaches us patience by His example (but it is not the only reason He went to the Cross).

My child, I came down from heaven for your salvation and took upon Myself your miseries, not out of necessity but out of love, that you might learn to be patient and bear the sufferings of this life without repining.[1] From the moment of My birth to My death on the cross, suffering did not leave Me. I suffered great want of temporal goods. Often I heard many complaints against Me. Disgrace and reviling I bore with patience. For My blessings I received ingratitude, for My miracles blasphemies, and for My teaching scorn.

The Disciple

O Lord, because You were patient in life, especially in fulfilling the design of the Father, it is fitting that I, a most miserable sinner, should live patiently according to Your will,[2] and, as long as You shall wish, bear the burden of this corruptible body for the welfare of my soul. For though this present life seems burdensome, yet by Your grace it becomes meritorious,[3] and it is made brighter and more endurable for the weak by Your example and the pathways of the saints. But it has also more consolation than formerly under the old law when the gates of heaven were closed, when the way thereto seemed darker than now, and when so few cared to seek the eternal kingdom. The just, the elect, could not enter heaven before Your sufferings and sacred death had paid the debt.[4]

Oh, what great thanks I owe You, Who have shown me and all the faithful the good and right way to Your everlasting kingdom! Your life is our way and in Your holy patience we come nearer to You Who are our crown. Had You not gone before and taught us, who would have cared to follow? Alas, how many would have remained far behind, had they not before their eyes Your holy example! Behold, even we who have heard of Your many miracles and teachings are still lukewarm; what would happen if we did not have such light by which to follow You?

2. Ultimately, Christ's sufferings and our sufferings come as the will of the Father.

3. Even the rewards in heaven are products of God's grace

4. The key reason for the death of Christ – the payment of our debt. A'Kempis postulates that the Old Testament elect saints could not enter heaven until after Christ died.

19. True Patience in Suffering

The Voice of Christ

What are you saying, My child? Think of My suffering and that of the saints, and cease complaining. You have not yet resisted to the shedding of blood.[1] What you suffer is very little compared with the great things they suffered who were so strongly tempted, so severely troubled, so tried and tormented in many ways. Well may you remember, therefore, the very painful woes of others, that you may bear your own little

1. Hebrews 12:1-4

2. This speaks to the demeanor by which suffering is endured. This is the major test of our spiritual maturity.

3. We must not complain about our trials and persecutions because ultimately they are ordained by God.

ones the more easily. And if they do not seem so small to you, examine if perhaps your impatience is not the cause of their apparent greatness; and whether they are great or small, try to bear them all patiently. The better you dispose yourself to suffer, the more wisely you act and the greater is the reward promised you.[2] Thus you will suffer more easily if your mind and habits are diligently trained to it.

Do not say: "I cannot bear this from such a man, nor should I suffer things of this kind, for he has done me a great wrong. He has accused me of many things of which I never thought. However, from someone else I will gladly suffer as much as I think I should."

Such a thought is foolish, for it does not consider the virtue of patience or the One Who will reward it, but rather weighs the person and the offense committed. The man who will suffer only as much as seems good to him, who will accept suffering only from those from whom he is pleased to accept it, is not truly patient. For the truly patient man does not consider from whom the suffering comes, whether from a superior, an equal, or an inferior, whether from a good and holy person or from a perverse and unworthy one; but no matter how great an adversity befalls him, no matter how often it comes or from whom it comes, he accepts it gratefully from the hand of God, and counts it a great gain.[3] For with God nothing that is suffered for His sake, no matter how small, can pass without reward. Be prepared for the fight, then, if you wish to gain the victory. Without struggle you cannot obtain the crown of patience, and if you refuse to suffer you are refusing the crown. But if you desire to be crowned, fight bravely and bear up patiently. Without labor there is no rest, and without fighting, no victory.

The Disciple

O Lord, let that which seems naturally impossible to me become possible through Your grace. You know that I can suffer very little, and that I am quickly discouraged when any small adversity arises. Let the torment of tribulation suffered for Your name be pleasant and desirable to me, since to suffer and be troubled for Your sake is very beneficial for my soul.

20. Confessing Our Weakness in the Miseries of Life

The Disciple

I will bring witness against myself to my injustice, and to You, O Lord, I will confess my weakness.[1]

Often it is a small thing that makes me downcast and sad. I propose to act bravely, but when even a small temptation comes I find myself in great straits. Sometimes it is the merest trifle which gives rise to grievous temptations. When I think myself somewhat safe and when I am not expecting it, I frequently find myself almost overcome by a slight wind. Look, therefore, Lord, at my lowliness and frailty which You know so well. Have mercy on me and snatch me out of the mire that I may not be caught in it and may not remain forever utterly despondent.

That I am so prone to fall and so weak in resisting my passions oppresses me frequently and confounds me in Your sight. While I do not fully consent to them, still their assault is very troublesome and grievous to me, and it wearies me exceedingly thus to live in daily strife. Yet from the fact that abominable fancies rush in upon me much more easily than they leave, my weakness becomes clear to me.

Oh that You, most mighty God of Israel, zealous Lover of faithful souls, would consider the labor and sorrow of Your servant, and assist him in all his undertakings! Strengthen me with heavenly courage lest the outer man, the miserable flesh, against which I shall be obliged to fight so long as I draw a

1. Every Christian must always be cognizant of his weakness. This is also humility.

2. The prayer for God's strength is essential and must be constant.

breath in this wretched life and which is not yet subjected to the spirit, prevail and dominate me.[2]

Alas! What sort of life is this, from which troubles and miseries are never absent, where all things are full of snares and enemies? For when one trouble or temptation leaves, another comes. Indeed, even while the first conflict is still raging, many others begin unexpectedly. How is it possible to love a life that has such great bitterness, that is subject to so many calamities and miseries? Indeed, how can it even be called life when it begets so many deaths and plagues? And yet, it is loved, and many seek their delight in it.

3. The world would have no power over us if the flesh within us wasn't reaching for it.

Many persons often blame the world for being false and vain, yet do not readily give it up because the desires of the flesh have such great power.[3] Some things draw them to love the world, others make them despise it. The lust of the flesh, the desire of the eyes, and the pride of life lead to love, while the pains and miseries, which are the just consequences of those things, beget hatred and weariness of the world.

4. The sweetness of God is contrasted with the bitter pleasures of the world.

Vicious pleasure overcomes the soul that is given to the world. She thinks that there are delights beneath these thorns, because she has never seen or tasted the sweetness of God or the internal delight of virtue.[4] They, on the other hand, who entirely despise the world and seek to live for God under the rule of holy discipline, are not ignorant of the divine sweetness promised to those who truly renounce the world. They see clearly how gravely the world errs, and in how many ways it deceives.

21. Above All Goods and All Gifts We Must Rest in God

The Disciple

Above all things and in all things, O my soul, rest always in God, for He is the everlasting rest of the saints.[1]

Grant, most sweet and loving Jesus, that I may seek my repose in You above every creature; above all health and beauty; above every honor and glory; every power and dignity; above all knowledge and cleverness, all riches and arts, all joy and gladness; above all fame and praise, all sweetness and consolation; above every hope and promise, every merit and desire; above all the gifts and favors that You can give or pour down upon me; above all the joy and exultation that the mind can receive and feel; and finally, above the angels and archangels and all the heavenly host; above all things visible and invisible; and may I seek my repose in You above everything that is not You, my God.[2]

For You, O Lord my God, are above all things the best. You alone are most high, You alone most powerful. You alone are most sufficient and most satisfying, You alone most sweet and consoling. You alone are most beautiful and loving, You alone most noble and glorious above all things. In You is every perfection that has been or ever will be. Therefore, whatever You give me besides Yourself, whatever You reveal to me concerning Yourself, and whatever You promise, is too small and insufficient when I do not see and fully enjoy You alone.[3] For my heart cannot rest or be fully content until, rising above all gifts and every created thing, it rests in You.

Who, O most beloved Spouse, Jesus Christ, most pure Lover, Lord of all creation, who shall give me the wings of true liberty that I may fly to rest in You? When shall freedom be fully given me to see how sweet You are, O Lord, my God? When shall I recollect myself entirely in You, so that because of Your love I may feel, not myself, but You alone above all sense and measure, in a manner known to none? But now I

1. To rest in God is the constant life of faith.

2. The highest value over all worldly honors and pleasures is to rest in Christ.

3. To enjoy God is to rest in Him – the highest value of life.

often lament and grieve over my unhappiness, for many evils befall me in this vale of miseries, often disturbing me, making me sad and overshadowing me, often hindering and distracting me, alluring and entangling me so that I neither have free access to You nor enjoy the sweet embraces which are ever ready for blessed souls.[4] Let my sighs and the manifold desolation here on earth move You.

4. Our trials can become distracting and we may lose a God-ward focus.

O Jesus, Splendor of eternal glory, Consolation of the pilgrim soul, with You my lips utter no sound and to You my silence speaks. How long will my Lord delay His coming? Let Him come to His poor servant and make him happy. Let Him put forth His hand and take this miserable creature from his anguish. Come, O come, for without You there will be no happy day or hour, because You are my happiness and without You my table is empty. I am wretched, as it were imprisoned and weighted down with fetters, until You fill me with the light of Your presence, restore me to liberty, and show me a friendly countenance.[5] Let others seek instead of You whatever they will, but nothing pleases me or will please me but You, my God, my Hope, my everlasting Salvation. I will not be silent, I will not cease praying until Your grace returns to me and You speak inwardly to me, saying: "Behold, I am here. Lo, I have come to you because you have called Me. Your tears and the desire of your soul, your humility and contrition of heart have inclined Me and brought Me to you."

5. The hardest time for the Christian is sensing a distance from God.

Lord, I have called You, and have desired You, and have been ready to spurn all things for Your sake. For You first spurred me on to seek You. May You be blessed, therefore, O Lord, for having shown this goodness to Your servant according to the multitude of Your mercies.

What more is there for Your servant to say to You unless, with his iniquity and vileness always in mind, he humbles himself before You? Nothing among all the wonders of heaven and earth is like to You. Your works are exceedingly good, Your judgments true, and Your providence rules the whole universe.[6] May You be praised and glorified, therefore, O Wisdom of the Father. Let my lips and my soul and all created things unite to praise and bless You.

6. God's sovereignty over all, perfect justice, and goodness are worthy of all praise.

22. Remember the Innumerable Gifts of God

The Disciple

Open my heart, O Lord, to Your law and teach me to walk in the way of Your commandments. Let me understand Your will. Let me remember Your blessings—all of them and each single one of them—with great reverence and care so that henceforth I may return worthy thanks for them.[1] I know that I am unable to give due thanks for even the least of Your gifts. I am unworthy of the benefits You have given me, and when I consider Your generosity my spirit faints away before its greatness. All that we have of soul and body, whatever we possess interiorly or exteriorly, by nature or by grace, are Your gifts and they proclaim Your goodness and mercy from which we have received all good things.[2]

1. Gratitude and obedience are the two basic functions of the new life in Christ.

If one receives more and another less, yet all are Yours and without You nothing can be received. He who receives greater things cannot glory in his own merit or consider himself above others or behave insolently toward those who receive less.[3] He who attributes less to himself and is the more humble and devout in returning thanks is indeed the greater and the better, while he who considers himself lower than all men and judges himself to be the least worthy, is the more fit to receive the greater blessing.

2. All good things come from God.

3. A'Kempis discards merit here, rightly seeing that all one can have only comes by God's grace.

He, on the other hand, who has received fewer gifts should not be sad or impatient or envious of the richer man. Instead he should turn his mind to You and offer You the greatest praise because You give so bountifully, so freely and willingly, without regard to persons.[4] All things come from You; therefore, You are to be praised in all things. You know what is good

4. Even the poor should be grateful because they have received all as God's gift.

5. A'Kempis notes merit, but he admits that we do not know why one receives more than another.

6. Finally, A'Kempis delights in God's will and sovereign decree as the best determinant for our condition and blessings.

1. The four steps to peace and liberty counter
1) self will
2) greed
3) self promotion
4) disobedience to God

for each of us; and why one should receive less and another more is not for us to judge, but for You Who have marked every man's merits.[5]

Therefore, O Lord God, I consider it a great blessing not to have many things which human judgment holds praiseworthy and glorious, for one who realizes his own poverty and vileness should not be sad or downcast at it, but rather consoled and happy because You, O God, have chosen the poor, the humble, and the despised in this world to be Your friends and servants. The truth of this is witnessed by Your Apostles, whom You made princes over all the world. Yet they lived in this world without complaining, so humble and simple, so free from malice and deceit, that they were happy even to suffer reproach for Your name and to embrace with great affection that which the world abhors.

A man who loves You and recognizes Your benefits, therefore, should be gladdened by nothing so much as by Your will, by the good pleasure of Your eternal decree.[6] With this he should be so contented and consoled that he would wish to be the least as others wish to be the greatest; that he would be as peaceful and satisfied in the last place as in the first, and as willing to be despised, unknown and forgotten, as to be honored by others and to have more fame than they. He should prefer Your will and the love of Your honor to all else, and it should comfort him more than all the benefits which have been, or will be, given him.

23. Four Things Which Bring Great Peace

The Voice of Christ

My child, I will teach you now the way of peace and true liberty.[1]

Seek, child, to do the will of others rather than your own.

Always choose to have less rather than more.

Look always for the last place and seek to be beneath all others.

Always wish and pray that the will of God be fully carried out in you.

Behold, such will enter into the realm of peace and rest.

The Disciple

O Lord, this brief discourse of Yours contains much perfection. It is short in words but full of meaning and abounding in fruit. Certainly if I could only keep it faithfully, I should not be so easily disturbed. For as often as I find myself troubled and dejected, I find that I have departed from this teaching. But You Who can do all things, and Who always love what is for my soul's welfare, give me increase of grace that I may keep Your words and accomplish my salvation.[2]

A Prayer Against Bad Thoughts

O Lord my God, be not far from me. O my God, hasten to help me, for varied thoughts and great fears have risen up within me, afflicting my soul.[3] How shall I escape them unharmed? How shall I dispel them?

"I will go before you," says the Lord, "and will humble the great ones of earth.[4] I will open the doors of the prison, and will reveal to you hidden secrets."

Do as You say, Lord, and let all evil thoughts fly from Your face. This is my hope and my only comfort—to fly to You in all tribulation, to confide in You, and to call on You from the depths of my heart and to await patiently for Your consolation.

A Prayer for Enlightening the Mind

Enlighten me, good Jesus, with the brightness of internal light, and take away all darkness from the habitation of my heart. Restrain my wandering thoughts and suppress the temptations which attack me so violently.[5] Fight strongly for me, and vanquish these evil beasts—the alluring desires of the flesh—so that peace may come through Your power and the fullness of Your praise resound in the holy courts, which is a

2. God's grace is what we need to work out our salvation. Reference Philippians 2:11,12.

3. Unfocused, flitting, random thoughts and fears are distressing to the Christian.

4. We need Christ to defend us from the devils who oppress us.

5. This prayer develops on the petition "Deliver us from evil."

6. The strongest tempests that blow are our own thoughts and demonic suggestions.

pure conscience. Command the winds and the tempests;[6] say to the sea: "Be still," and to the north wind, "Do not blow," and there will be a great calm.

Send forth Your light and Your truth to shine on the earth, for I am as earth, empty and formless until You illumine me. Pour out Your grace from above. Shower my heart with heavenly dew. Open the springs of devotion to water the earth, that it may produce the best of good fruits. Lift up my heart pressed down by the weight of sins, and direct all my desires to heavenly things, that having tasted the sweetness of supernal happiness, I may find no pleasure in thinking of earthly things.

Snatch me up and deliver me from all the passing comfort of creatures, for no created thing can fully quiet and satisfy my desires. Join me to Yourself in an inseparable bond of love; because You alone can satisfy him who loves You, and without You all things are worthless.

24. Avoiding Curious Inquiry About the Lives of Others

The Voice of Christ

My child, do not be curious. Do not trouble yourself with idle cares. What matters this or that to you? Follow Me. What is it to you if a man is such and such, if another does or says this or that? You will not have to answer for others, but you will have to give an account of yourself. Why, then, do you meddle in their affairs?[1]

1. We are to spend very little time thinking of what others are saying and doing.

Behold, I know all men. I see everything that is done under the sun, and I know how matters stand with each—what is in his mind and what in his heart and the end to which his intention is directed. Commit all things to Me, therefore, and keep yourself in good peace.[2] Let him who is disturbed be as restless as he will. Whatever he has said or done will fall upon himself, for he cannot deceive Me.

Do not be anxious for the shadow of a great name, for the close friendship of many, or for the particular affection of men.[3] These things cause distraction and cast great darkness about the heart. I would willingly speak My word and reveal My secrets to you, if you would watch diligently for My coming and open your heart to Me. Be prudent, then. Watch in prayer, and in all things humble yourself.

2. Christ keeps all things well in observation and under control.

3. More distractions from a relationship with Christ – being concerned about human relationships – the closeness or love or lack of love in these associations.

25. The Basis of Firm Peace of Heart and True Progress

The Voice of Christ

My child, I have said: "Peace I leave with you, My peace I give unto you: not as the world giveth, do I give unto you."[1]

All men desire peace but all do not care for the things that go to make true peace. My peace is with the humble and meek of heart: your peace will be in much patience. If you hear Me and follow My voice, you will be able to enjoy much peace.

1. John 14:27 Peace comes to the humble in heart.

The Disciple

What, then, shall I do, Lord?

The Voice of Christ

Watch yourself in all things, in what you do and what you say. Direct your every intention toward pleasing Me alone, and desire nothing outside of Me. Do not be rash in judging the deeds and words of others, and do not entangle yourself in affairs that are not your own.[2] Thus, it will come about that you will be disturbed little and seldom.

Yet, never to experience any disturbance or to suffer any hurt in heart or body does not belong to this present life, but rather to the state of eternal rest. Do not think, therefore, that you have found true peace if you feel no depression, or that all

2. A focus on others and pleasing others will not lead to peace. Focus on pleasing Christ.

3. Peace isn't the absence of trials and tribulations.

is well because you suffer no opposition.[3] Do not think that all is perfect if everything happens just as you wish. And do not imagine yourself great or consider yourself especially beloved if you are filled with great devotion and sweetness. For the true lover of virtue is not known by these things, nor do the progress and perfection of a man consist in them.

The Disciple

In what do they consist, Lord?

The Voice of Christ

They consist in offering yourself with all your heart to the divine will, not seeking what is yours either in small matters or great ones, either in temporal or eternal things, so that you will preserve equanimity and give thanks in both prosperity and adversity, seeing all things in their proper light.[4]

4. True virtue is heart submission to God's will.

If you become so brave and long-suffering in hope that you can prepare your heart to suffer still more even when all inward consolation is withdrawn, and if you do not justify yourself as though you ought not be made to suffer such great things,[5] but acknowledge Me to be just in all My works and praise My holy name—then you will walk in the true and right path of peace, then you may have sure hope of seeing My face again in joy. If you attain to complete contempt of self, then know that you will enjoy an abundance of peace, as much as is possible in this earthly life.

5. This submission to God's will is especially seen when one accepts suffering without complaint.

26. The Excellence of a Free Mind, Gained Through Prayer Rather Than By Study

The Disciple

It is the mark of a perfect man, Lord, never to let his mind relax in attention to heavenly things, and to pass through many cares as though he had none; not as an indolent man does, but having by the certain prerogative of a free mind no disorderly affection for any created being.[1]

Keep me, I beg You, most merciful God, from the cares of this life, lest I be too much entangled in them. Keep me from many necessities of the body, lest I be ensnared by pleasure. Keep me from all darkness of mind, lest I be broken by troubles and overcome. I do not ask deliverance from those things which worldly vanity desires so eagerly, but from those miseries which, by the common curse of humankind, oppress the soul of Your servant in punishment and keep him from entering into the liberty of spirit as often as he would.[2]

My God, Sweetness beyond words, make bitter all the carnal comfort that draws me from love of the eternal and lures me to its evil self by the sight of some delightful good in the present. Let it not overcome me, my God. Let not flesh and blood conquer me. Let not the world and its brief glory deceive me, nor the devil trip me by his craftiness. Give me courage to resist, patience to endure, and constancy to persevere. Give me the soothing unction of Your spirit rather than all the consolations of the world, and in place of carnal love, infuse into me the love of Your name.

Behold, eating, drinking, clothing, and other necessities that sustain the body are burdensome to the fervent soul. Grant me the grace to use such comforts temperately and not to become entangled in too great a desire for them.[3] It is not lawful to cast them aside completely, for nature must be sustained, but Your holy law forbids us to demand superfluous things and things that are simply for pleasure,[4] else the flesh would rebel against the spirit. In these matters, I beg, let

1. Disorderly affections are idolatrous and sinful affections that bring people into bondage (such as food, drink, or sex).

2. He doesn't ask for deliverance from disease and suffering but rather from the things that would enslave him (like pleasures).

3. Excessive desire for material things is the problem. This can displace our love for the Giver.

4. Gifts are meant for a grateful heart, not merely to stimulate lust, pleasure, or idolatry.

Your hand guide and direct me, so that I may not overstep the law in any way.

27. Self-Love is the Greatest Hindrance to the Highest Good

The Voice of Christ

My child, you should give all for all, and in no way belong to yourself.[1] You must know that self-love is more harmful to you than anything else in the world. In proportion to the love and affection you have for a thing, it will cling to you more or less. If your love is pure, simple, and well ordered, you will not be a slave to anything. Do not covet what you may not have. Do not possess anything that can hinder you or rob you of freedom.

It is strange that you do not commit yourself to Me with your whole heart, together with all that you can desire or possess. Why are you consumed with foolish sorrow? Why are you wearied with unnecessary care? Be resigned to My will and you will suffer no loss.[2]

If you seek this or that, if you wish to be in this place or that place, to have more ease and pleasure, you will never rest or be free from care, for some defect is found in everything and everywhere someone will vex you.[3] To obtain and multiply earthly goods, then, will not help you, but to despise them and root them out of your heart will aid. This, understand, is true not only of money and wealth, but also of ambition for honor and desire for empty praise, all of which will pass away with this world.

The place matters little if the spirit of fervor is not there; nor will peace be lasting if it is sought from the outside; if your heart has no true foundation, that is, if you are not founded in Me, you may change, but you will not better yourself. For

1. You are not your own. You are bought with a price.

2. Self will and desiring what self has determined it should have counter God's will and produce sorrow.

3. Seeking ease or heaven on earth is a futile effort.

when occasion arises and is accepted, you will find that from which you fled and worse.

A Prayer for Cleansing the Heart and Obtaining Heavenly Wisdom

Strengthen me by the grace of Your holy spirit, O God. Give me the power to be strengthened inwardly and to empty my heart of all vain care and anxiety, so that I may not be drawn away by many desires, whether for precious things or mean ones. Let me look upon everything as passing,[4] and upon myself as soon to pass away with them, because there is nothing lasting under the sun, where all is vanity and affliction of spirit.[5] How wise is he who thinks thus!

4. The disciple prays for a moderation of desires, especially when it comes to earthly blessings.

5. Ecclesiastes 2:17

Give me, Lord, heavenly wisdom to learn above all else to seek and find You, to enjoy and love You more than anything, and to consider other things as they are, as Your wisdom has ordered them. Grant me prudence to avoid the flatterer and to bear patiently with him who disagrees with me.[6] For it is great wisdom not to be moved by the sound of words, nor to give ear to the wicked, flattering siren. Then, I shall walk safely in the way I have begun.

6. Handling flattery and criticism rightly is core to wise living.

28. Strength Against Slander

The Voice of Christ

My child, do not take it to heart if some people think badly of you and say unpleasant things about you. You ought to think worse things of yourself and to believe that no one is weaker than yourself.[1] Moreover, if you walk in the spirit you will pay little heed to fleeting words. It is no small prudence to remain silent in evil times, to turn inwardly to Me, and not to be disturbed by human opinions. Do not let your peace depend on the words of men.[2] Their thinking well or badly of you does not make you different from what you are. Where are true peace and glory? Are they not in Me? He who neither

1. In reference to God we are far worse off than what man thinks.

2. This is a warning concerning people pleasing; concern over what man thinks should be much less than concern of what God thinks.

cares to please men nor fears to displease them will enjoy great peace, for all unrest and distraction of the senses arise out of disorderly love and vain fear.

29. How We Must Call Upon and Bless the Lord When Trouble Presses

The Disciple

Blessed be Your name forever, O Lord, Who have willed that this temptation and trouble come upon me. I cannot escape it, yet I must fly to You that You may help me and turn it to my good.[1] Now I am troubled, Lord, and my heart is not at rest, for I am greatly afflicted by this present suffering.

1. The believer both accepts the trial as the will of God and prays for help in the trial.

Beloved Father, what shall I say? I am straitened in harsh ways. Save me from this hour to which, however, I am come that You may be glorified when I am deeply humbled and freed by You. May it please You, then, to deliver me, Lord, for what can I, poor wretch that I am, do or where can I go without You? Give me patience, Lord, even now.[2] Help me, my God, and I will not be afraid however much I may be distressed.

2. What is needed most is humility and patience in the trial.

But here, in the midst of these troubles, what shall I say? Your will be done, Lord. I have richly deserved to be troubled and distressed. But I must bear it. Would that I could do so patiently, until the storm passes and calm returns! Yet Your almighty hand can take this temptation from me, or lighten its attack so that I do not altogether sink beneath it, as You, my God, my Mercy, have very often done for me before. And the more difficult my plight, the easier for You is this change of the right hand of the Most High.

30. The Quest of Divine Help and Confidence in Regaining Grace

The Voice of Christ

My child, I am the Lord Who gives strength in the day of trouble. Come to Me when all is not well with you. Your tardiness in turning to prayer is the greatest obstacle to heavenly consolation, for before you pray earnestly to Me you first seek many comforts and take pleasure in outward things.[1] Thus, all things are of little profit to you until you realize that I am the one Who saves those who trust in Me, and that outside of Me there is no worthwhile help, or any useful counsel or lasting remedy.

But now, after the tempest, take courage, grow strong once more in the light of My mercies; for I am near, says the Lord, to restore all things not only to the full but with abundance and above measure. Is anything difficult for Me? Or shall I be as one who promises and does not act? Where is your faith? Stand firm and persevere. Be a man of endurance and courage, and consolation will come to you in due time. Wait for Me; wait—and I will come to heal you.[2]

It is only a temptation that troubles you, a vain fear that terrifies you.

Of what use is anxiety about the future? Does it bring you anything but trouble upon trouble? Sufficient for the day is the evil thereof.[3] It is foolish and useless to be either grieved or happy about future things which perhaps may never happen. But it is human to be deluded by such imaginations, and the sign of a weak soul to be led on by suggestions of the enemy. For he does not care whether he overcomes you by love of the present or fear of the future.[4]

Let not your heart be troubled, therefore, nor let it be afraid.[5] Believe in Me and trust in My mercy. When you think you are far from Me, then often I am very near you. When you judge that almost all is lost, then very often you are in the way of gaining great merit.

1. The delay of prayer is the greatest hindrance in the Christian life.

2. The delay of prayer is the greatest hindrance in the Christian life.

3. Worry is useless. Reference Matthew 6:34.

4. The devil introduces fear of the future and an inordinate love of the present world where there should be a hope for the future.

5. John 14:1

All is not lost when things go contrary to your wishes. You ought not judge according to present feelings, nor give in to any trouble whenever it comes, or take it as though all hope of escape were lost. And do not consider yourself forsaken if I send some temporary hardship, or withdraw the consolation you desire. For this is the way to the kingdom of heaven, and without doubt it is better for you and the rest of My servants to be tried in adversities than to have all things as you wish.[6] I know your secret thoughts, and I know that it is profitable for your salvation to be left sometimes in despondency lest perhaps you be puffed up by success and fancy yourself to be what you are not.

6. The way into the kingdom of God is through much tribulation.

What I have given, I can take away and restore when it pleases Me. What I give remains Mine, and thus when I take it away I take nothing that is yours, for every good gift and every perfect gift is Mine.

If I send you trouble and adversity, do not fret or let your heart be downcast. I can raise you quickly up again and turn all your sorrow into joy.[7] I am no less just and worthy of great praise when I deal with you in this way.

7. Adversity is temporary, and Christ can turn sorrow into joy.

If you think aright and view things in their true light, you should never be so dejected and saddened by adversity, but rather rejoice and give thanks, considering it a matter of special joy that I afflict you with sorrow and do not spare you. "As the Father hath loved Me, so also I love you," I said to My disciples, and I certainly did not send them out to temporal joys but rather to great struggles, not to honors but to contempt, not to idleness, but to labors, not to rest but to bring forth much fruit in patience. Do you, My child, remember these words.

31. To Find the Creator, Forsake All Creatures

The Disciple

O Lord, I am in sore need still of greater grace if I am to arrive at the point where no man and no created thing can be an obstacle to me.[1] For as long as anything holds me back, I cannot freely fly to You. He that said "Oh that I had wings like a dove, that I might fly away and be at rest!" desired to fly freely to You. Who is more at rest than he who aims at nothing but God? And who more free than the man who desires nothing on earth?

It is well, then, to pass over all creation, perfectly to abandon self, and to see in ecstasy of mind that You, the Creator of all, have no likeness among all Your creatures, and that unless a man be freed from all creatures, he cannot attend freely to the Divine.[2] The reason why so few contemplative persons are found, is that so few know how to separate themselves entirely from what is transitory and created.

For this, indeed, great grace is needed, grace that will raise the soul and lift it up above itself. Unless a man be elevated in spirit, free from all creatures, and completely united to God, all his knowledge and possessions are of little moment. He who considers anything great except the one, immense, eternal good will long be little and lie groveling on the earth. Whatever is not God is nothing and must be accounted as nothing.[3]

There is great difference between the wisdom of an enlightened and devout man and the learning of a well-read and brilliant scholar, for the knowledge which flows down from divine sources is much nobler than that laboriously acquired by human industry.[4]

Many there are who desire contemplation, but who do not care to do the things which contemplation requires. It is also a great obstacle to be satisfied with externals and sensible things, and to have so little of perfect mortification. I know not what it is, or by what spirit we are led, or to what we pretend—we

1. Attention to man distracts from communion with God.

2. A'Kempis acknowledges a strong creature-Creator distinction.

3. God's presence is such that man's essence seems negligible.

4. A devout knowledge of God is vastly different from secular knowledge.

who wish to be called spiritual—that we spend so much labor and even more anxiety on things that are transitory and mean, while we seldom or never advert with full consciousness to our interior concerns.[5]

5. Spiritual men put time into meditation on the divine.

Alas, after very little recollection we falter, not weighing our deeds by strict examination. We pay no attention to where our affections lie, nor do we deplore the fact that our actions are impure.

Remember that because all flesh had corrupted its course, the great deluge followed. Since, then, our interior affection is corrupt, it must be that the action which follows from it, the index as it were of our lack of inward strength, is also corrupt. Out of a pure heart come the fruits of a good life.

People are wont to ask how much a man has done, but they think little of the virtue with which he acts. They ask: Is he strong? rich? handsome? a good writer? a good singer? or a good worker? They say little, however, about how poor he is in spirit, how patient and meek, how devout and spiritual.[6] Nature looks to his outward appearance; grace turns to his inward being. The one often errs, the other trusts in God and is not deceived.

6. The world is not interested in the values Jesus expresses.

32. Self-Denial and the Renunciation of Evil Appetites

The Voice of Christ

My child, you can never be perfectly free unless you completely renounce self, for all who seek their own interest and who love themselves are bound in fetters.[1] They are unsettled by covetousness and curiosity, always searching for ease and not for the things of Christ, often devising and framing that which will not last, for anything that is not of God will fail completely.

1. Self-love over self-denial is bondage.

Hold to this short and perfect advice, therefore: give up your desires and you will find rest.[2] Think upon it in your heart, and when you have put it into practice you will understand all things.

The Disciple

But this, Lord, is not the work of one day, nor is it mere child's play; indeed, in this brief sentence is included all the perfection of holy persons.

The Voice of Christ

My child, you should not turn away or be downcast when you hear the way of the perfect. Rather you ought to be spurred on the more toward their sublime heights, or at least be moved to seek perfection.

I would this were the case with you—that you had progressed to the point where you no longer loved self but simply awaited My bidding and his whom I have placed as father over you.[3] Then you would please Me very much, and your whole life would pass in peace and joy. But you have yet many things which you must give up, and unless you resign them entirely to Me you will not obtain that which you ask.

"I counsel thee to buy of me gold, fire-tried, that thou mayest be made rich"[4]—rich in heavenly wisdom which treads underfoot all that is low. Put aside earthly wisdom, all human self-complacency.

I have said: exchange what is precious and valued among men for that which is considered contemptible. For true heavenly wisdom—not to think highly of self and not to seek glory on earth—does indeed seem mean and small and is well-nigh forgotten, as many men praise it with their mouths but shy far away from it in their lives. Yet this heavenly wisdom is a pearl of great price, which is hidden from many.

2. Lusting and discontentment is never restful.

3. Self-love involves a self-will that doesn't submit to God's will and commands.

4. Revelation 3:18

33. Restlessness of Soul—Directing Our Final Intention Toward God

The Voice of Christ

My child, do not trust in your present feeling, for it will soon give way to another. As long as you live you will be subject to changeableness in spite of yourself. You will become merry at one time and sad at another, now peaceful but again disturbed, at one moment devout and the next indevout, sometimes diligent while at other times lazy, now grave and again flippant.[1]

1. Emotions are variable and cannot be trusted.

But the man who is wise and whose spirit is well instructed stands superior to these changes. He pays no attention to what he feels in himself or from what quarter the wind of fickleness blows, so long as the whole intention of his mind is conducive to his proper and desired end. For thus he can stand undivided, unchanged, and unshaken, with the singleness of his intention directed unwaveringly toward Me, even in the midst of so many changing events. And the purer this singleness of intention is, with so much the more constancy does he pass through many storms.[2]

2. A single focus on Christ and His kingdom is recommended.

But in many ways the eye of pure intention grows dim, because it is attracted to any delightful thing that it meets. Indeed, it is rare to find one who is entirely free from all taint of self-seeking.[3] The Jews of old, for example, came to Bethany to Martha and Mary, not for Jesus' sake alone, but in order to see Lazarus.

3. The impediment to the single eye is always self-seeking.

The eye of your intention, therefore, must be cleansed so that it is single and right. It must be directed toward Me, despite all the objects which may interfere.

34. God is Sweet Above All Things and in All Things to Those Who Love Him

The Disciple

Behold, my God and my all! What more do I wish for; what greater happiness can I desire? O sweet and delicious word! But sweet only to him who loves it, and not to the world or the things that are in the world.[1]

My God and my all! These words are enough for him who understands, and for him who loves it is a joy to repeat them often. For when You are present, all things are delightful; when You are absent, all things become loathsome. It is You Who give a heart tranquillity, great peace and festive joy. It is You Who make us think well of all things, and praise You in all things. Without You nothing can give pleasure for very long, for if it is to be pleasing and tasteful, Your grace and the seasoning of Your wisdom must be in it.[2] What is there that can displease him whose happiness is in You? And, on the contrary, what can satisfy him whose delight is not in You?

The wise men of the world, the men who lust for the flesh, are wanting in Your wisdom, because in the world is found the utmost vanity, and in the flesh is death.[3] But they who follow You by disdaining worldly things and mortifying the flesh are known to be truly wise, for they are transported from vanity to truth, from flesh to spirit. By such as these God is relished, and whatever good is found in creatures they turn to praise of the Creator.[4] But great—yes, very great, indeed—is the difference between delight in the Creator and in the creature, in eternity and in time, in Light uncreated and in the light that is reflected.

O Light eternal, surpassing all created brightness, flash forth the lightning from above and enlighten the inmost recesses of my heart. Cleanse, cheer, enlighten, and vivify my spirit with all its powers, that it may cleave to You in ecstasies of joy. Oh, when will that happy and wished-for hour come, that You may fill me with Your presence and become all in

1. An expression of delight in God.

2. Joy is found in God's grace and wisdom.

3. The lust of the flesh is vain and never satisfying.

4. The key to enjoying God's good gift is to turn all to praise.

all to me? So long as this is not given me, my joy will not be complete.

The old man, alas, yet lives within me. He has not yet been entirely crucified; he is not yet entirely dead. He still lusts strongly against the spirit, and he will not leave the kingdom of my soul in peace. But You, Who can command the power of the sea and calm the tumult of its waves, arise and help me. Scatter the nations that delight in war; crush them in Your sight. Show forth I beg, Your wonderful works and let Your right hand be glorified, because for me there is no other hope or refuge except in You, O Lord, my God.

35. There is No Security from Temptation in This Life

The Voice of Christ

My child, in this life you are never safe, and as long as you live the weapons of the spirit will ever be necessary to you. You dwell among enemies. You are subject to attack from the right and the left.[1] If, therefore, you do not guard yourself from every quarter with the shield of patience, you will not remain long unscathed.

1. The Christian life is a perpetual battle.

Moreover, if you do not steadily set your heart on Me, with a firm will to suffer everything for My sake, you will not be able to bear the heat of this battle or to win the crown of the blessed. You ought, therefore, to pass through all these things bravely and to oppose a strong hand to whatever stands in your way. For to him who triumphs heavenly bread is given, while for him who is too lazy to fight there remains much misery.[2]

2. The violent, those who will fight, will take the kingdom.

If you look for rest in this life, how will you attain to everlasting rest?[3] Dispose yourself, then, not for much rest but for great patience. Seek true peace, not on earth but in heaven; not in men or in other creatures but in God alone. For love of God you should undergo all things cheerfully, all labors and sor-

3. This life is not heaven.

rows, temptations and trials, anxieties, weaknesses, necessities, injuries, slanders, rebukes, humiliations, confusions, corrections, and contempt. For these are helps to virtue.[4] These are the trials of Christ's recruit. These form the heavenly crown. For a little brief labor I will give an everlasting crown, and for passing confusion, glory that is eternal.

4. The heart motive and disposition to face all opposition must be the love of God.

Do you think that you will always have spiritual consolations as you desire? My saints did not always have them. Instead, they had many afflictions, temptations of various kinds, and great desolation. Yet they bore them all patiently. They placed their confidence in God rather than in themselves, knowing that the sufferings of this life are not worthy to be compared with the glory that is to come. And you—do you wish to have at once that which others have scarcely obtained after many tears and great labors?[5]

5. Other saints have faced great tribulations. How are we different than they?

Wait for the Lord, act bravely, and have courage. Do not lose trust. Do not turn back but devote your body and soul constantly to God's glory. I will reward you most plentifully. I will be with you in every tribulation.

36. The Vain Judgments of Men

The Voice of Christ

My child, trust firmly in the Lord, and do not fear the judgment of men when conscience tells you that you are upright and innocent. For it is good and blessed to suffer such things, and they will not weigh heavily on the humble heart that trusts in God rather than in itself. Many men say many things, and therefore little faith is to be put in them.[1]

1. Trust in God and you will not care so much for the opinions and judgments of men.

Likewise, it is impossible to satisfy all men. Although Paul tried to please all in the Lord, and became all things to all men, yet he made little of their opinions. He labored abundantly for the edification and salvation of others, as much as lay in him and as much as he could, but he could not escape being sometimes judged and despised by others. Therefore, he committed all to God Who knows all things, and defended himself by his patience and humility against the tongues of those who spoke unjustly or thought foolish things and lies, or made accusations against him.[2] Sometimes, indeed, he did answer them, but only lest his silence scandalize the weak.

Who are you, then, that you should be afraid of mortal man? Today he is here, tomorrow he is not seen. Fear God and you will not be afraid of the terrors of men.[3] What can anyone do to you by word or injury? He hurts himself rather than you, and no matter who he may be he cannot escape the judgment of God. Keep God before your eyes, therefore, and do not quarrel with peevish words.

If it seems, then, that you are worsted and that you suffer undeserved shame, do not repine over it and do not lessen your crown by impatience. Look instead to heaven, to Me, Who have power to deliver you from all disgrace and injury, and to render to everyone according to his works.[4]

37. Pure and Entire Resignation of Self to Obtain Freedom of Heart

The Voice of Christ

My child, renounce self and you shall find Me. Give up your own self-will, your possessions, and you shall always gain.[1] For once you resign yourself irrevocably, greater grace will be given you.

The Disciple

How often, Lord, shall I resign myself? And in what shall I forsake myself?

The Voice of Christ

Always, at every hour, in small matters as well as great—I except nothing. In all things I wish you to be stripped of self. How otherwise can you be mine or I yours unless you be despoiled of your own will both inwardly and outwardly?[2] The

2. Don't waste time defending yourself before men. Appeal your case to the Higher Judge.

3. Fear God and you will not be afraid of the "paper tigers" of man.

4. Revelation 22:12

1. The Christian life is described as giving up self and abandoning possessions for Christ on an ongoing basis.

2. Self-will refuses obedience to the will of God.

sooner you do this the better it will be for you, and the more fully and sincerely you do it the more you will please Me and the greater gain you will merit.

Some there are who resign themselves, but with certain reservation; they do not trust fully in God and therefore they try to provide for themselves.[3] Others, again, at first offer all, but afterward are assailed by temptation and return to what they have renounced, thereby making no progress in virtue. These will not reach the true liberty of a pure heart nor the grace of happy friendship with Me unless they first make a full resignation and a daily sacrifice of themselves. Without this no fruitful union lasts nor will last.

I have said to you very often, and now I say again: forsake yourself, renounce yourself and you shall enjoy great inward peace.[4] Give all for all. Ask nothing, demand nothing in return. Trust purely and without hesitation in Me, and you shall possess Me. You will be free of heart and darkness will not overwhelm you.[5]

Strive for this, pray for this, desire this—to be stripped of all selfishness and naked to follow the naked Jesus, to die to self and live forever for Me.[6] Then all vain imaginations, all wicked disturbances and superfluous cares will vanish. Then also immoderate fear will leave you and inordinate love will die.

3. Resigning self here is equated to trusting fully in God.

4. Mark 8:34-35

5. Giving up self will gain everything for the believer.

6. Dying to self is to live for Christ.

38. The Right Ordering of External Affairs; Recourse to God in Dangers

The Voice of Christ

My child, you must strive diligently to be inwardly free, to have mastery over yourself everywhere, in every external act and occupation, that all things be subject to you and not you to them, that you be the master and director of your actions, not a slave or a mere hired servant.[1] You should be rather a free man and a true Hebrew, arising to the status and freedom of

1. Resist being controlled by power, politics, fame, and money. Ultimate slavery is enslavement to lusts and idolatry.

the children of God who stand above present things to contemplate those which are eternal; who look upon passing affairs with the left eye and upon those of heaven with the right; whom temporal things do not so attract that they cling to them, but who rather put these things to such proper service as is ordained and instituted by God, the great Workmaster, Who leaves nothing unordered in His creation.[2]

2. Use money and power for God's purposes, but keep your focus on the eternal inheritance.

If, likewise, in every happening you are not content simply with outward appearances, if you do not regard with carnal eyes things which you see and hear, but whatever be the affair, enter with Moses into the tabernacle to ask advice of the Lord, you will sometimes hear the divine answer and return instructed in many things present and to come. For Moses always had recourse to the tabernacle for the solution of doubts and questions, and fled to prayer for support in dangers and the evil deeds of men. So you also should take refuge in the secret chamber of your heart, begging earnestly for divine aid.[3]

3. Seek God's wisdom by prayer.

For this reason, as we read, Joshua and the children of Israel were deceived by the Gibeonites because they did not first seek counsel of the Lord, but trusted too much in fair words and hence were deceived by false piety.

39. A Man Should Not Be Unduly Solicitous About His Affairs

The Voice of Christ

My child, always commit your cause to Me. I will dispose of it rightly in good time.[1] Await My ordering of it and it will be to your advantage.

1. Roman 8:28

The Disciple

2. Trusting God's ordering of all things in the future is far better than worry.

Lord, I willingly commit all things to You, for my anxiety can profit me little.[2] But I would that I were not so concerned about the future, and instead offered myself without hesitation to Your good pleasure.

The Voice of Christ

My child, it often happens that a man seeks ardently after something he desires and then when he has attained it he begins to think that it is not at all desirable;[3] for affections do not remain fixed on the same thing, but rather flit from one to another. It is no very small matter, therefore, for a man to forsake himself even in things that are very small.

A man's true progress consists in denying himself, and the man who has denied himself is truly free and secure. The old enemy, however, setting himself against all good, never ceases to tempt them, but day and night plots dangerous snares to cast the unwary into the net of deceit. "Watch ye and pray," says the Lord, "that ye enter not into temptation."

3. Man does not even know what is good for him or what would constitute a good desire.

40. Man Has No Good in Himself and Can Glory in Nothing

The Disciple

Lord, what is man that You are mindful of him, or the son of man that You visit him?[1] What has man deserved that You should give him Your grace? What cause have I, Lord, to complain if You desert me, or what objection can I have if You do not do what I ask? This I may think and say in all truth: "Lord, I am nothing, of myself I have nothing that is good; I am lacking in all things, and I am ever tending toward nothing. And unless I have Your help and am inwardly strengthened by You, I become quite lukewarm and lax."[2]

But You, Lord, are always the same. You remain forever, always good, just, and holy; doing all things rightly, justly, and holily, disposing them wisely.[3] I, however, who am more ready to go backward than forward, do not remain always in one state, for I change with the seasons. Yet my condition quickly

1. Psalm 8:4

2. Anything good that we are or have is God's gift and undeserved grace.

3. A'Kempis compares us, in whom there is no natural good, with God, who is the essence of good.

improves when it pleases You and when You reach forth Your helping hand. For You alone, without human aid, can help me and strengthen me so greatly that my heart shall no more change but be converted and rest solely in You. Hence, if I knew well how to cast aside all earthly consolation, either to attain devotion or because of the necessity which, in the absence of human solace, compels me to seek You alone, then I could deservedly hope for Your grace and rejoice in the gift of new consolation.

Thanks be to You from Whom all things come, whenever it is well with me. In Your sight I am vanity and nothingness, a weak, unstable man. In what, therefore, can I glory, and how can I wish to be highly regarded? Is it because I am nothing? This, too, is utterly vain. Indeed, the greatest vanity is the evil plague of empty self-glory, because it draws one away from true glory and robs one of heavenly grace.[4] For when a man is pleased with himself he displeases You, when he pants after human praise he is deprived of true virtue. But it is true glory and holy exultation to glory in You and not in self, to rejoice in Your name rather than in one's own virtue, and not to delight in any creature except for Your sake.

4. Glorying in self is vain, empty, and robs us of grace and the realization of that which is truly glorious.

Let Your name, not mine, be praised. Let Your work, not mine, be magnified. Let Your holy name be blessed, but let no human praise be given to me.[5] You are my glory. You are the joy of my heart. In You I will glory and rejoice all the day, and for myself I will glory in nothing but my infirmities.

5. The spirit of the true, humble believer gives all glory to God and none to us.

Let the Jews seek the glory that comes from another. I will seek that which comes from God alone. All human glory, all temporal honor, all worldly position is truly vanity and foolishness compared to Your everlasting glory. O my Truth, my Mercy, my God, O Blessed Trinity, to You alone be praise and honor, power and glory, throughout all the endless ages of ages.

41. Contempt for All Earthly Honor

The Voice of Christ

My child, do not take it to heart if you see others honored and advanced, while you yourself are despised and humbled. Lift up your heart to Me in heaven and the contempt of men on earth will not grieve you.[1]

The Disciple

Lord, we are blinded and quickly misled by vanity. If I examine myself rightly, no injury has ever been done me by any creature; hence I have nothing for which to make just complaint to You. But I have sinned often and gravely against You; therefore is every creature in arms against me. Confusion and contempt should in justice come upon me, but to You due praise, honor, and glory.[2] And unless I prepare myself to be willingly despised and forsaken by every creature, to be considered absolutely nothing, I cannot have interior peace and strength, nor can I be enlightened spiritually or completely united with You.

1. The esteem of men should mean nothing to us when we have received the grace of Christ.

2. We deserve all contempt for our sin, thus we should never be upset when we are objects of contempt.

42. Peace is Not to Be Placed in Men

The Voice of Christ

My child, if you place your peace in any creature because of your own feeling or for the sake of his company, you will be unsettled and entangled. But if you have recourse to the ever-living and abiding Truth, you will not grieve if a friend should die or forsake you. Your love for your friend should be grounded in Me, and for My sake you should love whoever seems to be good and is very dear to you in this life. Without Me friendship has no strength and cannot endure.[1] Love which I do not bind is neither true nor pure.

You ought, therefore, to be so dead to such human affections as to wish as far as lies within you to be without the

1. Lasting friendships are those found in Christ.

2. A'Kempis is discouraging dependence on human friendships.

3. Our own righteousness is filthy rags. Dependence on our own goodness hinders God's grace.

4. Man's friendships and love pales in comparison to God's grace and love.

fellowship of men.[2] Man draws nearer to God in proportion as he withdraws farther from all earthly comfort. And he ascends higher to God as he descends lower into himself and grows more vile in his own eyes. He who attributes any good to himself hinders God's grace from coming into his heart, for the grace of the Holy Spirit seeks always the humble heart.[3]

If you knew how to annihilate yourself completely and empty yourself of all created love, then I should overflow in you with great grace.[4] When you look to creatures, the sight of the Creator is taken from you. Learn, therefore, to conquer yourself in all things for the sake of your Maker. Then will you be able to attain to divine knowledge. But anything, no matter how small, that is loved and regarded inordinately keeps you back from the highest good and corrupts the soul.

43. Beware Vain and Worldly Knowledge

The Voice of Christ

1. Man's words are compared to God's words.

My child, do not let the fine-sounding and subtle words of men deceive you.[1] For the kingdom of heaven consists not in talk but in virtue. Attend, rather, to My words which enkindle the heart and enlighten the mind, which excite contrition and abound in manifold consolations. Never read them for the purpose of appearing more learned or more wise. Apply yourself to mortifying your vices, for this will benefit you more than your understanding of many difficult questions.[2]

2. Mortifying your sin is more beneficial than theological arguings.

Though you shall have read and learned many things, it will always be necessary for you to return to this one principle: I am He who teaches man knowledge, and to the little ones I give a clearer understanding than can be taught by man. He to whom I speak will soon be wise and his soul will profit. But woe to those who inquire of men about many curious things, and care very little about the way they serve Me.

The time will come when Christ, the Teacher of teachers, the Lord of angels, will appear to hear the lessons of all— that is, to examine the conscience of everyone. Then He will search Jerusalem with lamps and the hidden things of darkness will be brought to light and the arguings of men's tongues be silenced.[3]

I am He Who in one moment so enlightens the humble mind that it comprehends more of eternal truth than could be learned by ten years in the schools.[4] I teach without noise of words or clash of opinions, without ambition for honor or confusion of argument.

I am He Who teaches man to despise earthly possessions and to loathe present things, to ask after the eternal, to hunger for heaven, to fly honors and to bear with scandals, to place all hope in Me, to desire nothing apart from Me, and to love Me ardently above all things.[5] For a certain man by loving Me intimately learned divine truths and spoke wonders. He profited more by leaving all things than by studying subtle questions.

To some I speak of common things, to others of special matters. To some I appear with sweetness in signs and figures, and to others I appear in great light and reveal mysteries. The voice of books is but a single voice, yet it does not teach all men alike, because I within them am the Teacher and the Truth, the Examiner of hearts, the Understander of thoughts, the Promoter of acts, distributing to each as I see fit.

3. The theological systems of men that have divided churches throughout the centuries will all be proven lacking when Christ the Teacher comes.

4. A'Kempis critiques seminaries, preferring Christ's teaching and the humbled mind.

5. This summary of the Christian faith is presented as the heavenly wisdom (vs. earthly systems of theological forms).

44. Do Not Be Concerned About Outward Things

The Voice of Christ

My child, there are many matters of which it is well for you to be ignorant, and to consider yourself as one who is dead upon the earth and to whom the whole world is crucified. There are many things, too, which it is well to pass by with a deaf ear, thinking, instead, of what is more to your peace. It is more profitable to turn away from things which displease you and to leave to every man his own opinion than to take part in

1. The man of God is to avoid all quarrels (1 Timothy 6:3-4).

quarrelsome talk.[1] If you stand well with God and look to His judgment, you will more easily bear being worsted.

The Disciple

2. Men tend to prioritize temporal honors and wealth rather than heavenly treasures and the eternal destiny of the soul.

To what have we come, Lord? Behold, we bewail a temporal loss. We labor and fret for a small gain, while loss of the soul is forgotten and scarcely ever returns to mind. That which is of little or no value claims our attention, whereas that which is of highest necessity is neglected—all because man gives himself wholly to outward things.[2] And unless he withdraws himself quickly, he willingly lies immersed in externals.

45. All Men Are Not to Be Believed, for It Is Easy to Err in Speech

The Disciple

1. Reliance on man is futile.

Grant me help in my needs, O Lord, for the aid of man is useless. How often have I failed to find faithfulness in places where I thought I possessed it! And how many times I have found it where I least expected it![1] Vain, therefore, is hope in men, but the salvation of the just is in You, O God. Blessed be Your name, O Lord my God, in everything that befalls us.

2. Our strongest position is in prayer, reaching out to God in childlike faith.

We are weak and unstable, quickly deceived and changed. Who is the man that is able to guard himself with such caution and care as not sometimes to fall into deception or perplexity? He who confides in You, O Lord, and seeks You with a simple heart does not fall so easily.[2] And if some trouble should come upon him, no matter how entangled in it he may be, he will be more quickly delivered and comforted by You. For You will not forsake him who trusts in You to the very end.

Rare is the friend who remains faithful through all his friend's distress. But You, Lord, and You alone, are entirely faithful in all things; other than You, there is none so faithful.

Oh, how wise is that holy soul who said: "My mind is firmly settled and founded in Christ."[3] If that were true of me, human fear would not so easily cause me anxiety, nor would the darts of words disturb. But who can foresee all things and provide against all evils? And if things foreseen have often hurt, can those which are unlooked for do otherwise than wound us gravely? Why, indeed, have I not provided better for my wretched self? Why, too, have I so easily kept faith in others? We are but men, however, nothing more than weak men, although we are thought by many to be, and are called, angels.

In whom shall I put my faith, Lord? In whom but You? You are the truth which does not deceive and cannot be deceived. Every man, on the other hand, is a liar, weak, unstable, and likely to err, especially in words, so that one ought not to be too quick to believe even that which seems, on the face of it, to sound true. How wise was Your warning to beware of men; that a man's enemies are those of his own household; that we should not believe if anyone says: "Behold he is here, or behold he is there."

I have been taught to my own cost, and I hope it has given me greater caution, not greater folly. "Beware," they say, "beware and keep to yourself what I tell you!" Then while I keep silent, believing that the matter is secret, he who asks me to be silent cannot remain silent himself, but immediately betrays both me and himself, and goes his way.[4] From tales of this kind and from such careless men protect me, O Lord, lest I fall into their hands and into their ways. Put in my mouth words that are true and steadfast and keep far from me the crafty tongue, because what I am not willing to suffer I ought by all means to shun.

Oh, how good and how peaceful it is to be silent about others, not to believe without discrimination all that is said, not easily to report it further, to reveal oneself to few, always to seek You as the discerner of hearts, and not to be blown away by every wind of words, but to wish that all things, within and beyond us, be done according to the pleasure of Thy will.[5]

3. It is wise to trust in Christ and Him alone – no other man.

4. Most people cannot bridle their tongues.

5. The peaceful, wise man will say little and be very careful how much he believes of what is said.

How conducive it is for the keeping of heavenly grace to fly the gaze of men, not to seek abroad things which seem to cause admiration, but to follow with utmost diligence those which give fervor and amendment of life! How many have been harmed by having their virtue known and praised too hastily! And how truly profitable it has been when grace remained hidden during this frail life, which is all temptation and warfare!

46. Trust in God Against Slander

The Voice of Christ

My child, stand firm and trust in Me. For what are words but words? They fly through the air but hurt not a stone. If you are guilty, consider how you would gladly amend. If you are not conscious of any fault, think that you wish to bear this for the sake of God. It is little enough for you occasionally to endure words, since you are not yet strong enough to bear hard blows.[1]

And why do such small matters pierce you to the heart, unless because you are still carnal and pay more heed to men than you ought? You do not wish to be reproved for your faults and you seek shelter in excuses because you are afraid of being despised.[2] But look into yourself more thoroughly and you will learn that the world is still alive in you, in a vain desire to please men. For when you shrink from being abased and confounded for your failings, it is plain indeed that you are not truly humble or truly dead to the world, and that the world is not crucified in you.

Listen to My word, and you will not value ten thousand words of men. Behold, if every malicious thing that could possibly be invented were uttered against you, what harm could it do if you ignored it all and gave it no more thought than you would a blade of grass? Could it so much as pluck one hair from your head?

1. Slander is not quite so hard a persecution as physical beatings.

2. The carnal, fleshly mindset is fearful of reproof and humbling.

He who does not keep his heart within him, and who does not have God before his eyes is easily moved by a word of disparagement. He who trusts in Me, on the other hand, and who has no desire to stand by his own judgment, will be free from the fear of men. For I am the judge and discerner of all secrets. I know how all things happen. I know who causes injury and who suffers it. From Me that word proceeded, and with My permission it happened, that out of many hearts thoughts may be revealed.[3] I shall judge the guilty and the innocent; but I have wished beforehand to try them both by secret judgment.

3. Even slander and criticism comes by God's sovereign order to test us.

The testimony of man is often deceiving, but My judgment is true—it will stand and not be overthrown. It is hidden from many and made known to but a few. Yet it is never mistaken and cannot be mistaken even though it does not seem right in the eyes of the unwise.

To Me, therefore, you ought to come in every decision, not depending on your own judgment. For the just man will not be disturbed, no matter what may befall him from God. Even if an unjust charge be made against him he will not be much troubled.[4] Neither will he exult vainly if through others he is justly acquitted. He considers that it is I Who search the hearts and inmost thoughts of men, that I do not judge according to the face of things or human appearances. For what the judgment of men considers praiseworthy is often worthy of blame in My sight.

4. Human injustices do not bother the just man because he is confident in the absolute justice of God.

The Disciple

O Lord God, just Judge, strong and patient, You Who know the weakness and depravity of men, be my strength and all my confidence, for my own conscience is not sufficient for me.[5] You know what I do not know, and, therefore, I ought to humble myself whenever I am accused and bear it meekly. Forgive me, then, in Your mercy for my every failure in this regard, and give me once more the grace of greater endurance. Better to me is Your abundant mercy in obtaining pardon than

5. A'Kempis includes a prayer of confession for failing to react properly to men's accusations.

6. We need God's mercy more than man's just treatment.

the justice which I imagine in defending the secrets of my conscience. And though I am not conscious to myself of any fault, yet I cannot thereby justify myself, because without Your mercy no man living will be justified in Your sight.[6]

47. Every Trial Must Be Borne for the Sake of Eternal Life

The Voice of Christ

My child, do not let the labors which you have taken up for My sake break you, and do not let troubles, from whatever source, cast you down; but in everything let My promise strengthen and console you. I am able to reward you beyond all means and measure.[1]

1. A'Kempis includes an encouragement for those working and serving Christ.

You will not labor here long, nor will you always be oppressed by sorrows. Wait a little while and you will see a speedy end of evils.[2] The hour will come when all labor and trouble shall be no more. All that passes away with time is trivial.

2. This life and our suffering are soon over.

What you do, do well. Work faithfully in My vineyard. I will be your reward. Write, read, sing, mourn, keep silence, pray, and bear hardships like a man. Eternal life is worth all these and greater battles. Peace will come on a day which is known to the Lord, and then there shall be no day or night as at present but perpetual light, infinite brightness, lasting peace, and safe repose. Then you will not say: "Who shall deliver me from the body of this death?"[3] nor will you cry: "Woe is me, because my sojourn is prolonged." For then death will be banished, and there will be health unfailing. There will be no anxiety then, but blessed joy and sweet, noble companionship.

3. Romans 7:24

If you could see the everlasting crowns of the saints in heaven, and the great glory wherein they now rejoice—they who were once considered contemptible in this world and, as it were, unworthy of life itself—you would certainly humble yourself at once to the very earth, and seek to be subject to all rather than to command even one.[4] Nor would you desire

4. Eternal glories make all the humbling on earth worthwhile.

the pleasant days of this life, but rather be glad to suffer for God, considering it your greatest gain to be counted as nothing among men.

Oh, if these things appealed to you and penetrated deeply into your heart, how could you dare to complain even once? Ought not all trials be borne for the sake of everlasting life? In truth, the loss or gain of God's kingdom is no small matter.

Lift up your countenance to heaven, then. Behold Me, and with Me all My saints. They had great trials in this life, but now they rejoice. They are consoled. Now they are safe and at rest. And they shall abide with Me for all eternity in the kingdom of My Father.

48. The Day of Eternity and the Distresses of This Life

The Disciple

O most happy mansion of the city above! O most bright day of eternity, which night does not darken, but which the highest truth ever enlightens! O day, ever joyful and ever secure, which never changes its state to the opposite! Oh, that this day shine forth, that all these temporal things come to an end! It envelops the saints all resplendent with heavenly brightness, but it appears far off as through a glass to us wanderers on the earth. The citizens of heaven know how joyful that day is, but the exiled sons of Eve mourn that this one is bitter and tedious.

The days of this life are short and evil, full of grief and distress. Here man is defiled by many sins, ensnared in many passions, enslaved by many fears, and burdened with many cares. He is distracted by many curiosities and entangled in many vanities, surrounded by many errors and worn by many labors, oppressed by temptations, weakened by pleasures, and tortured by want.[1]

1. The description of this world applies as much today as in A.D. 1441.

Oh, when will these evils end? When shall I be freed from the miserable slavery of vice? When, Lord, shall I think of You alone? When shall I fully rejoice in You? When shall I be without hindrance, in true liberty, free from every grievance of mind and body? When will there be solid peace, undisturbed and secure, inward peace and outward peace, peace secured on every side?[2] O good Jesus, when shall I stand to gaze upon You? When shall I contemplate the glory of Your kingdom? When will You be all in all to me? Oh, when shall I be with You in that kingdom of Yours, which You have prepared for Your beloved from all eternity?

I am left poor and exiled in a hostile land, where every day sees wars and very great misfortunes.[3] Console my banishment, assuage my sorrow. My whole desire is for You. Whatever solace this world offers is a burden to me. I desire to enjoy You intimately, but I cannot attain to it. I wish to cling fast to heavenly things, but temporal affairs and unmortified passions bear me down.[4] I wish in mind to be above all things, but I am forced by the flesh to be unwillingly subject to them. Thus, I fight with myself, unhappy that I am, and am become a burden to myself, while my spirit seeks to rise upward and my flesh to sink downward.[5] Oh, what inward suffering I undergo when I consider heavenly things; when I pray, a multitude of carnal thoughts rush upon me!

O my God, do not remove Yourself far from me, and depart not in anger from Your servant. Dart forth Your lightning and disperse them; send forth Your arrows and let the phantoms of the enemy be put to flight. Draw my senses toward You and make me forget all worldly things. Grant me the grace to cast away quickly all vicious imaginings and to scorn them. Aid me, O heavenly Truth, that no vanity may move me. Come, heavenly Sweetness, and let all impurity fly from before Your face.

Pardon me also, and deal mercifully with me, as often as I think of anything besides You in prayer. For I confess truly that I am accustomed to be very much distracted. Very often

2. Perfect peace will only be realized in glory.

3. The world is characterized as hostile, war-torn, and a wilderness in which we wander.

4. We are dragged down by unmortified lusts and worldly comforts.

5. Romans 7:12ff. We are often miserable when the spirit wars against the flesh.

I am not where bodily I stand or sit; rather, I am where my thoughts carry me. Where my thoughts are, there am I; and frequently my thoughts are where my love is. That which naturally delights, or is by habit pleasing, comes to me quickly. Hence You Who are Truth itself, have plainly said: "For where your treasure is, there is your heart also." If I love heaven, I think willingly of heavenly things. If I love the world, I rejoice at the happiness of the world and grieve at its troubles. If I love the flesh, I often imagine things that are carnal. If I love the spirit, I delight in thinking of spiritual matters. For whatever I love, I am willing to speak and hear about.[6]

6. We talk about and think of the things we love, either God or the things of the world.

Blessed is the man who for Your sake, O Lord, dismisses all creatures, does violence to nature, crucifies the desires of the flesh in fervor of spirit, so that with serene conscience he can offer You a pure prayer and, having excluded all earthly things inwardly and outwardly, becomes worthy to enter into the heavenly choirs.

49. The Desire of Eternal Life; the Great Rewards Promised to Those Who Struggle

The Voice of Christ

My child, when you feel the desire for everlasting happiness poured out upon you from above, and when you long to depart out of the tabernacle of the body that you may contemplate My glory without threat of change, open wide your heart and receive this holy inspiration with all eagerness. Give deepest thanks to the heavenly Goodness which deals with you so understandingly, visits you so mercifully, stirs you so fervently, and sustains you so powerfully lest under your own weight you sink down to earthly things. For you obtain this not by your own thought or effort, but simply by the condescension of heavenly grace and divine regard.[1] And the purpose of it is that you may advance in virtue and in greater humility, that you may prepare yourself for future trials, that you may strive

1. The yearning desire for heaven comes by God's grace.

2. This desire and hope for heaven helps us face trials on earth and faithfully serve Christ here.

3. Submit contentedly to God's will even if that means to continue here in trials and laborings.

4. Romans 8:18-25

5. God ordains this life for our sanctification.

to cling to Me with all the affection of your heart, and may serve Me with a fervent will.[2]

My child, often, when the fire is burning the flame does not ascend without smoke. Likewise, the desires of some burn toward heavenly things, and yet they are not free from temptations of carnal affection. Therefore, it is not altogether for the pure honor of God that they act when they petition Him so earnestly. Such, too, is often your desire which you profess to be so strong. For that which is alloyed with self-interest is not pure and perfect.

Ask, therefore, not for what is pleasing and convenient to yourself, but for what is acceptable to Me and is for My honor, because if you judge rightly, you ought to prefer and follow My will, not your own desire or whatever things you wish.[3]

I know your longings and I have heard your frequent sighs. Already you wish to be in the liberty of the glory of the sons of God.[4] Already you desire the delights of the eternal home, the heavenly land that is full of joy. But that hour is not yet come. There remains yet another hour, a time of war, of labor, and of trial. You long to be filled with the highest good, but you cannot attain it now. I am that sovereign Good. Await Me, until the kingdom of God shall come.

You must still be tried on earth, and exercised in many things. Consolation will sometimes be given you, but the complete fullness of it is not granted. Take courage, therefore, and be strong both to do and to suffer what is contrary to nature.

You must put on the new man. You must be changed into another man.[5] You must often do the things you do not wish to do and forego those you do wish. What pleases others will succeed; what pleases you will not. The words of others will be heard; what you say will be accounted as nothing. Others will ask and receive; you will ask and not receive. Others will gain great fame among men; about you nothing will be said. To others the doing of this or that will be entrusted; you will be judged useless. At all this nature will sometimes be sad, and it will be a great thing if you bear this sadness in silence. For in these and many similar ways the faithful servant of the Lord is wont to be tried, to see how far he can deny himself and break himself in all things.[6]

There is scarcely anything in which you so need to die to self as in seeing and suffering things that are against your will, especially when things that are commanded seem inconvenient or useless. Then, because you are under authority, and dare not resist the higher power, it seems hard to submit to the will of another and give up your own opinion entirely.[7]

But consider, my child, the fruit of these labors, how soon they will end and how greatly they will be rewarded, and you will not be saddened by them, but your patience will receive the strongest consolation. For instead of the little will that you now readily give up, you shall always have your will in heaven. There, indeed, you shall find all that you could desire. There you shall have possession of every good without fear of losing it. There shall your will be forever one with Mine. It shall desire nothing outside of Me and nothing for itself. There no one shall oppose you, no one shall complain of you, no one hinder you, and nothing stand in your way. All that you desire will be present there, replenishing your affection and satisfying it to the full. There I shall render you glory for the reproach you have suffered here; for your sorrow I shall give you a garment of praise, and for the lowest place a seat of power forever. There the fruit of glory will appear, the labor of penance rejoice, and humble subjection be gloriously crowned.

Bow humbly, therefore, under the will of all, and do not heed who said this or commanded that. But let it be your special care when something is commanded, or even hinted at, whether by a superior or an inferior or an equal, that you take it in good part and try honestly to perform it.[8] Let one person seek one thing and another something else. Let one glory in this, another in that, and both be praised a thousand times over. But as for you, rejoice neither in one or the other, but only in contempt of yourself and in My pleasure and honor.[9] Let this be your wish: That whether in life or in death God may be glorified in you.

6. The Lord gives us ample opportunity to humble ourselves and deny self.

7. The hardest test of self-denial is to submit to an authority with which you disagree.

8. Ephesians 5:21

9. Deny yourself and seek to glorify God. This is our main objective in the Christian life.

50. How a Desolate Person Ought to Commit Himself Into the Hands of God

The Disciple

1. The disciple's prayer now shifts from a Christ-ward direction to the Father.

Lord God, Holy Father, may You be blessed now and in eternity.[1] For as You will, so is it done; and what You do is good. Let Your servant rejoice in You—not in himself or in any other, for You alone are true joy. You are my hope and my crown. You, O Lord, are my joy and my honor.

2. All good possessed by us is by God's grace and unmerited favor.

What does Your servant possess that he has not received from You, and that without any merit of his own?[2] Yours are all the things which You have given, all the things which You have made.

I am poor and in labors since my youth, and my soul is sorrowful sometimes even to the point of tears. At times, also, my spirit is troubled because of impending sufferings. I long for the joy of peace. Earnestly I beg for the peace of Your children who are fed by You in the light of consolation. If You give peace, if You infuse holy joy, the soul of Your servant shall be filled with holy song and be devout in praising You.[3] But if

3. When God first gives us joy, peace, and the blessing of His presence, we are enabled to worship Him and obey Him.

You withdraw Yourself, as You so very often do, he will not be able to follow the way of Your commandments, but will rather be obliged to strike his breast and bend the knee, because his today is different from yesterday and the day before when Your light shone upon his head and he was protected in the shadow of Your wings from the temptations rushing upon him.

Just Father, ever to be praised, the hour is come for Your servant to be tried. Beloved Father, it is right that in this hour Your servant should suffer something for You. O Father, forever to be honored, the hour which You knew from all eternity is at hand, when for a short time Your servant should be outwardly oppressed, but inwardly should ever live with You.

4. A little suffering here is nothing to us in light of eternal glory.

Let him be a little slighted, let him be humbled, let him fail in the sight of men, let him be afflicted with sufferings and pains, so that he may rise again with You in the dawn of the new light and be glorified in heaven.[4]

Holy Father, You have so appointed and wished it. What has happened is what You commanded. For this is a favor to Your friend, to suffer and be troubled in the world for Your love, no matter how often and by whom You permit it to happen to him.

Nothing happens in the world without Your design and providence, and without cause.[5] It is well for me, O Lord, that You have humbled me, that I may learn the justice of Your judgments and cast away all presumption and haughtiness of heart. It is profitable for me that shame has covered my face that I may look to You rather than to men for consolation. Hereby I have learned also to fear Your inscrutable judgment falling alike upon the just and unjust yet not without equity and justice.

5. A'Kempis affirms the absolute sovereignty of God. God decrees and brings about all things.

Thanks to You that You have not spared me evils but have bruised me with bitter blows, inflicting sorrows, sending distress without and within.[6] Under heaven there is none to console me except You, my Lord God, the heavenly Physician of souls, Who wound and heal, Who cast down to hell and raise up again. Your discipline is upon me and Your very rod shall instruct me.

6. Afflictions for believers serve as God's chastisements.

Behold, beloved Father, I am in Your hands. I bow myself under Your correcting chastisement. Strike my back and my neck, that I may bend my crookedness to Your will. Make of me a pious and humble follower, as in Your goodness You are wont to do, that I may walk according to Your every nod.[7] Myself and all that is mine I commit to You to be corrected, for it is better to be punished here than hereafter.

7. Humility and obedience is the goal of God's corrections.

You know all things without exception, and nothing in man's conscience is hidden from You. Coming events You know before they happen, and there is no need for anyone to teach or admonish You of what is being done on earth. You know what will promote my progress, and how much tribulation will serve to cleanse away the rust of vice. Deal with me according to Your good pleasure and do not despise my sinful life, which is known to none so well or so clearly as to You alone.

Grant me, O Lord, the grace to know what should be known, to praise what is most pleasing to You, to esteem that which appears most precious to You, and to abhor what is unclean in Your sight.[8]

8. To love God is to love what He loves and hate what He hates.

Do not allow me to judge according to the light of my bodily eyes, nor to give sentence according to the hearing of ignorant men's ears. But let me distinguish with true judgment between things visible and spiritual, and always seek above all things Your good pleasure. The senses of men often err in their judgments, and the lovers of this world also err in loving only visible things. How is a man the better for being thought greater by men? The deceiver deceives the deceitful, the vain man deceives the vain, the blind deceives the blind, the weak deceives the weak as often as he extols them, and in truth his foolish praise shames them the more.[9] For, as the humble St. Francis says, whatever anyone is in Your sight, that he is and nothing more.

9. Men fail in judgment; therefore it is foolish to accept their praise.

51. When We Cannot Attain to the Highest, We Must Practice the Humble Works

The Voice of Christ

My child, you cannot always continue in the more fervent desire of virtue, or remain in the higher stage of contemplation, but because of humanity's sin you must sometimes descend to lower things and bear the burden of this corruptible life, albeit unwillingly and wearily.[1] As long as you wear a mortal body you will suffer weariness and heaviness of heart. You ought, therefore, to bewail in the flesh the burden of the flesh which keeps you from giving yourself unceasingly to spiritual exercises and divine contemplation.

1. Prayer and meditation gives us a break from temptations. But life, work, and relationships can awaken the sinful flesh in us.

In such condition, it is well for you to apply yourself to humble, outward works and to refresh yourself in good deeds, to await with unshaken confidence My heavenly visitation, patiently to bear your exile and dryness of mind until you are again visited by Me and freed of all anxieties.[2] For I will cause you to forget your labors and to enjoy inward quiet. I will spread before you the open fields of the Scriptures, so that with an open heart you may begin to advance in the way of My commandments. And you will say: the sufferings of this time are not worthy to be compared with the future glory which shall be revealed to us.[3]

2. Even when busy at work, you may anticipate time with Christ in the work.

3. Romans 8:18

52. A Man Ought Not to Consider Himself Worthy of Consolation, But Rather Deserving of Chastisement

The Disciple

Lord, I am not worthy of Your consolation or of any spiritual visitation. Therefore, You treat me justly when You leave me poor and desolate. For though I could shed a sea of tears, yet I should not be worthy of Your consolation. Hence, I deserve only to be scourged and punished because I have offended You often and grievously, and have sinned greatly in many things. In all justice, therefore, I am not worthy of any consolation.[1]

But You, O gracious and merciful God, Who do not will that Your works should perish,[2] deign to console Your servant beyond all his merit and above human measure, to show the riches of Your goodness toward the vessels of mercy. For Your consolations are not like the words of men.

What have I done, Lord, that You should confer on me any heavenly comfort? I remember that I have done nothing good, but that I have always been prone to sin and slow to amend. That is true. I cannot deny it. If I said otherwise You would stand against me, and there would be no one to defend

1. Keeping God's justice in mind humbles us and reminds us that we cannot earn God's good graces.

2. A'Kempis sees the believer as God's work of grace.

3. Romans 6:23

me. What have I deserved for my sins except hell and everlasting fire?[3]

In truth, I confess that I am deserving of all scorn and contempt. Neither is it fitting that I should be remembered among Your devoted servants. And although it is hard for me to hear this, yet for truth's sake I will allege my sins against myself, so that I may more easily deserve to beg Your mercy. What shall I say, guilty as I am and full of all confusion? My tongue can say nothing but this alone: "I have sinned, O Lord, I have sinned; have mercy on me and pardon me. Suffer me a little that I may pour out my grief, before I go to that dark land that is covered with the shadow of death."[4]

4. All we can do is confess our sin and plead His mercy.

What do you especially demand of a guilty and wretched sinner, except that he be contrite and humble himself for his sins? In true sorrow and humility of heart hope of forgiveness is born, the troubled conscience is reconciled, grace is found, man is preserved from the wrath to come, and God and the penitent meet with a holy kiss.[5]

5. Grace and forgiveness rush in when a man truly confesses his sins.

To You, O Lord, humble sorrow for sins is an acceptable sacrifice, a sacrifice far sweeter than the perfume of incense. This is also the pleasing ointment which You would have poured upon Your sacred feet, for a contrite and humble heart You have never despised.[6] Here is a place of refuge from the force of the enemy's anger. Here is amended and washed away whatever defilement has been contracted elsewhere.

6. Psalm 51:17

53. God's Grace Is Not Given to the Earthly Minded

The Voice of Christ

My child, my grace is precious. It does not allow itself to be mixed with external things or with earthly consolations. Cast away all obstacles to grace, therefore, if you wish to receive its infusion.

Seek to retire within yourself. Love to dwell alone with yourself. Seek no man's conversation, but rather pour forth devout prayer to God that you may keep your mind contrite and your heart pure.

Consider the whole world as nothing. Prefer attendance upon God to all outward occupation, for you cannot attend upon Me and at the same time take delight in external things.[1] You must remove yourself from acquaintances and from dear friends, and keep your mind free of all temporal consolation. Thus the blessed Apostle St. Peter begs the faithful of Christ to keep themselves as strangers and pilgrims in the world.

What great confidence at the hour of death shall be his who is not attached to this world by any affection. But the sickly soul does not know what it is to have a heart thus separated from all things, nor does the natural man know the liberty of the spiritual man. Yet, if he truly wishes to be spiritual, he must renounce both strangers and friends, and must beware of no one more than himself.

If you completely conquer yourself, you will more easily subdue all other things. The perfect victory is to triumph over self.[2] For he who holds himself in such subjection that sensuality obeys reason and reason obeys Me in all matters, is truly his own conqueror and master of the world.

Now, if you wish to climb to this high position you must begin like a man, and lay the ax to the root, in order to tear out and destroy any hidden unruly love of self or of earthly goods. From this vice of too much self-love comes almost every other vice that must be uprooted.[3] And when this evil is vanquished, and brought under control, great peace and quiet will follow at once.

But because few labor to die entirely to self, or tend completely away from self, therefore they remain entangled in self, and cannot be lifted in spirit above themselves. But he who desires to walk freely with Me must mortify all his low and inordinate affections, and must not cling with selfish love or desire to any creature.[4]

1. Love for God and communion with Him in private is to be preferred over all other communions with friends, etc.

2. To conquer self is to master the world.

3. The root of almost all vices is inordinate love of self (displacing a love for God).

4. The problem in relation to others is our self-oriented love.

54. The Different Motions of Nature and Grace

The Voice of Christ

My child, pay careful attention to the movements of nature and of grace,[1] for they move in very contrary and subtle ways, and can scarcely be distinguished by anyone except a man who is spiritual and inwardly enlightened. All men, indeed, desire what is good, and strive for what is good in their words and deeds. For this reason the appearance of good deceives many.

Nature is crafty and attracts many, ensnaring and deceiving them while ever seeking itself. But grace walks in simplicity, turns away from all appearance of evil, offers no deceits, and does all purely for God in whom she rests as her last end.[2]

Nature is not willing to die, or to be kept down, or to be overcome. Nor will it subdue itself or be made subject. Grace, on the contrary, strives for mortification of self. She resists sensuality, seeks to be in subjection, longs to be conquered, has no wish to use her own liberty, loves to be held under discipline, and does not desire to rule over anyone, but wishes rather to live, to stand, and to be always under God for Whose sake she is willing to bow humbly to every human creature.[3]

Nature works for its own interest and looks to the profit it can reap from another. Grace does not consider what is useful and advantageous to herself, but rather what is profitable to many. Nature likes to receive honor and reverence, but grace faithfully attributes all honor and glory to God. Nature fears shame and contempt, but grace is happy to suffer reproach for the name of Jesus.[4] Nature loves ease and physical rest. Grace, however, cannot bear to be idle and embraces labor willingly. Nature seeks to possess what is rare and beautiful, abhorring things that are cheap and coarse. Grace, on the contrary, delights in simple, humble things, not despising those that are rough, nor refusing to be clothed in old garments.

Nature has regard for temporal wealth and rejoices in earthly gains.[5] It is sad over a loss and irritated by a slight,

1. The contrast is between the natural man (the flesh) and the new man, who walks by grace.

2. Grace is simple, honest, and pure in its motive.

3. Grace is humble and willingly submits its will to others.

4. Grace is willing to suffer for Jesus and eschews honor for self.

5. Natural man is always seeking honor and wealth here over eternal treasures.

injurious word. But grace looks to eternal things and does not cling to those which are temporal, being neither disturbed at loss nor angered by hard words, because she has placed her treasure and joy in heaven where nothing is lost.

Nature is covetous, and receives more willingly than it gives. It loves to have its own private possessions. Grace, however, is kind and openhearted. Grace shuns private interest, is contented with little, and judges it more blessed to give than to receive.[6]

6. Grace sees little importance in personal possessions and wealth.

Nature is inclined toward creatures, toward its own flesh, toward vanities, and toward running about. But grace draws near to God and to virtue, renounces creatures, hates the desires of the flesh, restrains her wanderings and blushes at being seen in public.

Nature likes to have some external comfort in which it can take sensual delight, but grace seeks consolation only in God, to find her delight in the highest Good, above all visible things.[7]

7. Comforts for the one who lives by grace is found in God, not sensual delights and public attention.

Nature does everything for its own gain and interest. It can do nothing without pay and hopes for its good deeds to receive their equal or better, or else praise and favor. It is very desirous of having its deeds and gifts highly regarded. Grace, however, seeks nothing temporal, nor does she ask any recompense but God alone. Of temporal necessities she asks no more than will serve to obtain eternity.

Nature rejoices in many friends and kinsfolk, glories in noble position and birth, fawns on the powerful, flatters the rich, and applauds those who are like itself. But grace loves even her enemies and is not puffed up at having many friends.[8] She does not think highly of either position or birth unless there is also virtue there. She favors the poor in preference to the rich. She sympathizes with the innocent rather than with the powerful. She rejoices with the true man rather than with the deceitful, and is always exhorting the good to strive for better gifts, to become like the Son of God by practicing the virtues.

8. The natural man and the grace-endowed new man hold very different values. Grace values the poor, the sincere, the honest, and virtue over fame and worldly honor.

Nature is quick to complain of need and trouble; grace is stanch in suffering want.

Nature turns all things back to self. It fights and argues for self. Grace brings all things back to God in Whom they have their source.[9] To herself she ascribes no good, nor is she arrogant or presumptuous. She is not contentious. She does not prefer her own opinion to the opinion of others, but in every matter of sense and thought submits herself to eternal wisdom and the divine judgment.

9. Nature is self-oriented; grace is God-oriented and God-glorifying.

Nature has a relish for knowing secrets and hearing news. It wishes to appear abroad and to have many sense experiences. It wishes to be known and to do things for which it will be praised and admired. But grace does not care to hear news or curious matters, because all this arises from the old corruption of man, since there is nothing new, nothing lasting on earth. Grace teaches, therefore, restraint of the senses, avoidance of vain self-satisfaction and show, the humble hiding of deeds worthy of praise and admiration, and the seeking in every thing and in every knowledge the fruit of usefulness, the praise and honor of God.[10] She will not have herself or hers exalted, but desires that God Who bestows all simply out of love should be blessed in His gifts.

10. Doing good and honoring God is far more important than seeking honor and credit for what we do.

This grace is a supernatural light, a certain special gift of God, the proper mark of the elect and the pledge of everlasting salvation. It raises man up from earthly things to love the things of heaven. It makes a spiritual man of a carnal one.[11]

11. It is only this grace of God that can produce a spiritual man.

The more, then, nature is held in check and conquered, the more grace is given. Every day the interior man is reformed by new visitations according to the image of God.

55. The Corruption of Nature and the Efficacy of Divine Grace

The Disciple

O Lord, my God, Who created me to Your own image and likeness, grant me this grace which You have shown to be so great and necessary for salvation, that I may overcome my very evil nature that is drawing me to sin and perdition. For I feel in my flesh the law of sin contradicting the law of my mind and leading me captive to serve sensuality in many things.[1] I cannot resist the passions thereof unless Your most holy grace warmly infused into my heart assist me.[2]

1. Romans 7:23

There is need of Your grace, and of great grace, in order to overcome a nature prone to evil from youth. For through the first man, Adam, nature is fallen and weakened by sin, and the punishment of that stain has fallen upon all mankind. Thus nature itself, which You created good and right, is considered a symbol of vice and the weakness of corrupted nature, because when left to itself it tends toward evil and to baser things. The little strength remaining in it is like a spark hidden in ashes.[3] That strength is natural reason which, surrounded by thick darkness, still has the power of judging good and evil, of seeing the difference between true and false, though it is not able to fulfill all that it approves and does not enjoy the full light of truth or soundness of affection.

2. God's grace is completely essential for our sanctification.

3. Conscience is still somewhat capable of distinguishing right and wrong, yet it cannot change the heart or life.

Hence it is, my God, that according to the inward man I delight in Your law, knowing that Your command is good, just, and holy,[4] and that it proves the necessity of shunning all evil and sin. But in the flesh I keep the law of sin, obeying sensuality rather than reason. Hence, also, it is that the will to good is present in me, but how to accomplish it I know not.[5] Hence, too, I often propose many good things, but because the grace to help my weakness is lacking, I recoil and give up at the slightest resistance. Thus it is that I know the way of perfection and see clearly enough how I ought to act, but because

4. Romans 7:12

5. Romans 7:18

I am pressed down by the weight of my own corruption I do not rise to more perfect things.

6. Only the constant force of God's grace can give us the strength to do what is good and right.

How extremely necessary to me, O Lord, Your grace is to begin any good deed, to carry it on and bring it to completion![6] For without grace I can do nothing, but with its strength I can do all things in You. O Grace truly heavenly, without which our merits are nothing and no gifts of nature are to be esteemed!

7. Only the elect receive the grace of salvation from sin.

Before You, O Lord, no arts or riches, no beauty or strength, no wit or intelligence avail without grace. For the gifts of nature are common to good and bad alike, but the peculiar gift of Your elect is grace or love, and those who are signed with it are held worthy of everlasting life.[7] So excellent is this grace that without it no gift of prophecy or of miracles, no meditation be it ever so exalted, can be considered anything. Not even faith or hope or other virtues are acceptable to You without charity and grace.[8]

8. Only God's grace can enable us to faith and true love.

O most blessed grace, which makes the poor in spirit rich in virtues, which renders him who is rich in many good things humble of heart, come, descend upon me, fill me quickly with your consolation lest my soul faint with weariness and dryness of mind.

Let me find grace in Your sight, I beg, Lord, for Your grace is enough for me, even though I obtain none of the things which nature desires. If I am tempted and afflicted with many tribulations, I will fear no evils while Your grace is with me. This is my strength. This will give me counsel and help. This is more powerful than all my enemies and wiser than all the wise. This is the mistress of truth, the teacher of discipline, the light of the heart, the consoler in anguish, the banisher of sorrow, the expeller of fear, the nourisher of devotion, the producer of tears. What am I without grace, but dead wood, a useless branch, fit only to be cast away?

Let Your grace, therefore, go before me and follow me, O Lord, and make me always intent upon good works, through Jesus Christ, Your Son.

56. We Ought to Deny Ourselves and Imitate Christ Through Bearing the Cross

The Voice of Christ

My child, the more you depart from yourself, the more you will be able to enter into Me. As the giving up of exterior things brings interior peace, so the forsaking of self unites you to God. I will have you learn perfect surrender to My will, without contradiction or complaint.

Follow Me. I am the Way, the Truth, and the Life.[1] Without the Way, there is no going. Without the Truth, there is no knowing. Without the Life, there is no living. I am the Way which you must follow, the Truth which you must believe, the Life for which you must hope. I am the inviolable Way, the infallible Truth, the unending Life. I am the Way that is straight, the supreme Truth, the Life that is true, the blessed, the uncreated Life. If you abide in My Way you shall know the Truth, and the Truth shall make you free, and you shall attain life everlasting.

If you wish to enter into life, keep My commandments. If you will know the truth, believe in Me. If you will be perfect, sell all. If you will be My disciple, deny yourself.[2] If you will possess the blessed life, despise this present life. If you will be exalted in heaven, humble yourself on earth. If you wish to reign with Me, carry the Cross with Me. For only the servants of the Cross find the life of blessedness and of true light.[3]

The Disciple

Lord Jesus, because Your way is narrow and despised by the world, grant that I may despise the world and imitate You. For the servant is not greater than his Lord, nor the disciple above the Master.[4] Let Your servant be trained in Your life, for there is my salvation and true holiness. Whatever else I read or hear does not fully refresh or delight me.

1. John 14:6

2. Reference Matthew 19:17, 21, Matthew 16:24, and 2 Timothy 2:12.

3. Although not popular in the world, the Christian life is a cross, filled with self-denial, sacrifice, and keeping God's commandments.

4. John 13:16

The Voice of Christ

My child, now that you know these things and have read them all, happy will you be if you do them. He who has My commandments and keeps them, he it is that loves Me. And I will love him and will show Myself to him,[5] and will bring it about that he will sit down with Me in My Father's Kingdom.

5. John 14:21

The Disciple

Lord Jesus, as You have said, so be it, and what You have promised, let it be my lot to win. I have received the cross, from Your hand I have received it. I will carry it, carry it even unto death as You have laid it upon me. Truly, the life of a good religious man is a cross, but it leads to paradise. We have begun—we may not go back, nor may we leave off.

Take courage, brethren, let us go forward together and Jesus will be with us.[6] For Jesus' sake we have taken this cross. For Jesus' sake let us persevere with it. He will be our help as He is also our leader and guide. Behold, our King goes before us and will fight for us. Let us follow like men. Let no man fear any terrors. Let us be prepared to meet death valiantly in battle. Let us not suffer our glory to be blemished by fleeing from the Cross.

6. An encouragement to endure and persevere through the many tribulations and struggles in the Christian life.

57. A Man Should Not Be Too Downcast When He Falls Into Defects

The Voice of Christ

My child, patience and humility in adversity are more pleasing to Me than much consolation and devotion when things are going well.[1]

Why are you saddened by some little thing said against you? Even if it had been more you ought not to have been affected. But now let it pass. It is not the first, nor is it anything new, and if you live long it will not be the last.

You are manly enough so long as you meet no opposition. You give good advice to others, and you know how to

1. The greater measure of our piety is not our devotional life, but our reactions to adversity.

strengthen them with words, but when unexpected tribulation comes to your door, you fail both in counsel and in strength. Consider your great weakness, then, which you experience so often in small matters. Yet when these and like trials happen, they happen for your good.

Put it out of your heart as best you know how, and if it has touched you, still do not let it cast you down or confuse you for long. Bear it patiently at least, if you cannot bear it cheerfully. Even though you bear it unwillingly, and are indignant at it, restrain yourself and let no ill-ordered words pass your lips at which the weak might be scandalized.[2] The storm that is now aroused will soon be quieted and your inward grief will be sweetened by returning grace. "I yet live," says the Lord, "ready to help you and to console you more and more, if you trust in Me and call devoutly upon Me."

Remain tranquil and prepare to bear still greater trials. All is not lost even though you be troubled oftener or tempted more grievously. You are a man, not God. You are flesh, not an angel. How can you possibly expect to remain always in the same state of virtue when the angels in heaven and the first man in paradise failed to do so? I am He Who rescues the afflicted and brings to My divinity those who know their own weakness.[3]

The Disciple

Blessed be Your words, O Lord, sweeter to my mouth than honey and the honeycomb. What would I do in such great trials and anxieties, if You did not strengthen me with Your holy words? If I may but attain to the haven of salvation, what does it matter what or how much I suffer?[4] Grant me a good end. Grant me a happy passage out of this world. Remember me, my God, and lead me by the right way into Your kingdom.

2. The ability to remain silent and not respond in murmuring or anger under tribulation is a major step in Christian maturity.

3. Jesus is the Savior. This is basic.

4. The sufferings of this world are not worthy to be compared with the glory of heaven.

58. High Matters and the Hidden Judgments of God Are Not to Be Scrutinized

The Voice of Christ

My child, beware of discussing high matters and God's hidden judgments—why this person is so forsaken and why that one is favored with so great a grace, or why one man is so afflicted and another so highly exalted.[1] Such things are beyond all human understanding and no reason or disputation can fathom the judgments of God.

When the enemy puts such suggestions in your mind, therefore, or when some curious persons raise questions about them, answer with the prophet: "Thou art just, O Lord, and righteous are Thy judgments";[2] and this: "The judgments of the Lord are true and wholly righteous."[3] My judgments are to be feared, not discussed, because they are incomprehensible to the understanding of men.

In like manner, do not inquire or dispute about the merits of the saints, as to which is more holy, or which shall be greater in the kingdom of heaven. Such things often breed strife and useless contentions. They nourish pride and vainglory, whence arise envy and quarrels, when one proudly tries to exalt one saint and the other another. A desire to know and pry into such matters brings forth no fruit.[4] On the contrary, it displeases the saints, because I am the God, not of dissension, but of peace—of that peace which consists in true humility rather than in self-exaltation.

Some are drawn by the ardor of their love with greater affection to these saints or to those, but this affection is human and not divine. I am He who made all the saints. I gave them grace: I brought them to glory. I know the merits of each of them. I came before them in the blessings of My sweetness. I knew My beloved ones before the ages. I chose them out of the world—they did not choose Me. I called them by grace, I drew them on by mercy. I led them safely through various temptations. I poured into them glorious consolations. I gave

1. Here is a warning not to attempt to penetrate into the counsels of God, especially when it comes to afflictions.

2. Psalm 119:137

3. Psalm 19:9

4. Comparing and competing with each other only lead to pride. Reference James 3:14-15.

them perseverance and I crowned their patience. I know the first and the last. I embrace them all with love inestimable. I am to be praised in all My saints. I am to be blessed above all things, and honored in each of those whom I have exalted and predestined so gloriously without any previous merits of their own.[5]

He who despises one of the least of mine, therefore, does no honor to the greatest, for both the small and the great I made. And he who disparages one of the saints disparages Me also and all others in the kingdom of heaven. They are all one through the bond of charity. They have the same thought and the same will, and they mutually love one another; but, what is a much greater thing, they love Me more than themselves or their own merits. Rapt above themselves, and drawn beyond love of self, they are entirely absorbed in love of Me, in Whom they rest. There is nothing that can draw them away or depress them, for they who are filled with eternal truth burn with the fire of unquenchable love.

Therefore, let carnal and sensual men, who know only how to love their own selfish joys, forbear to dispute about the state of God's saints.[6] Such men take away and add according to their own inclinations and not as it pleases the Eternal Truth. In many this is sheer ignorance, especially in those who are but little enlightened and can rarely love anyone with a purely spiritual love. They are still strongly drawn by natural affection and human friendship to one person or another, and on their behavior in such things here below are based their imaginings of heavenly things. But there is an incomparable distance between the things which the imperfect imagine and those which enlightened men contemplate through revelation from above.

Be careful, then, My child, of treating matters beyond your knowledge out of curiosity. Let it rather be your business and aim to be found, even though the least, in the kingdom of God. For though one were to know who is more holy than another, or who is greater in the kingdom of heaven, of what val-

5. All saints through the ages are entirely recipients of God's grace, election, predestination, and His gift of perseverance.

6. Carnal men want to compare saints and find one better than another.

7. Since the "greatest" in the kingdom are the greatest recipients of grace, God is the One who is worthy of all the glory!

8. Praying to saints is an unbiblical practice common in the middle ages.

9. Revelation 4:10

10. Matthew 18:3

ue would this knowledge be to him unless out of it he should humble himself before Me and should rise up in greater praise of My name?[7]

The man who thinks of the greatness of his own sins and the littleness of his virtues, and of the distance between himself and the perfection of the saints, acts much more acceptably to God than the one who argues about who is greater or who is less. It is better to invoke the saints with devout prayers and tears, and with a humble mind to beg their glorious aid, than to search with vain inquisitiveness into their secrets.[8]

The saints are well and perfectly contented if men know how to content themselves and cease their useless discussions. They do not glory in their own merits, for they attribute no good to themselves but all to Me, because out of My infinite charity I gave all to them. They are filled with such love of God and with such overflowing joy, that no glory is wanting to them and they can lack no happiness. All the saints are so much higher in glory as they are more humble in themselves; nearer to Me, and more beloved by Me. Therefore, you find it written that they cast their crowns before God, and fell down upon their faces before the Lamb, and adored Him Who lives forever.[9]

Many ask who is the greater in the kingdom of heaven when they do not know whether they themselves shall be worthy of being numbered among its least. It is a great thing to be even the least in heaven where all are great because all shall be called, and shall be, the children of God. The least shall be as a thousand, and the sinner of a hundred years shall die. For when the disciples asked who should be greater in the kingdom of heaven they heard this response: "Unless you be converted and become as little children, you shall not enter into the kingdom of heaven. Therefore, whosoever shall humble himself as this little child, he is the greater in the kingdom of heaven."[10]

Woe to those, therefore, who disdain to humble themselves willingly with the little children, for the low gate of the heavenly kingdom will not permit them to enter. Woe also to the rich who have their consolations here, for when the poor enter into God's kingdom, they will stand outside lamenting.[11] Rejoice, you humble, and exult, you poor, for the kingdom of God is yours, if only you walk in the truth.

11. Luke 6:24

59. All Hope and Trust Are to Be Fixed In God Alone

The Disciple

What, Lord, is the trust which I have in this life, or what is my greatest comfort among all the things that appear under heaven? Is it not You, O Lord, my God, Whose mercies are without number?[1] Where have I ever fared well but for You? Or how could things go badly when You were present? I had rather be poor for Your sake than rich without You. I prefer rather to wander on the earth with You than to possess heaven without You. Where You are there is heaven, and where You are not are death and hell. You are my desire and therefore I must cry after You and sigh and pray. In none can I fully trust to help me in my necessities, but in You alone, my God. You are my hope. You are my confidence. You are my consoler, most faithful in every need.[2]

1. Psalm 73:25-28

2. God is alone our chief hope, consoler, and desire.

3. Romans 8:28

All seek their own interests. You, however, place my salvation and my profit first, and turn all things to my good.[3] Even though exposing me to various temptations and hardships, You Who are accustomed to prove Your loved ones in a thousand ways, order all this for my good. You ought not to be loved or praised less in this trial than if You had filled me with heavenly consolations.

In You, therefore, O Lord God, I place all my hope and my refuge. On You I cast all my troubles and anguish, because whatever I have outside of You I find to be weak and unstable. It will not serve me to have many friends, nor will powerful helpers be able to assist me, nor prudent advisers to give useful

4. There is no other refuge, comfort, or stable rest but in God.

answers, nor the books of learned men to console, nor any precious substance to win my freedom, nor any place, secret and beautiful though it be, to shelter me, if You Yourself do not assist, comfort, console, instruct, and guard me.[4] For all things which seem to be for our peace and happiness are nothing when You are absent, and truly confer no happiness.

You, indeed, are the fountain of all good, the height of life, the depth of all that can be spoken. To trust in You above all things is the strongest comfort of Your servants.

5. My soul is God's dwelling place.

My God, the Father of mercies, to You I look, in You I trust. Bless and sanctify my soul with heavenly benediction, so that it may become Your holy dwelling and the seat of Your eternal glory. And in this temple of Your dignity let nothing be found that might offend Your majesty.[5] In Your great goodness, and in the multitude of Your mercies, look upon me and listen to the prayer of Your poor servant exiled from You in the region of the shadow of death. Protect and preserve the soul of Your poor servant among the many dangers of this corruptible life, and direct him by Your accompanying grace, through the ways of peace, to the land of everlasting light.

Book 4
An Invitation to Holy Communion

The Voice of Christ

Come to Me, all you that labor and are burdened, and I will refresh you. The bread which I will give is My Flesh, for the life of the world. Take you and eat: this is My Body, which shall be delivered for you. Do this for the commemoration of Me. He that eateth My flesh, and drinketh My blood, abideth in Me, and I in him. The words that I have spoken to you are spirit and life.[1]

1. Reference Matthew 11:28, Matthew 26:26, and John 6:51,56, 63.

1. The Great Reverence With Which We Should Receive Christ

The Disciple

These are all Your words, O Christ, eternal Truth, though they were not all spoken at one time nor written together in one place. And because they are Yours and true, I must accept them all with faith and gratitude. They are Yours and You have spoken them; they are mine also because You have spoken them for my salvation. Gladly I accept them from Your lips that they may be the more deeply impressed in my heart.[1]

Words of such tenderness, so full of sweetness and love, encourage me; but my sins frighten me and an unclean conscience thunders at me when approaching such great myster-

1. A'Kempis is personally applying Jesus's words to himself. This is the believer's response to the words he reads in Scripture. He hears these words as though spoken of himself.

2. A'Kempis references 2 Chronicles 6:18: "But will God indeed dwell with men on the earth? Behold, heaven and the heaven of heavens cannot contain You. How much less this temple which I have built!"

3. Matthew 11:28

4. Our approach to the Lord's Table is one of humility and a deep sense of privilege. Who are we to enter relationship with the Creator of the Universe, the Holiest of the holies?

ies as these. The sweetness of Your words invites me, but the multitude of my vices oppresses me.

You command me to approach You confidently if I wish to have part with You, and to receive the food of immortality if I desire to obtain life and glory everlasting.

"Come to me," You say, "all you that labor and are burdened, and I will refresh you."

Oh, how sweet and kind to the ear of the sinner is the word by which You, my Lord God, invite the poor and needy to receive Your most holy Body! Who am I, Lord, that I should presume to approach You? Behold, the heaven of heavens cannot contain You,[2] and yet You say: "Come, all of you, to Me."[3]

What means this most gracious honor and this friendly invitation? How shall I dare to come, I who am conscious of no good on which to presume? How shall I lead You into my house, I who have so often offended in Your most kindly sight? Angels and archangels revere You, the holy and the just fear You, and You say: "Come to Me: all of you!" If You, Lord, had not said it, who would have believed it to be true? And if You had not commanded, who would dare approach?[4]

Behold, Noah, a just man, worked a hundred years building the ark that he and a few others might be saved; how, then, can I prepare myself in one hour to receive with reverence the Maker of the world?

Moses, Your great servant and special friend, made an ark of incorruptible wood which he covered with purest gold wherein to place the tables of Your law; shall I, a creature of corruption, dare so easily to receive You, the Maker of law and the Giver of life?

Solomon, the wisest of the kings of Israel, spent seven years building a magnificent temple in praise of Your name, and celebrated its dedication with a feast of eight days. He offered a thousand victims in Your honor and solemnly bore the Ark of the Covenant with trumpeting and jubilation to the place prepared for it; and I, unhappy and poorest of men, how shall I lead You into my house, I who scarcely can spend a half-hour devoutly—would that I could spend even that as I ought![5]

O my God, how hard these men tried to please You! Alas, how little is all that I do! How short the time I spend in preparing for Communion! I am seldom wholly recollected, and very seldom, indeed, entirely free from distraction. Yet surely in the presence of Your life-giving Godhead no unbecoming thought should arise and no creature possess my heart, for I am about to receive as my guest, not an angel, but the very Lord of angels.[6]

Very great, too, is the difference between the Ark of the Covenant with its treasures and Your most pure Body with its ineffable virtues, between these sacrifices of the law which were but figures of things to come and the true offering of Your Body which was the fulfillment of all ancient sacrifices.

Why, then, do I not long more ardently for Your adorable presence? Why do I not prepare myself with greater care to receive Your sacred gifts, since those holy patriarchs and prophets of old, as well as kings and princes with all their people, have shown such affectionate devotion for the worship of God?

The most devout King David danced before the ark of God with all his strength as he recalled the benefits once bestowed upon his fathers. He made musical instruments of many kinds. He composed psalms and ordered them sung with joy. He himself often played upon the harp when moved by the grace of the Holy Ghost. He taught the people of Israel to praise God with all their hearts and to raise their voices every day to bless and glorify Him. If such great devotion flourished in those days and such ceremony in praise of God before the Ark of the Covenant, what great devotion ought not I and all Christian people now show in the presence of this Sacrament; what reverence in receiving the most excellent Body of Christ![7]

Many people travel far to honor the relics of the saints, marveling at their wonderful deeds and at the building of magnificent shrines.[8] They gaze upon and kiss the sacred rel-

5. A'Kempis makes the point that we are even more privileged than Noah, Moses, and Solomon who were themselves privileged in that they were received by God (and their worship was received).

6. A'Kempis sees that communion is with the Lord Himself, and he regrets that he does not prepare himself very well for this blessed time.

7. A'Kempis points out David's passion for God at the mere presence of the Ark of the Covenant. This fact stirs his own heart at the Lord's table in love for Jesus.

8. Thomas A'Kempis refers to a practice common in the Middle Ages where many would make pilgrimages to see the ancient relics from the lives of the past saints. His passing comment seems to refer to this as futile and inconsequential compared to the privilege of coming to the Lord's Table.

9. A'Kempis does not specify what sort of present is involved. The reference to altar is a veiled reference to a sacrifice, which the Scripture does not confirm (except that Christ was crucified on a cross).

10. Faith, hope, and love are the right means by which we approach the Lord's Table.

11. The elect are those who receive Christ.

12. A'Kempis sees the Lord's Table as a means of grace.

13. A'Kempis rightly points out that it is by Christ's merits that we are saved, not our own merits.

ics encased in silk and gold; and behold, You are here present before me on the altar,[9] my God, Saint of saints, Creator of men, and Lord of angels!

Often in looking at such things, men are moved by curiosity, by the novelty of the unseen, and they bear away little fruit for the amendment of their lives, especially when they go from place to place lightly and without true contrition. But here in the Sacrament of the altar You are wholly present, my God, the man Christ Jesus, whence is obtained the full realization of eternal salvation, as often as You are worthily and devoutly received. To this, indeed, we are not drawn by levity, or curiosity, or sensuality, but by firm faith, devout hope, and sincere love.[10]

O God, hidden Creator of the world, how wonderfully You deal with us! How sweetly and graciously You dispose of things with Your elect to whom You offer Yourself to be received in this Sacrament![11] This, indeed, surpasses all understanding. This in a special manner attracts the hearts of the devout and inflames their love. Your truly faithful servants, who give their whole life to amendment, often receive in Holy Communion the great grace of devotion and love of virtue.

Oh, the wonderful and hidden grace of this Sacrament which only the faithful of Christ understand, which unbelievers and slaves of sin cannot experience! In it spiritual grace is conferred, lost virtue restored, and the beauty, marred by sin, repaired. At times, indeed, its grace is so great that, from the fullness of the devotion, not only the mind but also the frail body feels filled with greater strength.[12]

Nevertheless, our neglect and coldness is much to be deplored and pitied, when we are not moved to receive with greater fervor Christ in Whom is the hope and merit of all who will be saved.[13] He is our sanctification and redemption. He is our consolation in this life and the eternal joy of the blessed in heaven. This being true, it is lamentable that many pay so little heed to the salutary Mystery which fills the heavens with joy and maintains the whole universe in being.

Oh, the blindness and the hardness of the heart of man that does not show more regard for so wonderful a gift, but rather falls into carelessness from its daily use! If this most holy Sacrament were celebrated in only one place and consecrated by only one priest in the whole world, with what great desire, do you think, would men be attracted to that place, to that priest of God, in order to witness the celebration of the divine Mysteries! But now there are many priests and Mass is offered in many places,[14] that God's grace and love for men may appear the more clearly as the Sacred Communion is spread more widely through the world.

Thanks be to You, Jesus, everlasting Good Shepherd, Who have seen fit to feed us poor exiled people with Your precious Body and Blood,[15] and to invite us with words from Your own lips to partake of these sacred Mysteries: "Come to Me, all you who labor and are burdened, and I will refresh you."

14. Mass is a reference to the Lord's Supper, a word that comes from the Latin and was in use since the 6th century.

15. Protestants have differed on how or whether the body and blood of Christ are actually received at the table. The Reformed Westminster Larger Catechism teaches that believers "feed upon the body and blood of Christ, not after a corporal and carnal, but in a spiritual manner."

2. God's Great Goodness and Love is Shown to Man in This Sacrament

The Disciple

Trusting in Your goodness and great mercy, O Lord, I come as one sick to the Healer, as one hungry and thirsty to the Fountain of life, as one in need to the King of heaven, a servant to his Lord, a creature to his Creator, a soul in desolation to my gentle Comforter.

But whence is this to me, that You should come to me? Who am I that You should offer Yourself to me? How dares the sinner to appear in Your presence, and You, how do You condescend to come to the sinner? You know Your servant, and You know that he has nothing good in him that You should grant him this.

I confess, therefore, my unworthiness. I acknowledge Your goodness. I praise Your mercy, and give thanks for Your immense love. For it is because of Yourself that You do it, not for any merit of mine; so that Your goodness may be better known to me, that greater love may be aroused and more perfect humility born in me. Since, then, this pleases You and You have so willed it, Your graciousness pleases me also. Oh, that my sinfulness may not stand in the way!

O most sweet and merciful Jesus, what great reverence, thanks, and never-ending praise are due to You for our taking of Your sacred body,[1] whose dignity no man can express!

1. Communion is a partaking of the body of Christ, in the language of 1 Corinthians 10:16-17.

But on what shall I think in this Communion, this approach to my Lord, Whom I can never reverence as I ought, and yet Whom I desire devoutly to receive? What thought better, more helpful to me than to humble myself entirely in Your presence and exalt Your infinite goodness above myself?

2. A praise to God for His stooping to regard us, unworthy sinners.

I praise You, my God, and extol You forever![2] I despise myself and cast myself before You in the depths of my unworthiness. Behold, You are the Holy of holies, and I the scum of sinners! Behold, You bow down to me who am not worthy to look up to You! Behold, You come to me! You will to be with me! You invite me to Your banquet! You desire to give me heavenly food, the Bread of Angels to eat, none other than Yourself, the living Bread Who are come down from heaven and give life to the world.

Behold, whence love proceeds! What condescension shines forth! What great thanks and praise are due You for these gifts! Oh, how salutary and profitable was Your design in this institution! How sweet and pleasant the banquet when You gave Yourself as food!

How admirable is Your work, O Lord! How great Your power! How infallible Your truth! For You spoke and all things were made, and this, which You commanded, was done. It is a wonderful thing, worthy of faith, overpowering human understanding, that You, O Lord, my God, true God and man, are contained whole and entire under the appearance of a little bread and wine,[3] and without being consumed are eaten by him who receives You!

You, the Lord of the universe, Who have need of nothing, have willed to dwell in us by means of Your Sacrament. Keep my heart and body clean, so that with a joyous and spotless conscience I may be able often to celebrate Your Mysteries[4] and to receive for my eternal salvation what You have ordained and instituted for Your special honor and as an everlasting memorial.[5]

Rejoice, my soul, and give thanks to God for having left you so noble a gift and so special a consolation in this valley of tears. As often as you renew this Mystery and receive the Body of Christ, so often do you enact the work of redemption and become a sharer in all the merits of Christ, for the love of Christ never grows less and the wealth of His mercy is never exhausted.

Therefore, you should prepare yourself for it by constantly renewing your heart and pondering deeply the great mystery of salvation. As often as you celebrate or hear Mass,[6] it should seem as great, as new, as sweet to you as if on that very day Christ became man in the womb of the Virgin, or, hanging on the Cross, suffered and died for the salvation of man.

3. A'Kempis humbly realizes the incomprehensibility of this very deep subject. He does not equate the body to the bread here.

4. The English word "sacrament" is a translation of the Latin word "sacramentum." The Latin term "sacramentum" is traditionally applied to the ordinances of baptism and the Lord's Supper. Reference 1 Corinthians 4:1.

5. Thomas A'Kempis rightly points out that the Lord's Supper is an opportunity to remember the death of our Lord Jesus for the sins of His people. Reference Luke 22:19.

6. Mass is a term used by Lutherans, Anglicans, Methodists, and Catholics to refer to the liturgy, the Scriptures read, and the distribution of the elements in Communion.

3. It Is Profitable to Receive Communion Often

The Disciple

Behold, I come to You, Lord, that I may prosper by Your gift and be delighted at Your holy banquet which You, O God, in Your sweetness have prepared for Your poor. Behold, all that I can or ought to desire is in You. You are my salvation and my redemption, my hope and strength, my honor and glory.

Gladden, then, this day the soul of Your servant because I have raised my heart to You, O Lord Jesus. I long to receive You now, devoutly and reverently. I desire to bring You into my house that, with Zacheus, I may merit Your blessing[1] and be numbered among the children of Abraham.

My soul longs for Your Body; my heart desires to be united with You. Give me Yourself—it is enough; for without You there is no consolation. Without You I cannot exist, without Your visitation I cannot live.[2] I must often come to You, therefore, and receive the strength of my salvation lest, deprived of this heavenly food, I grow weak on the way.[3] Once, most merciful Jesus, while preaching to the people and healing their many ills, You said: "I will not send them away fasting, lest they faint in the way."[4] Deal with me likewise, You Who have left Yourself in this Sacrament for the consolation of the faithful. You are sweet refreshment to the soul, and he who eats You worthily will be a sharer in, and an heir to, eternal glory.

It is indeed necessary for me, who fall and sin so often, who so quickly become lax and weak, to renew, cleanse, and inflame myself through frequent prayer, confession, and the holy reception of Your Body, lest perhaps by abstaining too long, I fall away from my holy purpose. For from the days of his youth the senses of man are prone to evil, and unless divine aid strengthens him, he quickly falls deeper. But Holy Communion removes him from evil and confirms him in good.

If I am so often careless and lax when I celebrate or communicate, what would happen if I did not receive this remedy

1. The language of "merit" was common during A'Kempis' day, something unwise because it implies that man earns God's blessings. However, we come as unworthy sinners. Elsewhere, Thomas A'Kempis makes clear that we are unworthy to partake of Christ's saving benefits.

2. A'Kempis' language reflects the teaching of our Lord in John 15. "I am the vine, you are the branches. He who abides in Me, and I in him, bears much fruit; for without Me you can do nothing." (John 15:5)

3. Communion is a means by which we are strengthened in the Christian life.

4. Matthew 15:32

and seek so great a help? Although I am neither fit nor properly disposed to celebrate every day, yet I will do my best at proper times to receive the divine Mysteries and share in this great grace. This, indeed, is the one chief consolation of the faithful soul when separated from You by mortality, that often mindful of her God, she receives her Beloved with devout recollection.

Oh, wonderful condescension of Your affection toward us, that You, the Lord God, Creator and Giver of life to all, should see fit to come to a poor soul and to appease her hunger with all Your divinity and humanity! O happy mind and blessed soul which deserves to receive You, her Lord God, and in receiving You, is filled with spiritual joy! How great a Master she entertains, what a beloved guest she receives, how sweet a companion she welcomes, how true a friend she gains, how beautiful and noble is the spouse she embraces, beloved and desired above all things that can be loved and desired![5] Let heaven and earth and all their treasures stand silent before Your face, most sweetly Beloved, for whatever glory and beauty they have is of Your condescending bounty, and they cannot approach the beauty of Your name, Whose wisdom is untold.

5. A'Kempis emphasizes the individual communion with Christ. In truth, it is the church, the Bride of Christ, who communes together in the body and blood of Christ.

4. Many Blessings Are Given Those Who Receive Communion Worthily

The Disciple

O Lord my God, favor Your servant with the blessings of Your sweetness that I may merit to approach Your magnificent Sacrament worthily and devoutly. Lift up my heart to You and take away from me this heavy indolence. Visit me with Your saving grace that I may in spirit taste Your sweetness which lies hidden in this Sacrament like water in the depths of a spring. Enlighten my eyes to behold this great Mystery, and give me strength to believe in it with firm faith.

For it is Your work, not the power of man, Your sacred institution, not his invention. No man is able of himself to comprehend and understand these things which surpass even the keen vision of angels. How, then, shall I, an unworthy sinner who am but dust and ashes, be able to fathom and understand so great a mystery?

O Lord, I come to You at Your command in simplicity of heart, in good, firm faith, with hope and reverence, and I truly believe that You are present here in this Sacrament, God and man. It is Your will that I receive You and unite myself to You in love. Wherefore, I beg Your mercy and ask that special grace be given me, that I may be wholly dissolved in You and filled with Your love, no longer to concern myself with exterior consolations. For this, the highest and most worthy Sacrament, is the health of soul and body, the cure of every spiritual weakness. In it my defects are remedied, my passions restrained, and temptations overcome or allayed. In it greater grace is infused, growing virtue is nourished, faith confirmed, hope strengthened, and charity fanned into flame.[1]

You, my God, the protector of my soul, the strength of human weakness, and the giver of every interior consolation, have given and still do often give in this Sacrament great gifts to Your loved ones who communicate devoutly. Moreover, You give them many consolations amid their numerous troubles and lift them from the depths of dejection to the hope of Your protection. With new graces You cheer and lighten them within, so that they who are full of anxiety and without affection before Communion may find themselves changed for the better after partaking of this heavenly food and drink.

Likewise, You so deal with Your elect that they may truly acknowledge and plainly experience how weak they are in themselves and what goodness and grace they obtain from You. For though in themselves they are cold, obdurate,[2] and wanting in devotion, through You they become fervent, cheerful, and devout.

1. Thomas A'Kempis lists here the many benefits of partaking of communion. We learn here that A'Kempis does not believe the sacrament is merely a remembrance of Jesus Christ's death. It is also a means of spiritual nourishment and growth in grace.

2. Obdurate means stubborn or resistant to change.

Who, indeed, can humbly approach the fountain of sweetness and not carry away a little of it? Or who, standing before a blazing fire does not feel some of its heat? You are a fountain always filled with superabundance! You are a fire, ever burning, that never fails!

Therefore, while I may not exhaust the fullness of the fountain or drink to satiety,[3] yet will I put my lips to the mouth of this heavenly stream that from it I may receive at least some small drop to refresh my thirst and not wither away. And if I cannot as yet be all heavenly or as full of fire as the cherubim and seraphim, yet I will try to become more devout and prepare my heart so that I may gather some small spark of divine fire from the humble reception of this life-giving Sacrament.

Whatever is wanting in me, good Jesus, Savior most holy, do You in Your kindness and grace supply for me, You Who have been pleased to call all unto You, saying: "Come to Me all you that labor and are burdened and I will refresh you."[4]

I, indeed, labor in the sweat of my brow. I am torn with sorrow of heart. I am laden with sin, troubled with temptations, enmeshed and oppressed by many evil passions, and there is none to help me, none to deliver and save me but You, my Lord God and Savior, to Whom I entrust myself and all I have, that You may protect me and lead me to eternal life. For the honor and glory of Your name receive me, You Who have prepared Your Body and Blood as food and drink for me. Grant, O Lord, my God and Savior, that by approaching Your Mysteries frequently, the zeal of my devotion may increase.[5]

3. Satiety means the state of being fully satisfied.

4. Matthew 11:28

5. The end result A'Kempis looks for is the increase in the zeal of his devotion as he takes communion.

1. Nobody can say that he has merited or has earned the right to Communion to receive the life of Christ through His sacrifice.

2. Various church denominations hold that those ordained to the pastoral ministry of the church are the ones responsible for the administration of the sacraments (1 Cor. 4:1). The idea of priesthood was confined to the pastors within the Catholic Church, whereas 1 Peter 2:5-9 reminds us that all believers are priests to God.

3. Those who come to the Lord's Supper must believe that they commune with their Lord by faith (1 Cor. 10:16-17). As we partake and spiritually commune with our Lord, we can only receive Him by faith. If we come to the Lord's Supper without faith, the sacrament is of no benefit to us (1 Cor. 10:1-5).

4. A single bishop would ordain a pastor or priest during the late Middle Ages. The Scriptures teach an ordination by multiple bishops or elders: "Do not neglect the gift that is in you, which was given to you by prophecy with the laying on of the hands of the eldership." (1 Tim. 4:14)

5. The Dignity of the Sacrament and of the Priesthood

The Voice of Christ

Had you the purity of an angel and the sanctity of St. John the Baptist, you would not be worthy to receive or administer this Sacrament. It is not because of any human meriting that a man consecrates and administers the Sacrament of Christ, and receives the Bread of Angels for his food.[1] Great is the Mystery and great the dignity of priests to whom is given that which has not been granted the angels. For priests alone, rightly ordained in the Church, have power to celebrate Mass and consecrate the Body of Christ.[2]

The priest, indeed, is the minister of God, using the word of God according to His command and appointment. God, moreover, is there—the chief Author and invisible Worker to Whom all is subject as He wills, to Whom all are obedient as He commands.

In this most excellent Sacrament, therefore, you ought to believe in God rather than in your own senses or in any visible sign, and thus, with fear and reverence draw near to such a work as this.[3] Look to yourself and see whose ministry has been given you through the imposition of the bishop's hands.[4]

Behold, you have been made a priest, consecrated to celebrate Mass! See to it now that you offer sacrifice to God faithfully and devoutly at proper times,[5] and that you conduct yourself blamelessly. You have not made your burden lighter. Instead, you are now bound by stricter discipline and held to more perfect sanctity.[6]

A priest ought to be adorned with all virtues and show the example of a good life to others.[7] His way lies not among the vulgar and common habits of men but with the angels in heaven and the perfect men on earth. A priest clad in the sacred vestments acts in Christ's place, that he may pray to God both for himself and for all people in a suppliant and humble manner. He has before and behind him the sign of the Lord's cross that he may always remember the Passion of Christ.[8] It is before him, on the chasuble,[9] that he may look closely upon the footsteps of Christ and try to follow them fervently. It is behind him—he is signed with it—that he may gladly suffer for God any adversities inflicted by others.

He wears the cross before him that he may mourn his own sins, behind him, that in pity he may mourn the sins of others, and know that he is appointed to stand between God and the sinner, never to become weary of prayer and the holy offering until it is granted him to obtain grace and mercy.

When the priest celebrates Mass, he honors God, gladdens the angels, strengthens the Church, helps the living, brings rest to the departed, and wins for himself a share in all good things.

5. We do offer spiritual sacrifices of praise and thanksgiving. The Lord's Supper is not a bloody, physical sacrifice. It is a commemoration of the sacrifice once and for all offered for us on the cross.

6. Those who are ordained to the ministry of the gospel are held to a higher standard as teachers. According to the Apostle Paul, those who are ordained as elders/overseers in the church must be of an exemplary character (1 Tim. 3, Tit. 1). James writes, "My brethren, let not many of you become teachers, knowing that we shall receive a stricter judgment." (Jas. 3:1)

7. 1 Peter 5:2-3

8. A'Kempis is referring to the symbols inscribed on the vestments (clothing) of the priests. At this time, it appears that the priests wore clothing that would contain the symbol of the cross on both the front and back of the vestments.

9. Chasuble was a sleeveless outer vestment that goes around the head.

6. An Inquiry on the Proper Thing to Do Before Communion

The Disciple

When I consider Your dignity, O Lord, and my own meanness, I become very much frightened and confused. For if I do not receive, I fly from Life, and if I intrude unworthily, I incur Your displeasure. What, then, shall I do, my God, my Helper and Adviser in necessity? Teach me the right way. Place before me some short exercise suitable for Holy Communion, for it is good to know in what manner I ought to make my heart ready devoutly and fervently for You, to receive Your Sacrament for the good of my soul, or even to celebrate so great and divine a sacrifice.[1]

1. Here is a prayer to help the disciple in his preparations for this holy and awe-inspired time at the communion table.

7. The Examination of Conscience and the Resolution to Amend

The Voice of Christ

Above all, God's priest should approach the celebration and reception of this Sacrament with the deepest humility of heart and suppliant reverence, with complete faith and the pious intention of giving honor to God.

Carefully examine your conscience, then.[1] Cleanse and purify it to the best of your power by true contrition and humble confession, that you may have no burden, know of no remorse, and thus be free to come near.[2] Let the memory of all your sins grieve you, and especially lament and bewail your daily transgressions. Then if time permits, confess to God in the secret depths of your heart all the miseries your passions have caused.

Lament and grieve because you are still so worldly, so carnal, so passionate and unmortified, so full of roving lust, so careless in guarding the external senses, so often occupied in many vain fancies, so inclined to exterior things and so heed-

1. These are the recommended instructions for the preparation for the table. Reference 1 Corinthians 11:27-29.

2. Self-examination of the conscience should lead to a humble confession of sin to God.

less of what lies within, so prone to laughter and dissipation and so indisposed to sorrow and tears, so inclined to ease and the pleasures of the flesh and so cool to austerity and zeal, so curious to hear what is new and to see the beautiful and so slow to embrace humiliation and dejection, so covetous of abundance, so niggardly[3] in giving and so tenacious in keeping, so inconsiderate in speech, so reluctant in silence, so undisciplined in character, so disordered in action, so greedy at meals, so deaf to the Word of God, so prompt to rest and so slow to labor, so awake to empty conversation, so sleepy in keeping sacred vigils and so eager to end them, so wandering in your attention, so careless in saying the office, so lukewarm in celebrating, so heartless in receiving, so quickly distracted, so seldom fully recollected, so quickly moved to anger, so apt to take offense at others, so prone to judge, so severe in condemning, so happy in prosperity and so weak in adversity, so often making good resolutions and carrying so few of them into action.[4]

When you have confessed and deplored these and other faults with sorrow and great displeasure because of your weakness, be firmly determined to amend your life day by day and to advance in goodness.[5] Then, with complete resignation and with your entire will offer yourself upon the altar of your heart as an everlasting sacrifice to the honor of My name, by entrusting with faith both body and soul to My care, that thus you may be considered worthy to draw near and offer sacrifice to God and profitably receive the Sacrament of My Body. For there is no more worthy offering, no greater satisfaction for washing away sin than to offer yourself purely and entirely to God with the offering of the Body of Christ in Mass and Communion.[6]

If a man does what he can and is truly penitent, however often he comes to Me for grace and pardon, "As I live, saith the Lord God, I desire not the death of the wicked, but that the wicked turn from his way and live";[7] I will no longer remember his sins, but all will be forgiven him.

3. An old-fashioned word for miserly.

4. The paragraph contains a long list of our sinful tendencies that afflict all of us. These are the sins that so distress us, and call for confession to God.

5. After confessing the sin, there should be some resolution of heart and mind to forsake this sin.

6. A'Kempis' statement reflects an unbiblical perspective of the Lord's Supper. Christ's sacrifice on the cross was a sufficient atonement for sin. There is no need to add the sacrifice of ourselves or a re-sacrifice of Christ at the Communion table. Reference Romans 3:24-26.

7. Ezekiel 33:11

8. The Offering of Christ on the Cross; Our Offering

The Voice of Christ

As I offered Myself willingly to God the Father for your sins with hands outstretched and body naked on the cross, so that nothing remained in Me that had not become a complete sacrifice to appease the divine wrath, so ought you to be willing to offer yourself to Me day by day in the Mass as a pure and holy oblation, together with all your faculties and affections, with as much inward devotion as you can.

What more do I ask than that you give yourself entirely to Me? I care not for anything else you may give Me, for I seek not your gift but you. Just as it would not be enough for you to have everything if you did not have Me, so whatever you give cannot please Me if you do not give yourself.

Offer yourself to Me, therefore, and give yourself entirely for God—your offering will be accepted.[1] Behold, I offered Myself wholly to the Father for you, I even gave My whole Body and Blood for food that I might be all yours, and you Mine forever.

But if you rely upon self, and do not offer your free will to Mine, your offering will be incomplete and the union between us imperfect. Hence, if you desire to attain grace and freedom of heart, let the free offering of yourself into the hands of God precede your every action. This is why so few are inwardly free and enlightened—they know not how to renounce themselves entirely.

My word stands: "Everyone of you that doth not renounce all that he possesseth, cannot be My disciple."

If, therefore, you wish to be My disciple, offer yourself to Me with all your heart.[2]

1. We are called to offer ourselves as a "living sacrifice" to God in Romans 12:1. This sacrifice is not limited to the communion service. It is every day.

2. The "voice of Christ" here is based upon the words of our Lord when he calls us to total obedience to Him. "So likewise, whoever of you does not forsake all that he has cannot be My disciple." (Luke 14:33)

9. We Should Offer Ourselves and All That We Have to God, Praying for All

The Disciple

All things in heaven and on earth, O Lord, are Yours. I long to give myself to You as a voluntary offering to remain forever Yours. With a sincere heart I offer myself this day to You, O Lord, to Your eternal service, to Your homage, and as a sacrifice of everlasting praise.[1] Receive me with this holy offering of Your precious Body which also I make to You this day, in the presence of angels invisibly attending, for my salvation and that of all Your people.

O Lord, upon Your altar of expiation, I offer You all the sins and offenses I have committed in Your presence and in the presence of Your holy angels, from the day when I first could sin until this hour, that You may burn and consume them all in the fire of Your love, that You may wipe away their every stain, cleanse my conscience of every fault, and restore to me Your grace which I lost in sin[2] by granting full pardon for all and receiving me mercifully with the kiss of peace.

What can I do for all my sins but humbly confess and lament them, and implore Your mercy without ceasing? In Your mercy, I implore You, hear me when I stand before You, my God. All my sins are most displeasing to me. I wish never to commit them again. I am sorry for them and will be sorry as long as I live. I am ready to do penance and make satisfaction[3] to the utmost of my power.

Forgive me, O God, forgive me my sins for Your Holy Name. Save my soul which You have redeemed by Your most precious Blood. See, I place myself at Your mercy. I commit myself to Your hands. Deal with me according to Your goodness, not according to my malicious and evil ways.

I offer to You also all the good I have, small and imperfect though it be, that You may make it more pure and more holy, that You may be pleased with it, render it acceptable to Yourself, and perfect it more and more, and finally that You

---

1. This is the sacrifice we are to offer to God — a sacrifice of worship, a sacrifice of our whole life, every day. The expiation (wiping away of sins) and propitiation (shielding from the wrath of God) occurred by that sacrifice, not at the communion table.

2. Man lost a right relationship with God and the gracious fellowship of God when he fell into sin. Only Christ's sacrifice could provide full pardon and the "kiss of peace" reconciliation between God and man.

3. Doing penance took on an unbiblical connotation in the Middle Ages. While the Scriptures call for repentance and fruits worthy of repentance, this in no way merits salvation or a right standing with God. Clearly, it was the death of Christ that brought about the satisfaction of God. "[The LORD] shall see the labor of His soul, and be satisfied. By His knowledge My righteous Servant shall justify many, For he shall bear their iniquities." (Isaiah 53:11)

4. The disciple offers prayers for his friends and family members. However, the Bible does not commend prayer for those who have already died.

5. A'Kempis seems confused here in that we cannot offer a sacrifice of propitiation. That is what Christ did on the cross. It seems that he is praying for those who sin against him, asking that their sins would be forgiven (and Christ's propitiation would be theirs.)

may lead me, an indolent and worthless creature, to a good and happy end.

I offer You also all the holy desires of Your devoted servants, the needs of my parents, friends, brothers, sisters, and all who are dear to me;[4] of all who for Your sake have been kind to me or to others; of all who have wished and asked my prayers and Masses for them and theirs, whether they yet live in the flesh or are now departed from this world, that they may all experience the help of Your grace, the strength of Your consolation, protection from dangers, deliverance from punishment to come, and that, free from all evils, they may gladly give abundant thanks to You.

I offer You also these prayers and the Sacrifice of Propitiation[5] for those especially who have in any way injured, saddened, or slandered me, inflicted loss or pain upon me, and also for all those whom I have at any time saddened, disturbed, offended, and abused by word or deed, willfully or in ignorance. May it please You to forgive us all alike our sins and offenses against one another.

Take away from our hearts, O Lord, all suspicion, anger, wrath, contention, and whatever may injure charity and lessen brotherly love. Have mercy, O Lord, have mercy on those who ask Your mercy, give grace to those who need it, and make us such that we may be worthy to enjoy Your favor and gain eternal life.

10. Do Not Lightly Forego Holy Communion

The Voice of Christ

You must often return to the source of grace and divine mercy, to the fountain of goodness and perfect purity, if you wish to be free from passion and vice, if you desire to be made stronger and more watchful against all the temptations and deceits of the devil.

The enemy, knowing the great good and the healing power of Holy Communion, tries as much as he can by every manner and means to hinder and keep away the faithful and the devout. Indeed, there are some who suffer the worst assaults of Satan when disposing themselves to prepare for Holy Communion. As it is written in Job, this wicked spirit comes among the sons of God to trouble them by his wonted malice, to make them unduly fearful and perplexed, that thus he may lessen their devotion or attack their faith to such an extent that they perhaps either forego Communion altogether or receive with little fervor.[1]

No attention, however, must be paid to his cunning wiles, no matter how base and horrible—all his suggestions must be cast back upon his head. The wretch is to be despised and scorned. Holy Communion must not be passed by because of any assaults from him or because of the commotion he may arouse.

Oftentimes, also, too great solicitude for devotion and anxiety about confession hinder a person. Do as wise men do. Cast off anxiety and scruple, for it impedes the grace of God and destroys devotion of the mind.

Do not remain away from Holy Communion because of a small trouble or vexation but go at once to confession and willingly forgive all others their offenses.[2] If you have offended anyone, humbly seek pardon and God will readily forgive you.

What good is it to delay confession for a long time or to put off Holy Communion? Cleanse yourself at once, spit out the poison quickly. Make haste to apply the remedy and you

1. Satan is especially active when Christians gather for worship and the communion service. A reference is made to the book of Job and Satan's troubling of the sons of God (Job 1:6).

2. The Lord's Supper must not be taken by brothers and sisters who are holding something against each other. Reference Matthew 5:23-24.

will find it better than if you had waited a long time. If you put it off today because of one thing, perhaps tomorrow a greater will occur to you, and thus you will stay away from Communion for a long time and become even more unfit.

Shake off this heaviness and sloth as quickly as you can, for there is no gain in much anxiety, in enduring long hours of trouble, and in depriving yourself of the divine Mysteries because of these daily disturbances. Yes, it is very hurtful to defer Holy Communion long, for it usually brings on a lazy spiritual sleep.

How sad that some dissolute and lax persons are willing to postpone confession and likewise wish to defer Holy Communion, lest they be forced to keep a stricter watch over themselves! Alas, how little love and devotion have they who so easily put off Holy Communion!

How happy and acceptable to God is he who so lives, and keeps his conscience so pure, as to be ready and well disposed to communicate, even every day if he were permitted, and if he could do so unnoticed.

If, now and then, a man abstains by the grace of humility or for a legitimate reason, his reverence is commendable, but if laziness takes hold of him, he must arouse himself and do everything in his power, for the Lord will quicken his desire because of the good intention to which He particularly looks. When he is indeed unable to come, he will always have the good will and pious intention to communicate and thus he will not lose the fruit of the Sacrament.

3. A'Kempis is careful to maintain the mysterious nature of feeding on the body and blood of the Lord Jesus Christ. Scripture does not inform as to how it is done, merely that this is the partaking of His body and blood (1 Cor. 10:16-17).

Any devout person may at any hour on any day receive Christ in spiritual communion profitably and without hindrance. Yet on certain days and times appointed he ought to receive with affectionate reverence the Body of his Redeemer in this Sacrament, seeking the praise and honor of God rather than his own consolation.

For as often as he devoutly calls to mind the mystery and passion of the Incarnate Christ, and is inflamed with love for Him, he communicates mystically[3] and is invisibly refreshed.

He who prepares himself only when festivals approach or custom demands, will often find himself unprepared. Blessed is he who offers himself a sacrifice to the Lord as often as he celebrates or communicates.

Be neither too slow nor too fast in celebrating but follow the good custom common to those among whom you are. You ought not to cause others inconvenience or trouble, but observe the accepted rule as laid down by superiors, and look to the benefit of others rather than to your own devotion or inclination.[4]

4. "Therefore, my brethren, when you come together to eat, wait for one another. But if anyone is hungry, let him eat at home, lest you come together for judgment. And the rest I will set in order when I come." (1 Cor. 11:33-34)

11. The Body of Christ and Sacred Scripture Are Most Necessary to a Faithful Soul

The Disciple

O most sweet Lord Jesus, how great is the happiness of the devout soul that feasts upon You at Your banquet, where there is set before her to be eaten no other food but Yourself alone, her only Lover, most desired of all that her heart can desire!

To me it would be happiness, indeed, to shed tears in Your presence from the innermost depths of love, and like the pious Magdalen to wash Your feet with them.[1] But where now is this devotion, this copious shedding of holy tears? Certainly in Your sight, before Your holy angels, my whole heart ought to be inflamed and weep for joy.[2] For, hidden though You are beneath another form, I have You truly present in the Sacrament.

1. A'Kempis refers to the story of Mary Magdalene washing the feet of Jesus with her tears (John 12:1-3).

My eyes could not bear to behold You in Your own divine brightness, nor could the whole world stand in the splendor of the glory of Your majesty. In veiling Yourself in the Sacrament, therefore, You have regard for my weakness.

In truth, I possess and adore Him Whom the angels adore in heaven—I as yet by faith, they face to face unveiled. I must be content with the light of the true faith and walk in it until the day of eternal brightness dawns and the shadow of figures passes away. When, moreover, that which is perfect shall have

2. Given that Christ shares His very life with us, our response really should be tears of deep love and sheer joy. This represents the heart of Communion.

3. 1 Corinthians 13:9-10

come,[3] the need of sacraments shall cease, for the blessed in heavenly glory need no healing sacrament. Rejoicing endlessly in the presence of God, beholding His glory face to face, transformed from their own brightness to the brightness of the ineffable Deity, they taste the Word of God made flesh, as He was in the beginning and will remain in eternity.

Though mindful of these wonderful things, every spiritual solace becomes wearisome to me because so long as I do not plainly see the Lord in His glory, I consider everything I hear and see on earth of little account.

You are my witness, O God, that nothing can comfort me, no creature give me rest but You, my God, Whom I desire to contemplate forever. But this is not possible while I remain in mortal life, and, therefore, I must be very patient and submit myself to You in every desire.

Even Your saints, O Lord, who now rejoice with You in the kingdom of heaven, awaited the coming of Your glory with faith and great patience while they lived. What they believed, I believe. What they hoped for, I hope for, and whither they arrived, I trust I shall come by Your grace. Meanwhile I will walk in faith, strengthened by the example of the saints. I shall have, besides, for comfort and for the guidance of my life, the holy Books, and above all these, Your most holy Body for my special haven and refuge.[4]

4. The essential life preserving elements of the Christian life is the Bible (the holy Books) and Communion.

I feel there are especially necessary for me in this life two things without which its miseries would be unbearable. Confined here in this prison of the body I confess I need these two, food and light. Therefore, You have given me in my weakness Your sacred Flesh to refresh my soul and body, and You have set Your word as the guiding light for my feet. Without them I could not live aright, for the word of God is the light of my soul and Your Sacrament is the Bread of Life.

These also may be called the two tables, one here, one there, in the treasure house of holy Church. One is the table of the holy altar, having the holy Bread that is the precious Body of Christ. The other is the table of divine law, containing holy doctrine that teaches all the true faith and firmly leads them within the veil, the Holy of holies.

Thanks to You, Lord Jesus, Light of eternal light, for the table of Your holy teaching which You have prepared for us by Your servants, the prophets and Apostles and other learned men.

Thanks to You, Creator and Redeemer of men, Who, to declare Your love to all the world, have prepared a great supper in which You have placed before us as food not the lamb, the type of Yourself, but Your own most precious Body and Blood, making all the faithful glad in Your sacred banquet, intoxicating them with the chalice[5] of salvation in which are all the delights of paradise; and the holy angels feast with us but with more happiness and sweetness.

Oh, how great and honorable is the office of the priest, to whom is given the consecration of the Lord of majesty in sacred words, whose lips bless Him, whose hands hold Him,[6] whose tongue receives Him, and whose ministry it is to bring Him to others!

Oh, how clean those hands should be, how pure the lips, how sanctified the body, how immaculate the heart[7] of the priest to whom the Author of all purity so often comes. No word but what is holy, none but what is good and profitable ought to come from the lips of the priest who so often receives the Sacrament of Christ. Single and modest should be the eyes accustomed to looking upon the Body of Christ. Pure and lifted up to heaven the hands accustomed to handle the Creator of heaven and earth. To priests above all it is written in the law: "Be ye holy, for I, the Lord your God, am holy."[8]

Let Your grace, almighty God, assist us, that we who have undertaken the office of the priesthood may serve You worthily and devoutly in all purity and with a good conscience. And if we cannot live as innocently as we ought, grant us at least to lament duly the wrongs we have committed and in the spirit of humility and the purpose of a good will to serve You more fervently in the future.

5. A chalice is a large cup or goblet traditionally used in the sacrament of the Lord's Supper.

6. These words indicate that A'Kempis had received the doctrine of transubstantiation, the idea that the bread had turned into the body of Christ (the true human nature of Christ).

7. While we should desire complete holiness and complete conformity to the likeness of Christ (Eph. 4:13), we cannot expect perfect sinlessness until we are glorified in eternity (1 John 1:8).

8. 1 Peter 1:15-16

1. Pasch is another word for the "Passover" feast where our Lord instituted the Lord's Supper. This refers to Jesus's instruction to His disciples to prepare for the Passover meal the night before He was crucified.

2. The preparation for this Communion must take place in the room of your heart. Reference 1 Corinthians 5:7.

12. The Communicant Should Prepare Himself for Christ with Great Care

The Voice of Christ

I am the Lover of purity, the Giver of all holiness. I seek a pure heart and there is the place of My rest.

Prepare for Me a large room furnished and I with My disciples will keep the Pasch[1] with you.

If you wish that I come to you and remain with you, purge out the old leaven and make clean the dwelling of your heart.[2] Shut out the whole world with all the din of its vices. Sit as the sparrow lonely on the housetop, and think on your transgressions in bitterness of soul.

Everyone who loves prepares the best and most beautiful home for his beloved, because the love of the one receiving his lover is recognized thereby.

But understand that you cannot by any merit of your own make this preparation well enough, though you spend a year in doing it and think of nothing else. It is only by My goodness and grace that you are allowed to approach My table, as though a beggar were invited to dinner by a rich man and he had nothing to offer in return for the gift but to humble himself and give thanks.

Do what you can and do that carefully. Receive the Body of the Lord, your beloved God Who deigns to come to you, not out of habit or necessity, but with fear, with reverence, and with love.[3]

I am He that called you. I ordered it done. I will supply what you lack. Come and receive Me.

When I grant the grace of devotion, give thanks to God, not because you are worthy but because I have had mercy upon you. If you have it not and feel rather dry instead, continue in prayer, sigh and knock, and do not give up until you receive some crumb of saving grace.

You have need of Me. I do not need you. You do not come to sanctify Me but I come to sanctify you and make you better.

3. The right heart demeanor is one of fear, reverence, and love for Jesus balanced out in the believer.

You come to be sanctified and united with Me, to receive new grace and to be aroused anew to amend. Do not neglect this grace, but prepare your heart with all care, and bring into it your Beloved.

Not only should you prepare devoutly before Communion, but you should also carefully keep yourself in devotion after receiving the Sacrament.[4] The careful custody of yourself afterward is no less necessary than the devout preparation before, for a careful afterwatch is the best preparation for obtaining greater grace. If a person lets his mind wander to external comforts, he becomes quite indisposed.

Beware of much talking. Remain in seclusion and enjoy your God, for you have Him Whom all the world cannot take from you.

I am He to Whom you should give yourself entirely, that from now on you may live, not in yourself, but in Me, with all cares cast away.

4. The believer taking Communion should take heed to his devotional after the fact as well. Reference 1 Corinthians 10:7-11.

13. With All Her Heart the Devout Soul Should Desire Union with Christ in the Sacrament

The Disciple

Let it be granted me to find You alone, O Christ, to open to You my whole heart, to enjoy You as my soul desires, to be disturbed by no one, to be moved and troubled by no creature, that You may speak to me and I to You alone, as a lover speaks to his loved one, and friend converses with friend.

I pray for this, I desire this, that I may be completely united to You and may withdraw my heart from all created things, learning to relish the celestial[1] and the eternal through Holy Communion and the frequent celebration of Mass.

1. "Heavenly" bread come down from heaven. Reference John 6:51.

Ah Lord God, when shall I be completely united to You and absorbed by You, with self utterly forgotten? You in me and I in You? Grant that we may remain so together. You in truth are my Beloved, chosen from thousands, in Whom my soul is happy to dwell all the days of her life. You are in truth my pledge of peace, in Whom is the greatest peace and true rest, without Whom there is toil and sorrow and infinite misery.

You truly are the hidden God. Your counsel is not with the wicked, and Your conversation is rather with the humble and the simple.

O how kind is Your spirit, Lord, Who in order to show Your sweetness toward Your children, deign to feed them with the sweetest of bread, bread come down from heaven! Surely there is no other people so fortunate as to have their god near them, as You, our God, are present everywhere to the faithful, to whom You give Yourself to be eaten and enjoyed for their daily solace and the raising of their hearts to heaven.

Indeed, what other nation is so renowned as the Christian peoples? What creature under heaven is so favored as the devout soul to whom God comes, to feed her with His glorious Flesh? O unspeakable grace! O wonderful condescension! O love beyond measure, singularly bestowed upon man![2]

What return shall I make to the Lord for this love, this grace so boundless? There is nothing I can give more pleasing than to offer my heart completely to my God, uniting it closely with His. Then shall all my inner self be glad when my soul is perfectly united with God. Then will He say to me: "If you will be with Me, I will be with you." And I will answer Him: "Deign, O Lord, to remain with me. I will gladly be with You. This is my one desire, that my heart may be united with You."

2. The high privilege of receiving the life of God by the body and blood of the Son of God is beyond all comprehension! Angels do not receive this. Expressions of love, wonder, and praise must accompany the Table.

14. The Ardent Longing of Devout Men for the Body of Christ

The Disciple

How great is the abundance of Your kindness, O Lord, which You have hidden from those who fear You!

When I think how some devout persons come to Your Sacrament with the greatest devotion and love, I am frequently ashamed and confused that I approach Your altar and the table of Holy Communion so coldly and indifferently; that I remain so dry and devoid of heartfelt affection; that I am not completely inflamed in Your presence, O my God, nor so strongly drawn and attracted as many devout persons who, in their great desire for Communion and intense heart love, could not restrain their tears but longed from the depths of their souls and bodies to embrace You, the Fountain of Life. These were able to appease and allay their hunger in no other way than by receiving Your Body with all joy and spiritual eagerness. The faith of these men was true and ardent—convincing proof of Your sacred presence. They whose hearts burn so ardently within them when Jesus lives with them truly know their Lord in the breaking of bread.[1]

Such affection and devotion, such mighty love and zeal are often far beyond me. Be merciful to me, O sweet, good, kind Jesus, and grant me, Your poor suppliant, sometimes at least to feel in Holy Communion a little of the tenderness of Your love, that my faith may grow stronger, that my hope in Your goodness may increase, and that charity, once perfectly kindled within me by tasting heavenly manna, may never fail.[2]

Your mercy can give me the grace I long for and can visit me most graciously with fervor of soul according to Your good pleasure. For although I am not now inflamed with as great a desire as those who are singularly devoted to You, yet by Your grace I long for this same great flame, praying and seeking a place among all such ardent lovers that I may be numbered among their holy company.

1. Men and women have really testified that their spiritual hunger was satisfied by Christ in Communion with Him (at the Table, in prayer, and in His Word.)

2. These prayers get to very essential things — we need stronger faith, a true understanding of the love of Christ, and a fiery zeal.

15. The Grace of Devotion is Acquired Through Humility and Self-Denial

The Voice of Christ

You must seek earnestly the grace of devotion, ask for it fervently, await it patiently and hopefully, receive it gratefully, guard it humbly, cooperate with it carefully and leave to God, when it comes, the length and manner of the heavenly visitation.

When you feel little or no inward devotion, you should especially humiliate yourself, but do not become too dejected or unreasonably sad. In one short moment God often gives what He has long denied. At times He grants at the end what He has denied from the beginning of prayer. If grace were always given at once, or were present at our beck and call, it would not be well taken by weak humankind. Therefore, with good hope and humble patience await the grace of devotion.[1]

When it is not given, or for some unknown reason is taken away, blame yourself and your sins. Sometimes it is a small matter that hinders grace and hides it, if, indeed, that which prevents so great a good may be called little rather than great. But if you remove this hindrance, be it great or small, and if you conquer it perfectly, you shall have what you ask. As soon as you have given yourself to God with all your heart and seek neither this nor that for your own pleasure and purpose, but place yourself completely in His charge, you shall find yourself at peace, united with Him, because nothing will be so sweet, nothing will please you so much as the good pleasure of His will.

Anyone, therefore, who shall with simplicity of heart direct his intention to God and free himself from all inordinate love or dislike for any creature will be most fit to receive grace and will be worthy of the gift of devotion.[2] For where the Lord finds the vessel empty He pours down His blessing.

So also the more perfectly a man renounces things of this world, and the more completely he dies to himself through

1. When our hearts are cold to God's worship and to the love of Christ visibly demonstrated in the Lord's Supper, we should pray that the Lord would revive our hearts with love, with joy, and with awe. We find similar petitions to what Thomas A'Kempis describes here in the Psalms. "Revive me according to Your lovingkindness, so that I may keep the testimony of Your mouth." (Ps. 119:88) "Consider how I love Your precepts; revive me, O Lord, according to Your lovingkindness." (Ps. 119:159)

2. Inordinate focus on man, dependence on man, and bitterness or malice towards man can get in the way of our worship and Communion.

contempt of self, the more quickly this great grace comes to him,[3] the more plentifully it enters in, and the higher it uplifts the free heart.

Then shall he see and abound, then shall his heart marvel and be enlarged within him, because the Hand of the Lord is with him and in the hollow of that Hand he has placed himself forever. Thus shall the man be blessed who seeks God with all his heart and has not regarded his soul in vain. Such a one, receiving the Holy Eucharist, merits the grace of divine union because he looks not on his own thoughts, nor to his own comfort, but above all devotion and consolation to the glory and honor of God.

3. "Likewise you younger people, submit yourselves to your elders. Yes, all of you be submissive to one another, and be clothed with humility, for 'God resists the proud, but gives grace to the humble.'" (1 Pet. 5:5)

16. We Should Show Our Needs to Christ and Ask His Grace

The Disciple

O most kind, most loving Lord, Whom I now desire to receive with devotion, You know the weakness and the necessity which I suffer, in what great evils and vices I am involved, how often I am depressed, tempted, defiled, and troubled.

To You I come for help, to You I pray for comfort and relief. I speak to Him Who knows all things, to Whom my whole inner life is manifest, and Who alone can perfectly comfort and help me.

You know what good things I am most in need of and how poor I am in virtue. Behold I stand before You, poor and naked, asking Your grace and imploring Your mercy.

Feed Your hungry beggar.[1] Inflame my coldness with the fire of Your love. Enlighten my blindness with the brightness of Your presence. Turn all earthly things to bitterness for me, all grievance and adversity to patience, all lowly creation to contempt and oblivion. Raise my heart to You in heaven and suffer me not to wander on earth. From this moment to all eternity do You alone grow sweet to me, for You alone are

1. It should never to be forgotten that we are the beggars who have received mercy and continue to receive God's mercy.

my food and drink, my love and my joy, my sweetness and my total good.

Let Your presence wholly inflame me, consume and transform me into Yourself, that I may become one spirit with You by the grace of inward union and by the melting power of Your ardent love.

Suffer me not to go from You fasting and thirsty, but deal with me mercifully as You have so often and so wonderfully dealt with Your saints.

What wonder if I were completely inflamed by You to die to myself, since You are the fire ever burning and never dying, a love purifying the heart and enlightening the understanding.

17. The Burning Love and Strong Desire to Receive Christ

The Disciple

With greatest devotion and ardent love, with all affection and fervor of heart I wish to receive You, O Lord, as many saints and devout persons, most pleasing to You in their holiness of life and most fervent in devotion, desired You in Holy Communion.

O my God, everlasting love, my final good, my happiness unending, I long to receive You with as strong a desire and as worthy a reverence as any of the saints ever had or could have felt, and though I am not worthy to have all these sentiments of devotion, still I offer You the full affection of my heart as if I alone had all those most pleasing and ardent desires.

Yet, whatever a God-fearing mind can conceive and desire, I offer in its entirety to You with the greatest reverence and inward affection. I wish to keep nothing for self but to offer to You, willingly and most freely, myself and all that is mine.

O Lord God, my Creator and my Redeemer, I long to receive You this day with such reverence, praise, and honor, with such gratitude, worthiness and love, with such faith, hope, and purity as that with which Your most holy Mother, the glorious

Virgin Mary,[1] longed for and received You when she humbly and devoutly answered the angel who announced to her the mystery of the Incarnation: "Behold the handmaid of the Lord; be it done to me according to thy word."[2]

Likewise as Your blessed precursor, the most excellent of saints, John the Baptist, gladdened by Your presence, exulted in the Holy Ghost while yet enclosed in the womb of his mother, and afterward seeing Jesus walking among men, humbled himself and with devout love declared: "The friend of the bridegroom, who standeth and heareth him, rejoiceth with joy because of the bridegroom's voice,"[3] even so I long to be inflamed with great and holy desires and to give myself to You with all my heart.

Therefore I offer and present to You the gladness of all devout hearts, their ardent affection, their mental raptures, their supernatural illuminations and heavenly visions together with all the virtues and praises which have been or shall be celebrated by all creatures in heaven and on earth, for myself and all commended to my prayers, that You may be worthily praised and glorified forever.

Accept, O Lord my God, my promises and desires of giving You infinite praise and boundless benediction, which in the vastness of Your ineffable greatness are justly due You. This I render and desire to render every day and every moment of time, and in my loving prayers I invite and entreat all celestial spirits and all the faithful to join me in giving You praise and thanks.

Let all people, races, and tongues praise You and with the greatest joy and most ardent devotion magnify Your sweet and holy name.[4] And let all who reverently and devoutly celebrate this most great Sacrament and receive it in the fullness of faith, find kindness and mercy in You and humbly pray for me, a sinner. And when they have received the longed-for devotion and blissful union, and, well consoled and wonderfully refreshed, have retired from Your holy, Your celestial table, may they deign to remember my poor soul.

1. Mary is extended as an example of affection and love for Jesus. However, this language concerning Mary, the mother of Jesus, stems from common devotional perspectives during the Middle Ages that exalted Mary inordinately. Terms such as "holy" and "glorious" are reserved for the Father, the Son, and the Holy Spirit.

2. Luke 1:38

3. John the Baptist's joyous reception of the Christ is another example for us.
Reference John 3:29.

4. A'Kempis calls on all nations and peoples as well as angels to praise the Lord Jesus.

18. Man Should Not Scrutinize This Sacrament in Curiosity, But Humbly Imitate Christ and Submit Reason to Holy Faith

The Voice of Christ

Beware of curious and vain examination of this most profound Sacrament, if you do not wish to be plunged into the depths of doubt. He who scrutinizes its majesty too closely will be overwhelmed by its glory.[1]

God can do more than man can understand. A pious and humble search for truth He will allow, a search that is ever ready to learn and that seeks to walk in the reasonable doctrine of the fathers.

Blest is the simplicity that leaves the difficult way of dispute and goes forward on the level, firm path of God's commandments. Many have lost devotion because they wished to search into things beyond them.

Faith is required of you, and a sincere life, not a lofty intellect nor a delving into the mysteries of God. If you neither know nor understand things beneath you, how can you comprehend what is above you? Submit yourself to God and humble reason to faith, and the light of understanding will be given you so far as it is good and necessary for you. Some are gravely tempted concerning faith and the Sacrament but this disturbance is not laid to them but to the enemy.

Be not disturbed, dispute not in your mind, answer not the doubts sent by the devil, but believe the words of God, believe His saints and prophets and the evil enemy will flee from you. It is often very profitable for the servant of God to suffer such things. For Satan does not tempt unbelievers and sinners whom he already holds securely, but in many ways he does tempt and trouble the faithful servant.

Go forward, then, with sincere and unflinching faith, and with humble reverence approach this Sacrament. Whatever you cannot understand commit to the security of the all-powerful God, Who does not deceive you. The man, however,

1. Appropriately, A'Kempis ends with a warning concerning the profundity of this Sacrament. It is a great mystery (1 Cor. 10:16-17). Humility is most essential when discussing this doctrine. Where there is a lack of humility, there have been many schisms on the sacraments in the Christian church.

who trusts in himself is deceived. God walks with sincere men, reveals Himself to humble men, enlightens the understanding of pure minds, and hides His grace from the curious and the proud.

Human reason is weak and can be deceived. True faith, however, cannot be deceived. All reason and natural science ought to come after faith, not go before it, nor oppose it. For in this most holy and supremely excellent Sacrament, faith and love take precedence and work in a hidden manner.[2]

God, eternal, incomprehensible, and infinitely powerful, does great and inscrutable things in heaven and on earth, and there is no searching into His marvelous works. If all the works of God were such that human reason could easily grasp them, they would not be called wonderful or beyond the power of words to tell.[3]

2. Though we may not understand it, above all, we are to approach the Table in true faith. Trust in God, be humble, and He will bless you in the Communion.

3. We should approach the Lord's Supper with simple trust in God's promises. Whatever we cannot understand, we can safely leave in the hands of our loving Heavenly Father. "Lord, my heart is not haughty, nor my eyes lofty. Neither do I concern myself with great matters, nor with things too profound for me." (Ps. 131:1)

THE INSTITUTES
OF THE CHRISTIAN
RELIGION

John Calvin
AD 1559

Explanatory Notes by
Kevin Swanson and Joshua Schwisow

Introduction to *The Institutes of the Christian Religion*

John Calvin (1509-1564) was a great theologian and Church leader of the Reformation, whose influence still towers over all of Protestantism. In an age of both good and evil revolutions, Calvin was an organizer of theology and an organizer of the Church. He fought against Roman Catholicism on the one hand and against unbridled sectarianism on the other. He was not an innovator in theology, nor did he have a magnetic personality to draw followers to himself. Rather, he had a vision for a society that sought to be obedient to the rule of Christ in all things. It was this which attracted many people to him from all over Europe, and this made him a lightning rod for criticism.

Calvin was born in 1509 in Noyon, France, about sixty miles from Paris. His influential father wished for him to become a priest early on and then later pressed him to study law. Calvin, by all accounts, was a good student and was very religious. He studied grammar and rhetoric in Paris beginning in 1523. From 1528-1533, he studied first for the priesthood and then law at various universities in France. After his father's death, he studied humanities and theology, and it was during this time that he was recognized by his teachers as a fellow "doctor."

In 1523, he publicly rejected Roman Catholicism when he allied himself with the cause of the Reformers. For him, this was not a conversion to faith in Christ; he was devout before and afterwards. Rather, it was a conviction that the Roman Catholic Church had corrupted the most essential features of the Church, and therefore, he was justified to leave it for the true Church.

In 1536, the council of Geneva, Switzerland, with consent from the whole population, elected Calvin pastor and teacher to their town. Geneva had been on the brink of anarchy, and soon after Calvin's arrival, there was conflict. Calvin and his allies sought to institute Church discipline in Geneva, including mandatory subscription to a common confession, as well as giving the Church the ability to excommunicate the unrepentant. Because of this, many people feared that Calvin was just a new Protestant version of the pope. They were not yet willing to submit to this discipline, and so in 1538, they expelled him from the city along with his friends William Farel and Antoine Froment.

Calvin went to Strassburg where he had a productive time of writing and a fruitful ministry as pastor and professor. His most famous writing is the *Institutes of the Christian Religion*, which was written from 1536-1559 primarily in Latin. His series of commentaries on the Bible are also widely used to this day. It was during his time in Strassburg that he grew close to the fellow reformer Martin Bucer. It was also here that he married a widow named Idelette de Bure. Their only child died in infancy, and Idelette died less than ten years after marrying Calvin. But clearly Calvin appreciated her help in his ministry and said she had a great spirit.

By 1541, the political tide had turned in Geneva, and they sought to bring Calvin back. He felt duty bound to return, but he did so on the condition that this time, they would accept his plan of discipline. They did. For the next twenty-some years, until his death in 1564, he was the dominant figure in Geneva—not by office, but in influence. He still faced opposition and not everything went the way he thought it should, but it is nonetheless accurate to call the city at that time "Calvin's Geneva."

Calvin's theology was not just a matter for the intellect, it was a full-orbed vision for Christian society in submission to Christ. Alister McGrath, in the preface to *A Life of John Calvin*, writes, "To engage with Calvin and his legacy is thus to wrestle with one of the rare moments in modern history when Christianity moulded, rather than accommodated itself to, society... To speak of Calvin is to speak of Geneva[1]."

The question of whether or not Geneva was a theocracy has been much debated. Calvin was not a civil ruler; he was a pastor, teacher, and Church ruler. The Church was viewed as the moral adviser of the state, and the state was viewed as supporting the Church by keeping order in society. The ultimate degree of discipline by the Church was excommunication, and for the state, it was capital punishment. So while the Church and the state each had different governments, Christ's rule was acknowledged over both and the ultimate law for both was the Word of God.

It must be agreed that Calvin's legacy is huge no matter where one stands on the controversies surrounding his name. Today, "Calvinism" is often summarized in five points having to do with the issue of predestination, points that were first assembled at the Synod of Dort, half a century after Calvin's death. These points don't summarize all of Calvinism, which can briefly be described as a view of the entire world under the sovereignty of God. In addition to the issue of predestination, Calvin has been criticized for exercising the discipline he did in Geneva. Theodore Beza (1519-1605), Calvin's friend and successor in Geneva, acknowledged the criticism aimed at Calvin when he wrote, "I have been a witness of Calvin's life for sixteen years, and I think I am fully entitled to say that in this man there was exhibited to all a most beautiful example

1. Alister McGrath, *A Life of John Calvin: A Study in the Shaping of Western Culture* (Malden: Wiley-Blackwell, 1990), xii.

of the life and death of the Christian, which it will be as easy to calumniate as it will be difficult to emulate."

Geneva was a refuge for Protestants who fled from persecution, and it was an educational center where people came to study before returning to their homelands. This helped increase Calvin's influence throughout Europe; so much, in fact, that he was claimed as the father of French Huguenots, Dutch Burghers, English Puritans, Scottish Covenanters, and New England Pilgrims, all of whom strongly influenced the founders of America. Scottish Church leader and the Principle of the University of St. Andrews John Tulloch (1823-1886) wrote: "It was the Spirit bred by Calvin's discipline which, spreading into France and Holland and Scotland, maintained by its single strength the cause of a free Protestantism in all these lands. It was the same spirit which inspired the early and lived on in the later Puritans; which animated such men as Milton and Owen and Baxter; which armed the Parliament of England with strength against Charles I, and stirred the great soul of Cromwell in its proudest triumphs; and which, while it thus fed every source of political liberty in the Old World, burned undimmed in the gallant crew of the 'Mayflower'—the Pilgrim Fathers—who first planted the seeds of civilization in the great continent of the West." So the man known largely for his discipline has a legacy of instilling a love for true freedom. This should be expected... "For my yoke is easy and my burden is light." (Matt. 11:30)

John Calvin's *Institutes of the Christian Religion*, first published in 1536, represented a surprising shift from the theological literature of his day. In this work, he avoided the highly academic, stale, wooden dialectic so common among the late medieval scholastics in their attempts to explain Christian doctrine. Calvin's writing harks back to Augustine in style. His work is more devotional, with more biblical referencing and more testifying to a personal faith commitment to the doctrines of Scripture.

This classic work ranks among the top three most influential books in all of Christian history. In it Calvin presents a very strong biblical epistemology (a theory of knowledge). He also offers a biblical metaphysic (theory of reality) and a biblical ethic based on God's revelation. He presents the three uses of biblical law. He addresses the roles of the civil magistrate and the church. He affirms Augustine's view of God's absolute sovereignty and presents a clearer understanding of the distinct-but-not-separate relationship between faith and works in salvation. This distinction between justification and sanctification would become the major contribution of the Protestant Reformation.

In the *Institutes*, Calvin goes to great lengths to demonstrate the biblical basis of the doctrines of the Reformation. He points out that these ideas are not new but are instead solidly rooted in the church fathers. The reformers were not interested in creating a new sect or cult, although there were plenty of attempts to do just that around this time in Western history. These men wanted to recover the basic historical faith which had been concealed under layers of church traditions and falsehoods through the centuries. In a letter addressed to the king, Calvin argues: "So far are we from despising [the church fathers], that if this were the proper place, it would give us no trouble to support the greater part of the doctrines which we now hold by their suffrages."[2] Calvin often quotes the church fathers in the *Institutes* to buttress the orthodox Christian doctrines he defends.

2. https://www.ccel.org/ccel/calvin/institutes.ii.viii.html

The *Institutes* were written in part for Francis, king of France as an explanation and an apologetic for the Protestant Reformation occurring in France and elsewhere throughout Europe. All Christian leaders (and especially those attempting reform in the church) are subjected to misinterpretations, strawmen caricatures, and malicious slander. The 16th century reformers were no exception to this rule. King Francis was exposed to countless lies swirling through Paris regarding the Protestant reformers. Within his *Institutes*, Calvin hoped to set the heart of the king at rest concerning the true nature of the Reformation. He addressed his prefatory remarks to the king, stating:

> You yourself can bear witness, most noble King, with what lying slanders our teachings are daily accused unto you: as that they tend to no other end but to wrest from kings their scepters out of their hands, to throw down all judges' seats and judgments, to subvert all orders and civil governments, to trouble the peace and quiet of the people, to abolish all laws, to undo all proprieties and possessions; finally to turn all things upside down. And yet you hear but the smallest portion, for they spread among the people horrible things, which if they were true, the whole world might worthily judge our cause, with the maintainers thereof, worthy of a thousand fires and gallows.[3]

To this day, John Calvin and his fellow-reformers are castigated and slandered. Their doctrinal positions are misrepresented and calumniated. However, the more honest and charitable student would do well to pick up and read the reformer's writings for himself and consider these things, whether they be true, and true to Scripture.

3. Ibid.

Book 1
Chapter 1

The Knowledge of God and of Ourselves Mutually Connected. Nature of the Connection.

Our wisdom, in so far as it ought to be deemed true and solid Wisdom, consists almost entirely of two parts: the knowledge of God and of ourselves.[1] But as these are connected together by many ties, it is not easy to determine which of the two precedes and gives birth to the other. For, in the first place, no man can survey himself without forthwith turning his thoughts towards the God in whom he lives and moves; because it is perfectly obvious, that the endowments which we possess cannot possibly be from ourselves; nay, that our very being is nothing else than subsistence in God alone.[2] In the second place, those blessings which unceasingly distil to us from heaven, are like streams conducting us to the fountain. Here, again, the infinitude of good which resides in God becomes more apparent from our poverty. In particular, the miserable ruin into which the revolt of the first man has plunged us, compels us to turn our eyes upwards; not only that while hungry and famishing we may thence ask what we want, but being aroused by fear may learn humility. For as there exists in man something like a world of misery, and ever since we were stripped of the divine attire

1. Wisdom involves knowledge of God and man.

2. Right knowledge of men and God are equally necessary because our own life derives from God alone.

3. A sense of our own depravity, or lack of goodness in man, would urge us to contemplate God, the ultimate good.

4. Unless the impure can compare itself to Purity, it can not realize its impurity. Thus, knowledge of God is essential for us.

our naked shame discloses an immense series of disgraceful properties every man, being stung by the consciousness of his own unhappiness, in this way necessarily obtains at least some knowledge of God. Thus, our feeling of ignorance, vanity, want, weakness, in short, depravity and corruption, reminds us, that in the Lord, and none but He, dwell the true light of wisdom, solid virtue, exuberant goodness. We are accordingly urged by our own evil things to consider the good things of God; and, indeed, we cannot aspire to Him in earnest until we have begun to be displeased with ourselves. For what man is not disposed to rest in himself?[3] Who, in fact, does not thus rest, as long as he is unknown to himself; that is, as long as he is contented with his own endowments, and unconscious or unmindful of his misery? Every person, therefore, on coming to the knowledge of himself, is not only urged to seek God, but is also led as by the hand to find him.

On the other hand, it is evident that man never attains to a true self-knowledge until he has previously contemplated the face of God, and come down after such contemplation to look into himself. For (such is our innate pride) we always seem to ourselves just, and upright, and wise, and holy, until we are convinced, by clear evidence, of our injustice, vileness, folly, and impurity.[4] Convinced, however, we are not, if we look to ourselves only, and not to the Lord also —He being the only standard by the application of which this conviction can be produced. For, since we are all naturally prone to hypocrisy, any empty semblance of righteousness is quite enough to satisfy us instead of righteousness itself. And since nothing appears within us or around us that is not tainted with very great impurity, so long as we keep our mind within the confines of human pollution, anything which is in some small degree less defiled delights us as if it were most pure just as an eye, to which nothing but black had been previously presented, deems an object of a whitish, or even of a brownish hue, to be perfectly white. Nay, the bodily sense may furnish a still stronger illustration of the extent to which we are deluded in estimating the powers of the mind. If, at mid-day, we either look down to the ground, or on the surrounding objects which lie open to our view, we think ourselves endued with a very strong and piercing eyesight; but when we look up to the sun, and gaze at it unveiled, the sight which did excellently well for the earth is instantly so dazzled and confounded by the refulgence, as to oblige us to confess that our acuteness in discerning terrestrial objects is mere dimness when applied to the sun. Thus too, it happens in estimating our spiritual qualities. So long as we do not look beyond the earth, we are quite pleased with our own righteousness, wisdom, and virtue; we address ourselves in the most flattering terms, and seem only less than demigods.[5] But should we once begin to raise our thoughts to God, and reflect what kind of Being he is, and how absolute the perfection of that righteousness, and wisdom, and virtue, to which, as a standard, we are bound to be conformed, what formerly delighted us by its false show of righteousness will become polluted with the greatest iniquity; what strangely imposed upon us under the name of wisdom will disgust by its extreme folly; and what presented the appearance of virtuous energy will be condemned as the most miserable impotence.[6] So far are those qualities in us, which seem most perfect, from corresponding to the divine purity.

5. A lesser god in the pagan pantheon.

6. A right view of God in His holiness will yield a right view of ourselves in sin.

Hence that dread and amazement with which as Scripture uniformly relates, holy men were struck and overwhelmed whenever they beheld the presence of God. When we see those who previously stood firm and secure so quaking with terror, that the fear of death takes hold of them, nay, they are, in a manner, swallowed up and annihilated, the inference to be drawn is that men are never duly touched and impressed with a conviction of their insignificance, until they have contrasted themselves with the majesty of God. Frequent examples of this consternation occur both in the Book of Judges and the Prophetical Writings; so much so, that it was a common expression among the people of God, "We shall die, for we have seen the Lord." Hence the Book of Job, also, in hum-

7. Examples of O.T. saints who saw their feebleness and sinfulness in the presence of a holy God.

8. Calvin concludes that a proper approach is to study for a knowledge of God first.

bling men under a conviction of their folly, feebleness, and pollution, always derives its chief argument from descriptions of the Divine wisdom, virtue, and purity. Nor without cause: for we see Abraham the readier to acknowledge himself but dust and ashes the nearer he approaches to behold the glory of the Lord, and Elijah unable to wait with unveiled face for His approach; so dreadful is the sight.[7] And what can man do, man who is but rottenness and a worm, when even the Cherubim themselves must veil their faces in very terror? To this, undoubtedly, the Prophet Isaiah refers, when he says (Isaiah 24:23), "The moon shall be confounded, and the sun ashamed, when the Lord of Hosts shall reign;" i.e., when he shall exhibit his refulgence, and give a nearer view of it, the brightest objects will, in comparison, be covered with darkness. But though the knowledge of God and the knowledge of ourselves are bound together by a mutual tie, due arrangement requires that we treat of the former in the first place, and then descend to the latter.[8]

Book 1

Chapter 2

What it is to Know God, Tendency of this Knowledge.

By the knowledge of God, I understand that by which we not only conceive that there is some God, but also apprehend what it is for our interest, and conducive to his glory, what, in short, it is befitting to know concerning him. For, properly speaking, we cannot say that God is known where there is no religion or piety. I am not now referring to that species of knowledge by which men, in themselves lost and under curse, apprehend God as a Redeemer in Christ the Mediator. I speak only of that simple and primitive knowledge, to which the mere course of nature would have conducted us, had Adam stood upright. For although no man will now, in the present ruin of the human race, perceive God to be either a father, or the author of salvation, or propitious in any respect, until Christ interpose to make our peace; still it is one thing to perceive that God our Maker supports us by his power, rules us by his providence, fosters us by his goodness, and visits us with all kinds of blessings, and another thing to embrace the grace of reconciliation offered to us in Christ.[1] Since, then, the Lord first appears, as well in the creation of the world as in the general doctrine of Scripture, simply as a

1. Calvin distinguishes between a knowledge of God as powerful Creator and a knowledge of God as Redeemer in Christ.

Creator, and afterwards as a Redeemer in Christ,—a twofold knowledge of him hence arises: of these the former is now to be considered, the latter will afterwards follow in its order. But although our mind cannot conceive of God, without rendering some worship to him, it will not, however, be sufficient simply to hold that he is the only being whom all ought to worship and adore, unless we are also persuaded that he is the fountain of all goodness, and that we must seek everything in him, and in none but him. My meaning is: we must be persuaded not only that as he once formed the world, so he sustains it by his boundless power, governs it by his wisdom, preserves it by his goodness, in particular, rules the human race with justice and Judgment, bears with them in mercy, shields them by his protection; but also that not a particle of light, or wisdom, or justice, or power, or rectitude, or genuine truth, will anywhere be found, which does not flow from him, and of which he is not the cause; in this way we must learn to expect and ask all things from him, and thankfully ascribe to him whatever we receive.[2] For this sense of the divine perfections is the proper master to teach us piety, out of which religion springs. By piety I mean that union of reverence and love to God which the knowledge of his benefits inspires. For, until men feel that they owe everything to God, that they are cherished by his paternal care, and that he is the author of all their blessings, so that nought is to be looked for away from him, they will never submit to him in voluntary obedience; nay, unless they place their entire happiness in him, they will never yield up their whole selves to him in truth and sincerity.

2. It is not sufficient to believe/worship one God – He must be rightly assessed as all-good, the source of all wisdom and justice, and vitally involved in His rule over all.

Those, therefore, who, in considering this question, propose to inquire what the essence of God is, only delude us with frigid speculations,—it being much more our interest to know what kind of being God is, and what things are agreeable to his nature. For, of what use is it to join Epicures[3] in acknowledging some God who has cast off the care of the world, and only delights himself in ease? What avails it, in short, to know a God with whom we have nothing to do? The effect of

3. Epicures (341-270 BC), a Greek philosopher, who believed in no afterlife, only the present material world, configured a god who did not care about the world.

our knowledge rather ought to be, first, to teach us reverence and fear; and, secondly, to induce us, under its guidance and teaching, to ask every good thing from him, and, when it is received, ascribe it to him.[4] For how can the idea of God enter your mind without instantly giving rise to the thought, that since you are his workmanship, you are bound, by the very law of creation, to submit to his authority?—that your life is due to him?—that whatever you do ought to have reference to him? If so, it undoubtedly follows that your life is sadly corrupted, if it is not framed in obedience to him, since his will ought to be the law of our lives. On the other hand, your idea of his nature is not clear unless you acknowledge him to be the origin and fountain of all goodness. Hence would arise both confidence in him, and a desire of cleaving to him, did not the depravity of the human mind lead it away from the proper course of investigation.

4. Knowledge of God should yield reverence, worship, prayer, and thanksgiving rendered to Him.

For, first of all, the pious mind does not devise for itself any kind of God, but looks alone to the one true God; nor does it feign for him any character it pleases, but is contented to have him in the character in which he manifests himself always guarding, with the utmost diligences against transgressing his will, and wandering, with daring presumptions from the right path.[5] He by whom God is thus known perceiving how he governs all things, confides in him as his guardian and protector, and casts himself entirely upon his faithfulness,—perceiving him to be the source of every blessing, if he is in any strait or feels any want, he instantly recurs to his protection and trusts to his aid,—persuaded that he is good and merciful, he reclines upon him with sure confidence, and doubts not that, in the divine clemency, a remedy will be provided for his every time of need,—acknowledging him as his Father and his Lord he considers himself bound to have respect to his authority in all things, to reverence his majesty aim at the advancement of his glory, and obey his commands,—regarding him as a just judge, armed with severity to punish crimes, he keeps the Judgment-seat always in his view.[6] Standing in awe of it, he

5. A truly godly person will not want to invent a false caricature of God or transgress God's will.

6. The godly man fears the final Judgment of almighty God.

7. The man of true piety embraces God's glory: both in salvation and also in acts of righetous judgment.

8. True piety includes loving God, fearing God, and trusting God.

curbs himself, and fears to provoke his anger. Nevertheless, he is not so terrified by an apprehension of Judgment as to wish he could withdraw himself, even if the means of escape lay before him; nay, he embraces him not less as the avenger of wickedness than as the rewarder of the righteous; because he perceives that it equally appertains to his glory to store up punishment for the one, and eternal life for the other.[7] Besides, it is not the mere fear of punishment that restrains him from sin. Loving and revering God as his father, honoring and obeying him as his master, although there was no hell, he would revolt at the very idea of offending him. Such is pure and genuine religion, namely, confidence in God coupled with serious fear—fear, which both includes in it willing reverence, and brings along with it such legitimate worship as is prescribed by the law.[8] And it ought to be more carefully considered that all men promiscuously do homage to God, but very few truly reverence him. On all hands there is abundance of ostentatious ceremonies, but sincerity of heart is rare.

Book 1

Chapter 3

The Knowledge of God Naturally Implanted in the Human Mind

That there exists in the human minds and indeed by natural instinct, some sense of Deity, we hold to be beyond dispute, since God himself, to prevent any man from pretending ignorance, has endued all men with some idea of his Godhead,[1] the memory of which he constantly renews and occasionally enlarges, that all to a man being aware that there is a God, and that he is their Maker, may be condemned by their own conscience when they neither worship him nor consecrate their lives to his service. Certainly, if there is any quarter where it may be supposed that God is unknown, the most likely for such an instance to exist is among the dullest tribes farthest removed from civilization. But, as a heathen tells us, there is no nation so barbarous, no race so brutish, as not to be imbued with the conviction that there is a God. Even those who, in other respects, seem to differ least from the lower animals, constantly retain some sense of religion; so thoroughly has this common conviction possessed the mind, so firmly is it stamped on the breasts of all men. Since, then, there never has been, from the very first, any quarter of the globe, any city, any household even, without religion, this

1. Reference Romans 1:19-20. All men know that there is a Creator God.

2. Pagan idolatry itself proves man has a sense of God's existence.

amounts to a tacit confession, that a sense of Deity is inscribed on every heart. Nay, even idolatry is ample evidence of this fact.[2] For we know how reluctant man is to lower himself, in order to set other creatures above him. Therefore, when he chooses to worship wood and stone rather than be thought to have no God, it is evident how very strong this impression of a Deity must be; since it is more difficult to obliterate it from the mind of man, than to break down the feelings of his nature,—these certainly being broken down, when, in opposition to his natural haughtiness, he spontaneously humbles himself before the meanest object as an act of reverence to God.

Chapter 4

The Knowledge of God Stifled or Corrupted, Ignorantly or Maliciously

But though experience testifies that a seed of religion is divinely sown in all, scarcely one in a hundred is found who cherishes it in his heart, and not one in whom it grows to maturity so far is it from yielding fruit in its season. Moreover, while some lose themselves in superstitious observances, and others, of set purpose, wickedly revolt from God, the result is that, in regard to the true knowledge of him, all are so degenerate, that in no part of the world can genuine godliness be found.[1] In saying that some fall away into superstition, I mean not to insinuate that their excessive absurdity frees them from guilt; for the blindness under which they labor is almost invariably accompanied with vain pride and stubbornness. Mingled vanity and pride appear in this, that when miserable men do seek after God, instead of ascending higher than themselves as they ought to do, they measure him by their own carnal stupidity, and, neglecting solid inquiry, fly off to indulge their curiosity in vain speculation. Hence, they do not conceive of him in the character in which he is manifested, but imagine him to be whatever their own rashness has devised. This abyss standing open, they cannot move one foot-

1. Although all men have a sense of God's existence, they revolt against Him. Calvin holds that all men are ungodly (by nature).

2. Man will worship a god they invent in their own hearts.

3. The natural man's deception is self-imposed and willful.

4. Among the fools of Psalm 14:1, Calvin includes deists (those who believe God is absent and disengaged in His world).

5. Primarily, fallen man wants to get rid of the idea of a divine judgment.

step without rushing headlong to destruction. With such an idea of God, nothing which they may attempt to offer in the way of worship or obedience can have any value in his sight, because it is not him they worship, but, instead of him, the dream and figment of their own heart.[2] This corrupt procedure is admirably described by Paul, when he says, that "thinking to be wise, they became fools" (Rom. 1:22). He had previously said that "they became vain in their imaginations," but lest any should suppose them blameless, he afterwards adds that they were deservedly blinded, because, not contented with sober inquiry, because, arrogating to themselves more than they have any title to do, they of their own accord court darkness, nay, bewitch themselves with perverse, empty show.[3] Hence it is that their folly, the result not only of vain curiosity, but of licentious desire and overweening confidence in the pursuit of forbidden knowledge, cannot be excused.

The expression of David (Psalm 14:1, 53:1), "The fool hath said in his heart, There is no God," is primarily applied to those who, as will shortly farther appear, stifle the light of nature, and intentionally stupefy themselves. We see many, after they have become hardened in a daring course of sin, madly banishing all remembrance of God, though spontaneously suggested to them from within, by natural sense. To show how detestable this madness is, the Psalmist introduces them as distinctly denying that there is a God, because although they do not disown his essence, they rob him of his justice and providence, and represent him as sitting idly in heaven.[4] Nothing being less accordant with the nature of God than to cast off the government of the world, leaving it to chance, and so to wink at the crimes of men that they may wanton with impunity in evil courses; it follows, that every man who indulges in security, after extinguishing all fear of divine Judgment, virtually denies that there is a God.[5] As a just punishment of the wicked, after they have closed their own eyes, God makes their hearts dull and heavy, and hence, seeing, they see not. David, indeed, is the best interpreter of his own meaning, when he says elsewhere, the wicked has "no fear of God before his eyes," (Psalm 36:1); and, again, "He has said in his heart, God has forgotten; he hides his face; he will never see it." Thus although they are forced to acknowledge that there is some God, they, however, rob him of his glory by denying his power. For, as Paul declares, "If we believe not, he abides faithful, he cannot deny himself," (2 Tim. 2:13); so those who feign to themselves a dead and dumb idol, are truly said to deny God. It is, moreover, to be observed, that though they struggle with their own convictions, and would fain not only banish God from their minds, but from heaven also, their stupefaction is never so complete as to secure them from being occasionally dragged before the divine tribunal. Still, as no fear restrains them from rushing violently in the face of God, so long as they are hurried on by that blind impulse, it cannot be denied that their prevailing state of mind in regard to him is brutish oblivion.

In this way, the vain pretext which many employ to clothe their superstition is overthrown. They deem it enough that they have some kind of zeal for religion, how preposterous soever it may be, not observing that true religion must be conformable to the will of God as its unerring standard; that he can never deny himself, and is no spectra or phantom, to be metamorphosed at each individual's caprice.[6] It is easy to see how superstition, with its false glosses, mocks God, while it tries to please him. Usually fastening merely on things on which he has declared he sets no value, it either contemptuously overlooks, or even undisguisedly rejects, the things which he expressly enjoins, or in which we are assured that he takes pleasure. Those, therefore, who set up a fictitious worship, merely worship and adore their own delirious fancies; indeed, they would never dare so to trifle with God, had they not previously fashioned him after their own childish conceits. Hence that vague and wandering opinion of Deity is declared by an apostle to be ignorance of God: "Howbeit, then, when ye knew not God, ye did service unto them which by nature

6. Man then invents a god that fits him and worships this god according to his own fancies.

7. Galatians 4:8

8. Lanctantius was a church father from the 4th century.

are no gods."[7] And he elsewhere declares, that the Ephesians were "without God" (Eph. 2:12) at the time when they wandered without any correct knowledge of him. It makes little difference, at least in this respect, whether you hold the existence of one God, or a plurality of gods, since, in both cases alike, by departing from the true God, you have nothing left but an execrable idol. It remains, therefore, to conclude with Lactantius:[8] "No religion is genuine that is not in accordance with truth."

To this fault they add a second—viz. that when they do think of God it is against their will; never approaching him without being dragged into his presence, and when there, instead of the voluntary fear flowing from reverence of the divine majesty, feeling only that forced and servile fear which divine Judgment extorts Judgment which, from the impossibility of escape, they are compelled to dread, but which, while they dread, they at the same time also hate. To impiety, and to it alone, the saying of Statius properly applies: "Fear first brought gods into the world." Those whose inclinations are at variance with the justice of God, knowing that his tribunal has been erected for the punishment of transgression, earnestly wish that that tribunal were overthrown. Under the influence of this feeling they are actually warring against God, justice being one of his essential attributes. Perceiving that they are always within reach of his power, that resistance and evasion are alike impossible, they fear and tremble. Accordingly, to avoid the appearance of condemning a majesty by which all are overawed, they have recourse to some species of religious observance, never ceasing meanwhile to defile themselves with every kind of vice, and add crime to crime, until they have broken the holy law of the Lord in every one of its requirements, and set his whole righteousness at nought; at all events, they are not so restrained by their semblance of fear as not to luxuriate and take pleasure in iniquity, choosing rather to indulge their carnal propensities than to curb them with the bridle of the Holy Spirit. But since this shadow of religion (it scarcely even deserves to be called a shadow) is false and vain, it is easy to infer how much this confused knowledge of God differs from that piety which is instilled into the breasts of believers, and from which alone true religion springs. And yet hypocrites would fain, by means of tortuous windings, make a show of being near to God at the very time they are fleeing from him. For while the whole life ought to be one perpetual course of obedience, they rebel without fear in almost all their actions,[9] and seek to appease him with a few paltry sacrific- es; while they ought to serve him with integrity of heart and holiness of life, they endeavor to procure his favor by means of frivolous devices and punctilios of no value. Nay, they take greater license in their groveling indulgences,[10] because they imagine that they can fulfill their duty to him by preposterous expiations; in short, while their confidence ought to have been fixed upon him, they put him aside, and rest in themselves or the creatures. At length they bewilder themselves in such a maze of error, that the darkness of ignorance obscures, and ultimately extinguishes, those sparks which were designed to show them the glory of God. Still, however, the conviction that there is some Deity continues to exist, like a plant which can never be completely eradicated, though so corrupt, that it is only capable of producing the worst of fruit. Nay, we have still stronger evidence of the proposition for which I now con- tend—viz. that a sense of Deity is naturally engraved on the human heart, in the fact, that the very reprobate are forced to acknowledge it. When at their ease, they can jest about God, and talk pertly and loquaciously in disparagement of his pow- er; but should despair, from any cause, overtake them, it will stimulate them to seek him, and dictate ejaculatory prayers, proving that they were not entirely ignorant of God, but had perversely suppressed feelings which ought to have been ear- lier manifested.

9. Hypocrites are known by their immoral lives and cheap religious rites.

10. Calvin refers to the Roman Catholic indul- gences as examples of the "paltry sacrifices."

Book 1
Chapter 5

The Knowledge of God Conspicuous in the Creation, and Continual Government of the World

1. God's glory is evident in His creation everywhere. Nobody can miss it.

Since the perfection of blessedness consists in the knowledge of God, he has been pleased, in order that none might be excluded from the means of obtaining felicity, not only to deposit in our minds that seed of religion of which we have already spoken, but so to manifest his perfections in the whole structure of the universe, and daily place himself in our view, that we cannot open our eyes without being compelled to behold him. His essence, indeed, is incomprehensible, utterly transcending all human thought; but on each of his works his glory is engraved in characters so bright, so distinct, and so illustrious, that none, however dull and illiterate, can plead ignorance as their excuse.[1] Hence, with perfect truth, the Psalmist exclaims, "He covers himself with light as with a garment," (Psalm 104:2); as if he had said, that God for the first time was arrayed in visible attire when, in the creation of the world, he displayed those glorious banners, on which, to whatever side we turn, we behold his perfections visibly portrayed. In the same place, the Psalmist aptly compares the expanded heavens to his royal tent, and says, "He lays the beams of his chambers in the waters, makes the clouds his chariot, and walks upon the wings of the wind," sending forth the winds and lightning as his swift messengers. And because the glory of his power and wisdom is more refulgent in the firmament, it is frequently designated as his palace. And, first, wherever you turn your eyes, there is no portion of the world, however minute, that does not exhibit at least some sparks of beauty; while it is impossible to contemplate the vast and beautiful fabric as it extends around, without being overwhelmed by the immense weight of glory. Hence, the author of the Epistle to the Hebrews elegantly describes the visible worlds as images of the invisible (Heb. 11:3), the elegant structure of the world serving us as a kind of mirror, in which we may behold God, though otherwise invisible. For the same reason, the Psalmist attributes language to celestial objects, a language which all nations understand (Psalm 19:1), the manifestation of the Godhead being too clear to escape the notice of any people, however obtuse. The apostle Paul, stating this still more clearly, says, "That which may be known of God is manifest in them, for God has showed it unto them. For the invisible things of him from the creation of the world are clearly seen, being understood by the things that are made, even his eternal power and Godhead," (Rom. 1:20).

Bright, however, as is the manifestation which God gives both of himself and his immortal kingdom in the mirror of his works, so great is our stupidity, so dull are we in regard to these bright manifestations, that we derive no benefit from them.[2] For in regard to the fabric and admirable arrangement of the universe, how few of us are there who, in lifting our eyes to the heavens, or looking abroad on the various regions of the earth, ever think of the Creator? Do we not rather overlook Him, and sluggishly content ourselves with a view of his works? And then in regard to supernatural events, though these are occurring every day, how few are there who ascribe them to the ruling providence of God—how many who imagine that they are casual results produced by the blind evolutions of the wheel of chance?[3] Even when under the guidance and direc-

2. Calvin uses "we" to indicate the natural dullness in all men (to the evidences of God's glory in creation).

3. Instead of recognizing a personal God behind the extraordinary glory of His created works, people attribute it to blind chance.

tion of these events, we are in a manner forced to the contemplation of God (a circumstance which all must occasionally experience), and are thus led to form some impressions of Deity, we immediately fly off to carnal dreams and depraved fictions, and so by our vanity corrupt heavenly truth. This far, indeed, we differ from each other, in that every one appropriates to himself some peculiar error; but we are all alike in this, that we substitute monstrous fictions for the one living and true God—a disease not confined to obtuse and vulgar minds, but affecting the noblest, and those who, in other respects, are singularly acute. How lavishly in this respect have the whole body of philosophers betrayed their stupidity and want of sense? To say nothing of the others whose absurdities are of a still grosser description, how completely does Plato, the soberest and most religious of them all, lose himself in his round globe?[4] What must be the case with the rest, when the leaders, who ought to have set them an example, commit such blunders, and labor under such hallucinations? In like manner, while the government of the world places the doctrine of providence beyond dispute, the practical result is the same as if it were believed that all things were carried hither and thither at the caprice of chance; so prone are we to vanity and error. I am still referring to the most distinguished of the philosophers, and not to the common herd, whose madness in profaning the truth of God exceeds all bounds.

4. Calvin holds some respect for the "soberest" of the Greek philosophers – Plato. But this "most distinguished" philosopher also attributed the world to a blind chance.

In vain for us, therefore, does Creation exhibit so many bright lamps lighted up to show forth the glory of its Author. Though they beam upon us from every quarter, they are altogether insufficient of themselves to lead us into the right path. Some sparks, undoubtedly, they do throw out; but these are quenched before they can give forth a brighter effulgence. Wherefore, the apostle, in the very place where he says that the worlds are images of invisible things, adds that it is by faith we understand that they were framed by the word of God (Heb. 11:3); thereby intimating that the invisible Godhead is indeed represented by such displays, but that we have no eyes to perceive it until they are enlightened through faith by internal revelation from God. When Paul says that that which may be known of God is manifested by the creation of the world, he does not mean such a manifestation as may be comprehended by the wit of man (Rom. 1:19); on the contrary, he shows that it has no further effect than to render us inexcusable (Acts 17:27). And though he says, elsewhere, that we have not far to seek for God, inasmuch as he dwells within us, he shows, in another passage, to what extent this nearness to God is availing. God, says he, "in times past, suffered all nations to walk in their own ways. Nevertheless, he left not himself without witness, in that he did good, and gave us rain from heaven, and fruitful seasons, filling our hearts with food and gladness," (Acts 14:16, 17).[5] But though God is not left without a witness, while, with numberless varied acts of kindness, he woos men to the knowledge of himself, yet they cease not to follow their own ways, in other words, deadly errors.

5. God gives adequate witness to His power and goodness everywhere, but the problem is that man is in rebellion and refuses to look at it.

But though we are deficient in natural powers which might enable us to rise to a pure and clear knowledge of God, still, as the dullness which prevents us is within, there is no room for excuse. We cannot plead ignorance, without being at the same time convicted by our own consciences both of sloth and ingratitude. It were, indeed, a strange defense for man to pretend that he has no ears to hear the truth, while dumb creatures have voices loud enough to declare it; to allege that he is unable to see that which creatures without eyes demonstrate, to excuse himself on the ground of weakness of mind, while all creatures without reason are able to teach.[6] Wherefore, when we wander and go astray, we are justly shut out from every species of excuse, because all things point to the right path. But while man must bear the guilt of corrupting the seed of divine knowledge so wondrously deposited in his mind, and preventing it from bearing good and genuine fruit, it is still most true that we are not sufficiently instructed by that bare and simple, but magnificent testimony which the creatures bear to the glory of their Creator. For no sooner do

6. The problem is not weakness of mind with man.

7. Man's own mind creates deception and deflects the due praise of God the Creator elsewhere.

we, from a survey of the world, obtain some slight knowledge of Deity, than we pass by the true God, and set up in his stead the dream and phantom of our own brain, drawing away the praise of justice, wisdom, and goodness, from the fountain-head, and transferring it to some other quarter.[7] Moreover, by the erroneous estimate we form, we either so obscure or pervert his daily works, as at once to rob them of their glory and the author of them of his just praise.

Book 1
Chapter 6

The Need of Scripture, as a Guide and Teacher, in Coming to God as a Creator.

Therefore, though the effulgence which is presented to every eye, both in the heavens and on the earth, leaves the ingratitude of man without excuse, since God, in order to bring the whole human race under the same condemnation, holds forth to all, without exception, a mirror of his Deity in his works, another and better help must be given to guide us properly to God as a Creator.[1] Not in vain, therefore, has he added the light of his Word in order that he might make himself known unto salvation, and bestowed the privilege on those whom he was pleased to bring into nearer and more familiar relation to himself.[2] For, seeing how the minds of men were carried to and fro, and found no certain resting-place, he chose the Jews for a peculiar people, and then hedged them in that they might not, like others, go astray. And not in vain does he, by the same means, retain us in his knowledge, since but for this, even those who, in comparison of others, seem to stand strong, would quickly fall away. For as the aged, or those whose sight is defective, when any books however fair, is set before them, though they perceive that there is something written are scarcely able to make out two

1. Man is without excuse for his ingratitude to God. He is under condemnation.

2. A salvific knowledge of God cannot come by nature, but by the revealed Word.

3. Scripture is essential for the proper understanding of Deity because the fall has dulled the mind of natural man.

consecutive words, but, when aided by glasses, begin to read distinctly, so Scripture, gathering together the impressions of Deity, which, till then, lay confused in our minds, dissipates the darkness, and shows us the true God clearly.[3] God therefore bestows a gift of singular value, when, for the instruction of the Church, he employs not dumb teachers merely, but opens his own sacred mouth; when he not only proclaims that some God must be worshipped, but at the same time declares that He is the God to whom worship is due; when he not only teaches his elect to have respect to God, but manifests himself as the God to whom this respect should be paid.

Therefore, while it becomes man seriously to employ his eyes in considering the works of God, since a place has been assigned him in this most glorious theatre that he may be a spectator of them, his special duty is to give ear to the Word, that he may the better profit. Hence it is not strange that those who are born in darkness become more and more hardened in their stupidity; because the vast majority instead of confining themselves within due bounds by listening with docility to the Word, exult in their own vanity. If true religion is to beam upon us, our principle must be, that it is necessary to begin with heavenly teaching, and that it is impossible for any man to obtain even the minutest portion of right and sound doctrine without being a disciple of Scripture.[4] Hence, the first step in true knowledge is taken, when we reverently embrace the testimony which God has been pleased therein to give of himself. For not only does faith, full and perfect faith, but all correct knowledge of God, originate in obedience. And surely in this respect God has with singular Providence provided for mankind in all ages.

4. True knowledge of anything can only be obtained by the study of God's special revelation in His word.

For if we reflect how prone the human mind is to lapse into forgetfulness of God, how readily inclined to every kind of error, how bent every now and then on devising new and fictitious religions, it will be easy to understand how necessary it was to make such a depository of doctrine as would secure it from either perishing by the neglect, vanishing away amid the errors, or being corrupted by the presumptuous audacity of men.[5] It being thus manifest that God, foreseeing the inefficiency of his image imprinted on the fair form of the universe, has given the assistance of his Word to all whom he has ever been pleased to instruct effectually, we, too, must pursue this straight path, if we aspire in earnest to a genuine contemplation of God;—we must go, I say, to the Word, where the character of God, drawn from his works is described accurately and to the life; these works being estimated, not by our depraved Judgment, but by the standard of eternal truth. If, as I lately said, we turn aside from it, how great soever the speed with which we move, we shall never reach the goal, because we are off the course. We should consider that the brightness of the Divine countenance, which even an apostle declares to be inaccessible (1 Tim. 6:16), is a kind of labyrinth,—a labyrinth to us inextricable, if the Word do not serve us as a thread to guide our path; and that it is better to limp in the way, than run with the greatest swiftness out of it. Hence the Psalmist, after repeatedly declaring (Psalm 93, 96, 97, 99) that superstition should be banished from the world in order that pure religion may flourish, introduces God as reigning; meaning by the term, not the power which he possesses and which he exerts in the government of universal nature, but the doctrine by which he maintains his due supremacy: because error never can be eradicated from the heart of man until the true knowledge of God has been implanted in it.

5. Man is constantly given to forgetfulness and self-deception, heightening the need for a written revelation of God.

Book 1
Chapter 7

The Testimony of the Spirit Necessary to Give Full Authority to Scripture

Before proceeding farther, it seems proper to make some observations on the authority of Scripture, in order that our minds may not only be prepared to receive it with reverence, but be divested of all doubt. When that which professes to be the Word of God is acknowledged to be so, no person, unless devoid of common sense and the feelings of a man, will have the desperate hardihood to refuse credit to the speaker. But since no daily responses are given from heaven, and the Scriptures are the only records in which God has been pleased to consign his truth to perpetual remembrance, the full authority which they ought to possess with the faithful is not recognized, unless they are believed to have come from heaven, as directly as if God had been heard giving utterance to them. This subject well deserves to be treated more at large, and pondered more accurately. But my readers will pardon me for having more regard to what my plan admits than to what the extent of this topic requires.

It is necessary to attend to what I lately said, that our faith in doctrine is not established until we have a perfect conviction that God is its author. Hence, the highest proof of Scripture is uniformly taken from the character of him whose Word it is. The prophets and apostles boast not their own acuteness or any qualities which win credit to speakers, nor do they dwell on reasons; but they appeal to the sacred name of God, in order that the whole world may be compelled to submission.[1] The next thing to be considered is, how it appears not probable merely, but certain, that the name of God is neither rashly nor cunningly pretended. If, then, we would consult most effectually for our consciences, and save them from being driven about in a whirl of uncertainty, from wavering, and even stumbling at the smallest obstacle, our conviction of the truth of Scripture must be derived from a higher source than human conjectures, Judgments, or reasons; namely, the secret testimony of the Spirit.[2] It is true, indeed, that if we choose to proceed in the way of arguments it is easy to establish, by evidence of various kinds, that if there is a God in heaven, the Law, the Prophecies, and the Gospel, proceeded from him. Nay, although learned men, and men of the greatest talent, should take the opposite side, summoning and ostentatiously displaying all the powers of their genius in the discussion; if they are not possessed of shameless effrontery, they will be compelled to confess that the Scripture exhibits clear evidence of its being spoken by God, and, consequently, of its containing his heavenly doctrine. We shall see a little farther on, that the volume of sacred Scripture very far surpasses all other writings. Nay, if we look at it with clear eyes, and unblessed Judgment, it will forthwith present itself with a divine majesty which will subdue our presumptuous opposition, and force us to do it homage. Still, however, it is preposterous to attempt, by discussion, to rear up a full faith in Scripture. True, were I called to contend with the craftiest despisers of God, I trust, though I am not possessed of the highest ability or eloquence, I should not find it difficult to stop their obstreperous mouths; I could, without much ado, put down the boastings which they mutter in corners, were anything to be gained by refuting their cavils. But although we may maintain the sacred

1. The authors of scripture clearly ascribe their words to God as their source.

2. The Holy Spirit confirms that the Scriptures are the very Word of God.

3. Ungodly men cannot be convinced of the authority of God's word.

4. Human reason can not authenticate God's Word. A divine revelation can only be self-authenticated.

5. Only the Holy Spirit can enlighten the minds of unbelieving skeptics.

Word of God against gainsayers, it does not follow that we shall forthwith implant the certainty which faith requires in their hearts.[3] Profane men think that religion rests only on opinion, and, therefore, that they may not believe foolishly, or on slight grounds, desire and insist to have it proved by reason that Moses and the prophets were divinely inspired. But I answer, that the testimony of the Spirit[4] is superior to reason. For as God alone can properly bear witness to his own words, so these words will not obtain full credit in the hearts of men, until they are sealed by the inward testimony of the Spirit. The same Spirit, therefore, who spoke by the mouth of the prophets, must penetrate our hearts, in order to convince us that they faithfully delivered the message with which they were divinely entrusted. This connection is most aptly expressed by Isaiah in these words, "My Spirit that is upon thee, and my words which I have put in thy mouth, shall not depart out of thy mouth, nor out of the mouth of thy seed, nor out of the mouth of thy seed's seed, says the Lord, from henceforth and for ever," (Isa. 59:21). Some worthy persons feel disconcerted, because, while the wicked murmur with impunity at the Word of God, they have not a clear proof at hand to silence them, forgetting that the Spirit is called an earnest and seal to confirm the faith of the godly, for this very reason, that, until he enlightens their minds, they are tossed to and fro in a sea of doubts.[5]

Let it therefore be held as fixed, that those who are inwardly taught by the Holy Spirit acquiesce implicitly in Scripture; that Scripture, carrying its own evidence along with it, deigns not to submit to proofs and arguments, but owes the full conviction with which we ought to receive it to the testimony of the Spirit. Enlightened by him, we no longer believe, either on our own Judgment or that of others, that the Scriptures are from God; but, in a way superior to human Judgment, feel perfectly assured—as much so as if we beheld the divine image visibly impressed on it—that it came to us, by the instrumentality of men, from the very mouth of God. We ask not for proofs or probabilities on which to rest our Judgment, but we subject our intellect and Judgment to it as too transcendent for us to estimate.[6] This, however, we do, not in the manner in which some are wont to fasten on an unknown object, which, as soon as known, displeases, but because we have a thorough conviction that, in holding it, we hold unassailable truth; not like miserable men, whose minds are enslaved by superstition, but because we feel a divine energy living and breathing in it—an energy by which we are drawn and animated to obey it, willingly indeed, and knowingly, but more vividly and effectually than could be done by human will or knowledge. Hence, God most justly exclaims by the mouth of Isaiah, "Ye are my witnesses, saith the Lord, and my servant whom I have chosen, that ye may know and believe me, and understand that I am he," (Isa. 43:10). Such, then, is a conviction which asks not for reasons; such, a knowledge which accords with the highest reason, namely knowledge in which the mind rests more firmly and securely than in any reasons; such in fine, the conviction which revelation from heaven alone can produce. I say nothing more than every believer experiences in himself, though my words fall far short of the reality. I do not dwell on this subject at present, because we will return to it again: only let us now understand that the only true faith is that which the Spirit of God seals on our hearts. Nay, the modest and teachable reader will find a sufficient reason in the promise contained in Isaiah, that all the children of the renovated Church "shall be taught of the Lord," (Isaiah 54:13). This singular privilege God bestows on his elect only, whom he separates from the rest of mankind. For what is the beginning of true doctrine but prompt alacrity to hear the Word of God? And God, by the mouth of Moses, thus demands to be heard: "It is not in heavens that thou shouldest say, Who shall go up for us to heaven, and bring it unto us, that we may hear and do it? But the word is very nigh unto thee, in thy mouth and in thy heart," (Deut. 30:12, 14). God having been pleased to reserve the treasure of intelligence for his children, no wonder

6. Who are we to sit in judgment concerning God's word?

that so much ignorance and stupidity is seen in the generality of mankind. In the generality, I include even those specially chosen, until they are engrafted into the body of the Church. Isaiah, moreover, while reminding us that the prophetical doctrine would prove incredible not only to strangers, but also to the Jews, who were desirous to be thought of the household of God, subjoins the reason, when he asks, "To whom has the arm of the Lord been revealed?" (Isaiah 53:1). If at any time, then we are troubled at the small number of those who believe, let us, on the other hand, call to mind, that none comprehend the mysteries of God save those to whom it is given.

Book 1
Chapter 9

All the Principles of Piety Subverted by Fanatics, Who Substitute Revelations for Scripture

But what kind of Spirit did our Savior promise to send? One who should not speak of himself (John 16:13), but suggest and instill the truths which he himself had delivered through the word. Hence the office of the Spirit promised to us, is not to form new and unheard-of revelations, or to coin a new form of doctrine, by which we may be led away from the received doctrine of the gospel, but to seal on our minds the very doctrine which the gospel recommends.[1]

Hence it is easy to understand that we must give diligent heed both to the reading and hearing of Scripture, if we would obtain any benefit from the Spirit of God (just as Peter praises those who attentively study the doctrine of the prophets (2 Pet. 1:19), though it might have been thought to be superseded after the gospel light arose), and, on the contrary, that any spirit which passes by the wisdom of God's Word, and suggests any other doctrine, is deservedly suspected of vanity and falsehood. Since Satan transforms himself into an angel of light, what authority can the Spirit have with us if he be not ascertained by an infallible mark? And assuredly he is pointed out to us by the Lord with sufficient clearness; but these

1. The Holy Spirit Himself does not bring new revelation beyond what Christ left for us.

2. Thus, those who seek a revelation of the Holy Spirit apart from the Scriptures are "bent on their own destruction."

miserable men err as if bent on their own destruction, while they seek the Spirit from themselves rather than from Him.[2] But they say that it is insulting to subject the Spirit, to whom all things are to be subject, to the Scripture: as if it were disgraceful to the Holy Spirit to maintain a perfect resemblance throughout, and be in all respects without variation consistent with himself. True, if he were subjected to a human, an angelical, or to any foreign standard, it might be thought that he was rendered subordinate, or, if you will, brought into bondage, but so long as he is compared with himself, and considered in himself, how can it be said that he is thereby injured? I admit that he is brought to a test, but the very test by which it has pleased him that his majesty should be confirmed. It ought to be enough for us when once we hear his voice; but lest Satan should insinuate himself under his name, he wishes us to recognize him by the image which he has stamped on the Scriptures. The author of the Scriptures cannot vary, and change his likeness. Such as he there appeared at first, such he will perpetually remain. There is nothing contumelious to him in this, unless we are to think it would be honorable for him to degenerate, and revolt against himself.

There is nothing repugnant here to what was lately said that we have no great certainty of the word itself, until it be confirmed by the testimony of the Spirit. For the Lord has so knit together the certainty of his word and his Spirit, that our minds are duly imbued with reverence for the word when the Spirit shining upon it enables us there to behold the face of God;[3] and, on the other hand, we embrace the Spirit with no danger of delusion when we recognize him in his image, that is, in his word. Thus, indeed, it is. God did not produce his word before men for the sake of sudden display, intending to abolish it the moment the Spirit should arrive; but he employed the same Spirit, by whose agency he had administered the word, to complete his work by the efficacious confirmation of the word. In this way Christ explained to the two disciples (Luke 24:27), not that they were to reject the Scriptures and

3. The Holy Spirit illuminates the word for us.

trust to their own wisdom, but that they were to understand the Scriptures. In like manner, when Paul says to the Thessalonians, "Quench not the Spirit," he does not carry them aloft to empty speculation apart from the word; he immediately adds, "Despise not prophesying," (1 Thess. 5:19, 20).[4] By this, doubtless, he intimates that the light of the Spirit is quenched the moment prophesying falls into contempt. How is this answered by those swelling enthusiasts, in whose idea the only true illumination consists, in carelessly laying aside, and bidding adieu to the Word of God, while, with no less confidence than folly, they fasten upon any dreaming notion which may have casually sprung up in their minds? Surely a very different sobriety becomes the children of God. As they feel that without the Spirit of God they are utterly devoid of the light of truth, so they are not ignorant that the word is the instrument by which the illumination of the Spirit is dispensed. They know of no other Spirit than the one who dwelt and spoke in the apostles—the Spirit by whose oracles they are daily invited to the hearing of the word.

4. Calvin takes prophesying as an application of the Scriptures in the church.

Book 1
Chapter 13

The Unity of the Divine Essence in Three Persons Taught, in Scripture, from the Foundation of the World

1. Calvin sets out to prove the divinity and the person of the Son – the Word of God.

Before proceeding farther, it will be necessary to prove the divinity of the Son and the Holy Spirit. Thereafter, we shall see how they differ from each other. When the Word of God is set before us in the Scriptures,[1] it were certainly most absurd to imagine that it is only a fleeting and evanescent voice, which is sent out into the air, and comes forth beyond God himself, as was the case with the communications made to the patriarchs, and all the prophecies. The reference is rather to the wisdom ever dwelling with God, and by which all oracles and prophecies were inspired. For, as Peter testifies (1 Pet. 1:11), the ancient prophets spoke by the Spirit of Christ just as did the apostles, and all who after them were ministers of the heavenly doctrine. But as Christ was not yet manifested, we necessarily understand that the Word was begotten of the Father before all ages. But if that Spirit, whose organs the prophets were, belonged to the Word, the inference is irresistible, that the Word was truly God.[2] And this is clearly enough shown by Moses in his account of the creation, where he places the Word as intermediate. For why does he distinctly narrate that God, in creating each of his works, said, Let there be this—let there be that, unless that the

2. If the Word was revealed to the Old Testament prophets, He must be God.

unsearchable glory of God might shine forth in his image? I know prattlers would easily evade this, by saying that Word is used for order or command; but the apostles are better expositors, when they tell us that the worlds were created by the Son, and that he sustains all things by his mighty word (Heb. 1:2).[3] For we here see that word is used for the nod or command of the Son, who is himself the eternal and essential Word of the Father. And no man of sane mind can have any doubt as to Solomon's meaning, when he introduces Wisdom as begotten by God, and presiding at the creation of the world, and all other divine operations (Prov. 8:22). For it were trifling and foolish to imagine any temporary command at a time when God was pleased to execute his fixed and eternal counsel, and something more still mysterious. To this our Savior's words refer, "My Father worketh hitherto, and I work," (John 5:17).[4] In thus affirming, that from the foundation of the world he constantly worked with the Father, he gives a clearer explanation of what Moses simply touched. The meaning therefore is, that God spoke in such a manner as left the Word his peculiar part in the work, and thus made the operation common to both. But the clearest explanation is given by John, when he states that the Word—which was from the beginning, God and with God, was, together with God the Father, the maker of all things.[5] For he both attributes a substantial and permanent essence to the Word, assigning to it a certain peculiarity, and distinctly showing how God spoke the world into being. Therefore, as all revelations from heaven are duly designated by the title of the Word of God, so the highest place must be assigned to that substantial Word, the source of all inspiration, which, as being liable to no variation, remains for ever one and the same with God, and is God.

But as God has manifested himself more clearly by the advent of Christ, so he has made himself more familiarly known in three persons.[6] Of many proofs let this one suffice. Paul connects together these three, God, Faith, and Baptism, and reasons from the one to the other—viz. because there is

3. The New Testament confirms that the Son is the Creator and Sustainer of all things.

4. John 5:17 indicates a co-existence with the Father and Son prior to the incarnation.

5. 1 John 1:1-2 is the clearest biblical teaching on the divinity of the Son.

6. The New Testament more clearly manifests God in three persons.

one faith he infers that there is one God; and because there is one baptism he infers that there is one faith. Therefore, if by baptism we are initiated into the faith and worship of one God, we must of necessity believe that he into whose name we are baptized is the true God. And there cannot be a doubt that our Savior wished to testify, by a solemn rehearsal, that the perfect light of faith is now exhibited, when he said, "Go and teach all nations, baptizing them in the name of the Father, and of the Son, and of the Holy Spirit," (Mt. 28:19), since this is the same thing as to be baptized into the name of the one God, who has been fully manifested in the Father, the Son, and the Spirit.[7] Hence it plainly appears, that the three persons, in whom alone God is known, subsist in the Divine essence. And since faith certainly ought not to look hither and thither, or run up and down after various objects, but to look, refer, and cleave to God alone, it is obvious that were there various kinds of faith, there behaved also to be various gods.[8] Then, as the baptism of faith is a sacrament, its unity assures us of the unity of God. Hence also it is proved that it is lawful only to be baptized into one God, because we make a profession of faith in him in whose name we are baptized. What, then, is our Savior's meaning in commanding baptism to be administered in the name of the Father, and the Son, and the Holy Spirit, if it be not that we are to believe with one faith in the name of the Father, and the Son, and the Holy Spirit? But is this any thing else than to declare that the Father, Son, and Spirit, are one God? Wherefore, since it must be held certain that there is one God, not more than one, we conclude that the Word and Spirit are of the very essence of God.

On the other hand, the Scriptures demonstrate that there is some distinction between the Father and the Word, the Word and the Spirit; but the magnitude of the mystery reminds us of the great reverence and soberness which ought to be employed in discussing it.[9] It seems to me, that nothing can be more admirable than the words of Gregory Nanzianzen: "I cannot think of the unity without being irradiated by the Trin-

7. The single Name in Matthew 28:19 must point to the divinity of all 3 Persons.

8. "One faith" referred to in Ephesians 4:5 also implies one God.

9. The doctrine of the Trinity is a great mystery, calling for reverence in handling it.

ity: I cannot distinguish between the Trinity without being carried up to the unity." Therefore, let us beware of imagining such a Trinity of persons as will distract our thoughts, instead of bringing them instantly back to the unity. The words Father, Son, and Holy Spirit, certainly indicate a real distinction, not allowing us to suppose that they are merely epithets by which God is variously designated from his works. Still they indicate distinction only, not division. The passages we have already quoted show that the Son has a distinct subsistence from the Father, because the Word could not have been with God unless he were distinct from the Father; nor but for this could he have had his glory with the Father.[10] In like manner, Christ distinguishes the Father from himself when he says that there is another who bears witness of him (John 5:32; 8:16). To the same effect is it elsewhere said, that the Father made all things by the Word. This could not be, if he were not in some respect distinct from him. Besides, it was not the Father that descended to the earth, but he who came forth from the Father; nor was it the Father that died and rose again, but he whom the Father had sent. This distinction did not take its beginning at the incarnation: for it is clear that the only begotten Son previously existed in the bosom of the Father (John 1:18). For who will dare to affirm that the Son entered his Father's bosom for the first time, when he came down from heaven to assume human nature? Therefore, he was previously in the bosom of the Father, and had his glory with the Father. Christ intimates the distinction between the Holy Spirit and the Father, when he says that the Spirit proceeds from the Father, and between the Holy Spirit and himself, when he speaks of him as another as he does when he declares that he will send another Comforter; and in many other passages besides (John 14:6; 15:26; 14:16).[11]

10. Calvin provides proofs from Scripture that the Son is a distinct Person from the Father.

I am not sure whether it is expedient to borrow analogies from human affairs to express the nature of this distinction. The ancient fathers sometimes do so, but they at the same time admit that what they bring forward as analogous is very

11. Scriptural proofs distinguishing the Person of the Spirit from the Son.

widely different. And hence it is that I have a great dread of any thing like presumption here, lest some rash saying may furnish an occasion of calumny to the malicious, or of delusion to the unlearned. It were unbecoming, however, to say nothing of a distinction which we observe that the Scriptures have pointed out. This distinction is, that to the Father is attributed the beginning of action, the fountain and source of all things; to the Son, wisdom, counsel, and arrangement in action, while the energy and efficacy of action is assigned to the Spirit.[12] Moreover, though the eternity of the Father is also the eternity of the Son and Spirit, since God never could be without his own wisdom and energy; and though in eternity there can be no room for first or last, still the distinction of order is not unmeaning or superfluous, the Father being considered first, next the Son from him, and then the Spirit from both. For the mind of every man naturally inclines to consider, first, God, secondly, the wisdom emerging from him, and, lastly, the energy by which he executes the purpose of His counsel. For this reason, the Son is said to be of the Father only; the Spirit of both the Father and the Son. This is done in many passages, but in none more clearly than in the eighth chapter to the Romans, where the same Spirit is called indiscriminately the Spirit of Christ, and the Spirit of him who raised up Christ from the dead.[13] And not improperly. For Peter also testifies (1 Pet. 1:21), that it was the Spirit of Christ which inspired the prophets, though the Scriptures so often say that it was the Spirit of God the Father.[14]

Moreover, this distinction is so far from interfering with the most perfect unity of God, that the Son may thereby be proved to be one God with the Father, inasmuch as he constitutes one Spirit with him, and that the Spirit is not different from the Father and the Son, inasmuch as he is the Spirit of the Father and the Son. In each hypostasis[15] the whole nature is understood the only difference being that each has his own peculiar subsistence.[16] The whole Father is in the Son, and the whole Son in the Father, as the Son himself also de-

12. Calvin lists the functions or offices of the Persons in the Godhead.

13. Romans 8:11

14. These serve as proofs that the Spirit proceeds from Father and Son.

15. Hypostasis refers to the Persons.

16. Calvin sees each Person as God, yet having each their own "subsistence."

clares (John 14:10), "I am in the Father, and the Father in me;" nor do ecclesiastical writers admit that the one is separated from the other by any difference of essence. "By those names which denote distinctions", says Augustine, "is meant the relation which they mutually bear to each other, not the very substance by which they are one." In this way, the sentiments of the Father's, which might sometimes appear to be at variance with each other, are to be reconciled. At one time they teach that the Father is the beginning of the Son, at another they assert that the Son has both divinity and essence from himself, and therefore is one beginning with the Father. The cause of this discrepancy is well and clearly explained by Augustine, when he says, "Christ, as to himself, is called God, as to the Father he is called Son." And again, "The Father, as to himself, is called God, as to the Son he is called Father. He who, as to the Son, is called Father, is not Son; and he who, as to himself, is called Father, and he who, as to himself, is called Son, is the same God."[17] Therefore, when we speak of the Son simply, without reference to the Father, we truly and properly affirm that he is of himself, and, accordingly, call him the only beginning; but when we denote the relation which he bears to the Father, we correctly make the Father the beginning of the Son. Augustine's fifth book on the Trinity[18] is wholly devoted to the explanation of this subject. But it is far safer to rest contented with the relation as taught by him, than get bewildered in vain speculation by subtle prying into a sublime mystery.

Let those, then, who love soberness, and are contented with the measure of faith, briefly receive what is useful to be known. It is as follows:[19]—When we profess to believe in one God, by the name God is understood the one simple essence, comprehending three persons or hypostases;[20] and, accordingly, whenever the name of God is used indefinitely, the Son and Spirit, not less than the Father, is meant. But when the Son is joined with the Father, relation comes into view, and so we distinguish between the Persons. But as the Personal subsistence carry an order with them, the principle and origin being

17. Augustine grapples with the mystery of Christ's essential deity and His origin in the Father.

18. Augustine (a 5th century church father) wrote extensively on the Trinity.

19. Calvin summarizes the doctrine of the Trinity.

20. Hypostases refers to the persons, or "personal subsistence."

in the Father, whenever mention is made of the Father and Son, or of the Father and Spirit together, the name of God is specially given to the Father. In this way the unity of essence is retained, and respect is had to the order, which, however derogates in no respect from the divinity of the Son and Spirit. And surely since we have already seen how the apostles declare the Son of God to have been He whom Moses and the prophets declared to be Jehovah, we must always arrive at a unity of essence. We, therefore, hold it detestable blasphemy to call the Son a different God from the Father, because the simple name God admits not of relation, nor can God, considered in himself, be said to be this or that. Then, that the name Jehovah, taken indefinitely, may be applied to Christ, is clear from the words of Paul, "For this thing I besought the Lord thrice."[21] After giving the answer, "My grace is sufficient for thee," he subjoins, "that the power of Christ may rest upon me," (2 Cor. 12:8, 9). For it is certain that the name of Lord (Κυρίος) is there put for Jehovah, and, therefore, to restrict it to the person of the Mediator were puerile and frivolous, the words being used absolutely, and not with the view of comparing the Father and the Son. And we know that, in accordance with the received usage of the Greeks, the apostles uniformly substitute the word Κυρίος for Jehovah. Not to go far for an example, Paul besought the Lord in the same sense in which Peter quotes the passage of Joel, "Whosoever shall call upon the name of the Lord shall be saved,"[22] (Acts 2:21; Joel 2:28). Where this name is specially applied to the Son, there is a different ground for it, as will be seen in its own place; at present it is sufficient to remember, that Paul, after praying to God absolutely, immediately subjoins the name of Christ. Thus, too, the Spirit is called God absolutely by Christ himself. For nothing prevents us from holding that he is the entire spiritual essence of God, in which are comprehended Father, Son, and Spirit. This is plain from Scripture. For as God is there called a Spirit, so the Holy Spirit also, in so far as he is a hypostasis of the whole essence, is said to be both of God and from God.

21. Paul refers to "the Lord" here as God, Jehovah.

22. Here the reference to Jehovah God in the Old Testament is assigned to Jesus Christ.

Book 1

Chapter 14

In the Creation of the World, and All Things in it, the True God Distinguished by Certain Marks from Fictitious Gods

Since, being placed in this most beautiful theatre,[1] let us not decline to take a pious delight in the clear and manifest works of God. For, as we have elsewhere observed, though not the chief, it is, in point of order, the first evidence of faith, to remember to which side soever we turn, that all which meets the eye is the work of God, and at the same time to meditate with pious care on the end which God had in view in creating it.[2] Wherefore, in order that we may apprehend with true faith what it is necessary to know concerning God, it is of importance to attend to the history of the creation, as briefly recorded by Moses and afterwards more copiously illustrated by pious writers, more especially by Basil and Ambrose.[3] From this history we learn that God, by the power of his Word and his Spirit, created the heavens and the earth out of nothing; that thereafter he produced things inanimate and animate of every kind, arranging an innumerable variety of objects in admirable order, giving each kind its proper nature, office, place, and station; at the same time, as all things were liable to corruption, providing for the perpetuation of each single species, cherishing some by secret methods, and,

1. The universe is a "beautiful theater."

2. First signs of faith are found in the one who recognizes the work of God in creation.

3. Basil and Ambrose are 5th century church fathers, contemporary with Augustine.

4. Man is God's highest creation in the physical world.

as it were, from time to time instilling new vigor into them, and bestowing on others a power of continuing their race, so preventing it from perishing at their own death. Heaven and earth being thus most richly adorned, and copiously supplied with all things, like a large and splendid mansion gorgeously constructed and exquisitely furnished, at length man was made—man, by the beauty of his person and his many noble endowments, the most glorious specimen of the works of God.[4] But, as I have no intention to give the history of creation in detail, it is sufficient to have again thus briefly touched on it in passing. I have already reminded my reader, that the best course for him is to derive his knowledge of the subject from Moses and others who have carefully and faithfully transmitted an account of the creation.

It is unnecessary to dwell at length on the end that should be aimed at in considering the works of God. The subject has been in a great measure explained elsewhere, and in so far as required by our present work, may now be disposed of in a few words. Undoubtedly were one to attempt to speak in due terms of the inestimable wisdom, power, justice, and goodness of God, in the formation of the world, no grace or splendor of diction could equal the greatness of the subject. Still there can be no doubt that the Lord would have us constantly occupied with such holy meditation, in order that, while we contemplate the immense treasures of wisdom and goodness exhibited in the creatures as in so many mirrors, we may not only run our eye over them with a hasty, and, as it were, evanescent glance, but dwell long upon them, seriously and faithfully turn them in our minds, and every now and then bring

5. The creation requires of us deep meditation and constant reflection on God's works.

them to recollection.[5] But as the present work is of a didactic nature, we cannot fittingly enter on topics which require lengthened discourse. Therefore, in order to be compendious, let the reader understand that he has a genuine apprehension of the character of God as the Creator of the world; first, if he attends to the general rule, never thoughtlessly or obliviously to overlook the glorious perfections which God displays in his creatures; and, secondly, if he makes a self application of what he sees, so as to fix it deeply on his heart.[6] The former is exemplified when we consider how great the Architect must be who framed and ordered the multitude of the starry host so admirably, that it is impossible to imagine a more glorious sight, so stationing some, and fixing them to particular spots that they cannot move; giving a freer course to others yet setting limits to their wanderings; so tempering the movement of the whole as to measure out day and night, months, years, and seasons, and at the same time so regulating the inequality of days as to prevent every thing like confusion. The former course is, moreover, exemplified when we attend to his power in sustaining the vast mass, and guiding the swift revolutions of the heavenly bodies, &c.[7] These few examples sufficiently explain what is meant by recognizing the divine perfections in the creation of the world. Were we to attempt to go over the whole subject we should never come to a conclusion, there being as many miracles of divine power, as many striking evidences of wisdom and goodness, as there are classes of objects, nay, as there are individual objects, great or small, throughout the universe.

The other course which has a closer relation to faith remains to be considered—viz. that while we observe how God has destined all things for our good and salvation, we at the same time feel his power and grace, both in ourselves and in the great blessings which he has bestowed upon us; thence stirring up ourselves to confidence in him, to invocation, praise, and love. Moreover, as I lately observed, the Lord himself, by the very order of creation, has demonstrated that he created all things for the sake of man.[8] Nor is it unimportant to observe, that he divided the formation of the world into six days, though it had been in no respect more difficult to complete the whole work, in all its parts, in one moment than by a gradual progression.[9] But he was pleased to display his providence and paternal care towards us in this, that before he formed man, he provided whatever he foresaw would be useful

6. Examination of the natural world must include a view of God's character and a heart response of praise and love.

7. Astronomy especially demonstrates God's power and wisdom.

8. We ought to be especially thankful that so much of God's creation was made for man's benefit.

9. Calvin taught a 6 – 24 hour day creation, though he admits God could have done it all in "one moment."

and salutary to him. How ungrateful, then, were it to doubt whether we are cared for by this most excellent Parent, who we see cared for us even before we were born! How impious were it to tremble in distrust, lest we should one day be abandoned in our necessity by that kindness which, antecedent to our existence, displayed itself in a complete supply of all good things! Moreover, Moses tells us that everything which the world contains is liberally placed at our disposal. This God certainly did not that he might delude us with an empty form of donation. Nothing, therefore, which concerns our safety will ever be wanting. To conclude, in one word; as often as we call God the Creator of heaven and earth, let us remember that the distribution of all the things which he created are in his hand and power, but that we are his sons, whom he has undertaken to nourish and bring up in allegiance to him, that we may expect the substance of all good from him alone, and have full hope that he will never suffer us to be in want of things necessary to salvation, so as to leave us dependent on some other source; that in everything we desire we may address our prayers to him, and, in every benefit we receive, acknowledge his hand, and give him thanks; that thus allured by his great goodness and beneficence, we may study with our whole heart to love and serve him.

Book 1
Chapter 15

State in Which Man was Created. The Faculties of the Soul—The image of God—Free Will—Original Righteousness

We have now to speak of the creation of man, not only because of all the works of God it is the noblest, and most admirable specimen of his justice, wisdom, and goodness, but, as we observed at the outset, we cannot clearly and properly know God unless the knowledge of ourselves be added.[1] This knowledge is twofold,—relating, first, to the condition in which we were at first created; and, secondly, to our condition such as it began to be immediately after Adam's fall. For it would little avail us to know how we were created if we remained ignorant of the corruption and degradation of our nature in consequence of the fall. At present, however, we confine ourselves to a consideration of our nature in its original integrity. And, certainly, before we descend to the miserable condition into which man has fallen, it is of importance to consider what he was at first.[2] For there is need of caution, lest we attend only to the natural ills of man, and thereby seem to ascribe them to the Author of nature; impiety deeming it a sufficient defense if it can pretend that everything vicious in it proceeded in some sense from God, and not hesitating, when accused, to plead against God, and

1. Calvin's basic theory of knowledge — knowledge of God and knowledge of man are symbiotic for us.

2. To know ourselves, first we must understand man's nature pre-fall (God's original creation.)

throw the blame of its guilt upon Him. Those who would be thought to speak more reverently of the Deity catch at an excuse for their depravity from nature, not considering that they also, though more obscurely, bring a charge against God, on whom the dishonor would fall if anything vicious were proved to exist in nature. Seeing, therefore, that the flesh is continually on the alert for subterfuges, by which it imagines it can remove the blame of its own wickedness from itself to some other quarter, we must diligently guard against this depraved procedure, and accordingly treat of the calamity of the human race in such a way as may cut off every evasion, and vindicate the justice of God against all who would impugn it. We shall afterwards see, in its own place, how far mankind now are from the purity originally conferred on Adam. And, first, it is to be observed, that when he was formed out of the dust of the ground a curb was laid on his pride—nothing being more absurd than that those should glory in their excellence who not only dwell in tabernacles of clay, but are themselves in part dust and ashes. But God having not only deigned to animate a vessel of clay, but to make it the habitation of an immortal spirit, Adam might well glory in the great liberality of his Maker.

3. God created man as body and soul (2 parts). Calvin equates the spirit and soul.

Moreover, there can be no question that man consists of a body and a soul;[3] meaning by soul, an immortal though created essence, which is his nobler part. Sometimes he is called a spirit. But though the two terms, while they are used together differ in their meaning, still, when spirit is used by itself it is equivalent to soul, as when Solomon speaking of death says, that the spirit returns to God who gave it (Eccles. 12:7). And Christ, in commending his spirit to the Father, and Stephen his to Christ, simply mean, that when the soul is freed

4. A neoplatonic idea that the body is a prison-house for the soul.

from the prison-house of the body,[4] God becomes its perpetual keeper. Those who imagine that the soul is called a spirit because it is a breath or energy divinely infused into bodies, but devoid of essence, err too grossly, as is shown both by the nature of the thing, and the whole tenor of Scripture. It is true, indeed, that men cleaving too much to the earth are dull of apprehension, nay, being alienated from the Father of Lights, are so immersed in darkness as to imagine that they will not survive the grave; still the light is not so completely quenched in darkness that all sense of immortality is lost. Conscience, which, distinguishing, between good and evil, responds to the Judgment of God, is an undoubted sign of an immortal spirit.[5] How could motion devoid of essence penetrate to the Judgment-seat of God, and under a sense of guilt strike itself with terror? The body cannot be affected by any fear of spiritual punishment. This is competent only to the soul, which must therefore be endued with essence.[6] Then the mere knowledge of a God sufficiently proves that souls which rise higher than the world must be immortal, it being impossible that any evanescent vigor could reach the very fountain of life.

But our definition of the image seems not to be complete until it appears more clearly what the faculties are in which man excels, and in which he is to be regarded as a mirror of the divine glory. This, however, cannot be better known than from the remedy provided for the corruption of nature. It cannot be doubted that when Adam lost his first estate he became alienated from God. Wherefore, although we grant that the image of God was not utterly effaced and destroyed in him, it was, however, so corrupted, that any thing which remains is fearful deformity;[7] and, therefore, our deliverance begins with that renovation which we obtain from Christ, who is, therefore, called the second Adam, because he restores us to true and substantial integrity.[8] For although Paul, contrasting the quickening Spirit which believers receive from Christ, with the living soul which Adam was created (1 Cor. 15:45), commends the richer measure of grace bestowed in regeneration, he does not, however, contradict the statement, that the end of regeneration is to form us anew in the image of God. Accordingly, he elsewhere shows that the new man is renewed after the image of him that created him (Col. 3:19). To this corresponds another passage, "Put ye on the new man, who after

5. Certain unbelievers claim there is no eternality to the human soul, yet their consciences are still aware of a final judgment.

6. Calvin is insisting on the soul having essence and immortality.

7. Calvinist thinking does not see the image of God as completely disappearing in fallen man — rather it is a "fearful deformity."

8. Christ, the second Man, the new humanity restores us to a soundness of that divine image.

God is created," (Eph. 4:24). We must now see what particulars Paul comprehends under this renovation. In the first place, he mentions knowledge, and in the second, true righteousness and holiness. Hence we infer, that at the beginning the image of God was manifested by light of intellect, rectitude of heart, and the soundness of every part. For though I admit that the forms of expression are elliptical, this principle cannot be overthrown—viz. that the leading feature in the renovation of the divine image must also have held the highest place in its creation. To the same effect Paul elsewhere says, that beholding the glory of Christ with unveiled face, we are transformed into the same image. We now see how Christ is the most perfect image of God, into which we are so renewed as to bear the image of God in knowledge, purity, righteousness, and true holiness.[9] This being established, the imagination of Osiander,[10] as to bodily form, vanishes of its own accord. As to that passage of St Paul (1 Cor. 11:7), in which the man alone to the express exclusion of the woman, is called the image and glory of God, it is evident from the context, that it merely refers to civil order. I presume it has already been sufficiently proved, that the image comprehends everything which has any relation to the spiritual and eternal life. The same thing, in different terms, is declared by St John when he says, that the light which was from the beginning, in the eternal Word of God, was the light of man (John 1:4). His object being to extol the singular grace of God in making man excel the other animals, he at the same time shows how he was formed in the image of God, that he may separate him from the common herd, as possessing not ordinary animal existence, but one which combines with it the light of intelligence. Therefore, as the image of God constitutes the entire excellence of human nature, as it shone in Adam before his fall, but was afterwards vitiated and almost destroyed, nothing remaining but a ruin, confused, mutilated, and tainted with impurity, so it is now partly seen in the elect, in so far as they are regenerated by the Spirit. Its full luster, however, will be displayed in heaven.

9. This restoration that the Lord brings us points to the divine image in which man was created — knowledge, righteousness, and holiness.

10. Osiander (1498-1552) was a German protestant theologian who taught that the human body was made after the image of God. Calvin rather states that the spiritual part of man was reflective of the image of God.

Let us therefore hold, for the purpose of the present work, that the soul consists of two parts, the intellect and the will—the office of the intellect being to distinguish between objects, according as they seem deserving of being approved or disapproved;[11] and the office of the will, to choose and follow what the intellect declares to be good, to reject and shun what it declares to be bad.[12] We dwell not on the subtlety of Aristotle, that the mind has no motion of itself; but that the moving power is choice, which he also terms the appetite intellect. Not to lose ourselves in superfluous questions, let it be enough to know that the intellect is to us, as it were, the guide and ruler of the soul; that the will always follows its beck, and waits for its decision, in matters of desire. For which reason Aristotle truly taught, that in the appetite there is a pursuit and rejection corresponding in some degree to affirmation and negation in the intellect.[13] Moreover, it will be seen in another place, how surely the intellect governs the will. Here we only wish to observe, that the soul does not possess any faculty which may not be duly referred to one or other of these members. And in this way we comprehend sense under intellect. Others distinguish thus: They say that sense inclines to pleasure in the same way as the intellect to good; that hence the appetite of sense becomes concupiscence and lust, while the affection of the intellect becomes will. For the term appetite, which they prefer, I use that of will, as being more common.

Therefore, God has provided the soul of man with intellect, by which he might discern good from evil, just from unjust, and might know what to follow or to shun, reason going before with her lamp; whence philosophers, in reference to her directing power, have called her τὸ ἐγεμονικὸν.[14] To this he has joined will, to which choice belongs. Man excelled in these noble endowments in his primitive condition, when reason, intelligence, prudence, and Judgment, not only sufficed for the government of his earthly life, but also enabled him to rise up to God and eternal happiness. Thereafter choice was added to direct the appetites, and temper all the organic motions; the

11. Calvin leaves it to the mind as that which determines the ethical good or evil of something. The will then follows the mind.

12. Calvin does not include the affections or the heart in his breaking down of the soul into the intellect and the will.

13. Calvin disagrees with Aristotle, including "appetite" in the realm of the soul as distinct from the mind. Yet, the Lord distinguishes mind and heart in Matthew 22:37.

14. The stoic philosophers referred to the "imagination" (egemonikon) as the seat of the soul. Calvin sees this to be the mind.

15. In the original state, man was created with the mind dirtying the will and appetites to that which was good (per Calvin). The mind directs the will, and the will directs the appetites.

16. Man was created with the ability of free choice, and he had a mind uncorrupted by sin. Then he corrupted his own mind and will, and fell into sin.

17. The philosophers of men make a fatal mistake in that they assume man can still make a choice between good and evil, that somehow their minds and wills are not corrupted.

18. Even some Christians believe that man's nature has not been tainted, such that man can still make a free choice between good and evil.

will being thus perfectly submissive to the authority of reason. In this upright state, man possessed freedom of will, by which, if he chose, he was able to obtain eternal life.[15] It were here unseasonable to introduce the question concerning the secret predestination of God, because we are not considering what might or might not happen, but what the nature of man truly was. Adam, therefore, might have stood if he chose, since it was only by his own will that he fell; but it was because his will was pliable in either directions and he had not received constancy to persevere, that he so easily fell. Still he had a free choice of good and evil; and not only so, but in the mind and will there was the highest rectitude, and all the organic parts were duly framed to obedience, until man corrupted its good properties, and destroyed himself.[16] Hence the great darkness of philosophers who have looked for a complete building in a ruin, and fit arrangement in disorder. The principle they set out with was, that man could not be a rational animal unless he had a free choice of good and evil. They also imagined that the distinction between virtue and vice was destroyed, if man did not of his own counsel arrange his life. So far well, had there been no change in man. This being unknown to them, it is not surprising that they throw every thing into confusion.[17] But those who, while they profess to be the disciples of Christ, still seek for free-will in man, notwithstanding of his being lost and drowned in spiritual destruction, labor under manifold delusion, making a heterogeneous mixture of inspired doctrine and philosophical opinions, and so erring as to both.[18] But it will be better to leave these things to their own place. At present it is necessary only to remember, that man, at his first creation, was very different from all his posterity; who, deriving their origin from him after he was corrupted, received a hereditary taint. At first every part of the soul was formed to rectitude. There was soundness of mind and freedom of will to choose the good. If any one objects that it was placed, as it were, in a slippery position, because its power was weak, I answer, that the degree conferred was sufficient to take away every excuse. For surely the Deity could not be tied down to this condition,—to make man such, that he either could not or would not sin. Such a nature might have been more excellent; but to expostulate with God as if he had been bound to confer this nature on man, is more than unjust, seeing he had full right to determine how much or how little He would give.[19] Why He did not sustain him by the virtue of perseverance is hidden in his counsel; it is ours to keep within the bounds of soberness. Man had received the power, if he had the will, but he had not the will which would have given the power; for this will would have been followed by perseverance. Still, after he had received so much, there is no excuse for his having spontaneously brought death upon himself. No necessity was laid upon God to give him more than that intermediate and even transient will, that out of man's fall he might extract materials for his own glory.

19. Why God made Adam with the possibility of choosing sin, is a question we must not ask. This is seeking knowledge in the hidden will of God. Suffice it to say that man is without excuse for choosing to sin.

Book 1
Chapter 16

The World, Created by God, Still Cherished and Protected by Him. Each and all of its Parts Governed by His Providence

It were cold and lifeless to represent God as a momentary Creator, who completed his work once for all, and then left it. Here, especially, we must dissent from the profane, and maintain that the presence of the divine power is conspicuous, not less in the perpetual condition of the world then in its first creation. For, although even wicked men are forced, by the mere view of the earth and sky, to rise to the Creator, yet faith has a method of its own in assigning the whole praise of creation to God. To this effect is the passage of the Apostle already quoted that by faith we understand that the worlds were framed by the Word of God (Heb. 11:3); because, without proceeding to his Providence, we cannot understand the full force of what is meant by God being the Creator, how much soever we may seem to comprehend it with our mind, and confess it with our tongue. The carnal mind, when once it has perceived the power of God in the creation, stops there, and, at the farthest, thinks and ponders on nothing else than the wisdom, power, and goodness displayed by the Author of such a work (matters which rise spontaneously, and force themselves on the notice even of the unwilling), or on some general agency on which the power of motion depends, exercised in preserving and governing it.[1] In short, it imagines that all things are sufficiently sustained by the energy divinely infused into them at first. But faith must penetrate deeper. After learning that there is a Creator, it must forthwith infer that he is also a Governor and Preserver, and that, not by producing a kind of general motion in the machine of the globe as well as in each of its parts, but by a special providence sustaining, cherishing, superintending, all the things which he has made, to the very minutest, even to a sparrow. Thus David, after briefly premising that the world was created by God, immediately descends to the continual course of Providence, "By the word of the Lord were the heavens framed, and all the host of them by the breath of his mouth;" immediately adding, "The Lord looketh from heaven, he beholdeth the children of men," (Ps. 33:6, 13). He subjoins other things to the same effect. For although all do not reason so accurately, yet because it would not be credible that human affairs were superintended by God, unless he were the maker of the world, and no one could seriously believe that he is its Creator without feeling convinced that he takes care of his works; David with good reason, and in admirable order, leads us from the one to the other.[2] In general, indeed, philosophers teach, and the human mind conceives, that all the parts of the world are invigorated by the secret inspiration of God. They do not, however reach the height to which David rises taking all the pious along with him, when he says, "These wait all upon thee, that thou mayest give them their meat in due season. That thou givest them they gather: thou openest thine hand, they are filled with good. Thou hidest thy face, they are troubled: thou takest away their breath, they die, and return to their dust. Thou sendest forth thy Spirit, they are created, and thou renewest the face of the earth," (Ps. 104:27-30). Nay, though they subscribe to the sentiment of Paul, that in God "we live, and move, and have our being," (Acts 17:28), yet they are far from having a serious apprehension of the grace which he commends, because they

1. Men without faith might accept creation, but they cannot stand the idea of God's hand of providence still very intimately involved in His created world.

2. Christians must in faith receive both God's Creator role and Sustainer role at once.

3. Worldly philosophers are eager to push God away from their minds. Man by nature wants to think of God as a deist god, very uninvolved and very far away.

4. God does not merely set in motion His universe and walk away. His omnipotence and sovereign control is seen in every minute action and reaction going on everywhere.

have not the least relish for that special care in which alone the paternal favor of God is discerned.[3]

And truly God claims omnipotence to himself, and would have us to acknowledge it,—not the vain, indolent, slumbering omnipotence which sophists feign, but vigilant, efficacious, energetic, and ever active,—not an omnipotence which may only act as a general principle of confused motion, as in ordering a stream to keep within the channel once prescribed to it, but one which is intent on individual and special movements. God is deemed omnipotent, not because he can act though he may cease or be idle, or because by a general instinct he continues the order of nature previously appointed; but because, governing heaven and earth by his providence, he so overrules all things that nothing happens without his counsel.[4] For when it is said in the Psalms, "He has done whatsoever he has pleased," (Ps. 115:3), the thing meant is his sure and deliberate purpose. It were insipid to interpret the Psalmist's words in philosophic fashion, to mean that God is the primary agent, because the beginning and cause of all motion. This rather is the solace of the faithful, in their adversity, that every thing which they endure is by the ordination and command of God, that they are under his hand. But if the government of God thus extends to all his works, it is a childish cavil to confine it to natural influx. Those moreover who confine the providence of God within narrow limits, as if he allowed all things to be borne along freely according to a perpetual law of nature, do not more defraud God of his glory than themselves of a most useful doctrine; for nothing were more wretched than man if he were exposed to all possible movements of the sky, the air, the earth, and the water. We may add, that by this view the singular goodness of God towards each individual is unbecomingly impaired. David exclaims (Ps. 8:3), that infants hanging at their mothers breasts are eloquent enough to celebrate the glory of God, because, from the very moment of their births they find an aliment prepared for them by heavenly care. Indeed, if we do not shut our eyes and senses to the fact, we must see that some mothers have full provision for their infants, and others almost none, according as it is the pleasure of God to nourish one child more liberally, and another more sparingly. Those who attribute due praise to the omnipotence of God thereby derive a double benefit. He to whom heaven and earth belong, and whose nod all creatures must obey, is fully able to reward the homage which they pay to him, and they can rest secure in the protection of Him to whose control everything that could do them harm is subject, by whose authority, Satan, with all his furies and engines, is curbed as with a bridle, and on whose will everything adverse to our safety depends.[5] In this way, and in no other, can the immoderate and superstitious fears, excited by the dangers to which we are exposed, be calmed or subdued. I say superstitious fears. For such they are, as often as the dangers threatened by any created objects inspire us with such terror, that we tremble as if they had in themselves a power to hurt us, or could hurt at random or by chance; or as if we had not in God a sufficient protection against them. For example, Jeremiah forbids the children of God " to be dismayed at the signs of heaven, as the heathen are dismayed at them," (Jer. 10:2). He does not, indeed, condemn every kind of fear. But as unbelievers transfer the government of the world from God to the stars, imagining that happiness or misery depends on their decrees or presages, and not on the Divine will, the consequence is, that their fear, which ought to have reference to him only, is diverted to stars and comets. Let him, therefore, who would beware of such unbelief, always bear in mind, that there is no random power, or agency, or motion in the creatures, who are so governed by the secret counsel of God, that nothing happens but what he has knowingly and willingly decreed.[6]

First, then, let the reader remember that the providence we mean is not one by which the Deity, sitting idly in heaven, looks on at what is taking place in the world, but one by which he, as it were, holds the helms and overrules all events.[7] Hence his providence extends not less to the hand than to the

5. Even Satan, with all of his schemes, is under the constant, absolute control of God's hand.

6. When there is no sovereign God in mind, unbelievers will be caught in superstitious fear. They cannot control the stars and the comets, and they will conclude that these have control over their lives. Christians do not have these fears.

7. God's hand is on the helm (or the steering wheel) of every event.

eye. When Abraham said to his son, God will provide (Gen. 22:8), he meant not merely to assert that the future event was foreknown to God but to resign the management of an unknown business to the will of Him whose province it is to bring perplexed and dubious matters to a happy result. Hence it appears that providence consists in action. What many talk of bare prescience is the merest trifling. Those do not err quite so grossly who attribute government to God, but still, as I have observed, a confused and promiscuous government which consists in giving an impulse and general movement to the machine of the globe and each of its parts, but does not specially direct the action of every creature. It is impossible, however, to tolerate this error. For, according to its abettors, there is nothing in this providence, which they call universal, to prevent all the creatures from being moved contingently, or to prevent man from turning himself in this direction or in that, according to the mere freedom of his own will.[8] In this ways they make man a partner with God,—God, by his energy, impressing man with the movement by which he can act, agreeably to the nature conferred upon him while man voluntarily regulates his own actions. In short, their doctrine is, that the world, the affairs of men, and men themselves, are governed by the power, but not by the decree of God. I say nothing of the Epicureans (a pest with which the world has always been plagued), who dream of an inert and idle God, and others, not a whit sounder, who of old feigned that God rules the upper regions of the air, but leaves the inferior to Fortune.[9] Against such evident madness even dumb creatures lift their voice. My intention now is, to refute an opinion which has very generally obtained—an opinion which, while it concedes to God some blind and equivocal movement, withholds what is of principal moment—viz. the disposing and directing of every thing to its proper end by incomprehensible wisdom. By withholding government, it makes God the ruler of the world in name only, not in reality. For what, I ask, is meant by government, if it be not to preside so as to regulate the desti-

8. Calvin disagrees with those who limit God's sovereign order by granting men a free will out from under God's providential decree.

9. Some teach that God exists, but he leaves the world up to chance. Thus, the whole world is supposed to be run by indeterminate chance.

ny of that over which you preside? I do not, however, totally repudiate what is said of an universal providence, provided, on the other hand, it is conceded to me that the world is governed by God, not only because he maintains the order of nature appointed by him, but because he takes a special charge of every one of his works. It is true, indeed, that each species of created objects is moved by a secret instinct of nature, as if they obeyed the eternal command of God, and spontaneously followed the course which God at first appointed. And to this we may refer our Savior's words, that he and his Father have always been at work from the beginning (John 5:17); also the words of Paul, that "in him we live, and move, and have our being," (Acts 17:28); also the words of the author of the Epistle to the Hebrews, who, when wishing to prove the divinity of Christ, says, that he upholds "all things by the word of his power," (Heb. 1:3). But some, under pretext of the general, hide and obscure the special providence, which is so surely and clearly taught in Scripture, that it is strange how any one can bring himself to doubt of it. And, indeed, those who interpose that disguise are themselves forced to modify their doctrine, by adding that many things are done by the special care of God. This, however, they erroneously confine to particular acts. The thing to be proved, therefore, is, that single events are so regulated by God, and all events so proceed from his determinate counsel, that nothing happens fortuitously.

Those who would cast obloquy on this doctrine, calumniate it as the dogma of the Stoics concerning fate. The same charge was formerly brought against Augustine. We are unwilling to dispute about words; but we do not admit the term Fate, both because it is of the class which Paul teaches us to shun, as profane novelties (1 Tim. 6:20), and also because it is attempted, by means of an odious term, to fix a stigma on the truth of God. But the dogma itself is falsely and maliciously imputed to us. For we do not with the Stoics imagine a necessity consisting of a perpetual chain of causes, and a kind of involved series contained in nature, but we hold that God is

10. An excellent summary of what Calvin taught: God decrees all that He will do, and executes everything according to His decree.

11. Christians do not use the terms "Fortune" and "Chance." The Church Fathers, Basil of Caesarea (AD 330 - 379) and Augustine, both rejected these terms.

12. If God left anything up to chance, the whole world would be left up to chance. He would have no control over anything in this world.

the disposer and ruler of all things,—that from the remotest eternity, according to his own wisdom, he decreed what he was to do, and now by his power executes what he decreed.[10] Hence we maintain, that by his providence, not heaven and earth and inanimate creatures only, but also the counsels and wills of men are so governed as to move exactly in the course which he has destined. What, then, you will say, does nothing happen fortuitously, nothing contingently? I answer, it was a true saying of Basil the Great, that Fortune and Chance are heathen terms; the meaning of which ought not to occupy pious minds.[11] For if all success is blessing from God, and calamity and adversity are his curse, there is no place left in human affairs for fortune and chance. We ought also to be moved by the words of Augustine, "In my writings against the Academics," says he, "I regret having so often used the term Fortune; although I intended to denote by it not some goddess, but the fortuitous issue of events in external matters, whether good or evil. Hence, too, those words, Perhaps, Perchance, Fortuitously, which no religion forbids us to use, though everything must be referred to Divine Providence. Nor did I omit to observe this when I said, Although, perhaps, that which is vulgarly called Fortune, is also regulated by a hidden order, and what we call Chance is nothing else than that the reason and cause of which is secret. It is true, I so spoke, but I repent of having mentioned Fortune there as I did, when I see the very bad custom which men have of saying, not as they ought to do, 'So God pleased,' but, 'So Fortune pleased.'" In short, Augustine everywhere teaches, that if anything is left to fortune, the world moves at random.[12] And although he elsewhere declares that all things are carried on, partly by the free will of man, and partly by the Providence of God, he shortly after shows clearly enough that his meaning was, that men also are ruled by Providence, when he assumes it as a principle, that there cannot be a greater absurdity than to hold that anything is done without the ordination of God; because it would happen at random. For which reason, he also excludes the contingency which depends on human will, maintaining a little further on, in clearer terms, that no cause must be sought for but the will of God. When he uses the term permission, the meaning which he attaches to it will best appear from a single passage, where he proves that the will of God is the supreme and primary cause of all things, because nothing happens without his order or permission.[13] He certainly does not figure God sitting idly in a watch-tower, when he chooses to permit anything. The will which he represents as interposing is, if I may so express it, active (*actualis*), and but for this could not be regarded as a cause.

13. To use the term "God permitted this to happen," one must also affirm that He was the supreme cause in making it happen.

Book 1

Chapter 17

Use to be Made of the Doctrine of Providence

1. God's providential hand that works in all things will work with means, without means (without other secondary causes), and against means (miracles that defy scientific laws.)

Moreover, such is the proneness of the human mind to indulge in vain subtleties, that it becomes almost impossible for those who do not see the sound and proper use of this doctrine, to avoid entangling themselves in perplexing difficulties. It will, therefore, be proper here to advert to the end which Scripture has in view in teaching that all things are divinely ordained. And it is to be observed, first, that the Providence of God is to be considered with reference both to the past and the future; and, secondly, that in overruling all things, it works at one time with means, at another without means, and at another against means.[1] Lastly, the design of God is to show that He takes care of the whole human race, but is especially vigilant in governing the Church, which he favors with a closer inspection. Moreover, we must add, that although the paternal favor and beneficence, as well as the judicial severity of God, is often conspicuous in the whole course of his Providence, yet occasionally as the causes of events are concealed, the thought is apt to rise, that human affairs are whirled about by the blind impulse of Fortune, or our carnal nature inclines us to speak as if God were amusing himself by tossing men up and down like balls. It is true, indeed, that if with sedate and quiet minds we were disposed to learn, the issue would at length make it manifest, that the counsel of God was in accordance with the highest reason, that his purpose was either to train his people to patience, correct their depraved affections, tame their wantonness, inure them to self-denial, and arouse them from torpor; or, on the other hand, to cast down the proud, defeat the craftiness of the ungodly, and frustrate all their schemes. How much soever causes may escape our notice, we must feel assured that they are deposited with him, and accordingly exclaim with David, "Many, O Lord my God, are thy wonderful works which thou hast done, and thy thoughts which are to us-ward: if I would declare and speak of them, they are more than can be numbered," (Ps. 40:5). For while our adversities ought always to remind us of our sins, that the punishment may incline us to repentance, we see, moreover, how Christ declares there is something more in the secret counsel of his Father than to chastise every one as he deserves.[2] For he says of the man who was born blind, "Neither has this man sinned, nor his parents: but that the works of God should be made manifest in him," (John 9:3). Here, where calamity takes precedence even of birth, our carnal sense murmurs as if God were unmerciful in thus afflicting those who have not offended. But Christ declares that, provided we had eyes clear enough, we should perceive that in this spectacle the glory of his Father is brightly displayed. We must use modesty, not as it were compelling God to render an account, but so revering his hidden Judgments as to account his will the best of all reasons. When the sky is overcast with dense clouds, and a violent tempest arises, the darkness which is presented to our eye, and the thunder which strikes our ears, and stupefies all our senses with terror, make us imagine that every thing is thrown into confusion, though in the firmament itself all continues quiet and serene. In the same way, when the tumultuous aspect of human affairs unfits us for judging, we should still hold, that

2. We cannot know for sure all the reasons for calamity. There is more to calamity than our chastisement.

3. Even when hurricanes are raging down on the earth, the stratosphere is still calm and serene. This helps us to see that God is always in control and will bring all things to a good and proper end.

4. It is pride that demands to know God's purposes in all that He does.

5. Calvin now addresses the argument of the doctrine of God's absolute sovereignty — that this relieves us of responsibility to use precautions, or that this takes away moral responsibility for crime.

God, in the pure light of his justice and wisdom, keeps all these commotions in due subordination, and conducts them to their proper end.[3] And certainly in this matter many display monstrous infatuation, presuming to subject the works of God to their calculation, and discuss his secret counsels, as well as to pass a precipitate Judgment on things unknown, and that with greater license than on the doings of mortal men. What can be more preposterous than to show modesty toward our equals, and choose rather to suspend our Judgment than incur the blame of rashness, while we petulantly insult the hidden Judgments of God,[4] Judgments which it becomes us to look up to and revere.

The profane make such a bluster with their foolish puerilities, that they almost, according to the expression, confound heaven and earth. If the Lord has marked the moment of our death, it cannot be escaped,—it is vain to toil and use precaution.[5] Therefore, when one ventures not to travel on a road which he hears is infested by robbers; when another calls in the physician, and annoys himself with drugs, for the sake of his health; a third abstains from coarser food, that he may not injure a sickly constitution; and a fourth fears to dwell in a ruinous house; when all, in short, devise, and, with great eagerness of mind, strike out paths by which they may attain the objects of their desire; either these are all vain remedies, laid hold of to correct the will of God, or his certain decree does not fix the limits of life and death, health and sickness, peace and war, and other matters which men, according as they desire and hate, study by their own industry to secure or avoid. Nay, these trifles even infer, that the prayers of the faithful must be perverse, not to say superfluous, since they entreat the Lord to make a provision for things which he has decreed from eternity. And then, imputing whatever happens to the providence of God, they connive at the man who is known to have expressly designed it. Has an assassin slain an honest citizen? He has, say they, executed the counsel of God. Has some one committed theft or adultery? The deed having been provided and ordained by the Lord, he is the minister of his providence. Has a son waited with indifference for the death of his parent, without trying any remedy? He could not oppose God, who had so predetermined from eternity. Thus all crimes receive the name of virtues, as being in accordance with divine ordination.

As regards future events, Solomon easily reconciles human deliberation with divine providence. For while he derides the stupidity of those who presume to undertake anything without God, as if they were not ruled by his hand, he elsewhere thus expresses himself: "A man's heart deviseth his ways but the Lord directeth his steps," (Prov. 16:9); intimating, that the eternal decrees of God by no means prevent us from proceeding, under his will, to provide for ourselves, and arrange all our affairs. And the reason for this is clear. For he who has fixed the boundaries of our life, has at the same time entrusted us with the care of it, provided us with the means of preserving it, forewarned us of the dangers to which we are exposed, and supplied cautions and remedies, that we may not be overwhelmed unawares. Now, our duty is clear, namely, since the Lord has committed to us the defense of our life,[6]—to defend it; since he offers assistance,—to use it; since he forewarns us of danger,—not to rush on heedless; since he supplies remedies,—not to neglect them. But it is said, a danger that is not fatal will not hurt us, and one that is fatal cannot be resisted by any precaution. But what if dangers are not fatal, merely because the Lord has furnished you with the means of warding them off, and surmounting them? See how far your reasoning accords with the order of divine procedure: You infer that danger is not to be guarded against, because, if it is not fatal, you shall escape without precaution; whereas the Lord enjoins you to guard against it just because he wills it not to be fatal. These insane cavilers overlook what is plainly before their eyes—viz. that the Lord has furnished men with the artful of deliberation and caution, that they may employ them in subservience to his providence, in the pres-

6. While God is sovereign over what happens, we are still morally responsible to God to take care of our own lives — to obey His revealed will.

ervation of their life; while, on the contrary, by neglect and sloth, they bring upon themselves the evils which he has annexed to them. How comes it that a provident man, while he consults for his safety, disentangles himself from impending evils; while a foolish man, through unadvised temerity, perishes, unless it be that prudence and folly are, in either case, instruments of divine dispensation? God has been pleased to conceal from us all future events that we may prepare for them as doubtful, and cease not to apply the provided remedies until they have either been overcome, or have proved too much for all our care. Hence, I formerly observed, that the Providence of God does not interpose simply; but, by employing means, assumes, as it were, a visible form.[7]

At the same time, the Christian will not overlook inferior causes. For, while he regards those by whom he is benefited as ministers of the divine goodness, he will not, therefore, pass them by, as if their kindness deserved no gratitude, but feeling sincerely obliged to them, will willingly confess the obligation, and endeavor, according to his ability, to return it. In fine, in the blessings which he receives, he will revere and extol God as the principal author, but will also honor men as his ministers, and perceive, as is the truth, that by the will of God he is under obligation to those, by whose hand God has been pleased to show him kindness.[8] If he sustains any loss through negligence or imprudence, he will, indeed, believe that it was the Lord's will it should so be, but, at the same time, he will impute it to himself. If one for whom it was his duty to care, but whom he has treated with neglect, is carried off by disease, although aware that the person had reached a limit beyond which it was impossible to pass, he will not, therefore, extenuate his fault, but, as he had neglected to do his duty faithfully towards him, will feel as if he had perished by his guilty negligence.[9] Far less where, in the case of theft or murder, fraud and preconceived malice have existed, will he palliate it under the pretext of Divine Providence, but in the same crime will distinctly recognize the justice of God, and

7. God uses means to preserve life — warnings, men walking wisely, and remedies — as all part of His overarching plan.

8. We should be thankful for the means of God's goodness, the men who minister to us, as well as for the hand of God which is behind all good we receive.

9. If someone dies under our care, and we see that we neglected to help them, we must realize our own fault. At the same time, we also see that God's hand is ultimately in all these things.

the iniquity of man, as each is separately manifested. But in future events, especially, will he take account of such inferior causes. If he is not left destitute of human aid, which he can employ for his safety, he will set it down as a divine blessing; but he will not, therefore, be remiss in taking measures, or slow in employing the help of those whom he sees possessed of the means of assisting him. Regarding all the aids which the creatures can lend him, as hands offered him by the Lord, he will avail himself of them as the legitimate instruments of Divine Providence. And as he is uncertain what the result of any business in which he engages is to be (save that he knows, that in all things the Lord will provide for his good), he will zealously aim at what he deems for the best, so far as his abilities enable him. In adopting his measures, he will not be carried away by his own impressions, but will commit and resign himself to the wisdom of God, that under his guidance he may be led into the right path. However, his confidence in external aid will not be such that the presence of it will make him feel secure, the absence of it fill him with dismay, as if he were destitute. His mind will always be fixed on the Providence of God alone, and no consideration of present circumstances will be allowed to withdraw him from the steady contemplation of it. Thus Joab, while he acknowledges that the issue of the battle is entirely in the hand of God, does not therefore become inactive, but strenuously proceeds with what belongs to his proper calling, "Be of good courage," says he, "and let us play the men for our people, and for the cities of our God; and the Lord do that which seemeth him good," (2 Sam. 10:12).[10] The same conviction keeping us free from rashness and false confidence, will stimulate us to constant prayer, while at the same time filling our minds with good hope, it will enable us to feel secure, and bid defiance to all the dangers by which we are surrounded.

Here we are forcibly reminded of the inestimable felicity of a pious mind. Innumerable are the ills which beset human life, and present death in as many different forms. Not to go

10. Joab combines a belief in human responsibility with a confidence in Divine Providence.

beyond ourselves, since the body is a receptacle, nay the nurse, of a thousand diseases, a man cannot move without carrying along with him many forms of destruction. His life is in a manner interwoven with death. For what else can be said where heat and cold bring equal danger? Then, in what direction soever you turn, all surrounding objects not only may do harm, but almost openly threaten and seem to present immediate death. Go on board a ship, you are but a plank's breadth from death. Mount a horse, the stumbling of a foot endangers your life. Walk along the streets, every tile upon the roofs is a source of danger. If a sharp instrument is in your own hand, or that of a friend, the possible harm is manifest. All the savage beasts you see are so many beings armed for your destruction. Even within a high walled garden, where everything ministers to delight, a serpent will sometimes lurk. Your house, constantly exposed to fire, threatens you with poverty by day, with destruction by night. Your fields, subject to hail, mildew, drought, and other injuries, denounce barrenness, and thereby famine. I say nothing of poison, treachery, robbery, some of which beset us at home, others follow us abroad. Amid these perils, must not man be very miserable, as one who, more dead than alive, with difficulty draws an anxious and feeble breath, just as if a drawn sword were constantly suspended over his neck?[11] It may be said that these things happen seldom, at least not always, or to all, certainly never all at once. I admit it; but since we are reminded by the example of others, that they may also happen to us, and that our life is not an exception any more than theirs, it is impossible not to fear and dread as if they were to befall us. What can you imagine more grievous than such trepidation? Add that there is something like an insult to God when it is said, that man, the noblest of the creatures, stands exposed to every blind and random stroke of fortune. Here, however, we were only referring to the misery which man should feel, were he placed under the dominion of chance.

11. How can we possibly control all of the diseases, economic currents, criminals, and other risks to life in this word?

But when once the light of Divine Providence has illumined the believer's soul, he is relieved and set free, not only from the extreme fear and anxiety which formerly oppressed him, but from all care.[12] For as he justly shudders at the idea of chance, so he can confidently commit himself to God. This, I say, is his comfort, that his heavenly Father so embraces all things under his power—so governs them at will by his nod—so regulates them by his wisdom, that nothing takes place save according to his appointment; that received into his favor, and entrusted to the care of his angels neither fire, nor water, nor sword, can do him harm, except in so far as God their master is pleased to permit. For thus sings the Psalm, "Surely he shall deliver thee from the snare of the fowler, and from the noisome pestilence. He shall cover thee with his feathers, and under his wings shalt thou trust; his truth shall be thy shield and buckler. Thou shalt not be afraid for the terror by night; nor for the arrow that flieth by day; nor for the pestilence that walketh in darkness; nor for the destruction that wasteth at noonday" (Ps. 91:2-6). Hence the exulting confidence of the saints, "The Lord is on my side; I will not fear: what can man do unto me? The Lord taketh my part with them that help me." "Though an host should encamp against me, my heart shall not fear." "Yea, though I walk through the valley of the shadow of death, I will fear no evil." (Ps. 118:6; 27:3; 23:4).

How comes it, I ask, that their confidence never fails, but just that while the world apparently revolves at random, they know that God is every where at work, and feel assured that his work will be their safety? When assailed by the devil and wicked men, were they not confirmed by remembering and meditating on Providence, they should, of necessity, forthwith despond. But when they call to mind that the devil, and the whole train of the ungodly, are, in all directions, held in by the hand of God as with a bridle, so that they can neither conceive any mischief, nor plan what they have conceived, nor how much soever they may have planned, move a single finger to perpetrate, unless in so far as he permits, nay, unless in so far

12. The doctrine of God's providence relieves us of all anxiety over all the bad things that could happen to us.

as he commands; that they are not only bound by his fetters, but are even forced to do him service,—when the godly think of all these things they have ample sources of consolation.

Book 2

Chapter 1

Through the Fall and Revolt of Adam, the Whole Human Race Made Accursed and Degenerate. Of Original Sin

It was not without reason that the ancient proverb so strongly recommended to man the knowledge of himself. For if it is deemed disgraceful to be ignorant of things pertaining to the business of life, much more disgraceful is self-ignorance, in consequence of which we miserably deceive ourselves in matters of the highest moment, and so walk blindfold. But the more useful the precept is, the more careful we must be not to use it preposterously, as we see certain philosophers have done. For they, when exhorting man to know himself, state the motive to be, that he may not be ignorant of his own excellence and dignity. They wish him to see nothing in himself but what will fill him with vain confidence, and inflate him with pride.[1] But self-knowledge consists in this, first. When reflecting on what God gave us at our creation, and still continues graciously to give, we perceive how great the excellence of our nature would have been had its integrity remained, and, at the same time, remember that we have nothing of our own, but depend entirely on God, from whom we hold at pleasure whatever he has seen it meet to bestow;[2] secondly, When viewing our miserable condition since Ad-

1. Worldly philosophers are primarily interested in self-knowledge for pride's sake.

2. All good with which man was endued at creation was God's gift.

am's fall, all confidence and boasting are overthrown, we blush for shame, and feel truly humble. For as God at first formed us in his own image, that he might elevate our minds to the pursuit of virtue, and the contemplation of eternal life, so to prevent us from heartlessly burying those noble qualities which distinguish us from the lower animals, it is of importance to know that we were endued with reason and intelligence, in order that we might cultivate a holy and honorable life, and regard a blessed immortality as our destined aim. At the same time, it is impossible to think of our primeval dignity without being immediately reminded of the sad spectacle of our ignominy and corruption, ever since we fell from our original in the person of our first parent.[3] In this way, we feel dissatisfied with ourselves, and become truly humble, while we are inflamed with new desires to seek after God, in whom each may regain those good qualities of which all are found to be utterly destitute.

3. We are humbled to realize the great depth to which we fell from our original state.

In examining ourselves, the search which divine truth enjoins, and the knowledge which it demands, are such as may indispose us to every thing like confidence in our own powers, leave us devoid of all means of boasting, and so incline us to submission.[4] This is the course which we must follow, if we would attain to the true goal, both in speculation and practice. I am not unaware how much more plausible the view is, which invites us rather to ponder on our good qualities, than to contemplate what must overwhelm us with shame—our miserable destitution and ignominy. There is nothing more acceptable to the human mind than flattery, and, accordingly, when told that its endowments are of a high order, it is apt to be excessively credulous. Hence it is not strange that the greater part of mankind have erred so egregiously in this matter. Owing to the innate self-love by which all are blinded, we most willingly persuade ourselves that we do not possess a single quality which is deserving of hatred; and hence, independent of any countenance from without, general credit is given to the very foolish idea, that man is perfectly sufficient

4. True knowledge of self should leave us humbled and strongly aware of our shame and helpless condition.

of himself for all the purposes of a good and happy life.[5] If any are disposed to think more modestly, and concede somewhat to God, that they may not seem to arrogate every thing as their own, still, in making the division, they apportion matters so, that the chief ground of confidence and boasting always remains with themselves. Then, if a discourse is pronounced which flatters the pride spontaneously springing up in man's inmost heart, nothing seems more delightful. Accordingly, in every age, he who is most forward in extolling the excellence of human nature, is received with the loudest applause. But be this heralding of human excellence what it may, by teaching man to rest in himself, it does nothing more than fascinate by its sweetness, and, at the same time, so delude as to drown in perdition all who assent to it.[6] For what avails it to proceed in vain confidence, to deliberate, resolve, plan, and attempt what we deem pertinent to the purpose, and, at the very outset, prove deficient and destitute both of sound intelligence and true virtue, though we still confidently persist till we rush headlong on destruction? But this is the best that can happen to those who put confidence in their own powers. Whosoever, therefore, gives heed to those teachers, who merely employ us in contemplating our good qualities, so far from making progress in self-knowledge, will be plunged into the most pernicious ignorance.

While revealed truth concurs with the general consent of mankind in teaching that the second part of wisdom consists in self-knowledge, they differ greatly as to the method by which this knowledge is to be acquired. In the judgment of the flesh man deems his self-knowledge complete, when, with overweening confidence in his own intelligence and integrity, he takes courage, and spurs himself on to virtuous deeds, and when, declaring war upon vice, he uses his utmost endeavor to attain to the honorable and the fair. But he who tries himself by the standard of divine justice, finds nothing to inspire him with confidence; and hence, the more thorough his self-examination, the greater his despondency. Abandoning all depen-

5. Natural man is especially blinded to his depraved nature (blinded by self-love).

6. This self-confidence and faith in himself seals his condemnation.

dence on himself, he feels that he is utterly incapable of duly regulating his conduct. It is not the will of God, however, that we should forget the primeval dignity which he bestowed on our first parents—a dignity which may well stimulate us to the pursuit of goodness and justice. It is impossible for us to think of our first original, or the end for which we were created, without being urged to meditate on immortality, and to seek the kingdom of God. But such meditation, so far from raising our spirits, rather casts them down, and makes us humble. For what is our original? One from which we have fallen. What the end of our creation? One from which we have altogether strayed, so that, weary of our miserable lot, we groan, and groaning sigh for a dignity now lost. When we say that man should see nothing in himself which can raise his spirits, our meaning is, that he possesses nothing on which he can proudly plume himself. Hence, in considering the knowledge which man ought to have of himself, it seems proper to divide it thus, first, to consider the end for which he was created, and the qualities—by no means contemptible qualities—with which he was endued, thus urging him to meditate on divine worship and the future life; and, secondly, to consider his faculties, or rather want of faculties—a want which, when perceived, will annihilate all his confidence, and cover him with confusion. The tendency of the former view is to teach him what his duty is, of the latter, to make him aware how far he is able to perform it. We shall treat of both in their proper order.

We thus see that the impurity of parents is transmitted to their children, so that all, without exception, are originally depraved. The commencement of this depravity will not be found until we ascend to the first parent of all as the fountain head. We must, therefore, hold it for certain, that, in regard to human nature, Adam was not merely a progenitor, but, as it were, a root, and that, accordingly, by his corruption, the whole human race was deservedly vitiated. This is plain from the contrast which the Apostle draws between Adam and Christ, "Wherefore, as by one man sin entered into the world, and death by sin; and so death passed upon all men, for that all have sinned; even so might grace reign through righteousness unto eternal life by Jesus Christ our Lord," (Rom. 5:19–21). To what quibble will the Pelagians here recur?[7] That the sin of Adam was propagated by imitation! Is the righteousness of Christ then available to us only in so far as it is an example held forth for our imitation? Can any man tolerate such blasphemy? But if, out of all controversy, the righteousness of Christ, and thereby life, is ours by communication, it follows that both of these were lost in Adam that they might be recovered in Christ, whereas sin and death were brought in by Adam, that they might be abolished in Christ.[8] There is no obscurity in the words, "As by one man's disobedience many were made sinners, so by the obedience of one shall many be made righteous." Accordingly, the relation subsisting between the two is this: as Adam, by his ruin, involved and ruined us, so Christ, by his grace, restored us to salvation. In this clear light of truth I cannot see any need of a longer or more laborious proof. Thus, too, in the First Epistle to the Corinthians, when Paul would confirm believers in the confident hope of the resurrection, he shows that the life is recovered in Christ which was lost in Adam (1 Cor. 15:22). Having already declared that all died in Adam, he now also openly testifies, that all are imbued with the taint of sin. Condemnation, indeed, could not reach those who are altogether free from blame. But his meaning cannot be made clearer than from the other member of the sentence, in which he shows that the hope of life is restored in Christ. Every one knows that the only mode in which this is done is, when by a wondrous communication Christ transfuses into us the power of his own righteousness, as it is elsewhere said, "The Spirit is life because of righteousness," (1 Cor. 15:22). Therefore, the only explanation which can be given of the expression, "in Adam all died," is, that he by sinning not only brought disaster and ruin upon himself, but also plunged our nature into like destruction; and that not only in one fault, in a matter not pertaining to us, but by the corruption into which

7. The British monk Pelagius, who lived at the time of Augustine, rejected the doctrine of original sin.

8. Romans 5 clearly teaches that Adam's sin is imputed to all men, even as Christ's righteousness is imputed to those who are reborn in Him.

9. Adam's sin resulted in the corruption of the nature of all persons descending from him.

he himself fell, he infected his whole seed.[9] Paul never could have said that all are "by nature the children of wrath," (Eph. 2:3), if they had not been cursed from the womb. And it is obvious that the nature there referred to is not nature such as God created, but as vitiated in Adam; for it would have been most incongruous to make God the author of death. Adam, therefore, when he corrupted himself, transmitted the contagion to all his posterity. For a heavenly Judge, even our Savior himself, declares that all are by birth vicious and depraved, when he says that "that which is born of the flesh is fleshy" (John 3:6), and that therefore the gate of life is closed against all until they have been regenerated.

But lest the thing itself of which we speak be unknown or doubtful, it will be proper to define original sin. I have no intention, however, to discuss all the definitions which different writers have adopted, but only to adduce the one which seems to me most accordant with truth. Original sin, then, may be defined a hereditary corruption and depravity of our nature, extending to all the parts of the soul, which first makes us obnoxious to the wrath of God, and then produces in us works which in Scripture are termed works of the flesh. This corruption is repeatedly designated by Paul by the term sin (Gal. 5:19);[10] while the works which proceed from it, such as adultery, fornication, theft, hatred, murder, reveling, he terms, in the same way, the fruits of sin, though in various passages of Scripture, and even by Paul himself, they are also termed sins. The two things, therefore, are to be distinctly observed—viz. that being thus perverted and corrupted in all the parts of our nature, we are, merely on account of such corruption, deservedly condemned by God, to whom nothing is acceptable but righteousness, innocence, and purity. This is not liability for another's fault. For when it is said, that the sin of Adam has made us obnoxious to the justice of God, the meaning is not, that we, who are in ourselves innocent and blameless, are bearing his guilt, but that since by his transgression we are all placed under the curse, he is said to have brought us under

10. Adam's sin left all mankind corrupt and depraved in all parts of the soul.

obligation. Through him, however, not only has punishment been derived, but pollution instilled, for which punishment is justly due.[11] Hence Augustine, though he often terms it another's sin (that he may more clearly show how it comes to us by descent), at the same time asserts that it is each individual's own sin. And the Apostle most distinctly testifies, that "death passed upon all men, for that all have sinned," (Rom. 5:12); that is, are involved in original sin, and polluted by its stain.[12] Hence, even infants bringing their condemnation with them from their mother's womb, suffer not for another's, but for their own defect. For although they have not yet produced the fruits of their own unrighteousness, they have the seed implanted in them. Nay, their whole nature is, as it were, a seedbed of sin, and therefore cannot but be odious and abominable to God.[13] Hence it follows, that it is properly deemed sinful in the sight of God; for there could be no condemnation without guilt. Next comes the other point—viz. that this perversity in us never ceases, but constantly produces new fruits, in other words, those works of the flesh which we formerly described; just as a lighted furnace sends forth sparks and flames, or a fountain without ceasing pours out water. Hence, those who have defined original sin as the want of the original righteousness which we ought to have had, though they substantially comprehend the whole case, do not significantly enough express its power and energy. For our nature is not only utterly devoid of goodness, but so prolific in all kinds of evil, that it can never be idle. Those who term it concupiscence use a word not very inappropriate, provided it were added (this, however, many will by no means concede), that everything which is in man, from the intellect to the will, from the soul even to the flesh, is defiled and pervaded with this concupiscence; or, to express it more briefly, that the whole man is in himself nothing else than concupiscence.

11. We inherit both the guilt and the corruption of Adam's sin.

12. Somehow we were all "involved" in Adam's original sin.

13. Even infants are odious and abominable to God, a seed bed of sin, at birth.

Book 2

Chapter 2

Man Now Deprived of Freedom of Will, and Miserably Enslaved

I feel pleased with the well-known saying which has been borrowed from the writings of Augustine, that man's natural gifts were corrupted by sin, and his supernatural gifts withdrawn; meaning by supernatural gifts the light of faith and righteousness, which would have been sufficient for the attainment of heavenly life and everlasting felicity. Man, when he withdrew his allegiance to God, was deprived of the spiritual gifts by which he had been raised to the hope of eternal salvation. Hence it follows, that he is now an exile from the kingdom of God, so that all things which pertain to the blessed life of the soul are extinguished in him until he recover them by the grace of regeneration. Among these are faith, love to God, charity towards our neighbor, the study of righteousness and holiness. All these, when restored to us by Christ, are to be regarded as adventitious and above nature. If so, we infer that they were previously abolished. On the other hand, soundness of mind and integrity of heart were, at the same time, withdrawn, and it is this which constitutes the corruption of natural gifts.[1] For although there is still some residue of intelligence and judgment as well as will, we cannot call a mind sound and

1. Calvin distinguishes natural gifts of intelligence and will from supernatural gifts of faith, love of God, righteousness, and holiness.

entire which is both weak and immersed in darkness. As to the will, its depravity is but too well known. Therefore, since reason, by which man discerns between good and evil, and by which he understands and judges, is a natural gift, it could not be entirely destroyed; but being partly weakened and partly corrupted, a shapeless ruin is all that remains.[2] In this sense it is said (John 1:5), that "the light shineth in darkness, and the darkness comprehended it not;" these words clearly expressing both points—viz. that in the perverted and degenerate nature of man there are still some sparks which show that he is a rational animal, and differs from the brutes, inasmuch as he is endued with intelligence, and yet, that this light is so smothered by clouds of darkness that it cannot shine forth to any good effect. In like manner, the will, because inseparable from the nature of man, did not perish, but was so enslaved by depraved lusts as to be incapable of one righteous desire. The definition now given is complete, but there are several points which require to be explained. Therefore, proceeding agreeably to that primary distinction, by which we divided the soul into intellect and will, we will now inquire into the power of the intellect: To charge the intellect with perpetual blindness, so as to leave it no intelligence of any description whatever, is repugnant not only to the Word of God, but to common experience. We see that there has been implanted in the human mind a certain desire of investigating truth, to which it never would aspire unless some relish for truth antecedently existed. There is, therefore, now, in the human mind, discernment to this extent, that it is naturally influenced by the love of truth, the neglect of which in the lower animals is a proof of their gross and irrational nature.[3] Still it is true that this love of truth fails before it reaches the goal, forthwith falling away into vanity. As the human mind is unable, from dullness, to pursue the right path of investigation, and, after various wanderings, stumbling every now and then like one groping in darkness, at length gets completely bewildered, so its whole procedure proves how unfit it is to search the truth and find

2. All supernatural gifts were withdrawn, but man's mind was only "partly corrupted," per Calvin.

3. Calvin claims that the fallen mind still has some love of truth, which turns out to be a love-hate tension.

4. Humans are always seeking distractions and diversions from true knowledge.

5. Humanist, unbelieving philosophers will glance only briefly at the nature of God, but it is a fleeting knowledge quickly suppressed and mixed with lies.

it. Then it labors under another grievous defect, in that it frequently fails to discern what the knowledge is which it should study to acquire. Hence, under the influence of a vain curiosity, it torments itself with superfluous and useless discussions, either not adverting at all to the things necessary to be known, or casting only a cursory and contemptuous glance at them. At all events, it scarcely ever studies them in sober earnest.[4] Profane writers are constantly complaining of this perverse procedure, and yet almost all of them are found pursuing it. Hence Solomon, throughout the Book of Ecclesiastes, after enumerating all the studies in which men think they attain the highest wisdom, pronounces them vain and frivolous.

We must now explain what the power of human reason is, in regard to the kingdom of God, and spiritual discernments which consists chiefly of three things—the knowledge of God, the knowledge of his paternal favor towards us, which constitutes our salvation, and the method of regulating of our conduct in accordance with the Divine Law. With regard to the former two, but more properly the second, men otherwise the most ingenious are blinder than moles. I deny not, indeed, that in the writings of philosophers we meet occasionally with shrewd and apposite remarks on the nature of God, though they invariably savor somewhat of giddy imagination.[5] As observed above, the Lord has bestowed on them some slight perception of his Godhead that they might not plead ignorance as an excuse for their impiety, and has, at times, instigated them to deliver some truths, the confession of which should be their own condemnation. Still, though seeing, they saw not. Their discernment was not such as to direct them to the truth, far less to enable them to attain it, but resembled that of the bewildered traveler, who sees the flash of lightning glance far and wide for a moment, and then vanish into the darkness of the night, before he can advance a single step. So far is such assistance from enabling him to find the right path. Besides, how many monstrous falsehoods intermingle with those minute particles of truth scattered up and down in their writings as if by chance. In short, not one of them even made the least approach to that assurance of the divine favor, without which the mind of man must ever remain a mere chaos of confusion.[6] To the great truths, What God is in himself, and what he is in relation to us, human reason makes not the least approach.

6. The mind of the philosopher is a chaos of confusion. As pertaining to fundamental truths, the mind of man cannot begin to know.

Book 2
Chapter 3

Every Thing Proceeding from the Corrupt Nature of Man Damnable

1. Somehow natural man will devote himself to pursuing moral virtue.

2. Calvin says that God's grace provides an internal restraint to prevent men from fully expressing the evil nature within them in outward action.

Here, again we are met with a question very much the same as that which was previously solved. In every age there have been some who, under the guidance of nature, were all their lives devoted to virtue.[1] It is of no consequence, that many blots may be detected in their conduct; by the mere study of virtue, they evinced that there was somewhat of purity in their nature. The value which virtues of this kind have in the sight of God will be considered more fully when we treat of the merit of works. Meanwhile however, it will be proper to consider it in this place also, in so far as necessary for the exposition of the subject in hand. Such examples, then, seem to warn us against supposing that the nature of man is utterly vicious, since, under its guidance, some have not only excelled in illustrious deeds, but conducted themselves most honorably through the whole course of their lives. But we ought to consider, that, notwithstanding of the corruption of our nature, there is some room for divine grace, such grace as, without purifying it, may lay it under internal restraint.[2] For, did the Lord let every mind loose to wanton in its lusts, doubtless there is not a man who would not show that his nature is capable of all the crimes with which Paul charges it (Rom. 3 compared with Ps. 14:3). What? Can you exempt yourself from the number of those whose feet are swift to shed blood; whose hands are foul with rapine and murder; whose throats are like open sepulchers; whose tongues are deceitful; whose lips are venomous; whose actions are useless, unjust, rotten, deadly; whose soul is without God; whose inward parts are full of wickedness; whose eyes are on the watch for deception; whose minds are prepared for insult; whose every part, in short, is framed for endless deeds of wickedness? If every soul is capable of such abominations (and the Apostle declares this boldly), it is surely easy to see what the result would be, if the Lord were to permit human passion to follow its bent. No ravenous beast would rush so furiously, no stream, however rapid and violent, so impetuously burst its banks. In the elect, God cures these diseases in the mode which will shortly be explained; in others, he only lays them under such restraint as may prevent them from breaking forth to a degree incompatible with the preservation of the established order of things. Hence, how much soever men may disguise their impurity, some are restrained only by shame, others by a fear of the laws, from breaking out into many kinds of wickedness.[3] Some aspire to an honest life, as deeming it most conducive to their interest, while others are raised above the vulgar lot, that, by the dignity of their station, they may keep inferiors to their duty. Thus God, by his providence, curbs the perverseness of nature, preventing it from breaking forth into action, yet without rendering it inwardly pure.[4]

The objection, however, is not yet solved. For we must either put Cataline on the same footing with Camillus,[5] or hold Camillus to be an example that nature, when carefully cultivated, is not wholly void of goodness. I admit that the specious qualities which Camillus possessed were divine gifts, and appear entitled to commendation when viewed in themselves. But in what way will they be proofs of a virtuous nature? Must we not go back to the mind, and from it begin to reason thus?

3. These restraints include social shame and governmental laws.

4. The heart of the natural man is still essentially impure.

5. Cataline of the Roman Republic, (102-62 BC) is known for murdering his kin and conspiring to overthrow the government. Calvin contrasts him with the more noble Camillus (445 - 365 BC). He was known for his virtue, courage, etc. as one of the first generals of the Roman army.

If a natural man possesses such integrity of manners, nature is not without the faculty of studying virtue. But what if his mind was depraved and perverted, and followed anything rather than rectitude? Such it undoubtedly was, if you grant that he was only a natural man. How then will you laud the power of human nature for good, if, even where there is the highest semblance of integrity, a corrupt bias is always detected? Therefore, as you would not commend a man for virtue whose vices impose upon you by a show of virtue, so you will not attribute a power of choosing rectitude to the human will while rooted in depravity. Still, the surest and easiest answer to the objection is, that those are not common endowments of nature, but special gifts of God, which he distributes in divers forms, and, in a definite measure, to men otherwise profane. For which reason, we hesitate not, in common language, to say, that one is of a good, another of a vicious nature; though we cease not to hold that both are placed under the universal condition of human depravity. All we mean is that God has conferred on the one a special grace which he has not seen it meet to confer on the other.[6] When he was pleased to set Saul over the kingdom, he made him as it were a new man. This is the thing meant by Plato, when, alluding to a passage in the Iliad, he says, that the children of kings are distinguished at their birth by some special qualities—God, in kindness to the human race, often giving a spirit of heroism to those whom he destines for empire. In this way, the great leaders celebrated in history were formed. The same judgment must be given in the case of private individuals. But as those endued with the greatest talents were always impelled by the greatest ambitions (a stain which defiles all virtues and makes them lose all favor in the sight of God), so we cannot set any value on anything that seems praiseworthy in ungodly men.[7] We may add, that the principal part of rectitude is wanting, when there is no zeal for the glory of God, and there is no such zeal in those whom he has not regenerated by his Spirit. Nor is it without good cause said in Isaiah, that on Christ should rest "the spirit of

6. Camillus, though still subject to a depraved nature, must have received a special grace from God.

7. Natural man always taints his strong points with pride and ungodly ambition.

knowledge, and of the fear of the Lord," (Isa. 11:2); for by this we are taught that all who are strangers to Christ are destitute of that fear of God which is the beginning of wisdom (Ps. 111:10).[8] The virtues which deceive us by an empty show may have their praise in civil society and the common intercourse of life, but before the judgment-seat of God they will be of no value to establish a claim of righteousness.

When the will is enchained as the slave of sin, it cannot make a movement towards goodness, far less steadily pursue it.[9] Every such movement is the first step in that conversion to God, which in Scripture is entirely ascribed to divine grace. Thus Jeremiah prays, "Turn thou me, and I shall be turned," (Jer. 31:18). Hence, too, in the same chapter, describing the spiritual redemption of believers, the Prophet says, "The Lord has redeemed Jacob, and ransomed him from the hand of him that was stronger than he," (Jer. 31:11); intimating how close the fetters are with which the sinner is bound, so long as he is abandoned by the Lord, and acts under the yoke of the devil. Nevertheless, there remains a will which both inclines and hastens on with the strongest affection towards sin; man, when placed under this bondage, being deprived not of will, but of soundness of will.[10] Bernard says[11] not improperly, that all of us have a will; but to will well is proficiency, to will ill is defect. Thus simply to will is the part of man, to will ill the part of corrupt nature, to will well the part of grace. Moreover, when I say that the will, deprived of liberty, is led or dragged by necessity to evil, it is strange that any should deem the expression harsh, seeing there is no absurdity in it, and it is not at variance with pious use. It does, however, offend those who know not how to distinguish between necessity and compulsion.[12] Were any one to ask them, "Is not God necessarily good, is not the devil necessarily wicked," what answer would they give? The goodness of God is so connected with his Godhead, that it is not more necessary to be God than to be good; whereas the devil, by his fall, was so estranged from goodness, that he can do nothing but evil. Should any one give utterance to the

8. The greatest and most virtuous unbelievers still lack fear of God and a zeal for the glory of God.

9. Calvin's basic description of natural man: as a slave of sin, he cannot make a movement towards goodness.

10. The natural will tends always towards sin.

11. Reference to Bernard of Clairvaux (1090-1153)

12. Calvin draws a distinction between a will that draws to evil by necessity (of its corrupted nature), and that which would be compelled to do something against its wishes. To say that "God has to be good," does not mean that He is compelled by some outside force to be good.

13. Celestius was the primary disciple of Pelagius.

14. Quotations from Bernard's sermon "Super Cantica, #81."

15. Thus, man is bound by his own sinful nature, but acts freely in that he is not forced or compelled to sin.

profane jeer, that little praise is due to God for a goodness to which he is forced, is it not obvious to every man to reply, "It is owing not to violent impulse, but to his boundless goodness, that he cannot do evil?" Therefore, if the free will of God in doing good is not impeded, because he necessarily must do good; if the devil, who can do nothing but evil, nevertheless sins voluntarily; can it be said that man sins less voluntarily because he is under a necessity of sinning? This necessity is uniformly proclaimed by Augustine, who, even when pressed by the invidious cavil of Celestius,[13] hesitated not to assert it in the following terms: "Man through liberty became a sinner, but corruption, ensuing as the penalty, has converted liberty into necessity." Whenever mention is made of the subject, he hesitates not to speak in this way of the necessary bondage of sin. Let this, then, be regarded as the sum of the distinction. Man, since he was corrupted by the fall, sins not forced or unwilling, but voluntarily, by a most forward bias of the mind; not by violent compulsion, or external force, but by the movement of his own passion; and yet such is the depravity of his nature, that he cannot move and act except in the direction of evil. If this is true, the thing not obscurely expressed is, that he is under a necessity of sinning. Bernard, assenting to Augustine, thus writes: "Among animals, man alone is free, and yet sin intervening, he suffers a kind of violence, but a violence proceeding from his will, not from nature, so that it does not even deprive him of innate liberty."[14] For that which is voluntary is also free.[15] A little after he adds, "Thus, by some means strange and wicked, the will itself, being deteriorated by sin, makes a necessity; but so that the necessity, in as much as it is voluntary, cannot excuse the will, and the will, in as much as it is enticed, cannot exclude the necessity." For this necessity is in a manner voluntary. He afterwards says that "we are under a yoke, but no other yoke than that of voluntary servitude; therefore, in respect of servitude, we are miserable, and in respect of will, inexcusable; because the will, when it was free, made itself the slave of sin." At length he concludes,

"Thus the soul, in some strange and evil way, is held under this kind of voluntary, yet sadly free necessity, both bond and free; bond in respect of necessity, free in respect of will: and what is still more strange, and still more miserable, it is guilty because free, and enslaved because guilty, and therefore enslaved because free." My readers hence perceive that the doctrine which I deliver is not new, but the doctrine which of old Augustine delivered with the consent of all the godly, and which was afterwards shut up in the cloisters of monks for almost a thousand years. Lombard, by not knowing how to distinguish between necessity and compulsion, gave occasion to a pernicious error.[16]

16. Calvin points out that he is only advocating Augustine's theology, which was shut up for 1,000 years (likely from AD 500 to AD 1500) He blames the scholastics like Peter Lombard (1096-1160) for shutting up Augustine's theology.

On the other hand, it may be proper to consider what the remedy is which divine grace provides for the correction and cure of natural corruption. Since the Lord, in bringing assistance, supplies us with what is lacking, the nature of that assistance will immediately make manifest its converse—viz. our penury. When the Apostle says to the Philippians, "Being confident of this very thing, that he which has begun a good work in you, will perform it until the day of Jesus Christ," (Phil. 1:6), there cannot be a doubt, that by the good work thus begun, he means the very commencement of conversion in the will. God, therefore, begins the good work in us by exciting in our hearts a desire, a love, and a study of righteousness, or (to speak more correctly) by turning, training, and guiding our hearts unto righteousness; and he completes this good work by confirming us unto perseverance. But lest any one should cavil that the good work thus begun by the Lord consists in aiding the will, which is in itself weak, the Spirit elsewhere declares what the will, when left to itself, is able to do. His words are, "A new heart also will I give you, and a new spirit will I put within you: and I will take away the stony heart out of your flesh, and I will give you an heart of flesh. And I will put my Spirit within you, and cause you to walk in my statutes, and ye shall keep my judgments, and do them," (Ezek. 36:26, 27). How can it be said that the weakness of the human will

17. Calvin is addressing the semi-pelagian error here. Scripture does not speak of the will taken to a position of neutrality — where it could potentially choose good. The will is enabled to choose good and to actually do the commandments of God.

18. Calvin points out that the stony heart is constitutionally stone, and the change to flesh is fundamental.

19. God Himself must bring about a change in the will of man, if man will do any good.

is aided so as to enable it to aspire effectually to the choice of good, when the fact is, that it must be wholly transformed and renovated?[17] If there is any softness in a stone;[18] if you can make it tender, and flexible into any shape, then it may be said, that the human heart may be shaped for rectitude, provided that which is imperfect in it is supplemented by divine grace. But if the Spirit, by the above similitude, meant to show that no good can ever be extracted from our heart until it is made altogether new, let us not attempt to share with Him what He claims for himself alone. If it is like turning a stone into flesh when God turns us to the study of rectitude, everything proper to our own will is abolished, and that which succeeds in its place is wholly of God. I say the will is abolished, but not in so far as it is will, for in conversion everything essential to our original nature remains: I also say, that it is created anew, not because the will then begins to exist, but because it is turned from evil to good. This, I maintains is wholly the work of God, because, as the Apostle testifies, we are not "sufficient of ourselves to think any thing as of ourselves," (2 Cor. 3:5). Accordingly, he elsewhere says, not merely that God assists the weak or corrects the depraved will, but that he worketh in us to will[19] (Phil. 2:13). From this it is easily inferred, as I have said, that everything good in the will is entirely the result of grace. In the same sense, the Apostle elsewhere says, "It is the same God which worketh all in all," (1 Cor. 12:6). For he is not there treating of universal government, but declaring that all the good qualities which believers possess are due to God. In using the term "all," he certainly makes God the author of spiritual life from its beginning to its end. This he had previously taught in different terms, when he said that there is "one Lord Jesus Christ, by whom are all things, and we by him," (1 Cor. 8:6); thus plainly extolling the new creation, by which everything of our common nature is destroyed. There is here a tacit antithesis between Adam and Christ, which he elsewhere explains more clearly when he says, "We are his workmanship, created in Christ Jesus unto good works, which God has before ordained that we should walk in them," (Eph. 2:10). His meaning is to show in this way that our salvation is gratuitous because the beginning of goodness is from the second creation which is obtained in Christ. If any, even the minutest, ability were in ourselves, there would also be some merit. But to show our utter destitution, he argues that we merit nothing, because we are created in Christ Jesus unto good works, which God has prepared; again intimating by these words, that all the fruits of good works are originally and immediately from God. Hence the Psalmist, after saying that the Lord "has made us," to deprive us of all share in the work, immediately adds, "not we ourselves." That he is speaking of regeneration, which is the commencement of the spiritual life, is obvious from the context, in which the next words are, "we are his people, and the sheep of his pasture," (Psalm 100:3). Not contented with simply giving God the praise of our salvation, he distinctly excludes us from all share in it, just as if he had said that not one particle remains to man as a ground of boasting. The whole is of God.[20]

This movement of the will is not of that description which was for many ages taught and believed—viz. a movement which thereafter leaves us the choice to obey or resist it, but one which affects us efficaciously. We must, therefore, repudiate the oft-repeated sentiment of Chrysostom, "Whom he draws, he draws willingly;" insinuating that the Lord only stretches out his hand, and waits to see whether we will be pleased to take his aid.[21] We grant that, as man was originally constituted, he could incline to either side, but since he has taught us by his example how miserable a thing free will is if God works not in us to will and to do, of what use to us were grace imparted in such scanty measure? Nay, by our own ingratitude, we obscure and impair divine grace. The Apostle's doctrine is not, that the grace of a good will is offered to us if we will accept of it, but that God himself is pleased so to work in us as to guide, turn, and govern our heart by his Spirit, and reign in it as his own possession. Ezekiel promises that a

20. This is the crux of Calvin's doctrine. Salvation is of God from beginning to end. He is the first cause in regeneration and sanctification, dismissing all basis for boasting or merit.

21. Chrysostom (AD 349-407) of Constantinople was semi-pelagian, allowing man the choice as to whether he would receive God's aid.

22. Once God's salvific grace is applied, there is no possibility of a rejection of that grace or an abortion of the new life.

23. William of Ockham (AD 1285-1347) taught that a free "created will" could oppose God's decreed will. Calvin is addressing the idea that grace is offered to all but only received by the ones who want it.

new spirit will be given to the elect, not merely that they may be able to walk in his precepts, but that they may really walk in them (Ezek. 11:19; 36:27). And the only meaning which can be given to our Savior's words, "Every man, therefore, that has heard and learned of the Father, cometh unto me," (John 6:45), is, that the grace of God is effectual in itself.[22] This Augustine maintains in his book *De Prædestinatione Sancta*. This grace is not bestowed on all promiscuously, according to the common brocard (of Occam,[23] if I mistake not), that it is not denied to any one who does what in him lies. Men are indeed to be taught that the favor of God is offered, without exception, to all who ask it; but since those only begin to ask whom heaven by grace inspires, even this minute portion of praise must not be withheld from him. It is the privilege of the elect to be regenerated by the Spirit of God, and then placed under his guidance and government. Wherefore Augustine justly derides some who arrogate to themselves a certain power of willing, as well as censures others who imagine that that which is a special evidence of gratuitous election is given to all. He says, "Nature is common to all, but not grace;" and he calls it a showy acuteness "which shines by mere vanity, when that which God bestows, on whom he will is attributed generally to all." Elsewhere he says, "How came you? By believing. Fear, lest by arrogating to yourself the merit of finding the right way, you perish from the right way. I came, you say, by free choice, came by my own will. Why do you boast? Would you know that even this was given you? Hear Christ exclaiming, 'No man cometh unto me, except the Father which has sent me draw him.'" And from the words of John (6:44), he infers it to be an incontrovertible fact, that the hearts of believers are so effectually governed from above, that they follow with undeviating affection. "Whosoever is born of God does not commit sin; for his seed remaineth in him" (1 John 3:9). That intermediate movement which the sophists imagine, a movement which every one is free to obey or to reject, is obviously excluded by the doctrine of effectual perseverance.

Book 2

Chapter 6

Redemption for Man Lost to be Sought in Christ

The whole human race having been undone in the person of Adam, the excellence and dignity of our origin, as already described, is so far from availing us, that it rather turns to our greater disgrace, until God, who does not acknowledge man when defiled and corrupted by sin as his own work, appear as a Redeemer in the person of his only begotten Son. Since our fall from life unto death, all that knowledge of God the Creator, of which we have discoursed, would be useless, were it not followed up by faith, holding forth God to us as a Father in Christ.[1] The natural course undoubtedly was, that the fabric of the world should be a school in which we might learn piety, and from it pass to eternal life and perfect felicity. But after looking at the perfection beheld wherever we turn our eye, above and below, we are met by the divine malediction, which, while it involves innocent creatures in our fault, of necessity fills our own souls with despair. For although God is still pleased in many ways to manifest his paternal favor towards us, we cannot, from a mere survey of the world, infer that he is a Father. Conscience urging us within, and showing that sin is a just ground for our being forsaken,

1. Calvin defines the believer by His relationship with God (as adopted sons). Without faith in God as our Father in and through Jesus Christ, all knowledge of God is useless.

will not allow us to think that God accounts or treats us as sons. In addition to this are our sloth and ingratitude. Our minds are so blinded that they cannot perceive the truth, and all our senses are so corrupt that we wickedly rob God of his glory. Wherefore, we must conclude with Paul, "After that in the wisdom of God the world by wisdom knew not God, it pleased God by the foolishness of preaching to save them that believe," (1 Cor. 1:21). By the "wisdom of God," he designates this magnificent theatre of heaven and earth replenished with numberless wonders, the wise contemplation of which should have enabled us to know God. But this we do with little profit; and, therefore, he invites us to faith in Christ,—faith which, by a semblance of foolishness, disgusts the unbeliever. Therefore, although the preaching of the cross is not in accordance with human wisdom, we must, however, humbly embrace it if we would return to God our Maker, from whom we are estranged, that he may again become our Father.[2] It is certain that after the fall of our first parent, no knowledge of God without a Mediator was effectual to salvation. Christ speaks not of his own age merely, but embraces all ages, when he says "This is life eternal that they might know thee the only true God, and Jesus Christ, whom thou hast sent," (John 17:3). The more shameful therefore is the presumption of those who throw heaven open to the unbelieving and profane, in the absence of that grace which Scripture uniformly describes as the only door by which we enter into life. Should any confine our Savior's words to the period subsequent to the promulgation of the Gospel, the refutation is at hand; since on a ground common to all ages and nations, it is declared, that those who are estranged from God, and as such, are under the curse, the children of wrath, cannot be pleasing to God until they are reconciled.[3] To this we may add the answer which our Savior gave to the Samaritan woman "Ye worship ye know not what; we know what we worship: for salvation is of the Jews," (John 4:22). By these words, he both charges every Gentile religion with falsehood, and assigns the reason—viz. that under the

2. We become sons by faith, embracing the teaching of the cross of Christ.

3. Calvin rejects universal salvation on the basis of Ephesians 2:2,12, and he points out that salvation was not even offered to the Gentiles in the Old Testament era.

Law the Redeemer was promised to the chosen people only, and that, consequently, no worship was ever pleasing to God in which respect was not had to Christ. Hence also Paul affirms, that all the Gentiles were "without God," and deprived of the hope of life. Now, since John teaches that there was life in Christ from the beginning, and that the whole world had lost it (John 1:4), it is necessary to return to that fountain; And, accordingly, Christ declares that inasmuch as he is a propitiator, he is life. And, indeed, the inheritance of heaven belongs to none but the sons of God (John 15:6). Now, it were most incongruous to give the place and rank of sons to any who have not been engrafted into the body of the only begotten Son. And John distinctly testifies that those become the sons of God who believe in his name. But as it is not my intention at present formally to discuss the subject of faith in Christ, it is enough to have thus touched on it in passing.

Book 2

❀ Chapter 7

The Law Given, Not to Retain a People for Itself, But to Keep Alive the Hope of Salvation in Christ Until His Advent

But in order that a sense of guilt may urge us to seek for pardon, it is of importance to know how our being instructed in the Moral Law renders us more inexcusable. If it is true, that a perfect righteousness is set before us in the Law, it follows, that the complete observance of it is perfect righteousness in the sight of God; that is, a righteousness by which a man may be deemed and pronounced righteous at the divine tribunal. Wherefore Moses, after promulgating the Law, hesitates not to call heaven and earth to witness, that he had set life and death, good and evil, before the people. Nor can it be denied, that the reward of eternal salvation, as promised by the Lord, awaits the perfect obedience of the Law (Deut. 30:19). Again, however, it is of importance to understand in what way we perform that obedience for which we justly entertain the hope of that reward. For of what use is it to see that the reward of eternal life depends on the observance of the Law, unless it moreover appears whether it be in our power in that way to attain to eternal life? Herein, then, the weakness of the Law is manifested; for, in none of us is that righteousness of the Law manifested, and, therefore, being excluded from the promises of life, we again fall under the curse. I state not only what happens, but what must necessarily happen. The doctrine of the Law transcending our capacity, a man may indeed look from a distance at the promises held forth, but he cannot derive any benefit from them. The only thing, therefore, remaining for him is, from their excellence to form a better estimate of his own misery, while he considers that the hope of salvation is cut off, and he is threatened with certain death.[1] On the other hand, those fearful denunciations which strike not at a few individuals, but at every individual without exceptions rise up; rise up, I say, and, with inexorable severity, pursue us; so that nothing but instant death is presented by the Law.

1. An honest view of the law of God only leaves the unbeliever more self-conscious of his misery and the death sentence on his head.

Therefore, if we look merely to the Law, the result must be despondency, confusion, and despair, seeing that by it we are all cursed and condemned, while we are kept far away from the blessedness which it holds forth to its observers. Is the Lord, then, you will ask, only sporting with us? Is it not the next thing to mockery, to hold out the hope of happiness, to invite and exhort us to it, to declare that it is set before us, while all the while the entrance to it is precluded and quite shut up? I answer, although the promises, in so far as they are conditional, depend on a perfect obedience of the Law, which is nowhere to be found, they have not, however, been given in vain. For when we have learned, that the promises would be fruitless and unavailing, did not God accept us of his free goodness, without any view to our works, and when, having so learned, we, by faith, embrace the goodness thus offered in the gospel, the promises, with all their annexed conditions, are fully accomplished. For God, while bestowing all things upon us freely, crowns his goodness by not disdaining our imperfect obedience; forgiving its deficiencies, accepting it as if it were complete, and so bestowing upon us the full amount of what the Law has promised.[2] But as this point will be more fully discussed in treating of justification by faith, we shall not follow it further at present.

2. We are still given the promise of life despite our imperfect obedience. This is because of God's grace.

3. No Christian in this life has ever attained sinless perfection, as is present with angels.

I say, that if we go back to the remotest period, we shall not find a single saint who, clothed with a mortal body, ever attained to such perfection as to love the Lord with all his heart, and soul, and mind, and strength; and, on the other hand, not one who has not felt the power of concupiscence. Who can deny this? I am aware, indeed of a kind of saints whom a foolish superstition imagines, and whose purity the angels of heaven scarcely equal.[3] This, however, is repugnant both to Scripture and experience. But I say further, that no saint ever will attain to perfection, so long as he is in the body. Scripture bears clear testimony to this effect: "There is no man that sinneth not," saith Solomon (1 Kings 8:46). David says, "In thy sight shall no man living be justified," (Psalm 143:2). Job also, in numerous passages, affirms the same thing. But the clearest of all is Paul, who declares that "the flesh lusteth against the Spirit, and the Spirit against the flesh," (Gal. 5:17).

4. Calvin presents three uses for the law of God. The Law of God Use 1 — To convict of sin, to humble, to cause to abandon all self-derived righteousness. This use of the law is the unregenerate according to Calvin.

That the whole matter may be made clearer, let us take a succinct view of the office and use of the Moral Law. Now this office and use seems to me to consist of three parts.[4] First, by exhibiting the righteousness of God,—in other words, the righteousness which alone is acceptable to God,—it admonishes every one of his own unrighteousness, certiorates, convicts, and finally condemns him. This is necessary, in order that man, who is blind and intoxicated with self-love, may be brought at once to know and to confess his weakness and impurity. For until his vanity is made perfectly manifest, he is puffed up with infatuated confidence in his own powers, and never can be brought to feel their feebleness so long as he measures them by a standard of his own choice. So soon, however, as he begins to compare them with the requirements of the Law, he has something to tame his presumption. How high soever his opinion of his own powers may be, he immediately feels that they pant under the heavy load, then totter and stumble, and finally fall and give way. He, then, who is schooled by the Law, lays aside the arrogance which formerly blinded him. In like manner must he be cured of pride, the other disease under which we have said that he labors. So long as he is permitted to appeal to his own judgment, he substitutes a hypocritical for a real righteousness, and, contented with this, sets up certain factitious observances in opposition to the grace of God. But after he is forced to weigh his conduct in the balance of the Law, renouncing all dependence on this fancied righteousness, he sees that he is at an infinite distance from holiness, and, on the other hand, that he teems with innumerable vices of which he formerly seemed free. The recesses in which concupiscence lies hid are so deep and tortuous that they easily elude our view; and hence the Apostle had good reason for saying, "I had not known lust, except the law had said, Thou shalt not covet."[5] For, if it be not brought forth from its lurking places, it miserably destroys in secret before its fatal sting is discerned.

Thus the Law is a kind of mirror. As in a mirror we discover any stains upon our face, so in the Law we behold, first, our impotence; then, in consequence of it, our iniquity; and, finally, the curse, as the consequence of both.[6] He who has no power of following righteousness is necessarily plunged in the mire of iniquity, and this iniquity is immediately followed by the curse. Accordingly, the greater the transgression of which the Law convicts us, the severer the judgment to which we are exposed. To this effect is the Apostle's declaration, that "by the law is the knowledge of sin," (Rom. 3:20). By these words, he only points out the first office of the Law as experienced by sinners not yet regenerated. In conformity to this, it is said, "the law entered that the offence might abound;" and, accordingly, that it is "the ministration of death;" that it "worketh wrath" and kills (Rom. 5:20; 2 Cor. 3:7; Rom. 4:15). For there cannot be a doubt that the clearer the consciousness of guilt, the greater the increase of sin; because then to transgression a rebellious feeling against the Lawgiver is added.[7] All that remains for the Law, is to arm the wrath of God for the destruction of the sinner; for by itself it can do nothing but accuse, condemn, and destroy him. Thus Augustine says, "If the Spirit

5. Romans 7:7

6. The law is a mirror and shows us our sin and its curse. But no mirror can cleanse a dirty face, and neither can the law a befouled heart.

7. The law also adds to the guilt of it; because when one knows the law and still violates the law, his rebellion is accentuated.

of grace be absent, the law is present only to convict and slay us." But to say this neither insults the law, nor derogates in any degree from its excellence. Assuredly, if our whole will were formed and disposed to obedience, the mere knowledge of the law would be sufficient for salvation; but since our carnal and corrupt nature is at enmity with the Divine law, and is in no degree amended by its discipline, the consequence is, that the law which, if it had been properly attended to, would have given life, becomes the occasion of sin and death. When all are convicted of transgression, the more it declares the righteousness of God, the more, on the other hand, it discloses our iniquity; the more certainly it assures us that life and salvation are treasured up as the reward of righteousness, the more certainly it assures us that the unrighteous will perish. So far, however, are these qualities from throwing disgrace on the Law, that their chief tendency is to give a brighter display of the divine goodness.[8] For they show that it is only our weakness and depravity that prevents us from enjoying the blessedness which the law openly sets before us. Hence additional sweetness is given to divine grace, which comes to our aid without the law, and additional loveliness to the mercy which confers it, because they proclaim that God is never weary in doing good, and in loading us with new gifts.

8. The law is still holy, just, and good as a reflection of the good character of God. The problem is the sinful heart of man, not the law of God.

But while the unrighteousness and condemnation of all are attested by the law, it does not follow (if we make the proper use of it) that we are immediately to give up all hope and rush headlong on despair. No doubt, it has some such effect upon the reprobate, but this is owing to their obstinacy. With the children of God the effect is different. The Apostle testifies that the law pronounces its sentence of condemnation in order "that every mouth may be stopped, and all the world may become guilty before God," (Rom. 3:19). In another place, however, the same Apostle declares, that "God has concluded them all in unbelief;" not that he might destroy all, or allow all to perish, but that "he might have mercy upon all," (Rom. 11:32); in other words, that divesting themselves of an absurd opinion of their own virtue, they may perceive how they are wholly dependent on the hand of God;[9] that feeling how naked and destitute they are, they may take refuge in his mercy, rely upon it, and cover themselves up entirely with it; renouncing all righteousness and merit, and clinging to mercy alone, as offered in Christ to all who long and look for it in true faith. In the precepts of the law, God is seen as the rewarder only of perfect righteousness (a righteousness of which all are destitute), and, on the other hand, as the stern avenger of wickedness. But in Christ his countenance beams forth full of grace and gentleness towards poor unworthy sinners.

9. This conviction should drive us to see our dependence on the hand of God and seek the mercy of God in Christ.

The second office of the Law is, by means of its fearful denunciations and the consequent dread of punishment, to curb those who, unless forced, have no regard for rectitude and justice. Such persons are curbed not because their mind is inwardly moved and affected, but because, as if a bridle were laid upon them, they refrain their hands from external acts, and internally check the depravity which would otherwise petulantly burst forth.[10] It is true, they are not on this account either better or more righteous in the sight of God. For although restrained by terror or shame, they dare not proceed to what their mind has conceived, nor give full license to their raging lust, their heart is by no means trained to fear and obedience. Nay, the more they restrain themselves, the more they are inflamed, the more they rage and boil, prepared for any act or outbreak whatsoever were it not for the terror of the law. And not only so, but they thoroughly detest the law itself, and execrate the Lawgiver; so that if they could, they would most willingly annihilate him, because they cannot bear either his ordering what is right, or his avenging the despisers of his Majesty. The feeling of all who are not yet regenerate, though in some more, in others less lively, is, that in regard to the observance of the law, they are not led by voluntary submission, but dragged by the force of fear. Nevertheless, this forced and extorted righteousness is necessary for the good of society, its peace being secured by a provision but for which

10. The Law of God Use 2 – To restrain natural man by fear of punishment or social shaming from more destructive and egregious forms of sin.

11. This use of the law keeps society in a reasonably peaceful and survivable condition

all things would be thrown into tumult and confusion.[11] Nay, this tuition is not without its use, even to the children of God, who, previous to their effectual calling, being destitute of the Spirit of holiness, freely indulge the lusts of the flesh. When, by the fear of Divine vengeance, they are deterred from open outbreakings, though, from not being subdued in mind, they profit little at present, still they are in some measure trained to bear the yoke of righteousness, so that when they are called, they are not like mere novices, studying a discipline of which previously they had no knowledge. This office seems to be especially in the view of the Apostle, when he says, "That the law is not made for a righteous man, but for the lawless and disobedient, for the ungodly and for sinners, for unholy and profane, for murderers of fathers and murderers of mothers, for manslayers, for whoremongers, for them that defile themselves with mankind, for men-stealers, for liars, for perjured persons, and if there be any other thing that is contrary to sound doctrine," (1 Tim. 1:9, 10). He thus indicates that it is a restraint on unruly lusts that would otherwise burst all bonds.

12. The Law of God Use 3 — A rule of obedience for believers in whose heart the Holy Spirit dwells.

The third use of the Law (being also the principal use, and more closely connected with its proper end) has respect to believers in whose hearts the Spirit of God already flourishes and reigns.[12] For although the Law is written and engraved on their hearts by the finger of God, that is, although they are so influenced and actuated by the Spirit, that they desire to obey God, there are two ways in which they still profit in the Law. For it is the best instrument for enabling them daily to learn with greater truth and certainty what that will of the Lord is which they aspire to follow, and to confirm them in this knowledge;[13] just as a servant who desires with all his soul to approve himself to his master, must still observe, and be careful to ascertain his master's dispositions, that he may comport himself in accommodation to them. Let none of us deem ourselves exempt from this necessity, for none have as yet attained to such a degree of wisdom, as that they may not, by the daily instruction of the Law, advance to a purer knowledge of the

13. The law of God helps the Christian to know the will of God. His love for God motivates him to seek out what God desires of him.

Divine will. Then, because we need not doctrine merely, but exhortation also, the servant of God will derive this further advantage from the Law: by frequently meditating upon it, he will be excited to obedience, and confirmed in it, and so drawn away from the slippery paths of sin.[14] In this way must the saints press onward, since, however great the alacrity with which, under the Spirit, they hasten toward righteousness, they are retarded by the sluggishness of the flesh, and make less progress than they ought. The Law acts like a whip to the flesh, urging it on as men do a lazy sluggish ass. Even in the case of a spiritual man, inasmuch as he is still burdened with the weight of the flesh, the Law is a constant stimulus, pricking him forward when he would indulge in sloth. David had this use in view when he pronounced this high eulogium on the Law, "The law of the Lord is perfect, converting the soul: the testimony of the Lord is sure, making wise the simple. The statutes of the Lord are right, rejoicing the heart: the commandment of the Lord is pure, enlightening the eyes," (Ps. 19:7, 8). Again, "Thy word is a lamp unto my feet, and a light unto my path," (Ps. 119:105). The whole psalm abounds in passages to the same effect. Such passages are not inconsistent with those of Paul, which show not the utility of the law to the regenerate, but what it is able of itself to bestow. The object of the Psalmist is to celebrate the advantages which the Lord, by means of his law, bestows on those whom he inwardly inspires with a love of obedience. And he adverts not to the mere precepts, but also to the promise annexed to them, which alone makes that sweet which in itself is bitter. For what is less attractive than the law, when, by its demands and threatening, it overawes the soul, and fills it with terror? David specially shows that in the law he saw the Mediator, without whom it gives no pleasure or delight.[15]

14. The law of God also serves as a motivator to "excite us to obedience."

15. Apart from Christ, we could never achieve a delight for the law or a love for the law. However, if we love Christ, we will "keep His commandments."

Chapter 8

Exposition of the Moral Law

I believe it will not be out of place here to introduce the Ten Commandments of the Law. In this way it will be made more clear, that the worship which God originally prescribed is still in force (a point to which I have already adverted); and then a second point will be confirmed—viz. that the Jews not only learned from the law wherein true piety consisted, but from feeling their inability to observe it were overawed by the fear of judgments and so drawn, even against their will, towards the Mediator. In giving a summary of what constitutes the true knowledge of God, we showed that we cannot form any just conception of the character of God, without feeling overawed by his majesty, and bound to do him service.[1] In regard to the knowledge of ourselves, we showed that it principally consists in renouncing all idea of our own strength, and divesting ourselves of all confidence in our own righteousness, while, on the other hand, under a full consciousness of our wants, we learn true humility and self-abasement.[2] Both of these the Lord accomplishes by his Law, first, when, in assertion of the right which he has to our obedience, he calls us to reverence his majesty, and prescribes

1. Knowledge of God should yield reverence/ worship and a sense of obligation to serve Him.

2. Knowledge of ourselves should yield humility and a sense of spiritual need.

the conduct by which this reverence is manifested; and, secondly, when, by promulgating the rule of his justice (a rule, to the rectitude of which our nature, from being depraved and perverted, is continually opposed, and to the perfection of which our ability, from its infirmity and nervelessness for good, is far from being able to attain), he charges us both with impotence and unrighteousness.[3] Moreover, the very things contained in the two tables are, in a manner, dictated to us by that internal law, which, as has been already said, is in a manner written and stamped on every heart. For conscience, instead of allowing us to stifle our perceptions, and sleep on without interruption, acts as an inward witness and monitor, reminds us of what we owe to God, points out the distinction between good and evil, and thereby convicts us of departure from duty.[4] But man, being immured in the darkness of error, is scarcely able, by means of that natural law, to form any tolerable idea of the worship which is acceptable to God.[5] At all events, he is very far from forming any correct knowledge of it. In addition to this, he is so swollen with arrogance and ambition, and so blinded with self-love, that he is unable to survey, and, as it were, descend into himself, that he may so learn to humble and abase himself, and confess his misery. Therefore, as a necessary remedy, both for our dullness and our contumacy, the Lord has given us his written Law, which, by its sure attestations, removes the obscurity of the law of nature, and also, by shaking off our lethargy, makes a more lively and permanent impression on our minds.

It is now easy to understand the doctrine of the law—viz. that God, as our Creator, is entitled to be regarded by us as a Father and Master,[6] and should, accordingly, receive from us fear, love, reverence, and glory; nay, that we are not our own, to follow whatever course passion dictates, but are bound to obey him implicitly, and to acquiesce entirely in his good pleasure. Again, the Law teaches, that justice and rectitude are a delight, injustice an abomination to him, and, therefore, as we would not with impious ingratitude revolt from our Maker,

3. The law points out our sinfulness and our inability to obey.

4. The internal conscience in each person also witnesses the truth of the Ten Commandments.

5. This "natural law" in the human conscience is suppressed by error and by pride, necessitating the revealing of God's commandments in a special revelation.

6. Our relationship with God is characterized by sonship and servanthood - both.

our whole life must be spent in the cultivation of righteousness. For if we manifest becoming reverence only when we prefer his will to our own, it follows, that the only legitimate service to him is the practice of justice, purity, and holiness. Nor can we plead as an excuse, that we want the power, and, like debtors, whose means are exhausted, are unable to pay. We cannot be permitted to measure the glory of God by our ability; whatever we may be, he ever remains like himself, the friend of righteousness, the enemy of unrighteousness, and whatever his demands from us may be, as he can only require what is right, we are necessarily under a natural obligation to obey.[7] Our inability to do so is our own fault. If lust, in which sin has its dominion, so enthralls us, that we are not free to obey our Father, there is no ground for pleading necessity as a defense, since this evil necessity is within, and must be imputed to ourselves.

7. Natural inability is no excuse for our disobedience.

When, under the guidance of the Law, we have advanced thus far, we must, under the same guidance, proceed to descend into ourselves. In this way, we at length arrive at two results: First, contrasting our conduct with the righteousness of the Law, we see how very far it is from being in accordance with the will of God, and, therefore, how unworthy we are of holding our place among his creatures, far less of being accounted his sons; and, secondly, taking a survey of our powers, we see that they are not only unequal to fulfill the Law, but are altogether null. The necessary consequence must be, to produce distrust of our own ability, and also anxiety and trepidation of mind. Conscience cannot feel the burden of its guilt, without forthwith turning to the judgment of God, while the view of this judgment cannot fail to excite a dread of death.[8] In like manner, the proofs of our utter powerlessness must instantly beget despair of our own strength. Both feelings are productive of humility and abasement, and hence the sinner, terrified at the prospect of eternal death (which he sees justly impending over him for his iniquities), turns to the mercy of God as the only haven of safety. Feeling his utter inability to

8. The commandments of God produce a sense of guilt, inability, and dread of judgment in the mind

pay what he owes to the Law, and thus despairing of himself, he rethinks him of applying and looking to some other quarter for help.

But the Lord does not count it enough to inspire a reverence for his justice. To imbue our hearts with love to himself, and, at the same time, with hatred to iniquity, he has added promises and threatening. The eye of our mind being too dim to be attracted by the mere beauty of goodness, our most merciful Father has been pleased, in his great indulgence, to allure us to love and long after it by the hope of reward. He accordingly declares that rewards for virtue are treasured up with him, that none who yield obedience to his commands will labor in vain.[9] On the other hand, he proclaims not only that iniquity is hateful in his sight, but that it will not escape with impunity, because he will be the avenger of his insulted majesty. That he may encourage us in every way, he promises present blessings, as well as eternal felicity, to the obedience of those who shall have kept his commands, while he threatens transgressors with present suffering, as well as the punishment of eternal death. The promise, "Ye shall therefore keep my statutes, and my judgments; which if a man do, he shall live in them," (Lev. 18:5), and corresponding to this the threatening, "The souls that sinneth, it shall die," (Ezek. 18:4, 20); doubtless point to a future life and death, both without end. But though in every passage where the favor or anger of God is mentioned, the former comprehends eternity of life and the latter eternal destruction, the Law, at the same time, enumerates a long catalogue of present blessings and curses (Lev. 26:4; Deut. 28:1). The threatening attest the spotless purity of God, which cannot bear iniquity, while the promises attest at once his infinite love of righteousness (which he cannot leave unrewarded), and his wondrous kindness. Being bound to do him homage with all that we have, he is perfectly entitled to demand everything which he requires of us as a debt; and as a debt, the payment is unworthy of reward. He therefore foregoes his right, when he holds forth reward for

9. The Old Testament law includes warnings of God's judgments as well as promises of blessing if the law is kept. These promises give us a glimpse into God's mercies.

services which are not offered spontaneously, as if they were not due. The amount of these services, in themselves, has been partly described and will appear more clearly in its own place. For the present, it is enough to remember that the promises of the Law are no mean commendation of righteousness as they show how much God is pleased with the observance of them, while the threatening denounced are intended to produce a greater abhorrence of unrighteousness, lest the sinner should indulge in the blandishments of vice, and forget the judgment which the divine Lawgiver has prepared for him.

After we shall have expounded the Divine Law, what has been previously said of its office and use will be understood more easily, and with greater benefit. But before we proceed to the consideration of each separate commandment, it will be proper to take a general survey of the whole. At the outset, it was proved that in the Law human life is instructed not merely in outward decency but in inward spiritual righteousness. Though none can deny this, yet very few duly attend to it, because they do not consider the Lawgiver, by whose character that of the Law must also be determined. Should a king issue an edict prohibiting murder, adultery, and theft, the penalty, I admit, will not be incurred by the man who has only felt a longing in his mind after these vices, but has not actually committed them. The reason is, that a human lawgiver does not extend his care beyond outward order, and, therefore, his injunctions are not violated without outward acts.[10] But God,

10. Human governments are only interested in outward acts and punish the outward behavior. However, God's law is concerned more with the heart.

whose eye nothing escapes, and who regards not the outward appearance so much as purity of heart, under the prohibition of murder, adultery, and thefts includes wrath, hatred, lust, covetousness, and all other things of a similar nature. Being a spiritual Lawgiver, he speaks to the soul not less than the body. The murder which the soul commits is wrath and hatred; the theft, covetousness and avarice; and the adultery, lust. It may be alleged that human laws have respect to intentions and wishes, and not fortuitous events.[11] I admit this but then these must manifest themselves externally. They consider the

11. Men are concerned with motive, but only so far as the motive actually exercises an outward crime.

animus with which the act was done, but do not scrutinize the secret thoughts. Accordingly, their demand is satisfied when the hand merely refrains from transgression. On the contrary, the law of heaven being enacted for our minds, the first thing necessary to a due observance of the Law is to put them under restraint. But the generality of men, even while they are most anxious to conceal their disregard of the Law, only frame their hands and feet and other parts of their body to some kind of observance, but in the meanwhile keep the heart utterly estranged from everything like obedience. They think it enough to have carefully concealed from man what they are doing in the sight of God. Hearing the commandments, "Thou shalt not kill," "Thou shalt not commit adultery," "Thou shalt not steal," they do not unsheathe their sword for slaughter, nor defile their bodies with harlots, nor put forth their hands to other men's goods. So far well; but with their whole soul they breathe out slaughter, boil with lust, cast a greedy eye at their neighbor's property, and in wish devour it. Here the principal thing which the Law requires is wanting.[12] Whence then, this gross stupidity, but just because they lose sight of the Lawgiver, and form an idea of righteousness in accordance with their own disposition? Against this Paul strenuously protests, when he declares that the "law is spiritual" (Rom. 7:14); intimating that it not only demands the homage of the soul, and mind, and will, but requires an angelic purity, which, purified from all filthiness of the flesh, savors only of the Spirit.

12. Calvin sees the internal lust or hatred in the heart as the "principle" thing.

It will not now be difficult to ascertain the general end contemplated by the whole Law—viz. the fulfillment of righteousness, that man may form his life on the model of the divine purity. For therein God has so delineated his own character, that any one exhibiting in action what is commanded, would in some measure exhibit a living image of God.[13] Wherefore Moses, when he wished to fix a summary of the whole in the memory of the Israelites, thus addressed them, "And now, Israel, what does the Lord thy God require of thee, but to fear the Lord thy God, to walk in all his ways, and to

13. Man best represents the image of God when his life is conformed to God's law.

love him, and to serve the Lord thy God with all thy heart, and with all thy soul, to keep the commandments of the Lord and his statutes which I command thee this day for thy good?" (Deut. 10:12, 13). And he ceased not to reiterate the same thing, whenever he had occasion to mention the end of the Law. To this the doctrine of the Law pays so much regard, that it connects man, by holiness of life, with his God; and, as Moses elsewhere expresses it (Deut. 6:5; 11:13), and makes him cleave to him. Moreover, this holiness of life is comprehended under the two heads above mentioned. "Thou shalt love the Lord thy God with all thy heart, and with all thy soul, and with all thy mind, and with all thy strength, and thy neighbor as thyself." First, our mind must be completely filled with love to God, and then this love must forthwith flow out toward our neighbor.[14] This the Apostle shows when he says, "The end of the commandment is charity out of a pure heart, and a good conscience, and of faith unfeigned," (1 Tim. 1:5). You see that conscience and faith unfeigned are placed at the head, in other words, true piety; and that from this charity is derived. It is a mistake then to suppose, that merely the rudiments and first principles of righteousness are delivered in the Law, to form, as it were, a kind of introduction to good works, and not to guide to the perfect performance of them. For complete perfection, nothing more can be required than is expressed in these passages of Moses and Paul. How far, pray, would he wish to go, who is not satisfied with the instruction which directs man to the fear of God, to spiritual worship, practical obedience; in fine, purity of conscience, faith unfeigned, and charity? This confirms that interpretation of the Law which searches out, and finds in its precepts, all the duties of piety and charity. Those who merely search for dry and meager elements, as if it taught the will of God only by halves, by no means understand its end, the Apostle being witness.[15]

Let us therefore hold, that our life will be framed in best accordance with the will of God, and the requirements of his Law, when it is, in every respect, most advantageous to our

14. The whole law is comprehended or summarized under two commands - to love God and to love our neighbor.

15. These commandments convey the whole will of God for man — nothing is left out.

brethren. But in the whole Law, there is not one syllable which lays down a rule as to what man is to do or avoid for the advantage of his own carnal nature. And, indeed, since men are naturally prone to excessive self-love, which they always retain, how great soever their departure from the truth may be, there was no need of a law to inflame a love already existing in excess.[16] Hence it is perfectly plain, that the observance of the Commandments consists not in the love of ourselves, but in the love of God and our neighbor; and that he leads the best and holiest life who as little as may be studies and lives for himself; and that none lives worse and more unrighteous than he who studies and lives only for himself, and seeks and thinks only of his own. Nay, the better to express how strongly we should be inclined to love our neighbor, the Lord has made self-love as it were the standard, there being no feeling in our nature of greater strength and vehemence. The force of the expression ought to be carefully weighed. For he does not (as some sophists have stupidly dreamed) assign the first place to self-love, and the second to charity. He rather transfers to others the love which we naturally feel for ourselves. Hence the Apostle declares, that charity "seeketh not her own," (1 Cor. 13:5). Nor is the argument worth a straw, that the thing regulated must always be inferior to the rule. The Lord did not make self-love the rule, as if love towards others was subordinate to it; but whereas, through natural depravity, the feeling of love usually rests on ourselves, he shows that it ought to diffuse itself in another direction—that we should be prepared to do good to our neighbor with no less alacrity, ardor, and solicitude, than to ourselves.

Our Savior having shown, in the parable of the Samaritan (Luke 10:36), that the term neighbor comprehends the most remote stranger, there is no reason for limiting the precept of love to our own connections. I deny not that the closer the relation the more frequent our offices of kindness should be. For the condition of humanity requires that there be more duties in common between those who are more nearly connected by

16. Note, there is no command requiring us to love ourselves. We already know how to do that, and do it in "excess."

17. Love for neighbor, whoever he may be, must flow from our love for God. The one cannot happen without the other.

the ties of relationship, or friendship, or neighborhood. And this is done without any offence to God, by whose providence we are in a manner impelled to do it. But I say that the whole human race, without exception, are to be embraced with one feeling of charity: that here there is no distinction of Greek or Barbarian, worthy or unworthy, friend or foe, since all are to be viewed not in themselves, but in God. If we turn aside from this view, there is no wonder that we entangle ourselves in error. Wherefore, if we would hold the true course in love, our first step must be to turn our eyes not to man, the sight of whom might oftener produce hatred than love, but to God, who requires that the love which we bear to him be diffused among all mankind, so that our fundamental principle must ever be, let a man be what he may, he is still to be loved, because God is loved.[17]

Book 2

Chapter 9

Christ, Though Known to the Jews Under the Law, Yet Only Manifested Under the Gospel

We see the error of those who, in comparing the Law with the Gospel, represent it merely as a comparison between the merit of works, and the gratuitous imputation of righteousness.[1] The contrast thus made is by no means to be rejected, because, by the term Law, Paul frequently understands that rule of holy living in which God exacts what is his due, giving no hope of life unless we obey in every respect; and, on the other hand, denouncing a curse for the slightest failure. This Paul does when showing that we are freely accepted of God, and accounted righteous by being pardoned, because that obedience of the Law to which the reward is promised is nowhere to be found. Hence he appropriately represents the righteousness of the Law and the Gospel as opposed to each other. But the Gospel has not succeeded the whole Law in such a sense as to introduce a different method of salvation.[2] It rather confirms the Law, and proves that every thing which it promised is fulfilled. What was shadow, it has made substance. When Christ says that the Law and the Prophets were until John, he does not consign the fathers to the curse, which, as the slaves of the Law, they

1. Calvin addresses the idea that there was antithesis between the Old Testament revelation of Law and the Gospel, as the difference between a merit-based salvation, and justification by faith alone.

2. Calvin does not believe that the law offered a merit-based plan of salvation.

3. The New Testament Gospel must be seen as a clearer presentation of what was conveyed by the Old Testament Law (and prophets).

could not escape. He intimates that they were only imbued with the rudiments, and remained far beneath the height of the Gospel doctrine. Accordingly Paul, after calling the Gospel "the power of God unto salvation to every one that believeth," shortly after adds, that it was "witnessed by the Law and the Prophets," (Rom. 1:16; 3:21). And in the end of the same Epistle, though he describes "the preaching of Jesus Christ" as "the revelation of the mystery which was kept secret since the world began," he modifies the expression by adding, that it is "now made manifest" "by the scriptures of the prophets," (Rom. 16:25, 26). Hence we infer that when the whole Law is spoken of, the Gospel differs from it only in respect of clearness of manifestation.[3] Still, on account of the inestimable riches of grace set before us in Christ, there is good reason for saying, that by his advent the kingdom of heaven was erected on the earth (Mt. 12:28).

Book 2

✖ Chapter 12

Christ, to Perform the Office of Mediator, Behooved to Become Man

The work to be performed by the Mediator was of no common description: being to restore us to the divine favor, so as to make us, instead of sons of men, sons of God; instead of heirs of hell, heirs of a heavenly kingdom. Who could do this unless the Son of God should also become the Son of man, and so receive what is ours as to transfer to us what is his, making that which is his by nature to become ours by grace? Relying on this earnest, we trust that we are the sons of God, because the natural Son of God assumed to himself a body of our body, flesh of our flesh, bones of our bones, that he might be one with us; he declined not to take what was peculiar to us, that he might in his turn extend to us what was peculiarly his own, and thus might be in common with us both Son of God and Son of man. Hence that holy brotherhood which he commends with his own lips, when he says, "I ascend to my Father, and your Father, to my God, and your God," (John 20:17). In this way, we have a sure inheritance in the heavenly kingdom, because the only Son of God, to whom it entirely belonged, has adopted us as his brethren; and if brethren, then partners with him in the inher-

1. The Son of God takes upon Himself human nature so as to incorporate us into Him, and count us His brothers.

2. Our Savior must be divine because only the Source of life could destroy death; only the almighty power of God could overcome the power of the devil.

3. Our Savior must be human because it was the human that broke God's law. It must be a human who would obey the Father for the rest of us (even as Adam disobeyed as our representative).

4. God promised a redeemer by the Son of David and Abraham — thus our Savior had to take upon Himself that human nature.

itance[1] (Rom. 8:17). Moreover, it was especially necessary for this cause also that he who was to be our Redeemer should be truly God and man. It was his to swallow up death: who but Life could do so? It was his to conquer sin: who could do so save Righteousness itself? It was his to put to flight the powers of the air and the world: who could do so but the mighty power superior to both? But who possesses life and righteousness, and the dominion and government of heaven, but God alone? Therefore, God, in his infinite mercy, having determined to redeem us, became himself our Redeemer in the person of his only begotten Son.[2]

Another principal part of our reconciliation with God was, that man, who had lost himself by his disobedience, should, by way of remedy, oppose to it obedience, satisfy the justice of God, and pay the penalty of sin. Therefore, our Lord came forth very man, adopted the person of Adam, and assumed his name, that he might in his stead obey the Father; that he might present our flesh as the price of satisfaction to the just judgment of God, and in the same flesh pay the penalty which we had incurred.[3] Finally, since as God only he could not suffer, and as man only could not overcome death, he united the human nature with the divine, that he might subject the weakness of the one to death as an expiation of sin, and by the power of the other, maintaining a struggle with death, might gain us the victory. Those, therefore, who rob Christ of divinity or humanity either detract from his majesty and glory, or obscure his goodness. On the other hand, they are no less injurious to men, undermining and subverting their faith, which, unless it rest on this foundation, cannot stand. Moreover, the expected Redeemer was that son of Abraham and David whom God had promised in the Law and in the Prophets.[4] Here believers have another advantage. Tracing up his origin in regular series to David and Abraham, they more distinctly recognize him as the Messiah celebrated by so many oracles. But special attention must be paid to what I lately explained, namely, that a common nature is the pledge of our union with the Son of God; that, clothed with our flesh, he warred to death with sin that he might be our triumphant conqueror; that the flesh which he received of us he offered in sacrifice, in order that by making expiation he might wipe away our guilt, and appease the just anger of his Father.

❄ Chapter 14

How Two Natures Constitute the Person of the Mediator

When it is said that the Word was made flesh, we must not understand it as if he were either changed into flesh, or confusedly intermingled with flesh, but that he made choice of the Virgin's womb as a temple in which he might dwell. He who was the Son of God became the Son of man, not by confusion of substance, but by unity of person. For we maintain, that the divinity was so conjoined and united with the humanity, that the entire properties of each nature remain entire, and yet the two natures constitute only one Christ. If, in human affairs, any thing analogous to this great mystery can be found, the most apposite similitude seems to be that of man, who obviously consists of two substances, neither of which however is so intermingled with the other as that both do not retain their own properties. For neither is soul body, nor is body soul.[1] Wherefore that is said separately of the soul which cannot in any way apply to the body; and that, on the other hand, of the body which is altogether inapplicable to the soul; and that, again, of the whole man, which cannot be affirmed without absurdity either of the body or of the soul separately. Lastly, the proper-

1. Calvin uses the human body and soul as an analogy for the two natures of Christ in one person. This is the distinct but not separate relationship Calvin uses throughout the *Institutes*.

ties of the soul are transferred to the body, and the properties of the body to the soul, and yet these form only one man, not more than one. Such modes of expression intimate both that there is in man one person formed of two compounds, and that these two different natures constitute one person. Thus the Scriptures speak of Christ. They sometimes attribute to him qualities which should be referred specially to his humanity and sometimes qualities applicable peculiarly to his divinity, and sometimes qualities which embrace both natures, and do not apply specially to either. This combination of a twofold nature in Christ they express so carefully, that they sometimes communicate them with each other, a figure of speech which the ancients termed a communication of properties.

Book 2

Chapter 15

Three Things Briefly to be Regarded in Christ- Viz. His Offices of Prophet, King, and Priest

Though heretics pretend the name of Christ, truly does Augustine affirm that the foundation is not common to them with the godly, but belongs exclusively to the Church: for if those things which pertain to Christ be diligently considered, it will be found that Christ is with them in name only, not in reality. Thus in the present day, though the Papists have the words, Son of God, Redeemer of the world, sounding in their mouths, yet, because contented with an empty name, they deprive him of his virtue and dignity; what Paul says of "not holding the head," is truly applicable to them[1] (Col. 2:19). Therefore, that faith may find in Christ a solid ground of salvation, and so rest in him, we must set out with this principle, that the office which he received from the Father consists of three parts. For he was appointed Prophet, King, and Priest; though little were gained by holding the names unaccompanied by a knowledge of the end and use.

1. Calvin concludes that the Roman Catholics do not really hold to the Head (Christ). They are, in his words, "heretics."

Book 2

Chapter 16

How Christ Performed the Office of Redeemer in Procuring our Salvation. The Death, Resurrection, and Ascension of Christ

All that we have hitherto said of Christ leads to this one result, that condemned, dead, and lost in ourselves, we must in him seek righteousness, deliverance, life and salvation, as we are taught by the celebrated words of Peter, "Neither is there salvation in any other: for there is none other name under heaven given among men whereby we must be saved," (Acts 4:12). The name of Jesus was not given him at random, or fortuitously, or by the will of man, but was brought from heaven by an angel, as the herald of the supreme decree; the reason also being added, "for he shall save his people from their sins," (Matt. 1:21). In these words attention should be paid to what we have elsewhere observed that the office of Redeemer was assigned him in order that he might be our Savior.[1] Still, however, redemption would be defective if it did not conduct us by an uninterrupted progression to the final goal of safety. Therefore, the moment we turn aside from him in the minutest degree, salvation, which resides entirely in him, gradually disappears; so that all who do not rest in him voluntarily deprive themselves of all grace.[2] The observation of Bernard well deserves to be remembered:

1. This is core for the doctrine of salvation. Jesus (Savior) is His Name and He came to save us from our sins.

2. Very important to Calvin's doctrine: salvation is a complete, "uninterrupted progression to the final goal" of heaven. Any turning aside from Christ indicates there was no salvation.

"The name of Jesus is not only light but food also, yea, oil, without which all the food of the soul is dry; salt, without which as a condiment whatever is set before us is insipid; in fine, honey in the mouth, melody in the ear, joy in the heart, and, at the same time, medicine; every discourse where this name is not heard is absurd." But here it is necessary diligently to consider in what way we obtain salvation from him, that we may not only be persuaded that he is the author of it, but having embraced whatever is sufficient as a sure foundation of our faith, may eschew all that might make us waver. For seeing no man can descend into himself, and seriously consider what he is, without feeling that God is angry and at enmity with him, and therefore anxiously longing for the means of regaining his favor (this cannot be without satisfaction), the certainty here required is of no ordinary description,—sinners, until freed from guilt, being always liable to the wrath and curse of God, who, as he is a just judge, cannot permit his law to be violated with impunity, but is armed for vengeance.

But before we proceed farther, we must see in passing, how can it be said that God, who prevents us with his mercy, was our enemy until he was reconciled to us by Christ. For how could he have given us in his only-begotten Son a singular pledge of his love, if he had not previously embraced us with free favor? As there thus arises some appearance of contradiction, I will explain the difficulty. The mode in which the Spirit usually speaks in Scripture is, that God was the enemy of men until they were restored to favor by the death of Christ (Rom. 5:10); that they were cursed until their iniquity was expiated by the sacrifice of Christ (Gal. 3:10, 13); that they were separated from God, until by means of Christ's body they were received into union (Col. 1:21, 22). Such modes of expression are accommodated to our capacity, that we may the better understand how miserable and calamitous our condition is without Christ. For were it not said in clear terms, that Divine wrath, and vengeance, and eternal death,[3] lay upon us, we should be less sensible of our wretchedness without

3. Calvin takes the phrase "He descended into hell," to mean that Christ actually did engage "at close quarter with the powers of hell" and the "horrors of eternal death."

the mercy of God, and less disposed to value the blessing of deliverance.[4] For example, let a person be told, "Had God at the time you were a sinner hated you, and cast you off as you deserved, horrible destruction must have been your doom; but spontaneously and of free indulgence he retained you in his favor, not suffering you to be estranged from him, and in this way rescued you from danger,"—the person will indeed be affected, and made sensible in some degree how much he owes to the mercy of God. But again, let him be told, as Scripture teaches, that he was estranged from God by sin, an heir of wrath, exposed to the curse of eternal death, excluded from all hope of salvation, a complete alien from the blessing of God, the slave of Satan, captive under the yoke of sin; in fine, doomed to horrible destruction, and already involved in it; that then Christ interposed, took the punishment upon himself and bore what by the just judgment of God was impending over sinners; with his own blood expiated the sins which rendered them hateful to God, by this expiation satisfied and duly propitiated God the Father, by this intercession appeased his anger, on this basis founded peace between God and men, and by this tie secured the Divine benevolence toward them; will not these considerations move him the more deeply, the more strikingly they represent the greatness of the calamity from which he was delivered?[5] In short, since our mind cannot lay hold of life through the mercy of God with sufficient eagerness, or receive it with becoming gratitude, unless previously impressed with fear of the Divine anger, and dismayed at the thought of eternal death, we are so instructed by divine truth, as to perceive that without Christ God is in a manner hostile to us, and has his arm raised for our destruction.[6] Thus taught, we look to Christ alone for divine favor and paternal love.

When it is asked then how Christ, by abolishing sin, removed the enmity between God and us, and purchased a righteousness which made him favorable and kind to us, it may be answered generally, that he accomplished this by the whole course of his obedience. This is proved by the testimony of

4. To realize our state under God's wrath, and then to realize that God intervened and Christ interposed on our behalf ("while we were yet sinners"), is to better know the powerful love of God for us. These realizations should "move us more deeply."

5. Christ expiated our sin for us, which is a blotting out of sin. Christ was also a propitiation for us, a covering for us, shielding us from the wrath of God. Both expiation and propitiation result in reconciliation with God.

6. We receive these truths with a fear of God, and then also, a love for God as we view His wrath towards sin and His love for us.

7. Christ saves us by His obedience, by His whole life and death on the cross. He lived a life of obedience where Adam disobeyed.

Paul, "As by one man's disobedience many were made sinners, so by the obedience of one shall many be made righteous," (Rom. 5:19).[7] And indeed he elsewhere extends the ground of pardon which exempts from the curse of the law to the whole life of Christ, "When the fullness of the time was come, God sent forth his Son, made of a woman, made under the law, to redeem them that were under the law," (Gal. 4:4, 5). Thus even at his baptism he declared that a part of righteousness was fulfilled by his yielding obedience to the command of the Father. In short, from the moment when he assumed the form of a servant, he began, in order to redeem us, to pay the price of deliverance. Scripture, however, the more certainly to define the mode of salvation, ascribes it peculiarly and specially to the death of Christ. He himself declares that he gave his life a ransom for many (Mt. 20:28). Paul teaches that he died for our sins (Rom. 4:25). John Baptist exclaimed, "Behold the Lamb of God, which taketh away the sin of the world," (John 1:29). Paul in another passage declares, "that we are justified freely by his grace, through the redemption that is in Christ Jesus: whom God has set forth to be a propitiation through faith in his blood," (Rom. 3:25). "Again, being justified by his blood, we shall be saved from wrath through him" (Rom. 5:9). Again "He has made him to be sin for us, who knew no sin; that we might be made the righteousness of God in him," (2 Cor. 5:21). I will not search out all the passages, for the list would be endless, and many are afterwards to be quoted in their order. In the Confession of Faith, called the Apostles' Creed, the transition is admirably made from the birth of Christ to his death and resurrection, in which the completion of a perfect salvation consists. Still there is no exclusion of the other part of obedience which he performed in life. Thus Paul comprehends, from the beginning even to the end, his having assumed the form of a servant, humbled himself, and become obedient to death, even the death of the cross (Phil. 2:7). And, indeed, the first step in obedience was his voluntary subjection; for the sacrifice would have been unavailing to justification if not offered spontaneously. Hence our Lord, after testifying, "I lay down my life for the sheep," distinctly adds, "No man taketh it from me," (John 10:15, 18). In the same sense Isaiah says, "Like a sheep before her shearers is dumb, so he opened not his mouth," (Is. 53:7). The Gospel History relates that he came forth to meet the soldiers; and in presence of Pilate, instead of defending himself, stood to receive judgment. This, indeed, he did not without a struggle, for he had assumed our infirmities also, and in this way it behooved him to prove that he was yielding obedience to his Father.[8] It was no ordinary example of incomparable love towards us to struggle with dire terrors, and amid fearful tortures to cast away all care of himself that he might provide for us. We must bear in minds that Christ could not duly propitiate God without renouncing his own feelings and subjecting himself entirely to his Father's will. To this effect the Apostle appositely quotes a passage from the Psalms, "Lo, I come (in the volume of the book it is written of me) to do thy will, O God," (Heb. 10:5; Ps. 40:7, 8). Thus, as trembling consciences find no rest without sacrifice and ablution by which sins are expiated, we are properly directed thither, the source of our life being placed in the death of Christ.[9] Moreover, as the curse consequent upon guilt remained for the final judgment of God, one principal point in the narrative is his condemnation before Pontius Pilate, the governor of Judea, to teach us, that the punishment to which we were liable was inflicted on that Just One. We could not escape the fearful judgment of God; and Christ, that he might rescue us from it, submitted to be condemned by a mortal, nay, by a wicked and profane man. For the name of Governor is mentioned not only to support the credibility of the narrative, but to remind us of what Isaiah says, that "the chastisement of our peace was upon him;" and that "with his stripes we are healed," (Is. 53:5). For, in order to remove our condemnation, it was not sufficient to endure any kind of death. To satisfy our ransom, it was necessary to select a mode of death in which he might deliver us, both by giving himself

8. Jesus's refusal to offer a defense at His trial before Pilate is proof of His obedience to the Father.

9. Yet, it is "peculiarly and specially" the death of Christ in obedience to the Father that brought about our salvation.

10. Christ's death had to come about in the context of a judicial trial, albeit at the hands of wicked men. He was put in the place of an evildoer, representing us.

11. Christ was declared innocent (as He was) and declared guilty at the same time by Pilate — fitting for His position, taking the guilt of others upon Himself.

up to condemnations and undertaking our expiation. Had he been cut off by assassins, or slain in a seditious tumult, there could have been no kind of satisfaction in such a death. But when he is placed as a criminal at the bar, where witnesses are brought to give evidence against him, and the mouth of the judge condemns him to die, we see him sustaining the character of an offender and evil-doer.[10] Here we must attend to two points which had both been foretold by the prophets, and tend admirably to comfort and confirm our faith. When we read that Christ was led away from the judgment-seat to execution, and was crucified between thieves, we have a fulfillment of the prophecy which is quoted by the Evangelist, "He was numbered with the transgressors," (Is. 53:12; Mark 15:28). Why was it so? That he might bear the character of a sinner, not of a just or innocent person, inasmuch as he met death on account not of innocence, but of sin. On the other hand, when we read that he was acquitted by the same lips that condemned him (for Pilate was forced once and again to bear public testimony to his innocence), let us call to mind what is said by another prophet, "I restored that which I took not away," (Ps. 69:4). Thus we perceive Christ representing the character of a sinner and a criminal, while, at the same time, his innocence shines forth, and it becomes manifest that he suffers for another's and not for his own crime.[11] He therefore suffered under Pontius Pilate, being thus, by the formal sentence of the judge, ranked among criminals, and yet he is declared innocent by the same judge, when he affirms that he finds no cause of death in him. Our acquittal is in this that the guilt which made us liable to punishment was transferred to the head of the Son of God (Is. 53:12). We must specially remember this substitution in order that we may not be all our lives in trepidation and anxiety, as if the just vengeance which the Son of God transferred to himself, were still impending over us.

The very form of the death embodies a striking truth. The cross was cursed not only in the opinion of men, but by the enactment of the Divine Law. Hence Christ, while suspended on it, subjects himself to the curse.[12] And thus it behooved to be done, in order that the whole curse, which on account of our iniquities awaited us, or rather lay upon us, might be taken from us by being transferred to him. This was also shadowed in the Law, since the word by which sin itself is properly designated, was applied to the sacrifices and expiations offered for sin. By this application of the term, the Spirit intended to intimate, that they were a kind of purifications, bearing, by substitutions the curse due to sin.[13] But that which was represented figuratively in the Mosaic sacrifices is exhibited in Christ the archetype. Wherefore, in order to accomplish a full expiation, he made his soul a propitiatory victim for sin (as the prophet says, Is. 53:5, 10), on which the guilt and penalty being in a manner laid, ceases to be imputed to us. The Apostle declares this more plainly when he says, that "he made him to be sin for us, who knew no sin; that we might be made the righteousness of God in him," (2 Cor. 5:21). For the Son of God, though spotlessly pure, took upon him the disgrace and ignominy of our iniquities, and in return clothed us with his purity.[14] To the same thing he seems to refer, when he says, that he "condemned sin in the flesh," (Rom. 8:3), the Father having destroyed the power of sin when it was transferred to the flesh of Christ. This term, therefore, indicates that Christ, in his death, was offered to the Father as a propitiatory victim; that, expiation being made by his sacrifice, we might cease to tremble at the divine wrath. It is now clear what the prophet means when he says, that "the Lord has laid upon him the iniquity of us all," (Is. 53:6); namely, that as he was to wash away the pollution of sins, they were transferred to him by imputation. Of this the cross to which he was nailed was a symbol, as the Apostle declares, "Christ has redeemed us from the curse of the law, being made a curse for us: for it is written, Cursed is every one that hangeth on a tree: that the blessing of Abraham might come on the Gentiles through Jesus Christ," (Gal. 3:13, 14). In the same way Peter says, that he "bare our sins in his own body on the tree," (1 Peter 2:24), inasmuch as from

12. God's law had already declared the curse of crucifixion. Reference Deuteronomy 21:23.

13. The Old Testament sacrifices indicate that the shedding of blood was necessary to purify sinful man.

14. The innocent sacrificial victim (Christ) then bears the weight of the guilt and penalty of sin, and then clothes us with His purity and cleanses us with His blood.

15. Another benefit of Christ's work is that He broke the force of sin at the cross. Thus, the cross turns into a tremendous victory.

16. The blood of Christ has two benefits — propitiating the wrath of God and cleansing us from the defilement of sin.

the very symbol of the curse, we perceive more clearly that the burden with which we were oppressed was laid upon him. Nor are we to understand that by the curse which he endured he was himself overwhelmed, but rather that by enduring it he repressed, broke, annihilated all its force.[15] Accordingly, faith apprehends acquittal in the condemnation of Christ, and blessing in his curse. Hence it is not without cause that Paul magnificently celebrates the triumph which Christ obtained upon the cross, as if the cross, the symbol of ignominy, had been converted into a triumphal chariot. For he says, that he blotted out the handwriting of ordinances that was against us, which was contrary to us, and took it out of the way, nailing it to his cross: that "having spoiled principalities and powers he made a show of them openly, triumphing over them in it," (Col. 2:14, 15). Nor is this to be wondered at; for, as another Apostle declares, Christ, "through the eternal Spirit, offered himself without spot to God," (Heb. 9:14), and hence that transformation of the cross which were otherwise against its nature. But that these things may take deep root and have their seat in our inmost hearts, we must never lose sight of sacrifice and ablution. For, were not Christ a victim, we could have no sure conviction of his being our substitute-ransom and propitiation. And hence mention is always made of blood whenever scripture explains the mode of redemption: although the shedding of Christ's blood was available not only for propitiation, but also acted as a laver to purge our defilements.[16]

The Creed next mentions that he "was dead and buried." Here again it is necessary to consider how he substituted himself in order to pay the price of our redemption. Death held us under its yoke, but he in our place delivered himself into its power, that he might exempt us from it. This the Apostle means when he says, "that he tasted death for every man," (Heb. 2:9). By dying he prevented us from dying; or (which is the same thing) he by his death purchased life for us. But in this he differed from us, that in permitting himself to be overcome of death, it was not so as to be engulfed in its abyss but rather to annihilate it, as it must otherwise have annihilated us; he did not allow himself to be so subdued by it as to be crushed by its power; he rather laid it prostrate, when it was impending over us, and exulting over us as already overcome.[17] In fine, his object was, "that through death he might destroy him that had the power of death, that is, the devil, and deliver them who through fear of death were all their lifetime subject to bondage," (Heb. 2:14, 15). This is the first fruit which his death produced to us. Another is, that by fellowship with him he mortifies our earthly members that they may not afterwards exert themselves in action, and kill the old man, that he may not hereafter be in vigor and bring forth fruit. An effect of his burials moreover is that we as his fellows are buried to sin.[18] For when the Apostle says, that we are engrafted into the likeness of Christ's death and that we are buried with him unto sin, that by his cross the world is crucified unto us and we unto the world, and that we are dead with him, he not only exhorts us to manifest an example of his death, but declares that there is an efficacy in it which should appear in all Christians, if they would not render his death unfruitful and useless.[19] Accordingly in the death and burial of Christ a twofold blessing is set before us—viz. deliverance from death, to which we were enslaved, and the mortification of our flesh (Rom. 6:5; Gal. 2:19, 6:14; Col. 3:3).

But, apart from the Creed, we must seek for a surer exposition of Christ's descent to hell: and the word of God furnishes us with one not only pious and holy, but replete with excellent consolation. Nothing had been done if Christ had only endured corporeal death. In order to interpose between us and God's anger, and satisfy his righteous judgment, it was necessary that he should feel the weight of divine vengeance. Whence also it was necessary that he should engage, as it were, at close quarters with the powers of hell and the horrors of eternal death. We lately quoted from the Prophet, that the "chastisement of our peace was laid upon him" that he "was bruised for our iniquities" that he "bore our infirmities;"

17. By Christ's death, He went to war with death and conquered it for us.

18. Yet another benefit of the death of Christ — he kills the old man and disables the principle of sin in our lives (as we believe in Him and identify with His death).

19. There is more than an example of victory in His death. We actually share in His victory and obtain an efficacy from the cross in our own lives.

expressions which intimate, that, like a sponsor and surety for the guilty, and, as it were, subjected to condemnation, he undertook and paid all the penalties which must have been exacted from them, the only exception being, that the pains of death could not hold him. Hence there is nothing strange in its being said that he descended to hell, seeing he endured the death which is inflicted on the wicked by an angry God. It is frivolous and ridiculous to object that in this way the order is perverted, it being absurd that an event which preceded burial should be placed after it. But after explaining what Christ endured in the sight of man, the Creed appropriately adds the invisible and incomprehensible judgment which he endured before God, to teach us that not only was the body of Christ given up as the price of redemption, but that there was a greater and more excellent price—that he bore in his soul the tortures of condemned and ruined man.

Next follows the resurrection from the dead, without which all that has hitherto been said would be defective. For seeing that in the cross, death, and burial of Christ, nothing but weakness appears, faith must go beyond all these, in order that it may be provided with full strength. Hence, although in his death we have an effectual completion of salvation, because by it we are reconciled to God, satisfaction is given to his justice, the curse is removed, and the penalty paid; still it is not by his death, but by his resurrection, that we are said to be begotten again to a living hope (1 Pet. 1:3); because, as he, by rising again, became victorious over death, so the victory of our faith consists only in his resurrection.[20] The nature of it is better expressed in the words of Paul, "Who (Christ) was delivered for our offences, and was raised again for our justification," (Rom. 4:25); as if he had said, "By his death sin was taken away, by his resurrection righteousness was renewed and restored." For how could he by dying have freed us from death, if he had yielded to its power? How could he have obtained the victory for us, if he had fallen in the contest? Our salvation may be thus divided between the death and the

20. Calvin goes on to speak of the necessity of the resurrection. The victory of faith is seated in hope in the resurrection of our Lord Jesus Christ.

resurrection of Christ: by the former sin was abolished and death annihilated; by the latter righteousness was restored and life revived, the power and efficacy of the former being still bestowed upon us by means of the latter.[21] Paul accordingly affirms, that he was declared to be the Son of God by his resurrection (Rom. 1:4), because he then fully displayed that heavenly power which is both a bright mirror of his divinity, and a sure support of our faith; as he also elsewhere teaches, that "though he was crucified through weakness, yet he liveth by the power of God," (2 Cor. 13:4). In the same sense, in another passage, treating of perfection, he says, "That I may know him and the power of his resurrection," (Phil. 3:10). Immediately after he adds, "being made conformable unto his death." In perfect accordance with this is the passage in Peter, that God "raised him up from the dead, and gave him glory, that your faith and hope might be in God," (1 Pet. 1:21). Not that faith founded merely on his death is vacillating, but that the divine power by which he maintains our faith is most conspicuous in his resurrection. Let us remember, therefore, that when death only is mentioned, everything peculiar to the resurrection is at the same time included, and that there is a like synecdoche in the term resurrection, as often as it is used apart from death, everything peculiar to death being included. But as, by rising again, he obtained the victory, and became the resurrection and the life, Paul justly argues, "If Christ be not raised, your faith is vain; ye are yet in your sins," (1 Cor. 15:17). Accordingly, in another passage, after exulting in the death of Christ in opposition to the terrors of condemnation, he thus enlarges, "Christ that died, yea rather, that is risen again, who is even at the right hand of God, who also maketh intercession for us," (Rom. 8:34). Then, as we have already explained that the mortification of our flesh depends on communion with the cross, so we must also understand, that a corresponding benefit is derived from his resurrection. For as the Apostle says, "Like as Christ was raised up from the dead by the glory of the Father, even so we also should walk in newness of life,"

21. Our Lord's resurrection brought about righteousness and life for us — both justification and sanctification.

22. A sanctified life comes about in us by the resurrection of Christ — an enablement to rise up and walk in newness of life.

23. His resurrection assures us of the eternal, bodily resurrection of all of us who are found in Him.

24. Calvin moves on to explain the benefits of Christ's ascension.

25. By His ascension, Christ infuses His church with more power. He is given a position of authority over all things in heaven and earth. He sends His Holy Spirit to enable us and empower us.

(Rom. 6:4). Accordingly, as in another passage, from our being dead with Christ, he inculcates, "Mortify therefore your members which are upon the earth," (Col. 3:5); so from our being risen with Christ he infers, "seek those things which are above, where Christ sitteth at the right hand of God," (Col. 3:1). In these words we are not only urged by the example of a risen Savior to follow newness of life, but are taught that by his power we are renewed unto righteousness.[22] A third benefit derived from it is, that, like an earnest, it assures us of our own resurrection, of which it is certain that his is the surest representation. This subject is discussed at length (1 Cor. 15). But it is to be observed, in passing, that when he is said to have "risen from the dead," these terms express the reality both of his death and resurrection, as if it had been said, that he died the same death as other men naturally die, and received immortality in the same mortal flesh which he had assumed.[23]

The resurrection is naturally followed by the ascension into heaven.[24] For although Christ, by rising again, began fully to display his glory and virtue, having laid aside the abject and ignoble condition of a mortal life, and the ignominy of the cross, yet it was only by his ascension to heaven that his reign truly commenced. This the Apostle shows, when he says he ascended "that he might fill all things," (Eph. 4:10); thus reminding us, that under the appearance of contradiction, there is a beautiful harmony, inasmuch as though he departed from us, it was that his departure might be more useful to us than that presence which was confined in a humble tabernacle of flesh during his abode on the earth. Hence John, after repeating the celebrated invitation, "If any man thirst, let him come unto me and drink," immediately adds, "the Holy Ghost was not yet given; because that Jesus was not yet glorified," (John 7:37, 39). This our Lord himself also declared to his disciples, "It is expedient for you that I go away: for if I go not away the Comforter will not come unto you," (John 16:7).[25] To console them for his bodily absence, he tells them that he will not leave them comfortless, but will come again to them in a manner invisible indeed, but more to be desired, because they were then taught by a surer experience that the government which he had obtained, and the power which he exercises would enable his faithful followers not only to live well, but also to die happily. And, indeed we see how much more abundantly his Spirit was poured out, how much more gloriously his kingdom was advanced, how much greater power was employed in aiding his followers and discomfiting his enemies. Being raised to heaven, he withdrew his bodily presence from our sight, not that he might cease to be with his followers, who are still pilgrims on the earth, but that he might rule both heaven and earth more immediately by his power; or rather, the promise which he made to be with us even to the end of the world, he fulfilled by this ascension, by which, as his body has been raised above all heavens, so his power and efficacy have been propagated and diffused beyond all the bounds of heaven and earth.

Hence it is immediately added, that he "sitteth at the right hand of God the Father;" a similitude borrowed from princes, who have their assessors to whom they commit the office of ruling and issuing commands. Thus Christ, in whom the Father is pleased to be exalted, and by whose hand he is pleased to reign, is said to have been received up, and seated on his right hand (Mark 16:19); as if it had been said, that he was installed in the government of heaven and earth, and formally admitted to possession of the administration committed to him, and not only admitted for once, but to continue until he descend to judgment. For so the Apostle interprets, when he says, that the Father "set him at his own right hand in the heavenly places, far above all principality, and power, and might, and dominion, and every name that is named not only in this world, but also in that which is to come; and has put all things under his feet, and given him to be the head over all things to the Church."[26] You see to what end he is so seated namely, that all creatures both in heaven and earth should reverence his majesty, be ruled by his hand, do him implicit hom-

26. Ephesians 1:20-22

age, and submit to his power. All that the Apostles intends when they so often mention his seat at the Father's hand, is to teach, that every thing is placed at his disposal. Those, therefore, are in error, who supposes that his blessedness merely is indicated. We may observe, that there is nothing contrary to this doctrine in the testimony of Stephen, that he saw him standing (Acts 7:56), the subject here considered being not the position of his body, but the majesty of his empire, sitting meaning nothing more than presiding on the judgment-seat of heaven.[27]

27. Christ is ruling with all authority. Any perspective that diminishes this is a wrong view of reality and history.

From this doctrine faith derives manifold advantages. First, it perceives that the Lord, by his ascension to heaven, has opened up the access to the heavenly kingdom, which Adam had shut.[28] For having entered it in our flesh, as it were in our name, it follows, as the Apostle says, that we are in a manner now seated in heavenly places, not entertaining a mere hope of heaven, but possessing it in our head. Secondly, faith perceives that his seat beside the Father is not without great advantage to us. Having entered the temple not made with hands, he constantly appears as our advocate and intercessor in the presence of the Father; directs attention to his own righteousness, so as to turn it away from our sins; so reconciles him to us, as by his intercession to pave for us a way of access to his throne, presenting it to miserable sinners, to whom it would otherwise be an object of dread, as replete with grace and mercy.[29] Thirdly, it discerns his power, on which depend our strength, might, resources, and triumph over hell, "When he ascended up on high, he led captivity captive," (Eph. 4:8). Spoiling his foes, he gave gifts to his people, and daily loads them with spiritual riches. He thus occupies his exalted seat, that thence transferring his virtue unto us, he may quicken us to spiritual life, sanctify us by his Spirit, and adorn his Church with various graces, by his protection preserve it safe from all harm, and by the strength of his hand curb the enemies raging against his cross and our salvation; in fine, that he may possess all power in heaven and earth, until he have utterly routed all his foes,

28. Believing in Christ's ascension brings us the comfort that we are now invited into His heavenly kingdom.

29. His presence at the right hand of the Father assures us that He intercedes for us and pleads the merits of His blood for us.

who are also ours and completed the structure of his Church.[30] Such is the true nature of the kingdom, such the power which the Father has conferred upon him, until he arrive to complete the last act by judging the quick and the dead.

Christ, indeed, gives his followers no dubious proofs of present power, but as his kingdom in the world is in a manner veiled by the humiliation of a carnal condition, faith is most properly invited to meditate on the visible presence which he will exhibit on the last day.[31] For he will descend from heaven in visible form, in like manner as he was seen to ascend, and appear to all, with the ineffable majesty of his kingdom, the splendor of immortality, the boundless power of divinity, and an attending company of angels. Hence we are told to wait for the Redeemer against that day on which he will separate the sheep from the goats and the elect from the reprobate, and when not one individual either of the living or the dead shall escape his judgment. From the extremities of the universe shall be heard the clang of the trumpet summoning all to his tribunal; both those whom that day shall find alive, and those whom death shall previously have removed from the society of the living.[32]

It is most consolatory to think, that judgment is vested in him who has already destined us to share with him in the honor of judgment (Mt. 19:28); so far is it from being true, that he will ascend the judgment-seat for our condemnation. How could a most merciful prince destroy his own people? How could the head disperse its own members? How could the advocate condemn his clients?[33] For if the Apostle, when contemplating the interposition of Christ, is bold to exclaim, "Who is he that condemneth?" (Rom. 8:33), much more certain is it that Christ, the intercessor, will not condemn those whom he has admitted to his protection. It certainly gives no small security, that we shall be sifted at no other tribunal than that of our Redeemer, from whom salvation is to be expected; and that he who in the Gospel now promises eternal blessedness, will then as judge ratify his promise. The end for which

30. From His exalted position in heaven, our Lord continually overcomes His enemies and builds His church.

31. Christ's people can, with eyes of faith, witness His present power and authority. However, this sinful world veils the totality of it. This will be completely manifest on the day of Judgment.

32. His second coming will signal the final Judgment and the separation of the sheep and the goats, the reprobate and the elect.

33. For some the Lord Christ will be only a terrifying Judge. But, for His own, He is still their Head, their Shepherd, their Advocate, and their merciful Prince. How could an advocate or attorney condemn His own clients?

the Father has honored the Son by committing all judgment to him (John 5:22), was to pacify the consciences of his people when alarmed at the thought of judgment.

Hitherto I have followed the order of the Apostles' Creed,[34] because it states the leading articles of redemption in a few words, and may thus serve as a tablet in which the points of Christian doctrine, most deserving of attention, are brought separately and distinctly before us. I call it the Apostles' Creed, though I am by no means solicitous as to its authorship. The general consent of ancient writers certainly does ascribe it to the Apostles, either because they imagined it was written and published by them for common use, or because they thought it right to give the sanction of such authority to a compendium faithfully drawn up from the doctrine delivered by their hands. I have no doubt, that, from the very commencement of the Church, and, therefore, in the very days of the Apostles, it held the place of a public and universally received confession, whatever be the quarter from which it originally proceeded. It is not probable that it was written by some private individual, since it is certain that, from time immemorial, it was deemed of sacred authority by all Christians. The only point of consequence we hold to be incontrovertible—viz. that it gives, in clear and succinct order, a full statement of our faith, and in every thing which it contains is sanctioned by the sure testimony of Scripture. This being understood, it were to no purpose to labor anxiously, or quarrel with any one as to the authorship, unless, indeed, we think it not enough to possess the sure truth of the Holy Spirit, without, at the same time, knowing by whose mouth it was pronounced, or by whose hand it was written.

When we see that the whole sum of our salvation, and every single part of it, are comprehended in Christ, we must beware of deriving even the minutest portion of it from any other quarter.[35] If we seek salvation, we are taught by the very name of Jesus that he possesses it; if we seek any other gifts of the Spirit, we shall find them in his unction; strength in his

34. This entire chapter followed the order of the Apostle's Creed as it laid out the Gospel. Calvin says this contains the doctrines "most deserving" of our attention — the core faith.

35. A last warning — no part of our salvation may be derived from anywhere but by Jesus Christ.

government; purity in his conception; indulgence in his nativity, in which he was made like us in all respects, in order that he might learn to sympathize with us: if we seek redemption, we shall find it in his passion; acquittal in his condemnation; remission of the curse in his cross; satisfaction in his sacrifice; purification in his blood; reconciliation in his descent to hell; mortification of the flesh in his sepulcher; newness of life in his resurrection; immortality also in his resurrection; the inheritance of a celestial kingdom in his entrance into heaven; protection, security, and the abundant supply of all blessings, in his kingdom; secure anticipation of judgment in the power of judging committed to him. In fine, since in him all kinds of blessings are treasured up, let us draw a full supply from him, and none from any other quarter. Those who, not satisfied with him alone, entertain various hopes from others, though they may continue to look to him chiefly, deviate from the right path by the simple fact, that some portion of their thought takes a different direction. No distrust of this description can arise when once the abundance of his blessings is properly known.

Book 3
Chapter 1

The Benefits of Christ Made Available to us by the Secret Operation of the Spirit

1. Calvin informs the reader that he now takes up the application of Christ's redemption to poor and needy sinners in Book 3. Much of Book 3 will discuss God's saving work in the life of the believer.

2. Calvin lays down a foundational theological truth: unless we are united to Jesus Christ through faith, we cannot participate in any of His benefits. Therefore, Calvin's doctrine of salvation (what is called "soteriology") begins with union with Christ.

We must now see in what way we become possessed of the blessings which God has bestowed on his only-begotten Son, not for private use, but to enrich the poor and needy.[1] And the first thing to be attended to is, that so long as we are without Christ and separated from him, nothing which he suffered and did for the salvation of the human race is of the least benefit to us.[2] To communicate to us the blessings which he received from the Father, he must become ours and dwell in us. Accordingly, he is called our Head, and the first-born among many brethren, while, on the other hand, we are said to be engrafted into him and clothed with him, all which he possesses being, as I have said, nothing to us until we become one with him. And although it is true that we obtain this by faith, yet since we see that all do not indiscriminately embrace the offer of Christ which is made by the gospel, the very nature of the case teaches us to ascend higher, and inquire into the secret efficacy of the Spirit, to which it is owing that we enjoy Christ and all his blessings.[3] I have already treated of the eternal essence and divinity of the Spirit; let us at present attend to the special point, that Christ came by water and blood, as the Spirit testifies concerning him, that we might not lose the benefits of the salvation which he has purchased. For as there are said to be three witnesses in heaven, the Father, the Word, and the Spirit, so there are also three on the earth, namely, water, blood, and Spirit.[4] It is not without cause that the testimony of the Spirit is twice mentioned, a testimony which is engraved on our hearts by way of seal, and thus seals the cleansing and sacrifice of Christ. For which reason, also, Peter says, that believers are "elect" "through sanctification of the Spirit, unto obedience and sprinkling of the blood of Jesus Christ," (1 Pet. 1:2). By these words he reminds us, that if the shedding of his sacred blood is not to be in vain, our souls must be washed in it by the secret cleansing of the Holy Spirit. For which reason, also, Paul, speaking of cleansing and purification, says, "But ye are washed, but ye are sanctified, but ye are justified in the name of the Lord Jesus and by the Spirit of our God," (1 Cor. 6:11). The whole comes to this that the Holy Spirit is the bond by which Christ effectually binds us to himself. Here we may refer to what was said in the last Book concerning his anointing.

Here it will be proper to point out the titles which the Scripture bestows on the Spirit, when it treats of the commencement and entire renewal of our salvation. First, he is called the "Spirit of adoption," because he is witness to us of the free favor with which God the Father embraced us in his well-beloved and only-begotten Son, so as to become our Fathers and give us boldness of access to him; nays he dictates the very words, so that we can boldly cry, "Abba, Father." For the same reason, he is said to have "sealed us, and given the earnest of the Spirit in our hearts," because, as pilgrims in the world, and persons in a manner dead, he so quickens us from above as to assure us that our salvation is safe in the keeping of a faithful God. Hence, also, the Spirit is said to be "life because of righteousness." But since it is his secret irrigation

3. We are united to Christ through faith. But this faith must be sovereignly granted by the secret working of God's Holy Spirit giving us new life.

4. Here Calvin refers to the words of 1 John 5:7-8 where John describes the "earthly witnesses" of the Spirit, the water, and the blood that all testify to who Christ is. The identity of the "water" and the "blood" are disputed by commentators. Some think the water refers to Jesus' baptism where He was identified by the Father as the Son of God and anointed by the Spirit. The "blood" would likely refer to Jesus' crucifixion. Whatever the case, the main point Calvin wants to establish here is the vital importance of the Holy Spirit's work in salvation.

that makes us bud forth and produce the fruits of righteousness, he is repeatedly described as water. Thus in Isaiah "Ho, every one that thirsteth, come ye to the waters." Again, "I will pour water upon him that is thirsty, and floods upon the dry ground." Corresponding to this are the words of our Savior, to which I lately referred, "If any man thirst, let him come unto me and drink." Sometimes, indeed, he receives this name from his energy in cleansing and purifying, as in Ezekiel, where the Lord promises, "Then will I sprinkle you with clean water, and ye shall be clean." As those sprinkled with the Spirit are restored to the full vigor of life,[5] he hence obtains the names of "Oil" and "Unction." On the other hand, as he is constantly employed in subduing and destroying the vices of our concupiscence, and inflaming our hearts with the love of God and piety, he hence receives the name of Fire. In fine, he is described to us as a Fountain, whence all heavenly riches flow to us; or as the Hand by which God exerts his power, because by his divine inspiration he so breathes divine life into us, that we are no longer acted upon by ourselves, but ruled by his motion and agency, so that everything good in us is the fruit of his grace, while our own endowments without him are mere darkness of mind and perverseness of heart. Already, indeed, it has been clearly shown, that until our minds are intent on the Spirit, Christ is in a manner unemployed, because we view him coldly without us, and so at a distance from us. Now we know that he is of no avail save only to those to whom he is a head and the first-born among the brethren, to those, in fine, who are clothed with him. To this union alone it is owing that, in regard to us, the Savior has not come in vain. To this is to be referred that sacred marriage, by which we become bone of his bone, and flesh of his flesh, and so one with him (Eph. 5:30), for it is by the Spirit alone that he unites himself to us. By the same grace and energy of the Spirit we become his members, so that he keeps us under him, and we in our turn possess him.

5. What we learn here about the Spirit is that He is the giver of life. He grants us new life. He brings water to the desert of our souls. He subdues our old man (the flesh) and gives us a love for God. Everywhere we see the Spirit, as the third person of the Trinity, is life-giving. That is why the Nicene Creed describes the Holy Spirit as "the Lord, the giver of life."

Book 3

Chapter 2

Of Faith. The Definition of It. Its Particular Properties

The true knowledge of Christ consists in receiving him as he is offered by the Father, namely, as invested with his Gospel.[1] For, as he is appointed as the end of our faith, so we cannot directly tend towards him except under the guidance of the Gospel. Therein are certainly unfolded to us treasures of grace. Did these continue shut, Christ would profit us little. Hence Paul makes faith the inseparable attendant of doctrine in these words, "Ye have not so learned Christ; if so be that ye have heard him, and have been taught by him, as the truth is in Jesus," (Eph. 4:20, 21). Still I do not confine faith to the Gospel in such a sense as not to admit that enough was delivered to Moses and the Prophets to form a foundation of faith;[2] but as the Gospel exhibits a fuller manifestation of Christ, Paul justly terms it the doctrine of faith (1 Tim. 4:6). For which reason, also he elsewhere says, that, by the coming of faith, the Law was abolished (Rom. 10:4), including under the expression a new and unwonted mode of teaching, by which Christ, from the period of his appearance as the great Master, gave a fuller illustration of the Father's mercy, and testified more surely of our salvation. But an easier

1. In this chapter, Calvin describes the nature of saving faith. He begins by defining what the true knowledge of Christ consists in. It is to receive Christ, as offered by the Father to us, in the good news of Jesus' death and resurrection: the gospel.

2. Calvin clarifies that he is not saying that the way of salvation in Christ was completely hidden to the people of God in the Old Testament. They were saved the same way we are: by faith in God and in His promised redeemer (Rom. 4, Heb. 11). Nevertheless, with the coming of Christ, and the revelation of the New Testament, there is a "fuller manifestation" of Christ in the gospel. That which was once hidden and shadowy is made known clearly in the preaching of Christ and His Apostles.

3. This is always a wise way to approach difficult questions in theology. We begin with the clear and general teaching of God's Word. Then, we slowly navigate into the more complex particular questions. Beginning with what is clear sets our feet on solid ground. Here then, Calvin lays down some essential and general truths about faith.

4. Calvin points out that faith comes by the hearing of God's Word (Rom. 10:14-17). Without the Word of God revealing the gospel to us, faith has no proper object. Faith has nothing to rest in that will save.

5. Calvin does not deal here with the question of whether man (i.e. a preacher or teacher) is absolutely necessary for faith to hear the Word of God and believe. He simply points out that by whatever means the Word of God comes, saving faith must be resting in the Word of God, the revealed gospel, in order to be saving faith.

and more appropriate method will be to descend from the general to the particular.[3] First, we must remember, that there is an inseparable relation between faith and the word, and that these can no more be disconnected from each other than rays of light from the sun.[4] Hence in Isaiah the Lord exclaims, "Hear, and your soul shall live," (Is. 4:3). And John points to this same fountain of faith in the following words, "These are written that ye might believe," (John 20:31). The Psalmist also exhorting the people to faith says, "To-day, if ye will hear his voice," (Ps. 95:7), to hear being uniformly taken for to believe. In fine, in Isaiah the Lord distinguishes the members of the Church from strangers by this mark, "All thy children shall be taught of the Lord," (Is. 54:13); for if the benefit was indiscriminate, why should he address his words only to a few? Corresponding with this, the Evangelists uniformly employ the terms believers and disciples as synonymous. This is done especially by Luke in several passages of the Acts. He even applies the term disciple to a woman (Acts 9:36). Wherefore, if faith declines in the least degree from the mark at which it ought to aim, it does not retain its nature, but becomes uncertain credulity and vague wandering of mind. The same word is the basis on which it rests and is sustained. Declining from it, it falls. Take away the word, therefore, and no faith will remain. We are not here discussing, whether, in order to propagate the word of God by which faith is engendered, the ministry of man is necessary (this will be considered elsewhere); but we say that the word itself, whatever be the way in which it is conveyed to us, is a kind of mirror in which faith beholds God.[5] In this, therefore, whether God uses the agency of man, or works immediately by his own power, it is always by his word that he manifests himself to those whom he designs to draw to himself. Hence Paul designates faith as the obedience which is given to the Gospel (Rom. 1:5); and writing to the Philippians, he commends them for the obedience of faith (Phil. 2:17). For faith includes not merely the knowledge that God is, but also, nay chiefly, a perception of his will toward us. It concerns us to know not only what he is in himself, but also in what character he is pleased to manifest himself to us. We now see, therefore, that faith is the knowledge of the divine will[6] in regard to us, as ascertained from his word. And the foundation of it is a previous persuasion of the truth of God. So long as your mind entertains any misgivings as to the certainty of the word, its authority will be weak and dubious, or rather it will have no authority at all. Nor is it sufficient to believe that God is true, and cannot lie or deceive, unless you feel firmly persuaded that every word which him is sacred, inviolable truth.[7]

But since the heart of man is not brought to faith by every word of God,[8] we must still consider what it is that faith properly has respect to in the word. The declaration of God to Adam was, "Thou shalt surely die," (Gen. 2:17); and to Cain, "The voice of thy brother's blood crieth unto me from the ground," (Gen. 4:10); but these, so far from being fitted to establish faith, tend only to shake it. At the same time, we deny not that it is the office of faith to assent to the truth of God whenever, whatever, and in whatever way he speaks: we are only inquiring what faith can find in the word of God to lean and rest upon. When conscience sees only wrath and indignation, how can it but tremble and be afraid? And how can it avoid shunning the God whom it thus dreads? But faith ought to seek God, not shun him. It is evident, therefore, that we have not yet obtained a full definition of faith, it being impossible to give the name to every kind of knowledge of the divine will. Shall we, then, for "will", which is often the messenger of bad news and the herald of terror, substitute the benevolence or mercy of God? In this way, doubtless, we make a nearer approach to the nature of faith. For we are allured to seek God when told that our safety is treasured up in him;

6. In other words, just because a man knows God's Word and its threatenings against sin, this does not mean that he has saving faith. It is important to remember that the demons believe in God and they tremble (Jas. 2:19). But the demons are not saved by this kind of "faith" or "belief." Therefore, as Calvin points out, our definition of saving faith cannot merely mean "knowledge of God's will." We must also know and personally embrace God's mercy revealed in the gospel of His Son.

7. The Word of God is the essential foundation for faith. For this reason, attacks past and present on the authority and accuracy of God's Word are devastating to faith. Without a sure Word from the living God, how can we have any assurance that we will be saved? How can we have any assurance of the truth of the gospel and our interest in Jesus Christ unless the Word of God is, as Calvin describes it, "sacred, inviolable truth."

8. In what follows here, Calvin is arguing that God's Word contains both threats and promises. Of course, those who have faith in God's Word believe every word of Scripture. But God's law, contained in the Scriptures, condemns us in our sin. What then will faith "lean and rest upon?" Saving faith then, must look to God's mercy in Christ, in order to be saved.

9. "Propitious" here means "showing favor."

10. Calvin notes how frequently the Psalms connect God's mercy and God's truth. This is an indication that the believer, who speaks under God's inspiration in the Psalms, recognizes that faith is more than "knowing about God" but also involves a trust in God's mercy.

11. Apart from our Lord Jesus' saving work, we would all stand under the condemnation of the law. The law brings us under a curse (Gal. 3:10). But Christ is our peace (Eph. 2:14).

and we are confirmed in this when he declares that he studies and takes an interest in our welfare. Hence there is need of the gracious promise, in which he testifies that he is a propitious Father;[9] since there is no other way in which we can approach to him, the promise being the only thing on which the heart of man can recline. For this reason, the two things, mercy and truth, are uniformly conjoined in the Psalms as having a mutual connection with each other.[10] For it were of no avail to us to know that God is true, did He not in mercy allure us to himself; nor could we of ourselves embrace his mercy did not He expressly offer it. "I have declared thy faithfulness and thy salvation: I have not concealed thy loving-kindness and thy truth. Withhold not thy tender mercies from me, O Lord: let thy loving-kindness and thy truth continually preserve me," (Ps. 40:10, 11). "Thy mercy, O Lord, is in the heavens; and thy faithfulness reacheth unto the clouds," (Ps. 36:5). "All the paths of the Lord are mercy and truth unto such as keep his covenant and his testimonies," (Ps. 25:10). "His merciful kindness is great toward us: and the truth of the Lord endureth for ever," (Ps. 117:2). "I will praise thy name for thy loving-kindness and thy truth," (Ps. 138:2). I need not quote what is said in the Prophets, to the effect that God is merciful and faithful in his promises. It were presumptuous in us to hold that God is propitious to us, had we not his own testimony, and did he not prevent us by his invitation, which leaves no doubt or uncertainty as to his will. It has already been seen that Christ is the only pledge of love, for without him all things, both above and below speak of hatred and wrath.[11] We have also seen, that since the knowledge of the divine goodness cannot be of much importance unless it leads us to confide in it, we must exclude a knowledge mingled with doubt,—a knowledge which, so far from being firm, is continually wavering. But the human mind, when blinded and darkened, is very far from being able to rise to a proper knowledge of the divine will; nor can the heart, fluctuating with perpetual doubt, rest secure in such knowledge. Hence, in order that the word of

God may gain full credit, the mind must be enlightened, and the heart confirmed, from some other quarter. We shall now have a full definition of faith if we say that it is a firm and sure knowledge of the divine favor toward us, founded on the truth of a free promise in Christ, and revealed to our minds, and sealed on our hearts, by the Holy Spirit.[12]

Let us now again go over the parts of the definition separately: I should think that, after a careful examination of them, no doubt will remain. By knowledge we do not mean comprehension, such as that which we have of things falling under human sense. For that knowledge is so much superior, that the human mind must far surpass and go beyond itself in order to reach it. Nor even when it has reached it does it comprehend what it feels, but persuaded of what it comprehends not, it understands more from mere certainty of persuasion than it could discern of any human matter by its own capacity. Hence it is elegantly described by Paul as ability "to comprehend with all saints what is the breadth, and length, and depth, and height; and to know the love of Christ, which passeth knowledge," (Eph. 3:18, 19). His object was to intimate, that what our mind embraces by faith is every way infinite, that this kind of knowledge far surpasses all understanding. But because the "mystery which has been hid from ages and from generations" is now "made manifest to the saints," (Col. 1:26), faith is, for good reason, occasionally termed in Scripture understanding (Col. 2:2); and knowledge, as by John (1 John 3:2), when he declares that believers know themselves to be the sons of God. And certainly they do know, but rather as confirmed by a belief of the divine veracity than taught by any demonstration of reason. This is also indicated by Paul when he says, that "whilst we are at home in the body, we are absent from the Lord: (For we walk by faith, not by sight)," (2 Cor. 5:6, 7) thus showing, that what we understand by faith is yet distant from us and escapes our view. Hence we conclude that the knowledge of faith consists more of certainty than discernment.[13]

12. Here Calvin provides us with his definition of saving faith. It involves a "firm and sure knowledge" of God's favor to us, through Jesus Christ, revealed to our minds, and sealed on our hearts by God's Holy Spirit.

13. Calvin argues that the "knowledge" essential to faith is not a natural kind of knowledge, comparable to someone's knowledge of a subject or knowledge of mere facts. Rather, it is a divinely revealed knowledge of things beyond our comprehension. It is a certain knowledge of God's promises to us in the gospel. We know that these promises are ours by faith.

14. Calvin argues that in the definition of saving faith itself, there should be included this sure and firm persuasion in God's Word.

We add, that it is sure and firm, the better to express strength and constancy of persuasion.[14] For as faith is not contented with a dubious and fickle opinion, so neither is it contented with an obscure and ill-defined conception. The certainty which it requires must be full and decisive, as is usual in regard to matters ascertained and proved. So deeply rooted in our hearts is unbelief, so prone are we to it, that while all confess with the lips that God is faithful, no man ever believes it without an arduous struggle. Especially when brought to the test, we by our wavering betray the vice which lurked within. Nor is it without cause that the Holy Spirit bears such distinguished testimony to the authority of God, in order that it may cure the disease of which I have spoken, and induce us to give full credit to the divine promises: "The words of the Lord" (says David, Ps. 12:6) "are pure words, as silver tried in a furnace of earth purified seven times:" "The word of the Lord is tried: he is a buckler to all those that trust in him," (Ps. 18:30). And Solomon declares the same thing almost in the same words, "Every word of God is pure," (Prov. 30:5). But further quotation is superfluous, as the 119th Psalm is almost wholly occupied with this subject. Certainly, whenever God thus recommends his word, he indirectly rebukes our unbelief, the purport of all that is said being to eradicate perverse doubt from our hearts. There are very many also who form such an idea of the divine mercy as yields them very little comfort. For they are harassed by miserable anxiety while they doubt whether God will be merciful to them. They think, indeed, that they are most fully persuaded of the divine mercy, but they confine it within too narrow limits. The idea they entertain is, that this mercy is great and abundant, is shed upon many, is offered and ready to be bestowed upon all; but that it is uncertain whether it will reach to them individually, or rather whether they can reach to it. Thus their knowledge stopping short leaves them only mid-way; not so much confirming and tranquilizing the mind as harassing it with doubt and disquietude. Very different is that feeling of full assurance (πλεροφορία) which the Scriptures uniformly attribute to faith—an assurance which leaves no doubt that the goodness of God is clearly offered to us. This assurance we cannot have without truly perceiving its sweetness, and experiencing it in ourselves. Hence from faith the Apostle deduces confidence, and from confidence boldness. His words are, "In whom (Christ) we have boldness and access with confidence by the faith of him," (Eph. 3:12) thus undoubtedly showing that our faith is not true unless it enables us to appear calmly in the presence of God. Such boldness springs only from confidence in the divine favor and salvation. So true is this, that the term faith is often used as equivalent to confidence.[15]

The principal hinge on which faith turns is this: We must not suppose that any promises of mercy which the Lord offers are only true out of us, and not at all in us: we should rather make them ours by inwardly embracing them.[16] In this way only is engendered that confidence which he elsewhere terms peace (Rom. 5:1); though perhaps he rather means to make peace follow from it. This is the security which quiets and calms the conscience in the view of the judgment of God, and without which it is necessarily vexed and almost torn with tumultuous dread, unless when it happens to slumber for a moment, forgetful both of God and of itself. And verily it is but for a moment. It never long enjoys that miserable obliviousness, for the memory of the divine judgment, ever and anon recurring, stings it to the quick. In one word, he only is a true believer who, firmly persuaded that God is reconciled, and is a kind Father to him, hopes everything from his kindness, who, trusting to the promises of the divine favor, with undoubting confidence anticipates salvation; as the Apostle shows in these words, "We are made partakers of Christ, if we hold the beginning of our confidence steadfast unto the end," (Heb. 3:14). He thus holds, that none hope well in the Lord save those who confidently glory in being the heirs of the heavenly kingdom. No man, I say, is a believer but he who, trusting to the security of his salvation, confidently triumphs

15. "Faith" and "confidence" are sometimes used interchangeably in Scripture. In teaching that faith involves a full assurance and confidence, Calvin does not deny that faith may be assaulted. We all may struggle with degrees of doubt. Nevertheless, saving faith involves a firm confidence in God's promises (Heb. 10:22).

16. Faith is not just believing that God's promises are true in general. Rather, saving faith involves a personal embrace and resting in God's promises of salvation.

over the devil and death, as we are taught by the noble exclamation of Paul, "I am persuaded, that neither death, nor life, nor angels, nor principalities, nor powers, nor things present, nor things to come, nor height, nor depth, nor any other creature, shall be able to separate us from the love of God, which is in Christ Jesus our Lord," (Rom. 8:38). In like manner, the same Apostle does not consider that the eyes of our understanding are enlightened unless we know what is the hope of the eternal inheritance to which we are called (Eph. 1:18). Thus he uniformly intimates throughout his writings, that the goodness of God is not properly comprehended when security does not follow as its fruit.

But it will be said that this differs widely from the experience of believers, who, in recognizing the grace of God toward them, not only feel disquietude (this often happens), but sometimes tremble, overcome with terror, so violent are the temptations which assail their minds. This scarcely seems consistent with certainty of faith.[17] It is necessary to solve this difficulty, in order to maintain the doctrine above laid down. When we say that faith must be certain and secure, we certainly speak not of an assurance which is never affected by doubt, nor a security which anxiety never assails; we rather maintain that believers have a perpetual struggle with their own distrust, and are thus far from thinking that their consciences possess a placid quiet, uninterrupted by perturbation.[18] On the other hand, whatever be the mode in which they are assailed, we deny that they fall off and abandon that sure confidence which they have formed in the mercy of God.[19] Scripture does not set before us a brighter or more memorable example of faith than in David, especially if regard be had to the constant tenor of his life. And yet how far his mind was from being always at peace is declared by innumerable complaints, of which it will be sufficient to select a few. When he rebukes the turbulent movements of his soul, what else is it but a censure of his unbelief? "Why art thou cast down, my soul? And why art thou disquieted in me? Hope thou in God," (Psalm 42:6). His alarm

17. Calvin admits that what he said so far about the assurance and confidence of saving faith can sound far removed from the daily experience of believers. Don't we all deal with faith struggles? Calvin admits that we all deal with such "disquietude."

18. Things are not always "placid" in the Christian life. That is, they are not always perfectly peaceful and tranquil. And we deal with "perturbations" or "disturbances" to faith.

19. This is Calvin's clarification. Though faith may be assailed by doubts, saving faith is characterized by never abandoning its foundational confidence in God's promises.

was undoubtedly a manifest sign of distrust, as if he thought that the Lord had forsaken him. In another passage we have a fuller confession: "I said in my haste, I am cut off from before thine eyes," (Psalm 31:22). In another passage, in anxious and wretched perplexity, he debates with himself, nay, raises a question as to the nature of God: "Has God forgotten to be gracious? Has he in anger shut up his tender mercies?" (Psalm 77:9). What follows is still harsher: "I said this is my infirmity; but I will remember the years of the right hand of the Most High." As if desperate, he adjudges himself to destruction. He not only confesses that he is agitated by doubt, but as if he had fallen in the contest, leaves himself nothing in reserve,—God having deserted him, and made the hand which was wont to help him the instrument of his destruction. Wherefore, after having been tossed among tumultuous waves, it is not without reason he exhorts his soul to return to her quiet rest (Psalm 116:7). And yet (what is strange) amid those commotions, faith sustains the believer's heart, and truly acts the part of the palm tree, which supports any weights laid upon it, and rises above them; thus David, when he seemed to be overwhelmed, ceased not by urging himself forward to ascend to God. But he who anxiously contending with his own infirmity has recourse to faith, is already in a great measure victorious. This we may infer from the following passage, and others similar to it: "Wait on the Lord: be of good courage, and he shall strengthen thine heart: wait, I say, on the Lord," (Psalm 27:14). He accuses himself of timidity, and repeating the same thing twice, confesses that he is ever and anon exposed to agitation.[20] Still he is not only dissatisfied with himself for so feeling, but earnestly labors to correct it. Were we to take a nearer view of his case, and compare it with that of Ahaz, we should find a great difference between them. Isaiah is sent to relieve the anxiety of an impious and hypocritical king, and addresses him in these terms: "Take heed, and be quiet; fear not," (Isaiah 7:4). How did Ahab act? As has already been said, his heart was shaken as a tree is shaken by the wind: though he heard the promise,

20. Calvin turns to the Psalms to provide examples of faith being assailed, yet faith prevailing over those doubts. The Psalmists, such as David, evidence what believers know by personal experience. We can deal with trials of faith. Our confidence isn't in the quality of our faith. Instead our confidence is in God's infallible promises.

21. This is the result of unbelief: a trembling as a result of trials but no turning to God. Instead, unbelievers turn away from God.

22. Both believers and unbelievers face severe trials. But believers persevere in faith through them looking to God in prayer and holding fast to God's Word.

23. Calvin admits that due to the weakness of our flesh in this present life, our faith is never perfect. There is an imperfection to our faith, though it is real.

he ceased not to tremble. This, therefore, is the proper hire and punishment of unbelief,[21] so to tremble as in the day of trial to turn away from God, who gives access to himself only by faith. On the other hand, believers, though weighed down and almost overwhelmed with the burden of temptation, constantly rise up, though not without toil and difficulty; hence, feeling conscious of their own weakness, they pray with the Prophet, "Take not the word of truth utterly out of my mouths" (Psalm 119:43). By these words, we are taught that they at times become dumb, as if their faith were overthrown, and yet that they do not withdraw or turn their backs, but persevere in the contest, and by prayer stimulate their sluggishness, so as not to fall into stupor by giving way to it.[22]

To make this intelligible, we must return to the distinction between flesh and spirit, to which we have already adverted, and which here becomes most apparent. The believer finds within himself two principles: the one filling him with delight in recognizing the divine goodness, the other filling him with bitterness under a sense of his fallen state; the one leading him to recline on the promise of the Gospel, the other alarming him by the conviction of his iniquity; the one making him exult with the anticipation of life, the other making him tremble with the fear of death. This diversity is owing to imperfection of faith, since we are never so well in the course of the present life as to be entirely cured of the disease of distrust, and completely replenished and engrossed by faith.[23] Hence those conflicts: the distrust cleaving to the remains of the flesh rising up to assail the faith enlisting in our hearts. But if in the believer's mind certainty is mingled with doubt, must we not always be carried back to the conclusion, that faith consists not of a sure and clear, but only of an obscure and confused, understanding of the divine will in regard to us? By no means. Though we are distracted by various thoughts, it does not follow that we are immediately divested of faith. Though we are agitated and carried to and fro by distrust, we are not immediately plunged into the abyss; though we are shaken, we are not therefore driven from our place. The invariable issue of the contest is, that faith in the long run surmounts the difficulties by which it was beset and seemed to be endangered.[24]

The whole, then, comes to this: As soon as the minutest particle of faith[25] is instilled into our minds, we begin to behold the face of God placid, serene, and propitious; far off, indeed, but still so distinctly as to assure us that there is no delusion in it. In proportion to the progress we afterwards make (and the progress ought to be uninterrupted), we obtain a nearer and surer view, the very continuance making it more familiar to us. Thus we see that a mind illumined with the knowledge of God is at first involved in much ignorance,—ignorance, however, which is gradually removed. Still this partial ignorance or obscure discernment does not prevent that clear knowledge of the divine favor which holds the first and principal part in faith. For as one shut up in a prison, where from a narrow opening he receives the rays of the sun indirectly and in a manner divided, though deprived of a full view of the sun, has no doubt of the source from which the light comes, and is benefited by it; so believers, while bound with the fetters of an earthly body, though surrounded on all sides with much obscurity, are so far illumined by any slender light which beams upon them and displays the divine mercy as to feel secure.[26]

24. Calvin says that the test of real faith is whether it perseveres. It may be assailed, but in the long run does it overcome the difficulties?

25. By saying the "smallest particle" of faith, Calvin understands that faith may be very weak. But if it is a real trust in God, it is faith, however weak or small it may be.

26. Calvin provides a helpful illustration. Just as a man in prison might see just a few slender rays of light from the sun, so also do we behold God by faith, even though our faith may be weak, and at times it may be assailed.

1. Calvin indicates that the subject he will take up now is something that is a result of, or flows from, faith.

2. Calvin describes this as the summary of the gospel. For this summary, Calvin likely has in mind the summary recorded in the Gospel of Luke. "Then He said to them, 'Thus it is written, and thus it was necessary for the Christ to suffer and to rise from the dead the third day, and that repentance and remission of sins should be preached in His name to all nations, beginning at Jerusalem.'" (Luke 24:46-47)

3. Though faith and repentance should be distinguished, they must never be separated. In his preaching Paul summarized his message as calling people to faith and repentance (Acts 20:21).

4. Calvin argues that repentance is inseparable from faith. A man is justified by faith alone. Repentance doesn't "merit" us justification. But repentance will always be inseparably connected to faith.

5. Calvin argues that repentance is produced from faith. In this regard, we can say that repentance is one of the fruits of faith.

Book 3

Chapter 3

Regeneration by Faith. Of Repentance

A lthough we have already in some measure shown how faith possesses Christ, and gives us the enjoyment of his benefits, the subject would still be obscure were we not to add an exposition of the effects resulting from it.[1] The sum of the Gospel is, not without good reason, made to consist in repentance and forgiveness of sins;[2] and, therefore, where these two heads are omitted, any discussion concerning faith will be meager and defective,[3] and indeed almost useless. Now, since Christ confers upon us, and we obtain by faith, both free reconciliation and newness of life, reason and order require that I should here begin to treat of both. The shortest transition, however, will be from faith to repentance; for repentance being properly understood it will better appear how a man is justified freely by faith alone, and yet that holiness of life, real holiness, as it is called, is inseparable from the free imputation of righteousness.[4] That repentance not only always follows faith, but is produced by it, ought to be without controversy.[5] For since pardon and forgiveness are offered by the preaching of the Gospel, in order that the sinner, delivered from the tyranny of Satan, the yoke of sin, and the miserable bondage of iniquity, may pass into the kingdom of God, it is certain that no man can embrace the grace of the Gospel without retaking himself from the errors of his former life into the right path, and making it his whole study to practice repentance.[6] Those who think that repentance precedes faith instead of flowing from, or being produced by it, as the fruit by the tree, have never understood its nature, and are moved to adopt that view on very insufficient grounds.

6. It is not possible for a man to come to Christ by faith and not also repent of his former way of life.

Christ and John, it is said, in their discourses first exhort the people to repentance,[7] and then add, that the kingdom of heaven is at hand (Mt. 3:2; 4:17). Such too, is the message which the Apostles received and such the course which Paul followed, as is narrated by Luke (Acts 20:21). But clinging superstitiously to the juxtaposition of the syllables, they attend not to the coherence of meaning in the words. For when our Lord and John begin their preaching thus "Repent, for the kingdom of heaven is at hand," (Mt. 3:2), do they not deduce repentance as a consequence of the offer of grace and promise of salvation? The force of the words, therefore, is the same as if it were said, As the kingdom of heaven is at hand, for that reason repent. For Matthew, after relating that John so preached, says that therein was fulfilled the prophecy concerning the voice of one crying in the desert, "Prepare ye the way of the Lord, make straight in the desert a highway for our God," (Isaiah 40:3). But in the Prophet that voice is ordered to commence with consolation and glad tidings. Still, when we attribute the origin of repentance to faith, we do not dream of some period of time in which faith is to give birth to it: we only wish to show that a man cannot seriously engage in repentance unless he knows that he is of God.[8] But no man is truly persuaded that he is of God until he have embraced his offered favor. These things will be more clearly explained as we proceed. Some are perhaps misled by this, that not a few are subdued by terror of conscience, or disposed to obedience before they have been imbued with a knowledge, nay, before they have had any taste of the divine favor. This is that initial

7. Calvin notes that the very first words of Jesus and John the Baptist in their public ministry was a command to repent.

8. Calvin recognizes that we can't know the exact "mechanics" or "timing" of how faith produces repentance. This is a mystery. It is sufficient for us to know that the Scriptures present them as inseparable yet distinct.

9. A "neophyte" is a new convert to a religion.

10. Calvin argues that the idea of prescribing a period of repentance before someone can come into a state of favor with God is foolish. We come by faith. We don't merit our access to divine favor by works of penance.

11. "pride themselves" or "present themselves to be"

12. Calvin treats the Anabaptists and the Jesuits as similar in this regard. It is true that Anabaptists were radically different from the Roman Catholic Jesuits in some ways. But in their treatment of repentance as a first work necessary to receive God's grace that is somehow "completed," they were both in error.

13. It is an error to view repentance as a short period of days where we do various works and then it is over. Rather, repentance is to be a lifelong activity for a Christian. We continue to repent of our sins and put our trust in Jesus Christ daily.

14. Here Calvin gives us a key theological formula that can often protect us from falling into error: distinct but not separate.

fear which some writers class among the virtues, because they think it approximates to true and genuine obedience. But we are not here considering the various modes in which Christ draws us to himself, or prepares us for the study of piety: All I say is, that no righteousness can be found where the Spirit, whom Christ received in order to communicate it to his members, reigns not. Then, according to the passage in the Psalms, "There is forgiveness with thee, that thou mayest be feared," (Psalm 130:4), no man will ever reverence God who does not trust that God is propitious to him, no man will ever willingly set himself to observe the Law who is not persuaded that his services are pleasing to God. The indulgence of God in tolerating and pardoning our iniquities is a sign of paternal favor. This is also clear from the exhortation in Hosea, "Come, and let us return unto the Lord: for he has torn, and he will heal us; he has smitten, and he will bind us up," (Hos. 6:1); the hope of pardon is employed as a stimulus to prevent us from becoming reckless in sin. But there is no semblance of reason in the absurd procedure of those who, that they may begin with repentance, prescribe to their neophytes [9]certain days during which they are to exercise themselves in repentance, and after these are elapsed, admit them to communion in Gospel grace.[10] I allude to great numbers of Anabaptists, those of them especially who plume themselves[11] on being spiritual, and their associates the Jesuits,[12] and others of the same stamp. Such are the fruits which their giddy spirit produces, that repentance, which in every Christian man lasts as long as life, is with them completed in a few short days.[13]

Paul says in the Acts, that he was "testifying both to the Jews and also to the Greeks, repentance toward God, and faith toward our Lord Jesus Christ," (Acts 20:21). Here he mentions faith and repentance as two different things. What then? Can true repentance exist without faith? By no means. But although they cannot be separated, they ought to be distinguished.[14] As there is no faith without hope, and yet faith and hope are different, so repentance and faith, though constantly linked together, are only to be united, not confounded.[15] I am not unaware that under the term repentance is comprehended the whole work of turning to God, of which not the least important part is faith; but in what sense this is done will be perfectly obvious, when its nature and power shall have been explained. The term repentance is derived in the Hebrew from conversion, or turning again; and in the Greek from a change of mind and purpose; nor is the thing meant inappropriate to both derivations, for it is substantially this, that withdrawing from ourselves we turn to God, and laying aside the old, put on a new mind. Wherefore, it seems to me, that repentance may be not inappropriately defined thus: A real conversion of our life unto God, proceeding from sincere and serious fear of God; and consisting in the mortification of our flesh and the old man, and the quickening of the Spirit.[16] In this sense are to be understood all those addresses in which the prophets first, and the apostles afterwards, exhorted the people of their time to repentance. The great object for which they labored was, to fill them with confusion for their sins and dread of the divine judgment, that they might fall down and humble themselves before him whom they had offended, and, with true repentance, retake themselves to the right path. Accordingly, they use indiscriminately in the same sense, the expressions turning, or returning to the Lord; repenting, doing repentance. Whence, also, the sacred history describes it as repentance towards God, when men who disregarded him and wantoned in their lusts begin to obey his word, and are prepared to go whithersoever he may call them. And John Baptist and Paul, under the expression, bringing forth fruits meet for repentance,[17] described a course of life exhibiting and bearing testimony, in all its actions, to such a repentance.

But before proceeding farther, it will be proper to give a clearer exposition of the definition which we have adopted. There are three things, then, principally to be considered in it. First, in the conversion of the life to God, we require a transformation not only in external works, but in the soul itself,

15. The word "confounded" here means to mix together or to blur the distinction between. We must unite faith and repentance as both necessary, but keep them distinct from one another.

16. Calvin provides a brief definition of repentance. Repentance consists in (1) a turning to God, (2) the killing of the sinful flesh, and (3) the quickening of the Holy Spirit. The term "quickening" refers to the new life in Christ described in Scripture (Rom. 6:11-13).

17. It is important to distinguish between repentance itself and the fruits of repentance. When John the Baptist and Paul described "fruits in keeping with repentance" they meant fruits that were consistent with real repentance.

18. God must transform our soul and give us spiritual life. This is what is often called "regeneration" or the "new birth" as described in John 3. However, Calvin will use the word "regeneration" to describe more than just the initial act of re-creation by the work of God's Spirit.

19. It is important to remember that the outward physical sign of circumcision was designed to correspond to an inward spiritual reality. There was to be a circumcision of heart just as there had been a physical circumcision.

20. "Unfeigned repentance" is repentance that is real, not faked.

21. Not only must there be that re-creation of the soul by the Spirit. There must also be a fear of God for there to be true repentance.

which is able only after it has put off its old habits to bring forth fruits conformable to its renovation.[18] The prophet, intending to express this, enjoins those whom he calls to repentance to make them "a new heart and a new spirit," (Ezek. 18:31). Hence Moses, on several occasions, when he would show how the Israelites were to repent and turn to the Lord, tells them that it must be done with the whole heart, and the whole soul (a mode of expression of frequent recurrence in the prophets), and by terming it the circumcision of the heart, points to the internal affections. But there is no passage better fitted to teach us the genuine nature of repentance than the following: "If thou wilt return, O Israel, saith the Lord, return unto me." "Break up your fallow ground, and sow not among thorns. Circumcise yourselves to the Lord, and take away the foreskins of your heart," (Jer. 4:1-4). See how he declares to them that it will be of no avail to commence the study of righteousness unless impiety shall first have been eradicated from their inmost heart.[19] And to malice the deeper impression, he reminds them that they have to do with God, and can gain nothing by deceit, because he hates a double heart. For this reason Isaiah derides the preposterous attempts of hypocrites, who zealously aimed at an external repentance by the observance of ceremonies, but in the meanwhile cared not "to loose the bands of wickedness, to undo the heavy burdens, and to let the oppressed go free," (Isaiah 58:6). In these words he admirably shows wherein the acts of unfeigned repentance consist.[20]

The second part of our definition is, that repentance proceeds from a sincere fear of God.[21] Before the mind of the sinner can be inclined to repentance, he must be aroused by the thought of divine judgment; but when once the thought that God will one day ascend his tribunal to take an account of all words and actions has taken possession of his mind, it will not allow him to rest, or have one moment's peace, but will perpetually urge him to adopt a different plan of life, that he may be able to stand securely at that judgment-seat. Hence the Scripture, when exhorting to repentance, often introduces the subject of judgment, as in Jeremiah, "Lest my fury come forth like fire, and burn that none can quench it, because of the evil of your doings," (Jer. 4:4). Paul, in his discourse to the Athenians says, "The times of this ignorance God winked at; but now commandeth all men every where to repent: because he has appointed a day in the which he will judge the world in righteousness," (Acts 17:30, 31). The same thing is repeated in several other passages. Sometimes God is declared to be a judge, from the punishments already inflicted, thus leading sinners to reflect that worse awaits them if they do not quickly repent. There is an example of this in the 29th chapter of Deuteronomy. As repentance begins with dread and hatred of sin, the Apostle sets down godly sorrow as one of its causes (2 Cor. 7:10). By godly sorrow he means when we not only tremble at the punishment, but hate and abhor the sin, because we know it is displeasing to God.[22] It is not strange that this should be, for unless we are stung to the quick, the sluggishness of our carnal nature cannot be corrected; nay, no degree of pungency would suffice for our stupor and sloth, did not God lift the rod and strike deeper. There is, moreover, a rebellious spirit which must be broken as with hammers. The stern threatening which God employs are extorted from him by our depraved dispositions. For while we are asleep it were in vain to allure us by soothing measures. Passages to this effect are everywhere to be met with, and I need not quote them. But there is another reason why the fear of God lies at the root of repentance—viz. that though the life of man were possessed of all kinds of virtue, still if they do not bear reference to God, how much soever they may be lauded in the world, they are mere abomination in heaven,[23] inasmuch as it is the principal part of righteousness to render to God that service and honor of which he is impiously defrauded, whenever it is not our express purpose to submit to his authority.

We must now explain the third part of the definition, and show what is meant when we say that repentance consists of

22. Real repentance isn't proved by a person's sorrow. They may be sorrowful for the wrong reasons. They may be sorrowful because there are consequences. But if there is no fear of God, then it is not true repentance.

23. Calvin argues that for an action to be a "good work," it must be done for God and His glory.

24. This is sometimes expressed in the "put-off, put-on" principle. We put off sin (the old man) and we put on righteousness (the new man).

25. The word "mortify" means to kill. The old nature is to be completely slain, completely annihilated, and replaced with works of righteousness.

two parts—viz. the mortification of the flesh, and the quickening of the Spirit.[24] The prophets, in accommodation to a carnal people, express this in simple and homely terms, but clearly, when they say, "Depart from evil, and do good," (Ps. 34:14). "Wash you, make you clean, put away the evil of your doings from before mine eyes; cease to do evil; learn to do well; seek judgment; relieve the oppressed," &c. (Isaiah 1:16, 17). In dissuading us from wickedness they demand the entire destruction of the flesh, which is full of perverseness and malice. It is a most difficult and arduous achievement to renounce ourselves, and lay aside our natural disposition. For the flesh must not be thought to be destroyed unless every thing that we have of our own is abolished. But seeing that all the desires of the flesh are enmity against God (Rom. 8:7), the first step to the obedience of his law is the renouncement of our own nature. Renovation is afterwards manifested by the fruits produced by it—viz. justice, judgment, and mercy. Since it were not sufficient duly to perform such acts, were not the mind and heart previously endued with sentiments of justice, judgment, and mercy this is done when the Holy Spirit, instilling his holiness into our souls, so inspired them with new thoughts and affections, that they may justly be regarded as new. And, indeed, as we are naturally averse to God, unless self-denial precede, we shall never tend to that which is right. Hence we are so often enjoined to put off the old man, to renounce the world and the flesh, to forsake our lusts, and be renewed in the spirit of our mind. Moreover, the very name mortification reminds us how difficult it is to forget our former nature, because we hence infer that we cannot be trained to the fear of God, and learn the first principles of piety, unless we are violently smitten with the sword of the Spirit and annihilated, as if God were declaring, that to be ranked among his sons there must be a destruction of our ordinary nature.[25]

Both of these we obtain by union with Christ. For if we have true fellowship in his death, our old man is crucified by his power, and the body of sin becomes dead, so that the corruption of our original nature is never again in full vigor (Rom. 6:5, 6). If we are partakers in his resurrection, we are raised up by means of it to newness of life, which conforms us to the righteousness of God. In one word, then, by repentance I understand regeneration, the only aim of which is to form in us anew the image of God, which was sullied, and all but effaced by the transgression of Adam.[26] So the Apostle teaches when he says, "We all with open face beholding as in a glass the glory of the Lord, are changed into the same image from glory to glory, as by the Spirit of the Lord." Again, "Be renewed in the spirit of your minds" and "Put ye on the new man, which after God is created in righteousness and true holiness." Again, "Put ye on the new man, which is renewed in knowledge after the image of him that created him." Accordingly through the blessing of Christ we are renewed by that regeneration into the righteousness of God from which we had fallen through Adam, the Lord being pleased in this manner to restore the integrity of all whom he appoints to the inheritance of life. This renewal, indeed, is not accomplished in a moment, a day, or a year, but by uninterrupted, sometimes even by slow progress[27] God abolishes the remains of carnal corruption in his elect, cleanses them from pollution, and consecrates them as his temples, restoring all their inclinations to real purity, so that during their whole lives they may practice repentance,[28] and know that death is the only termination to this warfare.[29]

By regeneration the children of God are delivered from the bondage of sin, but not as if they had already obtained full possession of freedom, and no longer felt any annoyance from the flesh. Materials for an unremitting contest remain, that they may be exercised, and not only exercised, but may better understand their weakness. All writers of sound judgment agree in this, that, in the regenerate man, there is still a spring of evil which is perpetually sending forth desires that allure and stimulate him to sin. They also acknowledge that the saints are still so liable to the disease of concupiscence, that, though opposing it, they cannot avoid being ever and anon

26. Calvin indicates that his definition of regeneration also includes what some theologians distinguish as "sanctification." Regeneration remakes us into the image of God, which was damaged and twisted by the sin of Adam.

27. God's work of sanctification (renewing us in the image of God) is a lifelong process. It proceeds at different speeds according to the working of God's Spirit.

28. Repentance is not a once-for-all act in the Christian life. We are to daily repent of our sins and trust in Jesus Christ.

29. Our battle with sin and our pursuit of holiness ends only at death. Then, when we go to be with the Lord, we will be perfected in holiness.

30. Calvin disagrees with Augustine in this. Augustine thought that concupiscence only became sin when it was indulged or acted upon. Calvin argues that even the very desires of our sinful hearts are sin. The very nature of lusting after the things of the world is sin itself.

31. In other words, the remnants of indwelling sin in the soul of a believer are opposed to "rectitude" or "righteousness."

prompted and incited to lust, avarice, ambition, or other vices. It is unnecessary to spend much time in investigating the sentiments of ancient writers. Augustine alone may suffice, as he has collected all their opinions with great care and fidelity. Any reader who is desirous to know the sense of antiquity may obtain it from him. There is this difference apparently between him and us, that while he admits that believers, so long as they are in the body, are so liable to concupiscence that they cannot but feel it, he does not venture to give this disease the name of sin. He is contented with giving it the name of infirmity,[30] and says, that it only becomes sin when either external act or consent is added to conception or apprehension; that is, when the will yields to the first desire. We again regard it as sin whenever man is influenced in any degree by any desire contrary to the law of God; nay, we maintain that the very gravity which begets in us such desires is sin. Accordingly, we hold that there is always sin in the saints until they are freed from their mortal frame, because depraved concupiscence resides in their flesh, and is at variance with rectitude.[31] Augustine himself dose not always refrain from using the name of sin, as when he says, "Paul gives the name of sin to that carnal concupiscence from which all sins arise. This in regard to the saints loses its dominion in this world, and is destroyed in heaven." In these words he admits that believers, in so far as they are liable to carnal concupiscence, are chargeable with sin.

When it is said that God purifies his Church, so as to be "holy and without blemish," (Eph. 5:26, 27), that he promises this cleansing by means of baptism, and performs it in his elect, I understand that reference is made to the guilt rather than to the matter of sin. In regenerating his people God indeed accomplishes this much for them; he destroys the dominion of sin, by supplying the agency of the Spirit, which enables them to come off victorious from the contest. Sin, however, though it ceases to reign, ceases not to dwell in them. Accordingly, though we say that the old man is crucified, and the law of sin is abolished in the children of God (Rom. 6:6), the remains of sin survive, not to have dominion, but to humble them under a consciousness of their infirmity.[32] We admit that these remains, just as if they had no existence, are not imputed, but we, at the same time, contend that it is owing to the mercy of God that the saints are not charged with the guilt which would otherwise make them sinners before God. It will not be difficult for us to confirm this view, seeing we can support it by clear passages of Scripture. How can we express our view more plainly than Paul does in Rom. 7:6? We have elsewhere shown and Augustine by solid reasons proves, that Paul is there speaking in the person of a regenerated man.[33] I say nothing as to his use of the words evil and sin. However those who object to our view may quibble on these words, can any man deny that aversion to the law of God is an evil, and that hindrance to righteousness is sin? In short, who will not admit that there is guilt where there is spiritual misery? But all these things Paul affirms of this disease. Again, the law furnishes us with a clear demonstration by which the whole question may be quickly disposed of. We are enjoined to love God with all our heart, with all our soul, with all our strength. Since all the faculties of our soul ought thus to be engrossed with the love of God, it is certain that the commandment is not fulfilled by those who receive the smallest desire into their heart, or admit into their minds any thought whatever which may lead them away from the love of God to vanity.[34] What then? Is it not through the faculties of mind that we are assailed with sudden motions, that we perceive sensual, or form conceptions of mental objects? Since these faculties give admission to vain and wicked thoughts, do they not show that to that extent they are devoid of the love of God? He, then, who admits not that all the desires of the flesh are sins, and that that disease of concupiscence,[35] which they call a stimulus, is a fountain of sin, must of necessity deny that the transgression of the law is sin.

32. The word infirmity here does not mean sickness in terms of the modern use of the word. Rather, it refers to the "weakness" of our fallen condition.

33. The teaching of Romans 7 is hotly debated by interpreters. Some think that Paul is referring to the regenerate man and his ongoing battle with sin. Others think that Paul is speaking of an unregenerate man who is under the conviction of sin. Calvin and many other interpreters in the Reformed tradition held that Romans 7 speaks of the regenerate man.

34. If we are to love God with all of our heart, all of our soul, all of our mind, and all of our strength, then even the smallest desire contrary to this is sin.

35. The word "concupiscence" means "lust" or "desire." Calvin does not limit this term to "sexual lust." It includes all unlawful desires.

Book 3

Chapter 6

The Life of a Christian Man. Scriptural Arguments Exhorting to it

This is the place to address those who, having nothing of Christ but the name and sign, would yet be called Christians. How dare they boast of this sacred name? None have intercourse with Christ but those who have acquired the true knowledge of him from the Gospel. The Apostle denies that any man truly has learned Christ who has not learned to put off "the old man, which is corrupt according to the deceitful lusts, and put on Christ," (Eph. 4:22). They are convicted, therefore, of falsely and unjustly pretending a knowledge of Christ, whatever be the volubility and eloquence[1] with which they can talk of the Gospel. Doctrine is not an affair of the tongue, but of the life;[2] is not apprehended by the intellect and memory merely, like other branches of learning; but is received only when it possesses the whole soul, and finds its seat and habitation in the inmost recesses of the heart. Let them, therefore, either cease to insult God, by boasting that they are what they are not, or let them show themselves not unworthy disciples of their divine Master. To doctrine in which our religion is contained we have given the first place, since by it our salvation commences; but it must

1. The word "volubility" refers to a large quantity of speech. Calvin argues that it is not how much someone says they are a Christian or how eloquently they discourse about the faith that truly makes them a Christian. Like the character "Talkative" in Bunyan's *Pilgrim's Progress*, there are many who are good talkers but are not doers of the word.

2. The Apostle John says something similar in his letter. "My little children, let us not love in word or in tongue, but in deed and in truth." (1 John 3:18)

be transfused into the breast, and pass into the conduct, and so transform us into itself, as not to prove unfruitful. If philosophers are justly offended, and banish from their company with disgrace those who, while professing an art which ought to be the mistress of their conduct, convert it into mere loquacious sophistry,[3] with how much better reason shall we detest those flimsy sophists who are contented to let the Gospel play upon their lips, when, from its efficacy, it ought to penetrate the inmost affections of the heart, fix its seat in the soul, and pervade the whole man a hundred times more than the frigid discourses of philosophers?

I insist not that the life of the Christian shall breathe nothing but the perfect Gospel, though this is to be desired, and ought to be attempted.[4] I insist not so strictly on evangelical perfection, as to refuse to acknowledge as a Christian any man who has not attained it. In this way all would be excluded from the Church, since there is no man who is not far removed from this perfection, while many, who have made but little progress, would be undeservedly rejected. What then? Let us set this before our eye as the end at which we ought constantly to aim. Let it be regarded as the goal towards which we are to run. For you cannot divide the matter with God, undertaking part of what his word enjoins, and omitting part at pleasure. For, in the first place, God uniformly recommends integrity as the principal part of his worship, meaning by integrity real singleness of mind, devoid of gloss and fiction, and to this is opposed a double mind; as if it had been said, that the spiritual commencement of a good life is when the internal affections are sincerely devoted to God, in the cultivation of holiness and justice. But seeing that, in this earthly prison of the body, no man is supplied with strength sufficient to hasten in his course with due alacrity, while the greater number are so oppressed with weakness, that hesitating, and halting, and even crawling on the ground, they make little progress, let every one of us go as far as his humble ability enables him, and prosecute the journey once begun. No one will travel so badly as not daily

3. "Loquacious" is to talk a great deal. "Sophistry" is false speech, often in the form of words intended to deceive.

4. Calvin admits that there is not a single Christian who is perfect. But all Christians should aim for perfect holiness.

to make some degree of progress. This, therefore, let us never cease to do, that we may daily advance in the way of the Lord; and let us not despair because of the slender measure of success. How little soever the success may correspond with our wish, our labor is not lost when to-day is better than yesterday, provided with true singleness of mind we keep our aim, and aspire to the goal, not speaking flattering things to ourselves, nor indulging our vices, but making it our constant endeavor to become better, until we attain to goodness itself. If during the whole course of our life we seek and follow, we shall at length attain it, when relieved from the infirmity of flesh we are admitted to full fellowship with God.

Book 3

Chapter 7

A Summary of the Christian Life. Of Self-denial

Although the Law of God contains a perfect rule of conduct admirably arranged, it has seemed proper to our divine Master to train his people by a more accurate method, to the rule which is enjoined in the Law; and the leading principle in the method is, that it is the duty of believers to present their "bodies a living sacrifice, holy and acceptable unto God, which is their reasonable service," (Rom. 12:1). Hence he draws the exhortation: "Be not conformed to this world: but be ye transformed by the renewing of your mind, that ye may prove what is that good, and acceptable, and perfect will of God." The great point, then, is, that we are consecrated and dedicated to God, and, therefore, should not henceforth think, speak, design, or act, without a view to his glory.[1] What he hath made sacred cannot, without signal insult to him, be applied to profane use. But if we are not our own, but the Lord's, it is plain both what error is to be shunned, and to what end the actions of our lives ought to be directed. We are not our own; therefore, neither is our own

1. Calvin states that the law of God contained in Holy Scripture is a perfect guide. Yet, in the words of Romans 12, we have a simple summary statement that gives a brief and pointed command. We are commanded to yield our entire lives as a living sacrifice to God. We are to deny ourselves and do all to the glory of God.

2. Because we are bought with the precious blood of Christ, we now belong to God. Therefore, as slaves of righteousness, we cannot do anything according to our own rules and ideas. We are to do all for God and in obedience to God. "For none of us lives to himself, and no one dies to himself. For if we live, we live to the Lord; and if we die, we die to the Lord. Therefore, whether we live or die, we are the Lord's." (Rom. 14:7-8)

3. In the words of the hymn "Trust and Obey," there is no other way to be happy in Jesus but to "trust and obey." The safest path is the path of obedience to God. To obey our own will is to put ourselves on the path of destruction.

4. Not only should there be a verbal obedience given, but there should be a transformation or "renewal" of the mind. This itself is an act of obedience to God.

reason or will to rule our acts and counsels.[2] We are not our own; therefore, let us not make it our end to seek what may be agreeable to our carnal nature. We are not our own; therefore, as far as possible, let us forget ourselves and the things that are ours. On the other hand, we are God's; let us, therefore, live and die to him (Rom. 14:8). We are God's; therefore, let his wisdom and will preside over all our actions. We are God's; to him, then, as the only legitimate end, let every part of our life be directed. O how great the proficiency of him who, taught that he is not his own, has withdrawn the dominion and government of himself from his own reason that he may give them to God! For as the surest source of destruction to men is to obey themselves, so the only haven of safety is to have no other will, no other wisdom, than to follow the Lord wherever he leads.[3] Let this, then be the first step, to abandon ourselves, and devote the whole energy of our minds to the service of God. By service, I mean not only that which consists in verbal obedience, but that by which the mind, divested of its own carnal feelings, implicitly obeys the call of the Spirit of God.[4] This transformation (which Paul calls the renewing of the mind, Rom. 12:2; Eph. 4:23), though it is the first entrance to life, was unknown to all the philosophers. They give the government of man to reason alone, thinking that she alone is to be listened to; in short, they assign to her the sole direction of the conduct. But Christian philosophy bids her give place, and yield complete submission to the Holy Spirit, so that the man himself no longer lives, but Christ lives and reigns in him (Gal. 2:20).

Hence follows the other principle, that we are not to seek our own, but the Lord's will, and act with a view to promote his glory. Great is our proficiency, when, almost forgetting ourselves, certainly postponing our own reason, we faithfully make it our study to obey God and his commandments. For when Scripture enjoins us to lay aside private regard to ourselves, it not only divests our minds of an excessive longing for wealth, or power, or human favor, but eradicates all ambition and thirst for worldly glory, and other more secret pests. The Christian ought, indeed, to be so trained and disposed as to consider, that during his whole life he has to do with God. For this reason, as he will bring all things to the disposal and estimate of God, so he will religiously direct his whole mind to him. For he who has learned to look to God in everything he does, is at the same time diverted from all vain thoughts. This is that self-denial which Christ so strongly enforces on his disciples from the very outset (Mt. 16:24), which, as soon as it takes hold of the mind, leaves no place either, first, for pride, show, and ostentation; or, secondly, for avarice, lust, luxury, effeminacy, or other vices which are engendered by self love.[5] On the contrary, wherever it reigns not, the foulest vices are indulged in without shame; or, if there is some appearance of virtue, it is vitiated by a depraved longing for applause.[6] Show me, if you can, an individual who, unless he has renounced himself in obedience to the Lord's command, is disposed to do good for its own sake. Those who have not so renounced themselves have followed virtue at least for the sake of praise. The philosophers who have contended most strongly that virtue is to be desired on her own account, were so inflated with arrogance as to make it apparent that they sought virtue for no other reason than as a ground for indulging in pride. So far, therefore, is God from being delighted with these hunters after popular applause with their swollen breasts, that he declares they have received their reward in this world (Mt. 6:2), and that harlots and publicans are nearer the kingdom of heaven than they (Mt. 21:31). We have not yet sufficiently explained how great and numerous are the obstacles by which a man is impeded in the pursuit of rectitude, so long as he has not renounced himself. The old saying is true; there is a world of iniquity treasured up in the human soul. Nor can you find any other remedy for this than to deny yourself, renounce your own reason, and direct your whole mind to the pursuit of those things which the Lord requires of you, and which you are to seek only because they are pleasing to Him.

5. Calvin refers to the words of Jesus in Matthew 16. "Then Jesus said to His disciples, 'If anyone desires to come after Me, let him deny himself, and take up his cross, and follow Me. For whoever desires to save his life will lose it, but whoever loses his life for My sake will find it.'" (Matt. 16:24-25)

6. Calvin notes that sometimes there may be some "virtue," some outward "good works." But this is "vitiated" or negated by the desire for applause. That is, these good works are done for the praise of man, not for the glory of God. Jesus warns us in Matthew 6:1-4 not to do our righteousness to be seen by men. Otherwise, the only reward we will have is the praise of men.

How difficult it is to perform the duty of seeking the good of our neighbor! Unless you leave off all thought of yourself and in a manner cease to be yourself, you will never accomplish it. How can you exhibit those works of charity which Paul describes unless you renounce yourself, and become wholly devoted to others? "Charity (says he, 1 Cor. 13:4) suffereth long, and is kind; charity envieth not; charity vaunteth not itself, is not puffed up, doth not behave itself unseemly, seeketh not her own, is not easily provoked," &c. Were it the only thing required of us to seek not our own, nature would not have the least power to comply: she so inclines us to love ourselves only, that she will not easily allow us carelessly to pass by ourselves and our own interests that we may watch over the interests of others, nay, spontaneously to yield our own rights and resign it to another. But Scripture, to conduct us to this, reminds us, that whatever we obtain from the Lord is granted on the condition of our employing it for the common good of the Church, and that, therefore, the legitimate use of all our gifts is a kind and liberal communication of them with others. There cannot be a surer rule, nor a stronger exhortation to the observance of it, than when we are taught that all the endowments which we possess are divine deposits entrusted to us for the very purpose of being distributed for the good of our neighbor. But Scripture proceeds still farther when it likens these endowments to the different members of the body (1 Cor. 12:12). No member has its function for itself, or applies it for its own private use, but transfers it to its fellow-members; nor does it derive any other advantage from it than that which it receives in common with the whole body. Thus, whatever the pious man can do, he is bound to do for his brethren, not consulting his own interest in any other way than by striving earnestly for the common edification of the Church. Let this, then, be our method of showing good-will and kindness, considering that, in regard to everything which God has bestowed upon us, and by which we can aid our neighbor, we are his stewards, and are bound to give account of our stewardship;

moreover, that the only right mode of administration is that which is regulated by love. In this way, we shall not only unite the study of our neighbor's advantage with a regard to our own, but make the latter subordinate to the former. And lest we should have omitted to perceive that this is the law for duly administering every gift which we receive from God, he of old applied that law to the minutest expressions of his own kindness. He commanded the first-fruits to be offered to him as an attestation by the people that it was impious to reap any advantage from goods not previously consecrated to him (Exod. 22:29; 23:19). But if the gifts of God are not sanctified to us until we have with our own hand dedicated them to the Giver, it must be a gross abuse that does not give signs of such dedication. It is in vain to contend that you cannot enrich the Lord by your offerings. Though, as the Psalmist says "Thou art my Lord: my goodness extendeth not unto thee," yet you can extend it "to the saints that are in the earth," (Ps. 16:2, 3); and therefore a comparison is drawn between sacred oblations and alms as now corresponding to the offerings under the Law.

Moreover, that we may not weary in well-doing (as would otherwise forthwith and infallibly be the case), we must add the other quality in the Apostle's enumeration, "Charity suffereth long, and is kind, is not easily provoked," (1 Cor. 13:4). The Lord enjoins us to do good to all without exception, though the greater part, if estimated by their own merit, are most unworthy of it. But Scripture subjoins a most excellent reason, when it tells us that we are not to look to what men in themselves deserve, but to attend to the image of God, which exists in all, and to which we owe all honor and love. But in those who are of the household of faith, the same rule is to be more carefully observed, inasmuch as that image is renewed and restored in them by the Spirit of Christ. Therefore, whoever be the man that is presented to you as needing your assistance, you have no ground for declining to give it to him. Say he is a stranger. The Lord has given him a mark which ought to be familiar to you: for which reason he forbids you to despise your own flesh (Gal. 6:10). Say he is mean and of no consideration. The Lord points him out as one whom he has distinguished by the luster of his own image (Isaiah 58:7). Say that you are bound to him by no ties of duty. The Lord has substituted him as it were into his own place, that in him you may recognize the many great obligations under which the Lord has laid you to himself. Say that he is unworthy of your least exertion on his account; but the image of God, by which he is recommended to you, is worthy of yourself and all your exertions. But if he not only merits no good, but has provoked you by injury and mischief, still this is no good reason why you should not embrace him in love, and visit him with offices of love. He has deserved very differently from me, you will say. But what has the Lord deserved? Whatever injury he has done you, when he enjoins you to forgive him, he certainly means that it should be imputed to himself. In this way only we attain to what is not to say difficult but altogether against nature, to love those that hate us, render good for evil, and blessing for cursing, remembering that we are not to reflect on the wickedness of men, but look to the image of God in them, an image which, covering and obliterating their faults, should by its beauty and dignity allure us to love and embrace them.

7. If we are walking in love, our selfish nature will be put to death. Love for God and love for others is opposed to our natural bent to self-love. By loving God and neighbor, our self-love is crucified.

We shall thus succeed in mortifying ourselves if we fulfill all the duties of charity.[7] Those duties, however, are not fulfilled by the mere discharge of them, though none be omitted, unless it is done from a pure feeling of love. For it may happen that one may perform every one of these offices, in so far as the external act is concerned, and be far from performing them aright. For you see some who would be thought very liberal, and yet accompany every thing they give with insult, by the haughtiness of their looks, or the violence of their words. And to such a calamitous condition have we come in this unhappy age, that the greater part of men never almost give alms without contumely.[8] Such conduct ought not to have been tolerated even among the heathen; but from Christians something more is required than to carry cheerfulness in their looks, and

8. That is, men in Calvin's age would often give with insulting language and insolence.

give attractiveness to the discharge of their duties by courteous language. First, they should put themselves in the place of him whom they see in need of their assistance, and pity his misfortune as if they felt and bore it, so that a feeling of pity and humanity should incline them to assist him just as they would themselves. He who is thus minded will go and give assistance to his brethren, and not only not taint his acts with arrogance or upbraiding but will neither look down upon the brother to whom he does a kindness, as one who needed his help, or keep him in subjection as under obligation to him, just as we do not insult a diseased member when the rest of the body labors for its recovery, nor think it under special obligation to the other members, because it has required more exertion than it has returned. A communication of offices between members is not regarded as at all gratuitous, but rather as the payment of that which being due by the law of nature it were monstrous to deny. For this reason, he who has performed one kind of duty will not think himself thereby discharged, as is usually the case when a rich man, after contributing somewhat of his substance, delegates remaining burdens to others as if he had nothing to do with them. Every one should rather consider, that however great he is, he owes himself to his neighbors, and that the only limit to his beneficence is the failure of his means. The extent of these should regulate that of his charity.[9]

9. Since the life of the believer is to be a living sacrifice to God, we should not think our duty of charity done when we do our little portion. Instead, we should always be looking for the next opportunity to deny ourselves and serve others. As Calvin says, the only limit to a man's generosity should be the limitation of his means. Whatever God gives us, we should use generously.

Book 3

Chapter 8

Of Bearing the Cross-One Branch of Self-denial

1. Calvin further expounds the nature of self-denial in this chapter by pointing to the words of Jesus in Matthew 16:24. We must take up our "cross" and follow Jesus. Cross-bearing implies a life of suffering and trials as we follow in the footsteps of Jesus Christ. "To put to the proof" means "to put to the test." Our faith is tested through trials.

The pious mind must ascend still higher, namely, whither Christ calls his disciples when he says, that every one of them must "take up his cross," (Mt. 16:24). Those whom the Lord has chosen and honored with his intercourse must prepare for a hard, laborious, troubled life, a life full of many and various kinds of evils; it being the will of our heavenly Father to exercise his people in this way while putting them to the proof.[1] Having begun this course with Christ the first-born, he continues it towards all his children. For though that Son was dear to him above others, the Son in whom he was "well pleased," yet we see, that far from being treated gently and indulgently, we may say, that not only was he subjected to a perpetual cross while he dwelt on earth, but his whole life was nothing else than a kind of perpetual cross. The Apostle assigns the reason, "Though he was a Son, yet learned he obedience by the things which he suffered," (Heb. 5:8). Why then should we exempt ourselves from that condition to which Christ our Head behooved to submit; especially since he submitted on our account, that he might in his own person exhibit a model of patience? Wherefore, the Apostle declares, that all the children of God are destined to be conformed to him. Hence it affords us great consolation in hard and difficult circumstances, which men deem evil and adverse, to think that we are holding fellowship with the sufferings of Christ; that as he passed to celestial glory through a labyrinth of many woes, so we too are conducted thither through various tribulations.[2] For, in another passage, Paul himself thus speaks, "we must through much tribulation enter the kingdom of God," (Acts 14:22); and again, "that I may know him, and the power of his resurrection, and the fellowship of his sufferings, being made conformable unto his death," (Rom 8:29). How powerfully should it soften the bitterness of the cross, to think that the more we are afflicted with adversity, the surer we are made of our fellowship with Christ; by communion with whom our sufferings are not only blessed to us, but tend greatly to the furtherance of our salvation.

We may add, that the only thing which made it necessary for our Lord to undertake to bear the cross, was to testify and prove his obedience to the Father; whereas there are many reasons which make it necessary for us to live constantly under the cross. Feeble as we are by nature, and prone to ascribe all perfection to our flesh, unless we receive as it were ocular demonstration[3] of our weakness, we readily estimate our virtue above its proper worth, and doubt not that, whatever happens, it will stand unimpaired and invincible against all difficulties. Hence we indulge a stupid and empty confidence in the flesh, and then trusting to it wax proud against the Lord himself; as if our own faculties were sufficient without his grace. This arrogance cannot be better repressed than when He proves to us by experience, not only how great our weakness, but also our frailty is. Therefore, he visits us with disgrace, or poverty, or bereavement, or disease, or other afflictions. Feeling altogether unable to support them, we forthwith, in so far as regards ourselves, give way, and thus humbled learn to invoke his strength, which alone can enable us to bear up under a weight of affliction. Nay, even the holiest of men, however well aware

2. We can have comfort in suffering knowing that (1) we are appointed to go through such trials for the growth of our faith and (2) we know that we share in the fellowship of Christ's sufferings.

3. "Ocular" means that which is "visible" or evident to the eyes. In other words, trials make obvious our weaknesses. Without seeing our weakness, we might be tempted to ascribe "perfection" to our flesh.

that they stand not in their own strength, but by the grace of God, would feel too secure in their own fortitude and constancy, were they not brought to a more thorough knowledge of themselves by the trial of the cross. This feeling gained even upon David, "In my prosperity I said, I shall never be moved. Lord, by thy favor thou hast made my mountain to stand strong: thou didst hide thy face, and I was troubled," (Ps. 30:6, 7). He confesses that in prosperity his feelings were dulled and blunted, so that, neglecting the grace of God, on which alone he ought to have depended, he leant to himself, and promised himself perpetuity. If it so happened to this great prophet, who of us should not fear and study caution? Though in tranquility they flatter themselves with the idea of greater constancy and patience, yet, humbled by adversity, they learn the deception. Believers, I say, warned by such proofs of their diseases, make progress in humility, and, divesting themselves of a depraved confidence in the flesh, betake themselves to the grace of God, and, when they have so betaken themselves, experience the presence of the divine power, in which is ample protection.[4]

This Paul teaches when he says that tribulation works patience, and patience experience.[5] God having promised that he will be with believers in tribulation, they feel the truth of the promise; while supported by his hand, they endure patiently. This they could never do by their own strength. Patience, therefore, gives the saints an experimental proof that God in reality furnishes the aid which he has promised whenever there is need. Hence also their faith is confirmed, for it were very ungrateful not to expect that in future the truth of God will be, as they have already found it, firm and constant. We now see how many advantages are at once produced by the cross. Overturning the overweening opinion we form of our own virtue, and detecting the hypocrisy in which we delight, it removes our pernicious carnal confidence,[6] teaching us, when thus humbled, to recline on God alone, so that we neither are oppressed nor despond. Then victory is followed by hope, inasmuch as the Lord, by performing what he has promised, es-

4. We are humbled through adversity. This is good for us because we learn how weak we are, and we begin to more and more depend upon the grace of God.

5. Romans 5:3-5

6. Paul testifies in Galatians that it is in the cross alone that we should boast. "But God forbid that I should boast except in the cross of our Lord Jesus Christ, by whom the world has been crucified to me, and I to the world." (Gal. 6:14)

tablishes his truth in regard to the future. Were these the only reasons, it is surely plain how necessary it is for us to bear the cross. It is of no little importance to be rid of your self-love, and made fully conscious of your weakness; so impressed with a sense of your weakness as to learn to distrust yourself—to distrust yourself so as to transfer your confidence to God, re-clining on him with such heartfelt confidence as to trust in his aid, and continue invincible to the end, standing by his grace so as to perceive that he is true to his promises, and so assured of the certainty of his promises as to be strong in hope.

Another end which the Lord has in afflicting his people is to try their patience, and train them to obedience—not that they can yield obedience to him except in so far as he enables them; but he is pleased thus to attest and display striking proofs of the graces[7] which he has conferred upon his saints, lest they should remain within unseen and unemployed. Accordingly, by bringing forward openly the strength and constancy of en-durance with which he has provided his servants, he is said to try their patience. Hence the expressions that God tempted Abraham (Gen. 21:1, 12), and made proof of his piety by not declining to sacrifice his only son. Hence, too, Peter tells us that our faith is proved by tribulation, just as gold is tried in a furnace of fire. But who will say it is not expedient that the most excellent gift of patience which the believer has received from his God should be applied to uses by being made sure and manifest? Otherwise men would never value it according to its worth. But if God himself, to prevent the virtues which he has conferred upon believers from lurking in obscurity, nay, lying useless and perishing, does aright in supplying materials for calling them forth, there is the best reason for the afflic-tions of the saints, since without them their patience could not exist. I say, that by the cross they are also trained to obedience, because they are thus taught to live not according to their own wish, but at the disposal of God. Indeed, did all things proceed as they wish, they would not know what it is to follow God. Seneca mentions that there was an old proverb when any one

7. The Lord uses trib-ulation and afflictions in order to train us in obedience. This was the way the the Lord Jesus also learned obedience (Heb. 5:8). Likewise, we also learn obedience to God through affliction. The Psalmist writes, "It is good for me that I have been afflicted, that I may learn Your statutes" (Ps. 119:71). Calvin also notes that we need God's grace in order to obey. Therefore, when the Lord grows our obedi-ence through affliction, the affliction becomes an opportunity to mag-nify the grace of God.

8. Calvin notes here that when God is pouring out blessings upon us, we can begin to take them for granted and become spiritually lazy. This is what happened to Israel. They "grew fat" (Deut. 32:15) and they began to turn from God. The blessings of God in this life should lead us to gratitude and love for God. Such blessings should not produce a spiritual indolence.

9. "Petulance" refers to a bad temper.

10. For some of us, health and riches would be spiritually harmful for us. The Lord knows best what his children need. Calvin notes that not everyone needs the exact same discipline from the Lord's hand. It is good for us to know that our Heavenly Father is wise and loving. He may withhold things we think we should have because in reality, those things would not be good for us.

was exhorted to endure adversity, "Follow God;" thereby intimating, that men truly submitted to the yoke of God only when they gave their back and hand to his rod. But if it is most right that we should in all things prove our obedience to our heavenly Father, certainly we ought not to decline any method by which he trains us to obedience.

Still, however, we see not how necessary that obedience is, unless we at the same time consider how prone our carnal nature is to shake off the yoke of God whenever it has been treated with some degree of gentleness and indulgence.[8] It just happens to it as with refractory horses, which, if kept idle for a few days at hack and manger, become ungovernable, and no longer recognize the rider, whose command before they implicitly obeyed. And we invariably become what God complains of in the people of Israel—waxing gross and fat, we kick against him who reared and nursed us (Deut. 32:15). The kindness of God should allure us to ponder and love his goodness; but since such is our malignity, that we are invariably corrupted by his indulgence, it is more than necessary for us to be restrained by discipline from breaking forth into such petulance.[9] Thus, lest we become emboldened by an over-abundance of wealth; lest elated with honor, we grow proud; lest inflated with other advantages of body, or mind, or fortune, we grow insolent, the Lord himself interferes as he sees to be expedient by means of the cross, subduing and curbing the arrogance of our flesh, and that in various ways, as the advantage of each requires.[10] For as we do not all equally labor under the same disease, so we do not all need the same difficult cure. Hence we see that all are not exercised with the same kind of cross. While the heavenly Physician treats some more gently, in the case of others he employs harsher remedies, his purpose being to provide a cure for all. Still none is left free and untouched, because he knows that all, without a single exception, are diseased.

We may add, that our most merciful Father requires not only to prevent our weakness, but often to correct our past faults, that he may keep us in due obedience. Therefore, whenever we are afflicted we ought immediately to call to mind our past life. In this way we will find that the faults which we have committed are deserving of such castigation. And yet the exhortation to patience is not to be founded chiefly on the acknowledgment of sin. For Scripture supplies a far better consideration when it says, that in adversity "we are chastened of the Lord, that we should not be condemned with the world," (1 Cor. 11:32). Therefore, in the very bitterness of tribulation we ought to recognize the kindness and mercy of our Father, since even then he ceases not to further our salvation.[11] For he afflicts, not that he may ruin or destroy but rather that he may deliver us from the condemnation of the world. Let this thought lead us to what Scripture elsewhere teaches: "My son, despise not the chastening of the Lord; neither be weary of his correction: For whom the Lord loveth he correcteth; even as a father the son in whom he delighteth," (Prov. 3:11, 12). When we perceive our Father's rod, is it not our part to behave as obedient docile sons rather than rebelliously imitate desperate men, who are hardened in wickedness? God dooms us to destruction, if he does not, by correction, call us back when we have fallen off from him, so that it is truly said, "If ye be without chastisement," "then are ye bastards, and not sons," (Heb. 12:8). We are most perverse then if we cannot bear him while he is manifesting his good-will to us, and the care which he takes of our salvation. Scripture states the difference between believers and unbelievers to be, that the latter, as the slaves of inveterate and deep-seated iniquity, only become worse and more obstinate under the lash; whereas the former, like free-born sons turn to repentance. Now, therefore, choose your class. But as I have already spoken of this subject, it is sufficient to have here briefly adverted to it.

11. Calvin's statements are similar to what is described in Hebrews 12. "If you endure chastening, God deals with you as with sons; for what son is there whom a father does not chasten? But if you are without chastening, of which all have become partakers, then you are illegitimate and not sons." (Heb. 12:7-8)

Book 3

Chapter 9

Of Meditation on the Future Life

1. In this chapter, Calvin explains how meditation on the future life to come is such a vital discipline in the Christian life. The Christian faith has a future-orientation as we look, by faith, to the things yet to come, promised to us by God.

2. Afflictions are powerful wake-up calls for us. If all was perfectly easy and comfortable in this present life, we might become lethargic and not long for the life to come.

3. Jesus warns that for some, the Word of God has no lasting effect because the cares of this world and the deceitfulness of riches chokes the Word (Matt. 13:22).

Whatever be the kind of tribulation with which we are afflicted, we should always consider the end of it to be, that we may be trained to despise the present, and thereby stimulated to aspire to the future life.[1] For since God well knows how strongly we are inclined by nature to a slavish love of this world, in order to prevent us from clinging too strongly to it, he employs the fittest reason for calling us back, and shaking off our lethargy.[2] Every one of us, indeed, would be thought to aspire and aim at heavenly immortality during the whole course of his life. For we would be ashamed in no respect to excel the lower animals; whose condition would not be at all inferior to ours, had we not a hope of immortality beyond the grave. But when you attend to the plans, wishes, and actions of each, you see nothing in them but the earth. Hence our stupidity; our minds being dazzled with the glare of wealth, power, and honors, that they can see no farther. The heart also, engrossed with avarice, ambition, and lust, is weighed down and cannot rise above them.[3] In short, the whole soul, ensnared by the allurements of the flesh, seeks its happiness on the earth. To meet this disease, the Lord makes his people sensible of the vanity of the present life, by a constant proof of its miseries. Thus, that they may not promise themselves deep and lasting peace in it, he often allows them to be assailed by war, tumult, or rapine,[4] or to be disturbed by other injuries. That they may not long with too much eagerness after fleeting and fading riches, or rest in those which they already possess, he reduces them to want, or, at least, restricts them to a moderate allowance, at one time by exile, at another by sterility, at another by fire, or by other means. That they may not indulge too complacently in the advantages of married life, he either vexes them by the misconduct of their partners, or humbles them by the wickedness of their children, or afflicts them by bereavement. But if in all these he is indulgent to them, lest they should either swell with vain-glory, or be elated with confidence, by diseases and dangers he sets palpably before them how unstable and evanescent[5] are all the advantages competent to mortals. We duly profit by the discipline of the cross, when we learn that this life, estimated in itself, is restless, troubled, in numberless ways wretched, and plainly in no respect happy; that what are estimated its blessings are uncertain, fleeting, vain, and vitiated by a great admixture of evil. From this we conclude, that all we have to seek or hope for here is contest; that when we think of the crown we must raise our eyes to heaven. For we must hold, that our mind never rises seriously to desire and aspire after the future, until it has learned to despise the present life.

For there is no medium between the two things: the earth must either be worthless in our estimation, or keep us enslaved by an intemperate love of it. Therefore, if we have any regard to eternity, we must carefully strive to disencumber ourselves of these fetters. Moreover, since the present life has many enticements to allure us, and great semblance of delight, grace, and sweetness to soothe us, it is of great consequence to us to be now and then called off from its fascinations. For what, pray, would happen, if we here enjoyed an uninterrupted course of honor and felicity, when even the constant stimulus of afflic-

4. "Rapine" refers to the violent seizure of property.

5. "Evanescent" refers to that which soon disappears or evaporates.

tion cannot arouse us to a due sense of our misery? That human life is like smoke or a shadow is not only known to the learned; there is not a more trite proverb among the vulgar. Considering it a fact most useful to be known, they have recommended it in many well-known expressions. Still there is no fact which we ponder less carefully, or less frequently remember. For we form all our plans just as if we had fixed our immortality on the earth. If we see a funeral, or walk among graves, as the image of death is then present to the eye, I admit we philosophize admirably on the vanity of life. We do not indeed always do so, for those things often have no effect upon us at all. But, at the best, our philosophy is momentary. It vanishes as soon as we turn our back, and leaves not the vestige of remembrance behind; in short, it passes away, just like the applause of a theatre at some pleasant spectacle. Forgetful not only of death, but also of mortality itself, as if no rumor of it had ever reached us, we indulge in supine security as expecting a terrestrial immortality. Meanwhile, if any one breaks in with the proverb, that man is the creature of a day, we indeed acknowledge its truth, but, so far from giving heed to it, the thought of perpetuity still keeps hold of our minds. Who then can deny that it is of the highest importance to us all, I say not, to be admonished by words, but convinced by all possible experience of the miserable condition of our earthly life; since even when convinced we scarcely cease to gaze upon it with vicious, stupid admiration, as if it contained within itself the sum of all that is good? But if God finds it necessary so to train us, it must be our duty to listen to him when he calls, and shakes us from our torpor, that we may hasten to despise the world, and aspire with our whole heart to the future life.

Still the contempt which believers should train themselves to feel for the present life, must not be of a kind to beget hatred of it or ingratitude to God. This life, though abounding in all kinds of wretchedness, is justly classed among divine blessings which are not to be despised. Wherefore, if we do not recognize the kindness of God in it, we are chargeable with no little ingratitude towards him.[6] To believers, especially, it ought to be a proof of divine benevolence, since it is wholly destined to promote their salvation. Before openly exhibiting the inheritance of eternal glory, God is pleased to manifest himself to us as a Father by minor proofs—viz. the blessings which he daily bestows upon us. Therefore, while this life serves to acquaint us with the goodness of God, shall we disdain it as if it did not contain one particle of good? We ought, therefore, to feel and be affected towards it in such a manner as to place it among those gifts of the divine benignity which are by no means to be despised. Were there no proofs in Scripture (they are most numerous and clear), yet nature herself exhorts us to return thanks to God for having brought us forth into light, granted us the use of it, and bestowed upon us all the means necessary for its preservation. And there is a much higher reason when we reflect that here we are in a manner prepared for the glory of the heavenly kingdom. For the Lord hath ordained, that those who are ultimately to be crowned in heaven must maintain a previous warfare on the earth, that they may not triumph before they have overcome the difficulties of war, and obtained the victory. Another reason is, that we here begin to experience in various ways a foretaste of the divine benignity, in order that our hope and desire may be whetted for its full manifestation. When once we have concluded that our earthly life is a gift of the divine mercy, of which, agreeably to our obligation, it behooves us to have a grateful remembrance, we shall then properly descend to consider its most wretched condition, and thus escape from that excessive fondness for it, to which, as I have said, we are naturally prone.

6. Calvin clarifies that even when we deal with trials in this life, we have no right to hate God or be ungrateful to God. Even though this present life comes with many sorrows, there are still so many blessings from the Lord. Let us always be grateful for what God has given us though it be mixed with affliction.

Book 3
Chapter 10

How to Use the Present Life, and the Comforts of It

B y such rudiments we are at the same time well instructed by Scripture in the proper use of earthly blessings, a subject which, in forming a scheme of life, is by no mean to be neglected. For if we are to live, we must use the necessary supports of life; nor can we even shun those things which seem more subservient to delight than to necessity. We must therefore observe a mean, that we may use them with a pure conscience, whether for necessity or for pleasure.[1] This the Lord prescribes by his word, when he tells us that to his people the present life is a kind of pilgrimage by which they hasten to the heavenly kingdom. If we are only to pass through the earth, there can be no doubt that we are to use its blessings only in so far as they assist our progress, rather than retard it.[2] Accordingly, Paul, not without cause, admonishes us to use this world without abusing it, and to buy possessions as if we were selling them (1 Cor. 7:30, 31). But as this is a slippery place, and there is great danger of falling on either side, let us fix our feet where we can stand safely. There have been some good and holy men who, when they saw intemperance and luxury perpetually carried to excess, if not strictly curbed,

1. In this chapter, Calvin explains that we are to use the comforts of the present life in a particular way. He also notes that there are things of necessity (food and clothing for example). But there are also things God has created for our enjoyment and pleasure.

2. All things in the present life must be used in such a way that we progress in godliness rather than "retard" or slow down that progress.

and were desirous to correct so pernicious an evil, imagined that there was no other method than to allow man to use corporeal goods only in so far as they were necessaries: a counsel pious indeed, but unnecessarily austere; for it does the very dangerous thing of binding consciences in closer fetters than those in which they are bound by the word of God.[3] Moreover, necessity, according to them, was abstinence from every thing which could be wanted, so that they held it scarcely lawful to make any addition to bread and water. Others were still more austere, as is related of Cratetes the Theban, who threw his riches into the sea, because he thought, that unless he destroyed them they would destroy him. Many also in the present day, while they seek a pretext for carnal intemperance in the use of external things, and at the same time would pave the way for licentiousness, assume for granted, what I by no means concede, that this liberty is not to be restrained by any modification, but that it is to be left to every man's conscience to use them as far as he thinks lawful. I indeed confess that here consciences neither can nor ought to be bound by fixed and definite laws; but that Scripture having laid down general rules for the legitimate uses we should keep within the limits which they prescribe.[4]

Let this be our principle that we err not in the use of the gifts of Providence when we refer them to the end for which their author made and destined them, since he created them for our good, and not for our destruction.[5] No man will keep the true path better than he who shall have this end carefully in view. Now then, if we consider for what end he created food, we shall find that he consulted not only for our necessity, but also for our enjoyment and delight. Thus, in clothing, the end was, in addition to necessity, comeliness and honor; and in herbs, fruits, and trees, besides their various uses, gracefulness of appearance and sweetness of smell. Were it not so, the Prophet would not enumerate among the mercies of God "wine that maketh glad the heart of man, and oil to make his face to shine," (Ps. 104:15). The Scriptures would not ev-

3. The practice of "asceticism" has a long and troubled history in Christianity. Some have so despised the comforts of this present life as to confuse godliness with austerity and harshness. It is possible to enjoy God's good gifts in this life and not fall into covetousness and lust. The key is that we receive God's good gifts with thanksgiving (1 Tim. 4:4-5).

4. Calvin is concerned that our practice be guided by the principles of God's Word. We should not bind men's consciences to practices beyond what God's Word requires. We have liberty in Christ to have differing measures of wealth and possessions. The question is, are these things helping us to give thanks to God and seek the kingdom of God? Or are they leading us into covetousness?

5. God made all things for a purpose. We must look to His Word to understand the purpose behind His created order. It is foolish to call God's creation evil when it is fallen mankind that has perverted God's purposes. Food and sex are gifts from God. But they must be used the way God intended.

erywhere mention, in commendation of his benignity, that he had given such things to men. The natural qualities of things themselves demonstrate to what end, and how far, they may be lawfully enjoyed. Has the Lord adorned flowers with all the beauty which spontaneously presents itself to the eye, and the sweet odor which delights the sense of smell, and shall it be unlawful for us to enjoy that beauty and this odor? What? Has he not so distinguished colors as to make some more agreeable than others? Has he not given qualities to gold and silver, ivory and marble, thereby rendering them precious above other metals or stones? In short, has he not given many things a value without having any necessary use?

Have done, then, with that inhuman philosophy which, in allowing no use of the creatures but for necessity, not only maliciously deprives us of the lawful fruit of the divine beneficence, but cannot be realized without depriving man of all his senses, and reducing him to a block. But, on the other hand, let us with no less care guard against the lusts of the flesh, which, if not kept in order, break through all bounds, and are, as I have said, advocated by those who, under pretence of liberty, allow themselves every sort of license. First one restraint is imposed when we hold that the object of creating all things was to teach us to know their author, and feel grateful for his indulgence. Where is the gratitude if you so gorge or stupefy yourself with feasting and wine as to be unfit for offices of piety, or the duties of your calling? Where the recognition of God, if the flesh, boiling forth in lust through excessive indulgences infects the mind with its impurity, so as to lose the discernment of honor and rectitude? Where thankfulness to God for clothing, if on account of sumptuous raiment[6] we both admire ourselves and disdain others? If, from a love of show and splendor, we pave the way for immodesty? Where our recognition of God, if the glare of these things captivates our minds?[7] For many are so devoted to luxury in all their senses that their mind lies buried: many are so delighted with marble, gold, and pictures, that they become marble-heart-

6. "Sumptuous raiment" refers to splendid and expensive clothing.

7. Calvin gives a variety of illustrations of how food, sexuality, and clothing can be used according to God's intended purpose or how it can be twisted and become sinful.

ed—are changed as it were into metal, and made like painted figures. The kitchen, with its savory smells, so engrosses them that they have no spiritual savor. The same thing may be seen in other matters. Wherefore, it is plain that there is here great necessity for curbing licentious abuse, and conforming to the rule of Paul, "make not provision for the flesh to fulfill the lusts thereof," (Rom. 13:14). Where too much liberty is given to them, they break forth without measure or restraint.

There is no surer or quicker way of accomplishing this than by despising the present life and aspiring to celestial immortality. For hence two rules arise: First, "it remaineth, that both they that have wives be as though they had none;" "and they that use this world, as not abusing it," (1 Cor. 7:29, 31). Secondly, we must learn to be no less placid and patient in enduring penury,[8] than moderate in enjoying abundance. He who makes it his rule to use this world as if he used it not, not only cuts off all gluttony in regard to meat and drink, and all effeminacy, ambition, pride, excessive shows and austerity, in regard to his table, his house, and his clothes, but removes every care and affection which might withdraw or hinder him from aspiring to the heavenly life, and cultivating the interest of his soul. It was well said by Cato: Luxury causes great care, and produces great carelessness as to virtue; and it is an old proverb,—Those who are much occupied with the care of the body, usually give little care to the soul. Therefore while the liberty of the Christian in external matters is not to be tied down to a strict rule, it is, however, subject to this law—he must indulge as little as possible; on the other hand, it must be his constant aims not only to curb luxury, but to cut off all show of superfluous abundance, and carefully beware of converting a help into an hindrance.

Another rule is, that those in narrow and slender circumstances should learn to bear their wants patiently, that they may not become immoderately desirous of things,[9] the moderate use of which implies no small progress in the school of Christ. For in addition to the many other vices which accom-

8. "Penury" is extreme poverty.

9. Temptations to worldliness do not only affect those who are rich. Those in poverty can also be consumed by covetous desires. The Christian can pray, as Proverbs says, "Give me neither poverty nor riches" (Prov. 30:8).

pany a longing for earthly good, he who is impatient under poverty almost always betrays the contrary disease in abundance. By this I mean, that he who is ashamed of a sordid garment will be vain-glorious of a splendid one; he who not contented with a slender, feels annoyed at the want of a more luxurious supper, will intemperately abuse his luxury if he obtains it; he who has a difficulty, and is dissatisfied in submitting to a private and humble condition, will be unable to refrain from pride if he attain to honor. Let it be the aim of all who have any unfeigned desire for piety to learn, after the example of the Apostle, "both to be full and to be hungry, both to abound and to suffer need," (Phil. 4:12). Scripture, moreover, has a third rule for modifying the use of earthly blessings. We have already adverted to it when considering the offices of charity. For it declares that they have all been given us by the kindness of God, and appointed for our use under the condition of being regarded as trusts, of which we must one day give account. We must, therefore, administer them as if we constantly heard the words sounding in our ears, "Give an account of your stewardship." At the same time, let us remember by whom the account is to be taken—viz. by him who, while he so highly commends abstinence, sobriety, frugality, and moderation, abominates luxury, pride, ostentation, and vanity; who approves of no administration but that which is combined with charity, who with his own lips has already condemned all those pleasures which withdraw the heart from chastity and purity, or darken the intellect.

Book 3
Chapter 11

Of Justification by Faith. Both the Name and the Reality Defined

I trust I have now sufficiently shown how man's only resource for escaping from the curse of the law, and recovering salvation, lies in faith; and also what the nature of faith is, what the benefits which it confers, and the fruits which it produces. The whole may be thus summed up: Christ given to us by the kindness of God is apprehended and possessed by faith, by means of which we obtain in particular a twofold benefit; first, being reconciled by the righteousness of Christ, God becomes, instead of a judge, an indulgent Father; and, secondly, being sanctified by his Spirit, we aspire to integrity and purity of life. This second benefit—viz. regeneration, appears to have been already sufficiently discussed. On the other hand, the subject of justification was discussed more cursorily, because it seemed of more consequence first to explain that the faith by which alone, through the mercy of God, we obtain free justification, is not destitute of good works; and also to show the true nature of these good works on which this question partly turns. The doctrine of Justification is now to be fully discussed, and discussed under the conviction, that as it is the principal ground on which religion must be support-

1. The Reformer Martin Luther described justification as the doctrine on which the church stands or falls. Along with the doctrine of Scriptural authority, the doctrine of justification was one of the principal controversies of the Protestant Reformation. Calvin agrees with Luther's maxim. He calls it the "principal ground" on which religion is supported. The Reformers were keenly aware that doctrinal error with this doctrine would lead to deadly heresy. Justification answers one of the most crucial questions: how can a man be righteous before God?

2. If we do not rightly understand our justification before God, we lack a proper foundation to understand our relationship with God. We may doubt whether God is pleased with us, or whether God will eventually condemn us on the day of judgment. This is why justification is so important to understand.

ed,[1] so it requires greater care and attention. For unless you understand first of all what your position is before God, and what the judgment which he passes upon you, you have no foundation on which your salvation can be laid,[2] or on which piety towards God can be reared. The necessity of thoroughly understanding this subject will become more apparent as we proceed with it.

Lest we should stumble at the very threshold (this we should do were we to begin the discussion without knowing what the subject is), let us first explain the meaning of the expressions, To be justified in the sight of God, to be Justified by faith or by works. A man is said to be justified in the sight of God when in the judgment of God he is deemed righteous,[3] and is accepted on account of his righteousness; for as iniquity is abominable to God, so neither can the sinner find grace in his sight, so far as he is and so long as he is regarded as a sinner. Hence, wherever sin is, there also are the wrath and vengeance of God. He, on the other hand, is justified who is regarded not as a sinner, but as righteous, and as such stands acquitted at the judgment-seat of God, where all sinners are condemned. As an innocent man, when charged before an impartial judge, who decides according to his innocence, is said to be justified by the judge, as a man is said to be justified by God when, removed from the catalogue of sinners, he has God as the witness and assertor of his righteousness. In the same manner, a man will be said to be justified by works, if in his life there can be found a purity and holiness which merits an attestation of righteousness at the throne of God, or if by the perfection of his works he can answer and satisfy the divine justice. On the contrary, a man will be justified by faith when, excluded from the righteousness of works, he by faith lays hold of the righteousness of Christ, and clothed in it appears in the sight of God not as a sinner, but as righteous.

3. To be justified is to be "declared righteous." This is a legal declaration. As we will see in Calvin's treatment, the righteousness by which we are justified by God is not our own righteousness. It is the righteousness of Christ which is "imputed" or "reckoned" to our account.

Thus we simply interpret justification, as the acceptance with which God receives us into his favor as if we were righteous; and we say that this justification consists in the forgiveness of sins and the imputation of the righteousness of Christ.[4]

When Paul objects that the power of justifying exists not in faith, considered in itself, but only as receiving Christ, I willingly admit it. For did faith justify of itself, or (as it is expressed) by its own intrinsic virtue, as it is always weak and imperfect, its efficacy would be partial, and thus our righteousness being maimed would give us only a portion of salvation. We indeed imagine nothing of the kind, but say, that, properly speaking, God alone justifies. The same thing we likewise transfer to Christ, because he was given to us for righteousness; while we compare faith to a kind of vessel, because we are incapable of receiving Christ, unless we are emptied and come with open mouth to receive his grace.[5] Hence it follows, that we do not withdraw the power of justifying from Christ, when we hold that, previous to his righteousness, he himself is received by faith. Still, however, I admit not the tortuous figure of the sophist, that faith is Christ; as if a vessel of clay were a treasure, because gold is deposited in it. And yet this is no reason why faith, though in itself of no dignity or value, should not justify us by giving Christ; just as such a vessel filled with coin may give wealth. I say, therefore, that faith, which is only the instrument for receiving justification, is ignorantly confounded with Christ, who is the material cause, as well as the author and minister of this great blessing. This disposes of the difficulty—viz. how the term faith is to be understood when treating of justification.

Scripture, when it treats of justification by faith, leads us in a very different direction. Turning away our view from our own works, it bids us look only to the mercy of God and the perfection of Christ. The order of justification which it sets before us is this: first, God of his mere gratuitous goodness is pleased to embrace the sinner, in whom he sees nothing that can move him to mercy but wretchedness, because he sees him

4. Justification is not only the forgiveness of sins. It also includes the imputation of the righteousness of Christ to our account (2 Cor. 5:21).

5. Calvin provides an important clarification here. We are not justified by the "intrinsic" virtue of our faith. Faith is simply the "means" or the "instrument" by which we take hold of Christ. Faith is simply the "open mouth" that now can be fed.

6. Our justification involves no mixture of faith in Christ and our own works. We have no good works to bring. To rely on works in any way to be justified is foolish. The Apostle Paul repeatedly warns against this very thing in Galatians. "For as many as are of the works of the law are under the curse; for it is written, 'Cursed is everyone who does not continue in all things which are written in the book of the law, to do them.' But that no one is justified by the law in the sight of God is evident, for 'the just shall live by faith.'" (Gal. 3:10-11)

7. The gospel of God's grace in Christ is a free gift, received by faith alone. It is described as a "gift" free of price repeatedly in Scripture (Isa. 55:1-2, Rom. 3:24, 5:15-16, 6:23, Eph. 2:8-9).

8. Romans 10:5 provides a helpful distinction between the law and the gospel. The law is God's righteous standard. But it demands perfect righteousness. As fallen sinners, this is something we cannot do. For this reason, none of us can be justified by works. But the gospel gives us the righteousness of Christ, freely received by faith.

altogether naked and destitute of good works.[6] He, therefore, seeks the cause of kindness in himself, that thus he may affect the sinner by a sense of his goodness, and induce him, in distrust of his own works, to cast himself entirely upon his mercy for salvation. This is the meaning of faith by which the sinner comes into the possession of salvation, when, according to the doctrine of the Gospel, he perceives that he is reconciled by God; when, by the intercession of Christ, he obtains the pardon of his sins, and is justified; and, though renewed by the Spirit of God, considers that, instead of leaning on his own works, he must look solely to the righteousness which is treasured up for him in Christ. When these things are weighed separately, they will clearly explain our view, though they may be arranged in a better order than that in which they are here presented. But it is of little consequence, provided they are so connected with each other as to give us a full exposition and solid confirmation of the whole subject.

Here it is proper to remember the relation which we previously established between faith and the Gospel; faith being said to justify because it receives and embraces the righteousness offered in the Gospel. By the very fact of its being said to be offered by the Gospel,[7] all consideration of works is excluded. This Paul repeatedly declares, and in two passages, in particular, most clearly demonstrates. In the Epistle to the Romans, comparing the Law and the Gospel, he says, "Moses describeth the righteousness which is of the law, That the man which does those things shall live by them. But the righteousness which is of faith speaketh on this wise,—If thou shalt confess with thy mouth the Lord Jesus, and shalt believe in thine heart that God has raised him from the dead, thou shalt be saved," (Rom. 10:5, 6:9). Do you see how he makes the distinction between the Law and the Gospel to be, that the former gives justification to works, whereas the latter bestows it freely without any help from works?[8] This is a notable passage, and may free us from many difficulties if we understand that the justification which is given us by the Gospel is free from any terms of Law. It is for this reason he more than once places the promise in diametrical opposition to the Law. "If the inheritance be of the law, it is no more of promise," (Gal. 3:18). Expressions of similar import occur in the same chapter. Undoubtedly the Law also has its promises; and, therefore, between them and the Gospel promises there must be some distinction and difference, unless we are to hold that the comparison is inept. And in what can the difference consist unless in this that the promises of the Gospel are gratuitous,[9] and founded on the mere mercy of God, whereas the promises of the Law depend on the condition of works? But let no pester here allege that only the righteousness which men would obtrude upon God of their own strength and free will is repudiated; since Paul declares, without exceptions that the Law gained nothing by its commands, being such as none, not only of mankind in general, but none even of the most perfect, are able to fulfill. Love assuredly is the chief commandment in the Law, and since the Spirit of God trains us to love, it cannot but be a cause of righteousness in us, though that righteousness even in the saints is defective,[10] and therefore of no value as a ground of merit.

9. "Gratuitous" means "free" here.

10. Though the Holy Spirit produces in us a true righteousness, even the best works of the saints are not wholly perfect. Therefore, even our best works could not merit us anything.

Let us now consider the truth of what was said in the definition—viz. that justification by faith is reconciliation with God, and that this consists solely in the remission of sins. We must always return to the axioms that the wrath of God lies upon all men so long as they continue sinners. This is elegantly expressed by Isaiah in these words: "Behold, the Lord's hand is not shortened, that it cannot save; neither his ear heavy, that it cannot hear: but your iniquities have separated between you and your God, and your sins have hid his face from you, that he will not hear," (Isaiah 59:1, 2). We are here told that sin is a separation between God and man; that His countenance is turned away from the sinner; and that it cannot be otherwise, since, to have any intercourse with sin is repugnant to his righteousness. Hence the Apostle shows that man is at enmity with God until he is restored to favor by Christ (Rom.

5:8-10). When the Lord, therefore, admits him to union, he is said to justify him, because he can neither receive him into favor, nor unite him to himself, without changing his condition from that of a sinner into that of a righteous man. We add, that this is done by remission of sins. For if those whom the Lord has reconciled to himself are estimated by works, they will still prove to be in reality sinners, while they ought to be pure and free from sin. It is evident therefore, that the only way in which those whom God embraces are made righteous, is by having their pollutions wiped away by the remission of sins, so that this justification may be termed in one word the remission of sins.

Hence also it is proved, that it is entirely by the intervention of Christ's righteousness that we obtain justification before God. This is equivalent to saying that man is not just in himself, but that the righteousness of Christ is communicated to him by imputation,[11] while he is strictly deserving of punishment. Thus vanishes the absurd dogma, that man is justified by faith, inasmuch as it brings him under the influence of the Spirit of God by whom he is rendered righteous. This is so repugnant to the above doctrine that it never can be reconciled with it. There can be no doubt that he who is taught to seek righteousness out of himself does not previously possess it in himself. This is most clearly declared by the Apostle, when he says, that he who knew no sin was made an expiatory victim for sin, that we might be made the righteousness of God in him (2 Cor. 5:21). You see that our righteousness is not in ourselves, but in Christ; that the only way in which we become possessed of it is by being made partakers with Christ, since with him we possess all riches. There is nothing repugnant to this in what he elsewhere says: "God sending his own Son in the likeness of sinful flesh, and for sin condemned sin in the flesh: that the righteousness of the law might be fulfilled in us," (Rom. 8:3, 4). Here the only fulfillment to which he refers is that which we obtain by imputation. Our Lord Jesus Christ communicates his righteousness to us, and so by

11. "Imputation" is a legal reckoning. This can be contrasted with "infusion" or "impartation." To have something "infused" or "imparted" means it actually becomes a part of our nature. In sanctification, the Holy Spirit imparts grace to us and transforms our nature. But in justification, there is no such impartation. Instead, it is a legal declaration that we are righteous in Christ because we are united to Him by faith.

some wondrous ways in so far as pertains to the justice of God transfuses its power into us. That this was the Apostle's view is abundantly clear from another sentiment which he had expressed a little before: "As by one man's disobedience many were made sinners, so by the obedience of one shall many be made righteous," (Rom. 5:19). To declare that we are deemed righteous, solely because the obedience of Christ is imputed to us as if it where our own, is just to place our righteousness in the obedience of Christ.

Book 3

Chapter 12

Necessity of Contemplating the Judgement-Seat of God, in Order to be Seriously Convinced of the Doctrine of Gratuitous Justification

1. In this chapter, Calvin sets forth before us the reality of the judgment seat of God. As we contemplate the final judgment, we see how essential the doctrine of free justification is for each of us. With these words, Calvin reminds us that this is a heavenly court where the infinitely Holy God is the judge. We cannot use man's standard of righteousness. We must look to the righteousness of God.

Although the perfect truth of the above doctrine is proved by clear passages of Scripture, yet we cannot clearly see how necessary it is, before we bring distinctly into view the foundations on which the whole discussion ought to rest. First, then, let us remember that the righteousness which we are considering is not that of a human, but of a heavenly tribunal; and so beware of employing our own little standard to measure the perfection which is to satisfy the justice of God.[1] It is strange with what rashness and presumption this is commonly defined. Nay, we see that none talk more confidently, or, so to speak, more blusteringly, of the righteousness of works than those whose diseases are most palpable, and blemishes most apparent. This they do because they reflect not on the righteousness of Christ, which, if they had the slightest perception of it, they would never treat with so much insult. It is certainly undervalued, if not recognized to be so perfect that nothing can be accepted that is not in every respect entire and absolute, and tainted by no impurity; such indeed as never has been, and never will be, found in man. It is easy for any man, within the precincts of the schools, to talk of the sufficiency of works for justification; but when we come into the presence of God there must be a truce to such talk.[2] The matter is there discussed in earnest, and is no longer a theatrical logomachy.[3] Hither must we turn our minds if we would inquire to any purpose concerning true righteousness; the question must be: How shall we answer the heavenly Judge when he calls us to account? Let us contemplate that Judge, not as our own unaided intellect conceives of him, but as he is portrayed to us in Scripture (see especially the Book of Job), with a brightness which obscures the stars, a strength which melts the mountains, an anger which shakes the earth, a wisdom which takes the wise in their own craftiness, a purity before which all things become impure, a righteousness to which not even angels are equal (so far is it from making the guilty innocent), a vengeance which once kindled burns to the lowest hell (Ex. 34:7; Nah. 1:3; Deut. 32:22). Let Him, I say, sit in judgment on the actions of men, and who will feel secure in sisting himself before his throne? "Who among us," says the prophets "shall dwell with the devouring fire? Who among us shall dwell with everlasting burnings? He that walketh righteously, and speaketh uprightly," (Isaiah 33:14, 15). Let whoso will come forth. Nay, the answer shows that no man can. For, on the other hand, we hear the dreadful voice: "If thou, Lord, shouldst mark our iniquities, O Lord, who shall stand?" (Ps. 130:3). All must immediately perish, as Job declares, "Shall mortal man be more just than God? Shall a man be more pure than his Maker? Behold, he put no trust in his servants; and his angels he charged with folly: How much less in them that dwell in houses of clay, whose foundation is in the dust, which are crushed before the moth? They are destroyed from morning to evening," (Job 4:17-20). Again, "Behold, he putteth no trust in his saints; yea, the heavens are not clean in his sight. How much more abominable and filthy is man, which drinketh iniquity like water?" (Job 15:15, 16). I confess, indeed, that in the Book of Job reference is made to a righteousness of a more exalted description than the observance of the

2. That is, there must be an end to such talk. He notes that in the "schools" or universities of the day, men would discuss the sufficiency of works for justification. But on the day of judgment, all such discussions will be ended. "Every mouth will be stopped" (Rom. 3:19).

3. A "logomachy" is an argument over the meaning of words.

4. Our senses must be very dull if we are not filled with the fear of God as we contemplate the curses of the law against our sin. It is a fearful thing to fall into the hands of the living God! (Heb. 10:31)

5. That is, the whole discussion will be fruitless and vain unless we consider the judgment seat of God.

6. As long as we compare ourselves to others, we may think that we are very righteous. There are plenty of murderers and rapists we can compare ourselves to. If we aren't like them, doesn't that make us righteous? When viewed in the light of God's law, the answer must be a resounding no.

7. "Perspicacity" refers to the ability to see clearly.

Law. It is of importance to attend to this distinction; for even could a man satisfy the Law, he could not stand the scrutiny of that righteousness which transcends all our thoughts. Hence, although Job was not conscious of offending, he is still dumb with astonishment, because he sees that God could not be appeased even by the sanctity of angels, were their works weighed in that supreme balance. But to advert no farther to this righteousness, which is incomprehensible, I only say, that if our life is brought to the standard of the written law, we are lethargic indeed if we are not filled with dread at the many maledictions which God has employed for the purpose of arousing us,[4] and among others, the following general one: "Cursed be he that confirmeth not all the words of this law to do them," (Deut. 27:26). In short, the whole discussion of this subject will be insipid and frivolous,[5] unless we sist ourselves before the heavenly Judge, and anxious for our acquittal, voluntarily humble ourselves, confessing our nothingness.

Thus then must we raise our eyes that we may learn to tremble instead of vainly exulting. It is easy, indeed, when the comparison is made among men, for every one to plume himself on some quality which others ought not to despise; but when we rise to God, that confidence instantly falls and dies away.[6] The case of the soul with regard to God is very analogous to that of the body in regard to the visible firmament. The bodily eye, while employed in surveying adjacent objects, is pleased with its own perspicacity;[7] but when directed to the sun, being dazzled and overwhelmed by the refulgence, it becomes no less convinced of its weakness than it formerly was of its power in viewing inferior objects. Therefore, lest we deceive ourselves by vain confidence, let us recollect that even though we deem ourselves equal or superior to other men, this is nothing to God, by whose judgment the decision must be given. But if our presumption cannot be tamed by these considerations, he will answer us as he did the Pharisees, "Ye are they which justify yourselves before men; but God knoweth your hearts: for that which is highly esteemed among men is abomination in the sight of God," (Luke 16:15). Go now and make a proud boast of your righteousness among men, while God in heaven abhors it. But what are the feelings of the servants of God, of those who are truly taught by his Spirit? "Enter not into judgment with thy servant; for in thy sight shall no man living be justified," (Ps. 143:2). Another, though in a sense somewhat different, says, "How should man be just with God? If he will contend with him he cannot answer him one of a thousand," (Job 9:2, 3). Here we are plainly told what the righteousness of God is, namely, a righteousness which no human works can satisfy which charges us with a thousand sins, while not one sin can be excused. Of this righteousness Paul, that chosen vessel of God, had formed a just idea, when he declared, "I know nothing by myself, yet am I not hereby justified," (1 Cor. 4:4).

Therefore if we would make way for the call of Christ, we must put far from us all arrogance and confidence. The former is produced by a foolish persuasion of self-righteousness, when a man thinks that he has something in himself which deservedly recommends him to God; the latter may exist without any confidence in works. For many sinners, intoxicated with the pleasures of vice, think not of the judgment of God. Lying stupefied, as it were, by a kind of lethargy, they aspire not to the offered mercy. It is not less necessary to shake off torpor[8] of this description than every kind of confidence in ourselves, in order that we may haste to Christ unencumbered, and while hungry and empty be filled with his blessings. Never shall we have sufficient confidence in him unless utterly distrustful of ourselves; never shall we take courage in him until we first despond of ourselves; never shall we have full consolation in him until we cease to have any in ourselves. When we have entirely discarded all self-confidence, and trust solely in the certainty of his goodness, we are fit to apprehend and obtain the grace of God. "When," (as Augustine says), "forgetting our own merits, we embrace the gifts of Christ, because if he should seek for merits in us we should not obtain his gifts."

8. "Torpor" means a kind of lethargy or inactivity.

9. Calvin is referring to Bernard of Clairvaux (1090-1153). Bernard was an influential theologian in Europe during the Middle Ages. Calvin frequently quotes from Bernard in the *Institutes*. Calvin greatly respected Bernard for his writings.

With this Bernard admirably accords,[9] comparing the proud who presume in the least on their merits, to unfaithful servants, who wickedly take the merit of a favor merely passing through them, just as if a wall were to boast of producing the ray which it receives through the window. Not to dwell longer here, let us lay down this short but sure and general rule, That he is prepared to reap the fruits of the divine mercy who has thoroughly emptied himself, I say not of righteousness (he has none), but of a vain and blustering show of righteousness; for to whatever extent any man rests in himself, to the same extent he impedes the beneficence of God.

Book 3

Chapter 13

Two Things to be Observed in Gratuitous Justification

If we now inquire in what way the conscience can be quieted as in the view of God, we shall find that the only way is by having righteousness bestowed upon us freely by the gift of God. Let us always remember the words of Solomon, "Who can say I have made my heart clean, I am free from my sin?" (Prov. 20:9). Undoubtedly there is not one man who is not covered with infinite pollutions. Let the most perfect man descend into his own conscience, and bring his actions to account, and what will the result be? Will he feel calm and quiescent,[1] as if all matters were well arranged between himself and God; or will he not rather be stung with dire torment, when he sees that the ground of condemnation is within him if he be estimated by his works? Conscience, when it beholds God, must either have sure peace with his justice, or be beset by the terrors of hell. We gain nothing, therefore, by discoursing of righteousness, unless we hold it to be a righteousness stable enough to support our souls before the tribunal of God. When the soul is able to appear intrepidly[2] in the presence of God, and receive his sentence without dismay, then only let us know that we have found a righteousness that is not fictitious.

1. "Quiescent" means to be in a state of inactivity or dormancy. Here, the idea is that when your conscience does not accuse you before God, you are at peace internally.

2. To appear "intrepidly" means to enter the presence of God without fear.

3. To have faith is to have a sure foundation for our confidence before God. If we have faith in Christ, we can be assured that we will not be condemned by God. "Therefore, having been justified by faith, we have peace with God through our Lord Jesus Christ, through whom also we have access by faith into this grace in which we stand, and rejoice in hope of the glory of God." (Rom. 5:1-2)

It is not, therefore, without cause, that the Apostle insists on this matter. I prefer giving it in his words rather than my own: "If they which are of the law be heirs, faith is made void, and the promise made of no effect," (Rom. 4:14). He first infers that faith is made void if the promise of righteousness has respect to the merit of our works, or depends on the observance of the law. Never could any one rest securely in it, for never could he feel fully assured that he had fully satisfied the law; and it is certain that no man ever fully satisfied it by works. Not to go far for proof of this, every one who will use his eyes aright may be his own witness. Hence it appears how deep and dark the abyss is into which hypocrisy plunges the minds of men, when they indulge so securely as, without hesitations to oppose their flattery to the judgment of God, as if they were relieving him from his office as judge. Very different is the anxiety which fills the breasts of believers, who sincerely examine themselves. Every mind, therefore, would first begin to hesitate, and at length to despair, while each determined for itself with how great a load of debt it was still oppressed, and how far it was from coming up to the enjoined condition. Thus, then, faith would be oppressed and extinguished. To have faith is not to fluctuate, to vary, to be carried up and down, to hesitate, remain in suspense, vacillate, in fine, to despair; it is to possess sure certainty and complete security of mind, to have whereon to rest and fix your foot.[3]

Book 3

Chapter 14

The Beginning of Justification. In What Sense Progressive

In farther illustration of the subject, let us consider what kind of righteousness man can have, during the whole course of his life, and for this purpose let us make a fourfold division. Mankind, either endued with no knowledge of God, are sunk in idolatry; or, initiated in the sacraments, but by the impurity of their lives denying him whom they confess with their mouths, are Christians in name only; or they are hypocrites, who with empty glosses hide the iniquity of the heart; or they are regenerated by the Spirit of God, and aspire to true holiness. In the first place, when men are judged by their natural endowments, not an iota of good will be found from the crown of the head to the sole of the foot, unless we are to charge Scripture with falsehood, when it describes all the sons of Adam by such terms as these: "The heart is deceitful above all things, and desperately wicked."[1] "The imagination of man's heart is evil from his youth."[2] "The Lord knoweth the thoughts of man that they are vanity."[3] "They are all gone aside: they are altogether become filthy; there is none that does good, no, not one."[4] In short, that they are flesh, under which name are comprehended all those works which are enu-

1. Jer. 17:9
2. Gen. 8:21
3. Ps. 94:11

4. Rom. 3:12

5. This language means "to pride oneself."

6. While Calvin argues from Scripture that the depravity of man is "total" (affecting the entire nature). He does not deny that there is evidence of the image of God in man. There are "excellent endowments" in unbelievers. These are divine gifts that should be acknowledged as such.

7. Some of the Roman Emperors were considered wicked and cruel men such as Caligula, Nero, and Domitian. But Vespasian was considered a moderate man who did not descend into the wickedness of these other men. Calvin is willing to acknowledge that there are differences between them.

8. Even unbelievers who in some ways conform their lives to God's law will experience temporal blessings. These may include a longer life, better relationships, health, and prosperity. These do not equal eternal salvation of course. But they are still blessings from God.

merated by Paul; adultery, fornication, uncleanness, lasciviousness, idolatry, witchcraft, hatred, variance, emulation, wrath, strife, seditions, heresies, envying, murders, drunkenness, reveling, and all kinds of pollution and abomination which it is possible to imagine. Such, then, is the worth on which men are to plume themselves.[5] But if any among them possess an integrity of manners which presents some semblance of sanctity among men, yet because we know that God regards not the outward appearance, we must penetrate to the very source of action, if we would see how far works avail for righteousness. We must, I say, look within, and see from what affection of the heart these works proceed. This is a very wide field of discussion, but as the matter may be explained in few words, I will use as much brevity as I can.

First, then, I deny not, that whatever excellent endowments appear in unbelievers are divine gifts.[6] Nor do I set myself so much in opposition to common sense, as to contend that there was no difference between the justice, moderation, and equity of Titus and Trojan, and the rage, intemperance, and cruelty of Caligula, Nero, and Domitian; between the continence of Vespasian,[7] and the obscene lusts of Tiberius; and (not to dwell on single virtues and vices) between the observance of law and justice, and the contempt of them. So great is the difference between justice and injustice, that it may be seen even where the former is only a lifeless image. For what order would remain in the world if we were to confound them? Hence this distinction between honorable and base actions God has not only engraved on the minds of each, but also often confirms in the administration of his providence. For we see how he visits those who cultivate virtue with many temporal blessings.[8] Not that that external image of virtue in the least degree merits his favor, but he is pleased thus to show how much he delights in true righteousness, since he does not leave even the outward semblance of it to go unrewarded. Hence it follows, as we lately observed, that those virtues, or rather images of virtues, of whatever kind, are divine gifts, since there is nothing in any degree praiseworthy which proceeds not from him.[9]

Still the observation of Augustine is true, that all who are strangers to the true God, however excellent they may be deemed on account of their virtues are more deserving of punishment than of reward, because, by the pollution of their heart, they contaminate the pure gifts of God. For though they are instruments of God to preserve human society by justice, continence, friendship, temperance, fortitude, and prudence, yet they execute these good works of God in the worst manner, because they are kept from acting ill, not by a sincere love of goodness, but merely by ambition or self-love,[10] or some other sinister affection. Seeing then that these actions are polluted as in their very source, by impurity of heart, they have no better title to be classed among virtues than vices, which impose upon us by their affinity or resemblance to virtue. In short, when we remember that the object at which righteousness always aims is the service of God,[11] whatever is of a different tendency deservedly forfeits the name. Hence, as they have no regard to the end which the divine wisdom prescribes, although from the performance the act seems good, yet from the perverse motive it is sin.

Let us now see what kind of righteousness belongs to those persons whom we have placed in the fourth class.[12] We admits that when God reconciles us to himself by the intervention of the righteousness of Christ, and bestowing upon us the free pardon of sins regards us as righteous, his goodness is at the same time conjoined with mercy, so that he dwells in us by means of his Holy Spirit, by whose agency the lusts of our flesh are every day more and more mortified while that we ourselves are sanctified; that is consecrated to the Lord for true purity of life, our hearts being trained to the obedience of the law. It thus becomes our leading desire to obey his will, and in all things advance his glory only. Still, however while we walk in the ways of the Lord, under the guidance of the Holy Spirit, lest we should become unduly elated, and forget

9. "Every good gift and every perfect gift is from above, and comes down from the Father of lights, with whom there is no variation or shadow of turning." (Jas. 1:17)

10. Though unbelievers may do some outwardly good acts, those acts do not proceed from a love for God. They proceed from sinful motives. Paul tells us that whatever is done apart from faith is sin (Rom. 14:23).

11. The motive behind our actions is very important. Christians are to do all things to the glory of God (1 Cor. 10:31).

12. The fourth class described here are those who are true believers, indwelt by the Spirit of God.

ourselves, we have still remains of imperfection which serve to keep us humble: "There is no man that sinneth not," saith Scripture (1 Kings 8:46). What righteousness then can men obtain by their works? First, I say, that the best thing which can be produced by them is always tainted and corrupted by the impurity of the flesh, and has, as it were, some mixture of dross in it.[13] Let the holy servant of God, I say, select from the whole course of his life the action which he deems most excellent, and let him ponder it in all its parts; he will doubtless find in it something that savors of the rottenness of the flesh, since our alacrity in well-doing is never what it ought to be, but our course is always retarded by much weakness. Although we see theft the stains by which the works of the righteous are blemished, are by no means unapparent, still, granting that they are the minutest possible, will they give no offense to the eye of God, before which even the stars are not clean? We thus see, that even saints cannot perform one work which, if judged on its own merits, is not deserving of condemnation.

13. Though a believer will do good works as the Spirit works in them, they still have a degree of imperfection in those works. While their motive may be the glory of God, there might be a tinge of self-ambition still driving them. Perhaps an act of love is performed, but there is still some desire for the praise of man.

Even were it possible for us to perform works absolutely pure, yet one sin is sufficient to efface and extinguish all remembrance of former righteousness, as the prophet says (Ezek. 18:24). With this James agrees, "Whosoever shall keep the whole law, and yet offend in one point, is guilty of all," (James 2:10). And since this mortal life is never entirely free from the taint of sin, whatever righteousness we could acquire would ever and anon be corrupted, overwhelmed, and destroyed, by subsequent sins, so that it could not stand the scrutiny of God, or be imputed to us for righteousness. In short, whenever we treat of the righteousness of works, we must look not to the legal work but to the command. Therefore, when righteousness is sought by the Law, it is in vain to produce one or two single works; we must show an uninterrupted obedience.[14] God does not (as many foolishly imagine) impute that forgiveness of sins once for all, as righteousness; so that having obtained the pardon of our past life we may afterwards seek righteousness in the Law. This were only to mock and delude

14. Even as we grow in holiness, we still sin. And since the law demands perfect and uninterrupted obedience, it is obvious that none of us can stand before God by our own righteousness.

us by the entertainment of false hopes. For since perfection is altogether unattainable by us, so long as we are clothed with flesh, and the Law denounces death and judgment against all who have not yielded a perfect righteousness, there will always be ground to accuse and convict us unless the mercy of God interpose, and ever and anon absolve us by the constant remission of sins. Wherefore the statement which we set out is always true, If we are estimated by our own worthiness, in every thing that we think or devise, with all our studies and endeavors we deserve death and destruction.

We must strongly insist on these two things: That no believer ever performed one work which, if tested by the strict judgment of God, could escape condemnation; and, moreover, that were this granted to be possible (though it is not), yet the act being vitiated and polluted by the sins of which it is certain that the author of it is guilty, it is deprived of its merit.

When the saints repeatedly confirm and console themselves with the remembrance of their innocence and integrity, and sometimes even abstain not from proclaiming them, it is done in two ways: either because by comparing their good cause with the bad cause of the ungodly, they thence feel secure of victory, not so much from commendation of their own righteousness, as from the just and merited condemnation of their adversaries; or because, reviewing themselves before God, even without any comparison with others the purity of their conscience gives them some comfort and security. The former reason will afterwards be considered; let us now briefly show, in regard to the latter, how it accords with what we have above said, that we can have no confidence in works before the bar of God, that we cannot glory in any opinion of their worth. The accordance lies here, that when the point considered is the constitution and foundation of salvation, believers, without paying any respect to works, direct their eyes to the goodness of God alone. Nor do they turn to it only in the first instance, as to the commencement of blessedness, but rest in it as the completion. Conscience being thus founded, built

15. The good works we see in our lives are evidence of God's work within us. This can help to further our assurance of salvation.

16. It is inappropriate to look at our works as an "aid to salvation" or in any way meritorious. However, we can look to these works as evidence of God's sanctifying work in us.

17. To take something *a posteriori* means to reason after the effect. That is, when we look to the good works in our lives, from these we may deduce that God is at work in us. The opposite of this would be to reason *a priori*, before there is any evidence of good works.

up, and established is farther established by the consideration of works, inasmuch as they are proofs of God dwelling and reigning in us.[15] Since, then, this confidence in works has no place unless you have previously fixed your whole confidence on the mercy of God, it should not seem contrary to that on which it depends. Wherefore, when we exclude confidence in works, we merely mean, that the Christian mind must not turn back to the merit of works as an aid to salvation, but must dwell entirely on the free promise of justification. But we forbid no believer to confirm and support this faith by the signs of the divine favor towards him.[16] For if when we call to mind the gifts which God has bestowed upon us, they are like rays of the divine countenance, by which we are enabled to behold the highest light of his goodness; much more is this the case with the gift of good works, which shows that we have received the Spirit of adoption.

When believers therefore feel their faith strengthened by a consciousness of integrity, and entertain sentiments of exultation, it is just because the fruits of their calling convince them that the Lord has admitted them to a place among his children. Accordingly, when Solomon says, "In the fear of the Lord is strong confidence," (Prov. 14:26), and when the saints sometimes beseech the Lord to hear them, because they walked before his face in simplicity and integrity (Gen. 24:10; 2 Kings 20:3), these expressions apply not to laying the foundation of a firm conscience, but are of force only when taken *a posteriori*.[17] For there is no where such a fear of God as can give full security, and the saints are always conscious that any integrity which they may possess is mingled with many remains of the flesh. But as the fruits of regeneration furnish them with a proof of the Holy Spirit dwelling in them, experiencing God to be a Father in a matter of so much moment, they are strengthened in no slight degree to wait for his assistance in all their necessities. Even this they could not do, had they not previously perceived that the goodness of God is sealed to them by nothing but the certainty of the promise.

Should they begin to estimate it by their good works, nothing will be weaker or more uncertain; works, when estimated by themselves, no less proving the divine displeasure by their imperfection, than his good-will by their incipient purity. In short, while proclaiming the mercies of the Lord, they never lose sight of his free favor, with all its "breadth and length, and depth and height," testified by Paul (Eph. 3:18); as if he had said, Whithersoever the believer turns, however loftily he climbs, however far and wide his thoughts extend, he must not go farther than the love of Christ, but must be wholly occupied in meditating upon it, as including in itself all dimensions. Accordingly, he declares that it "passeth knowledge," that "to know the love of Christ" is to "be filled with all the fullness of God," (Eph. 3:19). In another passage, where he glories that believers are victorious in every contest, he adds the reason, "through him that loved us," (Rom. 8:37).

We now see that believers have no such confidence in works as to attribute any merit to them (since they regard them only as divine gifts, in which they recognize his goodness, and signs of calling, in which they discern their election); nor such confidence as to derogate in any respect[18] from the free righteousness of Christ; since on this it depends, and without this cannot subsist.

18. "Derogate" means "to detract from."

Book 3

Chapter 16

Refutation of Calumnies by Which it is Attempted to Throw Odium on This Doctrine

1. A "calumny" is a false and slanderous statement.

2. Calvin and the other Reformers were accused of detracting from the pursuit of good works because of their doctrine of justification. This is still a common charge brought against the doctrine of justification by faith alone. Some argue that it inclines people to be loose and sin freely with no consequences. This objection betrays an ignorance of the biblical doctrine as Calvin will show.

3. The Reformers insisted that justification is by faith alone, *but not by a faith that is alone*. Faith and works are distinct, but they cannot be separated (Jas. 2:14-26).

Our last sentence may refute the impudent calumny[1] of certain ungodly men, who charge us, first, with destroying good works[2] and leading men away from the study of them, when we say, that men are not justified, and do not merit salvation by works; and, secondly, with making the means of justification too easy, when we say that it consists in the free remission of sins, and thus alluring men to sin to which they are already too much inclined. These calumnies, I say, are sufficiently refuted by that one sentence; however, I will briefly reply to both. The allegation is that justification by faith destroys good works. I will not describe what kind of zealots for good works the persons are who thus charge us. We leave them as much liberty to bring the charge, as they take license to taint the whole world with the pollution of their lives. They pretend to lament that when faith is so highly extolled, works are deprived of their proper place. But what if they are rather ennobled and established? We dream not of a faith which is devoid of good works, nor of a justification which can exist without them: the only difference is, that while we acknowledge that faith and works are necessarily connected,[3] we, however, place justification in faith, not in works. How this is done is easily explained, if we turn to Christ only, to whom our faith is directed and from whom it derives all its power. Why, then, are we justified by faith? Because by faith we apprehend the righteousness of Christ, which alone reconciles us to God. This faith, however, you cannot apprehend without at the same time apprehending sanctification; for Christ "is made unto us wisdom, and righteousness, and sanctification, and redemption," (1 Cor. 1:30). Christ, therefore, justifies no man without also sanctifying him.[4] These blessings are conjoined by a perpetual and inseparable tie. Those whom he enlightens by his wisdom he redeems; whom he redeems he justifies; whom he justifies he sanctifies. But as the question relates only to justification and sanctification, to them let us confine ourselves. Though we distinguish between them, they are both inseparably comprehended in Christ. Would ye then obtain justification in Christ? You must previously possess Christ. But you cannot possess him without being made a partaker of his sanctification: for Christ cannot be divided.[5] Since the Lord, therefore, does not grant us the enjoyment of these blessings without bestowing himself, he bestows both at once but never the one without the other. Thus it appears how true it is that we are justified not without, and yet not by works, since in the participation of Christ, by which we are justified, is contained not less sanctification than justification.

4. It is the doctrine of union with Christ that ties these doctrines together. Because we are united to Christ by faith, we partake of all His saving benefits including justification, adoption, and sanctification (1 Cor. 1:30).

5. Any doctrine that separates justification from sanctification shows an ignorance or denial of the doctrine of union with Christ. You cannot divide Christ's saving benefits and only receive some of them.

Book 3

Chapter 17

The Promises of the Law and the Gospel Reconciled

Paul finds nothing stronger to prove justification by faith than that which is written of Abraham, he "believed God, and it was counted unto him for righteousness," (Rom. 4:3; Gal. 3:6). Therefore, when it is said that the achievement of Phinehas "was counted unto him for righteousness," (Ps. 106:30, 31), we may argue that what Paul contends for respecting faith applies also to works. Our opponents, accordingly, as if the point were proved, set it down that though we are not justified without faith, it is not by faith only; that our justification is completed by works. Here I beseech believers, as they know that the true standard of righteousness must be derived from Scripture alone, to consider with me seriously and religiously, how Scripture can be fairly reconciled with that view. Paul, knowing that justification by faith was the refuge of those who wanted righteousness of their own, confidently infers, that all who are justified by faith are excluded from the righteousness of works. But as it is clear that this justification is common to all believers, he with equal confidence infers that no man is justified by works; nay, more, that justification is without any help from works. But it is one thing to determine what power works have in themselves, and another to determine what place they are to hold after justification by faith has been established. If a price is to be put upon works according to their own worth, we hold that they are unfit to appear in the presence of God: that man, accordingly, has no works in which he can glory before God, and that hence, deprived of all aid from works, he is justified by faith alone. Justification, moreover, we thus define: The sinner being admitted into communion with Christ is, for his sake, reconciled to God; when purged by his blood he obtains the remission of sins, and clothed with righteousness, just as if it were his own, stands secure before the judgment-seat of heaven. Forgiveness of sins being previously given, the good works which follow have a value different from their merit, because whatever is imperfect in them is covered by the perfection of Christ, and all their blemishes and pollutions are wiped away by his purity, so as never to come under the cognizance of the divine tribunal. The guilt of all transgressions, by which men are prevented from offering God an acceptable service, being thus effaced, and the imperfection which is wont to sully even good works being buried,[1] the good works which are done by believers are deemed righteous, or; which is the same thing, are imputed for righteousness.

1. That is, our imperfections "sully" or "corrupt" even our good works.

In this way we can admit not only that there is a partial righteousness in works (as our adversaries maintain), but that they are approved by God as if they were absolutely perfect. If we remember on what foundation this is rested, every difficulty will be solved. The first time when a work begins to be acceptable is when it is received with pardon. And whence pardon, but just because God looks upon us and all that belongs to us as in Christ? Therefore, as we ourselves when engrafted into Christ appear righteous before God, because our iniquities are covered with his innocence; so our works are, and are deemed righteous, because every thing otherwise defective in them being buried by the purity of Christ is not imputed. Thus we may justly say, that not only ourselves, but our works

2. Even our good works must be covered in Christ, so that the remaining imperfections in them do not appear as unrighteous in God's sight. The 17th-century Westminster Confession of Faith says something similar: "Notwithstanding, the persons of believers being accepted through Christ, their good works also are accepted in him; not as though they were in this life wholly unblamable and unreprovable in God's sight; but that he, looking upon them in his Son, is pleased to accept and reward that which is sincere, although accompanied with many weaknesses and imperfections." (WCF 16.6)

3. Psalm 32:1-2

4. Psalm 112:1

5. Psalm 41:1

6. Psalm 1:1

7. Psalm 106:3

8. Matthew 5:3-12

9. "Approbation" means "approval" or "praise."

10. The state of blessedness described by the many Psalms and the Beatitudes owe their existence to this prior relationship between God and the believer. The man who is justified by faith will also experience many blessings that flow from a life of godly living.

also, are justified by faith alone.[2] Now, if that righteousness of works, whatever it be, depends on faith and free justification, and is produced by it, it ought to be included under it and, so to speak, made subordinate to it, as the effect to its cause; so far is it from being entitled to be set up to impair or destroy the doctrine of justification. Thus Paul, to prove that our blessedness depends not on our works, but on the mercy of God, makes special use of the words of David, "Blessed is he whose transgression is forgiven, whose sin is covered;" "Blessed is the man unto whom the Lord imputeth not iniquity."[3] Should any one here obtrude the numberless passages in which blessedness seems to be attributed to works, as, "Blessed is the man that feareth the Lord;"[4] "He that has mercy on the poor, happy is he;"[5] "Blessed is the man that walketh not in the counsel of the ungodly,"[6] and "that endureth temptation;" "Blessed are they that keep judgment,"[7] that are "pure in heart," "meek," "merciful,"[8] &c., they cannot make out that Paul's doctrine is not true. For seeing that the qualities thus extolled never all so exist in man as to obtain for him the approbation of God,[9] it follows, that man is always miserable until he is exempted from misery by the pardon of his sins. Since, then, all the kinds of blessedness extolled in the Scripture are vain so that man derives no benefit from them until he obtains blessedness by the forgiveness of sins, a forgiveness which makes way for them, it follows that this is not only the chief and highest, but the only blessedness, unless you are prepared to maintain that it is impaired by things which owe their entire existence to it.[10] There is much less to trouble us in the name of righteousness which is usually given to believers. I admit that they are so called from the holiness of their lives, but as they rather exert themselves in the study of righteousness than fulfill righteousness itself, any degree of it which they possess must yield to justification by faith, to which it is owing that it is what it is.

Book 3
Chapter 18

Of Christian Liberty

Christian liberty seems to me to consist of three parts. First, the consciences of believers, while seeking the assurance of their justification before God, must rise above the law, and think no more of obtaining justification by it.[1] For while the law, as has already been demonstrated, leaves not one man righteous, we are either excluded from all hope of justification, or we must be loosed from the law, and so loosed as that no account at all shall be taken of works. For he who imagines that in order to obtain justification he must bring any degree of works whatever, cannot fix any mode or limit, but makes himself debtor to the whole law. Therefore, laying aside all mention of the law, and all idea of works, we must in the matter of justification have recourse to the mercy of God only; turning away our regard from ourselves, we must look only to Christ. For the question is, not how we may be righteous, but how, though unworthy and unrighteous, we may be regarded as righteous. If consciences would obtain any assurance of this, they must give no place to the law. Still it cannot be rightly inferred from this that believers have no need of the law.[2] It ceases not to teach, exhort, and urge them to good, although it is not recognized by their consciences

1. Calvin argues that the doctrine of Christian liberty consists of three main points. The first point is this: believers no longer seek justification from law-keeping. They are set free from the law in this sense. They are, as Paul describes, "not under law but under grace" (Rom. 6:14).

2. Though believers are set free from the condemnation of the law, the law of God remains a guide for holiness. We are set free from the condemning power of the law in order to "bear fruit for God" (Rom. 7:4). Of course, we can only know what is "good fruit" by using the standard of God's law to define righteousness.

before the judgment-seat of God. The two things are very different, and should be well and carefully distinguished. The whole lives of Christians ought to be a kind of aspiration after piety, seeing they are called unto holiness (Eph. 1:4; 1 Thess. 4:5). The office of the law is to excite them to the study of purity and holiness, by reminding them of their duty. For when the conscience feels anxious as to how it may have the favor of God, as to the answer it could give, and the confidence it would feel, if brought to his judgment-seat, in such a case the requirements of the law are not to be brought forward, but Christ, who surpasses all the perfection of the law, is alone to be held forth for righteousness.

Another point which depends on the former is, that consciences obey the law, not as if compelled by legal necessity; but being free from the yoke of the law itself, voluntarily obey the will of God.[3] Being constantly in terror so long as they are under the dominion of the law, they are never disposed promptly to obey God, unless they have previously obtained this liberty. Our meaning shall be explained more briefly and clearly by an example. The command of the law is, "Thou shalt love the Lord thy God with all thine heart, and with all thy soul, and with all thy might," (Deut. 6:5). To accomplish this, the soul must previously be divested of every other thought and feeling, the heart purified from all its desires, all its powers collected and united on this one object. Those who, in comparison of others, have made much progress in the way of the Lord, are still very far from this goal. For although they love God in their mind, and with a sincere affection of heart, yet both are still in a great measure occupied with the lusts of the flesh, by which they are retarded and prevented from proceeding with quickened pace towards God. They indeed make many efforts, but the flesh partly enfeebles their strength, and partly binds them to itself. What can they do while they thus feel that there is nothing of which they are less capable than to fulfill the law? They wish, aspire, endeavor; but do nothing with the requisite perfection. If they look to the law, they see

3. We are no longer slaves to the law. The law is not our taskmaster. We are servants of Jesus Christ (Rom. 6:20-23).

that every work which they attempt or design is accursed. Nor can any one deceive himself by inferring that the work is not altogether bad, merely because it is imperfect, and, therefore, that any good which is in it is still accepted of God. For the law demanding perfect love condemns all imperfection, unless its rigor is mitigated. Let any man therefore consider his work which he wishes to be thought partly good, and he will find that it is a transgression of the law by the very circumstance of its being imperfect.

The third part of this liberty is that we are not bound before God to any observance of external things which are in themselves indifferent (ἀδιάφορα), but that we are now at full liberty either to use or omit them.[4] The knowledge of this liberty is very necessary to us; where it is wanting our consciences will have no rest, there will be no end of superstition. In the present day many think us absurd in raising a question as to the free eating of flesh, the free use of dress and holidays, and similar frivolous trifles, as they think them; but they are of more importance than is commonly supposed. For when once the conscience is entangled in the net, it enters a long and inextricable labyrinth, from which it is afterwards most difficult to escape. When a man begins to doubt whether it is lawful for him to use linen for sheets, shirts, napkins, and handkerchiefs, he will not long be secure as to hemp, and will at last have doubts as to tow; for he will revolve in his mind whether he cannot sup without napkins, or dispense with handkerchiefs. Should he deem a daintier food unlawful, he will afterwards feel uneasy for using loafbread and common eatables, because he will think that his body might possibly be supported on a still meaner food. If he hesitates as to a more genial wine, he will scarcely drink the worst with a good conscience; at last he will not dare to touch water if more than usually sweet and pure. In fine, he will come to this, that he will deem it criminal to trample on a straw lying in his way. For it is no trivial dispute that is here commenced, the point in debate being, whether the use of this thing or that is in accordance with the

4. The third part of Christian liberty is the freedom to observe or not observe matters that are defined as "indifferent" (adiaphora). These would include things that the Lord neither commands nor forbids in His Word such as what we eat and drink, whether we decide to observe certain days in a special manner, choice of clothing, and similar matters (see Rom. 14).

divine will, which ought to take precedence of all our acts and counsels. Here some must by despair be hurried into an abyss, while others, despising God and casting off his fear, will not be able to make a way for themselves without ruin. When men are involved in such doubts whatever be the direction in which they turn, every thing they see must offend their conscience.

"I know," says Paul, "that there is nothing unclean of itself," (by unclean meaning unholy); "but to him that esteemeth any thing to be unclean, to him it is unclean," (Rom. 14:14). By these words he makes all external things subject to our liberty, provided the nature of that liberty approves itself to our minds as before God. But if any superstitious idea suggests scruples,[5] those things which in their own nature were pure are to us contaminated. Wherefore the apostle adds, "Happy is he that condemneth not himself in that which he alloweth. And he that doubteth is damned if he eat, because he eateth not of faith: for whatsoever is not of faith is sin," (Rom. 14:22, 23). When men, amid such difficulties, proceed with greater confidence, securely doing whatever pleases them, do they not in so far revolt from God? Those who are thoroughly impressed with some fear of God, if forced to do many things repugnant to their consciences are discouraged and filled with dread. All such persons receive none of the gifts of God with thanksgiving, by which alone Paul declares that all things are sanctified for our use (1 Tim. 4:5). By thanksgiving I understand that which proceeds from a mind recognizing the kindness and goodness of God in his gifts. For many, indeed, understand that the blessings which they enjoy are the gifts of God, and praise God in their words; but not being persuaded that these have been given to them, how can they give thanks to God as the giver? In one word, we see whither this liberty tends—viz. that we are to use the gifts of God without any scruple of conscience, without any perturbation of mind, for the purpose for which he gave them: in this way our souls may both have peace with him, and recognize his liberality towards us.[6] For here are comprehended all ceremonies of free observance, so

5. A scruple is a doubt or hesitation as to the morality of a particular action. We each may have scruples about certain matters where our conscience convicts us of wrongdoing. However, our conscience needs to be constantly trained by the Word of God so we do not condemn lawful things as being unlawful.

6. All of God's gifts should be received with thanksgiving (1 Tim. 4:1-5). But we must be careful not to misuse God's gifts to fulfill our lusts or turn any of these things into idols. That is why some have scruples about certain foods or certain forms of entertainment. The Christian should always ask, can I give thanks to God while I do this, and does it help me in my pursuit of godliness?

that while our consciences are not to be laid under the necessity of observing them, we are also to remember that, by the kindness of God, the use of them is made subservient to edification.[7]

It is, however, to be carefully observed, that Christian liberty is in all its parts a spiritual matter, the whole force of which consists in giving peace to trembling consciences, whether they are anxious and disquieted as to the forgiveness of sins, or as to whether their imperfect works, polluted by the infirmities of the flesh, are pleasing to God, or are perplexed as to the use of things indifferent. It is, therefore, perversely interpreted by those who use it as a cloak for their lusts,[8] that they may licentiously abuse the good gifts of God, or who think there is no liberty unless it is used in the presence of men, and, accordingly, in using it pay no regard to their weak brethren. Under this head, the sins of the present age are more numerous. For there is scarcely any one whose means allow him to live sumptuously, who does not delight in feasting, and dress, and the luxurious grandeur of his house, who wishes not to surpass his neighbor in every kind of delicacy, and does not plume himself amazingly on his splendor. And all these things are defended under the pretext of Christian liberty. They say they are things indifferent: I admit it, provided they are used indifferently. But when they are too eagerly longed for, when they are proudly boasted of, when they are indulged in luxurious profusion, things which otherwise were in themselves lawful are certainly defiled by these vices.[9] Paul makes an admirable distinction in regard to things indifferent: "Unto the pure all things are pure: but unto them that are defiled and unbelieving is nothing pure; but even their mind and conscience is defiled" (Tit. 1:15). For why is a woe pronounced upon the rich who have received their consolation? (Luke 6:24), who are full, who laugh now, who "lie upon beds of ivory and stretch themselves upon their couches;" "join house to house," and "lay field to field;" "and the harp and the viol, the tablet and pipe, and wine, are in their feasts," (Amos 6:6;

7. Here, Calvin points out the importance of making our choices in such a way that we prioritize edification. Does this activity or practice edify me and others? Or is it unhelpful, even though it may not be unlawful?

8. To use the doctrine of Christian liberty as a justification for sin is to destroy the very purpose of Christian liberty: to enjoy freedom from sin and a conscience at peace. This is what Paul tells us in Galatians 5. "For you, brethren, have been called to liberty; only do not use liberty as an opportunity for the flesh, but through love serve one another." (Gal. 5:13)

9. Let us be on guard that we don't use the doctrine of Christian liberty to excuse our lustful and covetous behaviors. Clothing, food, beautiful homes, nice cars, are not unlawful. But if they become an idol, we must repent and put such things in their proper place.

10. "Plebeian" refers to the lower classes of Roman society. In this context, Calvin means even someone who enjoys a rather simple life with ordinary food and clothing, and not expensive and extravagant things, can still turn these things into an idol if they lack moderation.

11. Someone may appear modest due to their simple clothing and appearance. But the most important thing is the condition of their hearts: are they proud or humble?

Isa. 5:8, 10). Certainly ivory and gold, and riches, are the good creatures of God, permitted, nay destined, by divine providence for the use of man; nor was it ever forbidden to laugh, or to be full, or to add new to old and hereditary possessions, or to be delighted with music, or to drink wine. This is true, but when the means are supplied to roll and wallow in luxury, to intoxicate the mind and soul with present and be always hunting after new pleasures, is very far from a legitimate use of the gifts of God. Let them, therefore, suppress immoderate desire, immoderate profusion, vanity, and arrogance, that they may use the gifts of God purely with a pure conscience. When their mind is brought to this state of soberness, they will be able to regulate the legitimate use. On the other hand, when this moderation is wanting, even plebeian and ordinary delicacies are excessive.[10] For it is a true saying, that a haughty mind often dwells in a coarse and homely garb,[11] while true humility lurks under fine linen and purple. Let every one then live in his own station, poorly or moderately, or in splendor; but let all remember that the nourishment which God gives is for life, not luxury, and let them regard it as the law of Christian liberty, to learn with Paul in whatever state they are, "therewith to be content," to know "both how to be abased," and "how to abound," "to be full and to be hungry, both to abound and to suffer need," (Phil. 4:11).

Book 3
Chapter 20

Of Prayer-A Perpetual Exercise of Faith. The Daily Benefits Derived From It

From the previous part of the work we clearly see how completely destitute man is of all good, how devoid of every means of procuring his own salvation. Hence, if he would obtain succor in his necessity, he must go beyond himself, and procure it in some other quarter. It has farther been shown that the Lord kindly and spontaneously manifests himself in Christ, in whom he offers all happiness for our misery, all abundance for our want, opening up the treasures of heaven to us, so that we may turn with full faith to his beloved Son, depend upon him with full expectation, rest in him, and cleave to him with full hope. This, indeed, is that secret and hidden philosophy which cannot be learned by syllogisms: a philosophy thoroughly understood by those whose eyes God has so opened as to see light in his light (Ps. 36:9). But after we have learned by faith to know that whatever is necessary for us or defective in us is supplied in God and in our Lord Jesus Christ, in whom it hath pleased the Father that all fullness should dwell, that we may thence draw as from an inexhaustible fountain, it remains for us to seek and in prayer implore of him what we have learned to be in him.[1] To know God as the sovereign disposer of all good, inviting us to present our requests, and yet not to approach or ask of him, were so far from availing us, that it were just as if one told of a treasure

1. Calvin reminds the reader that we have already established how we can't do anything to save ourselves. It is Christ alone who can redeem us from our fallen sinful condition. But once we are united to Christ by faith, we still daily depend upon the Lord for help. This is why prayer is so basic to the Christian life.

were to allow it to remain buried in the ground. Hence the Apostle, to show that a faith unaccompanied with prayer to God cannot be genuine, states this to be the order: As faith springs from the Gospel, so by faith our hearts are framed to call upon the name of God (Rom. 10:14). And this is the very thing which he had expressed some time before—viz. that the Spirit of adoption, which seals the testimony of the Gospel on our hearts, gives us courage to make our requests known unto God, calls forth groanings which cannot be uttered, and enables us to cry, Abba, Father (Rom. 8:26). This last point, as we have hitherto only touched upon it slightly in passing, must now be treated more fully.

2. Prayer is the means by which we "penetrate" into the riches that our Heavenly Father has for us. What a gift prayer is! Through our Lord Jesus, we have direct access to the Father.

To prayer, then, are we indebted for penetrating to those riches which are treasured up for us with our heavenly Father.[2] For there is a kind of intercourse between God and men, by which, having entered the upper sanctuary, they appear before Him and appeal to his promises, that when necessity requires they may learn by experiences that what they believed merely on the authority of his word was not in vain. Accordingly, we see that nothing is set before us as an object of expectation from the Lord which we are not enjoined to ask of Him in prayer, so true it is that prayer digs up those treasures which the Gospel of our Lord discovers to the eye of faith. The necessity and utility of this exercise of prayer no words can sufficiently express. Assuredly it is not without cause our heavenly Father declares that our only safety is in calling upon his name, since by it we invoke the presence of his providence to watch over our interests, of his power to sustain us when weak and almost fainting, of his goodness to receive us into favor, though miserably loaded with sin; in fine, call upon him to manifest himself to us in all his perfections. Hence, admirable peace and tranquility are given to our consciences; for the straits by which we were pressed being laid before the Lord, we rest fully satisfied with the assurance that none of our evils are unknown to him, and that he is both able and willing to make the best provision for us.

But some one will say, Does he not know without a monitor both what our difficulties are, and what is meet for our interest, so that it seems in some measure superfluous to solicit him by our prayers, as if he were winking, or even sleeping, until aroused by the sound of our voice?[3] Those who argue thus attend not to the end for which the Lord taught us to pray. It was not so much for his sake as for ours.[4] He wills indeed, as is just, that due honor be paid him by acknowledging that all which men desire or feel to be useful, and pray to obtain, is derived from him. But even the benefit of the homage which we thus pay him redounds to ourselves. Hence the holy patriarchs, the more confidently they proclaimed the mercies of God to themselves and others felt the stronger incitement to prayer. It will be sufficient to refer to the example of Elijah, who being assured of the purpose of God had good ground for the promise of rain which he gives to Ahab, and yet prays anxiously upon his knees, and sends his servant seven times to inquire (1 Kings 18:42); not that he discredits the oracle, but because he knows it to be his duty to lay his desires before God, lest his faith should become drowsy or torpid. Wherefore, although it is true that while we are listless or insensible to our wretchedness, he wakes and watches for use and sometimes even assists us unasked; it is very much for our interest to be constantly supplicating him; first, that our heart may always be inflamed with a serious and ardent desire of seeking, loving and serving him, while we accustom ourselves to have recourse to him as a sacred anchor in every necessity; secondly, that no desires, no longing whatever, of which we are ashamed to make him the witness, may enter our minds, while we learn to place all our wishes in his sight, and thus pour out our heart before him; and, lastly, that we may be prepared to receive all his benefits with true gratitude and thanksgiving,[5] while our prayers remind us that they proceed from his hand. Moreover, having obtained what we asked, being persuaded that he has answered our prayers, we are led to long more earnestly for his favor, and at the same time have

3. This is a common objection. If the Lord already knows what we need, why do we need to ask Him for it? Will He not just take care of us without us having to ask?

4. That is, prayer was not designed to be the means of informing God of our requests which He otherwise would not have known. Instead, prayer is for our own benefit. In prayer, we give the honor to God due to His name. But we also receive a spiritual benefit from the act of prayer.

5. Through prayer we are reminded that it is God alone who is our help. We are strengthened in faith knowing that God hears us. And our gratitude may be increased as we contemplate God's goodness and give thanks to Him in prayer.

6. We receive much encouragement through answers to prayers. We see that God is indeed listening to us and providing the help we ask for.

greater pleasure in welcoming the blessings which we perceive to have been obtained by our prayers.[6] Lastly, use and experience confirm the thought of his providence in our minds in a manner adapted to our weakness, when we understand that he not only promises that he will never fail us, and spontaneously gives us access to approach him in every time of need, but has his hand always stretched out to assist his people, not amusing them with words, but proving himself to be a present aid. For these reasons, though our most merciful Father never slumbers nor sleeps, he very often seems to do so, that thus he may exercise us, when we might otherwise be listless and slothful, in asking, entreating, and earnestly beseeching him to our great good. It is very absurd, therefore, to dissuade men from prayer, by pretending that Divine Providence, which is always watching over the government of the universes is in vain importuned by our supplications, when, on the contrary, the Lord himself declares, that he is "nigh unto all that call upon him, to all that call upon him in truth" (Ps. 145:18). No better is the frivolous allegation of others that it is superfluous to pray for things which the Lord is ready of his own accord to bestow; since it is his pleasure that those very things which flow from his spontaneous liberality should be acknowledged as conceded to our prayers. This is testified by that memorable sentence in the psalms to which many others corresponds: "The eyes of the Lord are upon the righteous, and his ears are open unto their cry," (Ps. 34:15). This passage, while extolling the care which Divine Providence spontaneously exercises over the safety of believers, omits not the exercise of faith by which the mind is aroused from sloth. The eyes of God are awake to assist the blind in their necessity, but he is likewise pleased to listen to our groans, that he may give us the better proof of his love. And thus both things are true, "He that keepeth Israel shall neither slumber nor sleep," (Ps. 121:4); and yet whenever he sees us dumb and torpid, he withdraws as if he had forgotten us.

Let the first rule of right prayer then be, to have our heart and mind framed as becomes those who are entering into converse with God. This we shall accomplish in regard to the mind, if, laying aside carnal thoughts and cares which might interfere with the direct and pure contemplation of God, it not only be wholly intent on prayer, but also, as far as possible, be borne and raised above itself. I do not here insist on a mind so disengaged as to feel none of the gnawings of anxiety; on the contrary, it is by much anxiety that the fervor of prayer is inflamed. Thus we see that the holy servants of God betray great anguish, not to say solicitude, when they cause the voice of complaint to ascend to the Lord from the deep abyss and the jaws of death. What I say is, that all foreign and extraneous cares must be dispelled by which the mind might be driven to and fro in vague suspense, be drawn down from heaven, and kept groveling on the earth. When I say it must be raised above itself, I mean that it must not bring into the presence of God any of those things which our blind and stupid reason is wont to devise, nor keep itself confined within the little measure of its own vanity, but rise to a purity worthy of God.[7]

Both things are specially worthy of notice. First, let every one in professing to pray turn thither all his thoughts and feelings, and be not (as is usual) distracted by wandering thoughts; because nothing is more contrary to the reverence due to God than that levity which bespeaks a mind too much given to license and devoid of fear. In this matter we ought to labor the more earnestly the more difficult we experience it to be; for no man is so intent on prayer as not to feel many thoughts creeping in, and either breaking off the tenor of his prayer, or retarding it by some turning or digression.[8] Here let us consider how unbecoming it is when God admits us to familiar intercourse to abuse his great condescension by mingling things sacred and profane, reverence for him not keeping our minds under restraint; but just as if in prayer we were conversing with one like ourselves forgetting him, and allowing our thoughts to run to and fro. Let us know, then,

7. Calvin says that when we come to God in prayer, we need to first recognize the God to whom we speak. He is the Lord of all things, the creator of heaven and earth. We should be raised above our own carnal thoughts to remember that we are speaking to our great God.

8. Calvin encourages a focus and attention in prayer. Since we are speaking to the Lord, let us not be drawn away by distractions and cares.

9. Prayer is challenging work. We must strenuously labor to overcome distractions. We must seek to exert every thought and feeling into prayer. The missionary Samuel Zwemer called prayer the "gymnasium of the soul."

10. "Hardihood" means "bold" or "daring."

11. Calvin refers to the audacity of some men to bring their foolish and sinful desires to God in prayer, thinking that God will give them whatever they want. Such people do not pray according to God's will. James refers to those who "ask amiss" because they ask for the wrong things for the wrong reasons. "You ask and do not receive, because you ask amiss, that you may spend it on your pleasures." (Jas. 4:3)

12. "Jocular tales" are "joking" or "humorous" stories.

that none duly prepare themselves for prayer but those who are so impressed with the majesty of God that they engage in it free from all earthly cares and affections. The ceremony of lifting up our hands in prayer is designed to remind us that we are far removed from God, unless our thoughts rise upward: as it is said in the psalm, "Unto thee, O Lord, do I lift up my soul," (Psalm 25:1). And Scripture repeatedly uses the expression to raise our prayer, meaning that those who would be heard by God must not grovel in the mire. The sum is, that the more liberally God deals with us, condescendingly inviting us to disburden our cares into his bosom, the less excusable we are if this admirable and incomparable blessing does not in our estimation outweigh all other things, and win our affection, that prayer may seriously engage our every thought and feeling. This cannot be unless our mind, strenuously exerting itself against all impediments, rise upward.[9] Our second proposition was, that we are to ask only in so far as God permits. For though he bids us pour out our hearts (Ps. 62:8) he does not indiscriminately give loose reins to foolish and depraved affections; and when he promises that he will grant believers their wish, his indulgence does not proceed so far as to submit to their caprice. In both matters grievous delinquencies are everywhere committed. For not only do many without modesty, without reverence, presume to invoke God concerning their frivolities, but impudently bring forward their dreams, whatever they may be, before the tribunal of God. Such is the folly or stupidity under which they labor, that they have the hardihood[10] to obtrude upon God desires so vile, that they would blush exceedingly to impart them to their fellow men.[11] Profane writers have derided and even expressed their detestation of this presumption, and yet the vice has always prevailed. Hence, as the ambitious adopted Jupiter as their patron; the avaricious, Mercury; the literary aspirants, Apollo and Minerva; the warlike, Mars; the licentious, Venus: so in the present day, as I lately observed, men in prayer give greater license to their unlawful desires than if they were telling jocular tales[12] among their equals. God does not suffer his condescension to be thus mocked, but vindicating his own light, places our wishes under the restraint of his authority. We must, therefore, attend to the observation of John, "This is the confidence that we have in him, that if we ask any thing according to his will, he heareth us," (1 John 5:14). But as our faculties are far from being able to attain to such high perfection, we must seek for some means to assist them. As the eye of our mind should be intent upon God, so the affection of our heart ought to follow in the same course. But both fall far beneath this, or rather, they faint and fail, and are carried in a contrary direction. To assist this weakness, God gives us the guidance of the Spirit in our prayers to dictate what is right, and regulate our affections. For seeing "we know not what we should pray for as we ought," "the Spirit itself maketh intercession for us with groanings which cannot be uttered," (Rom. 8:26) not that he actually prays or groans, but he excites in us sighs, and wishes, and confidence, which our natural powers are not at all able to conceive. Nor is it without cause Paul gives the name of groanings which cannot be uttered to the prayers which believers send forth under the guidance of the Spirit. For those who are truly exercised in prayer are not unaware that blind anxieties so restrain and perplex them, that they can scarcely find what it becomes them to utter; nay, in attempting to lisp they halt and hesitate. Hence it appears that to pray aright is a special gift. We do not speak thus in indulgence to our sloth, as if we were to leave the office of prayer to the Holy Spirit, and give way to that carelessness to which we are too prone. Thus we sometimes hear the impious expression, that we are to wait in suspense until he take possession of our minds while otherwise occupied. Our meaning is, that, weary of our own heartlessness and sloth, we are to long for the aid of the Spirit.[13] Nor, indeed, does Paul, when he enjoins us to pray in the Spirit (1 Cor. 14:15), cease to exhort us to vigilance, intimating, that while the inspiration of the Spirit is effectual to the formation of prayer, it by no means impedes or retards our

13. The Spirit of God helps us in prayer. But this does not make us passive in our petitions to the Lord. The Spirit doesn't "take over" leaving us with nothing to do. Instead, the Spirit aids us by strengthening us in prayer.

14. Calvin says that prayer must be a sincere cry to God. It is not a perfunctory, rote exercise that we do as a mere ritual. Instead, our prayers should be the very cry of our hearts. We should come with heartfelt desire and great confidence in God.

15. Something that is done in a "perfunctory" way is an action done with little effort or reflection. This can happen in prayer when we always pray the same thing in a rote way with little thought given to the words we choose.

16. Our prayers should not be driven by mere custom or expectation. We should earnestly desire to bring our needs before the Father. Let us remember that we are speaking to God, the creator of all things. Our God is a personal God, not a vending machine.

17. God knows our hearts. He knows all the hypocrisy that is within us. Therefore, if we come asking for God to forgive our sins when we don't really believe we are sinners, this is a detestable hypocrisy in the sight of God.

own endeavors; since in this matter God is pleased to try how efficiently faith influences our hearts.

Another rule of prayer is, that in asking we must always truly feel our wants, and seriously considering that we need all the things which we ask, accompany the prayer with a sincere, nay, ardent desire of obtaining them.[14] Many repeat prayers in a perfunctory manner[15] from a set form, as if they were performing a task to God, and though they confess that this is a necessary remedy for the evils of their condition, because it were fatal to be left without the divine aid which they implore, it still appears that they perform the duty from custom,[16] because their minds are meanwhile cold, and they ponder not what they ask. A general and confused feeling of their necessity leads them to pray, but it does not make them solicitous as in a matter of present consequence, that they may obtain the supply of their need. Moreover, can we suppose anything more hateful or even more execrable to God than this fiction of asking the pardon of sins, while he who asks at the very time either thinks that he is not a sinner, or, at least, is not thinking that he is a sinner; in other words, a fiction by which God is plainly held in derision?[17] But mankind, as I have lately said, are full of depravity, so that in the way of perfunctory service they often ask many things of God which they think come to them without his beneficence, or from some other quarter, or are already certainly in their possession. There is another fault which seems less heinous, but is not to be tolerated. Some murmur out prayers without meditation, their only principle being that God is to be propitiated by prayer. Believers ought to be specially on their guard never to appear in the presence of God with the intention of presenting a request unless they are under some serious impression, and are, at the same time, desirous to obtain it. Nay, although in these things which we ask only for the glory of God, we seem not at first sight to consult for our necessity, yet we ought not to ask with less fervor and vehemence of desire. For instance, when we pray that his name be hallowed—that hallowing must, so to speak, be earnestly hungered and thirsted after.[18]

The third rule to be added is: that he who comes into the presence of God to pray must divest himself of all vainglorious thoughts, lay aside all idea of worth; in short, discard all self- confidence, humbly giving God the whole glory, lest by arrogating any thing, however little, to himself, vain pride cause him to turn away his face.[19] Of this submission, which casts down all haughtiness, we have numerous examples in the servants of God. The holier they are, the more humbly they prostrate themselves when they come into the presence of the Lord. Thus Daniel, on whom the Lord himself bestowed such high commendation, says, "We do not present our supplications before thee for our righteousness but for thy great mercies. O Lord, hear; O Lord, forgive; O Lord, hearken and do; defer not, for thine own sake, O my God: for thy city and thy people are called by thy name." This he does not indirectly in the usual manner, as if he were one of the individuals in a crowd: he rather confesses his guilt apart, and as a suppliant betaking himself to the asylum of pardon, he distinctly declares that he was confessing his own sin, and the sin of his people Israel (Dan. 9:18-20). David also sets us an example of this humility: "Enter not into judgment with thy servant: for in thy sight shall no man living be justified," (Psalm 143:2). In like manner, Isaiah prays, "Behold, thou art wroth; for we have sinned: in those is continuance, and we shall be saved. But we are all as an unclean thing, and all our righteousnesses are as filthy rags; and we all do fade as a leaf; and our iniquities, like the wind, have taken us away. And there is none that calleth upon thy name, that stirreth up himself to take hold of thee: for thou hast hid thy face from us, and hast consumed us, because of our iniquities. But now, O Lord, thou art our Father; we are the clay, and thou our potter; and we all are the work of thy hand. Be not wroth very sore,[20] O Lord, neither remember iniquity for ever: Behold, see, we beseech thee, we are all thy people." (Isa. 64:5-9). You see how they put no confidence in

18. Why pray if you don't really wish to receive an answer to your prayers? Calvin argues that we must pray with earnest, heartfelt desire.

19. The third rule Calvin lays down is this: we must come to God in prayer with humility. We don't come to God proudly thinking we deserve something from Him. God resists the proud, but He gives grace to the humble (1 Pet. 5:5).

20. "Do not be exceedingly angry."

21. Calvin quotes from the book of Baruch, one of the Apocryphal books. He does not quote Baruch here as an authority on the level of Holy Scripture. Rather, he uses Baruch as a pious example of the humility we should come to prayer with.

22. "Ingenuous" means "innocent" or "without deceit."

any thing but this: considering that they are the Lord's, they despair not of being the objects of his care. In the same way, Jeremiah says, "O Lord, though our iniquities testify against us, do thou it for thy name's sake," (Jer. 14:7). For it was most truly and piously written by the uncertain author (whoever he may have been) that wrote the book which is attributed to the prophet Baruch, "But the soul that is greatly vexed, which goeth stooping and feeble, and the eyes that fail, and the hungry soul, will give thee praise and righteousness, O Lord. Therefore, we do not make our humble supplication before thee, O Lord our God, for the righteousness of our fathers, and of our kings." "Hear, O Lord, and have mercy; for thou art merciful: and have pity upon us, because we have sinned before thee,"[21] (Baruch 2:18, 19; 3:2).

In fine, supplication for pardon, with humble and ingenuous[22] confession of guilt, forms both the preparation and commencement of right prayer. For the holiest of men cannot hope to obtain any thing from God until he has been freely reconciled to him. God cannot be propitious to any but those whom he pardons. Hence it is not strange that this is the key by which believers open the door of prayer, as we learn from several passages in The Psalms. David, when presenting a request on a different subject, says, "Remember not the sins of my youth, nor my transgressions; according to thy mercy remember me, for thy goodness sake, O Lord," (Psalm 25:7). Again, "Look upon my affliction and my pain, and forgive my sins," (Psalm 25:18). Here also we see that it is not sufficient to call ourselves to account for the sins of each passing day; we must also call to mind those which might seem to have been long before buried in oblivion. For in another passage the same prophet, confessing one grievous crime, takes occasion to go back to his very birth, "I was shapen in iniquity, and in sin did my mother conceive me," (Psalm 51:5); not to extenuate the fault by the corruption of his nature, but as it were to accumulate the sins of his whole life, that the stricter he was in condemning himself, the more placable God might be. But although the saints do not always in express terms ask forgiveness of sins, yet if we carefully ponder those prayers as given in Scripture, the truth of what I say will readily appear; namely, that their courage to pray was derived solely from the mercy of God, and that they always began with appeasing him. For when a man interrogates his conscience, so far is he from presuming to lay his cares familiarly before God, that if he did not trust to mercy and pardon, he would tremble at the very thought of approaching him. There is, indeed, another special confession. When believers long for deliverance from punishment, they at the same time pray that their sins may be pardoned; for it were absurd to wish that the effect should be taken away while the cause remains. For we must beware of imitating foolish patients who, anxious only about curing accidental symptoms, neglect the root of the disease.[23] Nay, our endeavor must be to have God propitious even before he attests his favor by external signs, both because this is the order which he himself chooses, and it were of little avail to experience his kindness, did not conscience feel that he is appeased, and thus enable us to regard him as altogether lovely. Of this we are even reminded by our Savior's reply. Having determined to cure the paralytic, he says, "Thy sins are forgiven thee;"[24] in other words, he raises our thoughts to the object which is especially to be desired—viz. admission into the favor of God, and then gives the fruit of reconciliation by bringing assistance to us. But besides that special confession of present guilt which believers employ, in supplicating for pardon of every fault and punishment, that general introduction which procures favor for our prayers must never be omitted, because prayers will never reach God unless they are founded on free mercy. To this we may refer the words of John, "If we confess our sins, he is faithful and just to forgive us our sins and to cleanse us from all unrighteousness," (1 John 1:9). Hence, under the law it was necessary to consecrate prayers by the expiation of blood, both that they might be accepted, and that the people might be warned that they were

23. Calvin gives us an illustration here. Just as a patient should want to get to the root problem of a disease, likewise, our fundamental ailment is sin. Therefore, confession of sin in prayer is essential.

24. Mark 2:5

unworthy of the high privilege until, being purged from their defilements, they founded their confidence in prayer entirely on the mercy of God.

The fourth rule of prayer is, that notwithstanding of our being thus abased and truly humbled, we should be animated to pray with the sure hope of succeeding.[25] There is, indeed, an appearance of contradiction between the two things, between a sense of the just vengeance of God and firm confidence in his favor, and yet they are perfectly accordant, if it is the mere goodness of God that raises up those who are overwhelmed by their own sins. For, as we have formerly shown that repentance and faith go hand in hand, being united by an indissoluble tie, the one causing terror, the other joy, so in prayer they must both be present. This concurrence David expresses in a few words: "But as for me, I will come into thy house in the multitude of thy mercy, and in thy fear will I worship toward thy holy temple," (Ps. 5:7). Under the goodness of God he comprehends faith, at the same time not excluding fear; for not only does his majesty compel our reverence, but our own unworthiness also divests us of all pride and confidence, and keeps us in fear. The confidence of which I speak is not one which frees the mind from all anxiety, and soothes it with sweet and perfect rest; such rest is peculiar to those who, while all their affairs are flowing to a wish are annoyed by no care, stung with no regret, agitated by no fear. But the best stimulus which the saints have to prayer is when, in consequence of their own necessities, they feel the greatest disquietude, and are all but driven to despair, until faith seasonably comes to their aid; because in such straits the goodness of God so shines upon them, that while they groan, burdened by the weight of present calamities, and tormented with the fear of greater, they yet trust to this goodness, and in this way both lighten the difficulty of endurance, and take comfort in the hope of final deliverance.[26] It is necessary therefore, that the prayer of the believer should be the result of both feelings, and exhibit the influence of both; namely, that while he groans

25. The fourth rule for prayer is this: we must have faith and hope in God. The Apostle John speaks of the confidence we should have in prayer. "Now this is the confidence that we have in Him, that if we ask anything according to His will, He hears us. And if we know that He hears us, whatever we ask, we know that we have the petitions that we have asked of Him." (1 John 5:14-15)

26. Calvin understands that this confidence doesn't mean that we come in prayer with zero anxiety whatsoever. The Psalms paint a very different picture. Often the Psalmist comes with doubt, uncertainty; even despair it seems. But by faith, the Psalmist rises above those challenges to trust in God. "Why are you cast down, O my soul? And why are you disquieted within me? Hope in God, for I shall yet praise Him For the help of His countenance." (Psalm. 42:5)

under present and anxiously dreads new evils, he should, at the same times have recourse to God, not at all doubting that God is ready to stretch out a helping hand to him. For it is not easy to say how much God is irritated by our distrust, when we ask what we expect not of his goodness. Hence, nothing is more accordant to the nature of prayer than to lay it down as a fixed rule, that it is not to come forth at random, but is to follow in the footsteps of faith. To this principle Christ directs all of us in these words, "Therefore, I say unto you, What things soever ye desire, when ye pray, believe that ye receive them, and ye shall have them," (Mark 11:24). The same thing he declares in another passage, "All things, whatsoever ye shall ask in prayer, believing, ye shall receive," (Mt. 21:22). In accordance with this are the words of James, "If any of you lack wisdom, let him ask of God, that giveth to all men liberally, and upbraideth not, and it shall be given him. But let him ask in faith, nothing wavering," (James 1:5). He most aptly expresses the power of faith by opposing it to wavering. No less worthy of notice is his additional statement, that those who approach God with a doubting, hesitating mind, without feeling assured whether they are to be heard or not, gain nothing by their prayers. Such persons he compares to a wave of the sea, driven with the wind and tossed. Hence, in another passage he terms genuine prayer "the prayer of faith," (James 5:15). Again, since God so often declares that he will give to every man according to his faith he intimates that we cannot obtain any thing without faith. In short, it is faith which obtains every thing that is granted to prayer. This is the meaning of Paul in the well known passage to which dull men give too little heed, "How then shall they call upon him in whom they have not believed? And how shall they believe in him of whom they have not heard?" "So then faith cometh by hearing, and hearing by the word of God," (Rom. 10:14, 17). Gradually deducing the origin of prayer from faith, he distinctly maintains that God cannot be invoked sincerely except by those to whom, by the preaching of the Gospel, his mercy and willingness have been made known, nay, familiarly explained.

Book 3
Chapter 21

Of the Eternal Election, by Which God has Predestinated Some to Salvation, and Others to Destruction

T he covenant of life is not preached equally to all, and among those to whom it is preached, does not always meet with the same reception. This diversity displays the unsearchable depth of the divine judgment, and is without doubt subordinate to God's purpose of eternal election. But if it is plainly owing to the mere pleasure of God that salvation is spontaneously offered to some, while others have no access to it, great and difficult questions immediately arise, questions which are inexplicable, when just views are not entertained concerning election and predestination. To many this seems a perplexing subject, because they deem it most incongruous that of the great body of mankind some should be predestinated to salvation, and others to destruction. How ceaselessly they entangle themselves will appear as we proceed. We may add, that in the very obscurity which deters them, we may see not only the utility of this doctrine, but also its most pleasant fruits. We shall never feel persuaded as we ought that our salvation flows from the free mercy of God as its fountain, until we are made acquainted with his eternal election, the grace of God being illustrated by the contrast—viz. that he does not adopt all promiscuously to the hope of salvation, but gives to some what he denies to others.[1] It is plain how greatly ignorance of this principle detracts from the glory of God, and impairs true humility. But though thus necessary to be known, Paul declares that it cannot be known unless God, throwing works entirely out of view, elect those whom he has predestined. His words are, "Even so then at this present time also, there is a remnant according to the election of grace. And if by grace, then it is no more of works: otherwise grace is no more grace. But if it be of works, then it is no more grace: otherwise work is no more work," (Rom. 11:6). If to make it appear that our salvation flows entirely from the good mercy of God, we must be carried back to the origin of election, then those who would extinguish it, wickedly do as much as in them lies to obscure what they ought most loudly to extol, and pluck up humility by the very roots.[2] Paul clearly declares that it is only when the salvation of a remnant is ascribed to gratuitous election, we arrive at the knowledge that God saves whom he wills of his mere good pleasure, and does not pay a debt, a debt which never can be due. Those who preclude access, and would not have any one to obtain a taste of this doctrine, are equally unjust to God and men, there being no other means of humbling us as we ought, or making us feel how much we are bound to him. Nor, indeed, have we elsewhere any sure ground of confidence. This we say on the authority of Christ, who, to deliver us from all fear, and render us invincible amid our many dangers, snares and mortal conflicts, promises safety to all that the Father has taken under his protection (John 10:26). From this we infer, that all who know not that they are the peculiar people of God, must be wretched from perpetual trepidation, and that those therefore, who, by overlooking the three advantages which we have noted, would destroy the very foundation of our safety, consult ill for themselves and for all the faithful. What? Do we not here find the very origin of the Church, which, as Bernard rightly teaches could not be found or recognized among the creatures, because it lies hid (in both

1. The doctrines of election and predestination should be handled with great care. Here, we enter into mysteries far above us. We should first submit to the plain teaching of Scripture. Whatever God has revealed, that we should believe. But we must be careful about prying into the mystery of God's purposes. The secret things belong to the Lord (Deut. 29:29).

2. The doctrine of election is a humbling doctrine. It reminds us that salvation is of the Lord. It is not owing to anything in us that we have salvation in Christ. It is the free mercy of God to bring us into an estate of salvation.

cases wondrously) within the lap of blessed predestination, and the mass of wretched condemnation? But before I enter on the subject, I have some remarks to address to two classes of men. The subject of predestination, which in itself is attended with considerable difficulty is rendered very perplexed and hence perilous by human curiosity, which cannot be restrained from wandering into forbidden paths and climbing to the clouds determined if it can that none of the secret things of God shall remain unexplored.[3] When we see many, some of them in other respects not bad men, every where rushing into this audacity and wickedness, it is necessary to remind them of the course of duty in this matter. First, then, when they inquire into predestination, let then remember that they are penetrating into the recesses of the divine wisdom, where he who rushes forward securely and confidently, instead of satisfying his curiosity will enter in inextricable labyrinth. For it is not right that man should with impunity pry into things which the Lord has been pleased to conceal within himself, and scan that sublime eternal wisdom which it is his pleasure that we should not apprehend but adore, that therein also his perfections may appear.[4] Those secrets of his will, which he has seen it meet to manifest, are revealed in his word—revealed in so far as he knew to be conducive to our interest and welfare.

"We have come into the way of faith," says Augustine: "let us constantly adhere to it. It leads to the chambers of the king, in which are hidden all the treasures of wisdom and knowledge. For our Lord Jesus Christ did not speak invidiously to his great and most select disciples when he said, 'I have yet many things to say unto you, but ye cannot bear them now,' (John 16:12). We must walk, advance, increase, that our hearts may be able to comprehend those things which they cannot now comprehend. But if the last day shall find us making progress, we shall there learn what here we could not." If we give due weight to the consideration, that the word of the Lord is the only way which can conduct us to the investigation of whatever it is lawful for us to hold with regard to him—is the only

3. Calvin points out that humans will seek to pry into God's purposes out of curiosity. But to do so is foolish. We are creatures. He is the potter. We are the clay (Jer. 18).

4. These mysteries of God's will are not to be fully understood by us. They should lead to adoration and praise. We should exclaim with Paul: "Oh, the depth of the riches both of the wisdom and knowledge of God! How unsearchable are His judgments and His ways past finding out!" (Rom. 11:33)

light which can enable us to discern what we ought to see with regard to him, it will curb and restrain all presumption. For it will show us that the moment we go beyond the bounds of the word we are out of the course, in darkness, and must every now and then stumble, go astray, and fall. Let it, therefore, be our first principle that to desire any other knowledge of predestination than that which is expounded by the word of God, is no less infatuated than to walk where there is no path, or to seek light in darkness. Let us not be ashamed to be ignorant in a matter in which ignorance is learning. Rather let us willingly abstain from the search after knowledge, to which it is both foolish as well as perilous, and even fatal to aspire. If an unrestrained imagination urges us, our proper course is to oppose it with these words, "It is not good to eat much honey: so for men to search their own glory is not glory," (Prov. 25:27). There is good reason to dread a presumption which can only plunge us headlong into ruin.

There are others who, when they would cure this disease, recommend that the subject of predestination should scarcely if ever be mentioned, and tell us to shun every question concerning it as we would a rock.[5] Although their moderation is justly commendable in thinking that such mysteries should be treated with moderation, yet because they keep too far within the proper measure, they have little influence over the human mind, which does not readily allow itself to be curbed. Therefore, in order to keep the legitimate course in this matter, we must return to the word of God, in which we are furnished with the right rule of understanding. For Scripture is the school of the Holy Spirit, in which as nothing useful and necessary to be known has been omitted, so nothing is taught but what it is of importance to know.[6] Every thing, therefore delivered in Scripture on the subject of predestination, we must beware of keeping from the faithful, lest we seem either maliciously to deprive them of the blessing of God, or to accuse and scoff at the Spirit, as having divulged what ought on any account to be suppressed. Let us, I say, al-

5. Some say that to even discuss election and predestination should be off limits. However, this option is not open for us. The Scriptures speak repeatedly of the doctrine (Rom. 8:28-30, Eph. 1). For this reason, we must seek to understand what the Scriptures reveal here. For Paul in Ephesians 1, the doctrine of election is a doctrine that brings forth praise to God.

6. This is an important point. If God saw fit to reveal something in Scripture, then it is for our benefit. We must not avoid any part of Scripture simply because it is difficult. The whole Word of God is for our salvation and edification (2 Tim. 3:16-17).

low the Christian to unlock his mind and ears to all the words of God which are addressed to him, provided he do it with this moderation—viz. that whenever the Lord shuts his sacred mouth, he also desists from inquiry. The best rule of sobriety is, not only in learning to follow wherever God leads, but also when he makes an end of teaching, to cease also from wishing to be wise. The danger which they dread is not so great that we ought on account of it to turn away our minds from the oracles of God. There is a celebrated saying of Solomon, "It is the glory of God to conceal a thing," (Prov. 25:2). But since both piety and common sense dictate that this is not to be understood of every thing, we must look for a distinction, lest under the pretence of modesty and sobriety we be satisfied with a brutish ignorance. This is clearly expressed by Moses in a few words, "The secret things belong unto the Lord our God: but those things which are revealed belong unto us, and to our children for ever," (Deut. 29:29). We see how he exhorts the people to study the doctrine of the law in accordance with a heavenly decree, because God has been pleased to promulgate it, while he at the same time confines them within these boundaries, for the simple reason that it is not lawful for men to pry into the secret things of God.

Although it is now sufficiently plain that God by his secret counsel chooses whom he will while he rejects others, his gratuitous election[7] has only been partially explained until we come to the case of single individuals, to whom God not only offers salvation, but so assigns it, that the certainty of the result remains not dubious or suspended. These are considered as belonging to that one seed of which Paul makes mention (Rom. 9:8; Gal. 3:16, &c). For although adoption was deposited in the hand of Abraham, yet as many of his posterity were cut off as rotten members, in order that election may stand and be effectual, it is necessary to ascend to the head in whom the heavenly Father has connected his elect with each other, and bound them to himself by an indissoluble tie. Thus in the adoption of the family of Abraham, God gave them a

7. The meaning of "gratuitous" here, as with the doctrine of "gratuitous justification" means "free." God freely chooses whom He will unto salvation. It is not done on the basis of our merit. It is the good pleasure of God (Eph. 1:5).

liberal display of favor which he has denied to others; but in the members of Christ there is a far more excellent display of grace, because those engrafted into him as their head never fail to obtain salvation. Hence Paul skillfully argues from the passage of Malachi which I quoted (Rom. 9:13; Mal. 1:2), that when God, after making a covenant of eternal life, invites any people to himself, a special mode of election is in part understood, so that he does not with promiscuous grace effectually elect all of them. The words, "Jacob have I loved," refer to the whole progeny of the patriarch,[8] which the prophet there opposes to the posterity of Esau. But there is nothing in this repugnant to the fact that in the person of one man is set before us a specimen of election, which cannot fail of accomplishing its object. It is not without cause Paul observes, that these are called a remnant (Rom. 9:27; 11:5); because experience shows that of the general body many fall away and are lost, so that often a small portion only remains. The reason why the general election of the people is not always firmly ratified, readily presents itself—viz. that on those with whom God makes the covenant, he does not immediately bestow the Spirit of regeneration, by whose power they persevere in the covenant even to the end. The external invitation, without the internal efficacy of grace which would have the effect of retaining them, holds a kind of middle place between the rejection of the human race and the election of a small number of believers. The whole people of Israel are called the Lord's inheritance, and yet there were many foreigners among them. Still, because the covenant which God had made to be their Father and Redeemer was not altogether null, he has respect to that free favor rather than to the perfidious defection[9] of many; even by them his truth was not abolished, since by preserving some residue to himself, it appeared that his calling was without repentance. When God ever and anon gathered his Church from among the sons of Abraham rather than from profane nations, he had respect to his covenant, which, when violated by the great body, he restricted to a few, that it might not entirely fail. In

8. In quoting Malachi 1:2, Calvin points out that God's rejection of Esau wasn't just a rejection of Esau the individual. Rather, Esau's line was rejected. God chose to give His covenant promises to Jacob (Israel) and his children. But Esau's people (Edom) were wholly rejected. This was not due to anything about Jacob or Esau themselves. It was so that the purpose of God according to election would stand (Rom. 9:11).

9. "Perfidious" means "deceitful" or "untrustworthy." The children of Israel had not kept covenant with the Lord and had "defected" from the true worship of God.

short, that common adoption of the seed of Abraham was a kind of visible image of a greater benefit which God deigned to bestow on some out of many. This is the reason why Paul so carefully distinguishes between the sons of Abraham according to the flesh and the spiritual sons who are called after the example of Isaac. Not that simply to be a son of Abraham was a vain or useless privilege (this could not be said without insult to the covenant), but that the immutable counsel of God, by which he predestinated to himself whomsoever he would, was alone effectual for their salvation. But until the proper view is made clear by the production of passages of Scripture, I advise my readers not to prejudge the question. We say, then, that Scripture clearly proves this much, that God by his eternal and immutable counsel determined once for all those whom it was his pleasure one day to admit to salvation, and those whom, on the other hand, it was his pleasure to doom to destruction. We maintain that this counsel, as regards the elect, is founded on his free mercy, without any respect to human worth, while those whom he dooms to destruction are excluded from access to life by a just and blameless, but at the same time incomprehensible judgment. In regard to the elect, we regard calling as the evidence of election, and justification as another symbol of its manifestation, until it is fully accomplished by the attainment of glory. But as the Lord seals his elect by calling and justification, so by excluding the reprobate either from the knowledge of his name or the sanctification of his Spirit, he by these marks in a manner discloses the judgment which awaits them. I will here omit many of the fictions which foolish men have devised to overthrow predestination. There is no need of refuting objections which the moment they are produced abundantly betray their hollowness. I will dwell only on those points which either form the subject of dispute among the learned, or may occasion any difficulty to the simple, or may be employed by impiety as specious pretexts for assailing the justice of God.

Book 3

Chapter 22

This Doctrine Confirmed by Proofs from Scripture

Many controvert all the positions which we have laid down, especially the gratuitous election of believers, which, however, cannot be overthrown. For they commonly imagine that God distinguishes between men according to the merits which he foresees that each individual is to have, giving the adoption of sons to those whom he foreknows will not be unworthy of his grace, and dooming those to destruction whose dispositions he perceives will be prone to mischief and wickedness.[1] Thus by interposing foreknowledge as a veil, they not only obscure election, but pretend to give it a different origin. Nor is this the commonly received opinion of the vulgar merely, for it has in all ages had great supporters. This I candidly confess, lest any one should expect greatly to prejudice our cause by opposing it with their names. The truth of God is here too certain to be shaken, too clear to be overborne by human authority.[2] Others who are neither versed in Scripture, nor entitled to any weight, assail

1. Some take the position that God's election is based on what He foresees that individual will do. For example, Arminians argue that God foresees who will believe in the gospel, and on that basis, chooses them unto salvation. Others might argue that God foresees who will be righteous or wicked, and on that basis "elects" them. However, neither of these positions fit the clear teaching of Scripture. In the case of Jacob and Esau, God's electing purpose had nothing to do with what they would do or what they would be like (Rom. 9:11).

2. These views of election are clearly contrary to Scripture. Ultimately, Calvin says, the truth of God is so clear in this matter that no human ideas will be able to overthrow the plain teaching of Scripture.

3. "Petulance." means "bad-tempered." "Improbity" means a lack of honesty. Calvin argues that those who oppose the doctrine of election are sometimes motivated by dishonesty in their handling of the Scriptures or even come with a personal revulsion to the doctrine. This is not to say all who oppose the biblical doctrine of election are driven by dishonesty or a bad temper.

4. This is a key point in the doctrinal debate over election. Is God free to act according to His own will? Or, is He bound by the decisions of His creatures? Paul describes us as the "pots" which are molded by the hand of the potter (Rom. 9:19-21).

5. To "expostulate" is to express disagreement.

6. "Effrontery" is rude or disrespectful behavior.

sound doctrine with a petulance and improbity[3] which it is impossible to tolerate. Because God of his mere good pleasure electing some passes by others, they raise a plea against him. But if the fact is certain, what can they gain by quarreling with God? We teach nothing but what experience proves to be true—viz. that God has always been at liberty[4] to bestow his grace on whom he would. Not to ask in what respect the posterity of Abraham excelled others if it be not in a worth, the cause of which has no existence out of God, let them tell why men are better than oxen or asses. God might have made them dogs when he formed them in his own image. Will they allow the lower animals to expostulate with God,[5] as if the inferiority of their condition were unjust? It is certainly not more equitable that men should enjoy the privilege which they have not acquired by any merit, than that he should variously distribute favors as seems to him meet. If they pass to the case of individuals where inequality is more offensive to them, they ought at least, in regard to the example of our Savior, to be restrained by feelings of awe from talking so confidently of this sublime mystery. He is conceived a mortal man of the seed of David; what, I would ask them, are the virtues by which he deserved to become in the very womb, the head of angels the only begotten Son of God, the image and glory of the Father, the light, righteousness, and salvation of the world? It is wisely observed by Augustine, that in the very head of the Church we have a bright mirror of free election, lest it should give any trouble to us the members—viz. that he did not become the Son of God by living righteously, but was freely presented with this great honor, that he might afterwards make others partakers of his gifts. Should any one here ask, why others are not what he was, or why we are all at so great a distance from him, why we are all corrupt while he is purity, he would not only betray his madness, but his effrontery also.[6] But if they are bent on depriving God of the free right of electing and reprobating, let them at the same time take away what has been given to Christ. It will now be proper to attend to what

Scripture declares concerning each. When Paul declares that we were chosen in Christ before the foundation of the world (Eph. 1:4), he certainly shows that no regard is had to our own worth; for it is just as if he had said, Since in the whole seed of Adam our heavenly Father found nothing worthy of his election, he turned his eye upon his own Anointed, that he might select as members of his body those whom he was to assume into the fellowship of life. Let believers, then, give full effect to this reason—viz. that we were in Christ adopted unto the heavenly inheritance, because in ourselves we were incapable of such excellence. This he elsewhere observes in another passage, in which he exhorts the Colossians to give thanks that they had been made meet to be partakers of the inheritance of the saints (Col. 1:12). If election precedes that divine grace by which we are made fit to obtain immortal life, what can God find in us to induce him to elect us? What I mean is still more clearly explained in another passage: God, says he, "has chosen us in him before the foundation of the world, that we might be holy and without blame before him in love: having predestinated us unto the adoption of children by Jesus Christ to himself, according to the good pleasure of his will," (Eph. 1:4, 5). Here he opposes the good pleasure of God to our merits of every description.

Wherever this good pleasure of God reigns, no good works are taken into account. The Apostle, indeed, does not follow out the antithesis, but it is to be understood, as he himself explains it in another passage, "Who has called us with a holy calling, not according to our works, but according to his own purpose and grace, which was given us in Christ Jesus before the world began," (2 Tim. 1:9). We have already shown that the additional words, "that we might be holy," remove every doubt. If you say that he foresaw they would be holy, and therefore elected them, you invert the order of Paul.[7] You may, therefore, safely infer, If he elected us that we might be holy, he did not elect us because he foresaw that we would be holy. The two things are evidently inconsistent—viz. that the pious

7. God's election is not based on His foreseeing anything in the creature. Instead, God determines to save His elect not because of anything in them, but because of the mere good pleasure of His will.

8. A "cavil" is an objection that has no real force or substance to it.

9. Since all mankind are fallen in sin and unable to have any holiness by their own power, obviously the holiness of the saints has its foundation in God's electing purpose. Our holiness flows from our election by God. This is in contrast to the view that God chooses some because they are foreseen to be holy in the future.

10. "To conciliate" means here to "gain God's favor."

owe it to election that they are holy, and yet attain to election by means of works. There is no force in the cavil[8] to which they are ever recurring, that the Lord does not bestow election in recompense of preceding, but bestows it in consideration of future merits. For when it is said that believers were elected that they might be holy, it is at the same time intimated that the holiness which was to be in them has its origin in election.[9] And how can it be consistently said, that things derived from election are the cause of election? The very thing which the Apostle had said, he seems afterwards to confirm by adding, "According to his good pleasure which he has purposed in himself," (Eph. 1:9); for the expression that God "purposed in himself," is the same as if it had been said, that in forming his decree he considered nothing external to himself; and, accordingly, it is immediately subjoined, that the whole object contemplated in our election is, that "we should be to the praise of his glory." Assuredly divine grace would not deserve all the praise of election, were not election gratuitous; and it would not be gratuitous did God in electing any individual pay regard to his future works. Hence, what Christ said to his disciples is found to be universally applicable to all believers, "Ye have not chosen me, but I have chosen you," (John 15:16). Here he not only excludes past merits, but declares that they had nothing in themselves for which they could be chosen except in so far as his mercy anticipated. And how are we to understand the words of Paul, "Who has first given to him, and it shall be recompensed unto him again?" (Rom. 11:35). His meaning obviously is, that men are altogether indebted to the preventing goodness of God, there being nothing in them, either past or future, to conciliate his favor.[10]

Book 3

Chapter 24

Election Confirmed by the Calling of God. The Reprobate Bring Upon Themselves the Righteous Destruction to Which They are Doomed

Therefore as those are in error who make the power of election dependent on the faith by which we perceive that we are elected, so we shall follow the best order, if, in seeking the certainty of our election, we cleave to those posterior signs which are sure attestations to it.[1] Among the temptations with which Satan assaults believers, none is greater or more perilous, than when disquieting them with doubts as to their election, he at the same time stimulates them with a depraved desire of inquiring after it out of the proper way. By inquiring out of the proper way,[2] I mean when puny man endeavors to penetrate to the hidden recesses of the divine wisdom, and goes back even to the remotest eternity, in order that he may understand what final determination God has made with regard to him. In this way he plunges headlong into an immense abyss, involves himself in numberless inextricable snares, and buries himself in the thickest darkness. For it is right that the stupidity of the human mind should be punished with fearful destruction, whenever it attempts to rise in its own strength to the height of divine wisdom. And this temptation is the more fatal, that it is the temptation to

1. The "posterior signs" Calvin refers to are those evidences of saving faith that attest to the reality of God's election.

2. Calvin says that one of Satan's temptations is to make believers find the certainty of their election in the wrong things.

3. We can't determine our election by trying to probe into the hidden counsels of God. Instead, we have assurance of faith by holding to the promises of God and seeing the evidence of God's grace in our life.

4. When rightly understood, the doctrine of election should give us great comfort. God's election reminds us that our salvation is secure and does not depend on us.

which of all others almost all of us are most prone. For there is scarcely a mind in which the thought does not sometimes rise, Whence your salvation but from the election of God? But what proof have you of your election? When once this thought has taken possession of any individual, it keeps him perpetually miserable, subjects him to dire torment, or throws him into a state of complete stupor.[3] I cannot wish a stronger proof of the depraved ideas, which men of this description form of predestination, than experience itself furnishes, since the mind cannot be infected by a more pestilential error than that which disturbs the conscience, and deprives it of peace and tranquility in regard to God. Therefore, as we dread shipwreck, we must avoid this rock, which is fatal to every one who strikes upon it. And though the discussion of predestination is regarded as a perilous sea, yet in sailing over it the navigation is calm and safe, nay pleasant, provided we do not voluntarily court danger. For as a fatal abyss engulfs those who, to be assured of their election, pry into the eternal counsel of God without the word, yet those who investigate it rightly, and in the order in which it is exhibited in the word, reap from it rich fruits of consolation.[4] Let our method of inquiry then be, to begin with the calling of God and to end with it. Although there is nothing in this to prevent believers from feeling that the blessings which they daily receive from the hand of God originate in that secret adoption, as they themselves express it in Isaiah, "Thou hast done wonderful things; thy counsels of old are faithfulness and truth," (Isa. 25:1). For with this as a pledge, God is pleased to assure us of as much of his counsel as can be lawfully known.

First, if we seek for the paternal mercy and favor of God, we must turn our eyes to Christ, in whom alone the Father is well pleased (Mt. 3:17). When we seek for salvation, life, and a blessed immortality, to him also must we retake ourselves, since he alone is the fountain of life and the anchor of salvation, and the heir of the kingdom of heaven. Then what is the end of election, but just that, being adopted as sons by the heavenly Father, we may by his favor obtain salvation and immortality? How much soever you may speculate and discuss you will perceive that in its ultimate object it goes no farther. Hence, those whom God has adopted as sons, he is said to have elected, not in themselves, but in Christ Jesus (Eph. 1:4); because he could love them only in him, and only as being previously made partakers with him, honor them with the inheritance of his kingdom. But if we are elected in him, we cannot find the certainty of our election in ourselves; and not even in God the Father, if we look at him apart from the Son.[5] Christ, then, is the mirror in which we ought, and in which, without deception, we may contemplate our election. For since it is into his body that the Father has decreed to engraft those whom from eternity he wished to be his, that he may regard as sons all whom he acknowledges to be his members, if we are in communion with Christ, we have proof sufficiently clear and strong that we are written in the Book of Life. Moreover, he admitted us to sure communion with himself, when, by the preaching of the gospel, he declared that he was given us by the Father, to be ours with all his blessings (Rom. 8:32). We are said to be clothed with him, to be one with him that we may live, because he himself lives. The doctrine is often repeated, "God so loved the world, that he gave his only begotten Son, that whosoever believeth in him should not perish, but have everlasting life," (John 3:16). He who believes in him is said to have passed from death unto life (John 5:24). In this sense he calls himself the bread of life, of which if a man eat, he shall never die (John 6:35). He, I say, was our witness, that all by whom he is received in faith will be regarded by our heavenly Father as sons. If we long for more than to be regarded as sons of God and heirs, we must ascend above Christ. But if this is our final goal, how infatuated is it to seek out of him what we have already obtained in him, and can only find in him? Besides, as he is the Eternal Wisdom, the Immutable Truth, the Determinate Counsel of the Father, there is no room for fear that any thing which he tells us will vary in

5. We are chosen "in the Son." If we would know whether we are elect, the simply question is: have we put our trust in Jesus Christ alone for salvation?

the minutest degree from that will of the Father after which we inquire. Nay, rather he faithfully discloses it to us as it was from the beginning, and always will be. The practical influence of this doctrine ought also to be exhibited in our prayers. For though a belief of our election animates us to involve God, yet when we frame our prayers, it were preposterous to obtrude it upon God, or to stipulate in this way, "O Lord, if I am elected, hear me." He would have us to rest satisfied with his promises, and not to inquire elsewhere whether or not he is disposed to hear us. We shall thus be disentangled from many snares, if we know how to make a right use of what is rightly written; but let us not inconsiderately wrest it to purposes different from that to which it ought to be confined.[6]

6. We don't have to sit around being tortured with the question, "am I elect. . . am I elect?" Instead, we simply must look to Christ by faith. If we are in communion with the Lord Jesus Christ then we can have certainty of our election.

Another confirmation tending to establish our confidence is, that our election is connected with our calling. For those whom Christ enlightens with the knowledge of his name, and admits into the bosom of his Church, he is said to take under his guardianship and protection. All whom he thus receives are said to be committed and entrusted to him by the Father that they may be kept unto life eternal. What would we have? Christ proclaims aloud that all whom the Father is pleased to save he has delivered into his protection (John 6:37-39, 17:6, 12). Therefore, if we would know whether God cares for our salvation, let us ask whether he has committed us to Christ, whom he has appointed to be the only Savior of all his people. Then, if we doubt whether we are received into the protection of Christ, he obviates the doubt when he spontaneously offers himself as our Shepherd, and declares that we are of the number of his sheep if we hear his voice[7] (John 10:3, 16). Let us, therefore, embrace Christ, who is kindly offered to us, and comes forth to meet us: he will number us among his flock, and keep us within his fold. But anxiety arises as to our future state. For as Paul teaches, that those are called who were previously elected, so our Savior shows that many are called, but few chosen (Mt. 22:14). Nay, even Paul himself dissuades us from security, when he says, "Let him that thinketh he stan-

7. This is another simple test of our election: have we been called by God? Do we hear the voice of Christ as His sheep?

deth take heed lest he fall," (1 Cor. 10:12). And again, "Well, because of unbelief they were broken off, and thou standest by faith. Be not high-minded, but fear: for if God spared not the natural branches, take heed lest he also spare not thee," (Rom. 11:20, 21). In fine, we are sufficiently taught by experience itself, that calling and faith are of little value without perseverance, which, however, is not the gift of all. But Christ has freed us from anxiety on this head; for the following promises undoubtedly have respect to the future: "All that the Father giveth me shall come to me, and him that comes to me I will in no wise cast out." Again, "This is the will of him that sent me, that of all which he has given me I should lose nothing; but should raise it up at the last day," (John 6:37, 39). Again "My sheep hear my voice, and I know them, and they follow me: and I give unto them eternal life, and they shall never perish, neither shall any man pluck them out of my hand. My Father which gave them me is greater than all: and no man is able to pluck them out of my Father's hand," (John 10:27, 28). Again, when he declares, "Every plant which my heavenly Father has not planted shall be rooted up," (Mt. 15:13), he intimates conversely that those who have their root in God can never be deprived of their salvation. Agreeable to this are the words of John, "If they had been of us, they would no doubt have continued with us," (1 John 2:19). Hence, also, the magnificent triumph of Paul over life and death, things present, and things to come (Rom. 8:38). This must be founded on the gift of perseverance.[8] There is no doubt that he employs the sentiment as applicable to all the elect. Paul elsewhere says, "Being confident of this very thing, that he who has begun a good work in you will perform it until the day of Jesus Christ," (Phil. 1:6). David, also, when his faith threatened to fail, leant on this support, "Forsake not the works of thy hands." Moreover, it cannot be doubted, that since Christ prays for all the elect, he asks the same thing for them as he asked for Peter—viz. that their faith fail not (Luke 22:32). Hence we infer, that there is no danger of their falling away, since the Son of God,

8. True believers will persevere to the end. But this perseverance is the gift of God. Our God preserves us faithful to the end (1 Cor. 1:7-9, Phil. 1:6, 1 Thess. 5:23-24).

who asks that their piety may prove constant, never meets with a refusal. What then did our Savior intend to teach us by this prayer, but just to confide, that whenever we are his our eternal salvation is secure?

9. Calvin acknowledges the experience many are familiar with. There are often members of the visible church who fall away from the faith. What should we make of this? What is the nature of apostasy? Calvin points out that those who fall away never had true saving faith (1 John 2:19). Jesus promises that none of His sheep will perish (John 6:39).

But it daily happens that those who seemed to belong to Christ revolt from him and fall away:[9] Nay, in the very passage where he declares that none of those whom the Father has given to him have perished, he excepts the son of perdition. This, indeed, is true; but it is equally true that such persons never adhered to Christ with that heartfelt confidence by which I say that the certainty of our election is established: "They went out from us," says John, "but they were not of us; for if they had been of us, they would, no doubt, have continued with us," (1 John 2:19). I deny not that they have signs of calling similar to those given to the elect; but I do not at all admit that they have that sure confirmation of election which I desire believers to seek from the word of the gospel. Wherefore, let not examples of this kind move us away from tranquil confidence in the promise of the Lord, when he declares that all by whom he is received in true faith have been given him by the Father, and that none of them, while he is their Guardian and Shepherd, will perish (John 3:16; 6:39). Of Judas we shall shortly speak. Paul does not dissuade Christians from security simply, but from careless, carnal security, which is accompanied with pride, arrogance, and contempt of others, which extinguishes humility and reverence for God, and produces a forgetfulness of grace received (Rom. 11:20). For he is addressing the Gentiles, and showing them that they ought not to exult proudly and cruelly over the Jews, in consequence of whose rejection they had been substituted in their stead. He also enjoins fear, not a fear under which they may waver in alarm, but a fear which, teaching us to receive the grace of God in humility, does not impair our confidence in it, as has elsewhere been said. We may add, that he is not speaking to individuals, but to sects in general (see 1 Cor. 10:12). The Church having been divided into two parties, and rivalries producing dissension,

Paul reminds the Gentiles that their having been substituted in the place of a peculiar and holy people was a reason for modesty and fear. For there were many vain-glorious persons among them, whose empty boasting it was expedient to repress. But we have elsewhere seen, that our hope extends into the future, even beyond death, and that nothing is more contrary to its nature than to be in doubt as to our future destiny.

Book 3
Chapter 25

Of the Last Resurrection

1. In this chapter, Calvin addresses our final hope of Christ's return and the resurrection. These topics in theology are traditionally classified as "eschatology" (the doctrine of the last things).

Although Christ, the Sun of righteousness, shining upon us through the gospel, has, as Paul declares, after conquering death, given us the light of life; and hence on believing we are said to have passed from "death unto life," being no longer strangers and pilgrims, but fellow citizens with the saints, and of the household of God, who has made us sit with his only begotten Son in heavenly places, so that nothing is wanting to our complete felicity; yet, lest we should feel it grievous to be exercised under a hard warfare, as if the victory obtained by Christ had produced no fruit, we must attend to what is elsewhere taught concerning the nature of hope.[1] For since we hope for what we see not, and faith, as is said in another passage, is "the evidence of things not seen" so long as we are imprisoned in the body we are absent from the Lord. For which reason Paul says, "Ye are dead, and your life is hid with Christ in God. When Christ, who is our life, shall appear, then shall ye also appear with him in glory." Our present condition, therefore, requires us to "live soberly, righteously, and godly;" "looking for that blessed hope, and the glorious appearing of the great God and our

Savior Jesus Christ."[2] Here there is need of no ordinary patience, lest, worn out with fatigue, we either turn backwards or abandon our post. Wherefore, all that has hitherto been said of our salvation calls upon us to raise our minds towards heaven, that, as Peter exhorts, though we now see not Christ, "yet believing," we may "rejoice with joy unspeakable and full of glory,"[3] receiving the end of our faith, even the salvation of our souls. For this reason Paul says, that the faith and charity of the saints have respect to the faith and hope which is laid up for them in heaven (Col. 1:5). When we thus keep our eyes fixed upon Christ in heaven, and nothing on earth prevents us from directing them to the promised blessedness, there is a true fulfillment of the saying, "where your treasure is, there will your heart be also," (Mt. 6:21). Hence the reason why faith is so rare in the world; nothing being more difficult for our sluggishness than to surmount innumerable obstacles in striving for the prize of our high calling. To the immense load of miseries which almost overwhelm us, are added the jeers of profane men, who assail us for our simplicity, when spontaneously renouncing the allurements of the present life we seem, in seeking a happiness which lies hid from us, to catch at a fleeting shadow. In short, we are beset above and below, behind and before, with violent temptations, which our minds would be altogether unable to withstand, were they not set free from earthly objects and devoted to the heavenly life, though apparently remote from us. Wherefore, he alone has made solid progress in the Gospel who has acquired the habit of meditating continually on a blessed resurrection.[4]

In ancient times philosophers discoursed, and even debated with each other, concerning the chief good: none, however, except Plato acknowledged that it consisted in union with God. He could not, however, form even an imperfect idea of its true nature; nor is this strange, as he had learned nothing of the sacred bond of that union. We even in this our earthly pilgrimage know wherein our perfect and only felicity consists,[5]—a felicity which, while we long for it, daily inflames

2. Titus 2:13

3. 1 Peter 1:8

4. It is the doctrine of the resurrection that gives us a solid foundation for hope. We should be steadfast, immovable, always abounding the work of the Lord, knowing that our labor is not in vain (1 Cor. 15:58). We are to be future-oriented, looking to the blessed hope of Christ's return and our resurrection (Tit. 2:13-14).

5. Our perfect and eternal "joy" or "happiness"

6. The term "conversation" here is translated in modern translations as "citizenship."

7. "Ardor" refers to our enthusiasm or passion. In light of the blessed hope we have, we know that we don't labor in vain. We are inheriting a kingdom that will never pass away. We serve a King who reigns over all things. One day, He will return and resurrect us from the dead.

our hearts more and more, until we attain to full fruition. Therefore I said, that none participate in the benefits of Christ save those who raise their minds to the resurrection. This, accordingly, is the mark which Paul sets before believers, and at which he says they are to aim, forgetting every thing until they reach it (Phil. 3:8). The more strenuously, therefore, must we contend for it, lest if the world engross us we be severely punished for our sloth. Accordingly, he in another passage distinguishes believers by this mark, that their conversation is in heaven,[6] from whence they look for the Savior (Phil. 3:20).

The very importance of the subject ought to increase our ardor.[7] Paul justly contends, that if Christ rise not the whole gospel is delusive and vain (1 Cor. 15:13-17); for our condition would be more miserable than that of other mortals, because we are exposed to much hatred and insult, and incur danger every hour; nay, are like sheep destined for slaughter; and hence the authority of the gospel would fail, not in one part merely, but in its very essence, including both our adoption and the accomplishment of our salvation. Let us, therefore, give heed to a matter of all others the most serious, so that no length of time may produce weariness. I have deferred the brief consideration to be given of it to this place, that my readers may learn, when they have received Christ, the author of perfect salvation, to rise higher, and know that he is clothed with heavenly immortality and glory in order that the whole body may be rendered conformable to the Head. For thus the Holy Spirit is ever setting before us in his person an example of the resurrection. It is difficult to believe that after our bodies have been consumed with rottenness, they will rise again at their appointed time. And hence, while many of the philosophers maintained the immortality of the soul, few of them assented to the resurrection of the body. Although in this they were inexcusable, we are thereby reminded that the subject is too difficult for human apprehension to reach it. To enable faith to surmount the great difficulty, Scripture furnishes two auxiliary proofs, the one the likeness of Christ's resurrection, and the other the omnipotence of God. Therefore, whenever the subject of the resurrection is considered, let us think of the case of our Savior, who, having completed his mortal course in our nature which he had assumed, obtained immortality, and is now the pledge of our future resurrection. For in the miseries by which we are beset, we always bear "about in the body the dying of the Lord Jesus, that the life also of Jesus might be made manifest in our mortal flesh," (2 Cor. 4:10). It is not lawful, it is not even possible, to separate him from us, without dividing him. Hence Paul's argument, "If there be no resurrection of the dead, then is Christ not risen," (1 Cor. 15:13); for he assumes it as an acknowledged principle, that when Christ was subjected to death, and by rising gained a victory over death, it was not on his own account, but in the Head was begun what must necessarily be fulfilled in all the members, according to the degree and order of each. For it would not be proper to be made equal to him in all respects. It is said in the psalm, "Neither wilt thou suffer thine Holy One to see corruption," (Ps. 16:10). Although a portion of this confidence appertain to us according to the measure bestowed on us, yet the full effect appeared only in Christ, who, free from all corruption, resumed a spotless body. Then, that there may be no doubt as to our fellowship with Christ in a blessed resurrection, and that we may be contented with this pledge, Paul distinctly affirms that he sits in the heavens, and will come as a judge on the last day for the express purpose of changing our vile body, "that it may be fashioned like unto his glorious body," (Phil. 3:21). For he elsewhere says that God did not raise up his Son from death to give an isolated specimen of his mighty power, but that the Spirit exerts the same efficacy in regard to them that believe; and accordingly he says, that the Spirit when he dwells in us is life, because the end for which he was given is to quicken our mortal body (Rom. 8:10, 11; Col. 3:4). I briefly glance at subjects which might be treated more copiously, and deserve to be adorned more splendidly, and yet in the little I have said I trust pious readers will find sufficient materials for building up their faith. Christ rose again that he might have us as partakers with him of future life. He was raised up by the Father, inasmuch as he was the Head of the Church, from which he cannot possibly be dissevered. He was raised up by the power of the Spirit, who also in us performs the office of quickening. In fine, he was raised up to be the resurrection and the life. But as we have said, that in this mirror we behold a living image of the resurrection, so it furnishes a sure evidence to support our minds, provided we faint not, nor grow weary at the long delay, because it is not ours to measure the periods of time at our own pleasure; but to rest patiently till God in his own time renew his kingdom. To this Paul refers when he says, "But every man in his own order: Christ the first-fruits; afterward they that are Christ's at his coming," (1 Cor. 15:23).

Book 4
Chapter 1

Of the True Church. Duty of Cultivating Unity With Her, as the Mother of All the Godly

In the last Book, it has been shown, that by the faith of the gospel Christ becomes ours, and we are made partakers of the salvation and eternal blessedness procured by him. But as our ignorance and sloth (I may add, the vanity of our mind) stand in need of external helps, by which faith may be begotten in us, and may increase and make progress until its consummation, God, in accommodation to our infirmity, has added such helps, and secured the effectual preaching of the gospel, by depositing this treasure with the Church.[1] He has appointed pastors and teachers, by whose lips he might edify his people (Eph. 4:11); he has invested them with authority, and, in short, omitted nothing that might conduce to holy consent in the faith, and to right order. In particular, he has instituted sacraments, which we feel by experience to be most useful helps in fostering and confirming our faith.[2] For seeing we are shut up in the prison of the body, and have not yet attained to the rank of angels, God, in accommodation to our capacity, has in his admirable providence provided a method by which, though widely separated, we might still draw near to him. Wherefore, due order requires that we first treat

1. In Book 4, Calvin gives his attention to the doctrine of the church. In the first chapter, Calvin explains how the church is the "mother of the godly." In the bosom of the church, we are nurtured in the faith and make progress in the faith until the consummation of all things.

2. Calvin will explain the nature of the sacraments in a later chapter. Here he points out that the sacraments are those visual and physical signs that enable us to "experience" the truths of the gospel. By the sacraments we are strengthened in faith.

of the Church, of its Government, Orders, and Power; next, of the Sacraments; and, lastly, of Civil Government;—at the same time guarding pious readers against the corruptions of the Papacy, by which Satan has adulterated all that God had appointed for our salvation. I will begin with the Church, into whose bosom God is pleased to collect his children, not only that by her aid and ministry they may be nourished so long as they are babes and children, but may also be guided by her maternal care until they grow up to manhood, and, finally, attain to the perfection of faith. What God has thus joined, let not man put asunder (Mark 10:9): to those to whom he is a Father, the Church must also be a mother.[3] This was true not merely under the Law, but even now after the advent of Christ; since Paul declares that we are the children of a new, even a heavenly Jerusalem (Gal. 4:26).

But as it is now our purpose to discourse of the visible Church, let us learn, from her single title of Mother, how useful, nay, how necessary the knowledge of her is, since there is no other means of entering into life unless she conceive us in the womb and give us birth, unless she nourish us at her breasts, and, in short, keep us under her charge and government, until, divested of mortal flesh, we become like the angels (Mt. 22:30). For our weakness does not permit us to leave the school until we have spent our whole lives as scholars.[4] Moreover, beyond the pale of the Church no forgiveness of sins, no salvation, can be hoped for, as Isaiah and Joel testify (Isa. 37:32; Joel 2:32). To their testimony Ezekiel subscribes, when he declares, "They shall not be in the assembly of my people, neither shall they be written in the writing of the house of Israel" (Ezek. 13:9); as, on the other hand, those who turn to the cultivation of true piety are said to inscribe their names among the citizens of Jerusalem. For which reason it is said in the psalm, "Remember me, O Lord, with the favor that thou bearest unto thy people: O visit me with thy salvation; that I may see the good of thy chosen, that I may rejoice in the gladness of thy nation, that I may glory with thine inheri-

3. The Lord has so ordered things that all those who are saved by Jesus Christ will be joined to the people of God (1 Cor. 12:13, Eph. 4:1-6). Of course, there may be exceptions where some who are true believers will not be joined to the visible church. This would be an exception to the pattern God sets forth in Scripture.

4. Calvin describes the church as a "school" in which we must learn until the very end of our lives. He also uses the picture of a mother. Just as a mother nurtures and trains her children, likewise the church is our mother on the way to heavenly Jerusalem.

tance" (Ps. 106:4, 5). By these words the paternal favor of God and the special evidence of spiritual life are confined to his peculiar people, and hence the abandonment of the Church is always fatal.[5]

The judgment which ought to be formed concerning the visible Church which comes under our observation, must, I think, be sufficiently clear from what has been said. I have observed that the Scriptures speak of the Church in two ways. Sometimes when they speak of the Church they mean the Church as it really is before God—the Church into which none are admitted but those who by the gift of adoption are sons of God, and by the sanctification of the Spirit true members of Christ.[6] In this case it not only comprehends the saints who dwell on the earth, but all the elect who have existed from the beginning of the world. Often, too, by the name of Church is designated the whole body of mankind scattered throughout the world, who profess to worship one God and Christ, who by baptism are initiated into the faith; by partaking of the Lord's Supper profess unity in true doctrine and charity, agree in holding the word of the Lord, and observe the ministry which Christ has appointed for the preaching of it.[7] In this Church there is a very large mixture of hypocrites, who have nothing of Christ but the name and outward appearance: of ambitious, avaricious, envious, evil-speaking men, some also of impure lives, who are tolerated for a time, either because their guilt cannot be legally established, or because due strictness of discipline is not always observed.[8] Hence, as it is necessary to believe the invisible Church, which is manifest to the eye of God only, so we are also enjoined to regard this Church which is so called with reference to man, and to cultivate its communion.

5. Many modern evangelicals read Calvin's words here and may be shocked by the importance Calvin assigns to the church. Some in the modern day treat the church as an optional add-on to the Christian life. In this view, the church is perhaps helpful, but not essential. This contradicts the plain teaching of Scripture that always describes the Christian life as a life lived in community with other believers in the church (see Rom. 12, Eph. 4-5, Col. 3, etc.).

6. Calvin introduces the distinction of the "visible" vs. the "invisible" church. This distinction is not meant to communicate that there are two different churches. Instead, it simply means that there are some within the visible church (as baptized members) who may not be truly united to Christ by faith. Only God knows the number of the elect. All that we can discern is the members of the visible church.

7. The "visible church" is defined as the people of God, professing a common faith, joined together in doctrine and love, holding to the Word, and partaking of the sacraments.

8. Within the visible church, there may be false professors. Their hypocrisy will eventually be exposed. But in this life, there is no church that is a perfectly pure church. All churches are subject to a mixture of error and corruption.

Accordingly, inasmuch as it was of importance to us to recognize it, the Lord has distinguished it by certain marks, and as it were symbols. It is, indeed, the special prerogative of God to know those who are his, as Paul declares in the passage already quoted (2 Tim. 2:19). And doubtless it has been so provided as a check on human rashness, the experience of every day reminding us how far his secret judgments surpass our apprehension. For even those who seemed most abandoned, and who had been completely despaired of, are by his goodness recalled to life, while those who seemed most stable often fall. Hence, as Augustine says, "In regard to the secret predestination of God, there are very many sheep without, and very many wolves within." For he knows, and has his mark on those who know neither him nor themselves. Of those again who openly bear his badge, his eyes alone see who of them are unfeignedly holy, and will persevere even to the end, which alone is the completion of salvation. On the other hand, foreseeing that it was in some degree expedient for us to know who are to be regarded by us as his sons, he has in this matter accommodated himself to our capacity. But as here full certainty was not necessary, he has in its place substituted the judgment of charity, by which we acknowledge all as members of the Church who by confession of faith, regularity of conduct, and participation in the sacraments, unite with us in acknowledging the same God and Christ. The knowledge of his body, inasmuch as he knew it to be more necessary for our salvation, he has made known to us by surer marks.

9. Calvin gives us two key marks of the church. The first is the faithful preaching of God's Word. The second is the faithful administration of the sacraments.

Hence the form of the Church appears and stands forth conspicuous to our view. Wherever we see the word of God sincerely preached and heard, wherever we see the sacraments administered according to the institution of Christ, there we cannot have any doubt that the Church of God has some existence,[9] since his promise cannot fail, "Where two or three are gathered together in my name, there am I in the midst of them" (Mt. 18:20). But that we may have a clear summary of this subject, we must proceed by the following steps:—The

Church universal is the multitude collected out of all nations, who, though dispersed and far distant from each other, agree in one truth of divine doctrine, and are bound together by the tie of a common religion. In this way it comprehends single churches, which exist in different towns and villages, according to the wants of human society, so that each of them justly obtains the name and authority of the Church; and also comprehends single individuals, who by a religious profession are accounted to belong to such churches, although they are in fact aliens from the Church, but have not been cut off by a public decision. There is, however, a slight difference in the mode of judging of individuals and of churches. For it may happen in practice that those whom we deem not altogether worthy of the fellowship of believers, we yet ought to treat as brethren, and regard as believers, on account of the common consent of the Church in tolerating and bearing with them in the body of Christ. Such persons we do not approve by our suffrage as members of the Church, but we leave them the place which they hold among the people of God, until they are legitimately deprived of it. With regard to the general body we must feel differently; if they have the ministry of the word, and honor the administration of the sacraments, they are undoubtedly entitled to be ranked with the Church, because it is certain that these things are not without a beneficial result. Thus we both maintain the Church universal in its unity, which malignant minds have always been eager to dissever, and deny not due authority to lawful assemblies distributed as circumstances require.

We have said that the symbols by which the Church is discerned are the preaching of the word and the observance of the sacraments, for these cannot anywhere exist without producing fruit and prospering by the blessing of God. I say not that wherever the word is preached fruit immediately appears; but that in every place where it is received, and has a fixed abode, it uniformly displays its efficacy. Be this as it may, when the preaching of the gospel is reverently heard, and the

10. If the church is a true church, then to disregard her authority, her admonitions, her counsels, and her rebukes is a serious thing. It is important that we each have a proper respect for the authority of the church, bestowed by our Lord Jesus, who is the head of the church. Our Lord Jesus walks among the churches (Rev. 2-3) to oversee and protect them. It is a foolish and dangerous thing to violate the church's unity and spurn its authority.

11. "Contumacy" is the stubborn refusal to obey or comply with authority. Calvin says that those who reject the church and separate themselves from it are refusing the lawful authority of Christ.

12. "No small praise is conferred"

13. The church is the bride of our Lord Jesus. Just as a husband will not allow the mistreatment and abuse of His bride by others, so also our Lord Jesus will protect His bride from the attacks of others.

sacraments are not neglected, there for the time the face of the Church appears without deception or ambiguity and no man may with impunity spurn her authority, or reject her admonitions, or resist her counsels, or make sport of her censures, far less revolt from her, and violate her unity.[10] For such is the value which the Lord sets on the communion of his Church, that all who contumaciously alienate themselves[11] from any Christian society, in which the true ministry of his word and sacraments is maintained, he regards as deserters of religion. So highly does he recommend her authority, that when it is violated he considers that his own authority is impaired. For there is no small weight in the designation given to her, "the house of God," "the pillar and ground of the truth" (1 Tim. 3:15). By these words Paul intimates, that to prevent the truth from perishing in the world. the Church is its faithful guardian, because God has been pleased to preserve the pure preaching of his word by her instrumentality, and to exhibit himself to us as a parent while he feeds us with spiritual nourishment, and provides whatever is conducive to our salvation. Moreover, no mean praise is conferred[12] on the Church when she is said to have been chosen and set apart by Christ as his spouse, "not having spot or wrinkle, or any such thing" (Eph. 5:27), as "his body, the fullness of him that filleth all in all" (Eph. 1:23). Whence it follows, that revolt from the Church is denial of God and Christ. Wherefore there is the more necessity to beware of a dissent so iniquitous; for seeing by it we aim as far as in us lies at the destruction of God's truth, we deserve to be crushed by the full thunder of his anger. No crime can be imagined more atrocious than that of sacrilegiously and perfidiously violating the sacred marriage which the only begotten Son of God has condescended to contract with us.[13]

Wherefore let these marks be carefully impressed upon our minds, and let us estimate them as in the sight of the Lord. There is nothing on which Satan is more intent than to destroy and efface one or both of them—at one time to delete and abolish these marks, and thereby destroy the true and genuine distinction of the Church; at another, to bring them into contempt, and so hurry us into open revolt from the Church. To his wiles it was owing that for several ages the pure preaching of the word disappeared, and now, with the same dishonest aim, he labors to overthrow the ministry, which, however, Christ has so ordered in his Church, that if it is removed the whole edifice must fall.[14] How perilous, then, nay, how fatal the temptation, when we even entertain a thought of separating ourselves from that assembly in which are beheld the signs and badges which the Lord has deemed sufficient to characterize his Church![15] We see how great caution should be employed in both respects. That we may not be imposed upon by the name of Church, every congregation which claims the name must be brought to that test as to a Lydian stone.[16] If it holds the order instituted by the Lord in word and sacraments there will be no deception; we may safely pay it the honor due to a church: on the other hand, if it exhibit itself without word and sacraments, we must in this case be no less careful to avoid the imposture than we were to shun pride and presumption in the other.

When we say that the pure ministry of the word and pure celebration of the sacraments is a fit pledge and earnest, so that we may safely recognize a church in every society in which both exist, our meaning is, that we are never to discard it so long as these remain, though it may otherwise teem with numerous faults. Nay, even in the administration of word and sacraments defects may creep in which ought not to alienate us from its communion. For all the heads of true doctrine are not in the same position. Some are so necessary to be known, that all must hold them to be fixed and undoubted as the proper essentials of religion: for instance, that God is one, that Christ is God, and the Son of God, that our salvation depends on the mercy of God, and the like. Others, again, which are the subject of controversy among the churches, do not destroy the unity of the faith; for why should it be regarded as a ground of dissension between churches, if one, without any spirit of

14. Let us not forget the spiritual battle that is waged over the church of Jesus Christ. Satan is out to destroy Christ's kingdom. It should not surprise us that people are led astray from recognizing the true marks of the church or by having contempt for the church.

15. If we recognize these Satanic temptations, let us be on guard against separating ourselves from the people of God. "Beware, brethren, lest there be in any of you an evil heart of unbelief in departing from the living God; but exhort one another daily, while it is called 'Today,' lest any of you be hardened through the deceitfulness of sin. For we have become partakers of Christ if we hold the beginning of our confidence steadfast to the end," (Heb. 3:12-14).

16. The "Lydian stone" was a flint slate used to test gold and silver. Gold or silver could be rubbed against the slate to test the quality of the gold or silver. Calvin says we can compare a church to these true marks to discern whether it is the real thing.

17. It is important that we learn to discern what is a "gnat" and what is a "camel" (Matt. 23:23-24). There are weightier matters in God's Word. It is important that we unify around those doctrines that are central and foundational. But when there are doctrinal and practical matters that are disputable, we should proceed with humility and not cause dissension in the church.

18. Calvin clarifies that he does not suggest we countenance or accept false doctrine. But no church is perfect, and we should not separate from a church over minor matters.

19. If we discern that error is being accepted in our church, we should strive in a humble and loving way to bring reform to those issues. Perhaps this means bringing the matter to the pastors/elders and asking them to address it. Perhaps it means using Scripture to explain why a particular doctrine or practice is in error.

20. Since we are all sinners redeemed by the blood of Christ, it is essential that we be patient with one another. We will sin against each other and our conduct will fall short.

contention or perverseness in dogmatizing, hold that the soul on quitting the body flies to heaven, and another, without venturing to speak positively as to the abode, holds it for certain that it lives with the Lord? The words of the Apostle are, "Let us therefore, as many as be perfect, be thus minded: and if in anything ye be otherwise minded, God shall reveal even this unto you" (Phil. 3:15). Does he not sufficiently intimate that a difference of opinion as to these matters which are not absolutely necessary, ought not to be a ground of dissension among Christians?[17] The best thing, indeed, is to be perfectly agreed, but seeing there is no man who is not involved in some mist of ignorance, we must either have no church at all, or pardon delusion in those things of which one may be ignorant, without violating the substance of religion and forfeiting salvation. Here, however, I have no wish to patronize even the minutest errors, as if I thought it right to foster them by flattery or connivance; what I say is, that we are not on account of every minute difference to abandon a church,[18] provided it retain sound and unimpaired that doctrine in which the safety of piety consists, and keep the use of the sacraments instituted by the Lord. Meanwhile, if we strive to reform what is offensive,[19] we act in the discharge of duty. To this effect are the words of Paul, "If anything be revealed to another that sitteth by, let the first hold his peace" (1 Cor. 14:30).

From this it is evident that to each member of the Church, according to his measure of grace, the study of public edification has been assigned, provided it be done decently and in order. In other words, we must neither renounce the communion of the Church, nor, continuing in it, disturb peace and discipline when duly arranged.

Our indulgence ought to extend much farther in tolerating imperfection of conduct.[20] Here there is great danger of falling, and Satan employs all his machinations to ensnare us. For there always have been persons who, imbued with a false persuasion of absolute holiness, as if they had already become a kind of aerial spirits, spurn the society of all in whom they see that something human still remains.[21] Such of old were the Cathari and the Donatists,[22] who were similarly infatuated. Such in the present day are some of the Anabaptists, who would be thought to have made superior progress.[23] Others, again, sin in this respect, not so much from that insane pride as from inconsiderate zeal. Seeing that among those to whom the gospel is preached, the fruit produced is not in accordance with the doctrine, they forthwith conclude that there no church exists. The offence is indeed well founded, and it is one to which in this most unhappy age we give far too much occasion. It is impossible to excuse our accursed sluggishness, which the Lord will not leave unpunished, as he is already beginning sharply to chastise us. Woe then to us who, by our dissolute license of wickedness, cause weak consciences to be wounded! Still those of whom we have spoken sin in their turn, by not knowing how to set bounds to their offence. For where the Lord requires mercy they omit it, and give themselves up to immoderate severity. Thinking there is no church where there is not complete purity and integrity of conduct, they, through hatred of wickedness, withdraw from a genuine church, while they think they are shunning the company of the ungodly. They allege that the Church of God is holy. But that they may at the same time understand that it contains a

21. In pride, some can consider themselves to attained perfect holiness. As a result, they reject fellowship with everyone else who falls short of the standard they have attained. This is a foolish and unbiblical perspective. Even for those who have attained some degree of holiness, they are still sinners.

22. Calvin mentions two sects in past church history. The Cathari were the more recent of the two groups, having gained some prominence during the late Middle Ages (12th to 14th centuries). The Cathari were also known as "Albigensians." They held to a number of heretical doctrines. Their theology revived many ancient Gnostic ideas that contradicted biblical teaching. The majority of Cathari resided in France. The Cathari were severely persecuted because of their heresies. A crusade was launched against the Cathari in 1209. This is sometimes called the "Crusade." By about 1350, most of the Cathari had been wiped out. The Donatists hail from a much earlier period of the church (4th and 5th centuries). They were a group that emphasized the purity of the church and would not re-admit those who had lapsed and denied the faith during persecution. They believed that the validity of the sacraments depended upon the holiness of the minister who administered them. The Donatist were "rigorists" who left little room for sinners to be a part of the church.

23. Calvin says that some of the Anabaptist groups were "perfectionistic" like the Cathari and Donatists of old.

mixture of good and bad, let them hear from the lips of our Savior that parable in which he compares the Church to a net in which all kinds of fishes are taken, but not separated until they are brought ashore. Let them hear it compared to a field which, planted with good seed, is by the fraud of an enemy mingled with tares, and is not freed of them until the harvest is brought into the barn. Let them hear, in fine, that it is a thrashing-floor in which the collected wheat lies concealed under the chaff, until, cleansed by the fanners and the sieve, it is at length laid up in the granary. If the Lord declares that the Church will labor under the defect of being burdened with a multitude of wicked until the Day of Judgment, it is in vain to look for a church altogether free from blemish (Mt. 13).[24]

24. Calvin alludes to the various parables of Jesus that describe the kingdom as a "mixed body." The church will contain both wheat and tares. This imperfection of the church will remain until the Day of Judgment when all will be sorted out by our Lord.

Still, however, even the good are sometimes affected by this inconsiderate zeal for righteousness, though we shall find that this excessive moroseness is more the result of pride and a false idea of sanctity, than genuine sanctity itself, and true zeal for it. Accordingly, those who are the most forward, and, as it were, leaders in producing revolt from the Church, have, for the most part, no other motive than to display their own superiority by despising all other men. Well and wisely, therefore, does Augustine say, "Seeing that pious reason and the mode of ecclesiastical discipline ought specially to regard the unity of the Spirit in the bond of peace, which the Apostle enjoins us to keep, by bearing with one another (for if we keep it not, the application of medicine is not only superfluous, but pernicious, and therefore proves to be no medicine); those bad sons who, not from hatred of other men's iniquities, but zeal for their own contentions, attempt altogether to draw away, or at least to divide, weak brethren ensnared by the glare of their name, while swollen with pride, stuffed with petulance, insidiously calumnious, and turbulently seditious, use the cloak of a rigorous severity, that they may not seem devoid of the light of truth, and pervert to sacrilegious schism, and purposes of excision, those things which are enjoined in the Holy Scriptures (due regard being had to sincere love, and the unity of peace), to correct a brother's faults by the appliance of a moderate cure."[25] To the pious and placid[26] his advice is, mercifully to correct what they can, and to bear patiently with what they cannot correct, in love lamenting and mourning until God either reform or correct, or at the harvest root up the tares, and scatter the chaff. Let all the godly study to provide themselves with these weapons, lest, while they deem themselves strenuous and ardent defenders of righteousness, they revolt from the kingdom of heaven, which is the only kingdom of righteousness. For as God has been pleased that the communion of his Church shall be maintained in this external society, any one who, from hatred of the ungodly, violates the bond of this society, enters on a downward course, in which he incurs great danger of cutting himself off from the communion of saints. Let them reflect, that in a numerous body there are several who may escape their notice, and yet are truly righteous and innocent in the eyes of the Lord. Let them reflect, that of those who seem diseased, there are many who are far from taking pleasure or flattering themselves in their faults, and who, ever and anon aroused by a serious fear of the Lord, aspire to greater integrity. Let them reflect, that they have no right to pass judgment on a man for one act, since the holiest sometimes make the most grievous fall. Let them reflect, that in the ministry of the word and participation of the sacraments, the power to collect the Church is too great to be deprived of its entire efficacy, by the fault of some ungodly men. Lastly, let them reflect, that in estimating the Church, divine is of more force than human judgment.[27]

Since they also argue that there is good reason for the Church being called holy, it is necessary to consider what the holiness is in which it excels, lest by refusing to acknowledge any church, save one that is completely perfect, we leave no church at all. It is true, indeed, as Paul says, that Christ "loved the church, and gave himself for it, that he might sanctify and cleanse it with the washing of water by the word, that he might present it to himself a glorious church, not having

25. This quote from Augustine contrasts the brother, who in pride, would divide the church by insisting on a perfect holiness and cast out his brothers that fall short. But the Scriptures teach us to restore our brother who falls with a spirit of gentleness (Gal. 6:1). The "cloak of religious severity" means that some use the standard of holiness as a "cover" or "cloak" for their proud and divisive behavior.

26. The "placid" are those who are peaceful and not easily upset or disturbed.

27. There is much wisdom to consider in this paragraph. Christians should remember how little they know about the true spiritual condition of the church. Let us leave judgment in the hands of God. We are responsible to restore those who fall (Gal. 6:1), and to call back those who are wandering (Jas. 5:19-20). But we must remember that we each stand or fall before our Master Jesus (Rom. 14:4). The Lord knows those who are His (2 Tim. 2:19).

28. The church is called holy, first because it is set apart by God as His treasured possession. But its holiness or purity is not yet perfect. The Lord is preparing the church to be without blemish as the bride of Christ. But that work will not be complete until the return of Christ.

spot, or wrinkle, or any such thing; but that it should be holy and without blemish" (Eph. 5:25-27). Nevertheless, it is true, that the Lord is daily smoothing its wrinkles, and wiping away its spots. Hence it follows, that its holiness is not yet perfect.[28] Such, then, is the holiness of the Church: it makes daily progress, but is not yet perfect; it daily advances, but as yet has not reached the goal, as will elsewhere be more fully explained. Therefore, when the Prophets foretell, "Then shall Jerusalem be holy, and there shall no strangers pass through her any more;"—"It shall be called, The way of holiness; the unclean shall not pass over it" (Joel 3:17; Isa. 35:8), let us not understand it as if no blemish remained in the members of the Church: but only that with their whole heart they aspire after holiness and perfect purity: and hence, that purity which they have not yet fully attained is, by the kindness of God, attributed to them. And though the indications of such a kind of holiness existing among men are too rare, we must understand, that at no period since the world began has the Lord been without his Church, nor ever shall be till the final consummation of all things. For although, at the very outset, the whole human race was vitiated and corrupted by the sin of Adam, yet of this kind of polluted mass he always sanctifies some vessels to honor, that no age may be left without experience of his mercy. This he has declared by sure promises, such as the following: "I have made a covenant with my chosen, I have sworn unto David my servant, Thy seed will I establish for ever, and build up thy throne to all generations" (Ps. 89:3, 4). "The Lord hath chosen Zion; he hath desired it for his habitation. This is my rest for ever; here will I dwell" (Ps. 132:13, 14). "Thus saith the Lord, which giveth the sun for a light by day, and the ordinances of the moon and of the stars for a light by night, which divideth the sea when the waves thereof roar; The Lord of hosts is his name: If those ordinances depart from before me, saith the Lord, then the seed of Israel also shall cease from being a nation before me for ever" (Jer. 31:35, 36).

Nor by remission of sins does the Lord only once for all elect and admit us into the Church, but by the same means he preserves and defends us in it. For what would it avail us to receive a pardon of which we were afterwards to have no use? That the mercy of the Lord would be vain and delusive if only granted once, all the godly can bear witness; for there is none who is not conscious, during his whole life, of many infirmities which stand in need of divine mercy. And truly it is not without cause that the Lord promises this gift specially to his own household, nor in vain that he orders the same message of reconciliation to be daily delivered to them. Wherefore, as during our whole lives we carry about with us the remains of sin, we could not continue in the Church one single moment were we not sustained by the uninterrupted grace of God in forgiving our sins. On the other hand, the Lord has called his people to eternal salvation, and therefore they ought to consider that pardon for their sins is always ready. Hence let us surely hold that if we are admitted and engrafted into the body of the Church, the forgiveness of sins has been bestowed, and is daily bestowed on us, in divine liberality, through the intervention of Christ's merits, and the sanctification of the Spirit.

Book 4

Chapter 2

Comparison Between the False Church and the True

1. Calvin says that we must give due weight to the ministry of the Word and sacraments. Where that ministry is taking place according to Christ's institution, we should acknowledge the church as a true church.

2. Calvin says that the fundamental truths of God's Word must be preached and the sacraments administered in a way that does not contradict Christ's institution of them. This can be difficult to ascertain in some cases. But this does serve as a basic guide for understanding the nature of the true church vs. the false church.

How much the ministry of the word and sacraments should weigh with us, and how far reverence for it should extend, so as to be a perpetual badge for distinguishing the Church, has been explained; for we have shown, first, that wherever it exists entire and unimpaired, no errors of conduct, no defects should prevent us from giving the name of Church; and, secondly, that trivial errors in this ministry ought not to make us regard it as illegitimate.[1] Moreover, we have shown that the errors to which such pardon is due, are those by which the fundamental doctrine of religion is not injured, and by which those articles of religion, in which all believers should agree, are not suppressed, while, in regard to the sacraments, the defects are such as neither destroy nor impair the legitimate institution of their Author.[2] But as soon as falsehood has forced its way into the citadel of religion, as soon as the sum of necessary doctrine is inverted, and the use of the sacraments is destroyed, the death of the Church undoubtedly ensues, just as the life of man is destroyed when his throat is pierced, or his vitals mortally wounded. This is clearly evinced by the words of Paul when he says, that the Church is "built upon the foundation of the apostles and prophets, Jesus Christ himself being the chief corner-stone" (Eph. 2:20). If the Church is founded on the doctrine of the apostles and prophets, by which believers are enjoined to place their salvation in Christ alone, then if that doctrine is destroyed, how can the Church continue to stand? The Church must necessarily fall whenever that sum of religion which alone can sustain it has given way. Again, if the true Church is "the pillar and ground of the truth" (1 Tim. 3:15), it is certain that there is no Church where lying and falsehood have usurped the ascendancy.

Since this is the state of matters under the Papacy, we can understand how much of the Church there survives.[3] There, instead of the ministry of the word, prevails a perverted government, compounded of lies, a government which partly extinguishes, partly suppresses, the pure light. In place of the Lord's Supper, the foulest sacrilege has entered,[4] the worship of God is deformed by a varied mass of intolerable superstitions; doctrine (without which Christianity exists not) is wholly buried and exploded, the public assemblies are schools of idolatry and impiety. Wherefore, in declining fatal participation in such wickedness, we run no risk of being dissevered from the Church of Christ.[5] The communion of the Church was not instituted to be a chain to bind us in idolatry, impiety, ignorance of God, and other kinds of evil, but rather to retain us in the fear of God and obedience of the truth. They, indeed, vaunt loudly of their Church, as if there was not another in the world; and then, as if the matter were ended, they make out that all are schismatics who withdraw from obedience to that Church which they thus depict, that all are heretics who presume to whisper against its doctrine. But by what arguments do they prove their possession of the true Church? They appeal to ancient records which formerly existed in Italy, France, and Spain, pretending to derive their origin from those holy men who, by sound doctrine, founded and raised up churches, confirmed the doctrine, and reared the edifice of the Church with their blood; they pretend that the Church

3. Calvin now turns to consider the Roman Catholic church in his day. He applies the test to the Roman church to ascertain whether it is a true church or not.

4. Calvin does not believe that the Roman Mass is the Lord's Supper. It is a sacrilege, a desecration of the sacrament of the Lord's Supper.

5. Calvin says that in light of the Roman church's apostasy, we don't run any risk of severing ourselves from the true church when we cease to participate in the Roman church.

thus consecrated by spiritual gifts and the blood of martyrs was preserved from destruction by a perpetual succession of bishops. They dwell on the importance which Irenæus, Tertullian, Origen, Augustine, and others, attached to this succession. How frivolous and plainly ludicrous these allegations are, I will enable any, who will for a little consider the matter with me, to understand without any difficulty. I would also exhort our opponents to give their serious attention, if I had any hope of being able to benefit them by instruction; but since they have laid aside all regard to truth, and make it their only aim to prosecute their own ends in whatever way they can, I will only make a few observations by which good men and lovers of truth may disentangle themselves from their quibbles. First, I ask them why they do not quote Africa, and Egypt, and all Asia, just because in all those regions there was a cessation of that sacred succession, by the aid of which they vaunt of having continued churches. They therefore fall back on the assertion, that they have the true Church, because ever since it began to exist it was never destitute of bishops, because they succeeded each other in an unbroken series. But what if I bring Greece before them? Therefore, I again ask them, Why they say that the Church perished among the Greeks, among whom there never was any interruption in the succession of bishops—a succession, in their opinion, the only guardian and preserver of the Church? They make the Greeks schismatics. Why? Because, by revolting from the Apostolic See, they lost their privilege. What? Do not those who revolt from Christ much more deserve to lose it? It follows, therefore, that the pretence of succession is vain, if posterity do not retain the truth of Christ, which was handed down to them by their fathers, safe and uncorrupted, and continue in it.[6]

6. The Roman church claims "apostolic succession." They claim that they have an unbroken line of succession of bishops going all the way back to the apostles. But as Calvin notes, if the truth of Christ's gospel was lost in the process, what would be the value of such a succession? The true church is not dependent upon an unbroken line of succession. Rather, the true church is "apostolic" if it holds to the teaching of Jesus and the Apostles.

Book 4
Chapter 3

Of the Teachers and Ministers of the Church. Their Election and Office

We are now to speak of the order in which the Lord has been pleased that his Church should be governed. For though it is right that he alone should rule and reign in the Church, that he should preside and be conspicuous in it, and that its government should be exercised and administered solely by his word; yet as he does not dwell among us in visible presence, so as to declare his will to us by his own lips, he in this (as we have said) uses the ministry of men, by making them, as it were, his substitutes, not by transferring his right and honor to them, but only doing his own work by their lips, just as an artificer uses a tool for any purpose.[1] What I have previously expounded I am again forced to repeat. God might have acted, in this respect, by himself, without any aid or instrument, or might even have done it by angels; but there are several reasons why he rather chooses to employ men. First, in this way he declares his condescension towards us, employing men to perform the function of his ambassadors in the world, to be the interpreters of his secret will; in short, to represent his own person.[2] Thus he shows by experience that it is not to no purpose he calls us

1. In this chapter, Calvin discusses the government of the church through its appointed officers. We must always remember that Jesus Christ is alone head of the church (Eph. 1, 5). Nevertheless, He has appointed offices for the government of this church through those set apart for these tasks (Eph. 4).

2. This is what ministers are: they are representatives of the Lord Jesus Christ.

3. To listen with "docility" means to listen submissively. If preachers represent our Lord Jesus and are ordained to speak in His name, then we must respect and honor them, and receive their Word as the Word of God, insofar as it is faithful to the Scriptures.

his temples, since by man's mouth he gives responses to men as from a sanctuary. Secondly, it forms a most excellent and useful training to humility, when he accustoms us to obey his word though preached by men like ourselves, or, it may be, our inferiors in worth. Did he himself speak from heaven, it were no wonder if his sacred oracles were received by all ears and minds reverently and without delay. For who would not dread his present power? Who would not fall prostrate at the first view of his great majesty? Who would not be overpowered by that immeasurable splendor? But when a feeble man, sprung from the dust, speaks in the name of God, we give the best proof of our piety and obedience, by listening with docility to his servant,[3] though not in any respect our superior. Accordingly, he hides the treasure of his heavenly wisdom in frail earthen vessels (2 Cor. 4:7), that he may have a more certain proof of the estimation in which it is held by us. Moreover, nothing was fitter to cherish mutual charity than to bind men together by this tie, appointing one of them as a pastor to teach the others who are enjoined to be disciples, and receive the common doctrine from a single mouth. For did every man suffice for himself, and stand in no need of another's aid (such is the pride of the human intellect), each would despise all others, and be in his turn despised. The Lord, therefore, has astricted his Church to what he foresaw would be the strongest bond of unity when he deposited the doctrine of eternal life and salvation with men, that by their hands he might communicate it to others. To this Paul had respect when he wrote to the Ephesians, "There is one body, and one Spirit, even as ye are called in one hope of your calling; one Lord, one faith, one baptism, one God and Father of all, who is above all, and through all, and in you all. But unto every one of us is given grace according to the measure of the gift of Christ. Wherefore he saith, When he ascended up on high, he led captivity captive, and gave gifts unto men. (Now that he ascended, what is it but that he also descended first into the lower parts of the earth? He that descended is the same also that ascended up far above all heavens, that he might fill all things.) And he gave some, apostles; and some, prophets; and some, evangelists; and some, pastors and teachers; for the perfecting of the saints, for the work of the ministry, for the edifying of the body of Christ: till we all come in the unity of the faith, and of the knowledge of the Son of God, unto a perfect man, unto the measure of the stature of the fullness of Christ: that we henceforth be no more children, tossed to and fro, and carried about with every wind of doctrine, by the sleight of men, and cunning craftiness, whereby they lie in wait to deceive; but speaking the truth in love, may grow up into him in all things, which is the head, even Christ: from whom the whole body fitly joined together and compacted by that which every joint supplieth, according to the effectual working in the measure of every part, maketh increase of the body unto the edifying of itself in love" (Eph 4:4-16).

By these words he shows that the ministry of men, which God employs in governing the Church, is a principal bond by which believers are kept together in one body.[4] He also intimates, that the Church cannot be kept safe, unless supported by those guards to which the Lord has been pleased to commit its safety. Christ "ascended up far above all heavens, that he might fill all things" (Eph. 4:10). The mode of filling is this: by the ministers to whom he has committed this office, and given grace to discharge it, he dispenses and distributes his gifts to the Church, and thus exhibits himself as in a manner actually present by exerting the energy of his Spirit in this his institution, so as to prevent it from being vain or fruitless. In this way, the renewal of the saints is accomplished, and the body of Christ is edified; in this way we grow up in all things unto Him who is the Head, and unite with one another; in this way we are all brought into the unity of Christ, provided prophecy flourishes among us, provided we receive his apostles, and despise not the doctrine which is administered to us. Whoever, therefore, studies to abolish this order and kind of government of which we speak, or disparages it as of minor

4. Our Lord Jesus uses His ministers to build us up in faith and love, so that we will further minister to one another, and stand fast in unity. This is the teaching of Ephesians 4.

5. Those who reject the government Christ has instituted, thinking that they will help the church are foolish. To do this is to attempt the overthrow of Christ's government in the church. Would we be so foolish as to question the wisdom of the Lord? There are groups who have done this very thing, such as the Society of Friends (Quakers) who rejected all church government.

importance, plots the devastation, or rather the ruin and destruction, of the Church.[5] For neither are the light and heat of the sun, nor meat and drink, so necessary to sustain and cherish the present life, as is the apostolic and pastoral office to preserve a Church in the earth.

Accordingly, I have observed above, that God has repeatedly commended its dignity by the titles which he has bestowed upon it, in order that we might hold it in the highest estimation, as among the most excellent of our blessings. He declares, that in raising up teachers, he confers a special benefit on men, when he bids his prophet exclaim, "How beautiful upon the mountains are the feet of him that bringeth good tidings, that publisheth peace" (Isa. 52:7); when he calls the apostles the light of the world and the salt of the earth (Mt. 5:13, 14). Nor could the office be more highly eulogized than when he said, "He that heareth you heareth me; and he that despiseth you despiseth me" (Luke 10:16). But the most striking passage of all is that in the Second Epistle to the Corinthians, where Paul treats as it were professedly of this question. He contends that there is nothing in the Church more noble and glorious than the ministry of the Gospel, seeing it is the administration of the Spirit of righteousness and eternal life. These and similar passages should have the effect of preventing that method of governing and maintaining the Church by ministers, a method which the Lord has ratified for ever, from seeming worthless in our eyes, and at length becoming obsolete by contempt. How very necessary it is, he has declared not only by words but also by examples. When he was pleased to shed the light of his truth in greater effulgence on Cornelius, he sent an angel from heaven to dispatch Peter to him (Acts 10:3). When he was pleased to call Paul to the knowledge of himself, and engraft him into the Church, he does not address him with his own voice, but sends him to a man from whom he may both obtain the doctrine of salvation and the sanctification of baptism (Acts 9:6-20). If it was not by mere accident that the angel, who is the interpreter of God, abstains from declaring the will of God, and orders a man to be called to declare it; that Christ, the only Master of believers, commits Paul to the teaching of a man, that Paul whom he had determined to carry into the third heaven, and honor with a wondrous revelation of things that could not be spoken (2 Cor. 12:2), who will presume to despise or disregard as superfluous that ministry, whose utility God has been pleased to attest by such evidence?

1. The "power of the keys" mentioned by Calvin comes from the words of our Lord in Matthew 16 and 18. In those two chapters, the Lord gives the "keys of the kingdom" to Peter (in Matthew 16) and to the rest of the apostles (Matthew 18). These keys are used to "bind" and "loose." This power is understood to reside in the discipline of the church.

2. Some object to this distinction due to the "priesthood of every believer." Every believer's status as priest is taught in 1 Peter 2:5. While it is true that we are each "priests" before God, this does not negate the biblical teaching that there are appointed leaders in the church, duly ordained to an office. These church offices are mentioned repeatedly in Scripture (Acts 20, Eph. 4, 1 Tim. 3, Tit. 1).

3. Calvin points out that discipline is necessary in the family How then would it make sense that the church would have no discipline whatsoever?

Book 4

Chapter 12

Of the Discipline of the Church, and Its Principal use in Censures and Excommunication

The discipline of the Church, the consideration of which has been deferred till now, must be briefly explained, that we may be able to pass to other matters. Now discipline depends in a very great measure on the power of the keys and on spiritual jurisdiction.[1] That this may be more easily understood, let us divide the Church into two principal classes—viz. clergy and people.[2] The term clergy I use in the common acceptation for those who perform a public ministry in the Church. We shall speak first of the common discipline to which all ought to be subject, and then proceed to the clergy, who have besides that common discipline one peculiar to themselves. But as some, from hatred of discipline, are averse to the very name, for their sake we observe,—If no society, nay, no house with even a moderate family, can be kept in a right state without discipline, much more necessary is it in the Church, whose state ought to be the best ordered possible.[3] Hence as the saving doctrine of Christ is the life of the Church, so discipline is, as it were, its sinews; for to it is owing that the members of the body adhere together, each in its own place. Wherefore, all who either wish that discipline were abolished, or who impede the restoration of it, whether they do this of design or through thoughtlessness, certainly aim at the complete devastation of the Church. For what will be the result if every one is allowed to do as he pleases? But this must happen if to the preaching of the gospel are not added private admonition,[4] correction, and similar methods of maintaining doctrine, and not allowing it to become lethargic. Discipline, therefore, is a kind of curb to restrain and tame those who war against the doctrine of Christ, or it is a kind of stimulus by which the indifferent are aroused; sometimes, also, it is a kind of fatherly rod, by which those who have made some more grievous lapse are chastised in mercy with the meekness of the spirit of Christ. Since, then, we already see some beginnings of a fearful devastation in the Church from the total want of care and method in managing the people, necessity itself cries aloud that there is need of a remedy. Now the only remedy is this which Christ enjoins, and the pious have always had in use.

The first foundation of discipline is to provide for private admonition; that is, if any one does not do his duty spontaneously, or behaves insolently, or lives not quite honestly, or commits something worthy of blame, he must allow himself to be admonished; and every one must study to admonish his brother when the case requires. Here especially is there occasion for the vigilance of pastors and presbyters,[5] whose duty is not only to preach to the people, but to exhort and admonish from house to house, whenever their hearers have not profited sufficiently by general teaching; as Paul shows, when he relates that he taught "publicly, and from house to house," and testifies that he is "pure from the blood of all men," because he had not shunned to declare "all the counsel of God" (Acts 20:20, 26, 27) Then does doctrine obtain force and authority, not only when the minister publicly expounds to all what they owe to Christ, but has the right and means of exacting this from those whom he may observe to be sluggish or disobedient to his doctrine. Should any one either perversely reject such admonitions, or by persisting in his faults, show that he contemns them, the injunction of Christ is, that after he has been a second time admonished before witnesses, he is to be

4. The discipline of the church is not just excommunication. There are other elements to this discipline. First of all, members of the church should privately admonish one another (Matt. 18:15).

5. When Calvin refers to "presbyters," he is referring to elders or "ruling elders" who govern in the church alongside the pastors who are ordained to the ministry of preaching the Word and the administration of the sacraments.

6. Calvin understands "telling the matter to the church" to refer to the elders of the church (Matt. 18:17). This view is considered a Presbyterian view of church government. Others believe that Matthew 18 is speaking of the whole congregation and that the congregation as a whole would vote on this matter of discipline. This perspective of church government is known as "congregationalism."

7. Calvin is referring to excommunication. If a member of the church will not submit to the discipline of the church, they are to be treated as a "heathen or tax collector."

8. "Captious" means raising petty objections or finding faults unnecessarily.

summoned to the bar of the Church, which is the consistory of elders,[6] and there admonished more sharply, as by public authority, that if he reverence the Church he may submit and obey (Mt. 18:15, 17). If even in this way he is not subdued, but persists in his iniquity, he is then, as a despiser of the Church, to be debarred from the society of believers.[7]

Put as our Savior is not there speaking of secret faults merely, we must attend to the distinction that some sins are private, others public or openly manifest. Of the former, Christ says to every private individual, "go and tell him his fault between thee and him alone" (Mt. 18:15). Of open sins Paul says to Timothy, "Those that sin rebuke before all, that others also may fear" (1 Tim. 5:20). Our Savior had previously used the words, "If thy brother shall trespass against thee." This clause, unless you would be captious,[8] you cannot understand otherwise than, If this happens in a manner known to yourself, others not being privy to it. The injunction which Paul gave to Timothy to rebuke those openly who sin openly, he himself followed with Peter (Gal. 2:14). For when Peter sinned so as to give public offence, he did not admonish him apart, but brought him forward in face of the Church. The legitimate course, therefore, will be to proceed in correcting secret faults by the steps mentioned by Christ, and in open sins, accompanied with public scandal, to proceed at once to solemn correction by the Church.[9]

Another distinction to be attended to is, that some sins are mere delinquencies, others crimes and flagrant iniquities.[10] In correcting the latter, it is necessary to employ not only admonition or rebuke, but a sharper remedy, as Paul shows when

9. Private sins should be kept private if possible. The second step in Matthew 18 is to bring in two or three witnesses. But if this step does not bring resolution, then the matter may be brought before the whole church. The case is different, however, when it comes to public sins. Sins that affect all should be rebuked in the presence of all.

10. Some sins are of a more serious nature and must be addressed more strongly. It is true that all sins equally deserve the judgment of God. But not all sins are equally heinous in the sight of God. Those that are leavenous to the church or scandalous, should be addressed using a sharper remedy.

he not only verbally rebukes the incestuous Corinthian, but punishes him with excommunication, as soon as he was informed of his crime (1 Cor. 5:4). Now then we begin better to perceive how the spiritual jurisdiction of the Church, which animadverts[11] on sins according to the word of the Lord, is at once the best help to sound doctrine, the best foundation of order, and the best bond of unity. Therefore, when the Church banishes from its fellowship open adulterers, fornicators, thieves, robbers, the seditious, the perjured, false witnesses, and others of that description; likewise the contumacious, who, when duly admonished for lighter faults, hold God and his tribunal in derision,[12] instead of arrogating to itself anything that is unreasonable, it exercises a jurisdiction which it has received from the Lord. Moreover, lest any one should despise the judgment of the Church, or count it a small matter to be condemned by the suffrages of the faithful, the Lord has declared that it is nothing else than the promulgation of his own sentence, and that that which they do on earth is ratified in heaven. For they act by the word of the Lord in condemning the perverse, and by the word of the Lord in taking the penitent back into favor (John 20:23). Those, I say, who trust that churches can long stand without this bond of discipline are mistaken, unless, indeed, we can with impunity dispense with a help which the Lord foresaw would be necessary. And, indeed, the greatness of the necessity will be better perceived by its manifold uses.

There are three ends to which the Church has respect in thus correcting and excommunicating.[13] The first is, that God may not be insulted by the name of Christians being given to those who lead shameful and flagitious lives,[14] as if his holy Church were a combination of the wicked and abandoned.[15] For seeing that the Church is the body of Christ, she cannot be defiled by such fetid and putrid members,[16] without bringing some disgrace on her Head. Therefore that there may be nothing in the Church to bring disgrace on his sacred name, those whose turpitude[17] might throw infamy on the name must be

11. The word "animadvert" means to "pass censure upon" or "speak out against."

12. The "contumacious" are those who despise the authority of the church. The "seditious" are those who incite or encourage such rebellion.

13. Calvin lists three purposes of church discipline.

14. "Flagitious" refers to "criminal" or "wicked" behavior.

15. The first purpose of discipline is to vindicate the name of God. When professing Christians sin flagrantly and do not repent, it brings shame to the holy name of Christ.

16. "Fetid" is an unpleasant smell. "Putrid" is something rotten and decaying. The terms are used metaphorically by Calvin to refer to those who are causing such harm to the body of Christ and defiling it. Just as a wound that smelled and was infected would cause harm to the body, so also such sinners who will not repent defile the church.

17. "Turpitude" means "depravity" or "wickedness."

18. To willfully admit profane, unrepentant sinners, to the Lord's table is to cast the Lord's body to dogs. This is how important the responsibility is to ministers to guard the holy table of the Lord.

19. The church father John Chrysostom (AD 349-407) is quoted here by Calvin. Chrysostom states that ministers should not fear man, even those in high authority, when barring some from the Lord's Table. As ministers of Jesus Christ, we have the authority to bar wicked men from the holy table of the Lord.

20. The second purpose of church discipline is to maintain the purity of the church.

21. The Apostle Paul, in 1 Corinthians 5, describes unrepentant sinners as "leaven" that will eventually affect the whole lump of bread. The purity of the church is damaged by letting sinners go on in their ways. Soon, their sins affect the rest of the church.

expelled from his family. And here, also, regard must be had to the Lord's Supper, which might he profaned by a promiscuous admission. For it is most true, that he who is entrusted with the dispensation of it, if he knowingly and willingly admits any unworthy person whom he ought and is able to repel, is as guilty of sacrilege as if he had cast the Lord's body to dogs.[18] Wherefore, Chrysostom bitterly inveighs against priests, who, from fear of the great, dare not keep any one back. "Blood will be required at your hands. If you fear man, he will mock you, but if you fear God, you will be respected also by men. Let us not tremble at fasces, purple, or diadems; our power here is greater.[19] Assuredly I will sooner give up my body to death, and allow my blood to be shed, than be a partaker of that pollution." Therefore, lest this most sacred mystery should be exposed to ignominy, great selection is required in dispensing it, and this cannot be except by the jurisdiction of the Church. A second end of discipline is, that the good may not, as usually happens, be corrupted by constant communication with the wicked.[20] For such is our proneness to go astray, that nothing is easier than to seduce us from the right course by bad example. To this use of discipline the apostle referred when he commanded the Corinthians to discard the incestuous man from their society. "A little leaven leaveneth the whole lump" (1 Cor. 5:6) And so much danger did he foresee here, that he prohibited them from keeping company with such persons.[21] "If any man that is called a brother be a fornicator, or covetous, or an idolater, or a railer, or a drunkard, or an extortioner; with such an one, no not to eat" (1 Cor. 5:11). A third end of discipline is, that the sinner may be ashamed, and begin to repent of his turpitude.[22] Hence it is for their interest also that their iniquity should be chastised, that whereas they would have become more obstinate by indulgence, they may be aroused by the rod. This the apostle intimates when he thus writes —"If

22. The third purpose of church discipline is to bring repentance and restoration to the sinner. This is what Paul describes in 1 Corinthians 5:5. Our desire in such discipline is that sinners will repent and be restored to the fellowship of the church.

any man obey not our word by this epistle, note that man, and have no company with him, that he may be ashamed" (2 Thess. 3:14). Again, when he says that he had delivered the Corinthian to Satan, "that the spirit may be saved in the day of the Lord Jesus" (1 Cor. 5:5); that is, as I interpret it, he gave him over to temporal condemnation, that he might be made safe for eternity. And he says that he gave him over to Satan because the devil is without the Church, as Christ is in the Church. Some interpret this of a certain infliction on the flesh, but this interpretation seems to me most improbable.

Book 4
❖ Chapter 14

Of the Sacraments

1. Calvin defines a sacrament as an external sign that seals the promises of God to us in order to strengthen our faith. In partaking of the sacraments, we also testify of our piety before God.

2. Calvin agrees with Augustine's basic definition: a visible sign of an invisible grace. But Calvin expands on Augustine's definition for the sake of clarity.

Akin to the preaching of the gospel, we have another help to our faith in the sacraments, in regard to which, it greatly concerns us that some sure doctrine should be delivered, informing us both of the end for which they were instituted, and of their present use. First, we must attend to what a sacrament is. It seems to me, then, a simple and appropriate definition to say, that it is an external sign, by which the Lord seals on our consciences his promises of good-will toward us, in order to sustain the weakness of our faith, and we in our turn testify our piety towards him, both before himself, and before angels as well as men.[1] We may also define more briefly by calling it a testimony of the divine favor toward us, confirmed by an external sign, with a corresponding attestation of our faith towards Him. You may make your choice of these definitions, which in meaning differ not from that of Augustine,[2] which defines a sacrament to be a visible sign of a sacred thing, or a visible form of an invisible grace, but does not contain a better or surer explanation. As its brevity makes it somewhat obscure, and thereby misleads the more illiterate, I wished to remove all doubt, and make the definition fuller by stating it at greater length.

From the definition which we have given, we perceive that there never is a sacrament without an antecedent promise, the sacrament being added as a kind of appendix, with the view of confirming and sealing the promise, and giving a better attestation, or rather, in a manner, confirming it.[3] In this way God provides first for our ignorance and sluggishness, and, secondly, for our infirmity; and yet, properly speaking, it does not so much confirm his word as establish us in the faith of it. For the truth of God is in itself sufficiently stable and certain, and cannot receive a better confirmation from any other quarter than from itself. But as our faith is slender and weak, so if it be not propped up on every side, and supported by all kinds of means, it is forthwith shaken and tossed to and fro, wavers, and even falls. And here, indeed, our merciful Lord, with boundless condescension, so accommodates himself to our capacity, that seeing how from our animal nature we are always creeping on the ground, and cleaving to the flesh, having no thought of what is spiritual, and not even forming an idea of it, he declines not by means of these earthly elements to lead us to himself.[4]

Nor are those to be listened to who oppose this view with a more subtle than solid dilemma. They argue thus: We either know that the word of God which precedes the sacrament is the true will of God, or we do not know it. If we know it, we learn nothing new from the sacrament which succeeds. If we do not know it, we cannot learn it from the sacrament, whose whole efficacy depends on the word. Our brief reply is: The seals which are affixed to diplomas, and other public deeds, are nothing considered in themselves, and would be affixed to no purpose if nothing was written on the parchment, and yet this does not prevent them from sealing and confirming when they are appended to writings.[5] It cannot be alleged that this comparison is a recent fiction of our own, since Paul himself used it, terming circumcision a seal (Rom. 4:11), where

3. The sacrament doesn't stand on its own as a "bare sign." Instead, baptism and the Lord's Supper point to God's promises. They signify and seal those promises to us and attest in visible form that God's promises are true.

4. Calvin points out that the Lord "condescends" to our earthly, physical frame and gives us visible and physical confirmations of His promises through the sacraments. Since we are prone to weakness, the sacraments are there to strengthen us in faith.

5. Calvin is dealing with a common objection. If the sacraments just point to the truth of God's Word, why not just have the Word? Why do we even need these physical and visible ordinances? Calvin provides an illustration for us. A public deed with a seal doesn't mean anything if there is no reality behind it. But the deed with a seal does matter when it is sealing something that is actually true. The sacraments have value in confirming the Word, and visibly showing forth the teaching of God's Word. Let us not despise what the Lord has wisely instituted.

he expressly maintains that the circumcision of Abraham was not for justification, but was an attestation to the covenant, by the faith of which he had been previously justified. And how, pray, can any one be greatly offended when we teach that the promise is sealed by the sacrament, since it is plain, from the promises themselves, that one promise confirms another? The clearer any evidence is, the fitter is it to support our faith. But sacraments bring with them the clearest promises, and, when compared with the word, have this peculiarity, that they represent promises to the life, as if painted in a picture. Nor ought we to be moved by an objection founded on the distinction between sacraments and the seals of documents—viz. that since both consist of the carnal elements of this world, the former cannot be sufficient or adequate to seal the promises of God, which are spiritual and eternal, though the latter may be employed to seal the edicts of princes concerning fleeting and fading things. But the believer, when the sacraments are presented to his eye, does not stop short at the carnal spectacle,[6] but by the steps of analogy which I have indicated, rises with pious consideration to the sublime mysteries which lie hidden in the sacraments.

As the Lord calls his promises covenants (Gen. 6:18; 9:9; 17:2), and sacraments signs of the covenants, so something similar may be inferred from human covenants. What could the slaughter of a hog effect, unless words were interposed or rather preceded? Swine are often killed without any interior or occult mystery. What could be gained by pledging the right hand, since hands are not infrequently joined in giving battle? But when words have preceded, then by such symbols of covenant sanction is given to laws, though previously conceived, digested, and enacted by words. Sacraments, therefore, are exercises which confirm our faith in the word of God; and because we are carnal, they are exhibited under carnal objects, that thus they may train us in accommodation to our sluggish capacity, just as nurses lead children by the hand.[7] And hence Augustine calls a sacrament a visible word, because it rep-

6. That is, the believer doesn't just look at the water of baptism or the elements of the Lord's Supper. The believer looks at them and by faith looks beyond to what these physical things point to: namely the saving work of Christ to cleanse us, and to restore us from our fallen state.

7. The sacraments are physical confirmations of God's covenant promises. They are given to us because we are weak and need such physical aids to teach us.

resents the promises of God as in a picture, and places them in our view in a graphic bodily form. We might refer to other similitudes, by which sacraments are more plainly designated, as when they are called the pillars of our faith. For just as a building stands and leans on its foundation, and yet is rendered more stable when supported by pillars, so faith leans on the word of God as its proper foundation, and yet when sacraments are added leans more firmly, as if resting on pillars. Or we may call them mirrors, in which we may contemplate the riches of the grace which God bestows upon us. For then, as has been said, he manifests himself to us in as far as our dullness can enable us to recognize him, and testifies his love and kindness to us more expressly than by word.

It is irrational to contend that sacraments are not manifestations of divine grace toward us, because they are held forth to the ungodly also, who, however, so far from experiencing God to be more propitious to them, only incur greater condemnation.[8] By the same reasoning, the gospel will be no manifestation of the grace of God, because it is spurned by many who hear it; nor will Christ himself be a manifestation of grace, because of the many by whom he was seen and known, very few received him. Something similar may be seen in public enactments. A great part of the body of the people deride and evade the authenticating seal, though they know it was employed by their sovereign to confirm his will; others trample it under foot, as a matter by no means appertaining to them; while others even execrate it: so that, seeing the condition of the two things to be alike, the appropriateness of the comparison which I made above ought to be more readily allowed. It is certain, therefore, that the Lord offers us his mercy, and a pledge of his grace, both in his sacred word and in the sacraments; but it is not apprehended save by those who receive the word and sacraments with firm faith: in like manner as Christ, though offered and held forth for salvation to all, is not, however, acknowledged and received by all. Augustine, when intending to intimate this, said that the efficacy of the

8. Another objection to the validity and importance of the sacraments is this: how can they really confirm anything if they are sometimes partaken of by the ungodly who don't truly receive the grace of God? Calvin replies this way: Some spurn the gospel preached in God's Word but this doesn't make that gospel untrue. Though something may be trampled underfoot, that in no way takes away from the truth of the gospel or the sacraments.

9. We do not believe that the sacraments have any effectiveness (efficacy) apart from faith. This can be contrasted with the Roman Catholic view of the sacraments. The Roman church teaches that the sacraments work ex opere operato ("from the work performed"). This means that even considered apart from the faith of the person receiving them, the sacraments are effective. But the Scriptures teach that baptism and the Lord's Supper are only efficacious for those who believe.

10. Jesus says something similar when He says that "the Spirit gives life, the flesh is of no help at all" (John 6:63).

11. "Aliment" means "food."

12. Calvin gives us an illustration. We see food as a gift from God and worship Him for it. We don't worship the food. Likewise, the sacraments are instruments by which God pledges to us His promises. We don't exalt the sacraments on their own. They are just instruments for us to see, taste, and touch God's promises.

word is produced in the sacrament, not because it is spoken, but because it is believed.[9]

The sacraments duly perform their office only when accompanied by the Spirit, the internal Master, whose energy alone penetrates the heart, stirs up the affections, and procures access for the sacraments into our souls. If he is wanting, the sacraments can avail us no more than the sun shining on the eyeballs of the blind, or sounds uttered in the ears of the deaf.[10] Wherefore, in distributing between the Spirit and the sacraments, I ascribe the whole energy to him, and leave only a ministry to them; this ministry, without the agency of the Spirit, is empty and frivolous, but when he acts within, and exerts his power, it is replete with energy.

To the other objection—viz. that when so much power is attributed to creatures, the glory of God is bestowed upon them, and thereby impaired—it is obvious to reply, that we attribute no power to the creatures. All we say is, that God uses the means and instruments which he sees to be expedient, in order that all things may be subservient to his glory, he being the Lord and disposer of all. Therefore, as by bread and other aliment[11] he feeds our bodies, as by the sun he illumines, and by fire gives warmth to the world, and yet bread, sun, and fire are nothing, save inasmuch as they are instruments under which he dispenses his blessings to us; so in like manner he spiritually nourishes our faith by means of the sacraments, whose only office is to make his promises visible to our eye, or rather, to be pledges of his promises. And as it is our duty in regard to the other creatures which the divine liberality and kindness has destined for our use, and by whose instrumentality he bestows the gifts of his goodness upon us, to put no confidence in them, nor to admire and extol them as the causes of our mercies; so neither ought our confidence to be fixed on the sacraments, nor ought the glory of God to be transferred to them, but passing beyond them all, our faith and confession should rise to Him who is the Author of the sacraments and of all things.[12]

Wherefore, let it be a fixed point, that the office of the sacraments differs not from the word of God; and this is to hold forth and offer Christ to us, and, in him, the treasures of heavenly grace.[13] They confer nothing, and avail nothing, if not received in faith, just as wine and oil, or any other liquor, however large the quantity which you pour out, will run away and perish unless there be an open vessel to receive it. When the vessel is not open, though it may be sprinkled all over, it will nevertheless remain entirely empty. We must be aware of being led into a kindred error by the terms, somewhat too extravagant, which ancient Christian writers have employed in extolling the dignity of the sacraments. We must not suppose that there is some latent virtue inherent in the sacraments by which they, in themselves, confer the gifts of the Holy Spirit upon us, in the same way in which wine is drunk out of a cup, since the only office divinely assigned them is to attest and ratify the benevolence of the Lord towards us; and they avail no farther than accompanied by the Holy Spirit to open our minds and hearts, and make us capable of receiving this testimony, in which various distinguished graces are clearly manifested.

13. The preaching of the Word and the sacraments have the same goal: to set forth Christ and the mercy of God in the gospel.

Book 4

❧ Chapter 15

Of Baptism

1. Calvin gives a brief summary of the meaning of baptism with these opening words. Baptism is the initiatory rite through which we become members of the church. We are engrafted into Christ and so become God's children. Calvin expands upon this brief summary in the paragraphs that follow.

2. The word "sacrament" comes from the Latin sacramentum. This Latin word was used to translate the Greek word mysterion (mystery). Hence, a sacrament is one of the mysteries of the gospel (see 1 Cor. 4:1).

3. The first meaning of baptism is the cleansing it shows forth. Obviously, the washing with water is intended to communicate that we are washed clean of our sins (see Acts 22:16).

Baptism is the initiatory sign by which we are admitted to the fellowship of the Church, that being engrafted into Christ we may be accounted children of God.[1] Moreover, the end for which God has given it (this I have shown to be common to all mysteries)[2] is, first, that it may be conducive to our faith in him; and, secondly, that it may serve the purpose of a confession among men. The nature of both institutions we shall explain in order. Baptism contributes to our faith three things, which require to be treated separately. The first object, therefore, for which it is appointed by the Lord, is to be a sign and evidence of our purification, or (better to explain my meaning) it is a kind of sealed instrument by which he assures us that all our sins are so deleted, covered, and effaced, that they will never come into his sight, never be mentioned, never imputed.[3] For it is his will that all who have believed, be baptized for the remission of sins. Hence those who have thought that baptism is nothing else than the badge and mark by which we profess our religion before men, in the same way as soldiers attest their profession by bearing the insignia of their commander, having not attended to what was the principal thing in baptism; and this is, that we are to receive it in connection with the promise, "He that believeth and is baptized shall be saved" (Mark 16:16).

In this sense is to be understood the statement of Paul, that "Christ loved the Church, and gave himself for it, that he might sanctify and cleanse it with the washing of water by the word" (Eph. 5:25, 26); and again, "not by works of righteousness which we have done, but according to his mercy he saved us, by the washing of regeneration and renewing of the Holy Ghost" (Titus 3:5). Peter also says that "baptism also doth now save us" (1 Peter 3:21). For he did not mean to intimate that our ablution and salvation[4] are perfected by water, or that water possesses in itself the virtue of purifying, regenerating, and renewing; nor does he mean that it is the cause of salvation, but only that the knowledge and certainty of such gifts are perceived in this sacrament. This the words themselves evidently show. For Paul connects together the word of life and baptism of water, as if he had said, by the gospel the message of our ablution and sanctification is announced; by baptism this message is sealed. And Peter immediately subjoins, that that baptism is "not the putting away of the filth of the flesh, but the answer of a good conscience toward God, which is of faith." Nay, the only purification which baptism promises is by means of the sprinkling of the blood of Christ, who is figured by water from the resemblance to cleansing and washing. Who, then, can say that we are cleansed by that water which certainly attests that the blood of Christ is our true and only laver?[5] So that we cannot have a better argument to refute the hallucination of those who ascribe the whole to the virtue of water than we derive from the very meaning of baptism, which leads us away as well from the visible element which is presented to our eye, as from all other means, that it may fix our minds on Christ alone.[6]

Nor is it to be supposed that baptism is bestowed only with reference to the past, so that, in regard to new lapses into which we fall after baptism, we must seek new remedies of expiation in other so-called sacraments, just as if the power of baptism had become obsolete.[7] To this error, in ancient times, it was owing that some refused to be initiated by baptism un-

4. "Ablution" means "washing."

5. A "laver" is a basin for washing, or a washbowl.

6. It isn't the physical water that saves us (1 Pet. 3:21). It is Christ who saves us and cleanses us from all sin. Baptism is a visible confirmation of God's promise to do this.

7. Baptism doesn't just cover sins committed before baptism. It is a promise from God to cleanse all past, present, and future sins through the blood of Christ.

8. It was common in some sectors of the early church to withhold baptism until later in life. This was due to an erroneous theological doctrine that suggested that sins committed after baptism would not be cleansed by that baptism.

9. When we do sin after our baptism, we should call to mind the baptism we received and know that God will surely forgive our sins through Christ. Our past baptism remains a valuable reminder for us.

til their life was in extreme danger, and they were drawing their last breath, that they might thus obtain pardon for all the past.[8] Against this preposterous precaution ancient bishops frequently inveigh in their writings. We ought to consider that at whatever time we are baptized, we are washed and purified once for the whole of life. Wherefore, as often as we fall, we must recall the remembrance of our baptism, and thus fortify our minds, so as to feel certain and secure of the remission of sins.[9] For though, when once administered, it seems to have passed, it is not abolished by subsequent sins. For the purity of Christ was therein offered to us, always is in force, and is not destroyed by any stain: it wipes and washes away all our defilements. Nor must we hence assume a license of sinning for the future (there is certainly nothing in it to countenance such audacity), but this doctrine is intended only for those who, when they have sinned, groan under their sins burdened and oppressed, that they may have wherewith to support and console themselves, and not rush headlong into despair. Thus Paul says that Christ was made a propitiation for us for the remission of sins that are past (Rom. 3:25). By this he denies not that constant and perpetual forgiveness of sins is thereby obtained even till death: he only intimates that it is designed by the Father for those poor sinners who, wounded by remorse of conscience, sigh for the physician. To these the mercy of God is offered. Those who, from hopes of impunity, seek a license for sin, only provoke the wrath and justice of God.

I know it is a common belief that forgiveness, which at our first regeneration we receive by baptism alone, is after baptism procured by means of penitence and the keys.[10] But those who entertain this fiction err from not considering that the

10. In the Roman church, the grace of justification gained through baptism can be lost by committing a mortal sin. Since that grace can be lost, Roman Catholics must use the sacrament of penance to regain that grace. They go to a priest, confess their sins, receive absolution (forgiveness), and then do works of satisfaction as an act of repentance. This is an unbiblical perspective however. We cannot lose our right standing before God. We should, however, confess our sins and remember that we are continually cleansed by the blood of Christ.

power of the keys, of which they speak, so depends on baptism, that it ought not on any account to be separated from it. The sinner receives forgiveness by the ministry of the Church; in other words, not without the preaching of the gospel. And of what nature is this preaching? That we are washed from our sins by the blood of Christ. And what is the sign and evidence of that washing if it be not baptism? We see, then, that that forgiveness has reference to baptism. This error had its origin in the fictitious sacrament of penance, on which I have already touched. What remains will be said at the proper place. There is no wonder if men who, from the grossness of their minds, are excessively attached to external things, have here also betrayed the defect,—if not contented with the pure institution of God, they have introduced new helps devised by themselves, as if baptism were not itself a sacrament of penance. But if repentance is recommended during the whole of life, the power of baptism ought to have the same extent. Wherefore, there can be no doubt that all the godly may, during the whole course of their lives, whenever they are vexed by a consciousness of their sins, recall the remembrance of their baptism, that they may thereby assure themselves of that sole and perpetual ablution[11] which we have in the blood of Christ.

Another benefit of baptism is, that it shows us our mortification in Christ and new life in him.[12] "Know ye not," says the apostle, "that as many of us as were baptized into Jesus Christ, were baptized into his death? Therefore we are buried with him by baptism into death," that we "should walk in newness of life" (Rom. 6:3, 4). By these words, he not only exhorts us to imitation of Christ, as if he had said, that we are admonished by baptism, in like manner as Christ died, to die to our lusts, and as he rose, to rise to righteousness; but he traces the matter much higher, that Christ by baptism has made us partakers of his death, engrafting us into it. And as the twig derives substance and nourishment from the root to which it is attached, so those who receive baptism with true faith truly feel the efficacy of Christ's death in the mortifica-

11. We are washed in baptism once. We receive the blood of Christ once for all, which serves to continually cleanse us of all sins. "But if we walk in the light as He is in the light, we have fellowship with one another, and the blood of Jesus Christ His Son cleanses us from all sin." (1 John 1:7)

12. This is the second point about baptism that Calvin explains. Baptism is evidence of our dying with Christ and rising again to newness of life.

tion of their flesh, and the efficacy of his resurrection in the quickening of the Spirit. On this he founds his exhortation, that if we are Christians we should be dead unto sin, and alive unto righteousness. He elsewhere uses the same argument—viz. that we are circumcised, and put off the old man, after we are buried in Christ by baptism (Col. 2:12). And in this sense, in the passage which we formerly quoted, he calls it "the washing of regeneration, and renewing of the Holy Ghost" (Tit. 3:5). We are promised, first, the free pardon of sins and imputation of righteousness; and, secondly, the grace of the Holy Spirit, to form us again to newness of life.

The last advantage which our faith receives from baptism is its assuring us not only that we are engrafted into the death and life of Christ, but so united to Christ himself as to be partakers of all his blessings.[13] For he consecrated and sanctified baptism in his own body, that he might have it in common with us as the firmest bond of union and fellowship which he deigned to form with us; and hence Paul proves us to be the sons of God, from the fact that we put on Christ in baptism (Gal. 3:27). Thus we see the fulfillment of our baptism in Christ, whom for this reason we call the proper object of baptism. Hence it is not strange that the apostles are said to have baptized in the name of Christ, though they were enjoined to baptize in the name of the Father and Spirit also (Acts 8:16; 19:5; Mt. 28:19). For all the divine gifts held forth in baptism are found in Christ alone. And yet he who baptizes into Christ cannot but at the same time invoke the name of the Father and the Spirit. For we are cleansed by his blood, just because our gracious Father, of his incomparable mercy, willing to receive us into favor, appointed him Mediator to effect our reconciliation with himself. Regeneration we obtain from his death and resurrection only, when sanctified by his Spirit we are imbued with a new and spiritual nature. Wherefore we obtain, and in a manner distinctly perceive, in the Father the cause, in the Son the matter, and in the Spirit the effect of our purification and regeneration. Thus first John baptized, and

13. This is the third point Calvin explains. Baptism assures us that we are united to Christ by faith and thus partake of all His saving benefits.

thus afterwards the apostles by the baptism of repentance for the remission of sins, understanding by the term repentance, regeneration, and by the remission of sins, ablution.

Now that the end to which the Lord had regard in the institution of baptism has been explained, it is easy to judge in what way we ought to use and receive it. For inasmuch as it is appointed to elevate, nourish, and confirm our faith, we are to receive it as from the hand of its author, being firmly persuaded that it is himself who speaks to us by means of the sign; that it is himself who washes and purifies us, and effaces the remembrance of our faults; that it is himself who makes us the partakers of his death, destroys the kingdom of Satan, subdues the power of concupiscence, nay, makes us one with himself, that being clothed with him we may be accounted the children of God.[14] These things, I say, we ought to feel as truly and certainly in our mind as we see our body washed, immersed, and surrounded with water. For this analogy or similitude furnishes the surest rule in the sacraments—viz. that in corporeal things we are to see spiritual, just as if they were actually exhibited to our eye, since the Lord has been pleased to represent them by such figures; not that such graces are included and bound in the sacrament, so as to be conferred by its efficacy, but only that by this badge the Lord declares to us that he is pleased to bestow all these things upon us. Nor does he merely feed our eyes with bare show; he leads us to the actual object, and effectually performs what he figures.

14. This is an important point to remember: baptism is about what God does to save us. It is a sign of God's saving work.

Book 4

Chapter 16

Pædobaptism. Its Accordance With the Institution of Christ, and the Nature of the Sign

1. This chapter provides a defense of the practice of paedobaptism (infant baptism). Paedobaptism is the practice of baptizing infants and young children of professing believers. This is done because children are members of the covenant people of God as well and recipients of God's covenant promises (Acts 2:38-39). In the opening words of this chapter, Calvin reminds the reader to look beyond the outward physical act of baptism and remember that it points us to God's covenant promises.

2. Calvin describes one of the modes of baptism as sprinkling. Calvin also believed that immersion or pouring were appropriate modes of baptism as well.

In the first place, then, it is a well-known doctrine, and one as to which all the pious are agreed,—that the right consideration of signs does not lie merely in the outward ceremonies, but depends chiefly on the promise and the spiritual mysteries, to typify which the ceremonies themselves are appointed. He, therefore, who would thoroughly understand the effect of baptism—its object and true character—must not stop short at the element and corporeal object but look forward to the divine promises which are therein offered to us, and rise to the internal secrets which are therein represented.[1] He who understands these has reached the solid truth, and, so to speak, the whole substance of baptism and will thence perceive the nature and use of outward sprinkling.[2] On the other hand, he who passes them by in contempt, and keeps his thoughts entirely fixed on the visible ceremony, will neither understand the force, nor the proper nature of baptism, nor comprehend what is meant, or what end is gained by the use of water. This is confirmed by passages of Scripture too numerous and too clear to make it necessary here to discuss them more at length. It remains, therefore, to inquire into the nature and efficacy of baptism, as evinced by the promises therein given. Scripture shows, first, that it points to that cleansing from sin which we obtain by the blood of Christ; and, secondly, to the mortification of the flesh which consists in participation in his death, by which believers are regenerated to newness of life, and thereby to the fellowship of Christ. To these general heads may be referred all that the Scriptures teach concerning baptism, with this addition, that it is also a symbol to testify our religion to men.[3]

Now, since prior to the institution of baptism, the people of God had circumcision in its stead, let us see how far these two signs differ, and how far they resemble each other.[4] In this way it will appear what analogy there is between them. When the Lord enjoins Abraham to observe circumcision (Gen. 17:10), he premises that he would be a God unto him and to his seed, adding, that in himself was a perfect sufficiency of all things, and that Abraham might reckon on his hand as a fountain of every blessing. These words include the promise of eternal life, as our Savior interprets when he employs it to prove the immortality and resurrection of believers: "God," says he, "is not the God of the dead, but of the living" (Mt. 22:32). Hence, too, Paul, when showing to the Ephesians how great the destruction was from which the Lord had delivered them, seeing that they had not been admitted to the covenant of circumcision, infers that at that time they were aliens from the covenant of promise, without God, and without hope (Eph. 2:12), all these being comprehended in the covenant. Now, the first access to God, the first entrance to immortal life, is the remission of sins. Hence it follows, that this corresponds to the promise of our cleansing in baptism. The Lord afterwards covenants with Abraham, that he is to walk before him in sincerity and innocence of heart: this applies to mortification or regeneration. And lest any should doubt whether circumcision were the sign of mortification, Moses explains more clearly elsewhere when he exhorts the people of Israel to circumcise the foreskin of their heart,[5] because the Lord had

3. Calvin points to the work of God promised in baptism first of all. But secondarily, he says that it also testifies our faith before others as well.

4. Just as circumcision served as a physical sign separating the people of God from those outside, there is now baptism which functions as a sign of covenant membership in the people of God. Calvin explains the similarities and differences between the Old Covenant sign of circumcision and the New Covenant sign of baptism.

5. Calvin alludes to Deuteronomy 10. "The LORD delighted only in your fathers, to love them; and He chose their descendants after them, you above all peoples, as it is this day. Therefore circumcise the foreskin of your heart, and be stiff-necked no longer" (Deut 10:15-16). This passage teaches us that circumcision wasn't just a physical sign. It was meant to point to a spiritual reality. It is the same with baptism. Though baptism is a physical, outward sign, it points to an inward spiritual reality.

chosen them for his own people, out of all the nations of the earth. As the Lord, in choosing the posterity of Abraham for his people, commands them to be circumcised, so Moses declares that they are to be circumcised in heart, thus explaining what is typified by that carnal circumcision. Then, lest any one should attempt this in his own strength, he shows that it is the work of divine grace. All this is so often inculcated by the prophets, that there is no occasion here to collect the passages which everywhere occur. We have, therefore, a spiritual promise given to the fathers in circumcision, similar to that which is given to us in baptism, since it figured to them both the forgiveness of sins and the mortification of the flesh. Besides, as we have shown that Christ, in whom both of these reside, is the foundation of baptism, so must he also be the foundation of circumcision. For he is promised to Abraham, and in him all nations are blessed. To seal this grace, the sign of circumcision is added.

There is now no difficulty in seeing wherein the two signs agree, and wherein they differ. The promise, in which we have shown that the power of the signs consists, is one in both—viz. the promise of the paternal favor of God, of forgiveness of sins, and eternal life. And the thing figured is one and the same—viz. regeneration. The foundation on which the completion of these things depends is one in both. Wherefore, there is no difference in the internal meaning, from which the whole power and peculiar nature of the sacrament is to be estimated.[6] The only difference which remains is in the external ceremony, which is the least part of it, the chief part consisting in the promise and the thing signified. Hence we may conclude that everything applicable to circumcision applies also to baptism, excepting always the difference in the visible ceremony.[7] To this analogy and comparison we are led by that rule of the apostle, in which he enjoins us to bring every interpretation of Scripture to the analogy of faith (Rom. 12:3, 6). And certainly in this matter the truth may almost be felt. For just as circumcision, which was a kind of badge to the Jews, assuring

6. Both circumcision and baptism pointed to the same realities: God's favor, forgiveness of sins, regeneration, eternal life, etc.

7. Obviously, circumcision and baptism differ in the way the external ceremony is administered. Another difference might be noted here. Circumcision was administered only to the male members of a household whereas baptism is for both male and female (Gal. 3:27-29).

them that they were adopted as the people and family of God, was their first entrance into the Church, while they, in their turn, professed their allegiance to God, so now we are initiated by baptism, so as to be enrolled among his people, and at the same time swear unto his name. Hence it is incontrovertible, that baptism has been substituted for circumcision, and performs the same office.[8]

Now, if we are to investigate whether or not baptism is justly given to infants, will we not say that the man trifles, or rather is delirious, who would stop short at the element of water, and the external observance, and not allow his mind to rise to the spiritual mystery? If reason is listened to, it will undoubtedly appear that baptism is properly administered to infants as a thing due to them. The Lord did not anciently bestow circumcision upon them without making them partakers of all the things signified by circumcision. He would have deluded his people with mere imposture, had he quieted them with fallacious symbols: the very idea is shocking. He distinctly declares, that the circumcision of the infant will be instead of a seal of the promise of the covenant. But if the covenant remains firm and fixed, it is no less applicable to the children of Christians in the present day, than to the children of the Jews under the Old Testament.[9] Now, if they are partakers of the thing signified, how can they be denied the sign? If they obtain the reality, how can they be refused the figure? The external sign is so united in the sacrament with the word, that it cannot be separated from it: but if they can be separated, to which of the two shall we attach the greater value? Surely, when we see that the sign is subservient to the word, we shall say that it is subordinate, and assign it the inferior place. Since, then, the word of baptism is destined for infants, why should we deny them the sign, which is an appendage of the word? This one reason, could no other be furnished, would be amply sufficient to refute all gainsayers. The objection, that there was a fixed day for circumcision, is a mere quibble. We admit that we are not now, like the Jews, tied down to certain

8. Calvin states clearly here that baptism is the New Covenant replacement or "substitute" for circumcision in the Old Covenant.

9. Calvin says that if children in the Old Covenant received the covenant sign which promised God's saving work, why would they not also receive the sign of the New Covenant?

10. The covenant promises made to Abraham extended to his descendants (Gen. 17:10-11). The covenant promises to Abraham are not abrogated in the New Covenant. Instead, they are extended and fulfilled (Gal. 3:27-29). The covenant promises are also extended to children of believers by the apostles when Peter preached on the Day of Pentecost (Acts 2:38-39).

11. Calvin points out that if children of believers are now excluded from the covenant promises, this would mean that the graciousness of the Old Covenant in including children is now diminished in the New Covenant. But the Scriptures present the New Covenant as better than the Old (Jer. 31, Heb. 8-9).

days; but when the Lord declares, that though he prescribes no day, yet he is pleased that infants shall be formally admitted to his covenant, what more do we ask?

Scripture gives us a still clearer knowledge of the truth. For it is most evident that the covenant, which the Lord once made with Abraham, is not less applicable to Christians now than it was anciently to the Jewish people, and therefore that word has no less reference to Christians than to Jews. Unless, indeed, we imagine that Christ, by his advent, diminished, or curtailed the grace of the Father—an idea not free from execrable blasphemy. Wherefore, both the children of the Jews, because, when made heirs of that covenant, they were separated from the heathen, were called a holy seed, and for the same reason the children of Christians, or those who have only one believing parent, are called holy, and, by the testimony of the apostle, differ from the impure seed of idolaters. Then, since the Lord, immediately after the covenant was made with Abraham, ordered it to be sealed in infants by an outward sacrament, how can it be said that Christians are not to attest it in the present day, and seal it in their children? Let it not be objected, that the only symbol by which the Lord ordered his covenant to be confirmed was that of circumcision, which was long ago abrogated. It is easy to answer, that, in accordance with the form of the old dispensation, he appointed circumcision to confirm his covenant, but that it being abrogated, the same reason for confirmation still continues, a reason which we have in common with the Jews. Hence it is always necessary carefully to consider what is common to both, and wherein they differed from us. The covenant is common, and the reason for confirming it is common. The mode of confirming it is so far different, that they had circumcision, instead of which we now have baptism. Otherwise, if the testimony by which the Jews were assured of the salvation of their seed is taken from us, the consequence will be, that, by the advent of Christ, the grace of God, which was formerly given to the Jews,[10] is more obscure and less perfectly attested to us.[11] If this cannot be said without extreme insult to Christ, by whom the infinite goodness of the Father has been more brightly and benignly than ever shed upon the earth, and declared to men, it must be confessed that it cannot be more confined, and less clearly manifested, than under the obscure shadows of the law.

It remains briefly to indicate what benefit redounds from the observance,[12] both to believers who bring their children to the church to be baptized, and to the infants themselves, to whom the sacred water is applied, that no one may despise the ordinance as useless or superfluous: though any one who would think of ridiculing baptism under this pretence, would also ridicule the divine ordinance of circumcision: for what can they adduce to impugn the one, that may not be retorted against the other?[13] Thus the Lord punishes the arrogance of those who forthwith condemn whatever their carnal sense cannot comprehend. But God furnishes us with other weapons to repress their stupidity.[14] His holy institution, from which we feel that our faith derives admirable consolation, deserves not to be called superfluous. For the divine symbol communicated to the child, as with the impress of a seal, confirms the promise given to the godly parent, and declares that the Lord will be a God not to him only, but to his seed; not merely visiting him with his grace and goodness, but his posterity also to the thousandth generation. When the infinite goodness of God is thus displayed, it, in the first place, furnishes most ample materials for proclaiming his glory, and fills pious breasts with no ordinary joy, urging them more strongly to love their affectionate Parent, when they see that, on their account, he extends his care to their posterity. I am not moved by the objection that the promise ought to be sufficient to confirm the salvation of our children. It has seemed otherwise to God, who, seeing our weakness, has herein been pleased to condescend to it. Let those, then, who embrace the promise of mercy to their children, consider it as their duty to offer them to the Church, to be sealed with the symbol of mercy, and animate themselves to surer confidence, on seeing with the

12. "Redounds" here means "come back upon." That is, Calvin is answering the question, what are the benefits that come from observing this ordinance?

13. If those who object to infant baptism would claim it is a useless practice, they would have to say the same thing about circumcision, Calvin suggests.

14. The reader may occasionally be shocked by the combative nature of Calvin's language. It is important to remember that Calvin lived in a very different historical context than we do. Debates over infant baptism were more than just matters of opinion. The Anabaptists, who rejected infant baptism, were often in great conflict with the Lutheran and the Reformed. They were also in conflict with the Roman church as well. These different viewpoints often resulted in significant conflict; even violence.

bodily eye the covenant of the Lord engraved on the bodies of their children. On the other hand, children derive some benefit from their baptism, when, being engrafted into the body of the Church, they are made an object of greater interest to the other members. Then when they have grown up, they are thereby strongly urged to an earnest desire of serving God, who has received them as sons by the formal symbol of adoption, before, from nonage, they were able to recognize him as their Father. In fine, we ought to stand greatly in awe of the denunciation, that God will take vengeance on every one who despises to impress the symbol of the covenant on his child (Gen. 17:15), such contempt being a rejection, and, as it were, abjuration of the offered grace.[15]

15. "Abjuration" is a "renouncing" or "rejection" of the offered grace of God in baptism.

Book 4
Chapter 17

Of the Lord's Supper, and the Benefits Conferred by it

After God has once received us into his family, it is not that he may regard us in the light of servants, but of sons, performing the part of a kind and anxious parent, and providing for our maintenance during the whole course of our lives.[1] And, not contented with this, he has been pleased by a pledge to assure us of his continued liberality.[2] To this end, he has given another sacrament to his Church by the hand of his only-begotten Son—viz. a spiritual feast, at which Christ testifies that he himself is living bread (John 6:51), on which our souls feed, for a true and blessed immortality. Now, as the knowledge of this great mystery is most necessary, and, in proportion to its importance, demands an accurate exposition, and Satan, in order to deprive the Church of this inestimable treasure, long ago introduced, first, mists, and then darkness, to obscure its light, and stirred up strife and contention to alienate the minds of the simple from a relish for this sacred food, and in our age, also, has tried the same artifice.[3] I will proceed, after giving a simple summary adapted to the capacity of the ignorant, to explain those difficulties by which Satan has tried to ensnare the world. First,

1. It is important to remember our identity in Christ: we are the children of God. As children, let us remember that we have a loving Heavenly Father. Just as our earthly father provided food and clothing, so also our Heavenly Father provides us grace sufficient for every day.

2. Calvin now turns to consider the sacrament of the Lord's Supper. It is a pledge of God's continued free grace to us.

3. An "artifice" is a clever, cunning strategy. Since the Lord's Supper is such a great blessing to Christ's church, it is no surprise that Satan has obscured this sacrament by stirring up confusion and disagreement about the nature and purpose of the Lord's Supper.

4. Calvin describes the Lord's Supper as our heavenly food. It sustains us and invigorates us during our pilgrimage to heaven. Calvin sees the sacrament as more than a mere sign, or just a remembrance of what Christ did. It is a nourishing, faith-strengthening sacrament.

5. The "corporeal" is that which is physical and bodily.

then, the signs are bread and wine, which represent the invisible food which we receive from the body and blood of Christ. For as God, regenerating us in baptism, engrafts us into the fellowship of his Church, and makes us his by adoption, so we have said that he performs the office of a provident parent, in continually supplying the food by which he may sustain and preserve us in the life to which he has begotten us by his word. Moreover, Christ is the only food of our soul, and, therefore, our heavenly Father invites us to him, that, refreshed by communion with him, we may ever and anon gather new vigor until we reach the heavenly immortality.[4] But as this mystery of the secret union of Christ with believers is incomprehensible by nature, he exhibits its figure and image in visible signs adapted to our capacity, nay, by giving, as it were, earnests and badges, he makes it as certain to us as if it were seen by the eye; the familiarity of the similitude giving it access to minds however dull, and showing that souls are fed by Christ just as the corporeal life[5] is sustained by bread and wine. We now, therefore, understand the end which this mystical benediction has in view—viz. to assure us that the body of Christ was once sacrificed for us, so that we may now eat it, and, eating, feel within ourselves the efficacy of that one sacrifice,—that his blood was once shed for us so as to be our perpetual drink. This is the force of the promise which is added, "Take, eat; this is my body, which is broken for you" (Mt. 26:26). The body which was once offered for our salvation we are enjoined to take and eat, that, while we see ourselves made partakers of it, we may safely conclude that the virtue of that death will be efficacious in us. Hence he terms the cup the covenant in his blood. For the covenant which he once sanctioned by his blood he in a manner renews, or rather continues, in so far as regards the confirmation of our faith, as often as he stretches forth his sacred blood as drink to us.

Pious souls can derive great confidence and delight from this sacrament, as being a testimony that they form one body with Christ, so that everything which is his they may call their own. Hence it follows, that we can confidently assure ourselves, that eternal life, of which he himself is the heir, is ours, and that the kingdom of heaven, into which he has entered, can no more be taken from us than from him; on the other hand, that we cannot be condemned for our sins, from the guilt of which he absolves us, seeing he has been pleased that these should be imputed to himself as if they were his own. This is the wondrous exchange made by his boundless goodness. Having become with us the Son of Man, he has made us with himself sons of God. By his own descent to the earth he has prepared our ascent to heaven. Having received our mortality, he has bestowed on us his immortality. Having undertaken our weakness, he has made us strong in his strength. Having submitted to our poverty, he has transferred to us his riches. Having taken upon himself the burden of unrighteousness with which we were oppressed, he has clothed us with his righteousness.[6]

To all these things we have a complete attestation in this sacrament, enabling us certainly to conclude that they are as truly exhibited to us as if Christ were placed in bodily presence before our view, or handled by our hands. For these are words which can never lie nor deceive—Take, eat, drink. This is my body, which is broken for you: this is my blood, which is shed for the remission of sins. In bidding us take, he intimates that it is ours: in bidding us eat, he intimates that it becomes one substance with us: in affirming of his body that it was broken, and of his blood that it was shed for us, he shows that both were not so much his own as ours, because he took and laid down both, not for his own advantage, but for our salvation. And we ought carefully to observe, that the chief, and almost the whole energy of the sacrament, consists in these words, It is broken for you: it is shed for you. It would not be of much importance to us that the body and blood of the Lord are now distributed, had they not once been set forth for our redemption and salvation. Wherefore they are represented under bread and wine, that we may learn that they are not

6. What love and mercy our Lord Jesus has bestowed upon us! Let us give thanks to our Lord for such love to make us who were poor now rich. Let us give thanks for His righteousness which is now ours by faith!

only ours, but intended to nourish our spiritual life; that is, as we formerly observed, by the corporeal things which are produced in the sacrament, we are by a kind of analogy conducted to spiritual things. Thus when bread is given as a symbol of the body of Christ, we must immediately think of this similitude. As bread nourishes, sustains, and protects our bodily life, so the body of Christ is the only food to invigorate and keep alive the soul. When we behold wine set forth as a symbol of blood, we must think that such use as wine serves to the body, the same is spiritually bestowed by the blood of Christ; and the use is to foster, refresh, strengthen, and exhilarate. For if we duly consider what profit we have gained by the breaking of his sacred body, and the shedding of his blood, we shall clearly perceive that these properties of bread and wine, agreeably to this analogy, most appropriately represent it when they are communicated to us.

Therefore, it is not the principal part of a sacrament simply to hold forth the body of Christ to us without any higher consideration, but rather to seal and confirm that promise by which he testifies that his flesh is meat indeed, and his blood drink indeed, nourishing us unto life eternal, and by which he affirms that he is the bread of life, of which, whosoever shall eat, shall live for ever—I say, to seal and confirm that promise, and in order to do so, it sends us to the cross of Christ, where that promise was performed and fulfilled in all its parts.[7] For we do not eat Christ duly and savingly unless as crucified, while with lively apprehension we perceive the efficacy of his death. When he called himself the bread of life, he did not take that appellation from the sacrament, as some perversely interpret; but such as he was given to us by the Father, such he exhibited himself when becoming partaker of our human mortality, he made us partakers of his divine immortality; when offering himself in sacrifice, he took our curse upon himself, that he might cover us with his blessing, when by his death he devoured and swallowed up death, when in his

7. Just as with baptism, Calvin reminds the reader to look beyond the sign itself to what the sign signifies and what it seals to us.

resurrection he raised our corruptible flesh, which he had put on, to glory and incorruption.

It only remains that the whole become ours by application. This is done by means of the gospel, and more clearly by the sacred Supper, where Christ offers himself to us with all his blessings, and we receive him in faith.[8] The sacrament, therefore, does not make Christ become for the first time the bread of life; but, while it calls to remembrance that Christ was made the bread of life that we may constantly eat him, it gives us a taste and relish for that bread, and makes us feel its efficacy. For it assures us, first, that whatever Christ did or suffered was done to give us life; and, secondly, that this quickening is eternal; by it we are ceaselessly nourished, sustained, and preserved in life. For as Christ would not have not been the bread of life to us if he had not been born, if he had not died and risen again; so he could not now be the bread of life, were not the efficacy and fruit of his nativity, death, and resurrection, eternal. All this Christ has elegantly expressed in these words, "The bread that I will give is my flesh, which I will give for the life of the world" (John 6:51); doubtless intimating, that his body will be as bread in regard to the spiritual life of the soul, because it was to be delivered to death for our salvation, and that he extends it to us for food when he makes us partakers of it by faith. Wherefore he once gave himself that he might become bread, when he gave himself to be crucified for the redemption of the world; and he gives himself daily, when in the word of the gospel he offers himself to be partaken by us, inasmuch as he was crucified, when he seals that offer by the sacred mystery of the Supper, and when he accomplishes inwardly what he externally designates. Moreover, two faults are here to be avoided. We must neither, by setting too little value on the signs, dissever them from their meanings to which they are in some degree annexed, nor by immoderately extolling them, seem somewhat to obscure the mysteries themselves. That Christ is the bread of life by which believers are nourished unto eternal life, no man is so utter-

8. Partaking of the Lord's Supper is of no spiritual benefit unless we are trusting in Christ alone. This is what Jesus says when he describes himself as the bread of life. We partake of His body and blood by faith. "And this is the will of Him who sent Me, that everyone who sees the Son and believes in Him may have everlasting life; and I will raise him up at the last day." (John 6:40)

ly devoid of religion as not to acknowledge. But all are not agreed as to the mode of partaking of him. For there are some who define the eating of the flesh of Christ, and the drinking of his blood, to be, in one word, nothing more than believing in Christ himself. But Christ seems to me to have intended to teach something more express and more sublime in that noble discourse, in which he recommends the eating of his flesh—viz. that we are quickened by the true partaking of him, which he designated by the terms eating and drinking, lest any one should suppose that the life which we obtain from him is obtained by simple knowledge. For as it is not the sight but the eating of bread that gives nourishment to the body, so the soul must partake of Christ truly and thoroughly, that by his energy it may grow up into spiritual life. Meanwhile, we admit that this is nothing else than the eating of faith, and that no other eating can be imagined. But there is this difference between their mode of speaking and mine. According to them, to eat is merely to believe; while I maintain that the flesh of Christ is eaten by believing, because it is made ours by faith, and that that eating is the effect and fruit of faith; or, if you will have it more clearly, according to them, eating is faith, whereas it rather seems to me to be a consequence of faith. The difference is little in words, but not little in reality. For, although the apostle teaches that Christ dwells in our hearts by faith (Eph. 3:17), no one will interpret that dwelling to be faith. All see that it explains the admirable effect of faith, because to it is owing that believers have Christ dwelling in them. In this way, the Lord was pleased, by calling himself the bread of life, not only to teach that our salvation is treasured up in the faith of his death and resurrection, but also, by virtue of true communication with him, his life passes into us and becomes ours, just as bread when taken for food gives vigor to the body.

The sum is, that the flesh and blood of Christ feed our souls just as bread and wine maintain and support our corporeal life. For there would be no aptitude in the sign, did not our souls find their nourishment in Christ.[9] This could not be,

9. Calvin believes that partaking of the elements of the Lord's Supper is more than just a memory exercise. He asserts that to partake of these elements by faith brings about an increase of spiritual life.

did not Christ truly form one with us, and refresh us by the eating of his flesh, and the drinking of his blood. But though it seems an incredible thing that the flesh of Christ, while at such a distance from us in respect of place, should be food to us, let us remember how far the secret virtue of the Holy Spirit surpasses all our conceptions, and how foolish it is to wish to measure its immensity by our feeble capacity.[10] Therefore, what our mind does not comprehend let faith conceive—viz. that the Spirit truly unites things separated by space. That sacred communion of flesh and blood by which Christ transfuses his life into us, just as if it penetrated our bones and marrow, he testifies and seals in the Supper, and that not by presenting a vain or empty sign,[11] but by there exerting an efficacy of the Spirit by which he fulfils what he promises. And truly the thing there signified he exhibits and offers[12] to all who sit down at that spiritual feast, although it is beneficially received by believers only who receive this great benefit with true faith and heartfelt gratitude. For this reason the apostle said, "The cup of blessing which we bless, is it not the communion of the blood of Christ? The bread which we break, is it not the communion of the body of Christ"? (1 Cor. 10:16.) There is no ground to object that the expression is figurative, and gives the sign the name of the thing signified. I admit, indeed, that the breaking of bread is a symbol, not the reality. But this being admitted, we duly infer from the exhibition of the symbol that the thing itself is exhibited. For unless we would charge God with deceit, we will never presume to say that he holds forth an empty symbol. Therefore, if by the breaking of bread the Lord truly represents the partaking of his body, there ought to be no doubt whatever that he truly exhibits and performs it. The rule which the pious ought always to observe is, whenever they see the symbols instituted by the Lord, to think and feel surely persuaded that the truth of the thing signified is also present. For why does the Lord put the symbol of his body into your hands, but just to assure you that you truly partake of him? If this is true let us feel as much assured that the visible

10. It is a mystery how we can be united and commune with Christ in the Lord's Supper, when in his human nature, we realize that He is at the right hand of God the Father in heaven. But Calvin explains that it is the Holy Spirit who makes this possible.

11. The elements are not just physical signs that do nothing more. Through them, the Spirit of God enables us to commune with our Lord Jesus.

12. For those who come to the sacrament in faith, they truly receive the spiritual benefits of Christ through the Lord's Supper.

sign is given us in seal of an invisible gift as that his body itself is given to us.

I hold then (as has always been received in the Church, and is still taught by those who feel aright), that the sacred mystery of the Supper consists of two things—the corporeal signs, which, presented to the eye, represent invisible things in a manner adapted to our weak capacity, and the spiritual truth, which is at once figured and exhibited by the signs. When attempting familiarly to explain its nature, I am accustomed to set down three things—the thing meant, the matter which depends on it, and the virtue or efficacy consequent upon both. The thing meant consists in the promises which are in a manner included in the sign. By the matter, or substance, I mean Christ, with his death and resurrection. By the effect, I understand redemption, justification, sanctification, eternal life, and all other benefits which Christ bestows upon us. Moreover, though all these things have respect to faith, I leave no room for the cavil, that when I say Christ is conceived by faith, I mean that he is only conceived by the intellect and imagination. He is offered by the promises, not that we may stop short at the sight or mere knowledge of him, but that we may enjoy true communion with him. And, indeed, I see not how any one can expect to have redemption and righteousness in the cross of Christ, and life in his death, without trusting first of all to true communion with Christ himself. Those blessings could not reach us, did not Christ previously make himself ours. I say then, that in the mystery of the Supper, by the symbols of bread and wine, Christ, his body and his blood, are truly exhibited to us, that in them he fulfilled all obedience, in order to procure righteousness for us— first that we might become one body with him; and, secondly, that being made partakers of his substance, we might feel the result of this fact in the participation of all his blessings.

They are greatly mistaken in imagining that there is no presence of the flesh of Christ in the Supper, unless it be placed in the bread.[13] They thus leave nothing for the secret operation

13. Calvin disagreed with the Roman church's view that the elements of bread and wine were actually transformed into the body and blood of Christ (the doctrine of transubstantiation). Calvin also disagreed with Luther's perspective that the human body of Christ was contained in the bread. He taught, instead, that the Spirit enables us to commune with the risen Christ.

of the Spirit, which unites Christ himself to us. Christ does not seem to them to be present unless he descends to us, as if we did not equally gain his presence when he raises us to himself. The only question, therefore, is as to the mode, they placing Christ in the bread, while we deem it unlawful to draw him down from heaven. Which of the two is more correct, let the reader judge. Only have done with the calumny that Christ is withdrawn from his Supper if he lurk not under the covering of bread. For seeing this mystery is heavenly, there is no necessity to bring Christ on the earth that he may be connected with us.

Now, should any one ask me as to the mode, I will not be ashamed to confess that it is too high a mystery either for my mind to comprehend or my words to express; and to speak more plainly, I rather feel than understand it.[14] The truth of God, therefore, in which I can safely rest, I here embrace without controversy. He declares that his flesh is the meat, his blood the drink, of my soul; I give my soul to him to be fed with such food. In his sacred Supper he bids me take, eat, and drink his body and blood under the symbols of bread and wine. I have no doubt that he will truly give and I receive. Only, I reject the absurdities which appear to be unworthy of the heavenly majesty of Christ, and are inconsistent with the reality of his human nature. Since they must also be repugnant to the word of God, which teaches both that Christ was received into the glory of the heavenly kingdom, so as to be exalted above all the circumstances of the world (Luke 24:26), and no less carefully ascribes to him the properties belonging to a true human nature. This ought not to seem incredible or contradictory to reason; because, as the whole kingdom of Christ is spiritual, so whatever he does in his Church is not to be tested by the wisdom of this world; or, to use the words of Augustine, "this mystery is performed by man like the others, but in a divine manner, and on earth, but in a heavenly manner." Such, I say, is the corporeal presence which the nature of the sacrament requires, and which we say is here displayed in such power and

14. It is wise with such mysteries to state what is clear in Scripture but leave areas of mystery as mysteries and not go beyond what is written. We cannot say how the Holy Spirit does this work. We only believe that He does.

efficacy, that it not only gives our minds undoubted assurance of eternal life, but also secures the immortality of our flesh, since it is now quickened by his immortal flesh, and in a manner shines in his immortality. Those who are carried beyond this with their hyperboles, do nothing more by their extravagancies than obscure the plain and simple truth. If any one is not yet satisfied, I would have him here to consider with himself that we are speaking of the sacrament, every part of which ought to have reference to faith. Now by participation of the body, as we have explained, we nourish faith not less richly and abundantly than do those who drag Christ himself from heaven. Still I am free to confess that that mixture or transfusion of the flesh of Christ with our soul, which they teach, I repudiate, because it is enough for us that Christ, out of the substance of his flesh, breathes life into our souls, nay, diffuses his own life into us, though the real flesh of Christ does not enter us. I may add that there can be no doubt that the analogy of faith by which Paul enjoins us to test every interpretation of Scripture, is clearly with us in this matter. Let those who oppose a truth so clear, consider to what standard of faith they conform themselves: "Ever spirit that confesseth not that Jesus Christ is come in the flesh is not of God" (1 John 4:3); 2 John ver. 7). These men, though they disguise the fact, or perceive it not, rob him of his flesh.

THE PILGRIM'S PROGRESS

John Bunyan
AD 1678

Explanatory Notes by
Joshua Schwisow

Introduction to
The Pilgrim's Progress

The *Pilgrim's Progress* was a book sure to maintain its place in history as a Christian classic when it was first published in 1678. It was an instant bestseller and has remained one of the most popular Christian books to this day. It has been translated into over 200 languages. In numerous missionary contexts, it has been one of the first books translated into other native languages after the Bible. This book is a remarkable testimony to God's providence. Who would have imagined that a poor English tinker (a repairer of metal household items) would produce one of the most influential literary works in the English language? Yet this is exactly what happened.

John Bunyan grew up in the small English village of Bedford (about sixty miles from London). During his youth, Bunyan was a profane and ungodly man. But in time, the Lord would call him out of darkness into His light. As a young man, Bunyan worked as a tinker in Bedford. When the English Civil War began in the 1640s, he served in the Parliamentary army, spending three years in the military.

Two years after his military service ended, Bunyan married. He was not a Christian at the time, but his wife was a godly woman. Through a series of events, Bunyan was convicted of his profanity, sabbath-breaking, and other sins. In one of the nonconformist assemblies in Bedford, Pastor John Gifford faithfully preached the gospel. Faith comes through the hearing of God's Word (Rom. 10:17), and Bunyan was soon converted to Christ under the teaching of this man and other faithful Christians. In later years, he recounted his life story in *Grace Abounding to the Chief of Sinners*.

Bunyan soon sensed a call to the gospel ministry. He began preaching regularly in the church in Bedford. When the monarchy was restored in 1660, a series of acts were passed that restricted the freedom of nonconformists such as Bunyan to gather for worship. Though Bunyan knew that he was risking much by going to preach, he kept preaching. Soon he was arrested and imprisoned in Bedford. Ultimately, he spent over a decade in prison. While there, he began writing *The Pilgrim's Progress*. In fact, when he recounts the dream he had while in "the den," he is likely referring to the Bedford Jail.

Bunyan wrote many works, but *The Pilgrim's Progress* has remained the most popular and enduring of his books. His deep knowledge of the Scriptures and imaginative allegorical portrayal of the Christian life displayed in this work have influenced Christians in every generation. Bunyan's characters and places such as "The Slough of Despond," "Doubting Castle," "The Celestial City," "Talkative," "Hopeful," and others have become standard vocabulary terms for Christians in every age and culture.

It has been pointed out that the Bible is not a textbook on systematic theology or just a list of rules and propositions. God reveals truth to mankind by means of stories, allegories, parables, and an occasional sermon. Thus, biblical truth is sometimes better portrayed in the organic form of a human story than it is in a series of well-structured propositions. Such forms of literature are often more memorable and fruitful. This is beautifully portrayed in Bunyan's classic work.

John Bunyan demonstrates a penetrating understanding of the human heart, the often-harrowing nature of the Christian life, and the many forms of deceit that lurk in the Christian Church then and now. Through Bunyan's timeless work, the good news of Jesus Christ shines forth in beauty and glory. His work speaks just as relevantly today as it did then, which may explain its popularity throughout the world.

The Author's Apology for His Book

When at the first I took my pen in hand
    Thus for to write, I did not understand
That I at all should make a little book
In such a mode: nay, I had undertook
To make another; which, when almost done,
Before I was aware I this begun.

And thus it was: I, writing of the way[1]
And race of saints[2] in this our gospel-day,
Fell suddenly into an allegory[3]
About their journey, and the way to glory,
In more than twenty things which I set down
This done, I twenty more had in my crown,
And they again began to multiply,
Like sparks that from the coals of fire do fly.
Nay, then, thought I, if that you breed so fast,
I'll put you by yourselves, lest you at last
Should prove ad infinitum,[4] and eat out
The book that I already am about.
Well, so I did; but yet I did not think
To show to all the world my pen and ink

1. It is not known which book Bunyan is referring to here. It may be his autobiographical work *Grace Abounding to the Chief of Sinners* or *The Heavenly Footman*.

2. Bunyan may have in mind the words of Paul: "Know ye not that they which run in a race run all, but one receiveth the prize? So run, that ye may obtain." (1 Cor. 9:24)

3. The literary form of allegory uses symbolic fictional characters and places that represent something else. In the *Pilgrim's Progress*, the people and places serve as symbols for those things in reality.

4. Latin: "again and again in the same way forever"

In such a mode; I only thought to make
I knew not what: nor did I undertake
Thereby to please my neighbor; no, not I;
I did it my own self to gratify.
Neither did I but vacant seasons spend
In this my scribble; nor did I intend
But to divert myself, in doing this,
From worser thoughts, which make me do amiss.
Thus I set pen to paper with delight,
And quickly had my thoughts in black and white;
For having now my method by the end,
Still as I pull'd, it came; and so I penned
It down; until it came at last to be,
For length and breadth, the bigness which you see.
Well, when I had thus put mine ends together
I show'd them others,[5] that I might see whether
They would condemn them, or them justify:
And some said, let them live; some, let them die:
Some said, John, print it; others said, Not so:
Some said, It might do good; others said, No.
Now was I in a strait, and did not see
Which was the best thing to be done by me:
At last I thought, Since ye are thus divided,
I print it will; and so the case decided.
For, thought I, some I see would have it done,
Though others in that channel do not run:
To prove, then, who advised for the best,
Thus I thought fit to put it to the test.
I further thought, if now I did deny
Those that would have it, thus to gratify;
I did not know, but hinder them I might
Of that which would to them be great delight.
For those which were not for its coming forth,
I said to them, Offend you, I am loath;
Yet since your brethren pleased with it be,
Forbear to judge, till you do further see.

5. John Bunyan explains that he shared the book with others to see whether it was worth publishing.

6. To allay concerns or satisfy

7. Bunyan's words are "dark" in that they are obscure. But they will produce "rain" and bring fruit to the reader's mind.

8. "Complain"

9. Valuable stones were believed to grow in the head of toads.

If that thou wilt not read, let it alone;
Some love the meat, some love to pick the bone.
Yea, that I might them better palliate,[6]
I did too with them thus expostulate:
May I not write in such a style as this?
In such a method too, and yet not miss
My end-thy good? Why may it not be done?
Dark clouds bring waters,[7] when the bright bring none.
Yea, dark or bright, if they their silver drops
Cause to descend, the earth, by yielding crops,
Gives praise to both, and carpeth[8] not at either,
But treasures up the fruit they yield together;
Yea, so commixes both, that in their fruit
None can distinguish this from that; they suit
Her well when hungry; but if she be full,
She spews out both, and makes their blessing null.
You see the ways the fisherman doth take
To catch the fish; what engines doth he make!
Behold how he engageth all his wits;
Also his snares, lines, angles, hooks, and nets:
Yet fish there be, that neither hook nor line,
Nor snare, nor net, nor engine can make thine:
They must be groped for, and be tickled too,
Or they will not be catch'd, whate'er you do.
How does the fowler seek to catch his game
By divers means! All which one cannot name.
His guns, his nets, his lime-twigs, light and bell:
He creeps, he goes, he stands; yea, who can tell
Of all his postures? Yet there's none of these
Will make him master of what fowls he please.
Yea, he must pipe and whistle, to catch this;
Yet if he does so, that bird he will miss.
If that a pearl may in toad's head dwell,[9]
And may be found too in an oyster-shell;
If things that promise nothing, do contain
What better is than gold; who will disdain,

That have an inkling of it, there to look,
That they may find it. Now my little book,
(Though void of all these paintings that may make
It with this or the other man to take,)
Is not without those things that do excel
What do in brave but empty notions dwell.
"Well, yet I am not fully satisfied
That this your book will stand, when soundly tried."
Why, what's the matter? "It is dark." What though?
"But it is feigned." What of that? I trow
Some men by feigned words, as dark as mine,
Make truth to spangle, and its rays to shine.
"But they want solidness." Speak, man, thy mind.
"They drown the weak; metaphors make us blind."
Solidity, indeed, becomes the pen
Of him that writeth things divine to men:
But must I needs want solidness, because
By metaphors I speak? Were not God's laws,
His gospel laws, in olden time held forth
By types, shadows, and metaphors?[10] Yet loth
Will any sober man be to find fault
With them, lest he be found for to assault
The highest wisdom! No, he rather stoops,
And seeks to find out what, by pins and loops,
By calves and sheep, by heifers, and by rams,
By birds and herbs, and by the blood of lambs,
God speaketh to him; and happy is he
That finds the light and grace that in them be.
But not too forward, therefore, to conclude
That I want solidness—that I am rude;
All things solid in show, not solid be;
All things in parable despise not we,
Lest things most hurtful lightly we receive,
And things that good are, of our souls bereave.
My dark and cloudy words they do but hold
The truth, as cabinets inclose the gold.[11]

10. Bunyan tells the reader that many portions of Scripture contain types, shadows, and metaphors. The Parables of Jesus are such an example of using imagery to communicate truth.

11. Even though this book is filled with "dark and cloudy words" it communicates the truth of God. The allegory of the book is intended by Bunyan to communicate not fiction, but the truth of God as revealed in Scripture.

12. Another term for the
Bible, the Holy Scriptures

The prophets used much by metaphors
To set forth truth: yea, who so considers
Christ, his apostles too, shall plainly see,
That truths to this day in such mantles be.
Am I afraid to say, that holy writ,[12]
Which for its style and phrase puts down all wit,
Is everywhere so full of all these things,
Dark figures, allegories? Yet there springs
From that same book, that lustre, and those rays
Of light, that turn our darkest nights to days.
Come, let my carper to his life now look,
And find there darker lines than in my book
He findeth any; yea, and let him know,
That in his best things there are worse lines too.
May we but stand before impartial men,
To his poor one I durst adventure ten,
That they will take my meaning in these lines
Far better than his lies in silver shrines.
Come, truth, although in swaddling-clothes, I find
Informs the judgment, rectifies the mind;
Pleases the understanding, makes the will
Submit, the memory too it doth fill

13. "If thou put the
brethren in remembrance
of these things, thou
shalt be a good minister
of Jesus Christ, nour-
ished up in the words of
faith and of good doc-
trine, whereunto thou
hast attained. But refuse
profane and old wives'
fables, and exercise
thyself rather unto godliness." (1 Timothy 4:6-7)

With what doth our imagination please;
Likewise it tends our troubles to appease.
Sound words, I know, Timothy is to use,
And old wives' fables he is to refuse;[13]
But yet grave Paul him nowhere doth forbid
The use of parables, in which lay hid
That gold, those pearls, and precious stones that were
Worth digging for, and that with greatest care.
Let me add one word more. O man of God,
Art thou offended? Dost thou wish I had
Put forth my matter in another dress?
Or that I had in things been more express?
Three things let me propound; then I submit
To those that are my betters, as is fit.

1. I find not that I am denied the use
Of this my method, so I no abuse
Put on the words, things, readers, or be rude
In handling figure or similitude,
In application; but all that I may
Seek the advance of truth this or that way.
Denied, did I say? Nay, I have leave,
(Example too, and that from them that have
God better pleased, by their words or ways,
Than any man that breatheth now-a-days,)
Thus to express my mind, thus to declare
Things unto thee that excellentest are.
2. I find that men as high as trees will write
Dialogue-wise; yet no man doth them slight
For writing so. Indeed, if they abuse
Truth, cursed be they, and the craft they use
To that intent; but yet let truth be free
To make her sallies upon thee and me,
Which way it pleases God: for who knows how,
Better than he that taught us first to plough,
To guide our minds and pens for his designs?
And he makes base things usher in divine.
3. I find that holy writ, in many places,
Hath semblance with this method, where the cases
Do call for one thing to set forth another:[14]
Use it I may then, and yet nothing smother
Truth's golden beams: nay, by this method may
Make it cast forth its rays as light as day.
And now, before I do put up my pen,
I'll show the profit of my book; and then
Commit both thee and it unto that hand
That pulls the strong down, and makes weak ones stand.[15]
This book it chalketh out before thine eyes
The man that seeks the everlasting prize:
It shows you whence he comes, whither he goes,
What he leaves undone; also what he does:

14. The Bible also repeatedly uses imagery to communicate truth. Therefore, there is nothing wrong with Bunyan using the same approach to communicate biblical truth.

15. The Lord has the power to reverse fortunes and bring down the proud and exalt the humble (see Ps. 75).

It also shows you how he runs, and runs,
Till he unto the gate of glory comes.
It shows, too, who set out for life amain,
As if the lasting crown they would obtain;
Here also you may see the reason why
They lose their labor, and like fools do die.
This book will make a traveler of thee,
If by its counsel thou wilt ruled be;
It will direct thee to the Holy Land,[16]
If thou wilt its directions understand
Yea, it will make the slothful active be;
The blind also delightful things to see.
Art thou for something rare and profitable?
Or would'st thou see a truth within a fable?
Art thou forgetful? Wouldest thou remember
From New-Year's day to the last of December?
Then read my fancies; they will stick like burs,
And may be, to the helpless, comforters.
This book is writ in such a dialect
As may the minds of listless men affect:
It seems a novelty, and yet contains
Nothing but sound and honest gospel strains.
Would'st thou divert thyself from melancholy?
Would'st thou be pleasant, yet be far from folly?
Would'st thou read riddles, and their explanation?
Or else be drowned in thy contemplation?
Dost thou love picking meat? Or would'st thou see
A man i' the clouds, and hear him speak to thee?
Would'st thou be in a dream, and yet not sleep?
Or would'st thou in a moment laugh and weep?
Would'st thou lose thyself and catch no harm,
And find thyself again without a charm?
Would'st read thyself, and read thou know'st not what,
And yet know whether thou art blest or not,
By reading the same lines? O then come hither,
And lay my book, thy head, and heart together.

16. The Promised Land of the Old Covenant was a type of the greater glory of the heavenly kingdom. In this book, Bunyan will call the heavenly kingdom the "Celestial City."

Book 1
Chapter 1

As I walked through the wilderness of this world, I lighted on a certain place where was a den,[1] and laid me down in that place to sleep; and as I slept, I dreamed a dream. I dreamed, and behold, I saw a man[2] clothed with rags,[3] standing in a certain place, with his face from his own house, a book in his hand,[4] and a great burden upon his back.[5] Isa 64:6; Luke 14:33; Psalm 38:4. I looked and saw him open the book, and read therein; and as he read, he wept and trembled;[6] and not being able longer to contain, he brake out with a lamentable cry, saying, "What shall I do?" Acts 2:37; 16:30; Habak 1:2,3.

In this plight, therefore, he went home, and restrained himself as long as he could, that his wife and children should not perceive his distress; but he could not be silent long, because that his trouble increased. Wherefore at length he brake his mind[7] to his wife and children; and thus he began to talk to them: "O, my dear wife," said he, "and you the children of my bowels, I, your dear friend, am in myself undone by reason

1. This is a reference to the prison in which Bunyan wrote much of The Pilgrim's Progress.

2. The man is not given a name here. Later in the book, we learn that Christian's name, before his conversion, was "Graceless."

3. This symbolizes the man's sinful condition.

4. The Bible

5. The debt of sin

6. The right response to our sins is to weep and tremble for God's judgment. But we must then look to the Savior Jesus Christ for salvation from the debt and corruption of sin.

7. "Brake" means to open his mind. The man decided to speak to his wife and children.

8. The man was undone by his sinful condition and could not remain in this condition any longer. He had to find a solution to his condition.

9. The "City of Destruction" lies under the judgment of God. Because all men are fallen in sin and guilty for their sins, we all, by nature, live in the City of Destruction. "Among whom also we all had our conversation in times past in the lusts of our flesh, fulfilling the desires of the flesh and of the mind; and were by nature the children of wrath, even as others." (Eph. 2:3)

10. "Greatly amazed"

11. "A feverish illness"

of a burden that lieth hard upon me;[8] moreover, I am certainly informed that this our city will be burnt with fire from heaven; in which fearful overthrow, both myself, with thee my wife, and you my sweet babes, shall miserably come to ruin,[9] except (the which yet I see not) some way of escape can be found whereby we may be delivered." At this his relations were sore amazed;[10] not for that they believed that what he had said to them was true, but because they thought that some frenzy distemper[11] had got into his head; therefore, it drawing towards night, and they hoping that sleep might settle his brains, with all haste they got him to bed.[12] But the night was as troublesome to him as the day; wherefore, instead of sleeping, he spent it in sighs and tears.[13] So when the morning was come, they would know how he did. He told them, "Worse and worse:" he also set to talking to them again; but they began to be hardened.[14] They also thought to drive away his distemper by harsh and surly carriage[15] to him; sometimes they would deride, sometimes they would chide, and sometimes they would quite neglect him. Wherefore he began to retire himself to his chamber to pray for and pity them, and also to condole his own misery; he would also walk solitarily

12. The man's wife and family did not believe his words. They thought he had gone crazy. Unfortunately, they did not see their own sinful condition and their need for salvation. Unless the Lord opens our eyes to our sinful condition and the way of salvation in Jesus Christ, we will not be able to see.

13. The man was under the conviction of sin. He understood the curse that lay upon him because of his sin. "For as many as are of the works of the law are under the curse: for it is written, Cursed is every one that continueth not in all things which are written in the book of the law to do them." (Gal. 3:10)

14. Rather than being softened to the truth, the man's family were hardened against the truth. The Word of God will either soften or harden the heart. In Bunyan's treatise *On the Fear of God*, he says, "Take heed of hardening thy heart at any time, against convictions or judgments. I bid you before to beware of a hard heart; now I bid you beware of hardening your soft heart."

15. "Harsh, bad-tempered, and unfriendly speech"

in the fields, sometimes reading, and sometimes praying: and thus for some days he spent his time.

Now I saw, upon a time, when he was walking in the fields, that he was (as he was wont) reading in his book, and greatly distressed in his mind; and as he read, he burst out, as he had done before, crying, "What shall I do to be saved?"[16] Acts 16:30,31.

I saw also that he looked this way, and that way, as if he would run; yet he stood still because (as I perceived) he could not tell which way to go. I looked then, and saw a man named Evangelist[17] coming to him, and he asked, "Wherefore dost thou cry?"

He answered, "Sir, I perceive, by the book in my hand, that I am condemned to die, and after that to come to judgment, Heb. 9:27; and I find that I am not willing to do the first, Job 10: 21,22 nor able to do the second." Ezek. 22:14.

Then said Evangelist, "Why not willing to die, since this life is attended with so many evils?" The man answered, "Because, I fear that this burden that is upon my back will sink me lower than the grave, and I shall fall into Tophet.[18] Isa. 30:33. And Sir, if I be not fit to go to prison, I am not fit to go to judgment, and from thence to execution; and the thoughts of these things make me cry."

16. The man repeats the question asked by the Philippian jailor (Acts 16:30-31). At this point, the man does not know the salvation of sin found in Jesus Christ. He is under the conviction of sin, but has not yet seen the solution.

17. Evangelist symbolizes the preacher of the gospel. The word "evangelist" refers to one who proclaims the gospel (Greek evangellion), the "good news" of Jesus Christ. So far, the man was under the conviction of sin and had no solution, but now the entrance into the "narrow way" through the wicket-gate is proclaimed by Evangelist.

18. The word "Tophet" refers to hell. In the prophet Jeremiah, we learn that Tophet was a place where many abominable sins were committed. Jeremiah warns that God will turn Tophet into a place of judgment. "And they have built the high places of Tophet, which is in the valley of the son of Hinnom, to burn their sons and their daughters in the fire; which I commanded them not, neither came it into my heart. Therefore, behold, the days come, saith the LORD, that it shall no more be called Tophet, nor the valley of the son of Hinnom, but the valley of slaughter: for they shall bury in Tophet, till there be no place." (Jer. 7:31-32)

19. The parchment contained not only this warning, "fly from the wrath to come," but it also contained God's promises because we find Christian comforting himself in the reading of the parchment roll later in the narrative. These promises of God were personally applied, giving Christian assurance of His salvation.

20. The gate is the entrance into the narrow way of salvation. "Enter ye in at the strait gate: for wide is the gate, and broad is the way, that leadeth to destruction, and many there be which go in thereat:..." (Matt. 7:13)

21. The light represents the Word of God, which gives light to the Christian's path.

Then said Evangelist, "If this be thy condition, why standest thou still?" He answered, "Because I know not whither to go." Then he gave him a parchment roll,[19] and there was written within, "Fly from the wrath to come." Matt. 3:7.

The man therefore read it, and looking upon Evangelist very carefully, said, "Whither must I fly?" Then said Evangelist, (pointing with his finger over a very wide field,) "Do you see yonder wicket-gate?"[20] Matt. 7:13,14. The man said, "No." Then said the other, "Do you see yonder shining light?"[21] Psalm 119:105; 2 Pet. 1:19. He said, "I think I do." Then said Evangelist, "Keep that light in your eye, and go up directly thereto, so shalt thou see the gate; at which, when thou knockest, it shall be told thee what thou shalt do." So I saw in my dream that the man began to run. Now he had not run far from his own door when his wife and children, perceiving it, began to cry after him to return; but the man put his fingers in his ears, and ran on crying, Life! life! eternal life! Luke 14:26. So he looked not behind him,[22] Gen. 19:17, but fled towards the middle of the plain.

The neighbors also came out to see him run, Jer. 20:10; and as he ran, some mocked, others threatened, and some cried after him to return; and among those that did so, there were two that were resolved to fetch him back by force. The name of the one was Obstinate[23] and the name of the other Pliable.[24] Now by this time the man was got a good distance from them; but, however, they were resolved to pursue him, which they did, and in a little time they overtook him. Then said the man, "Neighbors, wherefore are you come?" They said, "To persuade you to go back with us." But he said, "That can

22. When Lot and his family fled Sodom, they were commanded not to look back. To look back would indicate that they were not willing to fully part with the city. When we turn from the world, we must not look back with any yearning for the world's ways. Not to look back represents a whole-hearted repentance from the world's ways.

23. Obstinate and Pliable are the first allegorical characters in the story. Obstinate symbolizes the person who refuses to change their opinion, despite being attempted to do so by others.

24. Pliable symbolizes the person who is easily persuaded (pliable).

by no means be: you dwell," said he, "in the city of Destruction, the place also where I was born: I see it to be so; and dying there, sooner or later, you will sink lower than the grave, into a place that burns with fire and brimstone:[25] be content, good neighbors, and go along with me."

Obstinate: What, said Obstinate, and leave our friends and our comforts behind us![26]

Christian: Yes, said Christian, (for that was his name,) because that all which you forsake is not worthy to be compared with a little of that I am seeking to enjoy, 2 Cor. 4:18; and if you will go along with me, and hold it, you shall fare as I myself; for there, where I go, is enough and to spare. Luke 15:17. Come away, and prove my words.

Obstinate: What are the things you seek, since you leave all the world to find them?

Christian: I seek an inheritance incorruptible, undefiled, and that fadeth not away, 1 Peter 1:4; and it is laid up in heaven, and safe there, Heb. 11:16, to be bestowed, at the time appointed, on them that diligently seek it. Read it so, if you will, in my book.

Obstinate: Tush,[27] said Obstinate, away with your book; will you go back with us or no?

Christian: No, not I, said the other, because I have laid my hand to the plough. Luke 9:62.

Obstinate: Come then, neighbor Pliable, let us turn again, and go home without him: there is a company of these crazy-headed coxcombs,[28] that when they take a fancy by the end, are wiser in their own eyes than seven men that can render a reason.

Pliable: Then said Pliable, Don't revile; if what the good Christian says is true, the things he looks after[29] are better than ours: my heart inclines to go with my neighbor.

Obstinate: What, more fools still! Be ruled by me, and go back; who knows whither such a brain-sick fellow will lead you? Go back, go back, and be wise.

25. "But the fearful, and unbelieving, and the abominable, and murderers, and whoremongers, and sorcerers, and idolaters, and all liars, shall have their part in the lake which burneth with fire and brimstone: which is the second death." (Rev. 21:8)

26. To leave the world requires the sacrifice of self-denial. Jesus teaches that all who would become His disciples must deny himself and take up his cross, and follow Jesus (Matt. 16:24).

27. An exclamation expressing disapproval or dismissal

28. "Crazy fools"

29. "Things he looks for, or searches after"

Christian: Nay, but do thou come with thy neighbor Pliable; there are such things to be had which I spoke of, and many more glories besides. If you believe not me, read here in this book, and for the truth of what is expressed therein, behold, all is confirmed by the blood of Him that made it. Heb. 9: 17-21.

Pliable: Well, neighbor Obstinate, said Pliable, I begin to come to a point; I intend to go along with this good man, and to cast in my lot with him: but, my good companion, do you know the way to this desired place?

Christian: I am directed by a man whose name is Evangelist, to speed me to a little gate that is before us, where we shall receive instructions about the way.

Pliable: Come then, good neighbor, let us be going. Then they went both together.

Obstinate: And I will go back to my place, said Obstinate: I will be no companion of such misled, fantastical fellows.

Now I saw in my dream, that when Obstinate was gone back, Christian and Pliable went talking over the plain; and thus they began their discourse.

Christian: Come, neighbor Pliable, how do you do? I am glad you are persuaded to go along with me. Had even Obstinate himself but felt what I have felt of the powers and terrors of what is yet unseen, he would not thus lightly have given us the back.

Pliable: Come, neighbor Christian, since there are none but us two here, tell me now farther, what the things are, and how to be enjoyed, whither we are going.

Christian: I can better conceive of them with my mind, than speak of them with my tongue:[30] but yet, since you are desirous to know, I will read of them in my book.

Pliable: And do you think that the words of your book are certainly true?

Christian: Yes, verily; for it was made by Him that cannot lie.[31] Tit. 1:2.

Pliable: Well said; what things are they?

30. The glories to be revealed to the children of God are so great as to be inexpressible. The Apostle Peter says: "Whom having not seen, ye love; in whom, though now ye see him not, yet believing, ye rejoice with joy unspeakable and full of glory." (1 Pet. 1:8)

31. Because the Bible is the inspired Word of God (2 Tim. 3:16-17), it must be without error. This is so because God cannot lie (Tit. 1:2).

Christian: There is an endless kingdom to be inhabited, and everlasting life to be given us, that we may inhabit that kingdom for ever. Isa. 65:17; John 10: 27-29.

Pliable: Well said; and what else?

Christian: There are crowns of glory to be given us; and garments that will make us shine like the sun in the firmament of heaven. 2 Tim. 4:8; Rev. 22:5; Matt. 13:43.

Pliable: This is very pleasant; and what else?

Christian: There shall be no more crying, nor sorrow; for he that is owner of the place will wipe all tears from our eyes. Isa. 25:8; Rev 7:16, 17; 21:4.

Pliable: And what company shall we have there?

Christian: There we shall be with seraphims and cherubims, Isaiah 6:2; 1 Thess. 4:16,17; Rev. 5:11; creatures that will dazzle your eyes to look on them. There also you shall meet with thousands and ten thousands that have gone before us to that place; none of them are hurtful, but loving and holy; every one walking in the sight of God, and standing in his presence with acceptance for ever. In a word, there we shall see the elders with their golden crowns, Rev. 4:4; there we shall see the holy virgins with their golden harps, Rev. 14:1-5; there we shall see men, that by the world were cut in pieces, burnt in flames, eaten of beasts, drowned in the seas, for the love they bare to the Lord of the place, John 12:25; all well, and clothed with immortality as with a garment. 2 Cor. 5:2.

Pliable: The hearing of this is enough to ravish one's heart. But are these things to be enjoyed? How shall we get to be sharers thereof?

Christian: The Lord, the governor of the country, hath recorded that in this book, Isaiah 55:1,2; John 6:37; 7:37; Rev. 21:6; 22:17; the substance of which is, if we be truly willing to have it, he will bestow it upon us freely.[32]

Pliable: Well, my good companion, glad am I to hear of these things: come on, let us mend our pace.[33]

Christian: I cannot go as fast as I would, by reason of this burden that is on my back.[34]

32. The gospel is God's free grace bestowed on undeserving sinners. We receive God's free gift of salvation by faith. "For by grace are ye saved through faith; and that not of yourselves: it is the gift of God:..." (Eph. 2:8)

33. "Improve or speed up our pace"

34. Pliable is not conscious of the burden of sin. Christian, however, senses this burden, and it weighs him down.

35. A slough is an old English term for "swamp" or "bog." This "Slough of Despond" could also be called "the swamp of despondency." The word "despond" means to "become dejected and lose confidence."

36. Both Christian and Pliable were covered with a great deal of mud from the swamp.

37. The burden of sin continues to weigh down Christian and he begins to sink because of the despondency that sin produces.

38. "Slow speed"

39. Pliable was easily persuaded to join the pilgrimage with Christian. But just as he was easily persuaded to come (as his name implies) he was easily persuaded to give up at the first sign of difficulty.

40. Christian was driven by fear and this led to his falling into a state of despondency. God has not called us to fear, but to faith.

Now I saw in my dream, that just as they had ended this talk, they drew nigh to a very miry slough that was in the midst of the plain: and they being heedless, did both fall suddenly into the bog. The name of the slough was Despond.[35] Here, therefore, they wallowed for a time, being grievously bedaubed[36] with the dirt; and Christian, because of the burden that was on his back, began to sink in the mire.[37]

Pliable: Then said Pliable, Ah, neighbor Christian, where are you now?

Christian: Truly, said Christian, I do not know.

Pliable: At this Pliable began to be offended, and angrily said to his fellow, Is this the happiness you have told me all this while of? If we have such ill speed[38] at our first setting out, what may we expect between this and our journey's end? May I get out again with my life, you shall possess the brave country alone for me. And with that he gave a desperate struggle or two, and got out of the mire on that side of the slough which was next to his own house: so away he went, and Christian saw him no more.[39]

Wherefore Christian was left to tumble in the Slough of Despond alone; but still he endeavored to struggle to that side of the slough that was farthest from his own house, and next to the wicket-gate; the which he did, but could not get out because of the burden that was upon his back: but I beheld in my dream, that a man came to him, whose name was Help, and asked him what he did there.

Christian: Sir, said Christian, I was bid to go this way by a man called Evangelist, who directed me also to yonder gate, that I might escape the wrath to come. And as I was going thither, I fell in here.

Help: But why did not you look for the steps?

Christian: Fear followed me so hard[40] that I fled the next way, and fell in.

Help: Then, said he, Give me thine hand: so he gave him his hand, and he drew him out, Psalm 40:2, and he set him upon sound ground, and bid him go on his way.

Then I stepped to him[41] that plucked him out, and said, "Sir, wherefore, since over this place is the way from the city of Destruction to yonder gate, is it, that this plat is not mended,[42] that poor travellers might go thither with more security?" And he said unto me, "This miry slough is such a place as cannot be mended: it is the descent whither the scum and filth that attends conviction for sin doth continually run, and therefore it is called the Slough of Despond; for still, as the sinner is awakened about his lost condition, there arise in his soul many fears and doubts, and discouraging apprehensions, which all of them get together, and settle in this place: and this is the reason of the badness of this ground.[43]

"It is not the pleasure of the King that this place should remain so bad. Isa. 35:3,4. His laborers also have, by the direction of his Majesty's surveyors, been for above this sixteen hundred years[44] employed about this patch of ground, if perhaps it might have been mended: yea, and to my knowledge," said he, "there have been swallowed up at least twenty thousand cart loads, yea, millions of wholesome instructions, that have at all seasons been brought from all places of the King's dominions, (and they that can tell, say, they are the best materials to make good ground of the place,) if so be it might have been mended; but it is the Slough of Despond still, and so will be when they have done what they can.

"True, there are, by the direction of the Lawgiver, certain good and substantial steps,[45] placed even through the very midst of this slough; but at such time as this place doth much spew out its filth, as it doth against change of weather, these steps are hardly seen; or if they be, men, through the dizziness of their heads, step beside, and then they are bemired to purpose,[46] notwithstanding the steps be there: but the ground is good when they are once got in at the gate." 1 Sam. 12:23.

Now I saw in my dream, that by this time Pliable was got home to his house. So his neighbors came to visit him; and some of them called him wise man for coming back, and some called him fool for hazarding himself with Christian: others

41. The narrator (Bunyan) makes a rare appearance in the narrative in order to ask Help about the slough's existence.

42. A "plat" is a patch of ground.

43. The slough of despond cannot be mended because when a man comes under the conviction of sin, it necessarily produces fears, doubts, and discouragement. Unless a man apprehends God's mercy in Christ, he will slip into despondency. Our sinful condition is hopeless unless God brings us out of the "miry bog" and makes our steps secure (Ps. 40:1-2).

44. At the time Bunyan wrote, it had been around 1,600 years since the birth of Christ.

45. The way out of the despondency that comes with the conviction of sin is the promise of God's salvation. It is by these "steps" that one can come out of this despondency.

46. "Really stuck in the mire"

47. Pliable was ashamed because of the mockery of his neighbors.

48. "By chance to meet"

49. Mr. Worldly Wiseman symbolizes the legalist or moralist who believes that the good life can be attained through moral living, apart from the grace of God. The moralist sees no need for Christ's work on the cross. For him, the grace of God is unnecessary. In contrast to such a view, the Bible declares: "For as many as are of the works of the law are under the curse: for it is written, Cursed is every one that continueth not in all things which are written in the book of the law to do them." (Gal. 3:10)

50. "Worldly calculation"

51. "Close by"

52. Christian is still laboring under his heavy burden of sin.

again did mock at his cowardliness, saying, "Surely, since you began to venture, I would not have been so base as to have given out for a few difficulties:" so Pliable sat sneaking among them.[47] But at last he got more confidence, and then they all turned their tales, and began to deride poor Christian behind his back. And thus much concerning Pliable.

Now as Christian was walking solitary by himself, he espied one afar off come crossing over the field to meet him; and their hap was to meet[48] just as they were crossing the way of each other. The gentleman's name that met him was Mr. Worldly Wiseman:[49] he dwelt in the town of Carnal Policy,[50] a very great town, and also hard by[51] from whence Christian came. This man then, meeting with Christian, and having some inkling of him, (for Christian's setting forth from the city of Destruction was much noised abroad, not only in the town where he dwelt, but also it began to be the town-talk in some other places)—Mr. Worldly Wiseman, therefore, having some guess of him, by beholding his laborious going,[52] by observing his sighs and groans, and the like, began thus to enter into some talk with Christian.

Mr. Worldly Wiseman: How now, good fellow, whither away after this burdened manner?

Christian: A burdened manner indeed, as ever I think poor creature had! And whereas you ask me, Whither away? I tell you, sir, I am going to yonder wicket-gate before me; for there, as I am informed, I shall be put into a way to be rid of my heavy burden.

Mr. Worldly Wiseman: Hast thou a wife and children?

Christian: Yes; but I am so laden with this burden, that I cannot take that pleasure in them as formerly: methinks I am as if I had none. 1 Cor. 7:29.

Mr. Worldly Wiseman: Wilt thou hearken to me, if I give thee counsel?

Christian: If it be good, I will; for I stand in need of good counsel.

Mr. Worldly Wiseman: I would advise thee, then, that thou with all speed get thyself rid of thy burden; for thou wilt never be settled in thy mind till then: nor canst thou enjoy the benefits of the blessings which God hath bestowed upon thee till then.

Christian: That is that which I seek for, even to be rid of this heavy burden: but get it off myself I cannot, nor is there any man in our country that can take it off my shoulders; therefore am I going this way, as I told you, that I may be rid of my burden.

Mr. Worldly Wiseman: Who bid thee go this way to be rid of thy burden?

Christian: A man that appeared to me to be a very great and honorable person: his name, as I remember, is Evangelist.

Mr. Worldly Wiseman: I beshrew him for his counsel![53] there is not a more dangerous and troublesome way in the world than is that into which he hath directed thee; and that thou shalt find, if thou wilt be ruled by his counsel. Thou hast met with something, as I perceive, already; for I see the dirt of the Slough of Despond is upon thee: but that slough is the beginning of the sorrows that do attend those that go on in that way. Hear me; I am older than thou: thou art like to meet with, in the way which thou goest, wearisomeness, painfulness, hunger, perils, nakedness, sword, lions, dragons, darkness, and, in a word, death, and what not.[54] These things are certainly true, having been confirmed by many testimonies. And should a man so carelessly cast away himself, by giving heed to a stranger?

Christian: Why, sir, this burden on my back is more terrible to me than are all these things which you have mentioned: nay, methinks I care not what I meet with in the way, if so be I can also meet with deliverance from my burden.[55]

Mr. Worldly Wiseman: How camest thou by thy burden at first?

Christian: By reading this book in my hand.

53. "Curse him for his advice"

54. Worldly Wiseman is right about this: the Christian life is attended with many sufferings. As in Acts 14:22, we must enter the kingdom of God through many tribulations.

55. All the perils of the Christian life are worth it because it is the way of salvation. It is the only way that Christian can be free of the burden of sin.

56. Worldly Wiseman offers a much easier solution to Christian to get rid of his burden. But Christian will find that Worldly Wiseman lied to him.

57. Worldly Wiseman tells Christian that the way to get rid of his sin burden is to go to Legality. In other words, Worldly Wiseman tells Christian that by obeying God's commands and by being a moral person, he will remove his burden. Yet, according to Scripture, none of us can be justified (righteous in God's sight) by obeying the works of the law. Our sins need to be covered. As Hebrews 9:22 says, there is no remission (forgiveness of sins) without the shedding of blood.

58. Worldly Wiseman suggests that Christian and others like him are "crazed in their wits" over their burdens. In other words, Christian is taking the conviction of sin too seriously. Legality wants to help him by convincing him the burden was not very significant after all. Legality wants to try and ease Christian's conscience.

59. Christian will have a good reputation and be well thought of by his neighbors in the Town of Morality.

Mr. Worldly Wiseman: I thought so; and it has happened unto thee as to other weak men, who, meddling with things too high for them, do suddenly fall into thy distractions; which distractions do not only unman men, as thine I perceive have done thee, but they run them upon desperate ventures, to obtain they know not what.

Christian: I know what I would obtain; it is ease from my heavy burden.

Mr. Worldly Wiseman: But why wilt thou seek for ease this way, seeing so many dangers attend it? especially since (hadst thou but patience to hear me) I could direct thee to the obtaining of what thou desirest, without the dangers that thou in this way wilt run thyself into. Yea, and the remedy is at hand. Besides, I will add, that instead of those dangers, thou shalt meet with much safety, friendship, and content.[56]

Christian: Sir, I pray open this secret to me.

Mr. Worldly Wiseman: Why, in yonder village (the village is named Morality) there dwells a gentleman whose name is Legality,[57] a very judicious man, and a man of a very good name, that has skill to help men off with such burdens as thine is from their shoulders; yea to my knowledge, he hath done a great deal of good this way; aye, and besides, he hath skill to cure those that are somewhat crazed in their wits with their burdens.[58] To him, as I said, thou mayest go, and be helped presently. His house is not quite a mile from this place; and if he should not be at home himself, he hath a pretty young man to his son, whose name is Civility, that can do it (to speak on) as well as the old gentleman himself: there, I say, thou mayest be eased of thy burden; and if thou art not minded to go back to thy former habitation, (as indeed I would not wish thee,) thou mayest send for thy wife and children to this village, where there are houses now standing empty, one of which thou mayest have at a reasonable rate: provision is there also cheap and good; and that which will make thy life the more happy is, to be sure there thou shalt live by honest neighbors, in credit and good fashion.[59]

Now was Christian somewhat at a stand; but presently he concluded, If this be true which this gentleman hath said, my wisest course is to take his advice: and with that he thus farther spake.

Christian: Sir, which is my way to this honest man's house?

Mr. Worldly Wiseman: Do you see yonder high hill?[60]

Christian: Yes, very well.

Mr. Worldly Wiseman: By that hill you must go, and the first house you come at is his.

So Christian turned out of his way to go to Mr. Legality's house for help: but, behold, when he was got now hard by the hill, it seemed so high, and also that side of it that was next the way-side did hang so much over, that Christian was afraid to venture further, lest the hill should fall on his head; wherefore there he stood still, and wotted not what to do.[61] Also his burden now seemed heavier to him[62] than while he was in his way. There came also flashes of fire, Ex. 19:16, 18, out of the hill, that made Christian afraid that he should be burnt:[63] here therefore he did sweat and quake for fear. Heb. 12:21. And now he began to be sorry that he had taken Mr. Worldly Wiseman's counsel; and with that he saw Evangelist coming to meet him, at the sight also of whom he began to blush for shame. So Evangelist drew nearer and nearer; and coming up to him, he looked upon him, with a severe and dreadful countenance, and thus began to reason with Christian.

Evangelist: What doest thou here, Christian? said he: at which words Christian knew not what to answer; wherefore at present he stood speechless before him. Then said Evangelist farther, Art not thou the man that I found crying without the walls of the city of Destruction?

Christian: Yes, dear sir, I am the man.

Evangelist: Did not I direct thee the way to the little wicket-gate?

Christian: Yes, dear sir, said Christian.

Evangelist: How is it then thou art so quickly turned aside? For thou art now out of the way.

60. This hill symbolizes Mt. Sinai where Moses received the Ten Commandments. It stands as a symbol of the law of God, which condemns all men in their sins.

61. "Did not know what to do"

62. The law of God exposes our sin and increases the conviction of sin. Paul describes this effect of the law in Romans 7: "What shall we say then? Is the law sin? God forbid. Nay, I had not known sin, but by the law: for I had not known lust, except the law had said, Thou shalt not covet. But sin, taking occasion by the commandment, wrought in me all manner of concupiscence. For without the law sin was dead. For I was alive without the law once: but when the commandment came, sin revived, and I died." (Rom. 7:7-9)

63. Christian fears the torments of hell.

Christian: I met with a gentleman so soon as I had got over the Slough of Despond, who persuaded me that I might, in the village before me, find a man that could take off my burden.

Evangelist: What was he?

Christian: He looked like a gentleman, and talked much to me, and got me at last to yield: so I came hither; but when I beheld this hill, and how it hangs over the way, I suddenly made a stand, lest it should fall on my head.

Evangelist: What said that gentleman to you?

Christian: Why, he asked me whither I was going; and I told him.

Evangelist: And what said he then?

Christian: He asked me if I had a family; and I told him. But, said I, I am so laden with the burden that is on my back, that I cannot take pleasure in them as formerly.

Evangelist: And what said he then?

Christian: He bid me with speed get rid of my burden; and I told him it was ease that I sought. And, said I, I am therefore going to yonder gate, to receive farther direction how I may get to the place of deliverance. So he said that he would show me a better way, and short, not so attended with difficulties as the way, sir, that you set me in; which way, said he, will direct you to a gentleman's house that hath skill to take off these burdens: so I believed him, and turned out of that way into this, if haply I might be soon eased of my burden. But when I came to this place, and beheld things as they are, I stopped, for fear (as I said) of danger: but I now know not what to do.

Evangelist: Then said Evangelist, Stand still a little, that I show thee the words of God. So he stood trembling. Then said Evangelist, "See that ye refuse not Him that speaketh; for if they escaped not who refused him that spake on earth, much more shall not we escape, if we turn away from Him that speaketh from heaven." Heb. 12:25. He said, moreover, "Now the just shall live by faith; but if any man draw back, my soul shall have no pleasure in him." Heb. 10:38. He also did thus apply them: Thou art the man that art running into this misery; thou hast begun to reject the counsel of the Most High, and to draw back thy foot from the way of peace, even almost to the hazarding of thy perdition.[64]

Then Christian fell down at his feet as dead, crying, Woe is me, for I am undone! At the sight of which Evangelist caught him by the right hand, saying, "All manner of sin and blasphemies shall be forgiven unto men." Matt. 12:31. "Be not faithless, but believing." John 20:27. Then did Christian again a little revive, and stood up trembling, as at first, before Evangelist.

Then Evangelist proceeded, saying, Give more earnest heed to the things that I shall tell thee of. I will now show thee who it was that deluded thee, and who it was also to whom he sent thee. The man that met thee is one Worldly Wiseman, and rightly is he so called; partly because he savoreth only the doctrine of this world, 1 John 4:5, (therefore he always goes to the town of Morality to church;)[65] and partly because he loveth that doctrine best, for it saveth him best from the cross,[66] Gal. 6:12: and because he is of this carnal temper,[67] therefore he seeketh to pervert my ways, though right. Now there are three things in this man's counsel that thou must utterly abhor.

1. His turning thee out of the way.

2. His laboring to render the cross odious to thee.

3. And his setting thy feet in that way that leadeth unto the administration of death.[68]

First, Thou must abhor his turning thee out of the way; yea, and thine own consenting thereto; because this is to reject the counsel of God for the sake of the counsel of a Worldly Wiseman. The Lord says, "Strive to enter in at the straight gate," Luke 13:24, the gate to which I send thee; "for strait is the gate that leadeth unto life, and few there be that find it." Matt. 7:13,14. From this little wicket-gate, and from the way thereto, hath this wicked man turned thee, to the bringing of thee almost to destruction: hate, therefore, his turning thee out of the way, and abhor thyself for hearkening to him.

64. "Risk of your damnation"

65. We learn that Mr. Worldly Wiseman is a churchgoer who does not receive the gospel, but believes he will be saved by his good morality.

66. He does not have to receive Christ's sacrificial atonement on the cross, and he does not have to take up his own cross in following Jesus.

67. "Fleshly character"

68. Paul refers to the Law of Moses as a "ministry of death" in 2 Corinthians 3. "But if the ministration of death, written and engraven in stones, was glorious, so that the children of Israel could not stedfastly behold the face of Moses for the glory of his countenance; which glory was to be done away: How shall not the ministration of the spirit be rather glorious?" (2 Cor. 3:7-8)

Secondly, Thou must abhor his laboring to render the cross odious unto thee; for thou art to prefer it before the treasures of Egypt. Heb. 11:25,26. Besides, the King of glory hath told thee, that he that will save his life shall lose it. And he that comes after him, and hates not his father, and mother, and wife, and children, and brethren, and sisters, yea, and his own life also, he cannot be his disciple. Mark 8:38; John 12:25; Matt. 10:39; Luke 14:26. I say, therefore, for a man to labor to persuade thee that that shall be thy death, without which, the truth hath said, thou canst not have eternal life, this doctrine thou must abhor.

Thirdly, Thou must hate his setting of thy feet in the way that leadeth to the administration of death. And for this thou must consider to whom he sent thee, and also how unable that person was to deliver thee from thy burden.[69]

69. No one can remove the debt of sin by good works. As Paul says in Ephesians 2:9, "not of works, lest any man should boast."

He to whom thou wast sent for ease, being by name Legality, is the son of the bond-woman which now is, and is in bondage with her children, Gal. 4:21-27, and is, in a mystery, this Mount Sinai, which thou hast feared will fall on thy head. Now if she with her children are in bondage, how canst thou expect by them to be made free?[70] This Legality, therefore, is not able to set thee free from thy burden. No man was as yet ever rid of his burden by him; no, nor ever is like to be: ye cannot be justified by the works of the law; for by the deeds of the law no man living can be rid of his burden: Therefore Mr. Worldly Wiseman is an alien, and Mr. Legality is a cheat; and for his son Civility, notwithstanding his simpering looks,[71] he is but a hypocrite, and cannot help thee. Believe me, there is nothing in all this noise that thou hast heard of these sottish men, but a design to beguile thee of thy salvation, by turning thee from the way in which I had set thee. After this, Evangelist called aloud to the heavens for confirmation of what he had said; and with that there came words and fire out of the mountain under which poor Christian stood, which made the hair of his flesh stand up. The words were pronounced: "As many as are of the works of the law, are under the curse;

70. If those who rely on works of the law are under a curse (Gal. 3:10) and are enslaved, then there is no way that Legality could help Christian get rid of his burden.

71. "A smile or gesture in a fake or hypocritical way"

for it is written, Cursed is every one that continueth not in all things which are written in the book of the law to do them." Gal. 3:10.

Now Christian looked for nothing but death, and began to cry out lamentably; even cursing the time in which he met with Mr. Worldly Wiseman; still calling himself a thousand fools for hearkening to his counsel. He also was greatly ashamed to think that this gentleman's arguments, flowing only from the flesh, should have the prevalency with him so far as to cause him to forsake the right way. This done, he applied himself again to Evangelist in words and sense as follows.

Christian: Sir, what think you? Is there any hope? May I now go back, and go up to the wicket-gate? Shall I not be abandoned for this, and sent back from thence ashamed? I am sorry I have hearkened to this man's counsel; but may my sin be forgiven?

Evangelist: Then said Evangelist to him, Thy sin is very great, for by it thou hast committed two evils: thou hast forsaken the way that is good, to tread in forbidden paths. Yet will the man at the gate receive thee, for he has good-will for men; only, said he, take heed that thou turn not aside again, lest thou "perish from the way, when his wrath is kindled but a little." Psalm 2:12.

Book 1

Chapter 2

Then did Christian address himself to go back; and Evangelist, after he had kissed him, gave him one smile, and bid him God speed; So he went on with haste, neither spake he to any man by the way; nor if any asked him, would he vouchsafe them an answer. He went like one that was all the while treading on forbidden ground, and could by no means think himself safe, till again he was got into the way which he had left to follow Mr. Worldly Wiseman's counsel. So, in process of time, Christian got up to the gate. Now, over the gate there was written, "Knock, and it shall be opened unto you." Matt. 7:7.

He knocked, therefore, more than once or twice, saying,
"May I now enter here? Will he within
Open to sorry me, though I have been
An undeserving rebel? Then shall I
Not fail to sing his lasting praise on high."

At last there came a grave person[1] to the gate, named Goodwill, who asked who was there, and whence he came, and what he would have.

Christian: Here is a poor burdened sinner. I come from the city of Destruction, but am going to Mount Zion,[2] that I may be delivered from the wrath to come; I would therefore,

1. "A solemn or serious person"

2. The Celestial City is referred to here as Mount Zion, the heavenly Jerusalem. This language derives from the Book of Hebrews: "But ye are come unto mount Sion, and unto the city of the living God, the heavenly Jerusalem, and to an innumerable company of angels, to the general assembly and church of the firstborn, which are written in heaven, and to God the Judge of all, and to the spirits of just men made perfect,..." (Heb. 12:22-23)

sir, since I am informed that by this gate is the way thither, know if you are willing to let me in.

Goodwill: I am willing with all my heart,[3] said he; and with that he opened the gate.

So when Christian was stepping in, the other gave him a pull. Then said Christian, What means that? The other told him, A little distance from this gate there is erected a strong castle, of which Beelzebub[4] is the captain: from thence both he and they that are with him, shoot arrows at those that come up to this gate, if haply they may die before they can enter in.[5] Then said Christian, I rejoice and tremble. So when he was got in, the man of the Gate asked him who directed him thither.

Christian: Evangelist bid me come hither and knock, as I did: and he said, that you, sir, would tell me what I must do.

Goodwill: An open door is set before thee, and no man can shut it.[6]

Christian: Now I begin to reap the benefits of my hazards.

Goodwill: But how is it that you came alone?

Christian: Because none of my neighbors saw their danger as I saw mine.

Goodwill: Did any of them know of your coming?

Christian: Yes, my wife and children saw me at the first, and called after me to turn again: also, some of my neighbors stood crying and calling after me to return; but I put my fingers in my ears, and so came on my way.

Goodwill: But did none of them follow you, to persuade you to go back?

Christian: Yes, both Obstinate and Pliable; but when they saw that they could not prevail, Obstinate went railing back; but Pliable came with me a little way.

Goodwill: But why did he not come through?

3. Goodwill represents God's gracious response to sinners who come in faith and repentance. Even though Christian had sinned in turning away from the way and seeking to get rid of his burden in the Town of Morality, yet all those who come to Christ will not be refused. Our Lord says in John 6, "All that the Father giveth me shall come to me; and him that cometh to me I will in no wise cast out." (John 6:37)

4. "Beelzebub" is a Hebrew word meaning "Lord of the flies." Bunyan uses the word to refer to Satan. The word is used the same way in the Gospels (Matt. 12:24-27).

5. In the Parable of the Sower, Jesus refers to the seed sowed by the wayside. This seed is snatched quickly by Satan so that it cannot take root. "When any one heareth the word of the kingdom, and understandeth it not, then cometh the wicked one, and catcheth away that which was sown in his heart. This is he which received seed by the way side." (Matt. 13:19)

6. "I know thy works: behold, I have set before thee an open door, and no man can shut it: for thou hast a little strength, and hast kept my word, and hast not denied my name." (Rev. 3:8)

Christian: We indeed came both together until we came to the Slough of Despond, into the which we also suddenly fell. And then was my neighbor Pliable discouraged, and would not venture farther. Wherefore, getting out again on the side next to his own house, he told me I should possess the brave country alone for him: so he went his way, and I came mine; he after Obstinate, and I to this gate.

Goodwill: Then said Goodwill, Alas, poor man; is the celestial glory of so little esteem with him, that he counteth it not worth running the hazard of a few difficulties to obtain it?

Christian: Truly, said Christian, I have said the truth of Pliable; and if I should also say all the truth of myself, it will appear there is no betterment betwixt him and myself.[7] It is true, he went back to his own house, but I also turned aside to go in the way of death, being persuaded thereto by the carnal arguments of one Mr. Worldly Wiseman.

Goodwill: Oh, did he light upon you? What, he would have had you seek for ease at the hands of Mr. Legality! They are both of them a very cheat. But did you take his counsel?

Christian: Yes, as far as I durst. I went to find out Mr. Legality, until I thought that the mountain that stands by his house would have fallen upon my head; wherefore there I was forced to stop.

Goodwill: That mountain has been the death of many, and will be the death of many more: it is well you escaped being by it dashed in pieces.

Christian: Why truly I do not know what had become of me there, had not Evangelist happily met me again as I was musing in the midst of my dumps;[8] but it was God's mercy that he came to me again, for else I had never come hither. But now I am come, such a one as I am, more fit indeed for death by that mountain, than thus to stand talking with my Lord. But O, what a favor is this to me, that yet I am admitted entrance here!

Goodwill: We make no objections against any, notwithstanding all that they have done before they come hither; they

7. "I am not any better than he"

8. "Depressed" or "unhappy"

in no wise are cast out. John 6:37. And therefore good Christian, come a little way with me, and I will teach thee about the way thou must go. Look before thee; dost thou see this narrow way? That is the way thou must go. It was cast up by the patriarchs, prophets, Christ, and his apostles,[9] and it is as strait as a rule can make it; this is the way thou must go.

Christian: But, said Christian, are there no turnings nor windings, by which a stranger may lose his way?

Goodwill: Yes, there are many ways butt down upon this, and they are crooked and wide: but thus thou mayest distinguish the right from the wrong, the right only being strait and narrow.[10] Matt. 7:14.

Then I saw in my dream, that Christian asked him further, if he could not help him off with his burden that was upon his back. For as yet he had not got rid thereof; nor could he by any means get it off without help.

He told him, "As to thy burden, be content to bear it until thou comest to the place of deliverance; for there it will fall from thy back of itself."

Then Christian began to gird up his loins, and to address himself to his journey. So the other told him, that by that he was gone some distance from the gate, he would come to the house of the Interpreter,[11] at whose door he should knock, and he would show him excellent things. Then Christian took his leave of his friend, and he again bid him God speed.

Then he went on till he came at the house of the Interpreter, where he knocked over and over.[12] At last one came to the door, and asked who was there.

Christian: Sir, here is a traveller, who was bid by an acquaintance of the good man of this house to call here for my profit; I would therefore speak with the master of the house.

So he called for the master of the house, who, after a little time, came to Christian, and asked him what he would have.

Christian: Sir, said Christian, I am a man that am come from the city of Destruction, and am going to the Mount Zion; and I was told by the man that stands at the gate at the

9. The narrow way of salvation in Jesus Christ has been the same way of faith since the very beginning. Abraham and the other patriarchs were saved by faith (see Heb. 11). They trusted in God for the promised future Messiah. They walked the narrow path that Jesus refers to in Matthew 7:13-14.

10. Any detour off the narrow path is to be avoided by Christian. Only the narrow path that is straight is the way to the Celestial City.

11. Bunyan uses the "Interpreter" as a symbol of the Holy Spirit. The House of the Interpreter precedes Christian's conversion. Christian must first have a knowledge of divine truth revealed by the Spirit of God. At this house, Christian will learn some of the most important truths of Holy Scripture.

12. Jesus instructed us in Matthew 7: "Ask, and it shall be given you; seek, and ye shall find; knock, and it shall be opened unto you: For every one that asketh receiveth; and he that seeketh findeth; and to him that knocketh it shall be opened." (Matt. 7:7-8)

13. The Holy Spirit brings light to the dark soul, by revealing truth. "The entrance of thy words giveth light; It giveth understanding unto the simple." (Ps. 119:130)

14. The first image Christian encounters is this picture on the wall of a very grave (or sober) person, with his eyes lifted to heaven, the Bible in his hand, pleading with men. This is a picture of God's ministers of the gospel, called to preach the Word. Pastors ordained to this ministry are to be ministers of the Word, having the truth on their lips. They are to plead with the world "be ye reconciled to God." (2 Cor. 5:20)

15. God's ministers do not labor for worldly treasures or renown. Instead, from the Lord they will receive the "unfading crown of glory." (1 Pet. 5:4)

16. The Lord, in His mercy, gives us shepherd/teachers who can guide us on the pilgrim path to heaven. They minister the Word of God to us, showing us the way we should go (Eph. 4:11-16).

head of this way, that if I called here you would show me excellent things, such as would be helpful to me on my journey.

Interpreter: Then said Interpreter, Come in; I will show thee that which will be profitable to thee. So he commanded his man to light the candle,[13] and bid Christian follow him; so he had him into a private room, and bid his man open a door; the which when he had done, Christian saw the picture a very grave person hang up against the wall; and this was the fashion of it: It had eyes lifted up to heaven, the best of books in his hand, the law of truth was written upon its lips, the world was behind its back; it stood as if it pleaded with men, and a crown of gold did hang over its head.[14]

Christian: Then said Christian, What means this?

Interpreter: The man whose picture this is, is one of a thousand: he can beget children, 1 Cor. 4:15, travail in birth with children, Gal. 4:19, and nurse them himself when they are born. And whereas thou seest him with his eyes lift up to heaven, the best of books in his hand, and the law of truth writ on his lips: it is to show thee, that his work is to know, and unfold dark things to sinners; even as also thou seest him stand as if he pleaded with men. And whereas thou seest the world as cast behind him, and that a crown hangs over his head; that is to show thee, that slighting and despising the things that are present, for the love that he hath to his Master's service, he is sure in the world that comes next, to have glory for his reward.[15] Now, said the Interpreter, I have showed thee this picture first, because the man whose picture this is, is the only man whom the Lord of the place whither thou art going hath authorized to be thy guide in all difficult places[16] thou mayest meet with in the way: wherefore take good heed to what I have showed thee, and bear well in thy mind what thou hast seen, lest in thy journey thou meet with some that pretend to lead thee right,[17] but their way goes down to death.

Then he took him by the hand, and led him into a very large parlor that was full of dust, because never swept; the which after he had reviewed it a little while, the Interpreter called for a man to sweep. Now, when he began to sweep, the dust began so abundantly to fly about, that Christian had almost therewith been choked. Then said the Interpreter to a damsel that stood by, "Bring hither water, and sprinkle the room;" the which when she had done, it was swept and cleansed with pleasure.

Christian: Then said Christian, What means this?

Interpreter: The Interpreter answered, This parlor is the heart of a man that was never sanctified by the sweet grace of the Gospel. The dust is his original sin,[18] and inward corruptions, that have defiled the whole man. He that began to sweep at first, is the law; but she that brought water, and did sprinkle it, is the Gospel. Now whereas thou sawest, that so soon as the first began to sweep, the dust did so fly about that the room by him could not be cleansed, but that thou wast almost choked therewith; this is to show thee, that the law, instead of cleansing the heart (by its working) from sin, doth revive,[19] Rom. 7:9, put strength into, 1 Cor. 15:56, and increase

17. The Scriptures repeatedly warn against false teachers leading us astray. This is what the Apostle Paul warned about as he left Ephesus. "For I know this, that after my departing shall grievous wolves enter in among you, not sparing the flock. Also of your own selves shall men arise, speaking perverse things, to draw away disciples after them. Therefore watch, and remember, that by the space of three years I ceased not to warn every one night and day with tears." (Acts 20:29-31)

18. The Interpreter explains that the dust in the parlor is the remaining sin of the human heart. The law of God makes the dust to fly about the room, but doesn't remove the dust.

19. The law of God exposes our sin, but it has no power to cleanse the human heart. Paul describes this effect of the law upon his sin in Romans 7. "What shall we say then? Is the law sin? God forbid. Nay, I had not known sin, but by the law: for I had not known lust, except the law had said, Thou shalt not covet. But sin, taking occasion by the commandment, wrought in me all manner of concupiscence. For without the law sin was dead. For I was alive without the law once: but when the commandment came, sin revived, and I died." (Rom. 7:7-9)

20. The law itself gives no power to overcome sin. Apart from the Lord Jesus, each of us are naturally slaves to sin (John 8:34). It is only by faith in the sacrificial death of the Lord Jesus that our sin can be taken away. Jesus is the lamb of God who takes away the sins of the world (John 1:29).

21. When the cleansing water of the gospel comes into the heart, by the work of the Holy Spirit, it brings real power to subdue sin. As Paul writes in Romans 8, we mortify (kill) the sinful deeds of the flesh by the Spirit (Rom. 8:13).

22. Two characters are introduced by the names Passion and Patience. Passion represents the man whose fleshly desires rule him. He must have what he wants right away. According to the Interpreter, Passion is the men of this world who look for their hope in this life. But Patience is the heavenly man who looks to the world to come.

it in the soul, Rom. 5:20, even as it doth discover and forbid it; for it doth not give power to subdue.[20] Again, as thou sawest the damsel sprinkle the room with water, upon which it was cleansed with pleasure, this is to show thee, that when the Gospel comes in the sweet and precious influences thereof to the heart, then, I say, even as thou sawest the damsel lay the dust by sprinkling the floor with water, so is sin vanquished and subdued,[21] and the soul made clean, through the faith of it, and consequently fit for the King of glory to inhabit. John 15:3; Eph. 5:26; Acts 15:9; Rom. 16:25,26.

I saw moreover in my dream, that the Interpreter took him by the hand, and had him into a little room, where sat two little children, each one in his chair. The name of the eldest was Passion, and the name of the other Patience.[22] Passion seemed to be much discontented, but Patience was very quiet. Then Christian asked, "What is the reason of the discontent of Passion?" The Interpreter answered, "The governor of them would have him stay for his best things till the beginning of the next year, but he will have all now; but Patience is willing to wait."

Then I saw that one came to Passion, and brought him a bag of treasure, and poured it down at his feet: the which he took up, and rejoiced therein, and withal laughed Patience to scorn. But I beheld but a while, and he had lavished all away, and had nothing left him but rags.

Christian: Then said Christian to the Interpreter, Expound this matter more fully to me.

Interpreter: So he said, These two lads are figures; Passion of the men of this world, and Patience of the men of that which is to come; for, as here thou seest, passion will have all now, this year, that is to say, in this world; so are the men of this world: They must have all their good things now; they cannot stay till the next year, that is, until the next world, for their portion of good. That proverb, "A bird in the hand is worth two in the bush," is of more authority with them than are all the divine testimonies of the good of the world to come.

But as thou sawest that he had quickly lavished all away, and had presently left him nothing but rags, so will it be with all such men at the end of this world.

Christian: Then said Christian, Now I see that Patience has the best wisdom,[23] and that upon many accounts. 1. Because he stays for the best things. 2. And also because he will have the glory of his, when the other has nothing but rags.

Interpreter: Nay, you may add another, to wit, the glory of the next world will never wear out; but these are suddenly gone. Therefore Passion had not so much reason to laugh at Patience because he had his good things first, as Patience will have to laugh at Passion because he had his best things last; for first must give place to last, because last must have his time to come: but last gives place to nothing, for there is not another to succeed. He, therefore, that hath his portion first, must needs have a time to spend it; but he that hath his portion last, must have it lastingly: therefore it is said of Dives, "In thy lifetime thou receivedst thy good things, and likewise Lazarus evil things; but now he is comforted, and thou art tormented." Luke 16:25.

Christian: Then I perceive it is not best to covet things that are now, but to wait for things to come.

Interpreter: You say truth: for the things that are seen are temporal, but the things that are not seen are eternal. 2 Cor. 4:18. But though this be so, yet since things present and our fleshly appetite are such near neighbors one to another; and again, because things to come and carnal sense are such strangers one to another; therefore it is, that the first of these so suddenly fall into amity, and that distance is so continued between the second.

Then I saw in my dream, that the Interpreter took Christian by the hand, and led him into a place where was a fire burning against a wall, and one standing by it, always casting much water upon it, to quench it; yet did the fire burn higher and hotter.

23. Patience demonstrates his wisdom by looking to the things to come in glory. It is only those things that will really last. Ultimately, the men of this world will come to "rags" and suffer eternal destruction.

24. The effectual work of God's Holy Spirit in the heart cannot be extinguished. It is a fire that will burn forever, even though Satan tries his best to extinguish the flame of spiritual life.

25. The "oil" is the work of grace wherein our Lord Jesus Christ continually applies His work of redemption to us. We are promised in Scripture that Jesus will not lose any of his sheep (John 10:28-29). But we must remember that the work of grace in our hearts cannot be maintained by our own power. We need God's grace daily.

26. These are the men and women who have gone to glory.

Then said Christian, What means this?

The Interpreter answered, This fire is the work of grace[24] that is wrought in the heart; he that casts water upon it, to extinguish and put it out, is the devil: but in that thou seest the fire, notwithstanding, burn higher and hotter, thou shalt also see the reason of that. So he had him about to the back side of the wall, where he saw a man with a vessel of oil in his hand, of the which he did also continually cast (but secretly) into the fire.

Then said Christian, What means this?

The Interpreter answered, This is Christ, who continually, with the oil of his grace, maintains the work already begun in the heart;[25] by the means of which, notwithstanding what the devil can do, the souls of his people prove gracious still. 2 Cor. 12:9. And in that thou sawest that the man stood behind the wall to maintain the fire; this is to teach thee, that it is hard for the tempted to see how this work of grace is maintained in the soul.

I saw also, that the Interpreter took him again by the hand, and led him into a pleasant place, where was built a stately palace, beautiful to behold; at the sight of which Christian was greatly delighted. He saw also upon the top thereof certain persons walking, who were clothed all in gold.[26]

Then said Christian may we go in thither?

Then the Interpreter took him, and led him up towards the door of the palace; and behold, at the door stood a great company of men, as desirous to go in, but durst not. There also sat a man at a little distance from the door, at a table-side, with a book and his inkhorn before him, to take the names of them that should enter therein; he saw also that in the door-way stood many men in armor to keep it, being resolved to do to the men that would enter, what hurt and mischief they could. Now was Christian somewhat in amaze. At last, when every man started back for fear of the armed men, Christian saw a man of a very stout countenance come up to the man that sat there to write, saying, "Set down my name, sir;" the which when he had done, he saw the man draw his sword, and put a helmet on his head, and rush towards the door upon the armed men, who laid upon him with deadly force; but the man, not at all discouraged, fell to cutting and hacking most fiercely. So after he had received and given many wounds to those that attempted to keep him out, Matt. 11:12; Acts 14:22; he cut his way through them all, and pressed forward into the palace;[27] at which there was a pleasant voice heard from those that were within, even of those that walked upon the top of the palace, saying,

"Come in, come in,
Eternal glory thou shalt win."

So he went in, and was clothed with such garments as they. Then Christian smiled, and said, I think verily I know the meaning of this.

Now, said Christian, let me go hence. Nay, stay, said the Interpreter, till I have showed thee a little more, and after that thou shalt go on thy way. So he took him by the hand again, and led him into a very dark room, where there sat a man in an iron cage.[28]

Now the man, to look on, seemed very sad; he sat with his eyes looking down to the ground, his hands folded together, and he sighed as if he would break his heart. Then said Christian, What means this? At which the Interpreter bid him talk with the man.

Then said Christian to the man, What art thou? The man answered, I am what I was not once.

Christian: What wast thou once?

The Man: The man said, I was once a fair and flourishing professor,[29] Luke 8:13, both in mine own eyes, and also in the eyes of others: I once was, as I thought, fair for the celestial city, and had then even joy at the thoughts that I should get thither.

Christian: Well, but what art thou now?

The Man: I am now a man of despair, and am shut up in it, as in this iron cage. I cannot get out; Oh now I cannot!

27. The man who assaults the gates of heaven represents the "holy violence" with which we must press into the kingdom. Those who would inherit eternal glory must fight the good fight of faith (2 Tim. 4:7-8). Bunyan may have had in mind the words of Jesus from Matthew 11: "And from the days of John the Baptist until now the kingdom of heaven suffereth violence, and the violent take it by force." (Matt. 11:12)

28. This next symbol of the man in the iron cage is designed to teach Christian watchfulness and caution on the pilgrim path.

29. This man once professed the true faith, and even seemed to "flourish," but it was no longer his condition. Jesus describes the rocky ground in Luke 8: "They on the rock are they, which, when they hear, receive the word with joy; and these have no root, which for a while believe, and in time of temptation fall away." (Luke 8:13)

30. Bunyan uses this symbol of the man in the iron cage to illustrate the dangers of apostasy. The Scriptures describe those who appeared to have saving faith and may have even been baptized, professing members of the church for a time, but fall away. According to Hebrews 6, it is impossible to restore such a person. "For it is impossible for those who were once enlightened, and have tasted of the heavenly gift, and were made partakers of the Holy Ghost, And have tasted the good word of God, and the powers of the world to come, If they shall fall away, to renew them again unto repentance; seeing they crucify to themselves the Son of God afresh, and put him to an open shame." (Heb. 6:4-6)

Christian: But how camest thou into this condition?

The Man: I left off to watch and be sober: I laid the reins upon the neck of my lusts; I sinned against the light of the word, and the goodness of God; I have grieved the Spirit, and he is gone; I tempted the devil, and he is come to me; I have provoked God to anger, and he has left me: I have so hardened my heart, that I cannot repent.[30]

Then said Christian to the Interpreter, But is there no hope for such a man as this? Ask him, said the Interpreter.

Christian: Then said Christian, Is there no hope, but you must be kept in the iron cage of despair?

The Man: No, none at all.

Christian: Why, the Son of the Blessed is very pitiful.

The Man: I have crucified him to myself afresh, Heb. 6:6; I have despised his person, Luke 19:14; I have despised his righteousness; I have counted his blood an unholy thing; I have done despite to the spirit of grace, Heb. 10:29: therefore I have shut myself out of all the promises[31] and there now remains to me nothing but threatenings, dreadful threatenings, faithful threatenings of certain judgment and fiery indignation, which shall devour me as an adversary.

Christian: For what did you bring yourself into this condition?

The Man: For the lusts, pleasures, and profits of this world; in the enjoyment of which I did then promise myself much

31. The apostasy described here is a final and irremediable apostasy. It is important to remember that true believers may, for a time, fall away from the truth and sin against God. The Apostle Peter is one such example who publicly denied the Lord Jesus Christ. Yet, he was restored because he repented. There are some who, according to Hebrews 6 and Hebrews 10, apostatize and will never come to repentance.

delight: but now every one of those things also bite me, and gnaw me like a burning worm.[32]

Christian: But canst thou not now repent and turn?

The Man: God hath denied me repentance. His word gives me no encouragement to believe; yea, himself hath shut me up in this iron cage: nor can all the men in the world let me out. Oh eternity! eternity! how shall I grapple with the misery that I must meet with in eternity?

Interpreter: Then said the Interpreter to Christian, Let this man's misery be remembered by thee, and be an everlasting caution to thee.

Christian: Well, said Christian, this is fearful! God help me to watch and to be sober,[33] and to pray that I may shun the cause of this man's misery. Sir, is it not time for me to go on my way now?

Interpreter: Tarry till I shall show thee one thing more, and then thou shalt go on thy way.

So he took Christian by the hand again and led him into a chamber where there was one rising out of bed; and as he put on his raiment, he shook and trembled. Then said Christian, Why doth this man thus tremble? The Interpreter then bid him tell to Christian the reason of his so doing.

So he began, and said, "This night, as I was in my sleep, I dreamed, and behold the heavens grew exceeding black; also it thundered and lightened in most fearful wise, that it put me into an agony. So I looked up in my dream, and saw the clouds rack at an unusual rate; upon which I heard a great sound of a trumpet, and saw also a man sitting upon a cloud, attended with the thousands of heaven: they were all in flaming fire; also the heavens were in a burning flame. I heard then a voice, saying, 'Arise, ye dead, and come to judgment.' And with that the rocks rent, the graves opened, and the dead that were therein came forth: some of them were exceeding glad, and looked upward; and some sought to hide themselves under the mountains. Then I saw the man that sat upon the cloud open the book, and bid the world draw near. Yet there was, by

32. This man's love for the things of this world shows that his heart was never truly changed to begin with. He may have professed belief, but his heart was never changed. Ultimately, he did not love God but loved the things of this world. But the final end of his sinful lusts is eternal condemnation. The example of the man in the iron cage who cannot repent, as well as the biblical teaching of apostasy that cannot be remedied, can never be used as an excuse for others not to repent. We must always present the free grace of the gospel, even to the most hardened sinners. It is for God to grant repentance. These examples of apostasy are designed to warn us against a lack of watchfulness and sobriety.

33. That is, the man failed to be watchful and sober.

reason of a fierce flame that issued out and came from before him, a convenient distance between him and them, as between the judge and the prisoners at the bar. 1 Cor. 15; 1 Thess. 4:16; Jude 15; John 5: 28,29; 2 Thess. 1:8-10; Rev. 20:11-14; Isa. 26:21; Micah 7:16,17; Psa. 5:4; 50:1-3; Mal. 3:2,3; Dan. 7:9,10. I heard it also proclaimed to them that attended on the man that sat on the cloud, 'Gather together the tares, the chaff, and stubble, and cast them into the burning lake.' Matt. 3:12; 18:30; 24:30; Mal. 4:1. And with that the bottomless pit opened, just whereabout I stood; out of the mouth of which there came, in an abundant manner, smoke, and coals of fire, with hideous noises. It was also said to the same persons, 'Gather my wheat into the garner.' Luke 3:17. And with that I saw many catched up and carried away into the clouds, but I was left behind. 1 Thess. 4:16,17. I also sought to hide myself, but I could not, for the man that sat upon the cloud still kept his eye upon me; my sins also came into my mind, and my conscience did accuse me on every side. Rom. 2:14,15. Upon this I awakened from my sleep."

Christian: But what was it that made you so afraid of this sight?

The Man: Why, I thought that the day of judgment was come,[34] and that I was not ready for it: but this frightened me most, that the angels gathered up several, and left me behind; also the pit of hell opened her mouth just where I stood. My conscience too afflicted me; and, as I thought, the Judge had always his eye upon me, showing indignation in his countenance.

Then said the Interpreter to Christian, "Hast thou considered all these things?"

Christian: Yes, and they put me in hope and fear.[35]

Interpreter: Well, keep all things so in thy mind, that they may be as a goad in thy sides, to prick thee forward in the way thou must go. Then Christian began to gird up his loins, and to address himself to his journey. Then said the Interpreter, "The Comforter be always with thee, good Christian, to guide

34. This final symbol is of a man dreaming about the day of judgment. The warnings of divine judgment in Holy Scripture should cause us to be watchful, sober, and always ready for the final day. The day will come unexpectedly.

35. There is a healthy, godly fear of the Lord that Christians should cultivate. The Psalmist says in Psalm 119: "My flesh trembleth for fear of thee; and I am afraid of thy judgments" (Ps. 119:120). Yet godly fear must be mixed with the hope of the gospel and confidence of our salvation in Jesus.

thee in the way that leads to the city." So Christian went on
his way, saying,

"Here I have seen things rare and profitable,
Things pleasant, dreadful, things to make me stable
In what I have begun to take in hand:
Then let me think on them, and understand
Wherefore they showed me were, and let me be
Thankful, O good Interpreter, to thee."

Book 1
Chapter 3

1. Christian arrives at the foot of the cross of Jesus Christ. Below it is the "sepulchre," or the tomb where Christ was laid for three days.

2. The burden of sin has now fallen from the shoulders of Christian. Through the death and resurrection of Jesus Christ, the debt of sin is removed.

3. Christian's sins have been forgiven. He now experiences rest. Through the resurrection of Jesus Christ, he now has life. "Knowing this, that our old man is crucified with him, that the body of sin might be destroyed, that henceforth we should not serve sin. For he that is dead is freed from sin. Now if we be dead with Christ, we believe that we shall also live with him:..." (Rom. 6:6-8)

Now I saw in my dream, that the highway up which Christian was to go, was fenced on either side with a wall, and that wall was called Salvation. Isaiah 26:1. Up this way, therefore, did burdened Christian run, but not without great difficulty, because of the load on his back.

He ran thus till he came at a place somewhat ascending; and upon that place stood a cross, and a little below, in the bottom, a sepulchre.[1] So I saw in my dream, that just as Christian came up with the cross, his burden loosed from off his shoulders, and fell from off his back, and began to tumble, and so continued to do till it came to the mouth of the sepulchre, where it fell in, and I saw it no more.[2]

Then was Christian glad and lightsome, and said with a merry heart, "He hath given me rest by his sorrow, and life by his death."[3] Then he stood still a while, to look and wonder; for it was very surprising to him that the sight of the cross should thus ease him of his burden. He looked, therefore, and looked again, even till the springs that were in his head sent the waters down his cheeks. Zech. 12:10. Now as he stood looking and weeping, behold, three Shining Ones came to him, and saluted him with, "Peace be to thee." So the first said to him, "Thy sins be forgiven thee," Mark 2:5; the second stripped him of his rags, and clothed him with change of raiment, Zech.

3:4; the third also set a mark on his forehead, Eph. 1:13, and gave him a roll with a seal upon it,[4] which he bid him look on as he ran, and that he should give it in at the celestial gate: so they went their way. Then Christian gave three leaps for joy, and went on singing,

"Thus far did I come laden with my sin,
Nor could aught ease the grief that I was in,
Till I came hither. What a place is this!
Must here be the beginning of my bliss?
Must here the burden fall from off my back?
Must here the strings that bound it to me crack?
Blest cross! blest sepulchre! blest rather be
The Man that there was put to shame for me!"

I saw then in my dream, that he went on thus, even until he came at the bottom, where he saw, a little out of the way, three men fast asleep, with fetters upon their heels. The name of the one was Simple, of another Sloth, and of the third Presumption.[5]

Christian then seeing them lie in this case, went to them, if peradventure[6] he might awake them, and cried, you are like them that sleep on the top of a mast, Prov. 23:34, for the Dead Sea is under you, a gulf that hath no bottom: awake, therefore, and come away; be willing also, and I will help you off with your irons. He also told them, If he that goeth about like a roaring lion, 1 Pet. 5:8, comes by, you will certainly become a prey to his teeth. With that they looked upon him, and began to reply in this sort: Simple said, I see no danger;[7] Sloth said, Yet a little more sleep;[8] and Presumption said, Every tub must

4. Three angels appear and bestow three blessings of salvation in Christ. The first angel declares peace to Christian because his sins are forgiven. The second angel strips him of his "rags" symbolizing his old sins, and clothes him in the righteousness of Christ. The third angel seals him with a mark on his forehead. This seal is the sealing of the Holy Spirit (Eph. 1:13) guaranteeing as an "earnest" or "down-payment" of the salvation he received. Christian also receives a roll from the third angel. This roll would serve to assure him of his salvation. Later in the story, Christian will retrieve the roll from his bosom to "comfort" himself in the assurance of his salvation.

6. "If by chance"

---

5. Christian encounters three men sleeping who are designated as being "simple," "slothful," and "presumptive." Not only are they asleep, but they have "fetters" (chains) on their heels. This is the picture of men who do not esteem the great salvation of Christ, but due to their slothfulness, their presumption, or their simple-mindedness, are still asleep.

7. This man is "simple" because he foolishly does not consider the reality of the situation. He is fettered by his foolishness.

8. This man is fettered by his laziness. He cannot walk in the Christian life because he is a lazy man, bound in sin.

9. This means "every man must rely upon himself."

10. There is a spiritual battle going on. When people pretend as if there is no danger, they are in a very dangerous condition. Let us take seriously the warning of 1 Peter 5:8: "Be sober, be vigilant; because your adversary the devil walks about like a roaring lion, seeking whom he may devour."

11. These men are examples of people who have participated in the external elements of the faith such as attending church, praying, and reading the Scriptures, but they are not truly converted. They merely follow the "form," and they are hypocrites because they are not true believers in what they actually profess.

stand upon its own bottom.[9] And so they lay down to sleep again, and Christian went on his way.

Yet he was troubled to think that men in that danger[10] should so little esteem the kindness of him that so freely offered to help them, both by awakening of them, counselling of them, and proffering to help them off with their irons. And as he was troubled thereabout, he espied two men come tumbling over the wall, on the left hand of the narrow way; and they made up apace to him. The name of the one was Formalist, and the name of the other Hypocrisy.[11] So, as I said, they drew up unto him, who thus entered with them into discourse.

Christian: Gentlemen, whence came you, and whither do you go?

Formalist and Hypocrisy: We were born in the land of Vain-glory, and are going, for praise, to Mount Zion.[12]

Christian: Why came you not in at the gate which standeth at the beginning of the way? Know ye not that it is written, that "he that cometh not in by the door, but climbeth up some other way, the same is a thief and a robber?" John 10:1.

Formalist and Hypocrisy: They said, that to go to the gate for entrance was by all their countrymen counted too far about; and that therefore their usual way was to make a short cut of it, and to climb over the wall, as they had done.

Christian: But will it not be counted a trespass against the Lord of the city whither we are bound, thus to violate his revealed will?

Formalist and Hypocrisy: They told him, that as for that, he needed not to trouble his head thereabout: for what they did they had custom for, and could produce, if need were, testimony that would witness it for more than a thousand years.

Christian: But, said Christian, will you stand a trial at law?

12. Those who are not truly converted but make a show of religion are in it for the glory of man. They want the praise of man above all. This is what drove the Pharisees of Jesus' day. Jesus warns His followers not to seek the praise of man but the approval of God. "Therefore, when you do a charitable deed, do not sound a trumpet before you as the hypocrites do in the synagogues and in the streets, that they may have glory from men. Assuredly, I say to you, they have their reward." (Matt. 6:2)

Formalist and Hypocrisy: They told him, that custom, it being of so long standing as above a thousand years, would doubtless now be admitted as a thing legal[13] by an impartial judge: and besides, said they, if we get into the way, what matter is it which way we get in? If we are in, we are in: thou art but in the way, who, as we perceive, came in at the gate; and we also are in the way, that came tumbling over the wall: wherein now is thy condition better than ours?

Christian: I walk by the rule of my Master: you walk by the rude working of your fancies. You are counted thieves already by the Lord of the way: therefore I doubt you will not be found true men at the end of the way. You come in by yourselves without his direction, and shall go out by yourselves without his mercy.

To this they made him but little answer; only they bid him look to himself. Then I saw that they went on, every man in his way, without much conference one with another, save that these two men told Christian, that as to laws and ordinances, they doubted not but that they should as conscientiously do them as he. Therefore, said they, we see not wherein thou differest from us, but by the coat that is on thy back, which was, as we trow, given thee by some of thy neighbors, to hide the shame of thy nakedness.

Christian: By laws and ordinances you will not be saved, since you came not in by the door. Gal. 2:16. And as for this coat that is on my back,[14] it was given me by the Lord of the place whither I go; and that, as you say, to cover my nakedness with. And I take it as a token of kindness to me; for I had nothing but rags before. And besides, thus I comfort myself as I go. Surely, think I, when I come to the gate of the city, the Lord thereof will know me for good, since I have his coat on my back; a coat that he gave me freely in the day that he stripped me of my rags. I have, moreover, a mark in my forehead, of which perhaps you have taken no notice, which one of my Lord's most intimate associates fixed there in the day that my burden fell off my shoulders. I will tell you, moreover, that

13. Formalist and Hypocrisy believe their practice of climbing over the wall will be justified since so many have done it for thousands of years. They have come into this path not through faith in Jesus Christ, but by their own works. But when they come to the Celestial City, they will not be admitted. They do not know Christ. "Not everyone who says to Me, 'Lord, Lord,' shall enter the kingdom of heaven, but he who does the will of My Father in heaven. Many will say to Me in that day, 'Lord, Lord, have we not prophesied in Your name, cast out demons in Your name, and done many wonders in Your name?' And then I will declare to them, 'I never knew you; depart from Me, you who practice lawlessness!'" (Matt. 7:21-23)

14. Christian is assured that he will be able to enter the gate of the Celestial City because he is clothed in the righteousness of Christ. He is not trusting his own works. He has put his faith in Jesus Christ who has clothed him with new clothes.

I had then given me a roll sealed, to comfort me by reading as I go on the way; I was also bid to give it in at the celestial gate, in token of my certain going in after it: all which things I doubt you want, and want them because you came not in at the gate.

To these things they gave him no answer; only they looked upon each other, and laughed. Then I saw that they went all on, save that Christian kept before, who had no more talk but with himself, and that sometimes sighingly, and sometimes comfortably: also he would be often reading in the roll that one of the Shining Ones gave him, by which he was refreshed.

I beheld then, that they all went on till they came to the foot of the hill Difficulty, at the bottom of which there was a spring. There were also in the same place two other ways besides that which came straight from the gate: one turned to the left hand, and the other to the right, at the bottom of the hill; but the narrow way lay right up the hill, and the name of the going up the side of the hill is called Difficulty.[15] Christian now went to the spring, Isa. 49:10, and drank thereof to refresh himself, and then began to go up the hill, saying,

"The hill, though high, I covet to ascend;
The difficulty will not me offend;
For I perceive the way to life lies here:
Come, pluck up heart, let's neither faint nor fear.
Better, though difficult, the right way to go,
Than wrong, though easy, where the end is woe."[16]

The other two also came to the foot of the hill. But when they saw that the hill was steep and high, and that there were two other ways to go; and supposing also that these two ways might meet again with that up which Christian went, on the other side of the hill; therefore they were resolved to go in those ways. Now the name of one of those ways was Danger, and the name of the other Destruction. So the one took the way which is called Danger, which led him into a great wood; and the other took directly up the way to Destruction, which

15. Our Lord Jesus warns that the way of salvation is narrow and difficult. "Enter by the narrow gate; for wide is the gate and broad is the way that leads to destruction, and there are many who go in by it. Because narrow is the gate and difficult is the way which leads to life, and there are few who find it." (Matt. 7:13-14)

16. Christian reasons: it is better to take the difficult path that leads to life rather than the easy way that leads to destruction.

led him into a wide field, full of dark mountains, where he stumbled and fell, and rose no more.[17]

I looked then after Christian, to see him go up the hill, where I perceived he fell from running to going, and from going to clambering upon his hands and his knees, because of the steepness of the place. Now about the midway to the top of the hill was a pleasant Arbor,[18] made by the Lord of the hill for the refreshment of weary travellers. Thither, therefore, Christian got, where also he sat down to rest him: then he pulled his roll out of his bosom, and read therein to his comfort; he also now began afresh to take a review of the coat or garment that was given to him as he stood by the cross. Thus pleasing himself awhile, he at last fell into a slumber, and thence into a fast sleep, which detained him in that place until it was almost night; and in his sleep his roll fell out of his hand.[19] Now, as he was sleeping, there came one to him, and awaked him, saying, "Go to the ant, thou sluggard; consider her ways, and be wise." Prov. 6:6. And with that, Christian suddenly started up, and sped him on his way, and went apace till he came to the top of the hill.

Now when he was got up to the top of the hill, there came two men running amain;[20] the name of the one was Timorous, and of the other Mistrust:[21] to whom Christian said, Sirs, what's the matter? you run the wrong way. Timorous answered, that they were going to the city of Zion, and had got up that difficult place: but, said he, the farther we go, the more danger we meet with; wherefore we turned, and are going back again.

Yes, said Mistrust, for just before us lie a couple of lions in the way, whether sleeping or waking we know not; and we could not think, if we came within reach, but they would presently pull us in pieces.

Christian: Then said Christian, You make me afraid; but whither shall I fly to be safe? If I go back to mine own country, that is prepared for fire and brimstone, and I shall certainly perish there; if I can get to the celestial city, I am sure to be in safety there: I must venture. To go back is nothing but death:

17. When difficulty came, Formalist and Hypocrisy would not go on. They were not men of faith, and thus they did not persevere in this way.

18. This place was made by the Lord of the hill to refresh pilgrims who have ascended the Hill of Difficulty. Christian rests here, but soon falls asleep.

19. Christian is no longer watchful, having fallen asleep. As a result, he loses his roll. Frequently, the New Testament exhorts Christians to be "awake" and to be "sober." "And do this, knowing the time, that now it is high time to awake out of sleep; for now our salvation is nearer than when we first believed. The night is far spent, the day is at hand. Therefore let us cast off the works of darkness, and let us put on the armor of light." (Rom. 13:11-12)

20. "Running at full speed"

21. One who is "timorous" suffers from fear or nervousness. Fear and mistrust turn back from the way because due to fear, and a lack of trust in God, they will not go on.

22. Christian understands that to return to the City of Destruction means death. Though the Christian life is filled with many hazards and difficulty, it is the only path that leads to eternal life.

23. Christian's journey is stopped when he discovers that his roll was foolishly left in the Arbor.

24. This was the error of Christian. The Arbor was a place of rest intended for the relief of weary saints. It was established by the Lord. But Christian had "indulged the flesh" and thus fallen asleep. He was not awake to the spiritual realities in his sleep. He was not awake as we are called to be as "children of the day." "Therefore let us not sleep, as others do, but let us watch and be sober. For those who sleep, sleep at night, and those who get drunk are drunk at night. But let us who are of the day be sober, putting on the breastplate of faith and love, and as a helmet the hope of salvation." (1 Thess. 5:6-8)

to go forward is fear of death, and life everlasting beyond it: I will yet go forward.[22] So Mistrust and Timorous ran down the hill, and Christian went on his way. But thinking again of what he had heard from the men, he felt in his bosom for his roll, that he might read therein and be comforted; but he felt, and found it not. Then was Christian in great distress, and knew not what to do; for he wanted that which used to relieve him, and that which should have been his pass into the celestial city. Here, therefore, he began to be much perplexed, and knew not what to do. At last he bethought himself that he had slept in the arbor that is on the side of the hill; and falling down upon his knees, he asked God forgiveness for that foolish act, and then went back to look for his roll.[23] But all the way he went back, who can sufficiently set forth the sorrow of Christian's heart? Sometimes he sighed, sometimes he wept, and oftentimes he chid himself for being so foolish to fall asleep in that place, which was erected only for a little refreshment from his weariness. Thus, therefore, he went back, carefully looking on this side and on that, all the way as he went, if happily he might find his roll, that had been his comfort so many times in his journey. He went thus till he came again in sight of the arbor where he sat and slept; but that sight renewed his sorrow the more, by bringing again, even afresh, his evil of sleeping unto his mind. Rev. 2:4; 1 Thess. 5:6-8. Thus, therefore, he now went on, bewailing his sinful sleep, saying, O wretched man that I am, that I should sleep in the daytime! that I should sleep in the midst of difficulty! that I should so indulge the flesh as to use that rest for ease to my flesh which the Lord of the hill hath erected only for the relief of the spirits of pilgrims![24] How many steps have I taken in vain! Thus it happened to Israel; for their sin they were sent back again by the way of the Red Sea; and I am made to tread those steps with sorrow, which I might have trod with delight, had it not been for this sinful sleep. How far might I have been on my way by this time! I am made to tread those steps thrice over, which I needed not to have trod but once: yea, now also

I am like to be benighted, for the day is almost spent. O that I had not slept!

Now by this time he was come to the arbor again, where for a while he sat down and wept; but at last, (as Providence would have it,) looking sorrowfully down under the settle, there he espied his roll, the which he with trembling and haste catched up, and put it into his bosom. But who can tell how joyful this man was when he had gotten his roll again? For this roll was the assurance of his life, and acceptance at the desired haven. Therefore he laid it up in his bosom, gave thanks to God for directing his eye to the place where it lay, and with joy and tears betook himself again to his journey. But O how nimbly did he go up the rest of the hill! Yet before he got up, the sun went down upon Christian; and this made him again recall the vanity of his sleeping to his remembrance; and thus he again began to condole with himself: Oh thou sinful sleep! how for thy sake am I like to be benighted in my journey! I must walk without the sun, darkness must cover the path of my feet, and I must hear the noise of the doleful creatures, because of my sinful sleep! Now also he remembered the story that Mistrust and Timorous told him of, how they were frighted with the sight of the lions. Then said Christian to himself again, These beasts range in the night for their prey; and if they should meet with me in the dark, how should I shift them? how should I escape being by them torn in pieces? Thus he went on his way. But while he was bewailing his unhappy miscarriage,[25] he lift up his eyes, and behold there was a very stately palace before him, the name of which was Beautiful, and it stood by the highway-side.

So I saw in my dream that he made haste, and went forward, that if possible he might get lodging there. Now before he had gone far, he entered into a very narrow passage, which was about a furlong off the Porter's lodge, and looking very narrowly before him as he went, he espied two lions in the way. Now, thought he, I see the dangers that Mistrust and Timorous were driven back by. (The lions were chained, but

25. "His unhappy failure in duty"

26. Literary scholars debate the meaning of the lions in this part of Bunyan's allegory. Some believe it refers to the wicked of the world who oppose God's people. Others see a historical reference to the authorities of Bunyan's day who were persecuting nonconformists like Bunyan. We don't know what Bunyan had in mind for sure. Nevertheless, all Christians face "lions in the streets" that may seem powerful and dangerous. But when we are afraid, we put our trust in the Lord (Ps. 56:3). We must also remember, like these lions, anyone or anything that opposes us is under the control of God. Like these lions that are chained, nothing can happen to us apart from the sovereign will of God.

he saw not the chains.)[26] Then he was afraid, and thought also himself to go back after them; for he thought nothing but death was before him. But the Porter at the lodge, whose name is Watchful, perceiving that Christian made a halt, as if he would go back, cried unto him, saying, Is thy strength so small? Mark 4:40. Fear not the lions, for they are chained, and are placed there for trial of faith where it is,[27] and for discovery of those that have none: keep in the midst of the path, and no hurt shall come unto thee.

Then I saw that he went on, trembling for fear of the lions, but taking good heed to the directions of the Porter; he heard them roar, but they did him no harm. Then he clapped his hands, and went on till he came and stood before the gate where the Porter was. Then said Christian to the Porter, Sir, what house is this? and may I lodge here to-night? The Porter answered, This house was built by the Lord of the hill, and he built it for the relief and security of pilgrims.[28] The Porter also asked whence he was, and whither he was going.

Christian: I am come from the city of Destruction, and am going to Mount Zion: but because the sun is now set, I desire, if I may, to lodge here to-night.

The Porter: What is your name?

Christian: My name is now Christian, but my name at the first was Graceless:[29] I came of the race of Japheth, whom God will persuade to dwell in the tents of Shem.[30] Gen. 9:27.

27. Watchful tells Christian not to fear the lions. They were placed there intentionally as a test of faith. Indeed, the Lord may bring us through fearful circumstances so that we will learn to trust Him with our life. "The Lord is my light and my salvation; whom shall I fear? The Lord is the strength of my life; of whom shall I be afraid?" (Ps. 27:1)

28. Bunyan portrays a number of "locations" built by the Lord along the dangerous journey. The House Beautiful is one such place built for spiritual refreshment and protection. With these allegorical images Bunyan masterfully portrays the truth that the Lord is with us on this dangerous and difficult pilgrim journey. "You prepare a table before me in the presence of my enemies; you anoint my head with oil; my cup runs over." (Ps. 23:5)

29. Before his conversion, he was without the grace of God, without hope in the world.

30. This is a reference to Noah's prophecy of the line of Japheth dwelling in the tents of Shem. Bunyan interprets this as a prophecy of the race of the Gentiles becoming a part of God's people.

The Porter: But how does it happen that you come so late? The sun is set.

Christian: I had been here sooner, but that, wretched man that I am, I slept in the arbor that stands on the hill-side! Nay, I had, notwithstanding that, been here much sooner, but that in my sleep I lost my evidence, and came without it to the brow of the hill; and then feeling for it, and not finding it, I was forced with sorrow of heart to go back to the place where I slept my sleep, where I found it; and now I am come.

The Porter: Well, I will call out one of the virgins of this place, who will, if she likes your talk, bring you in to the rest of the family, according to the rules of the house. So Watchful the Porter rang a bell, at the sound of which came out of the door of the house a grave and beautiful damsel, named Discretion, and asked why she was called.[31]

The Porter answered, This man is on a journey from the city of Destruction to Mount Zion; but being weary and be-nighted, he asked me if he might lodge here to-night: so I told him I would call for thee, who, after discourse had with him, mayest do as seemeth thee good, even according to the law of the house.

Then she asked him whence he was, and whither he was going; and he told her. She asked him also how he got into the way; and he told her. Then she asked him what he had seen and met with in the way, and he told her. And at last she asked his name. So he said, It is Christian; and I have so much the more a desire to lodge here to-night, because, by what I perceive, this place was built by the Lord of the hill for the relief and security of pilgrims. So she smiled, but the water stood in her eyes; and after a little pause she said, I will call forth two or three more of the family. So she ran to the door, and called out Prudence, Piety, and Charity, who, after a little more discourse with him, had him into the family; and many of them meeting him at the threshold of the house, said, Come in, thou blessed of the Lord; this house was built by the Lord of the hill on purpose to entertain such pilgrims in.

31. "Grave" here means "solemn." There are four virgins presented in the narrative of the House Beautiful. They each represent different virtues of the Christian life.

32. Christian engages in spiritual conversation with Piety, Prudence, and Charity. The purpose of this discussion is for "the best improvement of time," i.e. spiritual edification. The Puritans often wrote about "spiritual conference." By this term they meant conversation that was directed to spiritual things for the purpose of edification. "And let us consider one another in order to stir up love and good works, not forsaking the assembling of ourselves together, as is the manner of some, but exhorting one another, and so much the more as you see the Day approaching." (Heb. 10:24-25)

33. Christian recounts his entire journey up to this point detailing the hazards of the journey and what he learned along the way.

Then he bowed his head, and followed them into the house. So when he was come in and sat down, they gave him something to drink, and consented together that, until supper was ready, some of them should have some particular discourse with Christian, for the best improvement of time;[32] and they appointed Piety, Prudence, and Charity to discourse with him: and thus they began.

Piety: Come, good Christian, since we have been so loving to you as to receive you into our house this night, let us, if perhaps we may better ourselves thereby, talk with you of all things that have happened to you in your pilgrimage.[33]

Christian: With a very good will; and I am glad that you are so well disposed.

Piety: What moved you at first to betake yourself to a pilgrim's life?

Christian: I was driven out of my native country by a dreadful sound that was in mine ears; to wit, that unavoidable destruction did attend me, if I abode in that place where I was.

Piety: But how did it happen that you came out of your country this way?

Christian: It was as God would have it; for when I was under the fears of destruction, I did not know whither to go; but by chance there came a man, even to me, as I was trembling and weeping, whose name is Evangelist, and he directed me to the Wicket-gate, which else I should never have found, and so set me into the way that hath led me directly to this house.

Piety: But did you not come by the house of the Interpreter?

Christian: Yes, and did see such things there, the remembrance of which will stick by me as long as I live, especially three things: to wit, how Christ, in despite of Satan, maintains his work of grace in the heart; how the man had sinned himself quite out of hopes of God's mercy; and also the dream of him that thought in his sleep the day of judgment was come.

Piety: Why, did you hear him tell his dream?

Christian: Yes, and a dreadful one it was, I thought; it made my heart ache as he was telling of it, but yet I am glad I heard it.

Piety: Was this all you saw at the house of the Interpreter?

Christian: No; he took me, and had me where he showed me a stately palace, and how the people were clad in gold that were in it; and how there came a venturous man, and cut his way through the armed men that stood in the door to keep him out; and how he was bid to come in, and win eternal glory. Methought those things did ravish my heart. I would have stayed at that good man's house a twelvemonth,[34] but that I knew I had farther to go.

Piety: And what saw you else in the way?

Christian: Saw? Why, I went but a little farther, and I saw One, as I thought in my mind, hang bleeding upon a tree; and the very sight of him made my burden fall off my back; for I groaned under a very heavy burden, but then it fell down from off me. It was a strange thing to me, for I never saw such a thing before: yea, and while I stood looking up, (for then I could not forbear looking,) three Shining Ones came to me. One of them testified that my sins were forgiven me; another stripped me of my rags, and gave me this broidered coat which you see; and the third set the mark which you see in my forehead, and gave me this sealed roll, (and with that he plucked it out of his bosom.)

Piety: But you saw more than this, did you not?

Christian: The things that I have told you were the best: yet some other I saw, as, namely, I saw three men, Simple, Sloth, and Presumption, lie asleep, a little out of the way, as I came, with irons upon their heels; but do you think I could awake them? I also saw Formality and Hypocrisy come tumbling over the wall, to go, as they pretended, to Zion; but they were quickly lost, even as I myself did tell them, but they would not believe. But, above all, I found it hard work to get up this hill, and as hard to come by the lions' mouths; and, truly, if it had not been for the good man, the porter that stands at the gate, I

34. That is, Christian would have stayed there an entire year if he could have. But Christian knew that he must continue on his journey.

35. Christian looks back on his past life with shame. He has no longing for the old ways of sin because he has a new nature implanted within.

36. This question by Prudence could be paraphrased in this way: "Do you still struggle with some of those past ways of life before your conversion?"

37. Christians do struggle with indwelling sin. But because a new nature has been implanted within them, they struggle against sin and seek to kill it. This is what Paul describes in Galatians 5. "I say then: Walk in the Spirit, and you shall not fulfill the lust of the flesh. For the flesh lusts against the Spirit, and the Spirit against the flesh; and these are contrary to one another, so that you do not do the things that you wish." (Gal. 5:16-17)

38. His "inward fleshly thoughts"

39. "Thoughts become warm"

do not know but that, after all, I might have gone back again; but I thank God I am here, and thank you for receiving me.

Then Prudence thought good to ask him a few questions, and desired his answer to them.

Prudence: Do you not think sometimes of the country from whence you came?

Christian: Yea, but with much shame and detestation.[35] Truly, if I had been mindful of that country from whence I came out, I might have had opportunity to have returned; but now I desire a better country, that is, a heavenly one. Heb. 11:15,16.

Prudence: Do you not yet bear away with you some of the things that then you were conversant withal?[36]

Christian: Yes, but greatly against my will;[37] especially my inward and carnal cogitations,[38] with which all my countrymen, as well as myself, were delighted. But now all those things are my grief; and might I but choose mine own things, I would choose never to think of those things more: but when I would be a doing that which is best, that which is worst is with me. Rom. 7:15, 21.

Prudence: Do you not find sometimes as if those things were vanquished, which at other times are your perplexity?

Christian: Yes, but that is but seldom; but they are to me golden hours in which such things happen to me.

Prudence: Can you remember by what means you find your annoyances at times as if they were vanquished?

Christian: Yes: when I think what I saw at the cross, that will do it; and when I look upon my broidered coat, that will do it; and when I look into the roll that I carry in my bosom, that will do it; and when my thoughts wax warm[39] about whither I am going, that will do it.

Prudence: And what is it that makes you so desirous to go to Mount Zion?

Christian: Why, there I hope to see Him alive that did hang dead on the cross; and there I hope to be rid of all those things that to this day are in me an annoyance to me: there they say there is no death, Isa. 25:8; Rev. 21:4; and there I shall dwell with such company as I like best. For, to tell you the truth, I love Him because I was by Him eased of my burden; and I am weary of my inward sickness. I would fain be where I shall die no more, and with the company that shall continually cry, Holy, holy, holy.

Then said Charity to Christian, Have you a family? Are you a married man?

Christian: I have a wife and four small children.

Charity: And why did you not bring them along with you?

Christian: Then Christian wept, and said, Oh, how willingly would I have done it! but they were all of them utterly averse to my going on pilgrimage.[40]

Charity: But you should have talked to them, and have endeavored to show them the danger of staying behind.

Christian: So I did; and told them also what God had shown to me of the destruction of our city; but I seemed to them as one that mocked, and they believed me not. Gen. 19:14.

Charity: And did you pray to God that he would bless your counsel to them?

Christian: Yes, and that with much affection; for you must think that my wife and poor children were very dear to me.

Charity: But did you tell them of your own sorrow, and fear of destruction? For I suppose that destruction was visible enough to you.

Christian: Yes, over, and over, and over. They might also see my fears in my countenance, in my tears, and also in my trembling under the apprehension of the judgment that did hang over our heads; but all was not sufficient to prevail with them to come with me.

Charity: But what could they say for themselves, why they came not?

Christian: Why, my wife was afraid of losing this world,[41] and my children were given to the foolish delights of youth; so, what by one thing, and what by another, they left me to wander in this manner alone.

40. Christian was heartbroken that his family must be left behind. Following Jesus may come at a high cost. But each of us must be willing to forsake father, mother, sister, and brother to walk with Christ. "If anyone comes to Me and does not hate his father and mother, wife and children, brothers and sisters, yes, and his own life also, he cannot be My disciple." (Luke 14:26)

41. The wife of Christian is an example of the "thorny ground hearer" in the Parable of the Sower. "Now he who received seed among the thorns is he who hears the word, and the cares of this world and the deceitfulness of riches choke the word, and he becomes unfruitful." (Matt. 13:22)

42. Bunyan is using the word "conversation" to refer to one's way of life.

43. Christians should frequently converse about their Lord Jesus Christ and what He has done for them. Much profit comes from contemplating our Lord and His glorious attributes.

Charity: But did you not, with your vain life, damp all that you, by words, used by way of persuasion to bring them away with you?

Christian: Indeed, I cannot commend my life, for I am conscious to myself of many failings therein. I know also, that a man, by his conversation,[42] may soon overthrow what, by argument or persuasion, he doth labor to fasten upon others for their good. Yet this I can say, I was very wary of giving them occasion, by any unseemly action, to make them averse to going on pilgrimage. Yea, for this very thing, they would tell me I was too precise, and that I denied myself of things (for their sakes) in which they saw no evil. Nay, I think I may say, that if what they saw in me did hinder them, it was my great tenderness in sinning against God, or of doing any wrong to my neighbor.

Charity: Indeed, Cain hated his brother, because his own works were evil, and his brother's righteous, 1 John, 3:12; and if thy wife and children have been offended with thee for this, they thereby show themselves to be implacable to good; thou hast delivered thy soul from their blood. Ezek. 3:19.

Now I saw in my dream, that thus they sat talking together until supper was ready. So when they had made ready, they sat down to meat. Now the table was furnished with fat things, and with wine that was well refined; and all their talk at the table was about the Lord of the hill;[43] as, namely, about what he had done, and wherefore he did what he did, and why he had builded that house; and by what they said, I perceived that he had been a great warrior, and had fought with and slain him that had the power of death, Heb. 2:14,15; but not without great danger to himself, which made me love him the more.

For, as they said, and as I believe, said Christian, he did it with the loss of much blood. But that which put the glory of grace into all he did, was, that he did it out of pure love to his country. And besides, there were some of them of the household that said they had been and spoke with him since he did die on the cross; and they have attested that they had it from his own lips, that he is such a lover of poor pilgrims, that the like is not to be found from the east to the west. They, moreover, gave an instance of what they affirmed; and that was, he had stripped himself of his glory that he might do this for the poor; and that they heard him say and affirm, that he would not dwell in the mountain of Zion alone. They said, moreover, that he had made many pilgrims princes, though by nature they were beggars born, and their original had been the dunghill. 1 Sam. 2:8; Psa. 113:7.

Thus they discoursed together till late at night; and after they had committed themselves to their Lord for protection, they betook themselves to rest. The pilgrim they laid in a large upper chamber, whose window opened towards the sun-rising. The name of the chamber was Peace,[44] where he slept till break of day, and then he awoke and sang,

"Where am I now? Is this the love and care
Of Jesus, for the men that pilgrims are,
Thus to provide that I should be forgiven,
And dwell already the next door to heaven!"

So in the morning they all got up; and, after some more discourse, they told him that he should not depart till they had shown him the rarities of that place. And first they had him into the study, where they showed him records of the greatest antiquity; in which, as I remember my dream, they showed him the pedigree of the Lord of the hill,[45] that he was the Son of the Ancient of days, and came by eternal generation.[46] Here also was more fully recorded the acts that he had done, and the

44. The Christian enjoys peace with God through the Lord Jesus Christ (Rom. 5:1). It is possible Bunyan had in mind the words of Psalm 4 with this image. "I will both lie down in peace, and sleep; for You alone, O LORD, make me dwell in safety." (Ps. 4:8)

45. A pedigree refers to one's ancestry or lineage.

46. This refers to the doctrine of the "eternal generation" of the Son of God. The Bible teaches that Jesus the Son of God has always existed as the Son, with the Father, before the universe and time came into existence. Jesus teaches this in John 17: "And now, O Father, glorify Me together with Yourself, with the glory which I had with You before the world was." (John 17:5)

47. Those who follow Jesus Christ have a place prepared for them that cannot be destroyed. "For we know that if our earthly house, this tent, is destroyed, we have a building from God, a house not made with hands, eternal in the heavens." (2 Cor. 5:1)

48. These words are a quotation from Hebrews 11. In Hebrews 11, the author recounts the acts of faith performed by God's people in past centuries.

49. The Lord has not left His servants without armor for the spiritual battle. The spiritual armor of the Christian is described in detail in Ephesians 6 and also mentioned in 1 Thessalonians 5.

50. The Lord does not leave any of his servants naked of armor in the battle. Bunyan describes how there is more than sufficient equipment in Christ's armory for each of His servants to go into battle.

51. The word "engines" here refers to the weapons or instruments used by God's people to do mighty acts of faith.

names of many hundreds that he had taken into his service; and how he had placed them in such habitations that could neither by length of days, nor decays of nature, be dissolved.[47]

Then they read to him some of the worthy acts that some of his servants had done; as how they had subdued kingdoms, wrought righteousness, obtained promises, stopped the mouths of lions, quenched the violence of fire, escaped the edge of the sword, out of weakness were made strong, waxed valiant in fight, and turned to flight the armies of the aliens.[48] Heb. 11:33,34.

Then they read again another part of the records of the house, where it was shown how willing their Lord was to receive into his favor any, even any, though they in time past had offered great affronts to his person and proceedings. Here also were several other histories of many other famous things, of all which Christian had a view; as of things both ancient and modern, together with prophecies and predictions of things that have their certain accomplishment, both to the dread and amazement of enemies, and the comfort and solace of pilgrims.

The next day they took him, and had him into the armory,[49] where they showed him all manner of furniture which their Lord had provided for pilgrims, as sword, shield, helmet, breastplate, all-prayer, and shoes that would not wear out. And there was here enough of this to harness out as many men for the service of their Lord as there be stars in the heaven for multitude.[50]

They also showed him some of the engines[51] with which some of his servants had done wonderful things. They showed him Moses' rod; the hammer and nail with which Jael slew Sisera; the pitchers, trumpets, and lamps too, with which Gideon put to flight the armies of Midian. Then they showed him the ox-goad wherewith Shamgar slew six hundred men. They showed him also the jawbone with which Samson did such mighty feats. They showed him moreover the sling and stone with which David slew Goliath of Gath; and the sword also with which their Lord will kill the man of sin, in the day that he shall rise up to the prey. They showed him besides many excellent things, with which Christian was much delighted. This done, they went to their rest again.

Then I saw in my dream, that on the morrow he got up to go forward, but they desired him to stay till the next day also; and then, said they, we will, if the day be clear, show you the Delectable Mountains;[52] which, they said, would yet farther add to his comfort, because they were nearer the desired haven than the place where at present he was; so he consented and stayed. When the morning was up, they had him to the top of the house, and bid him look south. So he did, and behold, at a great distance, he saw a most pleasant mountainous country, beautified with woods, vineyards, fruits of all sorts, flowers also, with springs and fountains, very delectable to behold. Isa. 33:16,17. Then he asked the name of the country. They said it was Immanuel's land; and it is as common, said they, as this hill is, to and for all the pilgrims. And when thou comest there, from thence thou mayest see to the gate of the celestial city, as the shepherds that live there will make appear.

Now he bethought himself of setting forward, and they were willing he should. But first, said they, let us go again into the armory. So they did; and when he came there, they harnessed him from head to foot with what was of proof, lest perhaps he should meet with assaults in the way.[53] He being therefore thus accoutred,[54] walked out with his friends to the gate; and there he asked the Porter if he saw any pilgrim pass by. Then the Porter answered, Yes.

Christian: Pray, did you know him? said he.

The Porter: I asked his name, and he told me it was Faithful.

Christian: O, said Christian, I know him; he is my townsman, my near neighbor; he comes from the place where I was born. How far do you think he may be before?

The Porter: He is got by this time below the hill.

Christian: Well, said Christian, good Porter, the Lord be with thee, and add to all thy plain blessings much increase for the kindness that thou hast showed me.

52. Delectable is used in the sense of "delightful." These mountains are very close to the Celestial City.

53. Before setting forth, Christian is equipped with the full armor of God. This armor will be his defense when he soon encounters the evil one. "Finally, my brethren, be strong in the Lord and in the power of His might. Put on the whole armor of God, that you may be able to stand against the wiles of the devil." (Eph. 6:10-11

54. Accoutred means "equipped"

Book 1

Chapter 4

Then he began to go forward; but Discretion, Piety, Charity, and Prudence would accompany him down to the foot of the hill. So they went on together, reiterating their former discourses, till they came to go down the hill. Then said Christian, As it was difficult coming up, so, so far as I can see, it is dangerous going down. Yes, said Prudence, so it is; for it is a hard matter for a man to go down into the valley of Humiliation, as thou art now, and to catch no slip by the way;[1] therefore, said they, we are come out to accompany thee down the hill. So he began to go down, but very warily; yet he caught a slip or two.

Then I saw in my dream, that these good companions, when Christian was got down to the bottom of the hill, gave him a loaf of bread, a bottle of wine, and a cluster of raisins; and then he went on his way,

"Whilst Christian is among his godly friends,
Their golden mouths make him sufficient mends
For all his griefs; and when they let him go,
He's clad with northern steel from top to toe."

But now, in this valley of Humiliation, poor Christian was hard put to it; for he had gone but a little way before he espied a foul fiend coming over the field to meet him: his name is Apollyon.[2] Then did Christian begin to be afraid, and to cast in his mind whether to go back, or to stand his ground. But

1. The four virgins tell Christian that it is hard for anyone to go down into the Valley of Humiliation without a few slips. The Lord may bring us through difficult valleys where our faith is tried. Yet, the Lord will sustain us through such difficulties. It may seem that our foot slips, but the Lord will make our steps secure. "I waited patiently for the Lord; And He inclined to me, And heard my cry. He also brought me up out of a horrible pit, Out of the miry clay, And set my feet upon a rock, And established my steps." (Ps. 40:1-2)

2. This title is given to the devil in Revelation 9:11. In Greek, the word "Apollyon" means "destroyer."

he considered again, that he had no armor for his back, and therefore thought that to turn the back to him might give him greater advantage with ease to pierce him with his darts; therefore he resolved to venture and stand his ground:[3] for, thought he, had I no more in mine eye than the saving of my life, it would be the best way to stand.

So he went on, and Apollyon met him. Now the monster was hideous to behold: he was clothed with scales like a fish, and they are his pride; he had wings like a dragon, and feet like a bear, and out of his belly came fire and smoke; and his mouth was as the mouth of a lion.[4] When he was come up to Christian, he beheld him with a disdainful countenance, and thus began to question him.

Apollyon: Whence came you, and whither are you bound?

Christian: I am come from the city of Destruction, which is the place of all evil, and I am going to the city of Zion.

Apollyon: By this I perceive thou art one of my subjects;[5] for all that country is mine, and I am the prince and god of it. How is it, then, that thou hast run away from thy king? Were it not that I hope thou mayest do me more service, I would strike thee now at one blow to the ground.

Christian: I was, indeed, born in your dominions,[6] but your service was hard,[7] and your wages such as a man could not live on; for the wages of sin is death, Rom. 6:23; therefore, when I was come to years, I did, as other considerate persons do, look out if perhaps I might mend myself.

3. We are called to stand in the day of evil, having been equipped with the whole armor of God. If we are equipped with this armor, the Bible promises that we will be able to stand. "Therefore take up the whole armor of God, that you may be able to withstand in the evil day, and having done all, to stand." (Eph. 6:13)

4. Bunyan mixes all different kinds of imagery from the Bible to depict the appearance of Apollyon. It includes some of the imagery of Leviathan from Job 41 and the various monsters in the Book of Revelation.

5. The devil says that Christian is one of his servants. In the City of Destruction (the world), people are in bondage to the "god of this world" (2 Cor. 4:3, Eph. 2:2). Jesus told the Jews, who were under the bondage of sin, that they were living under the service of the devil. "You are of your father the devil, and the desires of your father you want to do. He was a murderer from the beginning, and does not stand in the truth, because there is no truth in him. When he speaks a lie, he speaks from his own resources, for he is a liar and the father of it." (John 8:44)

6. Christian acknowledges that before his conversion he was born as a subject of Apollyon (Eph. 2:2). But now, he is no longer a servant of Satan or a servant of sin.

7. Satan is a liar and murderer. What he promises his servants is always a lie. Though he may promise freedom through sin, those who serve Satan will find that they only increase their bondage. "While they promise them liberty, they themselves are slaves of corruption; for by whom a person is overcome, by him also he is brought into bondage." (2 Pet. 2:19)

Apollyon: There is no prince that will thus lightly lose his subjects, neither will I as yet lose thee; but since thou complainest of thy service and wages, be content to go back, and what our country will afford I do here promise to give thee.

Christian: But I have let myself to another, even to the King of princes; and how can I with fairness go back with thee?

Apollyon: Thou hast done in this according to the proverb, "changed a bad for a worse;" but it is ordinary for those that have professed themselves his servants, after a while to give him the slip, and return again to me. Do thou so too, and all shall be well.

Christian: I have given him my faith, and sworn my allegiance to him; how then can I go back from this, and not be hanged as a traitor.

Apollyon: Thou didst the same by me, and yet I am willing to pass by all, if now thou wilt yet turn again and go back.

Christian: What I promised thee was in my non-age: and besides, I count that the Prince, under whose banner I now stand, is able to absolve me, yea, and to pardon also what I did as to my compliance with thee.[8] And besides, O thou destroying Apollyon, to speak truth, I like his service, his wages, his servants, his government, his company, and country, better than thine; therefore leave off to persuade me farther: I am his servant, and I will follow him.

Apollyon: Consider again, when thou art in cool blood, what thou art like to meet with in the way that thou goest. Thou knowest that for the most part his servants come to an ill end, because they are transgressors against me and my ways. How many of them have been put to shameful deaths! And besides, thou countest his service better than mine; whereas he never yet came from the place where he is, to deliver any that served him out of their enemies' hands: but as for me, how many times, as all the world very well knows, have I delivered, either by power or fraud, those that have faithfully served me, from him and his, though taken by them! And so will I deliver thee.[9]

8. Christian says that because he now serves the Lord Jesus Christ, he has the promises of the gospel. Christian will be pardoned of all his sins against the Lord. Now Christian prefers the wages, the servants, the government, company, and country of the Lord.

9. Satan lies to Christian. Satan does not deliver. Satan lies and murders. But Satan wants Christian to think that following Christ does not lead to life, but instead only leads to hardship.

Christian: His forbearing at present to deliver them, is on purpose to try their love,[10] whether they will cleave to him to the end: and as for the ill end thou sayest they come to, that is most glorious in their account. For, for present deliverance, they do not much expect it; for they stay for their glory; and then they shall have it, when their Prince comes in his and the glory of the angels.

Apollyon: Thou hast already been unfaithful in thy service to him; and how dost thou think to receive wages of him?[11]

Christian: Wherein, O Apollyon, have I been unfaithful to him?

Apollyon: Thou didst faint at first setting out, when thou wast almost choked in the gulf of Despond. Thou didst attempt wrong ways to be rid of thy burden, whereas thou shouldst have stayed till thy Prince had taken it off. Thou didst sinfully sleep, and lose thy choice things. Thou wast almost persuaded also to go back at the sight of the lions. And when thou talkest of thy journey, and of what thou hast seen and heard, thou art inwardly desirous of vainglory in all that thou sayest or doest.

Christian: All this is true,[12] and much more which thou hast left out; but the Prince whom I serve and honor is merciful, and ready to forgive. But besides, these infirmities possessed me in thy country, for there I sucked them in, and I have groaned under them, been sorry for them, and have obtained pardon of my Prince.

10. Christian defeats the lies of Satan by arguing that whatever trials a Christian may go through, it is for the testing of their faith and the growth of their love for God.

11. Apollyon seeks to discourage Christian. This is one of the strategic devices of Satan. He will attack us by showing our unfaithfulness to the Lord. He is the "accuser of the brethren" (Rev. 12:10). He will accuse us about our own sins. He will accuse other brothers and sisters of sins in our minds. We must not be ignorant of Satan's devices. The powerful promises of the gospel must be used as a weapon against the lies of the evil one.

12. When Satan accuses us, we acknowledge that we are indeed sinners. But we are no longer condemned. We are in Christ (Rom. 8:1). The Reformer Martin Luther saw these accusations of the devil as an opportunity to find comfort in the gospel. Luther wrote, "When the devil accuses us and says, 'You are a sinner and therefore damned,' we should answer, 'Because you say I am a sinner, I will be righteous and saved.' 'No,' says the devil, 'you will be damned.' And I reply, 'No, for I fly to Christ, who gave himself for my sins. Satan, you will not prevail against me when you try to terrify me by setting forth the greatness of my sins and try to bring me into heaviness, distrust, despair, hatred, contempt and blasphemy against God. On the contrary, when you say I am a sinner, you give me armor and weapons against yourself, so that with your own sword I may cut your throat and tread you under my feet, for Christ died for sinners. . . . As often as you object that I am a sinner, so often you remind me of the benefit of Christ my Redeemer, on whose shoulders, and not on mine, lie all my sins.'"

13. Satan flies into a furious rage. He cannot withstand the truth. Therefore, he flies into murderous attack against Christian.

Apollyon: Then Apollyon broke out into a grievous rage, saying, I am an enemy to this Prince; I hate his person, his laws, and people: I am come out on purpose to withstand thee.[13]

Christian: Apollyon, beware what you do, for I am in the King's highway, the way of holiness; therefore take heed to yourself.[14]

Apollyon: Then Apollyon straddled quite over the whole breadth of the way, and said, I am void of fear in this matter. Prepare thyself to die; for I swear by my infernal den, that thou shalt go no farther: here will I spill thy soul. And with that he threw a flaming dart at his breast; but Christian had a shield in his hand, with which he caught it, and so prevented the danger of that.[15]

Then did Christian draw, for he saw it was time to bestir him; and Apollyon as fast made at him, throwing darts as thick as hail; by the which, notwithstanding all that Christian could do to avoid it, Apollyon wounded him in his head, his

14. Bunyan may be alluding to the words of Isaiah 35:

A highway shall be there, and a road,
And it shall be called the Highway of Holiness.
The unclean shall not pass over it,
But it shall be for others.
Whoever walks the road, although a fool,
Shall not go astray.
No lion shall be there,
Nor shall any ravenous beast go up on it;
It shall not be found there.
But the redeemed shall walk there, (Isa. 35:8-9)

Apollyon is the one in danger. Christian is armed with the full armor of God and he is walking along the King's highway. As Luther wrote in his hymn "A Mighty Fortress is Our God," we need not fear "the Prince of Darkness Grim." We need not fear his rage because one little word shall "fell him."

15. "Above all, taking the shield of faith with which you will be able to quench all the fiery darts of the wicked one." (Eph. 6:16)

hand, and foot. This made Christian give a little back: Apollyon, therefore, followed his work amain,[16] and Christian again took courage, and resisted as manfully as he could. This sore combat lasted for above half a day, even till Christian was almost quite spent: for you must know, that Christian, by reason of his wounds, must needs grow weaker and weaker.

Then Apollyon, espying his opportunity, began to gather up close to Christian, and wrestling with him, gave him a dreadful fall; and with that Christian's sword flew out of his hand. Then said Apollyon, I am sure of thee now: and with that he had almost pressed him to death, so that Christian began to despair of life. But, as God would have it,[17] while Apollyon was fetching his last blow, thereby to make a full end of this good man, Christian nimbly reached out his hand for his sword, and caught it, saying, Rejoice not against me, O mine enemy: when I fall, I shall arise, Mic. 7:8; and with that gave him a deadly thrust, which made him give back, as one that had received his mortal wound. Christian perceiving that, made at him again, saying, Nay, in all these things we are more than conquerors, through Him that loved us. Rom. 8:37. And with that Apollyon spread forth his dragon wings, and sped him away, that Christian saw him no more.[18] James 4:7.

In this combat no man can imagine, unless he had seen and heard, as I did, what yelling and hideous roaring Apollyon made all the time of the fight; he spake like a dragon: and on the other side, what sighs and groans burst from Christian's heart. I never saw him all the while give so much as one pleasant look, till he perceived he had wounded Apollyon with his two-edged sword; then, indeed, he did smile, and look upward! But it was the dreadfullest sight that ever I saw.

So when the battle was over, Christian said, I will here give thanks to him[19] that hath delivered me out of the mouth of the lion, to him that did help me against Apollyon. And so he did, saying,

"Great Beelzebub, the captain of this fiend,
Designed my ruin; therefore to this end

16. "With full strength" or "with full speed"

17. Christian is not alone in the battle. Though the battle against the evil one is fierce, Apollyon will fail because of the power of God.

18. Christian resisted the devil, and as James 4:7 promises, the devil fled from him.

19. Christian acknowledges that the victory in this battle is from the Lord. Christian is convinced, just as David was, that the battle belongs to the Lord (1 Sam. 17:47).

20. A reference to the angel Michael mentioned in Revelation 12. "And war broke out in heaven: Michael and his angels fought with the dragon; and the dragon and his angels fought,..." (Rev. 12:7)

21. Though the battle with Apollyon has ended, Christian recognizes the need to remain watchful in the journey. "And take the helmet of salvation, and the sword of the Spirit, which is the word of God; praying always with all prayer and supplication in the Spirit, being watchful to this end with all perseverance and supplication for all the saints—" (Eph. 6:17-18)

He sent him harness'd out; and he, with rage
That hellish was, did fiercely me engage:
But blessed Michael helped me,[20] and I,
By dint of sword, did quickly make him fly:
Therefore to Him let me give lasting praise,
And thank and bless his holy name always."

Then there came to him a hand with some of the leaves of the tree of life, the which Christian took and applied to the wounds that he had received in the battle, and was healed immediately. He also sat down in that place to eat bread, and to drink of the bottle that was given him a little before: so, being refreshed, he addressed himself to his journey with his sword drawn in his hand;[21] for he said, I know not but some other enemy may be at hand. But he met with no other affront from Apollyon quite through this valley.

Now at the end of this valley was another, called the Valley of the Shadow of Death;[22] and Christian must needs go through it,[23] because the way to the Celestial City lay through the midst of it. Now, this valley is a very solitary place. The prophet Jeremiah thus describes it: "A wilderness, a land of deserts and pits, a land of drought, and of the Shadow of Death, a land that no man" (but a Christian) "passeth through, and where no man dwelt." Jer. 2:6.

Now here Christian was worse put to it than in his fight with Apollyon, as by the sequel you shall see.

22. This language is taken from Psalm 23.
"Yea, though I walk through the valley of the shadow of death,
I will fear no evil;
For You are with me;
Your rod and Your staff, they comfort me." (Ps. 23:4)

23. Christian could not avoid walking this dark road if he would go to the Celestial City. We will not make it to heaven without suffering, without passing through valleys and dark places. "And when they had preached the gospel to that city and made many disciples, they returned to Lystra, Iconium, and Antioch, strengthening the souls of the disciples, exhorting them to continue in the faith, and saying, "We must through many tribulations enter the kingdom of God." (Acts 14:21-22)

I saw then in my dream, that when Christian was got to the borders of the Shadow of Death, there met him two men,[24] children of them that brought up an evil report of the good land Num.13:32, making haste to go back; to whom Christian spake as follows.

Christian: Whither are you going?

The Two Men: They said, Back, back; and we would have you do so too, if either life or peace is prized by you.

Christian: Why, what's the matter? said Christian.

The Two Men: Matter! said they; we were going that way as you are going, and went as far as we durst: and indeed we were almost past coming back; for had we gone a little further, we had not been here to bring the news to thee.

Christian: But what have you met with? said Christian.

The Two Men: Why, we were almost in the Valley of the Shadow of Death, but that by good hap we looked before us, and saw the danger before we came to it. Psa. 44:19; 107:19.

Christian: But what have you seen? said Christian.

The Two Men: Seen! why the valley itself, which is as dark as pitch: we also saw there the hobgoblins, satyrs, and dragons of the pit: we heard also in that valley a continual howling and yelling, as of a people under unutterable misery, who there sat bound in affliction and irons: and over that valley hang the discouraging clouds of confusion: Death also doth always spread his wings over it. In a word, it is every whit dreadful, being utterly without order. Job 3:5; 10:22.

Christian: Then, said Christian, I perceive not yet, by what you have said, but that this is my way to the desired haven. Psalm 44:18,19; Jer. 2:6.

The Two Men: Be it thy way; we will not choose it for ours.

So they parted, and Christian went on his way, but still with his sword drawn in his hand, for fear lest he should be assaulted.

I saw then in my dream, so far as this valley reached, there was on the right hand a very deep ditch; that ditch is it into which the blind have led the blind in all ages, and have both

24. These two men are not named. But in biblical imagery and allusion, the spies returning from Canaan bringing a bad report seem to be in view (Num. 13).

25. In this valley, both sides of the path were deadly. A "quag" is a marshy or boggy place. Leland Ryken suggests that the ditch on the right represents error that leads to damnation while the other represents carnal sin. When Bunyan says "David" fell into this quag, he is referring to David's sin of adultery with Bathsheba and the murder of Uriah the Hittite (2 Sam. 11-12).

26. As Christian inches close to the mouth of hell in the midst of this valley, it is essential that he makes use of the weapon of prayer. In our darkest times, all we may be able to do is to cry out to the Lord of Heaven for deliverance. Prayer is a powerful weapon because in prayer we call upon the omnipotent God, the Almighty Lord. "Call upon Me in the day of trouble;
I will deliver you,
and you shall glorify
Me." (Ps. 50:15)

27. "Doleful" means "sorrowful" or "mournful."

there miserably perished. Again, behold, on the left hand there was a very dangerous quag,[25] into which, if even a good man falls, he finds no bottom for his foot to stand on: into that quag king David once did fall, and had no doubt therein been smothered, had not He that is able plucked him out. Psa. 69:14.

The pathway was here also exceeding narrow, and therefore good Christian was the more put to it; for when he sought, in the dark, to shun the ditch on the one hand, he was ready to tip over into the mire on the other; also, when he sought to escape the mire, without great carefulness he would be ready to fall into the ditch. Thus he went on, and I heard him here sigh bitterly; for besides the danger mentioned above, the pathway was here so dark, that ofttimes when he lifted up his foot to go forward, he knew not where, or upon what he should set it next.

About the midst of this valley I perceived the mouth of hell to be, and it stood also hard by the wayside. Now, thought Christian, what shall I do? And ever and anon the flame and smoke would come out in such abundance, with sparks and hideous noises, (things that cared not for Christian's sword, as did Apollyon before,) that he was forced to put up his sword, and betake himself to another weapon, called All-prayer,[26] Eph. 6:18; so he cried, in my hearing, O Lord, I beseech thee, deliver my soul. Psa. 116:4. Thus he went on a great while, yet still the flames would be reaching towards him; also he heard doleful voices,[27] and rushings to and fro, so that sometimes he thought he should be torn in pieces, or trodden down like mire in the streets. This frightful sight was seen, and these dreadful noises were heard by him for several miles together; and coming to a place where he thought he heard a company of fiends coming forward to meet him, he stopped, and began to muse what he had best to do. Sometimes he had half a thought to go back; then again he thought he might be half-way through the valley. He remembered also, how he had already vanquished many a danger; and that the danger of going back might be much more than for to go forward. So he resolved to go on; yet the fiends seemed to come nearer and nearer. But when they were come even almost at him, he cried out with a most vehement voice, I will walk in the strength of the Lord God. So they gave back, and came no farther.[28]

One thing I would not let slip. I took notice that now poor Christian was so confounded that he did not know his own voice; and thus I perceived it. Just when he was come over against the mouth of the burning pit, one of the wicked ones got behind him, and stepped up softly to him, and whisperingly suggested many grievous blasphemies to him, which he verily thought had proceeded from his own mind.[29] This put Christian more to it than any thing that he met with before, even to think that he should now blaspheme Him that he loved so much before. Yet if he could have helped it, he would not have done it; but he had not the discretion either to stop his ears, or to know from whence these blasphemies came.

When Christian had travelled in this disconsolate condition some considerable time, he thought he heard the voice of a man, as going before him, saying, Though I walk through the Valley of the Shadow of Death, I will fear no evil, for thou art with me. Psa. 23:4.

Then was he glad, and that for these reasons:[30]

First, Because he gathered from thence, that some who feared God were in this valley as well as himself.

Secondly, For that he perceived God was with them, though in that dark and dismal state. And why not, thought he, with me? though by reason of the impediment that attends this place, I cannot perceive it. Job 9:11.

Thirdly, For that he hoped (could he overtake them) to have company by and by.

So he went on, and called to him that was before; but he knew not what to answer, for that he also thought himself to be alone. And by and by the day broke: then said Christian, "He hath turned the shadow of death into the morning." Amos 5:8.

28. This is similar to what David writes in Psalm 18:
"He delivered me from my strong enemy,
From those who hated me, For they were too strong for me.
They confronted me in the day of my calamity,
But the Lord was my support." (Ps. 18:17-18)

29. In the midst of this darkness and fog, blasphemous thoughts are suggested to him by the demons. Due to the confusion of this place, Christian wonders whether this thought originated with his own mind. The devil and his demonic assistants will try to deceive us into believing such lies. Just because something comes into our mind does not mean it is our minds that produced it. We may be tempted and tried by wicked thoughts. It is important in the battle of the mind that we resist the devil and his temptations. We must expose his lies with the truth of God's Word.

30. Christian takes comfort and hope as he reviews the promises of God. In the valley of shadows, it is the promises of God that sustain us.

31. We dare not trust ourselves when we are in the valley since we cannot see clearly on our own. It is only by the light that God sends that we will see clearly in the valley. When we are in such perplexing, trying, dark times, let us entrust ourselves to the merciful care of God.
"Oh, send out Your light and Your truth!
Let them lead me;
Let them bring me to Your holy hill
And to Your taber-nacle." (Ps. 43:3)

32. The word "gin" refers to a kind of trap.

33. Pope and Pagan are responsible for the deaths of many. These two characters represent respectively (1) the Roman Catholic church, and (2) all pagan religions.

Now morning being come, he looked back, not out of desire to return, but to see, by the light of the day,[31] what hazards he had gone through in the dark. So he saw more perfectly the ditch that was on the one hand, and the quag that was on the other; also how narrow the way was which led betwixt them both. Also now he saw the hobgoblins, and satyrs, and dragons of the pit, but all afar off; for after break of day they came not nigh; yet they were discovered to him, according to that which is written, "He discovereth deep things out of darkness, and bringeth out to light the shadow of death." Job 12:22.

Now was Christian much affected with this deliverance from all the dangers of his solitary way; which dangers, though he feared them much before, yet he saw them more clearly now, because the light of the day made them conspicuous to him. And about this time the sun was rising, and this was another mercy to Christian; for you must note, that though the first part of the Valley of the Shadow of Death was dangerous, yet this second part, which he was yet to go, was, if possible, far more dangerous; for, from the place where he now stood, even to the end of the valley, the way was all along set so full of snares, traps, gins, and nets here,[32] and so full of pits, pitfalls, deep holes, and shelvings-down there, that had it now been dark, as it was when he came the first part of the way, had he had a thousand souls, they had in reason been cast away; but, as I said, just now the sun was rising. Then said he, "His Candle shineth on my head, and by his light I go through darkness." Job 29:3.

In this light, therefore, he came to the end of the valley. Now I saw in my dream, that at the end of the valley lay blood, bones, ashes, and mangled bodies of men, even of pilgrims that had gone this way formerly; and while I was musing what should be the reason, I espied a little before me a cave, where two giants, Pope and Pagan, dwelt in old times; by whose power and tyranny the men whose bones, blood, ashes, etc., lay there, were cruelly put to death.[33] But by this place Christian went without much danger, whereat I somewhat wondered;

but I have learnt since, that Pagan has been dead many a day; and as for the other, though he be yet alive, he is, by reason of age, and also of the many shrewd brushes that he met with in his younger days, grown so crazy and stiff in his joints that he can now do little more than sit in his cave's mouth, grinning at pilgrims as they go by, and biting his nails because he cannot come at them.[34]

So I saw that Christian went on his way; yet, at the sight of the old man that sat at the mouth of the cave, he could not tell what to think, especially because he spoke to him, though he could not go after him, saying, You will never mend, till more of you be burned. But he held his peace, and set a good face on it; and so went by, and catched no hurt. Then sang Christian,

"O world of wonders, (I can say no less,)
That I should be preserved in that distress
That I have met with here! O blessed be
That hand that from it hath delivered me!
Dangers in darkness, devils, hell, and sin,
Did compass me, while I this vale was in;
Yea, snares, and pits, and traps, and nets did lie
My path about, that worthless, silly I
Might have been catch'd, entangled, and cast down;
But since I live, let Jesus wear the crown."

34. Bunyan presents the Pope and Roman Catholicism as having grown weak and old. Though the Roman Catholic church had done much harm to God's people over centuries, by the time of Bunyan's writing, he saw it as weak and impotent.

Book 1
Chapter 5

1. This is a form of
greeting that would
have been familiar
to Bunyan's original
17th-century audience.

1. This is a form of
greeting that would
have been familiar
to Bunyan's original
17th-century audience.

2. This is a brief illustration of Proverbs 16:18:
"Pride goes before de-
struction, and a haughty
spirit before a fall."

3. Faithful plays the
role of the restorer as
described in Galatians
6:1. He restores his
brother after this fall.

4. "Blended" or "united" our spirits

N ow, as Christian went on his way, he came to a little
ascent, which was cast up on purpose that pilgrims
might see before them: up there, therefore, Christian went; and looking forward, he saw Faithful before him
upon his journey: Then said Christian aloud, Ho, ho; so-ho;[1]
stay, and I will be your companion. At that Faithful looked
behind him; to whom Christian cried again, Stay, stay, till I
come up to you. But Faithful answered, No, I am upon my life,
and the avenger of blood is behind me.

At this Christian was somewhat moved, and putting to
all his strength, he quickly got up with Faithful, and did also
overrun him; so the last was first. Then did Christian vainglo-
riously smile,[2] because he had gotten the start of his brother; but not taking good heed to his feet, he suddenly stumbled and fell, and could not rise again until Faithful came up
to help him.[3]

Then I saw in my dream, they went very lovingly on together, and had sweet discourse of all things that had happened to them in their pilgrimage; and thus Christian began.

Christian: My honored and well-beloved brother Faithful, I am glad that I have overtaken you, and that God has so
tempered our spirits[4] that we can walk as companions in this
so pleasant a path.

Faithful: I had thought, my dear friend, to have had your company quite from our town, but you did get the start of me; wherefore I was forced to come thus much of the way alone.

Christian: How long did you stay in the city of Destruction before you set out after me on your pilgrimage?

Faithful: Till I could stay no longer; for there was a great talk presently after you were gone out, that our city would, in a short time, with fire from heaven, be burnt down to the ground.

Christian: What, did your neighbors talk so?

Faithful: Yes, it was for a while in every body's mouth.

Christian: What, and did no more of them but you come out to escape the danger?

Faithful: Though there was, as I said, a great talk thereabout, yet I do not think they did firmly believe it; for, in the heat of the discourse, I heard some of them deridingly speak of you and of your desperate journey, for so they called this your pilgrimage. But I did believe, and do still, that the end of our city will be with fire and brimstone from above; and therefore I have made my escape.

Christian: Did you hear no talk of neighbor Pliable?

Faithful: Yes, Christian, I heard that he followed you till he came to the Slough of Despond, where, as some said, he fell in; but he would not be known to have so done: but I am sure he was soundly bedabbled with that kind of dirt.[5]

Christian: And what said the neighbors to him?

Faithful: He hath, since his going back, been had greatly in derision, and that among all sorts of people: some do mock and despise him, and scarce will any set him on work. He is now seven times worse than if he had never gone out of the city.

Christian: But why should they be so set against him, since they also despise the way that he forsook?

Faithful: O, they say, Hang him; he is a turncoat; he was not true to his profession! I think God has stirred up even His enemies to hiss at him, and make him a proverb, because he hath forsaken the way.[6] Jer. 29:18,19.

5. Pliable was thoroughly covered with the dirt from the Slough of Despond.

6. Though Pliable turned back to stay with the people of the City of Destruction, he now deals with the shame of having left the way of the world and then returned. Such is the way it is with the world. The world is not a loving place. Paul describes the way of life in the world in Titus 3. "For we ourselves were also once foolish, disobedient, deceived, serving various lusts and pleasures, living in malice and envy, hateful and hating one another." (Tit. 3:3)

7. He "sneaked" away on the other side.

8. The character Wanton represents the loose and forbidden woman described in Proverbs 5 and 7. She tempts Faithful to commit sexual immorality.

9. That is, Wanton promised Faithful sensual pleasures.
"I have perfumed my bed. With myrrh, aloes, and cinnamon.
Come, let us take our fill of love until morning;
Let us delight ourselves with love.
For my husband is not at home; He has gone on a long journey;
He has taken a bag of money with him,
And will come home on the appointed day." (Prov. 7:17-20)

10. The sexually immoral woman promises sensual pleasures. But the result of such sins will be a conscience struck with the guilt of sin.

11. This phrase seems to mean "I think/believe you did not consent to her desires?"

Christian: Had you no talk with him before you came out?

Faithful: I met him once in the streets, but he leered away on the other side,[7] as one ashamed of what he had done; So I spake not to him.

Christian: Well, at my first setting out I had hopes of that man; but now I fear he will perish in the overthrow of the city. For it has happened to him according to the true proverb, The dog is turned to his vomit again, and the sow that was washed to her wallowing in the mire. 2 Pet. 2:22.

Faithful: These are my fears of him too; but who can hinder that which will be?

Christian: Well, neighbor Faithful, said Christian, let us leave him, and talk of things that more immediately concern ourselves. Tell me now what you have met with in the way as you came; for I know you have met with some things, or else it may be writ for a wonder.

Faithful: I escaped the slough that I perceive you fell into, and got up to the gate without that danger; only I met with one whose name was Wanton, that had like to have done me mischief.[8]

Christian: It was well you escaped her net: Joseph was hard put to it by her, and he escaped her as you did; but it had like to have cost him his life. Gen. 39:11-13. But what did she do to you?

Faithful: You cannot think (but that you know something) what a flattering tongue she had; she lay at me hard to turn aside with her, promising me all manner of content.[9]

Christian: Nay, she did not promise you the content of a good conscience.[10]

Faithful: You know what I mean; all carnal and fleshly content.

Christian: Thank God that you escaped her: the abhorred of the Lord shall fall into her pit. Prov. 22:14.

Faithful: Nay, I know not whether I did wholly escape her or no.

Christian: Why, I trow you did not consent to her desires?[11]

Faithful: No, not to defile myself; for I remembered an old writing that I had seen, which said, "Her steps take hold on Hell." Prov. 5:5. So I shut mine eyes, because I would not be bewitched with her looks. Job 31:1. Then she railed on me, and I went my way.

Christian: Did you meet with no other assault as you came?

Faithful: When I came to the foot of the hill called Difficulty, I met with a very aged man, who asked me what I was, and whither bound. I told him that I was a pilgrim, going to the Celestial City. Then said the old man, Thou lookest like an honest fellow; wilt thou be content to dwell with me for the wages that I shall give thee? Then I asked his name, and where he dwelt? He said his name was Adam the First,[12] and that he dwelt in the town of Deceit. Eph. 4:22. I asked him then what was his work, and what the wages that he would give. He told me that his work was many delights; and his wages, that I should be his heir at last. I further asked him, what house he kept, and what other servants he had. So he told me that his house was maintained with all the dainties of the world, and that his servants were those of his own begetting. Then I asked how many children he had. He said that he had but three daughters, the Lust of the Flesh, the Lust of the Eyes, and the Pride of Life, 1 John, 2:16; and that I should marry them if I would. Then I asked, how long time he would have me live with him; And he told me, as long as he lived himself.

Christian: Well, and what conclusion came the old man and you to at last?

Faithful: Why, at first I found myself somewhat inclinable to go with the man, for I thought he spake very fair; but looking in his forehead, as I talked with him, I saw there written, "Put off the old man with his deeds."

Christian: And how then?

Faithful: Then it came burning hot into my mind, that, whatever he said, and however he flattered, when he got me home to his house he would sell me for a slave.[13] So I bid him forbear to talk, for I would not come near the door of his

12. Adam the first refers to fallen humanity (Rom. 5, 1 Cor. 15). His three daughters are the values of the world: the lust of the flesh, the lust of the eyes, and the pride of life (1 John 2:16).

13. To walk in the ways of the world is to indulge the flesh of the old man, which we are to put off. The wages of sin is death (Rom. 6:23).

14. The man who comes to beat Faithful is "Moses," representing the Law of God. The law convicts us of unrighteousness.

15. Paul refers to how the law of God "killed him" because it condemned his unrighteous acts. "I was alive once without the law, but when the commandment came, sin revived and I died. And the commandment, which was to bring life, I found to bring death. For sin, taking occasion by the commandment, deceived me, and by it killed me." (Rom. 7:9-11)

16. The law of God provides a guide for right and wrong. But it does not have the power to justify us before God, because we are unable to perfectly keep the law of God. "For as many as are of the works of the law are under the curse; for it is written, 'Cursed is everyone who does not continue in all things which are written in the book of the law, to do them.'" (Gal. 3:10)

house. Then he reviled me, and told me that he would send such a one after me that should make my way bitter to my soul. So I turned to go away from him; but just as I turned myself to go thence, I felt him take hold of my flesh, and give me such a deadly twitch back, that I thought he had pulled part of me after himself: this made me cry, "O wretched man." Rom. 7:24. So I went on my way up the hill.

Now, when I had got above half-way up, I looked behind me, and saw one coming after me, swift as the wind; so he overtook me just about the place where the settle stands.

Christian: Just there, said Christian, did I sit down to rest me; but being overcome with sleep, I there lost this roll out of my bosom.

Faithful: But, good brother, hear me out. So soon as the man overtook me, it was but a word and a blow; for down he knocked me, and laid me for dead. But when I was a little come to myself again I asked him wherefore he served me so. He said because of my secret inclining to Adam the First.[14] And with that he struck me another deadly blow on the breast, and beat me down backward; so I lay at his foot as dead as before.[15] So when I came to myself again I cried him mercy: but he said, I know not how to show mercy; and with that he knocked me down again. He had doubtless made an end of me, but that one came by and bid him forbear.

Christian: Who was that that bid him forbear?

Faithful: I did not know him at first: but as he went by, I perceived the holes in his hands and in his side: Then I concluded that he was our Lord. So I went up the hill.

Christian: That man that overtook you was Moses. He spareth none; neither knoweth he how to shew mercy to those that transgress the law.[16]

Faithful: I know it very well; it was not the first time that he has met with me. 'Twas he that came to me when I dwelt securely at home, and that told me he would burn my house over my head if I stayed there.

Christian: But did you not see the house that stood there on the top of the hill, on the side of which Moses met you?

Faithful: Yes, and the lions too, before I came at it. But, for the lions, I think they were asleep, for it was about noon; and because I had so much of the day before me, I passed by the Porter, and came down the hill.

Christian: He told me, indeed, that he saw you go by; but I wish you had called at the house, for they would have showed you so many rarities that you would scarce have forgot them to the day of your death. But pray tell me, Did you meet nobody in the Valley of Humility?

Faithful: Yes, I met with one Discontent, who would willingly have persuaded me to go back again with him: his reason was, for that the valley was altogether without honor. He told me, moreover, that to go there was the way to disoblige all my friends, as Pride, Arrogancy, Self-Conceit, Worldly Glory, with others, who he knew, as he said, would be very much offended if I made such a fool of myself as to wade through this valley.[17]

Christian: Well, and how did you answer him?

Faithful: I told him, that although all these that he named, might claim a kindred of me, and that rightly, (for indeed they were my relations according to the flesh,) yet since I became a pilgrim they have disowned me, and I also have rejected them; and therefore they were to me now no more than if they had never been of my lineage. I told him, moreover, that as to this valley, he had quite misrepresented the thing; for before honor is humility, and a haughty spirit before a fall. Therefore, said I, I had rather go through this valley to the honor that was so accounted by the wisest, than choose that which he esteemed most worthy of our affections.

Christian: Met you with nothing else in that valley?

Faithful: Yes, I met with Shame; but of all the men that I met with on my pilgrimage, he, I think, bears the wrong name. The other would be said nay, after a little argumenta-

17. Pride, arrogance, self-conceit, and worldly glory are all common vices that keep people from humbling themselves. But God says He resists the proud but gives grace to the humble (1 Pet. 5:5).

tion, and somewhat else; but this bold-faced Shame would never have done.

Christian: Why, what did he say to you?

Faithful: What? why, he objected against religion itself. He said it was a pitiful, low, sneaking business for a man to mind religion. He said, that a tender conscience was an unmanly thing; and that for a man to watch over his words and ways, so as to tie up himself from that hectoring liberty that the brave spirits of the times accustomed themselves unto, would make him the ridicule of the times. He objected also, that but few of the mighty, rich, or wise, were ever of my opinion; nor any of them neither, before they were persuaded to be fools, and to be of a voluntary fondness to venture the loss of all for nobody knows what. 1 Cor. 1:26; 3:18; Phil. 3:7-9; John 7:48. He, moreover, objected the base and low estate and condition of those that were chiefly the pilgrims of the times in which they lived; also their ignorance and want of understanding in all natural science. Yea, he did hold me to it at that rate also, about a great many more things than here I relate; as, that it was a shame to sit whining and mourning under a sermon, and a shame to come sighing and groaning home; that it was a shame to ask my neighbor forgiveness for petty faults, or to make restitution where I have taken from any. He said also, that religion made a man grow strange to the great, because of a few vices, which he called by finer names, and made him own and respect the base, because of the same religious fraternity: And is not this, said he, a shame?

Christian: And what did you say to him?

Faithful: Say? I could not tell what to say at first. Yea, he put me so to it, that my blood came up in my face;[18] even this Shame fetched it up, and had almost beat me quite off. But at last I began to consider, that that which is highly esteemed among men, is had in abomination with God. Luke 16:15. And I thought again, this Shame tells me what men are; but he tells me nothing what God, or the word of God is. And I thought, moreover, that at the day of doom we shall

18. At first Faithful was tempted to be ashamed of the way he had chosen. Shame tried to give him reasons to abandon the way of life because of worldly concerns such as the fear of man. The Christian is not concerned with what men think of him, but the Christian is concerned with what God thinks. "For do I now persuade men, or God? Or do I seek to please men? For if I still pleased men, I would not be a bondservant of Christ." (Gal. 1:10) Paul also says in Romans 1 that "he is not ashamed of the gospel" (Rom. 1:16).

not be doomed to death or life according to the hectoring spirits of the world, but according to the wisdom and law of the Highest. Therefore, thought I, what God says is best, is indeed best, though all the men in the world are against it. Seeing, then, that God prefers his religion; seeing God prefers a tender Conscience; seeing they that make themselves fools for the kingdom of heaven are wisest, and that the poor man that loveth Christ is richer than the greatest man in the world that hates him; Shame, depart, thou art an enemy to my salvation. Shall I entertain thee against my sovereign Lord? How then shall I look him in the face at his coming?[19] Mark 8:38. Should I now be ashamed of his ways and servants, how can I expect the blessing? But indeed this Shame was a bold villain; I could scarcely shake him out of my company; yea, he would be haunting of me, and continually whispering me in the ear, with some one or other of the infirmities that attend religion. But at last I told him, that it was but in vain to attempt farther in this business; for those things that he disdained, in those did I see most glory: and so at last I got past this importunate one.[20] And when I had shaken him off, then I began to sing,

"The trials that those men do meet withal,
That are obedient to the heavenly call,
Are manifold, and suited to the flesh,
And come, and come, and come again afresh;
That now, or some time else, we by them may
Be taken, overcome, and cast away.
O let the pilgrims, let the pilgrims then,
Be vigilant, and quit themselves like men."

Christian: I am glad, my brother, that thou didst withstand this villain so bravely; for of all, as thou sayest, I think he has the wrong name; for he is so bold as to follow us in the streets, and to attempt to put us to shame before all men; that is, to make us ashamed of that which is good. But if he was not himself audacious, he would never attempt to do as he does. But let us still resist him; for, notwithstanding all his bravadoes, he promoteth the fool, and none else. "The wise

19. Those who are ashamed of Christ at his coming show that they are not true followers of Jesus Christ. "For whoever is ashamed of Me and My words in this adulterous and sinful generation, of him the Son of Man also will be ashamed when He comes in the glory of His Father with the holy angels." (Mark 8:38)

20. Past this "persistent" one

21. One of the key ways to combat shame and fear is to cry out to the Lord for His strengthening power.

22. "The wicked flee when no one pursues, but the righteous are bold as a lion." (Prov. 28:1)

23. Talkative is a satirical character representing one who talks of spiritual things but has no spiritual life. This spiritual problem is described repeatedly in Scripture. We are not to love "in word or in tongue, but in deed and in truth" (1 John 3:18). We are to be "doers of the Word" and not "hearers only" (Jas. 1:22). He is "all talk but no walk."

shall inherit glory," said Solomon; "but shame shall be the promotion of fools." Prov. 3:35.

Faithful: I think we must cry to Him for help against Shame,[21] that would have us to be valiant for truth upon the earth.[22]

Christian: You say true; but did you meet nobody else in that valley?

Faithful: No, not I; for I had sunshine all the rest of the way through that, and also through the Valley of the Shadow of Death.

Christian: 'Twas well for you; I am sure it fared far otherwise with me. I had for a long season, as soon almost as I entered into that valley, a dreadful combat with that foul fiend Apollyon; yea, I thought verily he would have killed me, especially when he got me down, and crushed me under him, as if he would have crushed me to pieces; for as he threw me, my sword flew out of my hand: nay, he told me he was sure of me; but I cried to God, and he heard me, and delivered me out of all my troubles. Then I entered into the Valley of the Shadow of Death, and had no light for almost half the way through it. I thought I should have been killed there over and over; but at last day brake, and the sun rose, and I went through that which was behind with far more ease and quiet.

Moreover, I saw in my dream, that as they went on, Faithful, as he chanced to look on one side, saw a man whose name was Talkative,[23] walking at a distance beside them; for in this place there was room enough for them all to walk. He was a tall man, and something more comely at a distance than at hand. To this man Faithful addressed himself in this manner.

Faithful: Friend, whither away? Are you going to the heavenly country?

Talkative: I am going to the same place.

Faithful: That is well; then I hope we shall have your good company?

Talkative: With a very good will, will I be your companion.

Faithful: Come on, then, and let us go together, and let us spend our time in discoursing of things that are profitable.

Talkative: To talk of things that are good, to me is very acceptable, with you or with any other; and I am glad that I have met with those that incline to so good a work; for, to speak the truth, there are but few who care thus to spend their time as they are in their travels, but choose much rather to be speaking of things to no profit; and this hath been a trouble to me.

Faithful: That is, indeed, a thing to be lamented; for what thing so worthy of the use of the tongue and mouth of men on earth, as are the things of the God of heaven?

Talkative: I like you wonderful well, for your saying is full of conviction; and I will add, What thing is so pleasant, and what so profitable, as to talk of the things of God? What things so pleasant? that is, if a man hath any delight in things that are wonderful. For instance, if a man doth delight to talk of the history, or the mystery of things; or if a man doth love to talk of miracles, wonders, or signs, where shall he find things recorded so delightful, and so sweetly penned, as in the holy Scripture?

Faithful: That is true; but to be profited by such things in our talk, should be our chief design.[24]

Talkative: That's it that I said; for to talk of such things is most profitable; for by so doing a man may get knowledge of many things; as of the vanity of earthly things, and the benefit of things above. Thus in general; but more particularly, by this a man may learn the necessity of the new birth, the insufficiency of our works, the need of Christ's righteousness, etc. Besides, by this a man may learn what it is to repent, to believe, to pray, to suffer, or the like: by this, also, a man may learn what are the great promises and consolations of the Gospel, to his own comfort. Farther, by this a man may learn to refute false opinions, to vindicate the truth, and also to instruct the ignorant.[25]

Faithful: All this is true; and glad am I to hear these things from you.

24. Faithful notes that speaking of the things of God must lead to edification. If it does not lead to edification, it is not a profitable discussion. Paul warns of such discussions in 1 Timothy. "Nor give heed to fables and endless genealogies, which cause disputes rather than godly edification which is in faith." (1 Tim. 1:4)

25. Talkative finds it enjoyable to talk about the doctrines of the faith. He appears to be knowledgeable. But soon we will find that he has a mere intellectual understanding of these doctrines.

Talkative: Alas! the want of this is the cause that so few understand the need of faith, and the necessity of a work of grace in their soul, in order to eternal life; but ignorantly live in the works of the law, by which a man can by no means obtain the kingdom of heaven.

Faithful: But, by your leave, heavenly knowledge of these is the gift of God; no man attaineth to them by human industry, or only by the talk of them.

Talkative: All this I know very well; for a man can receive nothing, except it be given him from heaven: all is of grace, not of works. I could give you a hundred scriptures for the confirmation of this.

Faithful: Well, then, said Faithful, what is that one thing that we shall at this time found our discourse upon?

Talkative: What you will. I will talk of things heavenly, or things earthly; things moral, or things evangelical; things sacred, or things profane; things past, or things to come; things foreign, or things at home; things more essential, or things circumstantial: provided that all be done to our profit.[26]

Faithful: Now did Faithful begin to wonder; and stepping to Christian, (for he walked all this while by himself,) he said to him, but softly, What a brave companion have we got! Surely, this man will make a very excellent pilgrim.[27]

Christian: At this Christian modestly smiled, and said, This man, with whom you are so taken, will beguile with this tongue of his, twenty of them that know him not.

Faithful: Do you know him, then?

Christian: Know him? Yes, better than he knows himself.

Faithful: Pray what is he?

Christian: His name is Talkative: he dwelleth in our town. I wonder that you should be a stranger to him, only I consider that our town is large.

Faithful: Whose son is he? And whereabout doth he dwell?

Christian: He is the son of one Say-well. He dwelt in Prating-Row; and he is known to all that are acquainted with

26. Talkative says he will talk about anything. His main interest is talk on just about any subject.

27. Some are gifted at talking and showing interest in the doctrines of the faith. This can seem very impressive to us. But what matters to the Lord is not how much knowledge we have, but whether we love in deed and truth. Paul warns us about this in 1 Corinthians 8. "Now concerning things offered to idols: We know that we all have knowledge. Knowledge puffs up, but love edifies." (1 Cor. 8:1)

him by the name of Talkative of Prating-Row; and, notwithstanding his fine tongue, he is but a sorry fellow.[28]

Faithful: Well, he seems to be a very pretty man.

Christian: That is, to them that have not a thorough acquaintance with him, for he is best abroad; near home he is ugly enough. Your saying that he is a pretty man, brings to my mind what I have observed in the work of a painter, whose pictures show best at a distance; but very near, more unpleasing.

Faithful: But I am ready to think you do but jest, because you smiled.

Christian: God forbid that I should jest (though I smiled) in this matter, or that I should accuse any falsely. I will give you a further discovery of him. This man is for any company, and for any talk; as he talketh now with you, so will he talk when he is on the ale-bench; and the more drink he hath in his crown, the more of these things he hath in his mouth. Religion hath no place in his heart, or house, or conversation; all he hath lieth in his tongue, and his religion is to make a noise therewith.[29]

Faithful: Say you so? Then am I in this man greatly deceived.

Christian: Deceived! you may be sure of it. Remember the proverb, "They say, and do not;" but the kingdom of God is not in word, but in power. Matt. 23:3; 1 Cor. 4:20. He talketh of prayer, of repentance, of faith, and of the new birth; but he knows but only to talk of them. I have been in his family, and have observed him both at home and abroad; and I know what I say of him is the truth. His house is as empty of religion as the white of an egg is of savor. There is there neither prayer, nor sign of repentance for sin; yea, the brute, in his kind, serves God far better than he. He is the very stain, reproach, and shame of religion to all that know him, Rom. 2:24,25; it can hardly have a good word in all that end of the town where he dwells, through him. Thus say the common people that know him, "A saint abroad, and a devil at home." His poor family finds it so; he is such a churl, such a railer at, and so unreasonable with his servants, that they neither know how to do for

28. Bunyan paints a humorous picture of Talkative's origins. He is the son of "Say-well" and the street he lives on is "Prating-Row." The phrase "Prating-Row" in modern English means something like "Chattering Street."

29. Talkative is "all talk" but his way of life shows that religion doesn't go any further than conversation. There is no reality to what he says.

30. Talkative does not live a life of faith and repentance. He speaks of such things. But he shows himself to have a dead faith because it is not accompanied by works (Jas. 2). He mistreats his wife, he shouts at his servants, and he is unjust in his business dealings. His way of life shames the name of Christ before men. He is a false professor.

or speak to him. Men that have any dealings with him say, It is better to deal with a Turk than with him, for fairer dealings they shall have at their hands. This Talkative (if it be possible) will go beyond them, defraud, beguile, and overreach them. Besides, he brings up his sons to follow his steps; and if he finds in any of them a foolish timorousness, (for so he calls the first appearance of a tender conscience,) he calls them fools and blockheads, and by no means will employ them in much, or speak to their commendation before others. For my part, I am of opinion that he has, by his wicked life, caused many to stumble and fall; and will be, if God prevents not, the ruin of many more.[30]

Faithful: Well, my brother, I am bound to believe you, not only because you say you know him, but also because, like a Christian, you make your reports of men. For I cannot think that you speak these things of ill-will, but because it is even so as you say.

Christian: Had I known him no more than you, I might, perhaps, have thought of him as at the first you did; yea, had I received this report at their hands only that are enemies to religion, I should have thought it had been a slander-a lot that often falls from bad men's mouths upon good men's names and professions. But all these things, yea, and a great many more as bad, of my own knowledge, I can prove him guilty of. Besides, good men are ashamed of him; they can neither call him brother nor friend; the very naming of him among them makes them blush, if they know him.

Faithful: Well, I see that saying and doing are two things, and hereafter I shall better observe this distinction.

Christian: They are two things indeed, and are as diverse as are the soul and the body; for, as the body without the soul is but a dead carcass, so saying, if it be alone, is but a dead carcass also. The soul of religion is the practical part. "Pure religion and undefiled before God and the Father is this, to visit the fatherless and widows in their affliction, and to keep himself unspotted from the world." James 1:27; see also verses

22-26. This, Talkative is not aware of; he thinks that hearing and saying will make a good Christian; and thus he deceiveth his own soul. Hearing is but as the sowing of the seed; talking is not sufficient to prove that fruit is indeed in the heart and life. And let us assure ourselves, that at the day of doom men shall be judged according to their fruits. Matt. 13:23. It will not be said then, Did you believe? but, Were you doers, or talkers only? and accordingly shall they be judged. The end of the world is compared to our harvest, Matt. 13:30, and you know men at harvest regard nothing but fruit. Not that any thing can be accepted that is not of faith; but I speak this to show you how insignificant the profession of Talkative will be at that day.

Faithful: This brings to my mind that of Moses, by which he describeth the beast that is clean. Lev. 11; Deut. 14. He is such an one that parteth the hoof, and cheweth the cud; not that parteth the hoof only, or that cheweth the cud only. The hare cheweth the cud, but yet is unclean, because he parteth not the hoof. And this truly resembleth Talkative: he cheweth the cud, he seeketh knowledge; he cheweth upon the word, but he divideth not the hoof. He parteth not with the way of sinners; but, as the hare, he retaineth the foot of the dog or bear, and therefore he is unclean.

Christian: You have spoken, for aught I know, the true gospel sense of these texts.[31] And I will add another thing: Paul calleth some men, yea, and those great talkers too, sounding brass, and tinkling cymbals, 1 Cor. 13:1, 3; that is, as he expounds them in another place, things without life giving sound. 1 Cor. 14:7. Things without life; that is, without the true faith and grace of the gospel; and consequently, things that shall never be placed in the kingdom of heaven among those that are the children of life; though their sound, by their talk, be as if it were the tongue or voice of an angel.

Faithful: Well, I was not so fond of his company at first, but I am as sick of it now. What shall we do to be rid of him?

31. Faithful gives an allegorical interpretation of the clean and unclean animals and draws an analogy to Talkative's spiritual condition.

32. Once Talkative is confronted and challenged about the nature of true saving faith, he will soon dislike the company of Christian and Faithful.

Christian: Take my advice, and do as I bid you, and you shall find that he will soon be sick of your company too, except God shall touch his heart, and turn it.

Faithful: What would you have me to do?

Christian: Why, go to him, and enter into some serious discourse about the power of religion;[32] and ask him plainly, (when he has approved of it, for that he will,) whether this thing be set up in his heart, house, or conversation.

Faithful: Then Faithful stepped forward again, and said to Talkative, Come, what cheer? How is it now?

Talkative: Thank you, well: I thought we should have had a great deal of talk by this time.

Faithful: Well, if you will, we will fall to it now; and since you left it with me to state the question, let it be this: How doth the saving grace of God discover itself when it is in the heart of man?

Talkative: I perceive, then, that our talk must be about the power of things. Well, it is a very good question, and I shall be willing to answer you. And take my answer in brief, thus: First, where the grace of God is in the heart, it causeth there a great outcry against sin. Secondly-

Faithful: Nay, hold; let us consider of one at once. I think you should rather say, it shows itself by inclining the soul to abhor its sin.

Talkative: Why, what difference is there between crying out against, and abhorring of sin?

33. Faithful draws a distinction. It is one thing for a man to "cry out" against his sin. It is another thing for that man to actually hate his sin and then turn away from it.

Faithful: Oh! a great deal. A man may cry out against sin, of policy; but he cannot abhor it but by virtue of a godly antipathy against it.[33] I have heard many cry out against sin in the pulpit, who yet can abide it well enough in the heart, house, and conversation. Gen. 39:15. Joseph's mistress cried out with a loud voice, as if she had been very holy; but she would willingly, notwithstanding that, have committed uncleanness with him. Some cry out against sin, even as the mother cries out against her child in her lap, when she calleth it slut and naughty girl, and then falls to hugging and kissing it.

Talkative: You lie at the catch, I perceive.

Faithful: No, not I; I am only for setting things right. But what is the second thing whereby you would prove a discovery of a work of grace in the heart?

Talkative: Great knowledge of gospel mysteries.[34]

Faithful: This sign should have been first: but, first or last, it is also false; for knowledge, great knowledge, may be obtained in the mysteries of the Gospel, and yet no work of grace[35] in the soul. Yea, if a man have all knowledge, he may yet be nothing, and so, consequently, be no child of God. 1 Cor. 13:2. When Christ said, "Do you know all these things?" and the disciples answered, Yes, he added, "Blessed are ye if ye do them." He doth not lay the blessing in the knowing of them, but in the doing of them. For there is a knowledge that is not attended with doing: "He that knoweth his Master's will, and doeth it not." A man may know like an angel, and yet be no Christian: therefore your sign of it is not true. Indeed, to know is a thing that pleaseth talkers and boasters; but to do is that which pleaseth God. Not that the heart can be good without knowledge, for without that the heart is naught. There are, therefore, two sorts of knowledge, knowledge that resteth in the bare speculation of things, and knowledge that is accompanied with the grace of faith and love, which puts a man upon doing even the will of God from the heart: the first of these will serve the talker; but without the other, the true Christian is not content. "Give me understanding, and I shall keep thy law; yea, I shall observe it with my whole heart." Psa. 119:34.

Talkative: You lie at the catch again: this is not for edification.

Faithful: Well, if you please, propound another sign how this work of grace discovereth itself where it is.

Talkative: Not I, for I see we shall not agree.

Faithful: Well, if you will not, will you give me leave to do it?

Talkative: You may use your liberty.

34. Talkative argues that the work of grace in the heart will be evidenced by a great knowledge of doctrine. But Paul warns us that if we have all knowledge, but do not have love, we are nothing (1 Cor. 13:2).

35. Faithful's description of the evidence of saving grace in the soul includes the following: (1) a conviction of sin and shame from sin, and (2) a "closing with" (or receiving and resting in) Jesus the Savior as his only hope. To others this saving grace will be evidenced by (1) a confession of faith in Christ, and (2) a life of repentance and godliness that accords with that confession.

Faithful: A work of grace in the soul discovereth itself, either to him that hath it, or to standers-by.

To him that hath it, thus: It gives him conviction of sin, especially the defilement of his nature, and the sin of unbelief, for the sake of which he is sure to be damned, if he findeth not mercy at God's hand, by faith in Jesus Christ. This sight and sense of things worketh in him sorrow and shame for sin. Psa. 38:18; Jer. 31:19; John 16:8; Rom. 7:24; Mark 16:16; Gal. 2:16; Rev. 1:6. He findeth, moreover, revealed in him the Saviour of the world, and the absolute necessity of closing with him for life; at the which he findeth hungerings and thirstings after him; to which hungerings, etc., the promise is made. Now, according to the strength or weakness of his faith in his Saviour, so is his joy and peace, so is his love to holiness, so are his desires to know him more, and also to serve him in this world. But though, I say, it discovereth itself thus unto him, yet it is but seldom that he is able to conclude that this is a work of grace; because his corruptions now, and his abused reason, make his mind to misjudge in this matter: therefore in him that hath this work there is required a very sound judgment, before he can with steadiness conclude that this is a work of grace. John 16:9; Gal. 2:15,16; Acts 4:12; Matt. 5:6; Rev. 21:6.

To others it is thus discovered:

1. By an experimental confession of his faith in Christ. 2. By a life answerable to that confession; to wit, a life of holiness-heart-holiness, family-holiness, (if he hath a family,) and by conversation-holiness in the world; which in the general teacheth him inwardly to abhor his sin, and himself for that, in secret; to suppress it in his family, and to promote holiness in the world: not by talk only, as a hypocrite or talkative person may do, but by a practical subjection in faith and love to the power of the word. Job 42:5,6; Psa. 50:23; Ezek. 20:43; Matt. 5:8; John 14:15; Rom. 10:10; Ezek. 36:25; Phil. 1:27; 3:17-20. And now, sir, as to this brief description of the work of grace, and also the discovery of it, if you have aught to ob-

ject, object; if not, then give me leave to propound to you a second question.

Talkative: Nay, my part is not now to object, but to hear; let me, therefore, have your second question.

Faithful: It is this: Do you experience this first part of the description of it; and doth your life and conversation testify the same? Or standeth your religion in word or tongue, and not in deed and truth? Pray, if you incline to answer me in this, say no more than you know the God above will say Amen to, and also nothing but what your conscience can justify you in; for not he that commendeth himself is approved, but whom the Lord commendeth. Besides, to say I am thus and thus, when my conversation, and all my neighbors, tell me I lie, is great wickedness.

Then Talkative at first began to blush; but, recovering himself, thus he replied: You come now to experience, to conscience, and to God; and to appeal to him for justification of what is spoken. This kind of discourse I did not expect; nor am I disposed to give an answer to such questions, because I count not myself bound thereto, unless you take upon you to be a catechiser; and though you should so do, yet I may refuse to make you my judge. But I pray, will you tell me why you ask me such questions?

Faithful: Because I saw you forward to talk, and because I knew not that you had aught else but notion.[36] Besides, to tell you all the truth, I have heard of you that you are a man whose religion lies in talk, and that your conversation gives this your mouth-profession the lie. They say you are a spot among Christians, and that religion fareth the worse for your ungodly conversation; that some have already stumbled at your wicked ways, and that more are in danger of being destroyed thereby: your religion, and an ale-house, and covetousness, and uncleanness, and swearing, and lying, and vain company-keeping, etc., will stand together. The proverb is true of you which is said of a harlot, to wit, "That she is a shame to all women:" so are you a shame to all professors.

36. That is, Faithful knew Talkative to have nothing else but mere intellectual apprehension of the faith.

37. Peevish may mean "fretful, apt to mutter and complain, hard to please, etc."

38. "Having a form of godliness but denying its power. And from such people turn away!" (2 Tim. 3:5)

39. If Christians rightly understood the nature of saving faith and would call others to faith and repentance, it would help to purify the church of those who make false professions.

Talkative: Since you are so ready to take up reports, and to judge so rashly as you do, I cannot but conclude you are some peevish or melancholy man,[37] not fit to be discoursed with; and so adieu.

Then up came Christian, and said to his brother, I told you how it would happen; your words and his lusts could not agree. He had rather leave your company than reform his life. But he is gone, as I said: let him go; the loss is no man's but his own. He has saved us the trouble of going from him; for he continuing (as I suppose he will do) as he is, would have been but a blot in our company: besides, the apostle says, "From such withdraw thyself."[38]

Faithful: But I am glad we had this little discourse with him; it may happen that he will think of it again: however, I have dealt plainly with him, and so am clear of his blood if he perisheth.

Christian: You did well to talk so plainly to him as you did. There is but little of this faithful dealing with men now-a-days, and that makes religion to stink so in the nostrils of many as it doth; for they are these talkative fools, whose religion is only in word, and who are debauched and vain in their conversation, that (being so much admitted into the fellowship of the godly) do puzzle the world, blemish Christianity, and grieve the sincere. I wish that all men would deal with such as you have done; then should they either be made more conformable to religion, or the company of saints would be too hot for them.[39] Then did Faithful say,

"How Talkative at first lifts up his plumes!
How bravely doth he speak! How he presumes
To drive down all before him! But so soon
As Faithful talks of heart-work, like the moon
That's past the full, into the wane he goes;
And so will all but he that heart-work know."

Thus they went on, talking of what they had seen by the way, and so made that way easy, which would otherwise no doubt have been tedious to them, for now they went through a wilderness.

Book 1
Chapter 6

Now when they were got almost quite out of this wilderness, Faithful chanced to cast his eye back, and espied one[1] coming after them, and he knew him. Oh! said Faithful to his brother, who comes yonder? Then Christian looked, and said, It is my good friend Evangelist.[2] Aye, and my good friend too, said Faithful, for 'twas he that set me on the way to the gate. Now was Evangelist come up unto them, and thus saluted them.

Evangelist: Peace be with you, dearly beloved, and peace be to your helpers.

Christian: Welcome, welcome, my good Evangelist: the sight of thy countenance brings to my remembrance thy ancient kindness[3] and unwearied labors for my eternal good.[4]

Faithful: And a thousand times welcome, said good Faithful, thy company, O sweet Evangelist; how desirable is it to us poor pilgrims!

Evangelist: Then said Evangelist, How hath it fared with you, my friends, since the time of our last parting? What have you met with, and how have you behaved yourselves?

Then Christian and Faithful told him of all things that had happened to them in the way; and how, and with what difficulty, they had arrived to that place.

Right glad am I, said Evangelist, not that you have met with trials, but that you have been victors, and for that you

1. He "saw" someone.

2. Evangelist symbolizes the preacher of the gospel. The word "evangelist" refers to one who proclaims the gospel (Greek *evangellion*), the "good news" of Jesus Christ. Evangelist re-appears in Bunyan's narrative a number of times to help keep Christian pointed in the right direction as he journeys to the Celestial City.

3. To see Evangelist again is a reminder of Evangelist's kindness and labors for Christian.

4. It is important that preachers of the gospel remember that they are engaging in a work of eternal importance. To preach the gospel is to seek the eternal good of the hearers. We should all be thankful for the labors of faithful preachers of the good news.

have, notwithstanding many weaknesses, continued in the way to this very day.

I say, right glad am I of this thing, and that for mine own sake and yours: I have sowed, and you have reaped; and the day is coming, when "both he that soweth, and they that reap, shall rejoice together," John 4:36; that is, if you hold out: "for in due season ye shall reap, if ye faint not." Gal. 6:9. The crown is before you, and it is an incorruptible one; "so run that ye may obtain it." 1 Cor. 9:24-27. Some there be that set out for this crown, and after they have gone far for it, another comes in and takes it from them: "hold fast, therefore, that you have; let no man take your crown." Rev. 3:11. You are not yet out of the gunshot of the devil; "you have not resisted unto blood, striving against sin." Let the kingdom be always before you, and believe steadfastly concerning the things that are invisible. Let nothing that is on this side the other world get within you. And, above all, look well to your own hearts and to the lusts thereof; for they are "deceitful above all things, and desperately wicked." Set your faces like a flint;[5] you have all power in heaven and earth on your side.

Christian: Then Christian thanked him for his exhortations; but told him withal, that they would have him speak farther to them for their help the rest of the way; and the rather, for that they well knew that he was a prophet, and could tell them of things that might happen unto them, and also how they might resist and overcome them. To which request Faithful also consented. So Evangelist began as followeth.

Evangelist: My sons, you have heard in the word of the truth of the Gospel, that you must "through many tribulations enter into the kingdom of heaven;" and again, that "in every city, bonds and afflictions abide you;" and therefore you cannot expect that you should go long on your pilgrimage without them, in some sort or other. You have found something of the truth of these testimonies upon you already, and more will immediately follow: for now, as you see, you are almost out of this wilderness, and therefore you will soon come into a town

5. That is, Christian and Faithful should pursue their final destination with great determination, not looking to the right or to the left.

that you will by and by see before you; and in that town you will be hardly beset with enemies, who will strain hard but they will kill you; and be you sure that one or both of you must seal the testimony which you hold, with blood; but "be you faithful unto death, and the King will give you a crown of life." He that shall die there, although his death will be unnatural, and his pain, perhaps, great, he will yet have the better of his fellow; not only because he will be arrived at the Celestial City soonest, but because he will escape many miseries that the other will meet with in the rest of his journey. But when you are come to the town, and shall find fulfilled what I have here related, then remember your friend, and quit yourselves like men, and "commit the keeping of your souls to God in well doing, as unto a faithful Creator."[6]

Then I saw in my dream, that when they were got out of the wilderness, they presently saw a town before them, and the name of that town is Vanity; and at the town there is a fair kept, called Vanity Fair. It is kept all the year long. It beareth the name of Vanity Fair, because the town where it is kept is lighter than vanity,[7] Psa. 62:9; and also because all that is there sold, or that cometh thither, is vanity; as is the saying of the wise, "All that cometh is vanity." Eccl. 11:8; see also 1:2-14; 2:11-17; Isa. 40:17.

This fair is no new-erected business but a thing of ancient standing.[8] I will show you the original of it.

6. Evangelist warns the men they will soon enter a town. In that town, they will encounter fierce opposition and one of them will die. Evangelist speaks prophetically of what will soon happen. Christians should expect to encounter persecution from the world. But we can entrust our souls to God, who is faithful to preserve us from the ungodly.

7. The Book of Ecclesiastes provides the biblical background to the name "Vanity Fair." In Ecclesiastes, Solomon expounds the vanity (or emptiness) of the world (Eccl. 1:2).

8. In Bunyan's story, Vanity Fair is the representation of this fallen world and its cultural and social systems. The Christian faces three enemies: the world, the flesh, and the devil. Christian and Faithful experience the hostility of the world as they journey through the fair. Bunyan says that the fair is "of ancient standing." What Bunyan means is that this world system has existed since the fall of man. It is nothing new.

9. Bunyan indicates with this reference that he believes that the earth is relatively young, consistent with what we find provided in the genealogies of the Book of Genesis.

10. A "knave" is a dishonest or deceptive person. Rogue is a synonym of "knave."

11. The various "rows" or "streets" of the fair are named after different countries in Europe. In other words, the various divisions of Vanity Fair represent the world and the respective nations that are sold out to these worldly principles and attainments.

12. The "ware of Rome" refers to Roman Catholicism. Bunyan notes that the English church had rejected Roman Catholicism. This took place under King Henry VIII who separated the Church of England from the Pope of Rome.

Almost five thousand years ago[9] there were pilgrims walking to the Celestial City, as these two honest persons are: and Beelzebub, Apollyon, and Legion, with their companions, perceiving by the path that the pilgrims made, that their way to the city lay through this town of Vanity, they contrived here to set up a fair; a fair wherein should be sold all sorts of vanity, and that it should last all the year long. Therefore, at this fair are all such merchandise sold as houses, lands, trades, places, honors, preferments, titles, countries, kingdoms, lusts, pleasures; and delights of all sorts, as harlots, wives, husbands, children, masters, servants, lives, blood, bodies, souls, silver, gold, pearls, precious stones, and what not.

And moreover, at this fair there is at all times to be seen jugglings, cheats, games, plays, fools, apes, knaves, and rogues,[10] and that of every kind.

Here are to be seen, too, and that for nothing, thefts, murders, adulteries, false-swearers, and that of a blood-red color.

And, as in other fairs of less moment, there are the several rows and streets under their proper names, where such and such wares are vended; so here, likewise, you have the proper places, rows, streets, (namely, countries and kingdoms,) where the wares of this fair are soonest to be found. Here is the Britain Row, the French Row, the Italian Row, the Spanish Row, the German Row,[11] where several sorts of vanities are to be sold. But, as in other fairs, some one commodity is as the chief of all the fair; so the ware of Rome and her merchandise is greatly promoted in this fair; only our English nation, with some others, have taken a dislike thereat.[12]

Now, as I said, the way to the Celestial City lies just through this town, where this lusty fair is kept; and he that will go to the city, and yet not go through this town, "must needs go out of the world." 1 Cor. 5:10. The Prince of princes himself, when here, went through this town to his own country,[13] and that upon a fair-day too; yea, and, as I think, it was Beelzebub, the chief lord of this fair, that invited him to buy of his vanities, yea, would have made him lord of the fair, would he but have done him reverence as he went through the town. Yea, because he was such a person of honor, Beelzebub had him from street to street, and showed him all the kingdoms of the world in a little time, that he might, if possible, allure that blessed One to cheapen and buy some of his vanities; but he had no mind to the merchandise, and therefore left the town, without laying out so much as one farthing upon these vanities. Matt. 4:8,9; Luke 4:5-7. This fair, therefore, is an ancient thing, of long standing, and a very great fair.

Now, these pilgrims, as I said, must needs go through this fair. Well, so they did; but behold, even as they entered into the fair, all the people in the fair were moved; and the town itself, as it were, in a hubbub about them, and that for several reasons: for,

First, The Pilgrims were clothed with such kind of raiment as was diverse from the raiment of any that traded in that fair.[14] The people, therefore, of the fair made a great gazing upon them: some said they were fools; 1 Cor. 4:9,10; some, they were bedlams;[15] and some, they were outlandish men.

Secondly, And as they wondered at their apparel, so they did likewise at their speech; for few could understand what they said. They naturally spoke the language of Canaan;[16] but

13. Bunyan refers to the temptation of our Lord Jesus Christ. Jesus was taken through Vanity Fair when Satan promised to make Jesus the "lord" over the world. It is true that Satan has limited authority of the world. He is called the "god of this world" in Scripture (2 Cor. 4). However, Jesus has bound the strong man and robbed his house. The ruler of this world has been cast out (John 12:31).

14. "Raiment" is a reference to clothing. The clothing of the two pilgrims was different than any in the fair. Bunyan wants to communicate that God's people are to look and speak differently than people in the world. We are called to be a holy people, set apart from the world.

15. "Bedlams" is an old English term that refers to those who are mentally insane.

16. The people of God not only look different from the world. They also speak differently. Their speech is sanctified by the Holy Spirit. Christians are to be those who speak edifying words, and let no corrupting word come out of their mouth (Eph. 4:29, Col. 3:8).

17. Christians and non-Christians hold worldviews that are utterly opposed. Because of their different faith-commitments, their language will be different. In many cases, it can be difficult to find common ground or understand each other.

18. That is, the pilgrims did not care for the merchandise sold by the world. They were not interested in the lust of the flesh, the lust of the eyes, and the pride of life.

19. Jesus promised that the world would hate us because the world hates Christ (John 15:18-19). It should not surprise us when our Christian convictions create a stir and result in animosity towards us.

they that kept the fair were the men of this world: so that from one end of the fair to the other, they seemed barbarians each to the other.[17] 1 Cor. 2:7,8.

Thirdly, But that which did not a little amuse the merchandisers was, that these pilgrims set very light by all their wares.[18] They cared not so much as to look upon them; and if they called upon them to buy, they would put their fingers in their ears, and cry, "Turn away mine eyes from beholding vanity," Psa. 119:37, and look upward, signifying that their trade and traffic was in heaven. Phil. 3: 20,21.

One chanced, mockingly, beholding the carriage of the men, to say unto them, "What will ye buy?" But they, looking gravely upon him, said, "We buy the truth." Prov. 23:23. At that there was an occasion taken to despise the men the more; some mocking, some taunting, some speaking reproachfully, and some calling upon others to smite them. At last, things came to an hubbub and great stir in the fair, insomuch that all order was confounded. Now was word presently brought to the great one of the fair, who quickly came down, and deputed some of his most trusty friends to take those men into examination about whom the fair was almost overturned.[19] So the men were brought to examination; and they that sat upon them asked them whence they came, whither they went, and what they did there in such an unusual garb. The men told them they were pilgrims and strangers in the world, and that they were going to their own country, which was the heavenly Jerusalem, Heb. 11:13-16; and that they had given no occasion to the men of the town, nor yet to the merchandisers, thus to abuse them, and to let them in their journey, except it was for that, when one asked them what they would buy, they said they would buy the truth. But they that were appointed to examine them did not believe them to be any other than bedlams and mad, or else such as came to put all things into a confusion in the fair. Therefore they took them and beat them, and besmeared them with dirt, and then put them into the cage, that they might be made a spectacle to all the men of the fair. There, therefore, they lay for some time, and were made the objects of any man's sport, or malice, or revenge; the great one of the fair laughing still at all that befell them. But the men being patient, and "not rendering railing for railing, but contrariwise blessing," and giving good words for bad, and kindness for injuries done, some men in the fair, that were more observing and less prejudiced than the rest, began to check and blame the baser sort for their continual abuses done by them to the men. They, therefore, in an angry manner let fly at them again, counting them as bad as the men in the cage, and telling them that they seemed confederates, and should be made partakers of their misfortunes. The others replied that, for aught they could see, the men were quiet and sober, and intended nobody any harm; and that there were many that traded in their fair that were more worthy to be put into the cage, yea, and pillory too, than were the men that they had abused. Thus, after divers words had passed on both sides, (the men behaving themselves all the while very wisely and soberly before them,) they fell to some blows among themselves, and did harm one to another. Then were these two poor men brought before their examiners again, and were charged as being guilty of the late hubbub that had been in the fair. So they beat them pitifully, and hanged irons upon them, and led them in chains up and down the fair, for an example and terror to others, lest any should speak in their behalf, or join themselves unto them. But Christian and Faithful behaved themselves yet more wisely, and received the ignominy and shame that was cast upon them with so much meekness and patience,[20] that it won to their side (though but few in comparison of the rest) several of the men in the fair. This put the other party yet into a greater rage, insomuch that they concluded the death of these two men. Wherefore they threatened that neither cage nor irons should serve their turn, but that they should die for the abuse they had done, and for deluding the men of the fair.

20. Christians should be models of love and peace towards those who oppose them. Our Lord Jesus commanded us to love our enemies and do good to those who persecute us (Matt. 5:43-45). The Apostle Peter teaches us to not return injuries we receive, but instead to bless (1 Pet. 2:19-23).

21. They entrusted themselves to the Lord who would take care of their lives. Whether by life or by death, they would glorify Christ. "Therefore let those who suffer according to the will of God commit their souls to Him in doing good, as to a faithful Creator." (1 Pet. 4:19)

22. The judge and the jury are presented as biased characters who can hardly give a fair trial to Christian and Faithful. They are themselves committed to the values of the world. A Christian cannot expect to be treated fairly to those that oppose Jesus Christ and all righteousness.

23. Faithful notes that he is only following the laws of the Most High. Anything that opposes God he must also oppose. Christians are committed to the law of the highest lawmaker: Almighty God.

24. A "pickthank" is someone who seeks favor through flattery or gossip.

Then were they remanded to the cage again, until further order should be taken with them. So they put them in, and made their feet fast in the stocks.

Here, also, they called again to mind what they had heard from their faithful friend Evangelist, and were the more confirmed in their way and sufferings by what he told them would happen to them. They also now comforted each other, that whose lot it was to suffer, even he should have the best of it: therefore each man secretly wished that he might have that preferment. But committing themselves to the all-wise disposal of Him that ruleth all things,[21] with much content they abode in the condition in which they were, until they should be otherwise disposed of.

Then a convenient time being appointed, they brought them forth to their trial, in order to their condemnation. When the time was come, they were brought before their enemies and arraigned. The judge's name was Lord Hate-good;[22] their indictment was one and the same in substance, though somewhat varying in form; the contents whereof was this: "That they were enemies to, and disturbers of, the trade; that they had made commotions and divisions in the town, and had won a party to their own most dangerous opinions, in contempt of the law of their prince."

Then Faithful began to answer, that he had only set himself against that which had set itself against Him that is higher than the highest.[23] And, said he, as for disturbance, I make none, being myself a man of peace: the parties that were won to us, were won by beholding our truth and innocence, and they are only turned from the worse to the better. And as to the king you talk of, since he is Beelzebub, the enemy of our Lord, I defy him and all his angels.

Then proclamation was made, that they that had ought to say for their lord the king against the prisoner at the bar, should forthwith appear, and give in their evidence. So there came in three witnesses, to wit, Envy, Superstition, and Pickthank.[24]

They were then asked if they knew the prisoner at the bar; and what they had to say for their lord the king against him.

Then stood forth Envy, and said to this effect: My lord, I have known this man a long time, and will attest upon my oath before this honorable bench, that he is-

Judge: Hold; give him his oath.

So they sware him. Then he said, My lord, this man, notwithstanding his plausible name, is one of the vilest men in our country; he neither regardeth prince nor people, law nor custom, but doeth all that he can to possess all men with certain of his disloyal notions, which he in the general calls principles of faith and holiness. And in particular, I heard him once myself affirm, that Christianity and the customs of our town of Vanity were diametrically opposite, and could not be reconciled. By which saying, my lord, he doth at once not only condemn all our laudable doings, but us in the doing of them.

Then did the judge say to him, Hast thou any more to say?

Envy: My lord, I could say much more, only I would not be tedious to the court. Yet if need be, when the other gentlemen have given in their evidence, rather than any thing shall be wanting that will dispatch him, I will enlarge my testimony against him. So he was bid to stand by.

Then they called Superstition, and bid him look upon the prisoner. They also asked, what he could say for their lord the king against him. Then they sware him; so he began.

Superstition: My lord, I have no great acquaintance with this man, nor do I desire to have further knowledge of him. However, this I know, that he is a very pestilent fellow, from some discourse that I had with him the other day, in this town; for then, talking with him, I heard him say, that our religion was naught,[25] and such by which a man could by no means please God. Which saying of his, my lord, your lordship very well knows what necessarily thence will follow, to wit, that we still do worship in vain, are yet in our sins, and finally shall be damned: and this is that which I have to say.

25. This means that Faithful claimed that the religion of the worldly people of Vanity Fair was in vain or false.

26. Lechery refers to unrestrained or un-controlled practice of sexual desire

27. Despite the fact that Faithful has not spoken unkindly, they accuse him of this. He spoke the truth, and that itself was offensive. Likewise, Christians may be accused of bigotry, hatred, prejudice, and the like when they speak the truth.

28. This is false. There is no gentleness in this biased court against Faithful. But the Judge wishes to claim he is impartial and fair when he really is not.

Then was Pickthank sworn, and bid say what he knew in the behalf of their lord the king against the prisoner at the bar.

Pickthank: My lord, and you gentlemen all, this fellow I have known of a long time, and have heard him speak things that ought not to be spoken; for he hath railed on our noble prince Beelzebub, and hath spoken contemptibly of his honorable friends, whose names are, the Lord Old Man, the Lord Carnal Delight, the Lord Luxurious, the Lord Desire of Vain Glory, my old Lord Lechery,[26] Sir Having Greedy, with all the rest of our nobility: and he hath said, moreover, that if all men were of his mind, if possible, there is not one of these noblemen should have any longer a being in this town. Besides, he hath not been afraid to rail on you, my lord, who are now appointed to be his judge, calling you an ungodly villain, with many other such like vilifying terms, with which he hath bespattered most of the gentry of our town.[27]

When this Pickthank had told his tale, the judge directed his speech to the prisoner at the bar, saying, Thou runagate, heretic, and traitor, hast thou heard what these honest gentlemen have witnessed against thee?

Faithful: May I speak a few words in my own defence?

Judge: Sirrah, sirrah, thou deservest to live no longer, but to be slain immediately upon the place; yet, that all men may see our gentleness towards thee,[28] let us hear what thou, vile runagate, hast to say.

Faithful: 1. I say, then, in answer to what Mr. Envy hath spoken, I never said aught but this, that what rule, or laws, or custom, or people, were flat against the word of God, are diametrically opposite to Christianity. If I have said amiss in this, convince me of my error, and I am ready here before you to make my recantation.

2. As to the second, to wit, Mr. Superstition, and his charge against me, I said only this, that in the worship of God there is required a divine faith; but there can be no divine faith without a divine revelation of the will of God. Therefore, whatever is thrust into the worship of God that is not agreeable to di-

vine revelation, cannot be done but by a human faith;[29] which faith will not be profitable to eternal life.

3. As to what Mr. Pickthank hath said, I say, (avoiding terms, as that I am said to rail, and the like,) that the prince of this town, with all the rabblement, his attendants, by this gentleman named, are more fit for a being in hell than in this town and country. And so the Lord have mercy upon me.

Then the judge called to the jury, (who all this while stood by to hear and observe,) Gentlemen of the jury, you see this man about whom so great an uproar hath been made in this town; you have also heard what these worthy gentlemen have witnessed against him; also, you have heard his reply and confession: it lieth now in your breasts to hang him, or save his life; but yet I think meet to instruct you in our law.

There was an act made in the days of Pharaoh the Great, servant to our prince, that, lest those of a contrary religion should multiply and grow too strong for him, their males should be thrown into the river. Exod. 1:22. There was also an act made in the days of Nebuchadnezzar the Great, another of his servants, that whoever would not fall down and worship his golden image, should be thrown into a fiery furnace. Dan. 3:6. There was also an act made in the days of Darius,[30] that whoso for some time called upon any god but him, should be cast into the lion's den. Dan. 6:7. Now, the substance of these laws this rebel has broken, not only in thought, (which is not to be borne,) but also in word and deed; which must, therefore, needs be intolerable.

For that of Pharaoh, his law was made upon a supposition to prevent mischief, no crime being yet apparent; but here is a crime apparent. For the second and third, you see he disputeth against our religion; and for the treason that he hath already confessed, he deserveth to die the death.[31]

Then went the jury out, whose names were Mr. Blindman, Mr. No-good, Mr. Malice, Mr. Love-lust, Mr. Live-loose, Mr. Heady, Mr. High-mind, Mr. Enmity, Mr. Liar, Mr. Cruelty, Mr. Hate-light, and Mr. Implacable; who every one gave in

29. Faithful argues that any worship made to God that is not consistent with divine revelation (the Bible) is false worship. We cannot worship God in our own human way. We must worship the Lord as He has commanded us to worship. Jesus quotes Isaiah in Matthew 15: "These people draw near to Me with their mouth, And honor Me with their lips, But their heart is far from Me. And in vain they worship Me, Teaching as doctrines the commandments of men." (Matt. 15:8-9)

30. The law of Vanity Fair is defined by the past tyrants of this world, as mentioned in the Bible. This includes Pharaoh (Exodus), Nebuchadnezzar, and Darius (both in Daniel).

31. The jury has no real role here because the judge has already ruled that Faithful has broken the laws of the Fair.

his private verdict against him among themselves, and afterwards unanimously concluded to bring him in guilty before the judge. And first among themselves, Mr. Blindman, the foreman, said, I see clearly that this man is a heretic. Then said Mr. No-good, Away with such a fellow from the earth. Aye, said Mr. Malice, for I hate the very looks of him. Then said Mr. Love-lust, I could never endure him. Nor I, said Mr. Liveloose, for he would always be condemning my way. Hang him, hang him, said Mr. Heady. A sorry scrub, said Mr. High-mind. My heart riseth against him, said Mr. Enmity. He is a rogue, said Mr. Liar. Hanging is too good for him, said Mr. Cruelty. Let us dispatch him out of the way, said Mr. Hate-light. Then said Mr. Implacable, Might I have all the world given me, I could not be reconciled to him; therefore let us forthwith bring him in guilty of death.

And so they did; therefore he was presently condemned to be had from the place where he was, to the place from whence he came, and there to be put to the most cruel death that could be invented.

They therefore brought him out, to do with him according to their law; and first they scourged him, then they buffeted him, then they lanced his flesh with knives; after that, they stoned him with stones, then pricked him with their swords; and last of all, they burned him to ashes at the stake. Thus came Faithful to his end.

Now I saw, that there stood behind the multitude a chariot and a couple of horses waiting for Faithful, who (so soon as his adversaries had dispatched him) was taken up into it, and straightway was carried up through the clouds with sound of trumpet, the nearest way to the celestial gate.[32] But as for Christian, he had some respite, and was remanded back to prison: so he there remained for a space. But he who overrules all things, having the power of their rage in his own hand, so wrought it about, that Christian for that time escaped them, and went his way.

32. All Christians who die in the Lord go immediately to be with the Lord.

And as he went, he sang, saying,

"Well, Faithful, thou hast faithfully profest
Unto thy Lord, with whom thou shalt be blest,
When faithless ones, with all their vain delights,
Are crying out under their hellish plights:
Sing, Faithful, sing, and let thy name survive;
For though they killed thee, thou art yet alive."

Book 1

Chapter 7

1. Christian is not left without a companion in the ongoing journey of the Christian life. Hopeful was once a resident of Vanity Fair. But he was inspired by the words and actions of Christian and Faithful and converts to the faith.

Now I saw in my dream, that Christian went not forth alone; for there was one whose name was Hopeful, (being so made by the beholding of Christian and Faithful in their words and behavior, in their sufferings at the fair,) who joined himself unto him, and entering into a brotherly covenant, told him that he would be his companion.[1] Thus one died to bear testimony to the truth, and another rises out of his ashes to be a companion with Christian in his pilgrimage. This Hopeful also told Christian, that there were many more of the men in the fair that would take their time, and follow after.

So I saw, that quickly after they were got out of the fair, they overtook one that was going before them, whose name was By-ends;[2] so they said to him, What countryman, sir? and how far go you this way? He told them, that he came from the town of Fair-speech, and he was going to the Celestial City; but told them not his name.

2. This man is driven by self-interest in all his considerations.

From Fair-speech? said Christian; is there any good that lives there? Prov. 26:25.

By-Ends: Yes, said By-ends, I hope so.

Christian: Pray, sir, what may I call you? said Christian.

By-Ends: I am a stranger to you, and you to me: if you be going this way, I shall be glad of your company; if not, I must be content.

Christian: This town of Fair-speech, said Christian, I have heard of; and, as I remember, they say it's a wealthy place.

By-Ends: Yes, I will assure you that it is; and I have very many rich kindred there.

Christian: Pray, who are your kindred there, if a man may be so bold?

By-Ends: Almost the whole town; and in particular my Lord Turn-about, my Lord Time-server, my Lord Fair-speech, from whose ancestors that town first took its name; also, Mr. Smooth-man, Mr. Facing-both-ways, Mr. Any-thing; and the parson of our parish, Mr. Two-tongues, was my mother's own brother, by father's side; and, to tell you the truth, I am become a gentleman of good quality; yet my great-grandfather was but a waterman, looking one way and rowing another, and I got most of my estate by the same occupation.

Christian: Are you a married man?

By-Ends: Yes, and my wife is a very virtuous woman, the daughter of a virtuous woman; she was my Lady Feigning's daughter; therefore she came of a very honorable family, and is arrived to such a pitch of breeding, that she knows how to carry it to all, even to prince and peasant. 'Tis true, we somewhat differ in religion from those of the stricter sort, yet but in two small points: First, we never strive against wind and tide. Secondly, we are always most zealous when religion goes in his silver slippers; we love much to walk with him in the street, if the sun shines and the people applaud him.[3]

Then Christian stepped a little aside to his fellow Hopeful, saying, it runs in my mind that this is one By-ends, of Fair-speech; and if it be he, we have as very a knave[4] in our company as dwelleth in all these parts. Then said Hopeful, Ask him; methinks he should not be ashamed of his name. So Christian came up with him again, and said, Sir, you talk as if you knew something more than all the world doth; and, if I take not my mark amiss, I deem I have half a guess of you. Is not your name Mr. By-ends of Fair-speech?

3. By-ends and his extended family are examples of false religion. They are man-pleasers rather than lovers of God. By-ends explains that his religion consists in two unique principles. First, he never "strives against wind and tide." This means that he and his family never go against popular opinion. The second principle is to be zealous for religion when it goes "in his silver slippers." This means that whatever is most popular and praiseworthy among men is what he and his relatives are zealous for. Jesus warns us against such dangerous principles. "And He said to them, 'You are those who justify yourselves before men, but God knows your hearts. For what is highly esteemed among men is an abomination in the sight of God.'" (Luke 16:15)

4. A knave is a dishonest man.

5. By-ends received his name as a nickname because he always took whatever approach necessary to be popular and accepted.

6. The true path of following Christ will never be popular. Jesus told us the way to life is narrow and there are few who find it. Often, to be faithful to our Lord will bring us into contempt with others. Christian tells By-ends that if he would be their traveling companion, he must go against popular opinion.

By-Ends: This is not my name, but indeed it is a nickname that is given me by some that cannot abide me, and I must be content to bear it as a reproach, as other good men have borne theirs before me.

Christian: But did you never give an occasion to men to call you by this name?

By-Ends: Never, never! The worst that ever I did to give them an occasion to give me this name was, that I had always the luck to jump in my judgment with the present way of the times,[5] whatever it was, and my chance was to get thereby: but if things are thus cast upon me, let me count them a blessing; but let not the malicious load me therefore with reproach.

Christian: I thought, indeed, that you were the man that I heard of; and to tell you what I think, I fear this name belongs to you more properly than you are willing we should think it doth.

By-Ends: Well if you will thus imagine, I cannot help it; you shall find me a fair company-keeper, if you will still admit me your associate.

Christian: If you will go with us, you must go against wind and tide; the which, I perceive, is against your opinion: you must also own Religion in his rags,[6] as well as when in his silver slippers; and stand by him, too, when bound in irons, as well as when he walketh the streets with applause.

By-Ends: You must not impose, nor lord it over my faith; leave me to my liberty, and let me go with you.

Christian: Not a step farther, unless you will do, in what I propound, as we.

Then said By-ends, I shall never desert my old principles, since they are harmless and profitable. If I may not go with you, I must do as I did before you overtook me, even go by myself, until some overtake me that will be glad of my company.

Now I saw in my dream, that Christian and Hopeful forsook him, and kept their distance before him; but one of them, looking back, saw three men following Mr. By-ends; and, behold, as they came up with him, he made them a very low congee; and they also gave him a compliment. The men's names were, Mr. Hold-the-world, Mr. Money-love, and Mr. Save-all, men that Mr. By-ends had formerly been acquainted with; for in their minority they were schoolfellows, and taught by one Mr. Gripeman, a schoolmaster in Lovegain, which is a market-town in the county of Coveting, in the North. This Schoolmaster taught them the art of getting, either by violence, cozenage,[7] flattering, lying, or by putting on a guise of religion; and these four gentlemen had attained much of the art of their master, so that they could each of them have kept such a school themselves.

7. Cozenage means "to deceive" or "trick."

Well, when they had, as I said, thus saluted each other, Mr. Money-love said to Mr. By-ends, Who are they upon the road before us? For Christian and Hopeful were yet within view.

By-Ends: They are a couple of far country-men, that, after their mode, are going on pilgrimage.

Mr. Money-Love: Alas! why did they not stay, that we might have had their good company? for they, and we, and you, sir, I hope, are all going on pilgrimage.

By-Ends: We are so, indeed; but the men before us are so rigid, and love so much their own notions, and do also so lightly esteem the opinions of others, that let a man be ever so godly, yet if he jumps not with them in all things, they thrust him quite out of their company.

Mr. Save-All: That is bad; but we read of some that are righteous overmuch, and such men's rigidness prevails with them to judge and condemn all but themselves. But I pray, what, and how many, were the things wherein you differed?

By-Ends: Why, they, after their headstrong manner, conclude that it is their duty to rush on their journey all weathers, and I am for waiting for wind and tide. They are for hazarding all for God at a clap; and I am for taking all advantages to secure my life and estate.[8] They are for holding their notions, though all other men be against them; but I am for religion in what, and so far as the times and my safety will bear it. They are for religion when in rags and contempt; but I am for

8. By-ends will not give up that which is comfortable and popular in order to follow God. He will be religious if he can keep all of his personal interests. He is a man unwilling to deny self. Yet, our Lord Jesus said that if we will not deny ourselves, we cannot follow Him.

9. By-ends reveals the meaning of his name here. He argues that religion can be used as a cloak or a "means to an end" for personal gain. Paul seems to describe this kind of person in 1 Timothy: "If anyone teaches otherwise and does not consent to wholesome words, even the words of our Lord Jesus Christ, and to the doctrine which accords with godliness, he is proud, knowing nothing, but is obsessed with disputes and arguments over words, from which come envy, strife, reviling, evil suspicions, useless wranglings of men of corrupt minds and destitute of the truth, who suppose that godliness is a means of gain. From such withdraw yourself." (1 Tim. 6:3-5)

him when he walks in his silver slippers, in the sunshine, and with applause.

Mr. Hold-the-World: Aye, and hold you there still, good Mr. By-ends; for, for my part, I can count him but a fool, that having the liberty to keep what he has, shall be so unwise as to lose it. Let us be wise as serpents. It is best to make hay while the sun shines. You see how the bee lieth still in winter, and bestirs her only when she can have profit with pleasure. God sends sometimes rain, and sometimes sunshine: if they be such fools to go through the first, yet let us be content to take fair weather along with us. For my part, I like that religion best that will stand with the security of God's good blessings unto us; for who can imagine, that is ruled by his reason, since God has bestowed upon us the good things of this life, but that he would have us keep them for his sake? Abraham and Solomon grew rich in religion; and Job says, that a good man shall lay up gold as dust; but he must not be such as the men before us, if they be as you have described them.

Mr. Save-All: I think that we are all agreed in this matter; and therefore there needs no more words about it.

Mr. Money-Love: No, there needs no more words about this matter, indeed; for he that believes neither Scripture nor reason, (and you see we have both on our side,) neither knows his own liberty nor seeks his own safety.

By-Ends: My brethren, we are, as you see, going all on pilgrimage; and for our better diversion from things that are bad, give me leave to propound unto you this question.

Suppose a man, a minister, or a tradesman, etc., should have an advantage lie before him to get the good blessings of this life, yet so as that he can by no means come by them, except, in appearance at least, he becomes extraordinary zealous in some points of religion[9] that he meddled not with before; may he not use this means to attain his end, and yet be a right honest man?

Mr. Money-Love: I see the bottom of your question; and with these gentlemen's good leave, I will endeavor to shape you an answer. And first, to speak to your question as it concerneth a minister himself: suppose a minister, a worthy man, possessed but of a very small benefice, and has in his eye a greater, more fat and plump by far; he has also now an opportunity of getting it, yet so as by being more studious, by preaching more frequently and zealously, and, because the temper of the people requires it, by altering of some of his principles; for my part, I see no reason why a man may not do this, provided he has a call, aye, and more a great deal besides, and yet be an honest man. For why?

1. His desire of a greater benefice is lawful, (this cannot be contradicted,) since it is set before him by Providence; so then he may get it if he can, making no question for conscience' sake.

2. Besides, his desire after that benefice makes him more studious, a more zealous preacher, etc., and so makes him a better man, yea, makes him better improve his parts, which is according to the mind of God.

3. Now, as for his complying with the temper of his people, by deserting, to serve them, some of his principles, this argueth, 1. That he is of a self-denying temper. 2. Of a sweet and winning deportment. And, 3. So more fit for the ministerial function.

4. I conclude, then, that a minister that changes a small for a great, should not, for so doing, be judged as covetous; but rather, since he is improved in his parts and industry thereby, be counted as one that pursues his call, and the opportunity put into his hand to do good.[10]

And now to the second part of the question, which concerns the tradesman you mentioned. Suppose such an one to have but a poor employ in the world, but by becoming religious he may mend his market, perhaps get a rich wife, or more and far better customers to his shop; for my part, I see no reason but this may be lawfully done. For why?

1. To become religious is a virtue, by what means soever a man becomes so.

10. Mr. Money-love presents a minister who uses zeal in religion for personal gain. This man doesn't really have a zeal for God, but acts deceptively as if he does if it means more success for himself. Such men are dangerous hypocrites who have no real love for God. The scribes and Pharisees of the Gospels are examples of such hypocritical, insincere men who loved the praise of man rather than loving God.

11. The second example given by Mr. Money-love is that of a merchant who also uses religion as a means of personal gain. According to Mr. Money-love this is a good thing.

2. Nor is it unlawful to get a rich wife, or more custom to my shop.

3. Besides, the man that gets these by becoming religious, gets that which is good of them that are good, by becoming good himself; so then here is a good wife, and good customers, and good gain, and all these by becoming religious, which is good: therefore, to become religious to get all these is a good and profitable design.[11]

This answer, thus made by Mr. Money-love to Mr. By-ends' question, was highly applauded by them all; wherefore they concluded, upon the whole, that it was most wholesome and advantageous. And because, as they thought, no man was able to contradict it; and because Christian and Hopeful were yet within call, they jointly agreed to assault them with the question as soon as they overtook them; and the rather, because they had opposed Mr. By-ends before. So they called after them, and they stopped and stood still till they came up to them; but they concluded, as they went, that not Mr. By-ends, but old Mr. Hold-the-world should propound the question to them, because, as they supposed, their answer to him would be without the remainder of that heat that was kindled betwixt Mr. By-ends and them at their parting a little before.

So they came up to each other, and after a short salutation, Mr. Hold-the-world propounded the question to Christian and his fellow, and then bid them to answer if they could.

12. A man who thinks biblically and is filled with the Holy Spirit can easily answer such a foolish question. To use religion as a cloak for personal gain is ungodly.

Then said Christian, Even a babe in religion may answer ten thousand such questions.[12] For if it be unlawful to follow Christ for loaves, as it is, John 6:26; how much more abominable is it to make of him and religion a stalking-horse to get and enjoy the world! Nor do we find any other than heathens, hypocrites, devils, and wizards, that are of this opinion.

1. Heathens: for when Hamor and Shechem had a mind to the daughter and cattle of Jacob, and saw that there was no way for them to come at them but by being circumcised, they said to their companions, If every male of us be circumcised, as they are circumcised, shall not their cattle, and their substance,

and every beast of theirs be ours? Their daughters and their cattle were that which they sought to obtain, and their religion the stalking-horse they made use of to come at them. Read the whole story,[13] Gen. 34:20-24.

2. The hypocritical Pharisees were also of this religion: long prayers were their pretence, but to get widows' houses was their intent; and greater damnation was from God their judgment. Luke 20:46,47.

3. Judas the devil was also of this religion: he was religious for the bag, that he might be possessed of what was put therein; but he was lost, cast away, and the very son of perdition.

4. Simon the wizard was of this religion too; for he would have had the Holy Ghost, that he might have got money therewith: and his sentence from Peter's mouth was according. Acts 8:19-22.

5. Neither will it go out of my mind, but that that man who takes up religion for the world, will throw away religion for the world;[14] for so surely as Judas designed the world in becoming religious, so surely did he also sell religion and his Master for the same. To answer the question, therefore, affirmatively, as I perceive you have done, and to accept of, as authentic, such answer, is heathenish, hypocritical, and devilish; and your reward will be according to your works.

Then they stood staring one upon another, but had not wherewith to answer Christian. Hopeful also approved of the soundness of Christian's answer; so there was a great silence among them. Mr. By-ends and his company also staggered and kept behind, that Christian and Hopeful might outgo them. Then said Christian to his fellow, If these men cannot stand before the sentence of men, what will they do with the sentence of God? And if they are mute when dealt with by vessels of clay, what will they do when they shall be rebuked by the flames of a devouring fire?

Then Christian and Hopeful outwent them again, and went till they came at a delicate plain, called Ease, where they went with much content; but that plain was but narrow, so they

13. Christian refers to the story of Hamor and Shechem, who wanted to be circumcised in order to marry the daughters of Israel. These men didn't care for the God of Jacob. They just wanted to inter-marry.

14. This is an important point. If a man adopts religion to gain the approval of the world, when the world no longer approves of it, that man will reject religion. There is no commitment to God. Religion is just a tool for personal gain.

15. Lucre is an old English term for money. In Paul's list of qualifications for elders, this term is used in the King James Version. "Not given to wine, no striker, not greedy of filthy lucre; but patient, not a brawler, not covetous;..." (1 Tim. 3:3 KJV)

16. Those that fell into this silver mine of greed had been severely injured or killed. Paul gives such a warning in 1 Timothy: "But those who desire to be rich fall into temptation and a snare, and into many foolish and harmful lusts which drown men in destruction and perdition. For the love of money is a root of all kinds of evil, for which some have strayed from the faith in their greediness, and pierced themselves through with many sorrows." (1 Tim. 6:9-10)

17. This is a reference to Demas who is described as a man in love with the present world (2 Tim. 4:10).

18. Demas blushes because he knows he is telling a lie. This mine is a dangerous and deadly place.

were quickly got over it. Now at the farther side of that plain was a little hill, called Lucre,[15] and in that hill a silver-mine, which some of them that had formerly gone that way, because of the rarity of it, had turned aside to see; but going too near the brim of the pit, the ground, being deceitful under them, broke, and they were slain: some also had been maimed there, and could not, to their dying day, be their own men again.[16]

Then I saw in my dream, that a little off the road, over against the silver-mine, stood Demas[17] (gentleman-like) to call passengers to come and see; who said to Christian and his fellow, Ho! turn aside hither, and I will show you a thing.

Christian: What thing so deserving as to turn us out of the way to see it?

Demas: Here is a silver-mine, and some digging in it for treasure; if you will come, with a little pains you may richly provide for yourselves.

Hopeful: Then said Hopeful, let us go see.

Christian: Not I, said Christian: I have heard of this place before now, and how many there have been slain; and besides, that treasure is a snare to those that seek it, for it hindereth them in their pilgrimage.

Then Christian called to Demas, saying, Is not the place dangerous? Hath it not hindered many in their pilgrimage? Hosea 9:6.

Demas: Not very dangerous, except to those that are careless; but withal he blushed as he spake.[18]

Christian: Then said Christian to Hopeful, Let us not stir a step, but still keep on our way.

Hopeful: I will warrant you, when By-ends comes up, if he hath the same invitation as we, he will turn in thither to see.

Christian: No doubt thereof, for his principles lead him that way, and a hundred to one but he dies there.

Demas: Then Demas called again, saying, But will you not come over and see?

Christian: Then Christian roundly answered, saying, Demas, thou art an enemy to the right ways of the Lord of this way, and hast been already condemned for thine own turning aside, by one of his Majesty's judges, 2 Tim. 4:10; and why seekest thou to bring us into the like condemnation? Besides, if we at all turn aside, our Lord the King will certainly hear thereof, and will there put us to shame, where we would stand with boldness before him.

Demas cried again, that he also was one of their fraternity; and that if they would tarry a little, he also himself would walk with them.

Christian: Then said Christian, What is thy name? Is it not the same by which I have called thee?

Demas: Yes, my name is Demas; I am the son of Abraham.

Christian: I know you; Gehazi was your great-grandfather, and Judas your father, and you have trod in their steps; it is but a devilish prank that thou usest: thy father was hanged for a traitor, and thou deservest no better reward. 2 Kings 5:20-27; Matt.26:14,15; 27:3-5. Assure thyself, that when we come to the King, we will tell him of this thy behavior. Thus they went their way.

By this time By-ends and his companions were come again within sight, and they at the first beck went over to Demas. Now, whether they fell into the pit by looking over the brink thereof, or whether they went down to dig, or whether they were smothered in the bottom by the damps that commonly arise, of these things I am not certain; but this I observed, that they were never seen again in the way. Then sang Christian,

"By-ends and silver Demas both agree;[19]
One calls, the other runs, that he may be
A sharer in his lucre: so these two
Take up in this world, and no farther go."[20]

Now I saw that, just on the other side of this plain, the pilgrims came to a place where stood an old monument, hard by the highway-side, at the sight of which they were both concerned, because of the strangeness of the form thereof; for it seemed to them as if it had been a woman transformed into the shape of a pillar. Here, therefore, they stood looking and

19. This short song indicates that the principles that By-Ends and Demas live by are the same. They are both in love with the world and live by worldly principles.

20. These men love the riches of the world. But their wealth is only in this present life. One day, they will face the judgment of God.

looking upon it, but could not for a time tell what they should make thereof. At last Hopeful espied, written above upon the head thereof, a writing in an unusual hand; but he being no scholar, called to Christian (for he was learned) to see if he could pick out the meaning: so he came, and after a little laying of letters together, he found the same to be this, "Remember Lot's wife." So he read it to his fellow; after which they both concluded that that was the pillar of salt into which Lot's wife was turned, for her looking back with a covetous heart when she was going from Sodom for safety. Gen. 19:26. Which sudden and amazing sight gave them occasion for this discourse.[21]

21. Christian and Hopeful encounter the pillar of salt that was once Lot's wife. Lot's wife is a reminder of the dangers of a covetous heart in love with the world. Her monument stands as a warning to all travelers.

Christian: Ah, my brother, this is a seasonable sight: it came opportunely to us after the invitation which Demas gave us to come over to view the hill Lucre; and had we gone over, as he desired us, and as thou wast inclined to do, my brother, we had, for aught I know, been made, like this woman, a spectacle for those that shall come after to behold.

Hopeful: I am sorry that I was so foolish, and am made to wonder that I am not now as Lot's wife; for wherein was the difference betwixt her sin and mine? She only looked back, and I had a desire to go see. Let grace be adored;[22] and let me be ashamed that ever such a thing should be in mine heart.

22. Hopeful admits there was some temptation in his heart to look into the silver-mine. At times, Christians may be drawn to the allurements of the world. But those indwelt by the Spirit of God will turn away from such things because they love God. It was God's grace that preserved Hopeful. It is by God's grace that we are forgiven our remaining indwelling lusts.

Christian: Let us take notice of what we see here, for our help from time to come. This woman escaped one judgment, for she fell not by the destruction of Sodom; yet she was destroyed by another, as we see: she is turned into a pillar of salt.

Hopeful: True, and she may be to us both caution and example; caution, that we should shun her sin; or a sign of what judgment will overtake such as shall not be prevented by this caution: so Korah, Dathan, and Abiram, with the two hundred and fifty men that perished in their sin, did also become a sign or example to others to beware. Numb. 16:31,32; 26:9,10. But above all, I muse at one thing, to wit, how Demas and his fellows can stand so confidently yonder to look for that treasure, which this woman but for looking behind her after, (for we read not that she stepped one foot out of the way,) was turned into a pillar of salt; especially since the judgment which overtook her did make her an example within sight of where they are; for they cannot choose but see her, did they but lift up their eyes.[23]

Christian: It is a thing to be wondered at, and it argueth that their hearts are grown desperate in the case; and I cannot tell who to compare them to so fitly, as to them that pick pockets in the presence of the judge, or that will cut purses under the gallows. It is said of the men of Sodom, that they were "sinners exceedingly," because they were sinners "before the Lord," that is, in his eyesight, and notwithstanding the kindnesses that he had shown them; for the land of Sodom was now like the garden of Eden as heretofore. Gen. 13:10-13. This, therefore, provoked him the more to jealousy, and made their plague as hot as the fire of the Lord out of heaven could make it. And it is most rationally to be concluded, that such, even such as these are, that shall sin in the sight, yea, and that too in despite of such examples that are set continually before them, to caution them to the contrary, must be partakers of severest judgments.

Hopeful: Doubtless thou hast said the truth; but what a mercy is it, that neither thou, but especially I, am not made myself this example! This ministereth occasion to us to thank God, to fear before him, and always to remember Lot's wife.

I saw then that they went on their way to a pleasant river, which David the king called "the river of God;" but John, "the river of the water of life." Psa. 65:9; Rev. 22:1; Ezek. 47:1-9. Now their way lay just upon the bank of this river: here, therefore, Christian and his companion walked with great delight; they drank also of the water of the river, which was pleasant and enlivening to their weary spirits. Besides, on the banks of this river, on either side, were green trees with all manner of fruit; and the leaves they ate to prevent surfeits, and other diseases that are incident to those that heat their blood by travel. On either side of the river was also a meadow, curiously

23. This monument that stands as a warning is easily visible to those in love with the world. There are many warnings that God graciously gives. But those in love with the world suppress the truth and will not receive God's warnings.

beautified with lilies; and it was green all the year long. In this meadow they lay down and slept, for here they might lie down safely. Psa. 23:2; Isa. 14:30. When they awoke they gathered again of the fruit of the trees, and drank again of the water of the river, and then lay down again to sleep. Thus they did several days and nights. Then they sang;

"Behold ye, how these Crystal Streams do glide,
To comfort pilgrims by the highway-side.
The meadows green, besides their fragrant smell,
Yield dainties for them; And he that can tell
What pleasant fruit, yea, leaves these trees do yield,
Will soon sell all, that he may buy this field."

So when they were disposed to go on, (for they were not as yet at their journey's end,) they ate, and drank, and departed.

Now I beheld in my dream, that they had not journeyed far, but the river and the way for a time parted, at which they were not a little sorry; yet they durst not go out of the way. Now the way from the river was rough, and their feet tender by reason of their travels; so the souls of the pilgrims were much discouraged because of the way. Numb. 21:4. Wherefore, still as they went on, they wished for a better way. Now, a little before them, there was on the left hand of the road a meadow, and a stile to go over into it, and that meadow is called By-path meadow.[24] Then said Christian to his fellow, If this meadow lieth along by our wayside, let's go over into it. Then he went to the stile to see, and behold a path lay along by the way on the other side of the fence. It is according to my wish, said Christian; here is the easiest going; come, good Hopeful, and let us go over.

Hopeful: But how if this path should lead us out of the way?

Christian: That is not likely, said the other. Look, doth it not go along by the wayside? So Hopeful, being persuaded by his fellow, went after him over the stile. When they were gone over, and were got into the path, they found it very easy for their feet; and withal, they, looking before them, espied a man walking as they did, and his name was Vain-Confidence:[25] so

24. Because things got difficult, Christian and Hopeful leave the appointed way, hoping that this shortcut through By-path meadow will make progress easier. This choice of taking the "easy way" was foolish. It ends up bringing them into a dangerous place.

25. Vain-Confidence assures Christian and Hopeful that they can still go towards the Celestial City by taking this shortcut. But it was not true. Vain-Confidence is a picture of trusting in oneself. It was Christian's vain confidence that led him to go into By-path meadow.

they called after him, and asked him whither that way led. He said, To the Celestial Gate. Look, said Christian, did not I tell you so? by this you may see we are right. So they followed, and he went before them. But behold the night came on, and it grew very dark; so that they that went behind lost the sight of him that went before.

He therefore that went before, (Vain-Confidence by name,) not seeing the way before him, fell into a deep pit, which was on purpose there made, by the prince of those grounds, to catch vain-glorious fools withal, and was dashed in pieces with his fall. Isa. 9:16.

Now, Christian and his fellow heard him fall. So they called to know the matter, but there was none to answer, only they heard a groaning. Then said Hopeful, Where are we now? Then was his fellow silent, as mistrusting that he had led him out of the way; and now it began to rain, and thunder, and lighten in a most dreadful manner, and the water rose amain.

Then Hopeful groaned in himself, saying, Oh that I had kept on my way!

Christian: Who could have thought that this path should have led us out of the way?

Hopeful: I was afraid on't at the very first, and therefore gave you that gentle caution. I would have spoke plainer, but that you are older than I.

Christian: Good brother, be not offended; I am sorry I have brought thee out of the way, and that I have put thee into such imminent danger. Pray, my brother, forgive me; I did not do it of an evil intent.

Hopeful: Be comforted, my brother, for I forgive thee; and believe, too, that this shall be for our good.[26]

Christian: I am glad I have with me a merciful brother: but we must not stand here; let us try to go back again.

Hopeful: But, good brother, let me go before.

Christian: No, if you please, let me go first, that if there be any danger, I may be first therein, because by my means we are both gone out of the way.

26. Christian asks Hopeful to forgive him for foolishly bringing them into this dangerous place. Hopeful forgives Christian and is assured that God may still bring good out of the situation though it was a foolish decision.

698 – Great Christian Classics

27. Like the episode at the Arbor, Bunyan shows how falling asleep is a dangerous thing for a Christian, spiritually-speaking. We are to be awake and sober because the spiritual battle is always a present reality.

28. This castle is inhabited by Giant Despair and his wife Diffidence. Taking the three names together, Bunyan uses this place to describe a place of depression, doubt, despair, and a lack of confidence in God. The word "diffidence" refers to a lack of confidence. Leland Ryken suggests that Diffidence represents the lack of confidence in God to save, which the pilgrims suffer while in the dungeon.

29. A mean, forbidding, and bad-tempered voice.

Hopeful: No, said Hopeful, you shall not go first, for your mind being troubled may lead you out of the way again. Then for their encouragement they heard the voice of one saying, "Let thine heart be toward the highway, even the way that thou wentest: turn again." Jer. 31:21. But by this time the waters were greatly risen, by reason of which the way of going back was very dangerous. (Then I thought that it is easier going out of the way when we are in, than going in when we are out.) Yet they adventured to go back; but it was so dark, and the flood was so high, that in their going back they had like to have been drowned nine or ten times.

Neither could they, with all the skill they had, get again to the stile that night. Wherefore at last, lighting under a little shelter, they sat down there till the day brake; but being weary, they fell asleep.[27] Now there was, not far from the place where they lay, a castle, called Doubting Castle,[28] the owner whereof was Giant Despair, and it was in his grounds they now were sleeping: wherefore he, getting up in the morning early, and walking up and down in his fields, caught Christian and Hopeful asleep in his grounds. Then with a grim and surly voice,[29] he bid them awake, and asked them whence they were, and what they did in his grounds. They told him they were pilgrims, and that they had lost their way. Then said the giant, You have this night trespassed on me by trampling in and lying on my grounds, and therefore you must go along with me. So they were forced to go, because he was stronger than they. They also had but little to say, for they knew themselves in a fault. The giant, therefore, drove them before him, and put them into his castle, into a very dark dungeon, nasty and stinking to the spirits of these two men. Here, then, they lay from Wednesday morning till Saturday night, without one bit of bread, or drop of drink, or light, or any to ask how they did; they were, therefore, here in evil case, and were far from friends and acquaintance. Psa. 88:18. Now in this place Christian had double sorrow, because it was through his unadvised counsel that they were brought into this distress.

Now Giant Despair had a wife, and her name was Diffidence: so when he was gone to bed he told his wife what he had done, to wit, that he had taken a couple of prisoners, and cast them into his dungeon for trespassing on his grounds. Then he asked her also what he had best do further to them. So she asked him what they were, whence they came, and whither they were bound, and he told her. Then she counseled him, that when he arose in the morning he should beat them without mercy. So when he arose, he getteth him a grievous crab-tree cudgel,[30] and goes down into the dungeon to them, and there first falls to rating of them as if they were dogs,[31] although they gave him never a word of distaste. Then he falls upon them, and beats them fearfully, in such sort that they were not able to help themselves, or to turn them upon the floor. This done, he withdraws and leaves them there to condole their misery, and to mourn under their distress: so all that day they spent the time in nothing but sighs and bitter lamentations. The next night, she, talking with her husband further about them, and understanding that they were yet alive, did advise him to counsel them to make away with themselves.[32] So when morning was come, he goes to them in a surly manner, as before, and perceiving them to be very sore with the stripes that he had given them the day before, he told them, that since they were never like to come out of that place, their only way would be forthwith to make an end of themselves, either with knife, halter, or poison;[33] for why, said he, should you choose to live, seeing it is attended with so much bitterness? But they desired him to let them go. With that he looked ugly upon them, and rushing to them, had doubtless made an end of them himself, but that he fell into one of his fits, (for he sometimes in sunshiny weather fell into fits,)[34] and lost for a time the use of his hands; wherefore he withdrew, and left them as before to consider what to do. Then did the prisoners consult between themselves whether it was best to take his counsel or no; and thus they began to discourse:

30. A "cudgel" is a stick used as a weapon.

31. "Rating" means to "scold."

32. Diffidence counsels Giant Despair to advise the pilgrims to commit suicide.

33. The halter here is a "noose" used for hanging.

34. Giant Despair couldn't stand the light. He lived in the darkness.

Christian: Brother, said Christian, what shall we do? The life that we now live is miserable. For my part, I know not whether it is best to live thus, or to die out of hand. My soul chooseth strangling rather than life, and the grave is more easy for me than this dungeon. Job. 7:15. Shall we be ruled by the giant?

Hopeful: Indeed our present condition is dreadful, and death would be far more welcome to me than thus for ever to abide; but yet, let us consider, the Lord of the country to which we are going hath said, "Thou shalt do no murder,"[35] no, not to another man's person; much more, then, are we forbidden to take his counsel to kill ourselves. Besides, he that kills another, can but commit murder upon his body; but for one to kill himself, is to kill body and soul at once. And moreover, my brother, thou talkest of ease in the grave; but hast thou forgotten the hell whither for certain the murderers go? for "no murderer hath eternal life," etc. And let us consider again, that all the law is not in the hand of Giant Despair: others, so far as I can understand, have been taken by him as well as we, and yet have escaped out of his hands. Who knows but that God, who made the world, may cause that Giant Despair may die; or that, at some time or other, he may forget to lock us in; or that he may, in a short time, have another of his fits before us, and may lose the use of his limbs? And if ever that should come to pass again, for my part, I am resolved to pluck up the heart of a man, and to try my utmost to get from under his hand. I was a fool that I did not try to do it before. But, however, my brother, let us be patient, and endure a while: the time may come that may give us a happy release; but let us not be our own murderers. With these words Hopeful at present did moderate the mind of his brother; so they continued together in the dark that day, in their sad and doleful condition.[36]

Well, towards evening the giant goes down into the dungeon again, to see if his prisoners had taken his counsel. But when he came there he found them alive; and truly, alive was all; for now, what for want of bread and water, and by reason

35. To commit suicide is an act of murder. It is a sin.

36. "Doleful" means sorrowful or mournful.

of the wounds they received when he beat them, they could do little but breathe. But I say, he found them alive; at which he fell into a grievous rage, and told them, that seeing they had disobeyed his counsel, it should be worse with them than if they had never been born.

At this they trembled greatly, and I think that Christian fell into a swoon;[37] but coming a little to himself again, they renewed their discourse about the giant's counsel, and whether yet they had best take it or no. Now Christian again seemed for doing it; but Hopeful made his second reply as followeth:

Hopeful: My brother, said he, rememberest thou not how valiant thou hast been heretofore? Apollyon could not crush thee, nor could all that thou didst hear, or see, or feel, in the Valley of the Shadow of Death. What hardship, terror, and amazement hast thou already gone through; and art thou now nothing but fears! Thou seest that I am in the dungeon with thee, a far weaker man by nature than thou art. Also this giant hath wounded me as well as thee, and hath also cut off the bread and water from my mouth, and with thee I mourn without the light. But let us exercise a little more patience. Remember how thou playedst the man at Vanity Fair, and wast neither afraid of the chain nor cage, nor yet of bloody death: wherefore let us (at least to avoid the shame that it becomes not a Christian to be found in) bear up with patience as well as we can.

Now night being come again, and the giant and his wife being in bed, she asked him concerning the prisoners, and if they had taken his counsel: to which he replied, They are sturdy rogues; they choose rather to bear all hardships than to make away with themselves. Then said she, Take them into the castle-yard to-morrow, and show them the bones and skulls of those that thou hast already dispatched, and make them believe, ere a week comes to an end, thou wilt tear them in pieces, as thou hast done their fellows before them.[38]

So when the morning was come, the giant goes to them again, and takes them into the castle-yard, and shows them as

37. Christian fainted when Giant Despair threatened them.

38. Diffidence suggests that showing Christian and Hopeful the bones of those who had fallen under Giant Despair would lead them to despair of life and put them in a condition of fear.

39. Despair, or losing hope in God, is a dangerous condition. But prayer is the great means God has given us to call upon Him in the day of trouble and find deliverance. It is often recorded in the Psalms that God's people would sometimes fall into conditions of despair and hopelessness. But while in the pit, they called upon the Lord. "I will extol You, O LORD, for You have lifted me up, And have not let my foes rejoice over me. O LORD my God, I cried out to You, And You healed me. O LORD, You brought my soul up from the grave; You have kept me alive, that I should not go down to the pit." (Psalm 30:1-3)

40. The promises of God are infallibly certain because they are made by God who cannot lie. The promises of God can rescue us from the pit of despair. They give us hope in the midst of darkness. With this key, Christian and Hopeful can instantly unlock the dungeon and walk in freedom once again.

his wife had bidden him. These, said he, were pilgrims, as you are, once, and they trespassed on my grounds, as you have done; and when I thought fit I tore them in pieces; and so within ten days I will do you: get you down to your den again. And with that he beat them all the way thither. They lay, therefore, all day on Saturday in a lamentable case, as before. Now, when night was come, and when Mrs. Diffidence and her husband the giant was got to bed, they began to renew their discourse of their prisoners; and withal, the old giant wondered that he could neither by his blows nor counsel bring them to an end. And with that his wife replied, I fear, said she, that they live in hopes that some will come to relieve them; or that they have picklocks about them, by the means of which they hope to escape. And sayest thou so, my dear? said the giant; I will therefore search them in the morning.

Well, on Saturday, about midnight they began to pray, and continued in prayer till almost break of day.[39]

Now, a little before it was day, good Christian, as one half amazed, brake out into this passionate speech: What a fool, quoth he, am I, thus to lie in a stinking dungeon, when I may as well walk at liberty! I have a key in my bosom, called Promise,[40] that will, I am persuaded, open any lock in Doubting Castle. Then said Hopeful, That is good news; good brother, pluck it out of thy bosom, and try.

Then Christian pulled it out of his bosom, and began to try at the dungeon-door, whose bolt, as he turned the key, gave back, and the door flew open with ease, and Christian and Hopeful both came out. Then he went to the outward door that leads into the castle-yard, and with his key opened that door also. After he went to the iron gate, for that must be opened too; but that lock went desperately hard, yet the key did open it. They then thrust open the gate to make their escape with speed; but that gate, as it opened, made such a creaking, that it waked Giant Despair, who hastily rising to pursue his prisoners, felt his limbs to fail, for his fits took him again, so that he could by no means go after them. Then they went on, and came to the King's highway, and so were safe, because they were out of his jurisdiction.

Now, when they were gone over the stile, they began to contrive with themselves what they should do at that stile, to prevent those that shall come after from falling into the hands of Giant Despair. So they consented to erect there a pillar, and to engrave upon the side thereof this sentence: "Over this stile is the way to Doubting Castle, which is kept by Giant Despair, who despiseth the King of' the Celestial country, and seeks to destroy his holy pilgrims." Many, therefore, that followed after, read what was written, and escaped the danger. This done, they sang as follows:

"Out of the way we went, and then we found
What 'twas to tread upon forbidden ground:
And let them that come after have a care,
Lest heedlessness makes them as we to fare;
Lest they, for trespassing, his prisoners are,
Whose castle's Doubting, and whose name's Despair."

1. After facing such spiritual depths of despair in Doubting Castle, the pilgrims enter into the Delectable Mountains, a place of beauty and goodness not far from the Celestial City. The word "delectable" means "beautiful" or "pleasant" and "delightful."

They went then till they came to the Delectable Mountains,[1] which mountains belong to the Lord of that hill of which we have spoken before. So they went up to the mountains, to behold the gardens and orchards, the vineyards and fountains of water; where also they drank and washed themselves, and did freely eat of the vineyards. Now, there were on the tops of these mountains shepherds feeding their flocks, and they stood by the highway-side. The pilgrims, therefore, went to them, and leaning upon their staffs, (as is common with weary pilgrims when they stand to talk with any by the way,) they asked, Whose Delectable Mountains are these; and whose be the sheep that feed upon them?

The Shepherds: These mountains are Emmanuel's land, and they are within sight of his city; and the sheep also are his, and he laid down his life for them. John 10:11,15.

Christian: Is this the way to the Celestial City?

The Shepherds: You are just in your way.

Christian: How far is it thither?

The Shepherds: Too far for any but those who shall get thither indeed.

Christian: Is the way safe or dangerous?

The Shepherds: Safe for those for whom it is to be safe; but transgressors shall fall therein. Hos. 14:9.

Christian: Is there in this place any relief for pilgrims that are weary and faint in the way?

The Shepherds: The Lord of these mountains hath given us a charge not to be forgetful to entertain strangers, Heb. 13:2; therefore the good of the place is before you.

I saw also in my dream, that when the shepherds perceived that they were wayfaring men, they also put questions to them, (to which they made answer as in other places,) as, Whence came you? and, How got you into the way? and, By what means have you so persevered therein? for but few of them that begin to come hither, do show their face on these mountains. But when the shepherds heard their answers, being pleased therewith, they looked very lovingly upon them, and said, Welcome to the Delectable Mountains.

The shepherds, I say, whose names were Knowledge, Experience, Watchful, and Sincere, took them by the hand, and had them to their tents, and made them partake of that which was ready at present.[2] They said moreover, We would that you should stay here a while, to be acquainted with us, and yet more to solace yourselves with the good of these Delectable Mountains. Then they told them that they were content to stay. So they went to their rest that night, because it was very late.

Then I saw in my dream, that in the morning the shepherds called up Christian and Hopeful to walk with them upon the mountains. So they went forth with them, and walked a while, having a pleasant prospect on every side. Then said the shepherds one to another, Shall we show these pilgrims some wonders? So when they had concluded to do it, they had them first to the top of a hill called Error,[3] which was very steep on the farthest side, and bid them look down to the bottom. So Christian and Hopeful looked down, and saw at the bottom several men dashed all to pieces by a fall that they had had from the top. Then said Christian, What meaneth this? The shepherds answered, Have you not heard of them that were made to err, by hearkening to Hymenius and Philetus, as concerning the faith of the resurrection of

2. These shepherds indicate well what shepherds in the church should be like: men of knowledge and experience. They should be men who are watchful and sincerely keeping watch over God's flock. In the account that follows, these shepherds give some wise pastoral warnings to Christian and Hopeful.

3. This hill allegorically represents the dangers of heresies and false doctrine.

4. Those who fall into doctrinal error go beyond what is written in the Word of God. To construct doctrines that are contrary to or above the revealed words of God is dangerous. The characters mentioned here (Hymenius and Philetus) are mentioned in 2 Timothy as men who erred in their understanding of the doctrine of the resurrection. This error was deadly. Let us take heed that our doctrine and practice be based firmly upon the teaching of God's Word.

5. Christian and Hopeful were not cautious when they saw this other path near Doubting Castle. Because they wandered out of the path of righteousness, they faced Giant Despair. By God's grace, they were delivered from Doubting Castle. But these men now reflect with sorrow about the foolishness of that path they took.

the body? 2 Tim. 2:17,18. They answered, Yes. Then said the shepherds, Those that you see lie dashed in pieces at the bottom of this mountain are they; and they have continued to this day unburied, as you see, for an example to others to take heed how they clamber too high,[4] or how they come too near the brink of this mountain.

Then I saw that they had them to the top of another mountain, and the name of that is Caution, and bid them look afar off; which, when they did, they perceived, as they thought, several men walking up and down among the tombs that were there; and they perceived that the men were blind, because they stumbled sometimes upon the tombs, and because they could not get out from among them. Then said Christian, What means this?

The shepherds then answered, Did you not see, a little below these mountains, a stile that led into a meadow, on the left hand of this way? They answered, Yes. Then said the shepherds, From that stile there goes a path that leads directly to Doubting Castle, which is kept by Giant Despair; and these men (pointing to them among the tombs) came once on pilgrimage, as you do now, even until they came to that same stile. And because the right way was rough in that place, they chose to go out of it into that meadow, and there were taken by Giant Despair, and cast into Doubting Castle; where after they had a while been kept in the dungeon, he at last did put out their eyes, and led them among those tombs, where he has left them to wander to this very day, that the saying of the wise man might be fulfilled, "He that wandereth out of the way of understanding shall remain in the congregation of the dead." Prov. 21:16. Then Christian and Hopeful looked upon one another, with tears gushing out, but yet said nothing to the shepherds.[5]

Then I saw in my dream, that the shepherds had them to another place in a bottom, where was a door on the side of a hill; and they opened the door, and bid them look in. They looked in, therefore, and saw that within it was very dark and smoky; they also thought that they heard there a rumbling noise, as of fire, and a cry of some tormented, and that they smelt the scent of brimstone. Then said Christian, What means this? The shepherds told them, This is a by-way to hell, a way that hypocrites go in at; namely, such as sell their birthright, with Esau; such as sell their Master, with Judas; such as blaspheme the Gospel, with Alexander; and that lie and dissemble,[6] with Ananias and Sapphira his wife.

Then said Hopeful to the shepherds, I perceive that these had on them, even every one, a show of pilgrimage, as we have now; had they not?

The Shepherds: Yes, and held it a long time, too.

Hopeful: How far might they go on in pilgrimage in their day, since they, notwithstanding, were miserably cast away?

The Shepherds: Some farther, and some not so far as these mountains.

Then said the pilgrims one to the other, We had need to cry to the Strong for strength.[7]

The Shepherds: Aye, and you will have need to use it, when you have it, too.

By this time the pilgrims had a desire to go forward, and the shepherds a desire they should; so they walked together towards the end of the mountains. Then said the shepherds one to another, Let us here show the pilgrims the gates of the Celestial City, if they have skill to look through our perspective glass. The pilgrims lovingly accepted the motion: so they had them to the top of a high hill, called Clear, and gave them the glass to look.

Then they tried to look; but the remembrance of that last thing that the shepherds had shown them made their hands shake, by means of which impediment they could not look steadily through the glass; yet they thought they saw something like the gate, and also some of the glory of the place. Then they went away, and sang,

6. The word "dissemble" means to deceive by concealing one's true motives.

7. That is, Christian and Hopeful should call upon the Lord to give them strength and preserve them from all of these dangerous paths out of the way of life. When we see how many apostatize from the truth, this should make us sober and watchful. We must each remember that it is God's preserving grace that keeps us in the way of life. For this reason, we do not make the pilgrimage to the Celestial City in our own strength. We must cry out to the Lord for His strength.

8. The shepherds give the pilgrims some parting words of pastoral wisdom. One of the great blessings of having shepherds (pastors and elders in particular) in the Christian life is their role in helping guard against false doctrines and practices that would lead us astray.

"Thus by the shepherds secrets are reveal'd,
Which from all other men are kept concealed:
Come to the shepherds then, if you would see
Things deep, things hid, and that mysterious be."

When they were about to depart, one of the shepherds gave them a note of the way. Another of them bid them beware of the Flatterer. The third bid them take heed that they slept not upon Enchanted Ground. And the fourth bid them God speed.[8] So I awoke from my dream.

Book 1
Chapter 9

And I slept, and dreamed again, and saw the same two pilgrims going down the mountains along the highway towards the city. Now, a little below these mountains, on the left hand, lieth the country of Conceit, from which country there comes into the way in which the pilgrims walked, a little crooked lane. Here, therefore, they met with a very brisk lad that came out of that country, and his name was Ignorance.[1] So Christian asked him from what parts he came, and whither he was going.

Ignorance: Sir, I was born in the country that lieth off there, a little on the left hand, and I am going to the Celestial City.

Christian: But how do you think to get in at the gate, for you may find some difficulty there?

Ignorance: As other good people do,[2] said he.

Christian: But what have you to show at that gate, that the gate should be opened to you?

Ignorance: I know my Lord's will, and have been a good liver; I pay every man his own; I pray, fast, pay tithes, and give alms, and have left my country for whither I am going.

Christian: But thou camest not in at the wicket-gate, that is at the head of this way; thou camest in hither through that same crooked lane, and therefore I fear, however thou mayest think of thyself, when the reckoning-day shall come, thou wilt

1. Ignorance represents the person who thinks he is wise and understanding, but he is ultimately ignorant. He wants to take a shortcut to heaven, thinking that he can take any path he wants.

2. Ignorance believes he is a good person and that it is by one's own good works that one enters heaven. He is ignorant of his own sinfulness and the way of salvation.

3. "Most assuredly, I say to you, he who does not enter the sheepfold by the door, but climbs up some other way, the same is a thief and a robber." (John 10:1)

4. Ignorance thinks that religion is a matter of choice. Each person can choose what they believe, and no person's beliefs are better than another man's.

have laid to thy charge, that thou art a thief and a robber, instead of getting admittance into the city.[3]

Ignorance: Gentlemen, ye be utter strangers to me; I know you not: be content to follow the religion of your country, and I will follow the religion of mine.[4] I hope all will be well. And as for the gate that you talk of, all the world knows that is a great way off of our country. I cannot think that any man in all our parts doth so much as know the way to it; nor need they matter whether they do or no, since we have, as you see, a fine, pleasant, green lane, that comes down from our country, the next way into the way.

When Christian saw that the man was wise in his own conceit, he said to Hopeful whisperingly, "There is more hope of a fool than of him." Prov. 26:12. And said, moreover, "When he that is a fool walketh by the way, his wisdom faileth him, and he saith to every one that he is a fool. Eccles. 10:3. What, shall we talk farther with him, or outgo him at present, and so leave him to think of what he hath heard already, and then stop again for him afterwards, and see if by degrees we can do any good to him? Then said Hopeful,

"Let Ignorance a little while now muse
On what is said, and let him not refuse
Good counsel to embrace, lest he remain
Still ignorant of what's the chiefest gain.
God saith, those that no understanding have,
(Although he made them,) them he will not save."

Hopeful: He further added, It is not good, I think, to say so to him all at once; let us pass him by, if you will, and talk to him anon, even as he is able to bear it.

So they both went on, and Ignorance he came after. Now, when they had passed him a little way, they entered into a very dark lane, where they met a man whom seven devils had bound with seven strong cords, and were carrying him back to the door that they saw on the side of the hill. Matt. 12:45; Prov. 5:22. Now good Christian began to tremble, and so did Hopeful, his companion; yet, as the devils led away the man,

Christian looked to see if he knew him; and he thought it might be one Turn-away, that dwelt in the town of Apostacy. But he did not perfectly see his face, for he did hang his head like a thief that is found; but being gone past, Hopeful looked after him, and espied on his back a paper with this inscription, "Wanton professor, and damnable apostate."

Then said Christian to his fellow, Now I call to remembrance that which was told me of a thing that happened to a good man hereabout. The name of the man was Little-Faith; but a good man, and he dwelt in the town of Sincere. The thing was this. At the entering in at this passage, there comes down from Broadway-gate, a lane, called Dead-Man's lane; so called because of the murders that are commonly done there; and this Little-Faith going on pilgrimage, as we do now, chanced to sit down there and sleep. Now there happened at that time to come down the lane from Broadway-gate, three sturdy rogues, and their names were Faint-Heart, Mistrust, and Guilt, three brothers; and they, espying Little-Faith where he was, came galloping up with speed. Now the good man was just awaked from his sleep, and was getting up to go on his journey. So they came up all to him, and with threatening language bid him stand. At this, Little-Faith looked as white as a sheet, and had neither power to fight nor fly. Then said Faint-Heart, Deliver thy purse; but he making no haste to do it, (for he was loth to lose his money,) Mistrust ran up to him, and thrusting his hand into his pocket, pulled out thence a bag of silver. Then he cried out, Thieves, thieves! With that, Guilt, with a great club that was in his hand, struck Little-Faith on the head, and with that blow felled him flat to the ground, where he lay bleeding as one that would bleed to death. All this while the thieves stood by. But at last, they hearing that some were upon the road, and fearing lest it should be one Great-Grace, that dwells in the town of Good-Confidence, they betook themselves to their heels, and left this good man to shift for himself. Now, after a while, Little-Faith came to

5. A man of little faith is susceptible to the attacks of a faint heart, mistrust in God, and guilt. This man of little faith suffers because of his lack of faith in God. Yet, though he has little faith, he does have saving faith. These bandits that fall upon Little-Faith run when it sounds like Great Grace is coming on the road. The grace of God is great, and is sufficient to save and preserve even those of little faith who put their trust in Jesus Christ.

6. It is God's grace and providence that keeps us in the path of eternal life. We can rest in the hands of Jesus knowing that he will not lose any sheep from his hand (John 10:28).

himself, and getting up, made shift to scramble on his way. This was the story.[5]

Hopeful: But did they take from him all that ever he had?

Christian: No; the place where his jewels were they never ransacked; so those he kept still. But, as I was told, the good man was much afflicted for his loss; for the thieves got most of his spending-money. That which they got not, as I said, were jewels; also, he had a little odd money left, but scarce enough to bring him to his journey's end. Nay, (if I was not misinformed,) he was forced to beg as he went, to keep himself alive, for his jewels he might not sell; but beg and do what he could, he went, as we say, with many a hungry belly the most part of the rest of the way. 1 Pet. 4:18.

Hopeful: But is it not a wonder they got not from him his certificate, by which he was to receive his admittance at the Celestial Gate?

Christian: It is a wonder; but they got not that, though they missed it not through any good cunning of his; for he, being dismayed by their coming upon him, had neither power nor skill to hide any thing; so it was more by good providence than by his endeavor[6] that they missed of that good thing. 2 Tim. 1:12-14; 2 Pet. 2:9.

Hopeful: But it must needs be a comfort to him they got not this jewel from him.

Christian: It might have been great comfort to him, had he used it as he should; but they that told me the story said that he made but little use of it all the rest of the way, and that because of the dismay that he had in their taking away his money. Indeed, he forgot it a great part of the rest of his journey; and besides, when at any time it came into his mind, and he began to be comforted therewith, then would fresh thoughts of his loss come again upon him, and these thoughts would swallow up all.

Hopeful: Alas, poor man, this could not but be a great grief to him.

Christian: Grief? Aye, a grief indeed! Would it not have been so to any of us, had we been used as he, to be robbed and wounded too, and that in a strange place, as he was? It is a wonder he did not die with grief, poor heart. I was told that he scattered almost all the rest of the way with nothing but doleful and bitter complaints; telling, also, to all that overtook him, or that he overtook in the way as he went, where he was robbed, and how; who they were that did it, and what he had lost; how he was wounded, and that he hardly escaped with life.

Hopeful: But it is a wonder that his necessity did not put him upon selling or pawning some of his jewels, that he might have wherewith to relieve himself in his journey.

Christian: Thou talkest like one upon whose head is the shell to this very day. For what should he pawn them? or to whom should he sell them? In all that country where he was robbed, his jewels were not accounted of; nor did he want that relief which could from thence be administered to him. Besides, had his jewels been missing at the gate of the Celestial City, he had (and that he knew well enough) been excluded from an inheritance there, and that would have been worse to him than the appearance and villany of ten thousand thieves.

Hopeful: Why art thou so tart, my brother? Esau sold his birthright, and that for a mess of pottage, Heb. 12:16; and that birthright was his greatest jewel: and if he, why might not Little-Faith do so too?

Christian: Esau did sell his birthright indeed, and so do many besides, and by so doing exclude themselves from the chief blessing, as also that caitiff did;[7] but you must put a difference betwixt Esau and Little-Faith, and also betwixt their estates. Esau's birthright was typical; but Little-Faith's jewels were not so. Esau's belly was his god; but Little-Faith's belly was not so. Esau's want lay in his fleshy appetite; Little-Faith's did not so. Besides, Esau could see no further than to the fulfilling of his lusts: For I am at the point to die, said he: and what good will this birthright do me? Gen. 25:32. But Little-Faith, though it was his lot to have but a little faith, was by

7. The word "caitiff" means a cowardly or contemptible person.

8. Christian tells Hopeful that there is an important difference between Esau and Little-Faith. Though Little Faith could have "pawned his jewels" he did not because he was a man of faith. Little-Faith's "jewels" seem to function like Christian's "roll." It is a certificate or an assurance of his salvation. Esau gave up his birthright because he was not a man of faith. Later he cried because of the loss of his birthright, but his tears were not tears of true repentance. Little-Faith, though he is weak in faith, still has saving faith. Even the weakest of faith, if it is true faith, can look to Christ and be saved.

9. Christian and Hopeful become frustrated with one another due to this disagreement in their conversation. Bunyan reminds us here that in all discussions about matters of the faith, we must speak to one another with love and humility.

10. The men that assaulted Little-Faith are really cowards. But for those who are attacked by them, it does not feel that way. The trials brought by Faint-Heart, Mistrust, and Guilt can feel like enemies that cannot be defeated.

his little faith kept from such extravagances,[8] and made to see and prize his jewels more than to sell them, as Esau did his birthright. You read not any where that Esau had faith, no, not so much as a little; therefore no marvel, where the flesh only bears sway, (as it will in that man where no faith is to resist,) if he sells his birthright and his soul and all, and that to the devil of hell; for it is with such as it is with the ass, who in her occasion cannot be turned away, Jer. 2:24: when their minds are set upon their lusts, they will have them, whatever they cost. But Little-Faith was of another temper; his mind was on things divine; his livelihood was upon things that were spiritual, and from above: therefore, to what end should he that is of such a temper sell his jewels (had there been any that would have bought them) to fill his mind with empty things? Will a man give a penny to fill his belly with hay? or can you persuade the turtle-dove to live upon carrion, like the crow? Though faithless ones can, for carnal lusts, pawn, or mortgage, or sell what they have, and themselves outright to boot; yet they that have faith, saving faith, though but a little of it, cannot do so. Here, therefore, my brother, is thy mistake.

Hopeful: I acknowledge it; but yet your severe reflection had almost made me angry.[9]

Christian: Why, I did but compare thee to some of the birds that are of the brisker sort, who will run to and fro in untrodden paths with the shell upon their heads: but pass by that, and consider the matter under debate, and all shall be well betwixt thee and me.

Hopeful: But, Christian, these three fellows, I am persuaded in my heart, are but a company of cowards: would they have run else, think you, as they did, at the noise of one that was coming on the road? Why did not Little-Faith pluck up a greater heart? He might, methinks, have stood one brush with them, and have yielded when there had been no remedy.

Christian: That they are cowards, many have said, but few have found it so in the time of trial.[10] As for a great heart, Little-Faith had none; and I perceive by thee, my brother, hadst thou been the man concerned, thou art but for a brush, and then to yield. And verily, since this is the height of thy stomach now they are at a distance from us, should they appear to thee as they did to him, they might put thee to second thoughts.

But consider again, that they are but journeymen thieves; They serve under the king of the bottomless pit, who, if need be, will come to their aid himself, and his voice is as the roaring of a lion. 1 Pet. 5:8. I myself have been engaged as this Little-Faith was, and I found it a terrible thing. These three villains set upon me, and I beginning like a Christian to resist, they gave but a call, and in came their master. I would, as the saying is, have given my life for a penny, but that, as God would have it, I was clothed with armor of proof. Aye, and yet, though I was so harnessed, I found it hard work to quit myself like a man:[11] no man can tell what in that combat attends us, but he that hath been in the battle himself.

Hopeful: Well, but they ran, you see, when they did but suppose that one Great-Grace was in the way.

Christian: True, they have often fled, both they and their master, when Great-Grace hath but appeared; and no marvel, for he is the King's champion.[12] But I trow you will put some difference between Little-Faith and the King's champion. All the King's subjects are not his champions; nor can they, when tried, do such feats of war as he.[13] Is it meet to think that a little child should handle Goliath as David did? or that there should be the strength of an ox in a wren? Some are strong, some are weak; some have great faith, some have little: this man was one of the weak, and therefore he went to the wall.

Hopeful: I would it had been Great-Grace, for their sakes.

Christian: If it had been he, he might have had his hands full: for I must tell you, that though Great-Grace is excellent good at his weapons, and has, and can, so long as he keeps them at sword's point, do well enough with them; yet if they get within him, even Faint-Heart, Mistrust, or the other, it shall go hard but they will throw up his heels. And when a man is down, you know, what can he do?

11. This is patterned after the language of the KJV in 1 Corinthians 16. "Watch ye, stand fast in the faith, quit you like men, be strong" (1 Cor. 16:13 KJV). This means to "act like men" (ESV).

12. The grace of God is a powerful thing. What Jesus Christ has accomplished in His saving work through His life, death, and resurrection, is far greater than the reign of sin. "Moreover the law entered that the offense might abound. But where sin abounded, grace abounded much more, so that as sin reigned in death, even so grace might reign through righteousness to eternal life through Jesus Christ our Lord." (Rom. 5:20-21)

13. The Bible says that we are not those who conquer in our own strength. Romans 8 says we are more than conquerors through Christ (Rom. 8:37).

14. Christian mentions a number of instances in biblical history where certain men fell into despair by the attack of these three rogues. These include David, Heman (in Psalm 88), Hezekiah, and the Apostle Peter who denied that he knew Christ before just a servant girl.

15. The Lord is near, a very present help in times of trouble (Ps. 46:1-2). We must only call upon the name of the Lord, and He will help us.

Whoso looks well upon Great-Grace's face, will see those scars and cuts there that shall easily give demonstration of what I say. Yea, once I heard that he should say, (and that when he was in the combat,) We despaired even of life. How did these sturdy rogues and their fellows make David groan, mourn, and roar! Yea, Heman, Psa. 88, and Hezekiah too, though champions in their days, were forced to bestir them when by these assaulted; and yet, notwithstanding, they had their coats soundly brushed by them. Peter, upon a time, would go try what he could do; but though some do say of him that he is the prince of the apostles, they handled him so that they made him at last afraid of a sorry girl.[14]

Besides, their king is at their whistle;[15] he is never out of hearing; and if at any time they be put to the worst, he, if possible, comes in to help them; and of him it is said, "The sword of him that layeth at him cannot hold; the spear, the dart, nor the habergeon. He esteemeth iron as straw, and brass as rotten wood. The arrow cannot make him fly; sling-stones are turned with him into stubble. Darts are counted as stubble; he laugheth at the shaking of a spear." Job 41:26-29. What can a man do in this case? It is true, if a man could at every turn have Job's horse, and had skill and courage to ride him, he might do notable things. "For his neck is clothed with thunder. He will not be afraid as a grasshopper: the glory of his nostrils is terrible. He paweth in the valley, and rejoiceth in his strength; he goeth on to meet the armed men. He mocketh at fear, and is not affrighted; neither turneth he back from the sword. The quiver rattleth against him, the glittering spear and the shield. He swalloweth the ground with fierceness and rage; neither believeth he that it is the sound of the trumpet. He saith among the trumpets, Ha, ha! and he smelleth the battle afar off, the thunder of the captains, and the shoutings." Job 39:19-25.

But for such footmen as thee and I are, let us never desire to meet with an enemy, nor vaunt as if we could do better, when we hear of others that have been foiled, nor be tickled at the thoughts of our own manhood; for such commonly come by the worst when tried. Witness Peter, of whom I made mention before: he would swagger, aye, he would; he would, as his vain mind prompted him to say, do better and stand more for his Master than all men: but who so foiled and run down by those villains as he?

When, therefore, we hear that such robberies are done on the King's highway, two things become us to do.[16]

1. To go out harnessed, and be sure to take a shield with us: for it was for want of that, that he who laid so lustily at Leviathan could not make him yield; for, indeed, if that be wanting, he fears us not at all. Therefore, he that had skill hath said, "Above all, take the shield of faith, wherewith ye shall be able to quench all the fiery darts of the wicked." Eph. 6:16.

2. It is good, also, that we desire of the King a convoy, yea, that he will go with us himself. This made David rejoice when in the Valley of the Shadow of Death; and Moses was rather for dying where he stood, than to go one step without his God. Exod. 33:15.

O, my brother, if he will but go along with us, what need we be afraid of ten thousands that shall set themselves against us? Psa. 3:5-8; 27:1-3. But without him, the proud helpers fall under the slain. Isa. 10:4.

I, for my part, have been in the fray before now; and though (through the goodness of Him that is best) I am, as you see, alive, yet I cannot boast of any manhood.[17] Glad shall I be if I meet with no more such brunts; though I fear we are not got beyond all danger. However, since the lion and the bear have not as yet devoured me, I hope God will also deliver us from the next uncircumcised Philistine. Then sang Christian,

"Poor Little-Faith! hast been among the thieves?
Wast robb'd? Remember this, whoso believes,
And get more faith; then shall you victors be
Over ten thousand-else scarce over three."

So they went on, and Ignorance followed. They went then till they came at a place where they saw a way put itself into

16. When we see our fellow Christians assaulted by these enemies, it should be noted by us so we can be prepared and watchful for such robberies on the highway as well. The two things necessary to be safe on the highway is first to carry our shield (the shield of faith) and to have a "convoy" (God's presence) to go with us and protect us.

17. The strength to endure in the spiritual battles does not come from ourselves. It is the Lord who delivers us. "Our help is in the name of the LORD,
Who made heaven and earth." (Ps. 124:8)

18. This man is described as "black of flesh" but disguised in a white robe. This should not be read in any sense as "racist" when Bunyan describes this man as "black." Black here is used as a contrast between what the man appears to be. Blackness refers to sin while the white robe makes it appear that this is a holy man who is to be followed. Interpreters differ as to what this man represents. Some see this man as representing the robe of "self-righteousness" that externally looks good, but inwardly this man is full of sin. Jesus described the scribes and Pharisees as "whitewashed tombs" (Matt. 23:27). Another possible reference is to false teachers who, like Satan, disguise themselves as angels of light but are inwardly ravenous wolves (2 Cor. 11:13-14). The second of these options fits the context best based on what follows.

19. In light of this language, it is more likely that this man represents the false teacher who flatters with his lips but is really a deceiver.

their way, and seemed withal to lie as strait as the way which they should go; and here they knew not which of the two to take, for both seemed strait before them: therefore here they stood still to consider. And as they were thinking about the way, behold a man black of flesh, but covered with a very light robe,[18] come to them, and asked them why they stood there. They answered, they were going to the Celestial City, but knew not which of these ways to take. "Follow me," said the man, "it is thither that I am going." So they followed him in the way that but now came into the road, which by degrees turned, and turned them so far from the city that they desired to go to, that in a little time their faces were turned away from it; yet they follow him. But by and by, before they were aware, he led them both within the compass of a net, in which they were both so entangled that they knew not what to do; and with that the white robe fell off the black man's back. Then they saw where they were. Wherefore there they lay crying some time, for they could not get themselves out.

Christian: Then said Christian to his fellow, Now do I see myself in an error. Did not the shepherds bid us beware of the Flatterer?[19] As is the saying of the wise man, so we have found it this day: "A man that flattereth his neighbor, spreadeth a net for his feet." Prov. 29:5.

Hopeful: They also gave us a note of directions about the way, for our more sure finding thereof; but therein we have also forgotten to read, and have not kept ourselves from the paths of the destroyer. Here David was wiser than we; for saith he, "Concerning the works of men, by the word of thy lips I have kept me from the paths of the Destroyer." Psa. 17:4. Thus they lay bewailing themselves in the net. At last they espied a Shining One coming towards them with a whip of small cords in his hand. When he was come to the place where they were, he asked them whence they came, and what they did there. They told him that they were poor pilgrims going to Zion, but were led out of their way by a black man clothed in white, who bid us, said they, follow him, for he was going thither too. Then said he with the whip, It is Flatterer, a false apostle, that hath transformed himself into an angel of light. Dan. 11:32; 2 Cor. 11:13,14. So he rent the net, and let the men out. Then said he to them, Follow me, that I may set you in your way again. So he led them back to the way which they had left to follow the Flatterer. Then he asked them, saying, Where did you lie the last night? They said, With the shepherds upon the Delectable Mountains. He asked them then if they had not of the shepherds a note of direction for the way. They answered, Yes. But did you not, said he, when you were at a stand, pluck out and read your note? They answered, No. He asked them, Why? They said they forgot. He asked, moreover, if the shepherds did not bid them beware of the Flatterer. They answered, Yes; but we did not imagine, said they, that this fine-spoken man had been he. Rom. 16:17,18.

Then I saw in my dream, that he commanded them to lie down; which when they did, he chastised them sore,[20] to teach them the good way wherein they should walk, Deut. 25:2; 2 Chron. 6:27; and as he chastised them, he said, "As many as I love, I rebuke and chasten; be zealous, therefore, and repent." Rev. 3:19. This done, he bids them to go on their way, and take good heed to the other directions of the shepherds. So they thanked him for all his kindness, and went softly along the right way, singing,

"Come hither, you that walk along the way,
See how the pilgrims fare that go astray:
They catched are in an entangling net,
Cause they good counsel lightly did forget:
'Tis true, they rescued were; but yet, you see,
They're scouged to boot; let this your caution be."

Now, after awhile, they perceived afar off, one coming softly, and alone, all along the highway, to meet them. Then said Christian to his fellow, Yonder is a man with his back towards Zion, and he is coming to meet us.

Hopeful: I see him; let us take heed to ourselves now, lest he should prove a Flatterer also.[21] So he drew nearer and near-

20. The Shining One disciplines Christian and Hopeful for their lack of watchfulness. This is a loving rebuke in order to set the pilgrims on the right way again.

21. Once a Christian has experienced the danger of such deceivers, he is all the more wary of others who act the same. Let us not despise the hard experiences the Lord may providentially bring us through, since such experiences can be powerful teaching tools to prepare us for the future.

22. An atheist is one who denies the existence of God and scoffs at God's Word (Ps. 14:1).

23. Atheists are scoffers who are wise in their own eyes. They look down upon others as ignorant of the truth. Ironically and tragically, they themselves are the ones who have been deceived by the evil one. "But even if our gospel is veiled, it is veiled to those who are perishing, whose minds the god of this age has blinded, who do not believe, lest the light of the gospel of the glory of Christ, who is the image of God, should shine on them." (2 Cor. 4:3-4)

24. Christian and Hopeful caught a glimpse of Mount Zion from the Delectable Mountains. Atheist has been searching for the city for some twenty years but never found it. He could not see it, because he did not have faith. By faith, we walk, not by sight. But by faith we behold the future realities of Mount Zion.

er, and at last came up to them. His name was Atheist,[22] and he asked them whither they were going.

Christian: We are going to Mount Zion.

Then Atheist fell into a very great laughter.[23]

Christian: What's the meaning of your laughter?

Atheist: I laugh to see what ignorant persons you are, to take upon you so tedious a journey, and yet are like to have nothing but your travel for your pains.

Christian: Why, man, do you think we shall not be received?

Atheist: Received! There is not such a place as you dream of in all this world.

Christian: But there is in the world to come.

Atheist: When I was at home in mine own country I heard as you now affirm, and from that hearing went out to see, and have been seeking this city these twenty years, but find no more of it than I did the first day I set out. Eccles. 10:15; Jer. 17:15.

Christian: We have both heard, and believe, that there is such a place to be found.

Atheist: Had not I, when at home, believed, I had not come thus far to seek; but finding none, (and yet I should, had there been such a place to be found, for I have gone to seek it farther than you,) I am going back again, and will seek to refresh myself with the things that I then cast away for hopes of that which I now see is not.

Christian: Then said Christian to Hopeful his companion, Is it true which this man hath said?

Hopeful: Take heed, he is one of the Flatterers. Remember what it cost us once already for our hearkening to such kind of fellows. What! no Mount Zion? Did we not see from the Delectable Mountains the gate of the city?[24] Also, are we not now to walk by faith? 2 Cor. 5:7.

Let us go on, lest the man with the whip overtake us again. You should have taught me that lesson, which I will sound you in the ears withal: "Cease, my son, to hear the instruction that causeth to err from the words of knowledge." Prov. 19:27. I say, my brother, cease to hear him, and let us believe to the saving of the soul.

Christian: My brother, I did not put the question to thee, for that I doubted of the truth of our belief myself, but to prove thee, and to fetch from thee a fruit of the honesty of thy heart. As for this man, I know that he is blinded by the God of this world. Let thee and me go on, knowing that we have belief of the truth; and no lie is of the truth. 1 John, 5:21.

Hopeful: Now do I rejoice in hope of the glory of God. So they turned away from the man; and he, laughing at them, went his way.

I then saw in my dream, that they went on until they came into a certain country whose air naturally tended to make one drowsy, if he came a stranger into it. And here Hopeful began to be very dull, and heavy to sleep: wherefore he said unto Christian, I do now begin to grow so drowsy that I can scarcely hold open mine eyes; let us lie down here, and take one nap.

Christian: By no means, said the other; lest, sleeping, we never awake more.

Hopeful: Why, my brother? sleep is sweet to the laboring man; we may be refreshed, if we take a nap.

Christian: Do you not remember that one of the shepherds bid us beware of the Enchanted Ground? He meant by that, that we should beware of sleeping; wherefore "let us not sleep, as do others; but let us watch and be sober."[25] 1 Thess. 5:6.

Hopeful: I acknowledge myself in a fault; and had I been here alone, I had by sleeping run the danger of death. I see it is true that the wise man saith, "Two are better than one." Eccl. 4:9. Hitherto hath thy company been my mercy; and thou shalt have a good reward for thy labor.

Christian: Now, then, said Christian, to prevent drowsiness in this place, let us fall into good discourse.[26]

Hopeful: With all my heart, said the other.

Christian: Where shall we begin?

Hopeful: Where God began with us. But do you begin, if you please.

25. The Enchanted Ground is a very dangerous place for the Christian. It is a place of spiritual stupor, listlessness, and sleep. This is a treacherous condition for any Christian to fall into since we are called to be watchful and sober. We cannot sleep as those in the world sleep, numb to the spiritual realities all around them.

26. The Puritans often emphasized the importance of spiritual discourse (what they called "spiritual conference") in order to grow together spiritually and spur one another on to love and good works. In order to avoid the spiritual drowsiness produced by the Enchanted Ground, we must discourse with one another on spiritual things. "Beware, brethren, lest there be in any of you an evil heart of unbelief in departing from the living God; but exhort one another daily, while it is called 'Today,' lest any of you be hardened through the deceitfulness of sin." (Heb. 3:12-13)

27. The spiritual fellowship of the body of Christ is a gift from God. Through it, we are roused from spiritual sleep and exhorted to press on in the Christian life. Let us never despise the gift of Christ's body. Let us also contribute to the spiritual edification of Christ's body by being a source of spiritual encouragement for our brothers and sisters in Christ.

Christian: I will sing you first this song:
"When saints do sleepy grow, let them come hither,
And hear how these two pilgrims talk together;
Yea, let them learn of them in any wise,
Thus to keep open their drowsy, slumb'ring eyes.
Saints' fellowship, if it be managed well,
Keeps them awake, and that in spite of hell."[27]

Then Christian began, and said, I will ask you a question. How came you to think at first of doing what you do now?

Hopeful: Do you mean, how came I at first to look after the good of my soul?

Christian: Yes, that is my meaning.

Hopeful: I continued a great while in the delight of those things which were seen and sold at our fair; things which I believe now would have, had I continued in them still, drowned me in perdition and destruction.

Christian: What things were they?

Hopeful: All the treasures and riches of the world. Also I delighted much in rioting, reveling, drinking, swearing, lying, uncleanness, Sabbath-breaking, and what not, that tended to destroy the soul. But I found at last, by hearing and considering of things that are divine, which, indeed, I heard of you, as also of beloved Faithful, that was put to death for his faith and good living in Vanity Fair, that the end of these things is death, Rom. 6:21-23; and that for these things' sake, the wrath of God cometh upon the children of disobedience. Eph. 5:6.

Christian: And did you presently fall under the power of this conviction?

Hopeful: No, I was not willing presently to know the evil of sin, nor the damnation that follows upon the commission of it; but endeavored, when my mind at first began to be shaken with the word, to shut mine eyes against the light thereof.

Christian: But what was the cause of your carrying of it thus to the first workings of God's blessed Spirit upon you?

Hopeful: The causes were, 1. I was ignorant that this was the work of God upon me. I never thought that by awakenings for sin, God at first begins the conversion of a sinner. 2. Sin was yet very sweet to my flesh, and I was loth to leave it. 3. I could not tell how to part with mine old companions, their presence and actions were so desirable unto me. 4. The hours in which convictions were upon me, were such troublesome and such heart-affrighting hours, that I could not bear, no not so much as the remembrance of them upon my heart.[28]

Christian: Then, as it seems, sometimes you got rid of your trouble?

Hopeful: Yes, verily, but it would come into my mind again; and then I should be as bad, nay, worse than I was before.

Christian: Why, what was it that brought your sins to mind again?

Hopeful: Many things; as,

1. If I did but meet a good man in the streets; or,

2. If I have heard any read in the Bible; or,

3. If mine head did begin to ache; or,

4. If I were told that some of my neighbors were sick; or,

5. If I heard the bell toll for some that were dead; or,

6. If I thought of dying myself; or,

7. If I heard that sudden death happened to others.

8. But especially when I thought of myself, that I must quickly come to judgment.[29]

Christian: And could you at any time, with ease, get off the guilt of sin, when by any of these ways it came upon you?

Hopeful: No, not I; for then they got faster hold of my conscience; and then, if I did but think of going back to sin, (though my mind was turned against it,) it would be double torment to me.

Christian: And how did you do then?

Hopeful: I thought I must endeavor to mend my life; for else, thought I, I am sure to be damned.

Christian: And did you endeavor to mend?

Hopeful: Yes, and fled from, not only my sins, but sinful company too, and betook me to religious duties, as praying,

28. Hopeful was awakened by the Spirit of God to his sinful condition. Though he had not yet apprehended God's mercy in Christ, he could not shake off the conviction of sin.

29. The Lord providentially uses a variety of means to awaken a sinner to his or her spiritual condition and drive them to Christ for salvation.

30. The first step Hopeful took under the conviction of sin was to do good. He thought, for a time, that he could justify himself by good works. But eventually he realized that by works of the law, no man can be justified (Gal. 2:16). This mirrors John Bunyan's own experience as recorded in his autobiography, *Grace Abounding to the Chief of Sinners*. Like Hopeful, Bunyan was convicted of his sins, but tried to remedy his sinful condition by doing good works rather than looking to Jesus Christ the righteous one.

reading, weeping for sin, speaking truth to my neighbors, etc. These things did I, with many others, too much here to relate.

Christian: And did you think yourself well then?

Hopeful: Yes, for a while; but at the last my trouble came tumbling upon me again, and that over the neck of all my reformations.

Christian: How came that about, since you were now reformed?

Hopeful: There were several things brought it upon me, especially such sayings as these: "All our righteousnesses are as filthy rags." Isa. 64:6. "By the works of the law shall no flesh be justified." Gal. 2:16. "When ye have done all these things, say, We are unprofitable," Luke 17:10; with many more such like. From whence I began to reason with myself thus: If all my righteousnesses are as filthy rags; if by the deeds of the law no man can be justified; and if, when we have done all, we are yet unprofitable, then is it but a folly to think of heaven by the law. I farther thought thus: If a man runs a hundred pounds into the shopkeeper's debt, and after that shall pay for all that he shall fetch; yet if his old debt stands still in the book uncrossed, the shopkeeper may sue him for it, and cast him into prison, till he shall pay the debt.[30]

Christian: Well, and how did you apply this to yourself?

Hopeful: Why, I thought thus with myself: I have by my sins run a great way into God's book, and my now reforming will not pay off that score; therefore I should think still, under all my present amendments, But how shall I be freed from that damnation that I brought myself in danger of by my former transgressions?

Christian: A very good application: but pray go on.

Hopeful: Another thing that hath troubled me ever since my late amendments, is, that if I look narrowly into the best of what I do now, I still see sin, new sin, mixing itself with the best of that I do; so that now I am forced to conclude, that notwithstanding my former fond conceits of myself and duties, I have committed sin enough in one day to send me to hell,[31] though my former life had been faultless.

Christian: And what did you do then?

Hopeful: Do! I could not tell what to do, until I broke my mind to Faithful; for he and I were well acquainted. And he told me, that unless I could obtain the righteousness of a man that never had sinned, neither mine own, nor all the righteousness of the world, could save me.

Christian: And did you think he spake true?

Hopeful: Had he told me so when I was pleased and satisfied with my own amendments, I had called him fool for his pains; but now, since I see my own infirmity, and the sin which cleaves to my best performance, I have been forced to be of his opinion.[32]

Christian: But did you think, when at first he suggested it to you, that there was such a man to be found, of whom it might justly be said, that he never committed sin?

Hopeful: I must confess the words at first sounded strangely; but after a little more talk and company with him, I had full conviction about it.

Christian: And did you ask him what man this was, and how you must be justified by him?

Hopeful: Yes, and he told me it was the Lord Jesus, that dwelleth on the right hand of the Most High. Heb. 10:12-21. And thus, said he, you must be justified by him, even by trusting to what he hath done by himself in the days of his flesh, and suffered when he did hang on the tree. Rom. 4:5; Col. 1:14; 1 Pet. 1:19. I asked him further, how that man's righteousness could be of that efficacy, to justify another before God. And he told me he was the mighty God, and did what he did, and died the death also, not for himself, but for

31. The Reformation-era Heidelberg Catechism asks this question: "Q. 13: Can we ourselves make this payment?" The answer is then given: "Certainly not. On the contrary, we daily increase our debt." We can never pay for our sins through our own moral reformation. This cannot pay the debt of sin.

32. Those who are confident of their own righteousness will not see their need for the righteousness of Jesus Christ. A man must be humbled by his sinful condition before he will cry out to God for mercy. This is dramatically illustrated in the "Parable of the Pharisee and the Tax Collector" (Luke 18:9-14). In this parable, the Pharisee boasts of his own self-righteousness in his prayer to God. But the tax collector, humbled by the weight of his sin, doesn't even lift his eyes to heaven, beats his breast, and cries out "God be merciful to me the sinner." Jesus says that the tax collector went home justified rather than the proud pharisee.

33. The word "imputed" means "to credit" or "to reckon" to the account of another. When we put our faith in Jesus Christ, the perfect righteousness of Christ is imputed to us as if it were our own righteousness. "For He made Him who knew no sin to be sin for us, that we might become the righteousness of God in Him." (2 Cor. 5:21)

34. Hopeful casts aside his own righteousness and asks God to be merciful to Him and to impute the righteousness of Christ to his own account.

me; to whom his doings, and the worthiness of them, should be imputed, if I believed on him.[33]

Christian: And what did you do then?

Hopeful: I made my objections against my believing, for that I thought he was not willing to save me.

Christian: And what said Faithful to you then?

Hopeful: He bid me go to him and see. Then I said it was presumption. He said, No; for I was invited to come. Matt. 11:28. Then he gave me a book of Jesus' inditing, to encourage me the more freely to come; and he said concerning that book, that every jot and tittle thereof stood firmer than heaven and earth. Matt. 24:35. Then I asked him what I must do when I came; and he told me I must entreat upon my knees, Psa. 95:6; Dan. 6:10, with all my heart and soul, Jer. 29:12,13, the Father to reveal him to me. Then I asked him further, how I must make my supplications to him; and he said, Go, and thou shalt find him upon a mercy-seat, where he sits all the year long to give pardon and forgiveness to them that come. Exod. 25:22; Lev. 16:2; Num. 7:89; Heb. 4:16. I told him, that I knew not what to say when I came; and he bid say to this effect: God be merciful to me a sinner, and make me to know and believe in Jesus Christ; for I see, that if his righteousness had not been, or I have not faith in that righteousness, I am utterly cast away. Lord, I have heard that thou art a merciful God, and hast ordained that thy Son Jesus Christ should be the Saviour of the world; and moreover, that thou art willing to bestow him upon such a poor sinner as I am-and I am a sinner indeed. Lord, take therefore this opportunity, and magnify thy grace in the salvation of my soul, through thy Son Jesus Christ. Amen.[34]

Christian: And did you do as you were bidden?

Hopeful: Yes, over, and over, and over.

Christian: And did the Father reveal the Son to you?

Hopeful: Not at the first, nor second, nor third, nor fourth, nor fifth, no, nor at the sixth time neither.

Christian: What did you do then?

Hopeful: What? why I could not tell what to do.

Christian: Had you not thoughts of leaving off praying?

Hopeful: Yes; an hundred times twice told.

Christian: And what was the reason you did not?

Hopeful: I believed that it was true which hath been told me, to wit, that without the righteousness of this Christ, all the world could not save me; and therefore, thought I with myself, if I leave off, I die, and I can but die at the throne of grace. And withal this came into my mind, "If it tarry, wait for it; because it will surely come, and will not tarry." Hab. 2:3. So I continued praying until the Father showed me his Son.

Christian: And how was he revealed unto you?

Hopeful: I did not see him with my bodily eyes, but with the eyes of my understanding, Eph. 1:18,19; and thus it was. One day I was very sad, I think sadder than at any one time in my life; and this sadness was through a fresh sight of the greatness and vileness of my sins. And as I was then looking for nothing but hell, and the everlasting damnation of my soul, suddenly, as I thought, I saw the Lord Jesus looking down from heaven upon me, and saying, "Believe on the Lord Jesus Christ, and thou shalt be saved." Acts 16:31.

But I replied, Lord, I am a great, a very great sinner: and he answered, "My grace is sufficient for thee." 2 Cor. 12:9. Then I said, But, Lord, what is believing? And then I saw from that saying, "He that cometh to me shall never hunger, and he that believeth on me shall never thirst," John 6:35, that believing and coming was all one; and that he that came, that is, that ran out in his heart and affections after salvation by Christ, he indeed believed in Christ. Then the water stood in mine eyes, and I asked further, But, Lord, may such a great sinner as I am be indeed accepted of thee, and be saved by thee? And I heard him say, "And him that cometh to me, I will in no wise cast out." John 6:37. Then I said, But how, Lord, must I consider of thee in my coming to thee, that my faith may be placed aright upon thee? Then he said, "Christ Jesus came into the world to save sinners." 1 Tim. 1:15. He is the end of the law for righteousness to every one that believes. Rom.10:4, and chap.

35. The Son must reveal himself to the sinner for one to be saved. Hopeful for a time cried out for God's mercy, but he did not come to a full conviction of His salvation in Christ until the Lord revealed Himself to Hopeful through the promises of the Word of God.

36. This paragraph describes what true saving faith looks like. The Spirit of God produces a firm conviction in the truth of God's Word. The one who is saved knows the justice of God, his own sinfulness, and the beauty of Christ. The Spirit produces a love of righteousness, a love for Christ and the honor of His name, and the desire to give up everything for Jesus.

37. Ignorance is still following them at a distance.

4. He died for our sins, and rose again for our justification. Rom. 4:25. He loved us, and washed us from our sins in his own blood. Rev. 1:5. He is the Mediator between God and us. 1 Tim. 2:5. He ever liveth to make intercession for us. Heb. 7:25. From all which I gathered, that I must look for righteousness in his person, and for satisfaction for my sins by his blood: that what he did in obedience to his Father's law, and in submitting to the penalty thereof, was not for himself, but for him that will accept it for his salvation, and be thankful. And now was my heart full of joy, mine eyes full of tears, and mine affections running over with love to the name, people, and ways of Jesus Christ.

Christian: This was a revelation of Christ to your soul indeed.[35] But tell me particularly what effect this had upon your spirit.

Hopeful: It made me see that all the world, notwithstanding all the righteousness thereof, is in a state of condemnation. It made me see that God the Father, though he be just, can justly justify the coming sinner. It made me greatly ashamed of the vileness of my former life, and confounded me with the sense of mine own ignorance; for there never came a thought into my heart before now that showed me so the beauty of Jesus Christ. It made me love a holy life, and long to do something for the honor and glory of the name of the Lord Jesus. Yea, I thought that had I now a thousand gallons of blood in my body, I could spill it all for the sake of the Lord Jesus.[36]

I saw then in my dream, that Hopeful looked back, and saw Ignorance, whom they had left behind, coming after. Look, said he to Christian, how far yonder youngster loitereth behind.[37]

Christian: Aye, aye, I see him: he careth not for our company.

Hopeful: But I trow it would not have hurt him, had he kept pace with us hitherto.

Christian: That is true; but I warrant you he thinketh otherwise.

Hopeful: That I think he doth; but, however, let us tarry for him. (So they did.)

Then Christian said to him, Come away, man; why do you stay so behind?

Ignorance: I take my pleasure in walking alone, even more a great deal than in company, unless I like it the better.

Then said Christian to Hopeful, (but softly,) Did I not tell you he cared not for our company? But, however, said he, come up, and let us talk away the time in this solitary place. Then, directing his speech to Ignorance, he said, Come, how do you do? How stands it between God and your soul now?

Ignorance: I hope, well; for I am always full of good motions,[38] that come into my mind to comfort me as I walk.

Christian: What good motions? Pray tell us.

Ignorance: Why, I think of God and heaven.

Christian: So do the devils and damned souls.

Ignorance: But I think of them, and desire them.

Christian: So do many that are never like to come there. "The soul of the sluggard desireth, and hath nothing." Prov. 13:4.

Ignorance: But I think of them, and leave all for them.

Christian: That I doubt: for to leave all is a very hard matter; yea, a harder matter than many are aware of. But why, or by what, art thou persuaded that thou hast left all for God and heaven?

Ignorance: My heart tells me so.

Christian: The wise man says, "He that trusteth in his own heart is a fool." Prov. 28:26.

Ignorance: That is spoken of an evil heart; but mine is a good one.

Christian: But how dost thou prove that?

Ignorance: It comforts me in hopes of heaven.

Christian: That may be through its deceitfulness; for a man's heart may minister comfort to him in the hopes of that thing for which he has yet no ground to hope.

38. Ignorance sees himself as righteous. He thinks good thoughts and does good actions. He is ignorant of the poverty of his spiritual condition. He is like the church of Laodicea. "Because you say, 'I am rich, have become wealthy, and have need of nothing'—and do not know that you are wretched, miserable, poor, blind, and naked—" (Rev. 3:17)

39. Ignorance comforts himself with the hope of salvation because his own heart tells him so. But Christian warns Ignorance that our hearts can lead us astray. The Word of God is the only infallible witness on the matter. We can only have a well-grounded assurance if we are guided by God's Word.

Ignorance: But my heart and life agree together; and therefore my hope is well-grounded.

Christian: Who told thee that thy heart and life agree together?

Ignorance: My heart tells me so.

Christian: "Ask my fellow if I be a thief." Thy heart tells thee so! Except the word of God beareth witness in this matter,[39] other testimony is of no value.

Ignorance: But is it not a good heart that hath good thoughts? and is not that a good life that is according to God's commandments?

Christian: Yes, that is a good heart that hath good thoughts, and that is a good life that is according to God's commandments; but it is one thing indeed to have these, and another thing only to think so.

Ignorance: Pray, what count you good thoughts, and a life according to God's commandments?

Christian: There are good thoughts of divers kinds; some respecting ourselves, some God, some Christ, and some other things.

Ignorance: What be good thoughts respecting ourselves?

Christian: Such as agree with the word of God.

Ignorance: When do our thoughts of ourselves agree with the word of God?

40. Christian says that we must view ourselves as what the Word of God describes us to be. If we see ourselves as righteous, we are foolish because God's Word says that we are sinners.

Christian: When we pass the same judgment upon ourselves which the word passes.[40] To explain myself: the word of God saith of persons in a natural condition, "There is none righteous, there is none that doeth good." It saith also, that, "every imagination of the heart of man is only evil, and that continually." Gen. 6:5; Rom. 3. And again, "The imagination of man's heart is evil from his youth." Gen. 8:21. Now, then, when we think thus of ourselves, having sense thereof, then are our thoughts good ones, because according to the word of God.

Ignorance: I will never believe that my heart is thus bad.

Christian: Therefore thou never hadst one good thought concerning thyself in thy life. But let me go on. As the word passeth a judgment upon our hearts, so it passeth a judgment upon our ways; and when the thoughts of our hearts and ways agree with the judgment which the word giveth of both, then are both good, because agreeing thereto.

Ignorance: Make out your meaning.

Christian: Why, the word of God saith, that man's ways are crooked ways, not good but perverse; it saith, they are naturally out of the good way, that they have not known it. Psa. 125:5; Prov. 2:15; Rom. 3:12. Now, when a man thus thinketh of his ways, I say, when he doth sensibly, and with heart-humiliation, thus think, then hath he good thoughts of his own ways, because his thoughts now agree with the judgment of the word of God.

Ignorance: What are good thoughts concerning God?

Christian: Even, as I have said concerning ourselves, when our thoughts of God do agree with what the word saith of him; and that is, when we think of his being and attributes as the word hath taught, of which I cannot now discourse at large. But to speak of him with reference to us: then have we right thoughts of God when we think that he knows us better than we know ourselves, and can see sin in us when and where we can see none in ourselves; when we think he knows our inmost thoughts, and that our heart, with all its depths, is always open unto his eyes; also when we think that all our righteousness stinks in his nostrils, and that therefore he cannot abide to see us stand before him in any confidence, even in all our best performances.

Ignorance: Do you think that I am such a fool as to think that God can see no further than I; or that I would come to God in the best of my performances?

Christian: Why, how dost thou think in this matter?

Ignorance: Why, to be short, I think I must believe in Christ for justification.

41. Ignorance shows that he completely misunderstands the biblical doctrine of justification by faith. Ignorance believes that through Christ, his own obedience to God's law becomes meritorious. But the Scriptures say that by works of the law, no man will be justified (Gal. 2:16). Justification comes only by trusting in Christ and receiving Christ's perfect righteousness. Our works contribute nothing to our righteous standing before God.

Christian: How! think thou must believe in Christ, when thou seest not thy need of him! Thou neither seest thy original nor actual infirmities; but hast such an opinion of thyself, and of what thou doest, as plainly renders thee to be one that did never see the necessity of Christ's personal righteousness to justify thee before God. How, then, dost thou say, I believe in Christ?

Ignorance: I believe well enough, for all that.

Christian: How dost thou believe?

Ignorance: I believe that Christ died for sinners; and that I shall be justified before God from the curse, through his gracious acceptance of my obedience to his laws.[41] Or thus, Christ makes my duties, that are religious, acceptable to his Father by virtue of his merits, and so shall I be justified.

Christian: Let me give an answer to this confession of thy faith.

1. Thou believest with a fantastical faith; for this faith is nowhere described in the word.

2. Thou believest with a false faith; because it taketh justification from the personal righteousness of Christ, and applies it to thy own.

3. This faith maketh not Christ a justifier of thy person, but of thy actions; and of thy person for thy action's sake, which is false.

4. Therefore this faith is deceitful, even such as will leave thee under wrath in the day of God Almighty: for true justifying faith puts the soul, as sensible of its lost condition by the law, upon flying for refuge unto Christ's righteousness; (which righteousness of his is not an act of grace by which he maketh, for justification, thy obedience accepted with God, but his personal obedience to the law, in doing and suffering for us what that required at our hands;) this righteousness, I say, true faith accepteth; under the skirt of which the soul being shrouded, and by it presented as spotless before God, it is accepted, and acquitted from condemnation.

Ignorance: What! would you have us trust to what Christ in his own person has done without us? This conceit would loosen the reins of our lust,[42] and tolerate us to live as we list: for what matter how we live, if we may be justified by Christ's personal righteousness from all, when we believe it?

Christian: Ignorance is thy name, and as thy name is, so art thou: even this thy answer demonstrateth what I say. Ignorant thou art of what justifying righteousness is, and as ignorant how to secure thy soul, through the faith of it, from the heavy wrath of God. Yea, thou also art ignorant of the true effects of saving faith in this righteousness of Christ, which is to bow and win over the heart to God in Christ, to love his name, his word, ways, and people, and not as thou ignorantly imaginest.[43]

Hopeful: Ask him if ever he had Christ revealed to him from heaven.

Ignorance: What! you are a man for revelations! I do believe, that what both you and all the rest of you say about that matter, is but the fruit of distracted brains.

Hopeful: Why, man, Christ is so hid in God from the natural apprehensions of the flesh, that he cannot by any man be savingly known, unless God the Father reveals him to him.

Ignorance: That is your faith, but not mine, yet mine, I doubt not, is as good as yours, though I have not in my head so many whimsies as you.

Christian: Give me leave to put in a word. You ought not so slightly to speak of this matter: for this I will boldly affirm, even as my good companion hath done, that no man can know Jesus Christ but by the revelation of the Father: yea, and faith too, by which the soul layeth hold upon Christ, (if it be right,) must be wrought by the exceeding greatness of his mighty power, Matt. 11:27; 1 Cor. 12:3; Eph. 1:17-19; the working of which faith, I perceive, poor Ignorance, thou art ignorant of. Be awakened, then, see thine own wretchedness, and fly to the Lord Jesus; and by his righteousness, which is the righteous-

42. Ignorance thinks that the biblical doctrine of justification by faith will have the result of making men loose about sin. The Apostle Paul was charged with the same objection. "What shall we say then? Shall we continue in sin that grace may abound? Certainly not! How shall we who died to sin live any longer in it?" (Rom. 6:1-2)

43. Christian replies to Ignorance's false charge. True saving faith in Christ has the effect of winning the heart to God, to love God's name, God's Word, God's ways, and God's people.

ness of God, (for he himself is God,) thou shalt be delivered from condemnation.

Ignorance: You go so fast I cannot keep pace with you; do you go on before: I must stay a while behind.

Then they said,

"Well, Ignorance, wilt thou yet foolish be,
To slight good counsel, ten times given thee?
And if thou yet refuse it, thou shalt know,
Ere long, the evil of thy doing so.
Remember, man, in time: stoop, do not fear:
Good counsel, taken well, saves; therefore hear.
But if thou yet shalt slight it, thou wilt be
The loser, Ignorance, I'll warrant thee."

Book 1
Chapter 10

Then Christian addressed himself thus to his fellow:

Christian: Well, come, my good Hopeful, I perceive that thou and I must walk by ourselves again.

So I saw in my dream, that they went on apace before, and Ignorance he came hobbling after. Then said Christian to his companion, I much pity this poor man: it will certainly go ill with him at last.

Hopeful: Alas! there are abundance in our town in his condition, whole families, yea, whole streets, and that of pilgrims too; and if there be so many in our parts, how many, think you, must there be in the place where he was born?

Christian: Indeed, the word saith, "He hath blinded their eyes, lest they should see," etc.

But, now we are by ourselves, what do you think of such men? Have they at no time, think you, convictions of sin, and so, consequently, fears that their state is dangerous?

Hopeful: Nay, do you answer that question yourself, for you are the elder man.

Christian: Then I say, sometimes (as I think) they may; but they being naturally ignorant, understand not that such convictions tend to their good; and therefore they do desperately seek to stifle them, and presumptuously continue to flatter themselves in the way of their own hearts.

Hopeful: I do believe, as you say, that fear tends much to men's good, and to make them right at their beginning to go on pilgrimage.

Christian: Without all doubt it doth, if it be right; for so says the word, "The fear of the Lord is the beginning of wisdom." Job 28:28; Psalm 111:10; Prov. 1:7; 9:10.

Hopeful: How will you describe right fear?

Christian: True or right fear is discovered by three things:

1. By its rise; it is caused by saving convictions for sin.

2. It driveth the soul to lay fast hold of Christ for salvation.

3. It begetteth and continueth in the soul a great reverence of God, his word, and ways; keeping it tender, and making it afraid to turn from them, to the right hand or to the left, to any thing that may dishonor God, break its peace, grieve the Spirit, or cause the enemy to speak reproachfully.[1]

Hopeful: Well said; I believe you have said the truth. Are we now almost got past the Enchanted Ground?

Christian: Why? are you weary of this discourse?

Hopeful: No, verily, but that I would know where we are.

Christian: We have not now above two miles further to go thereon. But let us return to our matter.

Now, the ignorant know not that such conviction as tend to put them in fear, are for their good, and therefore they seek to stifle them.

Hopeful: How do they seek to stifle them?

Christian: 1. They think that those fears are wrought by the devil, (though indeed they are wrought of God,) and thinking so, they resist them, as things that directly tend to their overthrow. 2. They also think that these fears tend to the spoiling of their faith; when, alas for them, poor men that they are, they have none at all; and therefore they harden their hearts against them. 3. They presume they ought not to fear, and therefore, in despite of them, wax presumptuously confident. 4. They see that those fears tend to take away from them their pitiful old self-holiness, and therefore they resist them with all their might.

1. True fear of God is found in three characteristics. First, it involves a conviction of sin. Second, it drives a man to take hold of Christ by faith for salvation. Third, it then produces a reverence of God, a love for God, and a concern for the honor of God's name.

Hopeful: I know something of this myself; for before I knew myself it was so with me.

Christian: Well, we will leave, at this time, our neighbor Ignorance by himself, and fall upon another profitable question.

Hopeful: With all my heart; but you shall still begin.

Christian: Well then, did you not know, about ten years ago, one Temporary in your parts,[2] who was a forward man in religion then?

Hopeful: Know him! yes; he dwelt in Graceless, a town about two miles off of Honesty, and he dwelt next door to one Turnback.

Christian: Right; he dwelt under the same roof with him. Well, that man was much awakened once: I believe that then he had some sight of his sins, and of the wages that were due thereto.

Hopeful: I am of your mind, for (my house not being above three miles from him) he would oft-times come to me, and that with many tears. Truly I pitied the man, and was not altogether without hope of him; but one may see, it is not every one that cries, "Lord, Lord!"

Christian: He told me once that he was resolved to go on pilgrimage, as we go now; but all of a sudden he grew acquainted with one Save-self, and then he became a stranger to me.

Hopeful: Now, since we are talking about him, let us a little inquire into the reason of the sudden backsliding of him and such others.

Christian: It may be very profitable; but do you begin.

Hopeful: Well, then, there are, in my judgment, four reasons for it:

1. Though the consciences of such men are awakened, yet their minds are not changed: therefore, when the power of guilt weareth away, that which provoked them to be religious ceaseth; wherefore they naturally turn to their own course again; even as we see the dog that is sick of what he hath eaten, so long as his sickness prevails, he vomits and casts up all; not that he doth this of a free mind, (if we may say a dog

2. Temporary is the man who underwent some conviction of sin but was not ultimately converted. There was some temporary turning, but not a saving faith, which always perseveres.

has a mind,) but because it troubleth his stomach: but now, when his sickness is over, and so his stomach eased, his desires being not at all alienated from his vomit, he turns him about, and licks up all; and so it is true which is written, "The dog is turned to his own vomit again." 2 Pet. 2:22. Thus, I say, being hot for heaven, by virtue only of the sense and fear of the torments of hell, as their sense and fear of damnation chills and cools, so their desires for heaven and salvation cool also. So then it comes to pass, that when their guilt and fear is gone, their desires for heaven and happiness die, and they return to their course again.

2. Another reason is, they have slavish fears that do overmaster them: I speak now of the fears that they have of men; "For the fear of man bringeth a snare." Prov. 29:25. So then, though they seem to be hot for heaven so long as the flames of hell are about their ears, yet, when that terror is a little over, they betake themselves to second thoughts, namely, that it is good to be wise and not to run (for they know not what) the hazard of losing all, or at least of bringing themselves into unavoidable and unnecessary troubles; and so they fall in with the world again.

3. The shame that attends religion lies also as a block in their way: they are proud and haughty, and religion in their eye is low and contemptible: therefore when they have lost their sense of hell and the wrath to come, they return again to their former course.

4. Guilt, and to meditate terror, are grievous to them; they like not to see their misery before they come into it; though perhaps the sight of it at first, if they loved that sight, might make them fly whither the righteous fly and are safe; but because they do, as I hinted before, even shun the thoughts of guilt and terror, therefore, when once they are rid of their awakenings about the terrors and wrath of God, they harden their hearts gladly, and choose such ways as will harden them more and more.[3]

---

3. There are a number of reasons people are not savingly converted even though they undergo some conviction of sin. Hopeful gives four reasons in this section. First, men may be awakened to a sense of their sins, but if their minds are not changed, they eventually turn back to the way of sin again. Secondly, men may be overcome by a fear of man. Third, men do not want to deal with the shame that comes with following the way of truth. Fourth, men do not want to think about their guilt and the judgment to come. So they harden their hearts and turn away from that conviction of sin.

Christian: You are pretty near the business, for the bottom of all is for want of a change in their mind and will.[4] And therefore they are but like the felon that standeth before the judge: he quakes and trembles, and seems to repent most heartily, but the bottom of all is the fear of the halter:[5] not that he hath any detestation of the offence, as it is evident; because, let but this man have his liberty, and he will be a thief, and so a rogue still; whereas, if his mind was changed, he would be otherwise.

Hopeful: Now I have showed you the reason of their going back, do you show me the manner thereof.

Christian: So I will willingly.

1. They draw off their thoughts, all that they may, from the remembrance of God, death, and judgment to come.

2. Then they cast off by degrees private duties, as closet prayer, curbing their lusts, watching, sorrow for sin, and the like.

3. Then they shun the company of lively and warm Christians.

4. After that, they grow cold to public duty, as hearing, reading, godly conference, and the like.[6]

5. They then begin to pick holes, as we say, in the coats of some of the godly,[7] and that devilishly, that they may have a seeming color to throw religion (for the sake of some infirmities they have espied in them) behind their backs.

6. Then they begin to adhere to, and associate themselves with, carnal, loose, and wanton men.

7. Then they give way to carnal and wanton discourses in secret; and glad are they if they can see such things in any that are counted honest, that they may the more boldly do it through their example.

8. After this they begin to play with little sins openly.

9. And then, being hardened, they show themselves as they are. Thus, being launched again into the gulf of misery, unless a miracle of grace prevent it, they everlastingly perish in their own deceivings.[8]

4. That is, there is no change in their mind and will. This is why they go back to their sin.

5. Christian gives an illustration. It is like a felon convicted by the law and standing before the judge. The felon may not have any true remorse for what he has done. He may appear repentant, but this is not because he detests his own criminal actions. Instead, he fears "the halter" (the noose). He fears the consequences of his sinful actions, but the repentance is not Godward.

6. "Godly conference" was a term used by the Puritans to refer to edifying conversation between Christians.

7. It is a sign of a dangerous spiritual condition when professing Christians begin to criticize and tear down their fellow brothers and sisters ("picking holes in their coats.")

8. Christian outlines the progress of apostasy (falling away). It starts in a seemingly "small" way. But eventually those who apostatize from the truth end by rejecting God and sinning willfully. The ultimate end of apostasy is eternal destruction.

9. The country of Beulah is the last region the pilgrims travel through before entering the Celestial City. The word "Beulah" means "married" in the Hebrew (Isa. 62:4). The language Bunyan uses is derived from Isaiah 62. This chapter describes the Lord's restoration of His people from a state of desolation to a state of spiritual exaltation. It is a fitting name for the pleasant land very near the Celestial City.

Now I saw in my dream, that by this time the pilgrims were got over the Enchanted Ground, and entering into the country of Beulah, whose air was very sweet and pleasant,[9] Isaiah 62:4-12; Song 2:10-12; the way lying directly through it, they solaced themselves there for a season. Yea, here they heard continually the singing of birds, and saw every day the flowers appear in the earth, and heard the voice of the turtle in the land. In this country the sun shineth night and day: wherefore this was beyond the Valley of the Shadow of Death, and also out of the reach of Giant Despair; neither could they from this place so much as see Doubting Castle. Here they were within sight of the city they were going to; also here met them some of the inhabitants thereof; for in this land the shining ones commonly walked, because it was upon the borders of heaven. In this land also the contract between the Bride and the Bridegroom was renewed; yea, here, "as the bridegroom rejoiceth over the bride, so doth God rejoice over them." Here they had no want of corn and wine; for in this place they met with abundance of what they had sought for in all their pilgrimage. Here they heard voices from out of the city, loud voices, saying, "Say ye to the daughter of Zion, Behold, thy salvation cometh! Behold, his reward is with him!" Here all the inhabitants of the country called them "the holy People, the redeemed of the Lord, sought out," etc.

Now, as they walked in this land, they had more rejoicing than in parts more remote from the kingdom to which they were bound; and drawing near to the city, they had yet a more perfect view thereof: It was builded of pearls and precious stones, also the streets thereof were paved with gold; so that, by reason of the natural glory of the city, and the reflection of the sunbeams upon it, Christian with desire fell sick; Hopeful also had a fit or two of the same disease: wherefore here they lay by it a while, crying out because of their pangs, "If you see my Beloved, tell him that I am sick of love."[10]

But, being a little strengthened, and better able to bear their sickness, they walked on their way, and came yet nearer

10. Bunyan uses the language of the Song of Songs to describe the relationship between Jesus Christ and his bride (the church).

and nearer, where were orchards, vineyards, and gardens, and their gates opened into the highway. Now, as they came up to these places, behold the gardener stood in the way; to whom the pilgrims said, Whose goodly vineyards and gardens are these? He answered, they are the King's, and are planted here for his own delight, and also for the solace of pilgrims. So the gardener had them into the vineyards, and bid them refresh themselves with the dainties, Deut. 23:24; he also showed them there the King's walks and arbors where he delighted to be: And here they tarried and slept.

Now I beheld in my dream, that they talked more in their sleep at this time than ever they did in all their journey; and, being in a muse thereabout, the gardener said even to me, Wherefore musest thou at the matter? It is the nature of the fruit of the grapes of these vineyards, "to go down so sweetly as to cause the lips of them that are asleep to speak." Song 7:9.

So I saw that when they awoke, they addressed themselves to go up to the city. But, as I said, the reflection of the sun upon the city (for the city was pure gold, Rev. 21:18,) was so extremely glorious, that they could not as yet with open face behold it, but through an instrument made for that purpose. 2 Cor. 3:18. So I saw, that as they went on, there met them two men in raiment that shone like gold, also their faces shone as the light.

These men asked the pilgrims whence they came; and they told them. They also asked them where they had lodged, what difficulties and dangers, what comforts and pleasures, they had met with in the way; and they told them. Then said the men that met them, You have but two difficulties more to meet with, and then you are in the City.

Christian then and his companion asked the men to go along with them: so they told them that they would; But, said they, you must obtain it by your own faith. So I saw in my dream, that they went on together till they came in sight of the gate.

Now I further saw, that betwixt them and the gate was a river;[11] but there was no bridge to go over, and the river was

11. In order to enter the Celestial City, Christian and Hopeful must cross the river. This river symbolizes death by which we pass from this life into glory. The biblical type that Bunyan may have had in mind is the River Jordan, which the children of Israel crossed in order to enter the Promised Land.

12. Facing death can be frightening, even to the Christian. But Christians face death with gospel hope. They know that to depart and be with Christ is "far better" (Phil. 1:23). To be absent from the body is to be with the Lord (2 Cor. 5:8).

13. Only Enoch and Elijah were translated to be with the Lord without dying. The path of all other saints has been through death.

14. Passing through death to be with the Lord is temporary. When Jesus Christ returns, the resurrection will occur and there will be no more death (1 Thess. 4:13-18).

15. The water's depth would depend upon the faith of those who pass through. Those with weaker faith would find death to be a greater test of faith, and it would feel as if the waters would swallow them up and they would drown. But for those strong in faith, the river of death does not pose so great a challenge.

16. "Deep calls unto deep at the noise of Your waterfalls; All Your waves and billows have gone over me." (Ps. 42:7)

very deep. At the sight, therefore, of this river the pilgrims were much stunned; but the men that went with them said, You must go through, or you cannot come at the gate.[12]

The pilgrims then began to inquire if there was no other way to the gate. To which they answered, Yes; but there hath not any, save two, to wit, Enoch and Elijah,[13] been permitted to tread that path since the foundation of the world, nor shall until the last trumpet shall sound.[14] The pilgrims then, especially Christian, began to despond in their mind, and looked this way and that, but no way could be found by them by which they might escape the river. Then they asked the men if the waters were all of a depth. They said, No; yet they could not help them in that case; for, said they, you shall find it deeper or shallower as you believe in the King of the place.[15]

Then they addressed themselves to the water, and entering, Christian began to sink, and crying out to his good friend Hopeful, he said, I sink in deep waters; the billows go over my head; all his waves go over me.[16] Selah.

Then said the other, Be of good cheer, my brother: I feel the bottom, and it is good. Then said Christian, Ah! my friend, the sorrows of death have compassed me about, I shall not see the land that flows with milk and honey. And with that a great darkness and horror fell upon Christian, so that he could not see before him. Also here he in a great measure lost his senses, so that he could neither remember nor orderly talk of any of those sweet refreshments that he had met with in the way of his pilgrimage. But all the words that he spoke still tended to discover that he had horror of mind, and heart-fears that he should die in that river, and never obtain entrance in at the gate. Here also, as they that stood by perceived, he was much in the troublesome thoughts of the sins that he had committed, both since and before he began to be a pilgrim. It was also observed that he was troubled with apparitions of hobgoblins and evil spirits; for ever and anon he would intimate so much by words.[17]

Hopeful therefore here had much ado to keep his brother's head above water; yea, sometimes he would be quite gone down, and then, ere a while, he would rise up again half dead. Hopeful did also endeavor to comfort him, saying, Brother, I see the gate, and men standing by to receive us; but Christian would answer, It is you, it is you they wait for; for you have been hopeful ever since I knew you. And so have you, said he to Christian. Ah, brother, (said he,) surely if I was right he would now arise to help me; but for my sins he hath brought me into the snare, and hath left me. Then said Hopeful, My brother, you have quite forgot the text where it is said of the wicked, "There are no bands in their death, but their strength is firm; they are not troubled as other men, neither are they plagued like other men." Psa. 73:4,5. These troubles and distresses that you go through in these waters, are no sign that God hath forsaken you; but are sent to try you,[18] whether you will call to mind that which heretofore you have received of his goodness, and live upon him in your distresses.

Then I saw in my dream, that Christian was in a muse a while. To whom also Hopeful added these words, Be of good cheer, Jesus Christ maketh thee whole.[19] And with that Christian brake out with a loud voice, Oh, I see him again; and he tells me, "When thou passest through the waters, I will be with thee; and through the rivers, they shall not overflow thee." Isa. 43:2. Then they both took courage, and the enemy was after that as still as a stone, until they were gone over. Christian, therefore, presently found ground to stand upon, and so it followed that the rest of the river was but shallow. Thus they got over.

Now, upon the bank of the river, on the other side, they saw the two shining men again, who there waited for them. Wherefore, being come out of the river, they saluted them, saying, We are ministering spirits, sent forth to minister for

17. The river of death brings fear and despair to Christian's heart. He feels again the guilt of his sins, and he is attacked by the demonic powers who would tempt him to doubt.

18. Hopeful helps to keep his brother Christian's head afloat. Christian begins to despair and think that he has no hope of entering at the gate. But Hopeful reminds Christian of the promises of God. God has sent the waters of affliction, the river of death, to try Christian's faith. These waters are not meant to destroy Christian.

19. On the day of our death, we cannot put any trust in ourselves. We have no righteousness of our own to commend us to God. We must simply look to Jesus Christ by faith. He is our righteousness. He is our salvation. Jesus Christ makes us whole. Martin Luther understood this well. His dying words were simply: "We are all beggars, this is true."

those that shall be the heirs of salvation. Thus they went along towards the gate.

Now you must note, that the city stood upon a mighty hill; but the pilgrims went up that hill with ease, because they had these two men to lead them up by the arms: they had likewise left their mortal garments behind them in the river;[20] for though they went in with them, they came out without them. They therefore went up here with much agility and speed, though the foundation upon which the city was framed was higher than the clouds; they therefore went up through the region of the air, sweetly talking as they went, being comforted because they safely got over the river, and had such glorious companions to attend them.

The talk that they had with the shining ones was about the glory of the place; who told them that the beauty and glory of it was inexpressible. There, said they, is "Mount Sion, the heavenly Jerusalem, the innumerable company of angels, and the spirits of just men made perfect." Heb. 12:22-24. You are going now, said they, to the paradise of God, wherein you shall see the tree of life, and eat of the never-fading fruits thereof: and when you come there you shall have white robes given you, and your walk and talk shall be every day with the King, even all the days of eternity. Rev. 2:7; 3:4,5; 22:5. There you shall not see again such things as you saw when you were in the lower region upon earth; to wit, sorrow, sickness, affliction, and death; "For the former things are passed away." Rev. 21:4. You are going now to Abraham, to Isaac, and Jacob, and to the prophets, men that God hath taken away from the evil to come, and that are now "resting upon their beds, each one walking in his righteousness." The men then asked, What must we do in the holy place? To whom it was answered, You must there receive the comfort of all your toil, and have joy for all your sorrow; you must reap what you have sown, even the fruit of all your prayers, and tears, and sufferings for the King by the way. Gal. 6:7,8. In that place you must wear crowns of gold, and enjoy the perpetual sight and vision of the Holy

20. Christian and Hopeful now moved with agility since they left behind their weak, mortal flesh.

One; for "there you shall see him as he is." 1 John, 3:2. There also you shall serve him continually with praise, with shouting and thanksgiving, whom you desired to serve in the world, though with much difficulty, because of the infirmity of your flesh. There your eyes shall be delighted with seeing, and your ears with hearing the pleasant voice of the Mighty One. There you shall enjoy your friends again that are gone thither before you; and there you shall with joy receive even every one that follows into the holy place after you. There also you shall be clothed with glory and majesty, and put into an equipage fit to ride out with the King of Glory. When he shall come with sound of trumpet in the clouds, as upon the wings of the wind, you shall come with him; and when he shall sit upon the throne of judgment, you shall sit by him; yea, and when he shall pass sentence upon all the workers of iniquity, let them be angels or men, you also shall have a voice in that judgment, because they were his and your enemies. Also, when he shall again return to the city, you shall go too with sound of trumpet, and be ever with him. 1 Thess. 4:14-17; Jude 14,15; Dan. 7:9,10; 1 Cor. 6:2,3.

Now, while they were thus drawing towards the gate, behold a company of the heavenly host came out to meet them: to whom it was said by the other two shining ones, These are the men that have loved our Lord when they were in the world, and that have left all for his holy name; and he hath sent us to fetch them, and we have brought them thus far on their desired journey, that they may go in and look their Redeemer in the face with joy. Then the heavenly host gave a great shout, saying, "Blessed are they that are called to the marriage-supper of the Lamb." Rev. 19:9. There came out also at this time to meet them several of the King's trumpeters, clothed in white and shining raiment, who, with melodious noises and loud, made even the heavens to echo with their sound. These trumpeters saluted Christian and his fellow with ten thousand welcomes from the world; and this they did with shouting and sound of trumpet.

This done, they compassed them round on every side; some went before, some behind, and some on the right hand, and some on the left, (as it were to guard them through the upper regions,) continually sounding as they went, with melodious noise, in notes on high; so that the very sight was to them that could behold it as if heaven itself was come down to meet them. Thus, therefore, they walked on together; and, as they walked, ever and anon these trumpeters, even with joyful sound, would, by mixing their music with looks and gestures, still signify to Christian and his brother how welcome they were into their company, and with what gladness they came to meet them. And now were these two men, as it were, in heaven, before they came to it, being swallowed up with the sight of angels, and with hearing of their melodious notes. Here also they had the city itself in view; and they thought they heard all the bells therein to ring, to welcome them thereto. But, above all, the warm and joyful thoughts that they had about their own dwelling there with such company, and that for ever and ever; oh, by what tongue or pen can their glorious joy be expressed! Thus they came up to the gate.

Now when they were come up to the gate, there was written over it, in letters of gold,

"Blessed are they that do his commandments, that they may have right to the tree of life, and may enter in through the gates into the city."

Then I saw in my dream, that the shining men bid them call at the gate: the which when they did, some from above looked over the gate, to wit, Enoch, Moses, and Elijah, etc., to whom it was said, These pilgrims are come from the City of Destruction, for the love that they bear to the King of this place; and then the pilgrims gave in unto them each man his certificate, which they had received in the beginning: those therefore were carried in unto the King, who, when he had read them, said, Where are the men? To whom it was answered, They are standing without the gate. The King then commanded to open the gate, "That the righteous nation (said he) that keepeth the truth may enter in." Isa. 26:2.

Now I saw in my dream, that these two men went in at the gate; and lo, as they entered, they were transfigured; and they had raiment put on that shone like gold. There were also that met them with harps and crowns, and gave them to them; the harps to praise withal, and the crowns in token of honor. Then I heard in my dream, that all the bells in the city rang again for joy, and that it was said unto them,

"Enter ye into the joy of your lord."

I also heard the men themselves, that they sang with a loud voice, saying,

"Blessing, and honor, and glory, and power, be unto him that sitteth upon the throne, and unto the lamb, for ever and ever."

Now, just as the gates were opened to let in the men, I looked in after them, and behold the city shone like the sun; the streets also were paved with gold; and in them walked many men, with crowns on their heads, palms in their hands, and golden harps, to sing praises withal.[21]

There were also of them that had wings, and they answered one another without intermission, saying, Holy, holy, holy is the Lord. And after that they shut up the gates; which, when I had seen, I wished myself among them.

Now, while I was gazing upon all these things, I turned my head to look back, and saw Ignorance come up to the river side;[22] but he soon got over, and that without half the difficulty which the other two men met with. For it happened that there was then in that place one Vain-Hope, a ferryman,[23] that with his boat helped him over; so he, as the other I saw, did ascend the hill, to come up to the gate; only he came alone, neither did any man meet him with the least encouragement. When he was come up to the gate, he looked up to the writing that was above, and then began to knock, supposing that entrance should have been quickly administered to him; but he was asked by the men that looked over the top of the gate,

21. John Bunyan brings together a rich litany of biblical images to describe the heavenly land. Many of the images Bunyan uses here are drawn from the Book of Revelation.

22. Ignorance had been following Christian and Hopeful making his way to the Celestial City. But all along Ignorance has had a false hope of entrance into eternal life. Bunyan closes Book 1 with the fate of Ignorance. This is done in order to warn the reader of false paths of salvation.

23. This ferryman was to bring Ignorance over the river of death without having to pass through the waters.

24. Ignorance is turned away at the gate. He has no right to enter the Celestial City. He had not put his trust in Christ. He had put his trust in himself. This language comes from Jesus' Parable of the Wedding Feast. "But when the king came in to see the guests, he saw a man there who did not have on a wedding garment. So he said to him, 'Friend, how did you come in here without a wedding garment?' And he was speechless. Then the king said to the servants, 'Bind him hand and foot, take him away, and cast him into outer darkness; there will be weeping and gnashing of teeth.' For many are called, but few are chosen." (Matt. 22:11-14)

25. John Bunyan's narrative began as a "dream" which he saw. That dream now ends with the final vision of Ignorance's fate in hell. As readers of this beautiful narrative, the question is now put to us: what will we learn from what we have read? John Bunyan has set before us the way of life and death. Are we in that path of life tread by Christian, or are we like Ignorance who was mistaken about his spiritual condition?

Whence come you? and what would you have? He answered, I have ate and drank in the presence of the King, and he has taught in our streets. Then they asked him for his certificate, that they might go in and show it to the King: so he fumbled in his bosom for one, and found none. Then said they, Have you none? but the man answered never a word. So they told the King, but he would not come down to see him, but commanded the two shining ones, that conducted Christian and Hopeful to the city, to go out and take Ignorance, and bind him hand and foot,[24] and have him away. Then they took him up, and carried him through the air to the door that I saw in the side of the hill, and put him in there. Then I saw that there was a way to hell, even from the gate of heaven, as well as from the City of Destruction. So I awoke, and behold it was a dream.[25]

Now, reader, I have told my dream to thee,
See if thou canst interpret it to me,

Or to thyself, or neighbor: but take heed
Of misinterpreting; for that, instead
Of doing good, will but thyself abuse:
By misinterpreting, evil ensues.
Take heed, also, that thou be not extreme
In playing with the outside of my dream;
Nor let my figure or similitude
Put thee into a laughter, or a feud.

Leave this for boys and fools; but as for thee,
Do thou the substance of my matter see.[26]
Put by the curtains, look within my veil,
Turn up my metaphors, and do not fail.
There, if thou seekest them, such things thou'lt find
As will be helpful to an honest mind.
What of my dross thou findest there, be bold
To throw away, but yet preserve the gold.[27]
What if my gold be wrapped up in ore?
None throw away the apple for the core:
But if thou shalt cast all away as vain,
I know not but 't will make me dream again.

26. John Bunyan closes with a poem exhorting the reader to have a right understanding of what he has written. He exhorts us to understand the "substance" of what he wrote. He doesn't want us to get caught up in over-interpreting or mis-interpreting his allegorical symbols. If we will read and apply this allegory well, we need to understand the spiritual meaning of Bunyan's allegory.

27. John Bunyan admits we may find some error (dross) in his book. Be sure to cast away any mistakes but preserve that which is good (in accord with Scripture).

Book 2
The Author's Way

Go, now, my little Book, to every place
Where my first Pilgrim has but shown his face:

Call at their door: if any say, Who's there?
Then answer thou, Christiana is here.
If they bid thee come in, then enter thou,
With all thy boys; and then, as thou know'st how,
Tell who they are, also from whence they came;
Perhaps they'll know them by their looks, or name:
But if they should not, ask them yet again,
If formerly they did not entertain
One Christian, a Pilgrim? If they say
They did, and were delighted in his way;
Then let them know that these related were
Unto him; yea, his wife and children are.
Tell them, that they have left their house and home;
Are turned Pilgrims; seek a world to come;[1]
That they have met with hardships in the way;
That they do meet with troubles night and day;
That they have trod on serpents; fought with devils;
Have also overcome a many evils;
Yea, tell them also of the next who have,
Of love to pilgrimage, been stout and brave
Defenders of that way; and how they still

1. Bunyan tells us that part 2 will recount the journey of Christian's wife and children. Christiana and her boys have now joined the pilgrim pathway.

Refuse this world to do their Father's will.
Go tell them also of those dainty things
That pilgrimage unto the Pilgrim brings.
Let them acquainted be, too, how they are
Beloved of their King, under his care;
What goodly mansions he for them provides;
Though they meet with rough winds and swelling tides,
How brave a calm they will enjoy at last,
Who to their Lord, and by his ways hold fast.
Perhaps with heart and hand they will embrace
Thee, as they did my firstling; and will grace
Thee and thy fellows with such cheer and fare,
As show well, they of Pilgrims lovers are.

OBJECTION I

But how if they will not believe of me
That I am truly thine? 'cause some there be
That counterfeit the Pilgrim and his name,
Seek, by disguise, to seem the very same;
And by that means have wrought themselves into
The hands and houses of I know not who.

ANSWER

'Tis true, some have, of late, to counterfeit
My Pilgrim, to their own my title set;
Yea, others half my name, and title too,
Have stitched to their books, to make them do.
But yet they, by their features, do declare
Themselves not mine to be, whose'er they are.[2]
If such thou meet'st with, then thine only way
Before them all, is, to say out thy say
In thine own native language, which no man
Now useth, nor with ease dissemble can.
If, after all, they still of you shall doubt,
Thinking that you, like gypsies, go about,

2. The objection is made that there are false pilgrims that look like the real thing. How can we tell true pilgrims apart from false pilgrims? The answer is that there are certain characteristics or features of the true pilgrim. The Bible gives us a description of what a true Christian looks like. By using this God-inspired standard, we can discern the true from the false.

In naughty wise the country to defile;
Or that you seek good people to beguile
With things unwarrantable; send for me,
And I will testify you pilgrims be;
Yea, I will testify that only you
My Pilgrims are, and that alone will do.

OBJECTION II

But yet, perhaps, I may enquire for him
Of those who wish him damned life and limb.[3]
What shall I do, when I at such a door
For Pilgrims ask, and they shall rage the more?

3. Bunyan's first book was controversial with many who did not like the theology of the book.

ANSWER

Fright not thyself, my Book, for such bugbears[4]
Are nothing else but groundless fears.
My Pilgrim's book has traveled sea and land,
Yet could I never come to understand
That it was slighted or turned out of door
By any Kingdom, were they rich or poor.
In France and Flanders,[5] where men kill each other,
My Pilgrim is esteemed a friend, a brother.
In Holland, too, 'tis said, as I am told,
My Pilgrim is with some, worth more than gold.
Highlanders and wild Irish[6] can agree
My Pilgrim should familiar with them be.
'Tis in New England under such advance,
Receives there so much loving countenance,[7]
As to be trimm'd, newcloth'd, and deck'd with gems,
That it might show its features, and its limbs.
Yet more: so comely doth my Pilgrim walk,
That of him thousands daily sing and talk.
If you draw nearer home, it will appear
My Pilgrim knows no ground of shame or fear:
City and country will him entertain,

4. "Bugbears" are the equivalent of "boogey-men." They are only in the imagination.

5. Bunyan details how the first book was translated and went into many different lands.

6. The term "high-landers" refers to those who live in the Scottish highlands.

7. Bunyan's first book was very popular in New England. The inhabitants of New England had often styled them-selves as "pilgrims."

With Welcome, Pilgrim; yea, they can't refrain
From smiling, if my Pilgrim be but by,
Or shows his head in any company.

8. "Brave gallants" refers to dashing or daring young men.

Brave gallants do my Pilgrim hug and love,[8]
Esteem it much, yea, value it above
Things of greater bulk; yea, with delight

9. David Hawkes interprets this in the following way: "A dainty, apparently trivial dish is preferable to a hearty but indigestible repast [meal]."

Say, my lark's leg is better than a kite.[9]
Young ladies, and young gentlewomen too,
Do not small kindness to my Pilgrim show;
Their cabinets, their bosoms, and their hearts,
My Pilgrim has; 'cause he to them imparts
His pretty riddles in such wholsome strains,
As yield them profit double to their pains
Of reading; yea, I think I may be bold
To say some prize him far above their gold.
The very children that do walk the street,
If they do but my holy Pilgrim meet,
Salute him will; will wish him well, and say,

10. "Stripling" means "young man."

He is the only stripling of the day.[10]
They that have never seen him, yet admire
What they have heard of him, and much desire
To have his company, and hear him tell
Those Pilgrim stories which he knows so well.
Yea, some that did not love him at first,

11. "Noddy" refers to a foolish or silly person.

But call'd him fool and noddy,[11] say they must,
Now they have seen and heard him, him commend
And to those whom they love they do him send.
Wherefore, my Second Part, thou need'st not be
Afraid to show thy head: none can hurt thee,
That wish but well to him that went before;
'Cause thou com'st after with a second store
Of things as good, as rich, as profitable,
For young, for old, for stagg'ring, and for stable.

OBJECTION III

But some there be that say, He laughs too loud
And some do say, His Head is in a cloud.
Some say, His words and stories are so dark,
They know not how, by them, to find his mark.

ANSWER

One may, I think, say, Both his laughs and cries
May well be guess'd at by his wat'ry eyes.
Some things are of that nature, as to make
One's fancy chuckle, while his heart doth ache:
When Jacob saw his Rachel with the sheep,
He did at the same time both kiss and weep.
Whereas some say, A cloud is in his head;
That doth but show his wisdom's covered
With its own mantles—and to stir the mind
To search well after what it fain would find,
Things that seem to be hid in words obscure
Do but the godly mind the more allure
To study what those sayings should contain,
That speak to us in such a cloudy strain.
I also know a dark similitude
Will on the curious fancy more intrude,[12]
And will stick faster in the heart and head,
Than things from similes not borrowed.
Wherefore, my Book, let no discouragement
Hinder thy travels. Behold, thou art sent
To friends, not foes; to friends that will give place
To thee, thy pilgrims, and thy words embrace.
Besides, what my first Pilgrim left conceal'd,
Thou, my brave second Pilgrim, hast reveal'd;
What Christian left lock'd up, and went his way,
Sweet Christiana opens with her key.

12. Bunyan says that using "similitudes," that is, casting his story in the form of allegory will make the truth "stick faster" in the heart and head.

OBJECTION IV

But some love not the method of your first:
Romance they count it; throw't away as dust.
If I should meet with such, what should I say?
Must I slight them as they slight me, or nay?

ANSWER

My Christiana, if with such thou meet,
By all means, in all loving wise them greet;
Render them not reviling for revile,
But, if they frown, I prithee on them smile:[13]
Perhaps 'tis nature, or some ill report,
Has made them thus despise, or thus retort.
Some love no fish, some love no cheese, and some
Love not their friends, nor their own house or home;
Some start at pig, slight chicken, love not fowl
More than they love a cuckoo or an owl.
Leave such, my Christiana, to their choice,[14]
And seek those who to find thee will rejoice;
By no means strive, but, in most humble wise,
Present thee to them in thy Pilgrim's guise.
Go then, my little Book, and show to all
That entertain and bid thee welcome shall,
What thou shalt keep close shut up from the rest;
And wish what thou shalt show them may be bless'd
To them for good, and make them choose to be
Pilgrims, by better far than thee or me.
Go, then, I say, tell all men who thou art:
Say, I am Christiana; and my part
Is now, with my four sons, to tell you what
It is for men to take a Pilgrim's lot.[15]
Go, also, tell them who and what they be
That now do go on pilgrimage with thee;
Say, Here's my neighbor Mercy: she is one
That has long time with me a pilgrim gone:

13. Christiana, the main character of the second part, is to "smile back" at those who may not like the form of the story. "Prithee" means "ask you to."

14. Bunyan acknowledges that not everyone will like his story. Not all receive the truth. But there will be some who understand and identify with the story.

15. The purpose of Bunyan's allegory of Christiana and her four sons is to tell the reader what it looks like to be a pilgrim follower of Jesus.

Come, see her in her virgin face, and learn
'Twixt idle ones and pilgrims to discern.
Yea, let young damsels learn of her to prize
The world which is to come, in any wise.
When little tripping maidens follow God,
And leave old doting sinners to his rod,
'Tis like those days wherein the young ones cried
Hosanna! when the old ones did deride.[16]
Next tell them of old Honest, whom you found
With his white hairs treading the Pilgrim's ground;
Yea, tell them how plain-hearted this man was;
How after his good Lord he bare the cross.
Perhaps with some gray head, this may prevail
With Christ to fall in love, and sin bewail.
Tell them also, how Master Fearing went
On pilgrimage, and how the time he spent
In solitariness, with fears and cries;
And how, at last, he won the joyful prize.
He was a good man, though much down in spirit;
He is a good man, and doth life inherit.
Tell them of Master Feeble-Mind also,
Who not before, but still behind would go.
Show them also, how he had like been slain,
And how one Great-Heart did his life regain.
This man was true of heart; though weak in grace,
One might true godliness read in his face.
Then tell them of Master Ready-to-Halt,
A man with crutches, but much without fault.
Tell them how Master Feeble-Mind and he
Did love, and in opinion much agree.
And let all know, though weakness was their chance,
Yet sometimes one could sing, the other dance.
Forget not Master Valiant-for-the-Truth,
That man of courage, though a very youth:
Tell every one his spirit was so stout,
No man could ever make him face about;

16. Bunyan is referring to Jesus' triumphal entry into Jerusalem. Many of the children welcomed Jesus into the city while the Pharisees scoffed at and criticized Jesus.

And how Great-Heart and he could not forbear,
But pull down Doubting-Castle, slay Despair!
Overlook not Master Despondency,
Nor Much-afraid, his daughter, though they lie
Under such mantles, as may make them look
(With some) as if their God had them forsook.
They softly went, but sure; and, at the end,
Found that the Lord of Pilgrims was their friend.
When thou hast told the world of all these things,
Then turn about, my Book, and touch these strings;
Which, if but touched, will such music make,
They'll make a cripple dance, a giant quake.
Those riddles that lie couched within thy breast,
Freely propound, expound; and for the rest
Of thy mysterious lines, let them remain
For those whose nimble fancies shall them gain.[17]
Now may this little Book a blessing be
To those who love this little Book and me;
And may its buyer have no cause to say,
His money is but lost or thrown away.
Yea, may this second Pilgrim yield that fruit
As may with each good Pilgrim's fancy suit;
And may it some persuade, that go astray,
To turn their feet and heart to the right way.[18]

17. Bunyan previews for the reader many of the characters of this second part.

18. Bunyan desires to persuade the reader to also follow the pilgrim path to the Celestial City. He has an evangelistic purpose in writing the second part of *The Pilgrim's Progress.*

Book 2
To the Reader

Courteous companions,
    Some time since, to tell you my dream that I had of Christian the pilgrim, and of his dangerous journey towards the Celestial country, was pleasant to me and profitable to you. I told you then also what I saw concerning his wife and children, and how unwilling they were to go with him on pilgrimage; insomuch that he was forced to go on his progress without them; for he durst not run the danger of that destruction which he feared would come by staying with them in the City of Destruction: wherefore, as I then showed you, he left them and departed.

Now it hath so happened, through the multiplicity of business, that I have been much hindered and kept back from my wonted travels into those parts whence he went, and so could not, till now, obtain an opportunity to make further inquiry after those whom he left behind, that I might give you an account of them. But having had some concerns that way of late, I went down again thitherward. Now, having taken up my lodging in a wood about a mile off the place, as I slept, I dreamed again.[1]

And as I was in my dream, behold, an aged gentleman came by where I lay; and, because he was to go some part of the way that I was traveling, methought I got up and went

1. Like the first part, Bunyan casts the allegory in the form of a dream he had of the story events.

2. One who is "sagacious" has good discernment and judgment.

3. "Quoth I" means "said I."

4. This is an illustration of what Proverbs 10 says: "The memory of the righteous is blessed,
But the name of the wicked will rot." (Prov. 10:7)

with him. So, as we walked, and as travelers usually do, I was as if we fell into a discourse; and our talk happened to be about Christian and his travels; for thus I began with the old man:

Sir, said I, what town is that there below, that lieth on the left hand of our way?

Then said Mr. Sagacity,[2] (for that was his name,) It is the City of Destruction, a populous place, but possessed with a very ill-conditioned and idle sort of people.

I thought that was that city, quoth I; I went once myself through that town; and therefore know that this report you give of it is true.

Mr. Sagacity: Too true! I wish I could speak truth in speaking better of them that dwell therein.

Well, sir, quoth I,[3] then I perceive you to be a well-meaning man, and so one that takes pleasure to hear and tell of that which is good. Pray, did you never hear what happened to a man some time ago of this town, (whose name was Christian,) that went on a pilgrimage up towards the higher regions?

Mr. Sagacity: Hear of him! Aye, and I also heard of the molestations, troubles, wars, captivities, cries, groans, frights, and fears, that he met with and had on his journey. Besides, I must tell you, all our country rings of him; there are but few houses that have heard of him and his doings, but have sought after and got the records of his pilgrimage; yea, I think I may say that his hazardous journey has got many well-wishers to his ways; for, though when he was here he was fool in every man's mouth, yet now he is gone he is highly commended of all.[4] For 'tis said he lives bravely where he is: yea, many of them that are resolved never to run his hazards, yet have their mouths water at his gains.

They may, quoth I, well think, if they think any thing that is true, that he liveth well where he is; for he now lives at, and in the fountain of life, and has what he has without labor and sorrow, for there is no grief mixed therewith. But, pray what talk have the people about him?

Mr. Sagacity: Talk! the people talk strangely about him: some say that he now walks in white, Rev. 3:4; that he has a chain of gold about his neck; that he has a crown of gold, beset with pearls, upon his head: others say, that the shining ones, who sometimes showed themselves to him in his journey, are become his companions, and that he is as familiar with them where he is, as here one neighbor is with another. Besides, it is confidently affirmed concerning him, that the King of the place where he is has bestowed upon him already a very rich and pleasant dwelling at court, and that he every day eateth and drinketh, and walketh and talketh with him, and receiveth of the smiles and favors of him that is Judge of all there. Zech. 3:7; Luke 14:14,15. Moreover, it is expected of some, that his Prince, the Lord of that country, will shortly come into these parts, and will know the reason, if they can give any, why his neighbors set so little by him, and had him so much in derision, when they perceived that he would be a pilgrim.[5] Jude, 14,15.

For they say, that now he is so in the affections of his Prince, that his Sovereign is so much concerned with the indignities that were cast upon Christian when he became a pilgrim, that he will look upon all as if done unto himself, Luke 10:16; and no marvel, for it was for the love that he had to his Prince that he ventured as he did.[6]

I dare say, quoth I; I am glad on't; I am glad for the poor man's sake, for that now he has rest from his labor, and for that he now reapeth the benefit of his tears with joy; and for that he has got beyond the gun-shot of his enemies, and is out of the reach of them that hate him. Rev. 14:13; Psa. 126:5,6. I also am glad for that a rumor of these things is noised abroad in this country;[7] who can tell but that it may work some good effect on some that are left behind? But pray, sir, while it is fresh in my mind, do you hear anything of his wife and children? Poor hearts! I wonder in my mind what they do.

Mr. Sagacity: Who? Christiana and her sons? They are like to do as well as Christian did himself; for though they all

5. Mr. Sagacity recounts many of the blessings of eternal life with the Lord referencing many Scripture passages that speak of the eternal state with the Lord.

6. Christians endure the sufferings and sorrow of the Christian life because they love their Lord Jesus and will hazard all to be with him. It is the love of Christ that constrains us.

7. The narrator (Bunyan) is glad to hear that the news of Christian's journey and eventual entrance to Zion is discussed abroad. The life testimony of Christians may be used by the Lord to bring others to saving faith.

played the fool at first, and would by no means be persuaded by either the tears or entreaties of Christian, yet second thoughts have wrought wonderfully with them: so they have packed up, and are also gone after him.

Better and better, quoth I: but, what! wife and children, and all?

Mr. Sagacity: It is true: I can give you an account of the matter, for I was upon the spot at the instant, and was thoroughly acquainted with the whole affair.

Then, said I, a man, it seems, may report it for a truth.

Mr. Sagacity: You need not fear to affirm it: I mean, that they are all gone on pilgrimage, both the good woman and her four boys. And being we are, as I perceive, going some considerable way together, I will give you an account of the whole matter.

This Christiana, (for that was her name from the day that she with her children betook themselves to a pilgrim's life,) after her husband was gone over the river, and she could hear of him no more, her thoughts began to work in her mind. First, for that she had lost her husband, and for that the loving bond of that relation was utterly broken betwixt them. For you know, said he to me, nature can do no less but entertain the living with many a heavy cogitation,[8] in the remembrance of the loss of loving relations. This, therefore, of her husband did cost her many a tear. But this was not all; for Christiana did also begin to consider with herself, whether her unbecoming behavior towards her husband was not one cause that she saw him no more, and that in such sort he was taken away from her. And upon this came into her mind, by swarms, all her unkind, unnatural, and ungodly carriage[9] to her dear friend; which also clogged her conscience, and did load her with guilt.[10] She was, moreover, much broken with recalling to remembrance the restless groans, brinish tears,[11] and self-bemoanings of her husband, and how she did harden her heart against all his entreaties and loving persuasions of her and her sons to go with him; yea, there was not any thing that Christian either said to

8. With many heavy, sorrowful thoughts

9. The word "carriage" refers to one's conduct or pattern of life.

10. Christiana falls under the conviction of her sin.

11. "Brinish tears" refers to "salty tears."

her, or did before her, all the while that his burden did hang on his back, but it returned upon her like a flash of lightning, and rent the caul of her heart in sunder;[12] especially that bitter outcry of his, "What shall I do to be saved?" did ring in her ears most dolefully.

Then said she to her children, Sons, we are all undone. I have sinned away your father, and he is gone: he would have had us with him, but I would not go myself: I also have hindered you of life. With that the boys fell into tears, and cried out to go after their father. Oh, said Christiana, that it had been but our lot to go with him! then had it fared well with us, beyond what it is like to do now. For, though I formerly foolishly imagined, concerning the troubles of your father, that they proceeded of a foolish fancy[13] that he had, or for that he was overrun with melancholy humors;[14] yet now it will not out of my mind, but that they sprang from another cause; to wit, for that the light of life was given him,[15] James 1:23-25; John 8:12; by the help of which, as I perceive, he has escaped the snares of death. Prov. 14:27. Then they all wept again, and cried out, Oh, woe worth the day!

The next night Christiana had a dream; and, behold, she saw as if a broad parchment was opened before her, in which were recorded the sum of her ways; and the crimes, as she

12. This language comes from Hosea 13: "I will meet them as a bear that is bereaved of her whelps, And will rend the caul of their heart, And there will I devour them like a lion: The wild beast shall tear them." (Hos. 13:8) The caul is a membrane within an organ. The idea is that Christiana's heart was torn in two by her decision.

13. That is, Christiana believed that Christian's decision to go on pilgrimage was from a foolish imagination of the danger he was in.

14. "Humors" is not used in the modern sense of something humorous. It here refers to a mental disposition. That is, Christiana thought Christian was dealing with feelings of melancholy that influenced him to leave.

15. Before her eyes were opened, Christiana believed that Christian had made a foolish decision to believe a fable. But now she saw the truth and herself was convicted to leave the City of Destruction and walk on the path to eternal life.

16. Christiana adopts the words of the humbled tax collector in Jesus' parable. "And the tax collector, standing afar off, would not so much as raise his eyes to heaven, but beat his breast, saying, 'God, be merciful to me a sinner!'" (Luke 18:13)

17. This refers to two demons. This is indicated by their conversation. They want to take her away from thinking about her sins and about the way of salvation.

18. The character Secret may represent the Holy Spirit who reveals to us the things of God. "These things we also speak, not in words which man's wisdom teaches but which the Holy Spirit teaches, comparing spiritual things with spiritual. But the natural man does not receive the things of the Spirit of God, for they are foolishness to him; nor can he know them, because they are spiritually discerned." (1 Cor. 2:13-14)

thought looked very black upon her. Then she cried out aloud in her sleep, "Lord, have mercy upon me a sinner!" Luke 18:13; and the little children heard her.[16]

After this she thought she saw two very ill-favored ones[17] standing by her bedside, and saying, What shall we do with this woman? for she cries out for mercy, waking and sleeping: if she be suffered to go on as she begins, we shall lose her as we have lost her husband. Wherefore we must, by one way or other, seek to take her off from the thoughts of what shall be hereafter, else all the world cannot help but she will become a pilgrim.

Now she awoke in a great sweat, also a trembling was upon her: but after a while she fell to sleeping again. And then she thought she saw Christian, her husband, in a place of bliss among many immortals, with a harp in his hand, standing and playing upon it before One that sat on a throne with a rainbow about his head. She saw also, as if he bowed his head with his face to the paved work that was under his Prince's feet, saying, "I heartily thank my Lord and King for bringing me into this place." Then shouted a company of them that stood round about, and harped with their harps; but no man living could tell what they said but Christian and his companions.

Next morning, when she was up, had prayed to God, and talked with her children a while, one knocked hard at the door; to whom she spake out, saying, "If thou comest in God's name, come in." So he said, "Amen;" and opened the door, and saluted her with, "Peace be to this house." The which when he had done, he said, "Christiana, knowest thou wherefore I am come?" Then she blushed and trembled; also her heart began to wax warm with desires to know from whence he came, and what was his errand to her. So he said unto her, "My name is Secret; I dwell with those that are on high.[18] It is talked of where I dwell as if thou hadst a desire to go thither: also there is a report that thou art aware of the evil thou hast formerly done to thy husband, in hardening of thy heart against his way, and in keeping of these babes in their ignorance. Christiana, the Merciful One has sent me to tell thee, that he is a God ready to forgive, and that he taketh delight to multiply the pardon of offences.[19] He also would have thee to know, that he inviteth thee to come into his presence, to his table, and that he will feed thee with the fat of his house, and with the heritage of Jacob thy father.

"There is Christian, thy husband that was, with legions more, his companions, ever beholding that face that doth minister life to beholders; and they will all be glad when they shall hear the sound of thy feet step over thy Father's threshold."

Christiana at this was greatly abashed in herself,[20] and bowed her head to the ground. This visitor proceeded, and said, "Christiana, here is also a letter for thee, which I have brought from thy husband's King." So she took it, and opened it, but it smelt after the manner of the best perfume. Song 1:3. Also it was written in letters of gold. The contents of the letter were these, That the King would have her to do as did Christian her husband; for that was the way to come to his city, and to dwell in his presence with joy for ever. At this the good woman was quite overcome; so she cried out to her visitor, Sir, will you carry me and my children with you, that we also may go and worship the King?

Then said the visitor, Christiana, the bitter is before the sweet.[21] Thou must through troubles, as did he that went before thee, enter this Celestial City. Wherefore I advise thee to do as did Christian thy husband: go to the Wicket-gate yonder, over the plain, for that stands at the head of the way up which thou must go; and I wish thee all good speed. Also I advise that thou put this letter in thy bosom, that thou read therein to thyself and to thy children until you have got it by heart; for it is one of the songs that thou must sing while thou art in this house of thy pilgrimage, Psalm 119:54; also this thou must deliver in at the further gate.

Now I saw in my dream, that this old gentleman, as he told me the story, did himself seem to be greatly affected therewith. He moreover proceeded, and said, So Christiana

19. This is the grace and mercy of God. He is a God ready to forgive. Even though sinners may harden themselves against him and continue in their sins, He is ready to receive those who turn and repent. The Parable of the Prodigal Son gives us this picture: a father ready and willing to forgive and restore.

20. "Abashed" means "ashamed" or "embarrassed."

21. The path of eternal life is filled with tribulations and sorrows. We must enter the kingdom of God through many tribulations (Acts 14:22).

22. Christiana understands that her natural fallen condition, and the condition of her sons, is a state of sin and misery. The Apostle Paul describes this condition in Ephesians as being "children of wrath" (Eph. 2:3) and being without hope and without God in the world (Eph. 2:12).

23. A change has occurred in Christiana such that her neighbors are stunned by her new way of speaking.

24. Mrs. Timorous is a fearful, apprehensive woman.

called her sons together, and began thus to address herself unto them: "My sons, I have, as you may perceive, been of late under much exercise in my soul about the death of your father: not for that I doubt at all of his happiness, for I am satisfied now that he is well. I have also been much affected with the thoughts of my own state and yours, which I verily believe is by nature miserable.[22] My carriage also to your father in his distress is a great load to my conscience; for I hardened both mine own heart and yours against him, and refused to go with him on pilgrimage.

The thoughts of these things would now kill me outright, but that for a dream which I had last night, and but that for the encouragement which this stranger has given me this morning. Come, my children, let us pack up, and begone to the gate that leads to the Celestial country, that we may see your father, and be with him and his companions in peace, according to the laws of that land.

Then did her children burst out into tears, for joy that the heart of their mother was so inclined. So their visitor bid them farewell; and they began to prepare to set out for their journey.

But while they were thus about to be gone, two of the women that were Christiana's neighbors came up to her house, and knocked at her door. To whom she said as before, If you come in God's name, come in. At this the women were stunned; for this kind of language they used not to hear, or to perceive to drop from the lips of Christiana.[23] Yet they came in: but behold, they found the good woman preparing to be gone from her house.

So they began, and said, Neighbor, pray what is your meaning by this?

Christiana answered, and said to the eldest of them, whose name was Mrs. Timorous,[24] I am preparing for a journey.

This Timorous was daughter to him that met Christian upon the Hill of Difficulty, and would have had him go back for fear of the lions.

Timorous: For what journey, I pray you?

Christiana: Even to go after my good husband. And with that she fell a weeping.

Timorous: I hope not so, good neighbor; pray, for your poor children's sake, do not so unwomanly cast away yourself.

Christiana: Nay, my children shall go with me; not one of them is willing to stay behind.

Timorous: I wonder in my very heart what or who has brought you into this mind!

Christiana: O neighbor, knew you but as much as I do, I doubt not but that you would go along with me.

Timorous: Prithee, what new knowledge hast thou got, that so worketh off thy mind from thy friends, and that tempteth thee to go nobody knows where?

Christiana: Then Christiana replied, I have been sorely afflicted since my husband's departure from me; but especially since he went over the river. But that which troubleth me most is, my churlish carriage to him[25] when he was under his distress. Besides, I am now as he was then; nothing will serve me but going on pilgrimage. I was a dreaming last night that I saw him. O that my soul was with him! He dwelleth in the presence of the King of the country; he sits and eats with him at his table; he is become a companion of immortals, and has a house now given him to dwell in, to which the best palace on earth, if compared, seems to me but a dunghill.[26] 2 Cor. 5:1-4. The Prince of the place has also sent for me, with promise of entertainment, if I shall come to him; his messenger was here even now, and has brought me a letter, which invites me to come. And with that she plucked out her letter, and read it, and said to them, What now will you say to this?

Timorous: Oh, the madness that has possessed thee and thy husband, to run yourselves upon such difficulties! You have heard, I am sure what your husband did meet with, even in a manner at the first step that he took on his way, as our neighbor Obstinate can yet testify, for he went along with him; yea, and Pliable too, until they, like wise men, were afraid to go any further. We also heard, over and above, how he met with

25. "Rude behavior"

26. When the glories of heaven are compared with this earth, even the greatest glories of the earth are nothing in comparison.

the lions, Apollyon, the Shadow of Death, and many other things. Nor is the danger that he met with at Vanity Fair to be forgotten by thee. For if he, though a man, was so hard put to it, what canst thou, being but a poor woman, do? Consider also, that these four sweet babes are thy children, thy flesh and thy bones. Wherefore, though thou shouldest be so rash as to cast away thyself, yet, for the sake of the fruit of thy body, keep thou at home.

But Christiana said unto her, Tempt me not, my neighbor: I have now a price put into my hands to get gain, and I should be a fool of the greatest size if I should have no heart to strike in with the opportunity. And for that you tell me of all these troubles which I am like to meet with in the way, they are so far from being to me a discouragement, that they show I am in the right. The bitter must come before the sweet, and that also will make the sweet the sweeter. Wherefore, since you came not to my house in God's name, as I said, I pray you to be gone, and not to disquiet me further.

Then Timorous reviled her, and said to her fellow, Come, neighbor Mercy, let us leave her in her own hands, since she scorns our counsel and company. But Mercy was at a stand, and could not so readily comply with her neighbor; and that for a two fold reason. 1. Her bowels yearned over Christiana. So she said within herself, if my neighbor will needs be gone, I will go a little way with her, and help her. 2. Her bowels yearned over her own soul; for what Christiana had said had taken some hold upon her mind. Wherefore she said within herself again, I will yet have more talk with this Christiana; and, if I find truth and life in what she shall say, I myself with my heart shall also go with her. Wherefore Mercy began thus to reply to her neighbor Timorous:

Mercy: Neighbor, I did indeed come with you to see Christiana this morning; and since she is, as you see, taking of her last farewell of the country, I think to walk this sunshiny morning a little with her, to help her on her way. But she told her not of her second reason, but kept it to herself.

Timorous: Well, I see you have a mind to go a fooling too; but take heed in time, and be wise: while we are out of danger, we are out; but when we are in, we are in.

So Mrs. Timorous returned to her house, and Christiana betook herself to her journey. But when Timorous was got home to her house she sends for some of her neighbors, to wit, Mrs. Bat's-Eyes, Mrs. Inconsiderate, Mrs. Light-Mind, and Mrs. Know-Nothing.[27] So when they were come to her house, she falls to telling of the story of Christiana, and of her intended journey. And thus she began her tale:

Timorous: Neighbors, having had little to do this morning, I went to give Christiana a visit; and when I came at the door I knocked, as you know it is our custom; and she answered, If you come in God's name, come in. So in I went, thinking all was well; but, when I came in I found her preparing herself to depart the town, she, and also her children. So I asked her what was her meaning by that. And she told me, in short, that she was now of a mind to go on pilgrimage, as did her husband. She told me also of a dream that she had, and how the King of the country where her husband was, had sent an inviting letter to come thither.

Then said Mrs. Know-Nothing, And what, do you think she will go?

Timorous: Aye, go she will, whatever comes on't; and methinks I know it by this; for that which was my great argument to persuade her to stay at home, (to wit, the troubles she was like to meet with on the way,) is one great argument with her to put her forward on her journey. For she told me in so many words, The bitter goes before the sweet; yea, and forasmuch as it doth, it makes the sweet the sweeter.

Mrs. Bat's-Eyes: Oh, this blind and foolish woman! said she; and will she not take warning by her husband's afflictions? For my part, I see, if he were here again, he would rest himself content in a whole skin, and never run so many hazards for nothing.

27. The names given to these various women are similar. They are characterized by foolishness, ignorance, and blindness.

28. "Dumpish" means "sad" or "depressed."

29. "Lechery" refers to lustful desire or unlawful sexual desire.

Mrs. Inconsiderate also replied, saying, Away with such fantastical fools from the town: a good riddance, for my part, I say, of her; should she stay where she dwells, and retain this her mind, who could live quietly by her? for she will either be dumpish,[28] or unneighborly, or talk of such matters as no wise body can abide. Wherefore, for my part, I shall never be sorry for her departure; let her go, and let better come in her room: it was never a good world since these whimsical fools dwelt in it.

Then Mrs. Light-Mind added as followeth: Come, put this kind of talk away. I was yesterday at Madam Wanton's, where we were as merry as the maids. For who do you think should be there but I and Mrs. Love-the-Flesh, and three or four more, with Mrs. Lechery,[29] Mrs. Filth, and some others: so there we had music and dancing, and what else was meet to fill up the pleasure. And I dare say, my lady herself is an admirable well-bred gentlewoman, and Mr. Lechery is as pretty a fellow.

Book 2

Chapter 1

By this time Christiana was got on her way, and Mercy went along with her: so as they went, her children being there also, Christiana began to discourse. And, Mercy, said Christiana, I take this as an unexpected favor, that thou shouldest set forth out of doors with me to accompany me a little in the way.

Mercy: Then said young Mercy, (for she was but young,) If I thought it would be to purpose to go with you, I would never go near the town any more.

Christiana: Well, Mercy, said Christiana, cast in thy lot with me: I well know what will be the end of our pilgrimage: my husband is where he would not but be for all the gold in the Spanish mines. Nor shalt thou be rejected, though thou goest but upon my invitation. The King, who hath sent for me and my children, is one that delighteth in mercy. Besides, if thou wilt, I will hire thee, and thou shalt go along with me as my servant. Yet we will have all things in common betwixt thee and me: only go along with me.

Mercy: But how shall I be ascertained that I also should be entertained?[1] Had I this hope but from one that can tell, I would make no stick at all, but would go, being helped by Him that can help, though the way was never so tedious.

1. Mercy is asking, "How can I know that I will also be received by the King?"

Christiana: Well, loving Mercy, I will tell thee what thou shalt do: go with me to the Wicket-gate, and there I will further inquire for thee; and if there thou shalt not meet with encouragement, I will be content that thou return to thy place: I will also pay thee for thy kindness which thou showest to me and my children, in the accompanying of us in the way that thou dost.

Mercy: Then will I go thither, and will take what shall follow; and the Lord grant that my lot may there fall, even as the King of heaven shall have his heart upon me.

Christiana then was glad at heart, not only that she had a companion, but also for that she had prevailed with this poor maid to fall in love with her own salvation. So they went on together, and Mercy began to weep. Then said Christiana, Wherefore weepeth my sister so?

Mercy: Alas! said she, who can but lament, that shall but rightly consider what a state and condition my poor relations are in, that yet remain in our sinful town? And that which makes my grief the more heavy is, because they have no instructor, nor any to tell them what is to come.[2]

Christiana: Pity becomes pilgrims; and thou dost weep for thy friends, as my good Christian did for me when he left me: he mourned for that I would not heed nor regard him; but his Lord and ours did gather up his tears, and put them into his bottle;[3] and now both I and thou, and these my sweet babes, are reaping the fruit and benefit of them. I hope, Mercy, that these tears of thine will not be lost; for the truth hath said, that "they that sow in tears shall reap in joy." And "he that goeth forth and weepeth, bearing precious seed, shall doubtless come again with rejoicing, bringing his sheaves with him." Psa. 126:5,6.

Then said Mercy,
"Let the Most Blessed be my guide,
   If it be his blessed will,
Unto his gate, into his fold,
   Up to his holy hill.

2. Mercy weeps over those left in the City of Destruction. Our hearts should go out with compassion to those who are lost in their sins and blinded by the god of this world. "Rivers of water run down from my eyes, because men do not keep Your law." (Ps. 119:136)

3. "You number my wanderings; Put my tears into Your bottle; Are they not in Your book?" (Ps. 56:8)

And let him never suffer me
    To swerve, or turn aside
From his free-grace and holy ways,
    Whate'er shall me betide.
And let him gather them of mine
    That I have left behind;
Lord, make them pray they may be thine,
    With all their heart and mind."

Now my old friend proceeded, and said, But when Christiana came to the Slough of Despond, she began to be at a stand; For, said she, this is the place in which my dear husband had like to have been smothered with mud. She perceived, also, that notwithstanding the command of the King to make this place for pilgrims good, yet it was rather worse than formerly. So I asked if that was true. Yes, said the old gentleman, too true; for many there be that pretend to be the King's laborers, and that say they are for mending the King's highways, who bring dirt and dung instead of stones, and so mar instead of mending. Here Christiana therefore, with her boys, did make a stand. But said Mercy, Come, let us venture; only let us be wary.[4] Then they looked well to their steps, and made a shift to get staggering over.

Yet Christiana had like to have been in, and that not once or twice. Now they had no sooner got over, but they thought they heard words that said unto them, "Blessed is she that believeth; for there shall be a performance of those things which were told her from the Lord." Luke 1:45.

Then they went on again; and said Mercy to Christiana, had I as good ground to hope for a loving reception at the Wicket-gate as you, I think no Slough of Despond would discourage me.

Well, said the other, you know your sore, and I know mine; and, good friend, we shall all have enough evil before we come to our journey's end. For can it be imagined that the people who design to attain such excellent glories as we do, and who are so envied that happiness as we are, but that we shall meet

4. By faith, Christiana, Mercy, and the boys cross the Slough of Despond. They are sustained and kept safe by their faith in the Lord.

5. The narrator is no longer hearing the story recounted by Mr. Sagacity. He is continuing to watch the goings of the pilgrims on his own.

6. Bunyan alludes to Jesus' words: "Ask, and it will be given to you; seek, and you will find; knock, and it will be opened to you. For everyone who asks receives, and he who seeks finds, and to him who knocks it will be opened." (Matt. 7:7-8)

7. In the first part of the book, Christian encountered flying arrows from the enemy at the Wicket-gate. This time, the dogs bark to scare away pilgrims from entering the narrow path of salvation. As Jesus said in the Parable of the Sower, the enemy would like to steal the Word of God sown from the heart so that people will not believe. But the pilgrims keep knocking until the door opens.

8. Christiana bowed low to the man.

with what fears and snares, with what troubles and afflictions they can possibly assault us with that hate us?

And now Mr. Sagacity left me to dream out my dream by myself.[5] Wherefore, methought I saw Christiana, and Mercy, and the boys, go all of them up to the gate: to which, when they were come, they betook themselves to a short debate about how they must manage their calling at the gate, and what should be said unto him that did open to them: so it was concluded, since Christiana was the eldest, that she should knock for entrance, and that she should speak to him that did open, for the rest. So Christiana began to knock, and as her poor husband did, she knocked and knocked again.[6] But instead of any that answered, they all thought they heard as if a dog came barking upon them; a dog, and a great one too; and this made the women and children afraid. Nor durst they for a while to knock any more, for fear the mastiff should fly upon them. Now, therefore, they were greatly tumbled up and down in their minds, and knew not what to do: knock they durst not, for fear of the dog; go back they durst not, for fear the keeper of that gate should espy them as they so went, and should be offended with them; at last they thought of knocking again, and knocked more vehemently than they did at first. Then said the keeper of the gate, Who is there? So the dog left off to bark, and he opened unto them.[7]

Then Christiana made low obeisance,[8] and said, Let not our Lord be offended with his handmaidens, for that we have knocked at his princely gate. Then said the keeper, Whence come ye? And what is it that you would have?

Christiana answered, We are come from whence Christian did come, and upon the same errand as he; to wit, to be, if it shall please you, graciously admitted by this gate into the way that leads unto the Celestial City. And I answer, my Lord, in the next place, that I am Christiana, once the wife of Christian, that now is gotten above.

With that the keeper of the gate did marvel, saying, What, is she now become a pilgrim that but a while ago abhorred that life? Then she bowed her head, and said, Yea; and so are these my sweet babes also.

Then he took her by the hand and led her in, and said also, Suffer little children to come unto me;[9] and with that he shut up the gate. This done, he called to a trumpeter that was above, over the gate, to entertain Christiana with shouting, and the sound of trumpet for joy.[10] So he obeyed, and sounded, and filled the air with his melodious notes.

9. This is an allusion to Jesus' words who would not allow the disciples to prevent the children from coming to him (Matt. 19:14).

Now all this while poor Mercy did stand without, trembling and crying, for fear that she was rejected. But when Christiana had got admittance for herself and her boys, then she began to make intercession for Mercy.

Christiana: And she said, My Lord, I have a companion that stands yet without, that is come hither upon the same account as myself: one that is much dejected in her mind, for that she comes, as she thinks, without sending for; whereas I was sent for by my husband's King to come.

10. As our Lord Jesus said, there is more joy in heaven over one sinner who repents (Luke 15:7).

Now Mercy began to be very impatient, and each minute was as long to her as an hour; wherefore she prevented Christiana from a fuller interceding for her, by knocking at the gate herself. And she knocked then so loud that she made Christiana to start. Then said the keeper of the gate, Who is there? And Christiana said, It is my friend.

So he opened the gate, and looked out, but Mercy was fallen down without in a swoon,[11] for she fainted, and was afraid that no gate should be opened to her.

11. To "swoon" means to "faint."

Then he took her by the hand, and said, Damsel, I bid thee arise.

Oh, sir, said she, I am faint; there is scarce life left in me. But he answered, that one once said, "When my soul fainted within me I remembered the Lord: and my prayer came unto thee, into thy holy temple." Jonah 2:7. Fear not, but stand upon thy feet, and tell me wherefore thou art come.

Mercy: I am come for that unto which I was never invited, as my friend Christiana was. Hers was from the King, and mine was but from her. Wherefore I fear I presume.

12. Thanks be to God that there is an abundance of grace in our Lord Jesus Christ. He is a sufficient Savior to save all who come to Him by faith. Whoever comes to Jesus Christ will not be turned away (John 6:37).

Keep: Did she desire thee to come with her to this place?

Mercy: Yes; and, as my Lord sees, I am come. And if there is any grace and forgiveness of sins to spare,[12] I beseech that thy poor handmaid may be a partaker thereof.

Then he took her again by the hand, and led her gently in, and said, I pray for all them that believe on me, by what means soever they come unto me. Then said he to those that stood by, Fetch something and give it to Mercy to smell on, thereby to stay her faintings; so they fetched her a bundle of myrrh, and a while after she was revived.

And now were Christiana and her boys, and Mercy, received of the Lord at the head of the way, and spoken kindly unto by him. Then said they yet further unto him, We are sorry for our sins, and beg of our Lord his pardon, and further information what we must do.

I grant pardon, said he, by word and deed; by word in the promise of forgiveness, by deed in the way I obtained it. Take the first from my lips with a kiss, and the other as it shall be revealed. Song 1:2; John 20:20.

13. The "deed" mentioned here is the death of Jesus on the cross.

Now I saw in my dream, that he spake many good words unto them, whereby they were greatly gladdened. He also had them up to the top of the gate, and showed them by what deed they were saved;[13] and told them withal, that that sight they would have again as they went along in the way, to their comfort.

So he left them awhile in a summer parlor below, where they entered into talk by themselves; and thus Christiana began. O how glad am I that we are got in hither.

Mercy: So you well may; but I, of all, have cause to leap for joy.

Christiana: I thought one time, as I stood at the gate, because I had knocked and none did answer, that all our labor had been lost, especially when that ugly cur[14] made such a heavy barking against us.

14. A "cur" is an aggressive dog.

Mercy: But my worst fear was after I saw that you was taken into his favor, and that I was left behind. Now, thought I, it is fulfilled which is written, "Two women shall be grinding at the mill; the one shall be taken, and the other left." Matt. 24:41. I had much ado to forbear crying out, Undone! And afraid I was to knock any more; but when I looked up to what was written over the gate, I took courage. I also thought that I must either knock again, or die; so I knocked, but I cannot tell how, for my spirit now struggled between life and death.

Christiana: Can you not tell how you knocked? I am sure your knocks were so earnest that the very sound of them made me start; I thought I never heard such knocking in all my life; I thought you would come in by a violent hand, or take the kingdom by storm.[15] Matt. 11:12.

Mercy: Alas! to be in my case, who that so was could but have done so? You saw that the door was shut upon me, and there was a most cruel dog thereabout. Who, I say, that was so faint-hearted as I, would not have knocked with all their might? But pray, what said my Lord to my rudeness? Was he not angry with me?

Christiana: When he heard your lumbering noise, he gave a wonderful innocent smile; I believe what you did pleased him well,[16] for he showed no sign to the contrary. But I marvel in my heart why he keeps such a dog: had I known that before, I should not have had heart enough to have ventured myself in this manner. But now we are in, we are in, and I am glad with all my heart.

Mercy: I will ask, if you please, next time he comes down, why he keeps such a filthy cur in his yard; I hope he will not take it amiss.

Do so, said the children, and persuade him to hang him; for we are afraid he will bite us when we go hence.

So at last he came down to them again, and Mercy fell to the ground on her face before him, and worshiped, and said, "Let my Lord accept the sacrifice of praise which I now offer unto him with the calves of my lips."

So he said unto her, Peace be to thee; stand up. But she continued upon her face, and said, "Righteous art thou, O

15. Mercy earnestly desired to enter through the Wicket-gate. She was one, as described by Jesus, who stormed the gates of heaven, and took the kingdom of heaven by storm (Matt. 11:12).

16. The Lord invites us to seek His face and to seek Him earnestly. In Jesus' parable of the persistent widow in Luke 18, he presents a widow who is importunate and continues asking for justice. We are to be like the widow who keeps crying to God night and day.

Lord, when I plead with thee; yet let me talk with thee of thy judgments." Jer. 12:1. Wherefore dost thou keep so cruel a dog in thy yard, at the sight of which such women and children as we are ready to fly from thy gate for fear?

17. The dog does not belong to the Lord at the Wicket-gate. It belongs to the evil one who tries to scare away pilgrims.

He answered and said, That dog has another owner;[17] he also is kept close in another man's ground, only my pilgrims hear his barking; he belongs to the castle which you see there at a distance, but can come up to the walls of this place. He has frighted many an honest pilgrim from worse to better, by the great voice of his roaring. Indeed, he that owneth him doth not keep him out of any good-will to me or mine, but with intent to keep the pilgrims from coming to me, and that they may be afraid to come and knock at this gate for entrance. Sometimes also he has broken out, and has worried some that I loved; but I take all at present patiently. I also give my pilgrims timely help, so that they are not delivered to his power, to do with them what his doggish nature would prompt him to. But what

18. "I trow" means "I think" or "I believe."

my purchased one, I trow,[18] hadst thou known never so much beforehand, thou wouldest not have been afraid of a dog. The beggars that go from door to door, will, rather than lose a supposed alms, run the hazard of the bawling, barking, and biting too of a dog; and shall a dog, a dog in another man's yard, a dog whose barking I turn to the profit of pilgrims, keep any from coming to me? I deliver them from the lions, and my darling from the power of the dog. Psa. 22:21,22.

Mercy: Then said Mercy, I confess my ignorance; I spake what I understood not; I acknowledge that thou doest all things well.

Then Christiana began to talk of their journey, and to inquire after the way. So he fed them and washed their feet, and set them in the way of his steps, according as he had dealt with her husband before.

Book 2
Chapter 2

S o I saw in my dream, that they walked on their way, and had the weather very comfortable to them.

Then Christiana began to sing, saying,

Blessed be the day that I began
   A pilgrim for to be;
And blessed also be the man
   That thereto moved me.
'Tis true, 't was long ere I began
   To seek to live for ever;
But now I run fast as I can:
   'Tis better late than never.
Our tears to joy, our fears to faith,
   Are turned, as we see;
Thus our beginning (as one saith)
   Shows what our end will be.

Now there was, on the other side of the wall that fenced in the way up which Christiana and her companions were to go, a garden, and that garden belonged to him whose was that barking dog,[1] of whom mention was made before. And some of the fruit-trees that grew in that garden shot their branches over the wall; and being mellow, they that found them did gather them up, and eat of them to their hurt. So Christiana's boys, as boys are apt to do, being pleased with the trees, and

1. This garden belonged to the evil one.

2. The "ill-favored ones" in part 1 referred to demons. Here, the term refers to ungodly men who wish to assault the women.

3. Christiana was angry and kicked the men away.

with the fruit that hung thereon, did pluck them, and began to eat. Their mother did also chide them for so doing, but still the boys went on.

Well, said she, my sons, you transgress, for that fruit is none of ours; but she did not know that it belonged to the enemy: I'll warrant you, if she had she would have been ready to die for fear. But that passed, and they went on their way. Now, by that they were gone about two bow-shots from the place that led them into the way, they espied two very ill-favored ones[2] coming down apace to meet them. With that, Christiana and Mercy her friend covered themselves with their veils, and so kept on their journey: the children also went on before; so that at last they met together. Then they that came down to meet them, came just up to the women, as if they would embrace them; but Christiana said, stand back, or go peaceably as you should. Yet these two, as men that are deaf, regarded not Christiana's words, but began to lay hands upon them: at that Christiana waxing very wroth,[3] spurned at them with her feet. Mercy also, as well as she could, did what she could to shift them. Christiana again said to them, Stand back, and be gone, for we have no money to lose, being pilgrims, as you see, and such too as live upon the charity of our friends.

Ill-Favored Ones: Then said one of the two men, We make no assault upon you for money, but are come out to tell you, that if you will but grant one small request which we shall ask, we will make women of you for ever.

Christiana: Now Christiana, imagining what they should mean, made answer again, We will neither hear, nor regard, nor yield to what you shall ask. We are in haste, and cannot stay; our business is a business of life and death. So again she and her companion made a fresh essay to go past them; but they letted them in their way.

Ill-Favored Ones: And they said, We intend no hurt to your lives; it is another thing we would have.

Christiana: Aye, quoth Christiana, you would have us body and soul, for I know it is for that you are come; but we will die rather upon the spot, than to suffer ourselves to be brought into such snares as shall hazard our well-being hereafter. And with that they both shrieked out, and cried, Murder! murder! and so put themselves under those laws that are provided for the protection of women.[4] Deut. 22:25-27. But the men still made their approach upon them, with design to prevail against them. They therefore cried out again.

Now they being, as I said, not far from the gate in at which they came, their voice was heard from whence they were, thither: wherefore some of the house came out, and knowing that it was Christiana's tongue, they made haste to her relief. But by that they were got within sight of them, the women were in a very great scuffle; the children also stood crying by. Then did he that came in for their relief call out to the ruffians, saying, What is that thing you do? Would you make my Lord's people to transgress? He also attempted to take them, but they did make their escape over the wall into the garden of the man to whom the great dog belonged; so the dog became their protector. This Reliever then came up to the women, and asked them how they did. So they answered, We thank thy Prince, pretty well, only we have been somewhat affrighted: we thank thee also for that thou camest in to our help, otherwise we had been overcome.

Reliever: So, after a few more words, this Reliever said as followeth: I marveled much, when you were entertained at the gate above, seeing ye knew that ye were but weak women, that you petitioned not the Lord for a conductor;[5] then might you have avoided these troubles and dangers; for he would have granted you one.

Christiana: Alas! said Christiana, we were so taken with our present blessing, that dangers to come were forgotten by us. Besides, who could have thought, that so near the King's palace there could have lurked such naughty ones? Indeed, it had been well for us had we asked our Lord for one; but since our Lord knew it would be for our profit, I wonder he sent not one along with us.

4. These men desire to sexually assault the women along the way. Both Christiana and Mercy cry out for help. Bunyan mentions the law in Deuteronomy which describes this situation. "But if a man finds a betrothed young woman in the countryside, and the man forces her and lies with her, then only the man who lay with her shall die. But you shall do nothing to the young woman; there is in the young woman no sin deserving of death, for just as when a man rises against his neighbor and kills him, even so is this matter. For he found her in the countryside, and the betrothed young woman cried out, but there was no one to save her." (Deut. 22:25-27)

5. Reliever asks why the women did not request a "conductor." The word "conductor" here refers to a guide and protector along the path. This element of Bunyan's story is different from part 1. The women and the boys are guarded by a conductor along the path of their journey.

Reliever: It is not always necessary to grant things not asked for, lest by so doing they become of little esteem; but when the want of a thing is felt, it then comes under, in the eyes of him that feels it, that estimate that properly is its due, and so consequently will be thereafter used. Had my Lord granted you a conductor, you would not either so have bewailed that oversight of yours, in not asking for one, as now you have occasion to do. So all things work for good, and tend to make you more wary.[6]

6. Christiana wonders why the Lord did not provide a conductor right at the beginning of their journey. The Reliever points out that they would not have been grateful for the conductor unless they saw the grave dangers on the path. This made the women wary of the dangers and more desirous to have such a conductor.

Christiana: Shall we go back again to my Lord, and confess our folly, and ask one?

Reliever: Your confession of your folly I will present him with. To go back again, you need not, for in all places where you shall come, you will find no want at all; for in every one of my Lord's lodgings, which he has prepared for the reception of his pilgrims, there is sufficient to furnish them against all attempts whatsoever. But, as I said, He will be inquired of by them, to do it for them. Ezek. 36:37. And 'tis a poor thing that is not worth asking for. When he had thus said, he went back to his place, and the pilgrims went on their way.

Mercy: Then said Mercy, What a sudden blank is here! I made account that we had been past all danger, and that we should never see sorrow more.

Christiana: Thy innocency, my sister, said Christiana to Mercy, may excuse thee much; but as for me, my fault is so much the greater, for that I saw this danger before I came out of the doors, and yet did not provide for it when provision might have been had. I am much to be blamed.

Mercy: Then said Mercy, How knew you this before you came from home? Pray open to me this riddle.

7. The sexual sin that Christiana could have fallen into could have kept her from the way of eternal life. Such is the exceeding danger of sin.

Christiana: Why, I will tell you. Before I set foot out of doors, one night as I lay in my bed I had a dream about this; for methought I saw two men, as like these as ever any in the world could look, stand at my bed's feet, plotting how they might prevent my salvation.[7] I will tell you their very words. They said, (it was when I was in my troubles,) What shall we do with this woman? for she cries out, waking and sleeping, for forgiveness: if she be sufferet do go on as she begins, we shall lose her as we have lost her husband. This you know might have made me take heed, and have provided when provision might have been had.

Mercy: Well, said Mercy, as by this neglect we have an occasion ministered unto us to behold our own imperfections, so our Lord has taken occasion thereby to make manifest the riches of his grace; for he, as we see, has followed us with unasked kindness, and has delivered us from their hands that were stronger than we, of his mere good pleasure.

Thus now, when they had talked away a little more time, they drew near to a house which stood in the way, which house was built for the relief of pilgrims, as you will find more fully related in the first part of these records of the Pilgrim's Progress. So they drew on towards the house, (the house of the Interpreter;) and when they came to the door, they heard a great talk in the house. Then they gave ear, and heard, as they thought, Christiana mentioned by name; for you must know that there went along, even before her, a talk of her and her children's going on pilgrimage. And this was the most pleasing to them, because they had heard that she was Christian's wife, that woman who was some time ago so unwilling to hear of going on pilgrimage. Thus, therefore, they stood still, and heard the good people within commending her who they little thought stood at the door. At last Christiana knocked, as she had done at the gate before. Now, when she had knocked, there came to the door a young damsel, and opened the door, and looked, and behold, two women were there.

The Damsel: Then said the damsel to them, With whom would you speak in this place?

Christiana: Christiana answered, We understand that this is a privileged place for those that are become pilgrims, and we now at this door are such: wherefore we pray that we may be partakers of that for which we at this time are come; for the

8. They did not wish to go any further that night.

day, as thou seest, is very far spent, and we are loth to-night to go any further.[8]

The Damsel: Pray, what may I call your name, that I may tell it to my Lord within.

Christiana: My name is Christiana; I was the wife of that pilgrim that some years ago did travel this way, and these be his four children. This maiden also is my companion, and is going on pilgrimage too.

Innocent: Then Innocent ran in, (for that was her name,) and said to those within, Can you think who is at the door? There is Christiana and her children, and her companion, all waiting for entertainment here. Then they leaped for joy, and went and told their Master. So he came to the door and looking upon her, he said, Art thou that Christiana whom Christian the good man left behind him when he betook himself to a pilgrim's life.

Christiana: I am that woman that was so hard-hearted as to slight my husband's troubles, and that left him to go on in his journey alone, and these are his four children; but now I also am come, for I am convinced that no way is right but this.

Interpreter: Then is fulfilled that which is written of the man that said to his son, "Go work to-day in my vineyard; and he said to his father, I will not: but afterwards repented and went."[9] Matt. 21:29.

9. The parable of Jesus in Matthew 21 is referenced here. In that story, the Lord tells us that even though one of the servants initially was unwilling to obey his master, he did eventually repent and then went and did the master's will.

Christiana: Then said Christiana, So be it: Amen. God made it a true saying upon me, and grant that I may be found at the last of him in peace, without spot, and blameless.

Interpreter: But why standest thou thus at the door? Come in, thou daughter of Abraham; we were talking of thee but now, for tidings have come to us before how thou art become a pilgrim. Come, children, come in; come, maiden, come in. So he had them all into the house.

So when they were within, they were bidden to sit down and rest them; the which when they had done, those that attended upon the pilgrims in the house came into the room to see them. And one smiled, and another smiled, and they all smiled for joy that Christiana was become a pilgrim: They also looked upon the boys; they stroked them over their faces with the hand, in token of their kind reception of them: they also carried it lovingly to Mercy, and bid them all welcome into their Master's house.

After a while, because supper was not ready, the Interpreter took them into his Significant Rooms, and showed them what Christian, Christiana's husband, had seen some time before. Here, therefore, they saw the man in the cage, the man and his dream, the man that cut his way through his enemies, and the picture of the biggest of them all, together with the rest of those things that were then so profitable to Christian.[10]

This done, and after those things had been somewhat digested by Christiana and her company, the Interpreter takes them apart again, and has them first into a room where was a man that could look no way but downwards, with a muck-rake in his hand. There stood also one over his head with a celestial crown in his hand, and proffered him that crown for his muck-rake;[11] but the man did neither look up nor regard, but raked to himself the straws, the small sticks, and dust of the floor.

Then said Christiana, I persuade myself that I know somewhat the meaning of this; for this is a figure of a man of this world: is it not, good sir?

Interpreter: Thou hast said right,[12] said he; and his muck-rake doth show his carnal mind. And whereas thou seest him rather give heed to rake up straws and sticks, and the dust of the floor, than to do what He says that calls to him from above with the celestial crown in his hand; it is to show, that heaven is but as a fable to some, and that things here are counted the only things substantial. Now, whereas it was also showed thee that the man could look no way but downwards, it is to let thee know that earthly things, when they are with power upon men's minds, quite carry their hearts away from God.[13]

Christiana: Then said Christiana, O deliver me from this muck-rake. Prov. 30:8.

10. The Interpreter is a character who sets forth the basic truths of God's Word to Christian, and now to Christiana and her companions. He explains the difference between true and false conversion.

11. The man with the muck-rake is offered a crown. But he did not wish to have the crown. He was too busy with his muck-rake, raking the straw, sticks, and dust.

12. Christiana understands that this is a picture of the men of the world. The people of this world are offered a crown through salvation in Christ Jesus, but they are content to remain wedded to the things of this world that do not profit. Worldly people count the only things "substantial" or "real" to be the things of this life.

13. The worldly man is in love with the things of this life. Therefore, he can't even look up to see heavenly things.

14. Few wish to have neither poverty nor riches (Prov. 30:7-9). It is rare to see someone turn away from the covetousness of this life to heavenly things instead.

Interpreter: That prayer, said the Interpreter, has lain by till it is almost rusty: "Give me not riches," is scarce the prayer of one in ten thousand.[14] Straws, and sticks, and dust, with most, are the great things now looked after.

With that Christiana and Mercy wept, and said, It is, alas! too true.

When the Interpreter had shown them this, he had them into the very best room in the house; a very brave room it was. So he bid them look round about, and see if they could find any thing profitable there. Then they looked round and round; for there was nothing to be seen but a very great spider on the wall, and that they overlooked.

Mercy: Then said Mercy, Sir, I see nothing; but Christiana held her peace.

Interpreter: But, said the Interpreter, look again. She therefore looked again, and said, Here is not any thing but an ugly spider, who hangs by her hands upon the wall. Then said he, Is there but one spider in all this spacious room? Then the water stood in Christiana's eyes, for she was a woman quick of apprehension; and she said, Yea, Lord, there are more here than one; yea, and spiders whose venom is far more destructive than that which is in her. The Interpreter then looked pleasantly on her, and said, Thou hast said the truth. This made Mercy to blush, and the boys to cover their faces; for they all began now to understand the riddle.[15]

15. Though there was one "actual" spider in the room, the purpose of the spider was to remind the visitors that they all had the "venom of sin" within them. But by God's grace, though that is our natural condition, we can still dwell in God's house and take hold of the best rooms.

Then said the Interpreter again, "The spider taketh hold with her hands," as you see, "and is in kings' palaces." Prov. 30:28. And wherefore is this recorded, but to show you, that, how full of the venom of sin soever you be, yet you may, by the hand of Faith, lay hold of and dwell in the best room that belongs to the King's house above?

Christiana: I thought, said Christiana, of something of this; but I could not imagine it at all. I thought that we were like spiders, and that we looked like ugly creatures, in what fine room soever we were: but that by this spider, that venomous and ill-favored creature, we were to learn how to act faith, that came not into my thoughts; and yet she had taken hold with her hands, and, as I see, dwelleth in the best room in the house. God has made nothing in vain.

Then they seemed all to be glad; but the water stood in their eyes; yet they looked one upon another, and also bowed before the Interpreter.

He had them into another room, where were a hen and chickens, and bid them observe a while. So one of the chickens went to the trough to drink, and every time she drank she lifted up her head and her eyes towards heaven. See, said he, what this little chick doth, and learn of her to acknowledge whence your mercies come, by receiving them with looking up. Yet again, said he, observe and look: so they gave heed, and perceived that the hen did walk in a fourfold method towards her chickens: 1. She had a common call, and that she hath all the day long. 2. She had a special call, and that she had but sometimes. 3. She had a brooding note. Matt. 23:37. And, 4. She had an outcry.

Now, said he, compare this hen to your King and these chickens to his obedient ones; for, answerable to her, he himself hath his methods which he walketh in towards his people. By his common call, he gives nothing; by his special call, he always has something to give; he has also a brooding voice, for them that are under his wing; and he has an outcry, to give the alarm when he seeth the enemy come. I choose, my darlings, to lead you into the room where such things are, because you are women, and they are easy for you.

Christiana: And, sir, said Christiana, pray let us see some more. So he had them into the slaughter-house, where was a butcher killing a sheep; and behold, the sheep was quiet, and took her death patiently. Then said the Interpreter, You must learn of this sheep to suffer and to put up with wrongs without murmurings and complaints. Behold how quietly she takes her death, and, without objecting, she suffereth her skin to be pulled over her ears. Your King doth call you his sheep.[16]

16. The Apostle Peter writes, "For what credit is it if, when you are beaten for your faults, you take it patiently? But when you do good and suffer, if you take it patiently, this is commendable before God. For to this you were called, because Christ also suffered for us, leaving us an example, that you should follow His steps: 'Who committed no sin, Nor was deceit found in His mouth'; who, when He was reviled, did not revile in return; when He suffered, He did not threaten, but committed Himself to Him who judges righteously; who Himself bore our sins in His own body on the tree, that we, having died to sins, might live for righteousness—by whose stripes you were healed. For you were like sheep going astray, but have now returned to the Shepherd and Overseer of your souls." (1 Pet. 2:20-25)

17. This mirrors some of Jesus' sayings in the parables as well as the words of John the Baptist. That which does not bear fruit is rooted out and thrown into the fire. Christiana and Mercy are to apply these things to themselves. True saving faith will bear fruit in good works.

18. The robin is used as a picture of the person who professes saving faith in Jesus (a "professor") and associates with God's people. On the outside, they look good. But inwardly, they are really hypocrites. They "swallow down sin" with few pangs of conscience. True believers, however, will have a life that is consistent both inwardly and outwardly. What we do when alone, away from the seeing eyes of others, is a key test of the reality of our profession. Do we have a religion that merely exists to please men? Or, do we have a true faith in God and love for God?

After this he led them into his garden, where was great variety of flowers; and he, said, Do you see all these? So Christiana said, Yes. Then said he again, Behold, the flowers are diverse in stature, in quality, and color, and smell, and virtue; and some are better than others; also, where the gardener has set them, there they stand, and quarrel not one with another.

Again, he had them into his field, which he had sown with wheat and corn: but when they beheld, the tops of all were cut off, and only the straw remained. He said again, This ground was dunged, and ploughed, and sowed, but what shall we do with the crop? Then said Christiana, Burn some, and make muck of the rest. Then said the Interpreter again, Fruit, you see, is that thing you look for; and for want of that you condemn it to the fire, and to be trodden under foot of men: beware that in this you condemn not yourselves.[17]

Then, as they were coming in from abroad, they espied a little robin with a great spider in his mouth. So the Interpreter said, Look here. So they looked, and Mercy wondered, but Christiana said, What a disparagement is it to such a pretty little bird as the robin-red-breast; he being also a bird above many, that loveth to maintain a kind of sociableness with men! I had thought they had lived upon crumbs of bread, or upon other such harmless matter: I like him worse than I did.

The Interpreter then replied, This robin is an emblem, very apt to set forth some professors by; for to sight they are, as this robin, pretty of note, color, and carriage. They seem also to have a very great love for professors that are sincere; and, above all others, to desire to associate with them, and to be in their company, as if they could live upon the good man's crumbs. They pretend also, that therefore it is that they frequent the house of the godly, and the appointments of the Lord: but when they are by themselves, as the robin, they can catch and gobble up spiders; they can change their diet, drink iniquity, and swallow down sin like water.[18]

So, when they were come again into the house, because supper as yet was not ready, Christiana again desired that the

Interpreter would either show or tell some other things that
are profitable.

Then the Interpreter began, and said, The fatter the sow
is, the more she desires the mire; the fatter the ox is, the more
gamesomely[19] he goes to the slaughter; and the more healthy
the lustful man is, the more prone he is unto evil. There is a
desire in women to go neat and find; and it is a comely thing
to be adorned with that which in God's sight is of great price.
'T is easier watching a night or two, than to sit up a whole year
together: so 't is easier for one to begin to profess well, than to
hold out as he should to the end. Every shipmaster, when in a
storm, will willingly cast that overboard which is of the smallest value in the vessel; but who will throw the best out first?
None but he that feareth not God. One leak will sink a ship,
and one sin will destroy a sinner. He that forgets his friend is
ungrateful unto him; but he that forgets his Saviour is unmerciful to himself. He that lives in sin, and looks for happiness
hereafter, is like him that soweth cockle,[20] and thinks to fill
his barn with wheat or barley. If a man would live well, let
him fetch his last day to him, and make it always his company-keeper.[21] Whispering, and change of thoughts, prove that
sin is in the world. If the world, which God sets light by, is
counted a thing of that worth with men, what is heaven, that
God commendeth? If the life that is attended with so many
troubles, is so loth to be let go by us, what is the life above?
Every body will cry up the goodness of men; but who is there
that is, as he should be, affected with the goodness of God?
We seldom sit down to meat, but we eat, and leave. So there is
in Jesus Christ more merit and righteousness than the whole
world has need of.

When the Interpreter had done, he takes them out into
his garden again, and had them to a tree whose inside was
all rotten and gone, and yet it grew and had leaves. Then said
Mercy, What means this? This tree, said he, whose outside is
fair, and whose inside is rotten, is that to which many may
be compared that are in the garden of God; who with their

19. "Gamesome-ly" means "merrily" or "playfully."

20. "Cockle" is a type of weed. In other words, he who sows weeds will not reap wheat or barley. He will harvest more weeds.

21. If a man would live wisely, he should keep before himself the reality of the coming day of judgment. This encourages us to walk with sobriety before the Lord. Jonathan Edwards resolved in his *Resolutions*: "Resolved, to endeavor to my utmost to act as I can think I should do, if I had already seen the happiness of heaven, and hell torments."

22. This picture of the tree rotten inside is similar to the robin. It is a picture of the hypocrite who has a nice looking exterior, but inwardly they are spiritually bankrupt.

mouths speak high in behalf of God, but indeed will do nothing for him; whose leaves are fair, but their heart good for nothing but to be tinder for the devil's tinder-box.[22]

Now supper was ready, the table spread, and all things set on the board: so they sat down, and did eat, when one had given thanks. And the Interpreter did usually entertain those that lodged with him with music at meals; so the minstrels played. There was also one that did sing, and a very fine voice he had. His song was this:

"The Lord is only my support,
  And he that doth me feed;
How can I then want any thing
  Whereof I stand in need?"[23]

23. This song reminds us of the opening words of Psalm 23: "The LORD is my shepherd; I shall not want. He makes me to lie down in green pastures; He leads me beside the still waters." (Ps. 23:1-2)

When the song and music were ended, the Interpreter asked Christiana what it was that at first did move her thus to betake herself to a pilgrim's life. Christiana answered, First, the loss of my husband came into my mind, at which I was heartily grieved; but all that was but natural affection. Then after that came the troubles and pilgrimage of my husband into my mind, and also how like a churl[24] I had carried it to him as to that. So guilt took hold of my mind, and would have drawn me into the pond, but that opportunely I had a dream of the well-being of my husband, and a letter sent me by the King of that country where my husband dwells, to come to him. The dream and the letter together so wrought upon my mind that they forced me to this way.

24. A churl is a "mean-spirited" person.

Interpreter: But met you with no opposition before you set out of doors?

Christiana: Yes, a neighbor of mine, one Mrs. Timorous: she was akin to him that would have persuaded my husband to go back, for fear of the lions. She also befooled me, for, as she called it, my intended desperate adventure; she also urged what she could to dishearten me from it, the hardships and troubles that my husband met with in the way; but all this I got over pretty well. But a dream that I had of two ill-looking ones, that I thought did plot how to make me miscarry[25] in my

25. "Miscarry" is here used in the sense of "fail to attain."

journey, that hath troubled me much: yea, it still runs in my mind, and makes me afraid of every one that I meet, lest they should meet me to do me a mischief, and to turn me out of my way. Yea, I may tell my Lord, though I would not have every body know of it, that between this and the gate by which we got into the way, we were both so sorely assaulted that we were made to cry out murder; and the two that made this assault upon us, were like the two that I saw in my dream.

Then said the Interpreter, Thy beginning is good; thy latter end shall greatly increase. So he addressed himself to Mercy, and said unto her, And what moved thee to come hither, sweet heart?

Mercy: Then Mercy blushed and trembled, and for a while continued silent.

Interpreter: Then said he, Be not afraid; only believe, and speak thy mind.

Mercy: So she began, and said, Truly, sir, my want of experience is that which makes me covet to be in silence, and that also that fills me with fears of coming short at last. I cannot tell of visions and dreams, as my friend Christiana can; nor know I what it is to mourn for my refusing the counsel of those that were good relations.

Interpreter: What was it, then, dear heart, that hath prevailed with thee to do as thou hast done?

Mercy: Why, when our friend here was packing up to be gone from our town, I and another went accidentally to see her. So we knocked at the door and went in. When we were within, and seeing what she was doing, we asked her what was her meaning. She said she was sent for to go to her husband; and then she up and told us how she had seen him in a dream, dwelling in a curious place, among immortals, wearing a crown, playing upon a harp, eating and drinking at his Prince's table, and singing praises to him for bringing him thither, etc. Now, methought, while she was telling these things unto us, my heart burned within me. And I said in my heart, If this be true, I will leave my father and my mother, and the land of my nativity, and will, if I may, go along with Christiana. So I asked her further of the truth of these things, and if she would let me go with her; for I saw now that there was no dwelling, but with the danger of ruin, any longer in our town. But yet I came away with a heavy heart; not for that I was unwilling to come away, but for that so many of my relations were left behind. And I am come with all the desire of my heart, and will go, if I may, with Christiana unto her husband and his King.

Interpreter: Thy setting out is good, for thou hast given credit to the truth; thou art a Ruth, who did, for the love she bare to Naomi and to the Lord her God, leave father and mother, and the land of her nativity, to come out and go with a people she knew not heretofore.[26] "The Lord recompense thy work, and a full reward be given thee of the Lord God of Israel, under whose wings thou art come to trust." Ruth 2:11,12.

Now supper was ended, and preparation was made for bed; the women were laid singly alone, and the boys by themselves. Now when Mercy was in bed, she could not sleep for joy, for that now her doubts of missing at last were removed further from her than ever they were before. So she lay blessing and praising God, who had such favor for her.

In the morning they arose with the sun, and prepared themselves for their departure; but the Interpreter would have them tarry a while; For, said he, you must orderly go from hence. Then said he to the damsel that first opened unto them, Take them and have them into the garden to the bath, and there wash them and make them clean from the soil which they had gathered by traveling. Then Innocent the damsel took them and led them into the garden, and brought them to the bath; so she told them that there they must wash and be clean, for so her Master would have the women to do that called at his house as they were going on pilgrimage. Then they went in and washed, yea, they and the boys, and all; and they came out of that bath, not only sweet and clean, but also much enlivened and strengthened in their joints. So when

26. Like Ruth, Mercy left her own land and joined with Christiana to walk with God. As Ruth said, "Your people will be my people and your God will be my God."

they came in, they looked fairer a deal than when they went out to the washing.

When they were returned out of the garden from the bath, the Interpreter took them and looked upon them, and said unto them, "Fair as the moon." Then he called for the seal wherewith they used to be sealed that were washed in his bath. So the seal was brought, and he set his mark upon them, that they might be known in the places whither they were yet to go. Now the seal was the contents and sum of the passover which the children of Israel did eat, Exod. 13:8-10, when they came out of the land of Egypt; and the mark was set between their eyes.[27] This seal greatly added to their beauty, for it was an ornament to their faces. It also added to their gravity, and made their countenance more like those of angels.

Then said the Interpreter again to the damsel that waited upon these women, Go into the vestry, and fetch out garments for these people. So she went and fetched out white raiment,[28] and laid it down before him; so he commanded them to put it on: it was fine linen, white and clean. When the women were thus adorned, they seemed to be a terror one to the other; for that they could not see that glory each one had in herself, which they could see in each other. Now therefore they began to esteem each other better than themselves.[29] For, You are fairer than I am, said one; and, You are more comely than I am, said another. The children also stood amazed, to see into what fashion they were brought.

27. The seal set upon their foreheads is a reminder of God's saving work. The children of Israel were to have a memorial of God's deliverance in the Passover (Ex. 13:8-10).

28. Christiana and Mercy are clothed in the beautiful white robes of Christ's saving work. "Then one of the elders answered, saying to me, 'Who are these arrayed in white robes, and where did they come from?' And I said to him, 'Sir, you know.' So he said to me, 'These are the ones who come out of the great tribulation, and washed their robes and made them white in the blood of the Lamb.'" (Rev. 7:13-15)

29. "Let nothing be done through selfish ambition or conceit, but in lowliness of mind let each esteem others better than himself." (Phil. 2:3)

Book 2
Chapter 3

The Interpreter then called for a man-servant of his, one Great-Heart, and bid him take a sword, and helmet, and shield; and, Take these my daughters, said he, conduct them to the house called Beautiful, at which place they will rest next. So he took his weapons, and went before them; and the Interpreter said, God speed. Those also that belonged to the family, sent them away with many a good wish. So they went on their way, and sang,

> This place hath been our second stage:
>> Here we have heard, and seen
> Those good things, that from age to age
>> To others hid have been.
> The dunghill-raker, spider, hen,
>> The chicken, too, to me
> Have taught a lesson: let me then
>> Conformed to it be.[1]
> The butcher, garden, and the field,
>> The robin and his bait,
> Also the rotten tree, doth yield
>> Me argument of weight,
> To move me for to watch and pray,
>> To strive to be sincere;
> To take my cross up day by day,

1. The pilgrims desire to take the lessons learned in the House of the Interpreter and live in light of such important lessons.

And serve the Lord with fear.

Now I saw in my dream, that they went on, and Great-Heart before them. So they went, and came to the place where Christian's burden fell off his back and tumbled into a sepulchre. Here then they made a pause; and here also they blessed God. Now, said Christiana, it comes to my mind what was said to us at the gate, to wit, that we should have pardon by word and deed: by word, that is, by the promise; by deed, to wit, in the way it was obtained. What the promise is, of that I know something; but what is it to have pardon by deed, or in the way that it was obtained, Mr. Great-Heart, I suppose you know; wherefore, if you please, let us hear your discourse thereof.[2]

Mr. Great-Heart: Pardon by the deed done, is pardon obtained by some one for another that hath need thereof; not by the person pardoned, but in the way, saith another, in which I have obtained it. So then, to speak to the question more at large, the pardon that you, and Mercy, and these boys have attained, was obtained by another;[3] to wit, by him that let you in at the gate. And he hath obtained it in this double way; he hath performed righteousness to cover you, and spilt his blood to wash you in.[4]

Christiana: But if he parts with his righteousness to us, what will he have for himself?

Mr. Great-Heart: He has more righteousness than you have need of, or than he needeth himself.

Christiana: Pray make that appear.

Mr. Great-Heart: With all my heart: but first I must premise, that he of whom we are now about to speak, is one that has not his fellow: He has two natures in one person, plain to be distinguished, impossible to be divided.[5] Unto each of these natures a righteousness belongeth, and each righteousness is essential to that nature; so that one may as easily cause that nature to be extinct, as to separate its justice or righteousness from it. Of these righteousnesses therefore, we are not made partakers, so as that they, or any of them, should be put upon us, that we might be made just, and live thereby. Besides

2. The band of pilgrims arrive at the foot of the cross and the open tomb where Christian had his burden of sin removed from his back. At this point, Christiana requests that Great-Heart discourse on the meaning of this place. What follows is an extended conversation on the righteousness of Jesus Christ.
3. Great-Heart explains that the pardon (forgiveness or remission) of sin that the pilgrims have received is not by their own works. That pardon comes through the saving work of Jesus Christ.
4. The salvation attained is attained in a "double way." What this refers to is the perfect righteousness of Jesus Christ who obeyed the law on our behalf (Rom. 5:19). Jesus also took our debt of sin when he went to the cross, dying for us, and securing for us redemption through His blood (Eph. 1:7).
5. Great-Heart explains what is unique about Jesus Christ who is both God and man. The orthodox doctrine of Christ's nature is this: He has both a divine and human nature in one person. These natures can be distinguished, but they cannot be divided or separated.

these, there is a righteousness which this person has, as these two natures are joined in one. And this is not the righteousness of the Godhead, as distinguished from the manhood; nor the righteousness of the manhood, as distinguished from the Godhead; but a righteousness which standeth in the union of both natures, and may properly be called the righteousness that is essential to his being prepared of God to the capacity of the mediatory office, which he was to be entrusted with. If he parts with his first righteousness, he parts with his Godhead; if he parts with his second righteousness, he parts with the purity of his manhood; if he parts with his third, he parts with that perfection that capacitates him to the office of mediation. He has therefore another righteousness, which standeth in performance, or obedience to a revealed will; and that is what he puts upon sinners, and that by which their sins are covered. Wherefore he saith, "As by one man's disobedience many were made sinners, so by the obedience of one shall many be made righteous." Rom. 5:19.

Christiana: But are the other righteousnesses of no use to us?

Mr. Great-Heart: Yes; for though they are essential to his natures and office, and cannot be communicated unto another, yet it is by virtue of them that the righteousness that justifies is for that purpose efficacious. The righteousness of his Godhead gives virtue to his obedience; the righteousness of his manhood giveth capability to his obedience to justify; and the righteousness that standeth in the union of these two natures to his office, giveth authority to that righteousness to do the work for which it was ordained.

So then here is a righteousness that Christ, as God, has no need of; for he is God without it: Here is a righteousness that Christ, as man, has no need of to make him so; for he is perfect man without it. Again, here is a righteousness that Christ, as God-man, has no need of; for he is perfectly so without it. Here then is a righteousness that Christ, as God, and as God-man, has no need of, with reference to himself, and therefore he can spare it; a justifying righteousness, that he for himself wanteth not, and therefore giveth it away: Hence it is called the gift of righteousness. This righteousness, since Christ Jesus the Lord has made himself under the law, must be given away; for the law doth not only bind him that is under it, to do justly, but to use charity. Rom. 5:17. Wherefore he must, or ought by the law, if he hath two coats, to give one to him that hath none. Now, our Lord indeed hath two coats, one for himself, and one to spare; wherefore he freely bestows one upon those that have none.[6] And thus, Christiana and Mercy, and the rest of you that are here, doth your pardon come by deed, or by the work of another man. Your Lord Christ is he that worked, and hath given away what he wrought for, to the next poor beggar he meets.

But again, in order to pardon by deed, there must something be paid to God as a price, as well as something prepared to cover us withal. Sin has delivered us up to the just curse of a righteous law: now from this curse[7] we must be justified by way of redemption, a price being paid for the harms we have done; and this is by the blood of your Lord, who came and stood in your place and stead, and died your death for your transgressions: Thus has he ransomed you from your transgressions by blood, and covered your polluted and deformed souls with righteousness, Rom. 8:34; for the sake of which, God passeth by you and will not hurt you when he comes to judge the world.[8] Gal. 3:13.

Christiana: This is brave![9] Now I see that there was something to be learned by our being pardoned by word and deed. Good Mercy, let us labor to keep this in mind: and, my children, do you remember it also. But, sir, was not this it that made my good Christian's burden fall from off his shoulder, and that made him give three leaps for joy?

Mr. Great-Heart: Yes, it was the belief of this that cut those strings that could not be cut by other means;[10] and it was to give him a proof of the virtue of this, that he was suffered to carry his burden to the cross.

6. Great-Heart explains that Jesus Christ has sufficient righteousness to spare for poor needy sinners. He shows charity by giving a "coat" of righteousness to us who have no righteousness of our own.

7. Paul describes this curse in Galatians 3: "For as many as are of the works of the law are under the curse; for it is written, 'Cursed is everyone who does not continue in all things which are written in the book of the law, to do them.'" (Gal. 3:10)

8. In the verses that follow in Galatians 3, Paul tells us the glorious good news of our salvation in Christ: "Christ has redeemed us from the curse of the law, having become a curse for us (for it is written, 'Cursed is everyone who hangs on a tree')" (Gal. 3:13)

9. "This is splendid or glorious."

10. There was no other way for Christian to lose that burden of sin except by believing in Jesus Christ and resting in His righteousness. "For by grace you have been saved through faith, and that not of yourselves; it is the gift of God,..." (Eph. 2:8)

11. No matter how great the debt of sin, Jesus Christ's redemption is sufficient to cover it and set a man free from that guilt. "Blithe" means to be "happy" or "joyous."

12. Great-Heart notes that receiving Christ's saving work by faith not only frees us from the guilt and bondage of sin, but it also produces in our hearts a great love for the Lord Jesus who saved us. Paul remarks in 1 Corinthians that love for the Lord Jesus Christ is a key sign of a true follower. "If anyone does not love the Lord Jesus Christ, let him be accursed. O Lord, come!" (1 Cor. 16:22)

13. That is, "there were some that stood by" when Jesus was crucified but did not receive Him by faith.

Christiana: I thought so; for though my heart was lightsome and joyous before, yet it is ten times more lightsome and joyous now. And I am persuaded by what I have felt, though I have felt but little as yet, that if the most burdened man in the world was here, and did see and believe as I now do, it would make his heart the more merry and blithe.[11]

Mr. Great-Heart: There is not only comfort and the ease of a burden brought to us by the sight and consideration of these, but an endeared affection begot in us by it: for who can, if he doth but once think that pardon comes not only by promise but thus, but be affected with the way and means of his redemption, and so with the man that hath wrought it for him?[12]

Christiana: True; methinks it makes my heart bleed to think that he should bleed for me. Oh, thou loving One: Oh, thou blessed One. Thou deservest to have me; thou hast bought me. Thou deservest to have me all: thou hast paid for me ten thousand times more than I am worth. No marvel that this made the tears stand in my husband's eyes, and that it made him trudge so nimbly on. I am persuaded he wished me with him: but, vile wretch that I was, I let him come all alone. Oh, Mercy, that thy father and mother were here; yea, and Mrs. Timorous also: nay, I wish now with all my heart that here was Madam Wanton too. Surely, surely, their hearts would be affected; nor could the fear of the one, nor the powerful lusts of the other, prevail with them to go home again, and to refuse to become good pilgrims.

Mr. Great-Heart: You speak now in the warmth of your affections; will it, think you, be always thus with you? Besides, this is not communicated to every one, nor to every one that did see your Jesus bleed. There were that stood by,[13] and that saw the blood run from the heart to the ground, and yet were so far off this, that instead of lamenting, they laughed at him, and, instead of becoming his disciples, did harden their hearts against him. So that all that you have, my daughters, you have by peculiar impression made by a divine contemplating upon what I have spoken to you. Remember, that 'twas told you, that the hen, by her common call, gives no meat to her chickens. This you have therefore by a special grace.[14]

Now I saw in my dream, that they went on until they were come to the place that Simple, and Sloth, and Presumption, lay and slept in when Christian went by on pilgrimage: and behold, they were hanged up in irons a little way off on the other side.[15]

Mercy: Then said Mercy to him that was their guide and conductor, what are these three men; and for what are they hanged there?

Mr. Great-Heart: These three men were men of very bad qualities; they had no mind to be pilgrims themselves, and whomsoever they could, they hindered. They were sloth and folly themselves, and whomsoever they could persuade they made so too, and withal taught them to presume that they should do well at last. They were asleep when Christian went by; and now you go by, they are hanged.

Mercy: But could they persuade any to be of their opinion?

Mr. Great-Heart: Yes, they turned several out of the way. There was Slow-pace that they persuaded to do as they. They also prevailed with one Short-wind, with one No-heart, with one Linger-after-Lust, and with one Sleepy-head, and with a young woman, her name was Dull, to turn out of the way and become as they. Besides, they brought up an ill report of your Lord, persuading others that he was a hard taskmaster. They also brought up an evil report of the good Land, saying, it was not half so good as some pretended it was. They also began to vilify his servants, and to count the best of them meddlesome, troublesome busybodies. Further, they would call the bread of God husks; the comforts of his children, fancies; the travel and labor of pilgrims, things to no purpose.[16]

Christiana: Nay, said Christiana, if they were such, they shall never be bewailed by me: they have but what they deserve; and I think it is well that they stand so near the highway, that others may see and take warning. But had it not been

14. It is a grace of God that the pilgrims can see (spiritually speaking) with eyes of faith whereas many hear the gospel but do not believe. Jesus said in Matthew 11: "All things have been delivered to Me by My Father, and no one knows the Son except the Father. Nor does anyone know the Father except the Son, and the one to whom the Son wills to reveal Him." (Matt. 11:27)

15. Some of the characters in Part II are new to this part while others are re-presented with new lessons. Simple, Sloth, and Presumption re-appear in the same location as part I. However, now they are hanged for their crimes.

16. These three men despised God and His ways and convinced others to do the same.

well if their crimes had been engraven in some plate of iron or brass, and left here where they did their mischiefs, for a caution to other bad men?

Mr. Great-Heart: So it is, as you may well perceive, if you will go a little to the wall.

Mercy: No, no; let them hang, and their names rot, and their crimes live forever against them. I think it a high favor that they were hanged before we came hither: who knows else what they might have done to such poor women as we are? Then she turned it into a song, saying,

"Now then you three hang there, and be a sign
To all that shall against the truth combine.
And let him that comes after, fear this end,
If unto pilgrims he is not a friend.
And thou, my soul, of all such men beware,
That unto holiness opposers are."[17]

Thus they went on till they came to the foot of the hill Difficulty, where again the good Mr. Great-Heart took an occasion to tell them what happened there when Christian himself went by. So he had them first to the spring. Lo, saith he, this is the spring that Christian drank of before he went up this hill: and then it was clear and good; but now it is dirty with the feet of some that are not desirous that pilgrims here should quench their thirst.[18] Ezek. 34:18,19. Thereat Mercy said, And why so envious, trow?[19] But, said their guide, it will do, if taken up and put into a vessel that is sweet and good; for then the dirt will sink to the bottom, and the water come out by itself more clear.[20] Thus therefore Christiana and her companions were compelled to do. They took it up, and put it into an earthen pot, and so let it stand till the dirt was gone to the bottom, and then they drank thereof.

Next he showed them the two by-ways that were at the foot of the hill, where Formality and Hypocrisy lost themselves. And, said he, these are dangerous paths. Two were here cast away when Christian came by; and although, as you see these ways are since stopped up with chains, posts, and a ditch,

17. When we see God's fearsome judgment upon those who oppose the gospel, it should produce in us a sobriety and a fear of the Lord. Such providential warnings help us to understand the dire consequences of sin.

18. A spring sat at the bottom of the Hill Difficulty. It provided refreshment for weary pilgrims before they ascended that arduous hill. But others who did not want to see the success of pilgrims had intentionally dirtied the waters.

19. "And why where they so envious, do you think?"

20. "To the pure all things are pure, but to those who are defiled and unbelieving nothing is pure; but even their mind and conscience are defiled." (Tit. 1:15)

yet there are those that will choose to adventure here rather than take the pains to go up this hill.

Christiana: "The way of transgressors is hard." Prov. 13:15. It is a wonder that they can get into these ways without danger of breaking their necks.

Mr. Great-Heart: They will venture: yea, if at any time any of the King's servants do happen to see them, and do call upon them, and tell them that they are in the wrong way, and do bid them beware of the danger, then they railingly return them answer, and say, "As for the word that thou hast spoken unto us in the name of the King, we will not hearken unto thee; but we will certainly do whatsoever thing goeth out of our own mouths." Jer. 44:16,17. Nay, if you look a little further, you shall see that these ways are made cautionary enough, not only by these posts, and ditch, and chain, but also by being hedged up: yet they will choose to go there.[21]

Christiana: They are idle; they love not to take pains; uphill way is unpleasant to them. So it is fulfilled unto them as it is written, "The way of the slothful man is full of thorns." Prov. 15:19. Yea, they will rather choose to walk upon a snare than to go up this hill, and the rest of this way to the city.

Then they set forward, and began to go up the hill, and up the hill they went. But before they got to the top, Christiana began to pant, and said, I dare say this is a breathing hill; no marvel if they that love their ease more than their souls choose to themselves a smoother way.

Then said Mercy, I must sit down: also the least of the children began to cry. Come, come, said Great-Heart, sit not down here; for a little above is the Prince's arbor.[22] Then he took the little boy by the hand, and led him up thereto.

When they were come to the arbor, they were very willing to sit down, for they were all in a pelting heat. Then said Mercy, "How sweet is rest to them that labor." Matt. 11:28; and how good is the Prince of pilgrims to provide such resting-places for them! Of this arbor I have heard much; but I

21. There are warnings signs posted all over the dangerous path. Even with all the warnings, sinners still go on and are destroyed. Likewise, reader, in God's mercy you will receive warnings against the paths of sin from your parents, your pastors, and by other means in your life. Will you take heed to the way of your feet or will you follow the path of transgressors and be destroyed? God's warning signs are merciful. Let us heed them.

22. The Hill of Difficulty is an appropriate name. It is a hard hill to climb. In the same way, the Christian life is filled with times of difficulty. We may be tempted to give up in our combat against our sinful flesh, against the world, and against the evil one. But we must persevere by faith. "For you have need of endurance, so that after you have done the will of God, you may receive the promise:..." (Heb. 10:36)

23. "I was disheartened and exhausted."

24. The way of eternal life is the narrow and hard path. The way to hell is an easy and broad path which many travel (Matt. 7:13-14).

never saw it before. But here let us beware of sleeping; for, as I have heard, it cost poor Christian dear.

Then said Mr. Great-Heart to the little ones, Come, my pretty boys, how do you do? What think you now of going on pilgrimage? Sir, said the least, I was almost beat out of heart;[23] but I thank you for lending me a hand at my need. And I remember now what my mother hath told me, namely, that the way to heaven is as a ladder, and the way to hell is as down a hill. But I had rather go up the ladder to life, than down the hill to death.[24]

Then said Mercy, But the proverb is, "To go down the hill is easy." But James said, (for that was his name,) The day is coming when, in my opinion, when going down the hill will be the hardest of all. 'Tis a good boy, said his master; thou hast given her a right answer. Then Mercy smiled, but the little boy did blush.

Christiana: Come, said Christiana, will you eat a bit to sweeten your mouths, while you sit here to rest your legs? for I have here a piece of pomegranate which Mr. Interpreter put into my hand just when I came out of his door; he gave me also a piece of an honeycomb, and a little bottle of spirits. I thought he gave you something, said Mercy, because he called you aside. Yes, so he did, said the other; but, said Christiana, it shall be still as I said it should, when at first we came from home; thou shalt be a sharer in all the good that I have, because thou so willingly didst become my companion. Then she gave to them, and they did eat, both Mercy and the boys. And said Christiana to Mr. Great-Heart, Sir, will you do as we? But he answered, You are going on pilgrimage, and presently I shall return; much good may what you have do you: at home I eat the same every day.

Book 2
Chapter 4

Now when they had eaten and drank, and had chatted a little longer, their guide said to them, The day wears away; if you think good, let us prepare to be going. So they got up to go, and the little boys went before; But Christiana forgot to take her bottle of spirits with her,[1] so she sent her little boy back to fetch it. Then said Mercy, I think this is a losing place: here Christian lost his roll, and here Christiana left her bottle behind her. Sir, what is the cause of this?[2] So their guide made answer, and said, The cause is sleep, or forgetfulness: some sleep when they should keep awake, and some forget when they should remember; and this is the very cause why often, at the resting-places, some pilgrims in some things come off losers. Pilgrims should watch, and remember what they have already received, under their greatest enjoyments; but for want of doing so, oftentimes their rejoicing ends in tears, and their sunshine in a cloud: witness the story of Christian at this place.

When they were come to the place where Mistrust and Timorous met Christian, to persuade him to go back for fear of the lions, they perceived as it were a stage, and before it, towards the road, a broad plate with a copy of verses written thereon, and underneath the reason of raising up that stage in that place rendered. The verses were,

1. Like Christian who forgot his roll here, Christiana forgets her bottle of spirits.

2. The cause of pilgrims losings things in the arbor is a lack of watchfulness. Pilgrims come to rest, but they fall asleep and forget. Pilgrims must always remain watchful and sober. The Lord may graciously give us seasons of rest and peace on this pilgrim journey, but this does not mean we can leave off being watchful and awake.

"Let him that sees this stage, take heed
  Unto his heart and tongue;
Lest, if he do not, here he speed
  As some have long agone."

The words underneath the verses were, "This stage was built to punish those upon, who, through timorousness or mistrust, shall be afraid to go further on pilgrimage. Also, on this stage both Mistrust and Timorous were burned through the tongue with a hot iron, for endeavoring to hinder Christian on his journey."

Then said Mercy, This is much like to the saying of the Beloved: "What shall be given unto thee, or what shall be done unto thee, thou false tongue? Sharp arrows of the mighty, with coals of juniper? Psa. 120:3,4.

So they went on till they came within sight of the lions. Now Mr. Great-Heart was a strong man, so he was not afraid of a lion: But yet when they were come up to the place where the lions were, the boys, that went before, were now glad to cringe behind, for they were afraid of the lions; so they stepped back, and went behind. At this their guide smiled, and said, How now, my boys; do you love to go before when no danger doth approach, and love to come behind so soon as the lions appear?

Now, as they went on, Mr. Great-Heart drew his sword, with intent to make a way for the pilgrims in spite of the lions. Then there appeared one that, it seems, had taken upon him to back the lions;[3] and he said to the pilgrims' guide, What is the cause of your coming hither? Now the name of that man was Grim, or Bloody-man because of his slaying of pilgrims; and he was of the race of the giants.

Mr. Great-Heart: Then said the pilgrims' guide, These women and children are going on pilgrimage, and this is the way they must go; and go it they shall, in spite of thee and the lions.

3. Another character appears in the narrative with the lions named "Grim" or "Bloody Man." He "backs" or supports the lions in opposing the pilgrims. Some commentators interpret this character as a reference to those persecuting authorities who went after non-conformists like John Bunyan who did not submit to the Church of England. Whatever reference Bunyan had in mind, he represents for all time those who persecute and kill God's people.

Grim: This is not their way, neither shall they go therein. I am come forth to withstand them, and to that end will back the lions.

Now, to say the truth, by reason of the fierceness of the lions, and of the grim carriage of him that did back them, this way had of late lain much unoccupied, and was almost grown over with grass.[4]

Christiana: Then said Christiana, Though the highways have been unoccupied heretofore, and though the travellers have been made in times past to walk through by-paths, it must not be so now I am risen, now I am risen a mother in Israel.[5] Judges 5:6,7.

Grim: Then he swore by the lions that it should; and therefore bid them turn aside, for they should not have passage there.

But Great-Heart their guide made first his approach unto Grim, and laid so heavily on him with his sword that he forced him to retreat.

Grim: Then said he that attempted to back the lions, Will you slay me upon mine own ground?

Mr. Great-Heart: It is the King's highway that we are in, and in this way it is that thou hast placed the lions; but these women, and these children, though weak, shall hold on their way in spite of thy lions. And with that he gave him again a downright blow, and brought him upon his knees. With this blow also he broke his helmet, and with the next he cut off an arm. Then did the giant roar so hideously that his voice frightened the women, and yet they were glad to see him lie sprawling upon the ground.[6] Now the lions were chained, and so of themselves could do nothing.[7] Wherefore, when old Grim, that intended to back them, was dead, Mr. Great-Heart said to the pilgrims, Come now, and follow me, and no hurt shall happen to you from the lions. They therefore went on, but the women trembled as they passed by them; the boys also looked as if they would die; but they all got by without further hurt.

4. Bunyan tells us that so fierce was the opposition of the lions and the bloody man that few had courage to go on this path. Thus the path had become overgrown with grass because no one would tread upon it.

5. Christiana adopts the language of Deborah, one of the judges in Israel (Judg. 5:6-7). Like Deborah, she is a woman of faith and courage. She will oppose the enemies of God.

6. The bloody man (Grim), the persecutor of God's people is slain by Great-Heart. He can do nothing to hurt the pilgrims any longer. Though we may at times be frightened by the world's attempt to persecute us, we can overcome by faith and not fear those who can only kill the body but cannot kill the soul (Matt. 10:28).

7. All Christians face "lions in the streets" that may seem powerful and dangerous. But when we are afraid, we put our trust in the Lord (Ps. 56:3). We must also remember, like these lions, anyone or anything that opposes us is under the control of God. Like these lions that are chained, nothing can happen to us apart from the sovereign will of God.

Now, when they were within sight of the Porter's lodge, they soon came up unto it; but they made the more haste after this to go thither, because it is dangerous traveling there in the night. So when they were come to the gate, the guide knocked, and the Porter cried, Who is there? But as soon as the guide had said, It is I, he knew his voice, and came down, for the guide had oft before that come thither as a conductor of pilgrims. When he was come down, he opened the gate; and seeing the guide standing just before it, (for he saw not the women, for they were behind him,) he said unto him, How now, Mr. Great-Heart, what is your business here so late at night? I have brought, said he, some pilgrims hither, where, by my Lord's commandment, they must lodge: I had been here some time ago, had I not been opposed by the giant that did use to back the lions. But I, after a long and tedious combat with him, have cut him off, and have brought the pilgrims hither in safety.

The Porter: Will you not go in, and stay till morning?

Mr. Great-Heart: No, I will return to my Lord to-night.

Christiana: O, sir, I know not how to be willing you should leave us in our pilgrimage: you have been so faithful and loving to us, you have fought so stoutly for us, you have been so hearty in counselling of us, that I shall never forget your favor towards us.

Mercy: Then said Mercy, O that we might have thy company to our journey's end! How can such poor women as we hold out in a way so full of troubles as this way is, without a friend and defender?

James: Then said James, the youngest of the boys, Pray, sir, be persuaded to go with us, and help us, because we are so weak, and the way so dangerous as it is.[8]

Mr. Great-Heart: I am at my Lord's commandment; if he shall allot me to be your guide quite through, I will willingly wait upon you. But here you failed at first; for when he bid me come thus far with you, then you should have begged me of him to have gone quite through with you, and he would have

8. Christiana, Mercy, and James all plead with Mr. Great-Heart to remain with them for the duration of their journey. How important it is that we have spiritual guides in the Christian life to help conduct us in our journey to heaven! Pastors, elders, parents, and other wise Christians all can serve in this role. Elders are particularly given the title and role of shepherds (Acts 20:28).

granted your request.[9] However, at present I must withdraw; and so, good Christiana, Mercy, and my brave children, adieu.

Then the Porter, Mr. Watchful, asked Christiana of her country, and of her kindred. And she said, I came from the city of Destruction. I am a widow woman, and my husband is dead, his name was Christian, the pilgrim. How! said the Porter, was he your husband? Yes, said she, and these are his children and this, pointing to Mercy, is one of my town's-women. Then the Porter rang his bell, as at such times he is wont, and there come to the door one of the damsels, whose name was Humble-Mind; and to her the Porter said, Go tell it within, that Christiana, the wife of Christian, and her children, are come hither on pilgrimage. She went in, therefore, and told it. But oh, what noise for gladness was there within when the damsel did but drop that out of her mouth![10]

So they came with haste to the Porter, for Christana stood still at the door. Then some of the most grave[11] said unto her, Come in, Christiana, come in, thou wife of that good man; come in, thou blessed woman, come in, with all that are with thee. So she went in, and they followed her that were her children and companions. Now when they were gone in, they were had into a large room, where they were bidden to sit down: so they sat down, and the chief of the house were called to see and welcome the guests. Then they came in, and understanding who they were, did salute each other with a kiss, and said, Welcome, ye vessels of the grace of God; welcome to us, your friends.

Now, because it was somewhat late, and because the pilgrims were weary with their journey, and also made faint with the sight of the fight, and of the terrible lions, they desired, as soon as might be, to prepare to go to rest. Nay, said those of the family, refresh yourselves first with a morsel of meat; for they had prepared for them a lamb, with the accustomed sauce belonging thereto, Exod. 12:21; John 1:29; for the Porter had heard before of their coming, and had told it to them with-

9. Until this point, the pilgrims had not requested Great-Heart to remain with them through the entire journey. If they had done so, they would surely have had their request granted. As James says, "You do not have because you do not ask." (Jas. 4:2)

10. There was great joy when those in the house heard that Christiana had repented, put her faith in Christ, and was now on the same journey her husband undertook. This reflects the joy in heaven when a sinner repents (Luke 15:7).

11. "Grave" here refers to one who is solemn or sober.

in. So when they had supped, and ended their prayer with a psalm, they desired they might go to rest.

But let us, said Christiana, if we may be so bold as to choose, be in that chamber that was my husband's when he was here; so they had them up thither, and they all lay in a room. When they were at rest, Christiana and Mercy entered into discourse about things that were convenient.

Christiana: Little did I think once, when my husband went on pilgrimage, that I should ever have followed him.

Mercy: And you as little thought of lying in his bed, and in his chamber to rest, as you do now.

Christiana: And much less did I ever think of seeing his face with comfort, and of worshiping the Lord the King with him; and yet now I believe I shall.

Mercy: Hark, don't you hear a noise?

Christiana: Yes, it is, as I believe, a noise of music, for joy that we are here.[12]

Mercy: Wonderful! Music in the house, music in the heart, and music also in heaven, for joy that we are here! Thus they talked a while, and then betook themselves to sleep.

So in the morning when they were awake, Christiana said to Mercy, What was the matter that you did laugh in your sleep to-night? I suppose you were in a dream.

Mercy: So I was, and a sweet dream it was; but are you sure I laughed?

Christiana: Yes, you laughed heartily; but prithee, Mercy, tell me thy dream.

Mercy: I was a dreaming that I sat all alone in a solitary place, and was bemoaning of the hardness of my heart. Now I had not sat there long but methought many were gathered about me to see me, and to hear what it was that I said. So they hearkened, and I went on bemoaning the hardness of my heart. At this, some of them laughed at me, some called me fool, and some began to thrust me about. With that, methought I looked up and saw one coming with wings towards me. So he came directly to me, and said, Mercy, what aileth thee? Now

12. Music is an essential part of the Christian life. Just as there is music in heaven, so also the House Beautiful contains music of joy. "Let the word of Christ dwell in you richly in all wisdom, teaching and admonishing one another in psalms and hymns and spiritual songs, singing with grace in your hearts to the Lord." (Col. 3:16)

when he had heard me make my complaint, he said, Peace be to thee; he also wiped my eyes with his handkerchief, and clad me in silver and gold. Ezek. 16:8-11. He put a chain about my neck, and ear-rings in mine ears, and a beautiful crown upon my head. Then he took me by the hand, and said, Mercy, come after me. So he went up, and I followed till we came at a golden gate. Then he knocked; and when they within had opened, the man went in, and I followed him up to a throne, upon which one sat; and he said to me, Welcome, daughter. The place looked bright and twinkling, like the stars, or rather like the sun, and I thought that I saw your husband there; so I awoke from my dream. But did I laugh?

Christiana: Laugh! aye, and well you might to see yourself so well. For you must give me leave to tell you that it was a good dream; and that, as you have begun to find the first part true, so you shall find the second at last. "God speaks once, yea, twice, yet man perceiveth it not; in a dream, in a vision of the night, when deep sleep falleth upon men, in slumberings upon the bed." Job 33:14,15. We need not, when abed, to lie awake to talk with God; he can visit us while we sleep, and cause us then to hear his voice. Our heart oftentimes wakes when we sleep, and God can speak to that, either by words, by proverbs, by signs and similitudes, as well as if one was awake.

Mercy: Well, I am glad of my dream; for I hope ere long to see it fulfilled, to the making me laugh again.

Christiana: I think it is now high time to rise, and to know what we must do.

Mercy: Pray, if they invite us to stay a while, let us willingly accept of the proffer. I am the more willing to stay a while here, to grow better acquainted with these maids: methinks Prudence, Piety, and Charity, have very comely and sober countenances.

Christiana: We shall see what they will do.

So when they were up and ready, they came down, and they asked one another of their rest, and if it was comfortable or not.

13. The pilgrims lodge in the House Beautiful for about a month. This house serves as a place of spiritual instruction and refreshment. The time spent in this home was not wasted. It prepared the pilgrims for their arduous and dangerous journey ahead.

14. This discourse between Prudence and Christiana's boys is unique to Part II. This conversation illustrates the importance that Bunyan and other Puritans placed upon Christian instruction. "Catechesis" is a particular method of teaching by using questions and answers to impart teaching. The Puritans wrote and used numerous catechisms such as the *Westminster Shorter Catechism*.

15. James wisely answers that God saved Him. All three persons of the Holy Trinity saved him by the Father's grace, by the Son's saving work, and by the Holy Spirit's illumination, renovation, and preservation.

Mercy: Very good, said Mercy: it was one of the best night's lodgings that ever I had in my life.

Then said Prudence and Piety, If you will be persuaded to stay here a while, you shall have what the house will afford.

Charity: Aye, and that with a very good will, said Charity. So they consented, and stayed there about a month or above,[13] and became very profitable one to another. And because Prudence would see how Christiana had brought up her children, she asked leave of her to catechise them.[14] So she gave her free consent. Then she began with her youngest, whose name was James.

Prudence: And she said, Come, James, canst thou tell me who made thee?

James: God the Father, God the Son, and God the Holy Ghost.

Prudence: Good boy. And canst thou tell who saved thee?[15]

James: God the Father, God the Son, and God the Holy Ghost.

Prudence: Good boy still. But how doth God the Father save thee?

James: By his grace.

Prudence: How doth God the Son save thee?

James: By his righteousness, death and blood, and life.

Prudence: And how doth God the Holy Ghost save thee?

James: By his illumination, by his renovation, and by his preservation.

Then said Prudence to Christiana, You are to be commended for thus bringing up your children. I suppose I need not ask the rest these questions, since the youngest of them can answer them so well. I will therefore now apply myself to the next youngest.

Prudence: Then she said, Come, Joseph, (for his name was Joseph,) will you let me catechise you?

Joseph: With all my heart.

Prudence: What is man?

Joseph: A reasonable creature, so made by God, as my brother said.

Prudence: What is supposed by this word, saved?

Joseph: That man, by sin, has brought himself into a state of captivity and misery.

Prudence: What is supposed by his being saved by the Trinity?

Joseph: That sin is so great and mighty a tyrant that none can pull us out of its clutches but God; and that God is so good and loving to man, as to pull him indeed out of this miserable state.

Prudence: What is God's design in saving poor men?

Joseph: The glorifying of his name, of his grace, and justice, etc., and the everlasting happiness of his creature.[16]

Prudence: Who are they that will be saved?

Joseph: They that accept of his salvation.

Prudence: Good boy, Joseph; thy mother hath taught thee well, and thou hast hearkened unto what she has said unto thee.

Then said Prudence to Samuel, who was the eldest but one,

Prudence: Come, Samuel, are you willing that I should catechise you?

Samuel: Yes, forsooth, if you please.[17]

Prudence: What is heaven?

Samuel: A place and state most blessed, because God dwelleth there.

Prudence: What is hell?

Samuel: A place and state most woeful, because it is the dwelling-place of sin, the devil, and death.

Prudence: Why wouldst thou go to heaven?

Samuel: That I may see God, and serve him without weariness; that I may see Christ, and love him everlastingly; that I may have that fullness of the Holy Spirit in me which I can by no means here enjoy.

Prudence: A very good boy, and one that has learned well.

16. God purposes to save His chosen ones for the glory of His own name and for the everlasting benefit of His creatures. Our purpose is to "glorify God and enjoy Him forever" (Westminster Shorter Catechism Q. 1).

17. "Yes indeed, if you wish."

18. Prudence is asking whether there was any thing or any being that existed before God.

19. Prudence is asking whether there was any thing or any being that existed before God.

20. Matthew humbly admits that there are portions of the Bible he does not yet understand.

21. This is a wise practice. We must be humble to remember that God knows more than we do and that He is wiser than us. But we should also pray for illumination to better understand God's Word. This is the prayer of the Psalmist in Psalm 119. "Open my eyes, that I may see wondrous things from Your law." (Ps. 119:18)

22. Prudence alludes to God's two forms of revelation. General revelation is God's revelation of Himself revealed in the created order. Special revelation is God's revelation of Himself in the Word of God (the Bible).

23. All conversation for the Christian should lead to edification. "Let no corrupt word proceed out of your mouth, but what is good for necessary edification, that it may impart grace to the hearers." (Eph. 4:29)

Then she addressed herself to the eldest, whose name was Matthew; and she said to him, Come, Matthew, shall I also catechise you?

Matthew: With a very good will.

Prudence: I ask then, if there was ever any thing that had a being antecedent to or before God?[18]

Matthew: No, for God is eternal;[19] nor is there any thing, excepting himself, that had a being until the beginning of the first day. For in six days the Lord made heaven and earth, the sea, and all that in them is.

Prudence: What do you think of the Bible?

Matthew: It is the holy word of God.

Prudence: Is there nothing written therein but what you understand?

Matthew: Yes, a great deal.[20]

Prudence: What do you do when you meet with places therein that you do not understand?

Matthew: I think God is wiser than I. I pray also that he will please to let me know all therein that he knows will be for my good.[21]

Prudence: How believe you as touching the resurrection of the dead?

Matthew: I believe they shall rise the same that was buried; the same in nature, though not in corruption. And I believe this upon a double account: first, because God has promised it; secondly, because he is able to perform it.

Then said Prudence to the boys, You must still hearken to your mother; for she can teach you more. You must also diligently give ear to what good talk you shall hear from others: for your sakes do they speak good things. Observe also, and that with carefulness, what the heavens and the earth do teach you; but especially be much in the meditation of that book[22] which was the cause of your father's becoming a pilgrim. I, for my part, my children, will teach you what I can while you are here, and shall be glad if you will ask me questions that tend to godly edifying.[23]

Now by that these pilgrim's had been at this place a week, Mercy had a visitor that pretended some good-will unto her, and his name was Mr. Brisk;[24] a man of some breeding, and that pretended to religion, but a man that stuck very close to the world. So he came once or twice, or more, to Mercy, and offered love unto her. Now Mercy was of a fair countenance, and therefore the more alluring.

Her mind also was to be always busying of herself in doing; for when she had nothing to do for herself, she would be making hose and garments for others, and would bestow them upon those that had need. And Mr. Brisk not knowing where or how she disposed of what she made, seemed to be greatly taken, for that he found her never idle. I will warrant her a good housewife, quoth he to himself.[25]

Mercy then revealed the business to the maidens that were of the house, and inquired of them concerning him, for they did know him better than she. So they told her that he was a very busy young man, and one who pretended to religion, but was, as they feared, a stranger to the power of that which is good.[26]

Nay then, said Mercy, I will look no more on him; for I purpose never to have a clog to my soul.[27]

Prudence then replied, that there needed no matter of great discouragement to be given to him; her continuing so as she had begun to do for the poor, would quickly cool his courage.[28]

24. A visitor arrives at the House Beautiful by the name of Mr. Brisk. This man seeks to court Mercy for marriage. However, the narrator describes him as a man who "pretended to religion." Mr. Brisk represents the man who uses religion as a means of personal gain but is really in love with the world.

25. "He said to himself."

26. Paul warns about such men. "For men will be lovers of themselves, lovers of money, boasters, proud, blasphemers, disobedient to parents, unthankful, unholy, unloving, unforgiving, slanderers, without self-control, brutal, despisers of good, traitors, headstrong, haughty, lovers of pleasure rather than lovers of God, having a form of godliness but denying its power. And from such people turn away! For of this sort are those who creep into households and make captives of gullible women loaded down with sins, led away by various lusts,..." (2 Tim. 3:2-6)

27. Christians are those concerned to guard their hearts. Therefore, any people, places, or opportunities that lead us away from the Lord must be turned away from. "Keep your heart with all diligence, for out of it spring the issues of life." (Prov. 4:23) In the case of Mr. Brisk, Mercy recognized that he was an ungodly man who would be bad company for her to keep.

28. Mercy's practice of true religion would eventually repel Mr. Brisk since he was a pretender at religion.

29. Once Mr. Brisk saw that Mercy was doing good for those in need, not for money, but laying up treasures in heaven, he was no longer interested in her.

30. Mr. Brisk will begin to speak poorly of Mercy to others since he is repulsed by her godliness and he himself is not a godly man.

31. Prudence is saying that in those days, mercy was often mentioned in talk, but it was not frequently practiced.

32. Mercy finds herself still unmarried. As she is a merciful woman practicing mercy, few wish to marry her and join her in that way of life. Worldly people will not be attracted to true religion. The true practice of works of mercy requires the crucifixion of the sinful flesh. This is something the worldly person will not do.

33. Prudence asks whether the husband of Bountiful professed to be a believer. The answer was yes, but his faith was not real.

So the next time he comes he finds her at her old work, making things for the poor. Then said he, What, always at it? Yes, said she, either for myself or for others. And what canst thou earn a day? said he. I do these things, said she, that I may be rich in good works, laying up in store for myself a good foundation against the time to come, that I may lay hold on eternal life. 1 Tim. 6:17-19. Why, prithee, what doest thou with them? said he. Clothe the naked, said she. With that his countenance fell. So he forbore to come at her again.[29] And when he was asked the reason why, he said, that Mercy was a pretty lass, but troubled with ill conditions.

When he had left her, Prudence said, Did I not tell thee that Mr. Brisk would soon forsake thee? yea, he will rise up an ill report of thee;[30] for, notwithstanding his pretence to religion, and his seeming love to Mercy, yet Mercy and he are of tempers so different that I believe they will never come together.

Mercy: I might have had husbands before now, though I spoke not of it to any; but they were such as did not like my conditions, though never did any of them find fault with my person. So they and I could not agree.

Prudence: Mercy in our days is but little set by any further than as to its name:[31] the practice which is set forth by thy conditions, there are but few that can abide.[32]

Mercy: Well, said Mercy, if nobody will have me, I will die unmarried, or my conditions shall be to me as a husband: for I cannot change my nature; and to have one who lies cross to me in this, that I purpose never to admit of as long as I live. I had a sister named Bountiful, that was married to one of these churls, but he and she could never agree; but because my sister was resolved to do as she had begun, that is, to show kindness to the poor, therefore her husband first cried her down at the cross, and then turned her out of his doors.

Prudence: And yet he was a professor, I warrant you?[33]

Mercy: Yes, such a one as he was, and of such as he the world is now full: but I am for none of them all.

Now Matthew, the eldest son of Christiana, fell sick,[34] and his sickness was sore upon him, for he was much pained in his bowels, so that he was with it at times pulled, as it were, both ends together. There dwelt also not far from thence one Mr. Skill, an ancient and well-approved physician. So Christiana desired it, and entered the room, and had a little observed the boy, he concluded that he was sick of the gripes.[35] Then he said to his mother, What diet has Matthew of late fed upon? Diet! said Christiana, nothing but what is wholesome. The physician answered, This boy has been tampering with something that lies in his stomach undigested, and that will not away without means. And I tell you he must be purged, or else he will die.

Samuel: Then said Samuel, Mother, what was that which my brother did gather up and eat as soon as we were come from the gate that is at the head of this way? You know that there was an orchard on the left hand, on the other side of the wall, and some of the trees hung over the wall, and my brother did pluck and eat.

Christiana: True, my child, said Christiana, he did take thereof, and did eat: naughty boy as he was, I chid him,[36] and yet he would eat thereof.

Mr. Skill: I knew he had eaten something that was not wholesome food; and that food, to wit, that fruit, is even the most hurtful of all. It is the fruit of Beelzebub's orchard. I do marvel that none did warn you of it; many have died thereof.

Christiana: Then Christiana began to cry; and she said, Oh, naughty boy! and Oh, careless mother! what shall I do for my son?

Mr. Skill: Come, do not be too much dejected; the boy may do well again, but he must purge and vomit.

Christiana: Pray, sir, try the utmost of your skill with him, whatever it costs.

Mr. Skill: Nay, I hope I shall be reasonable. So he made him a purge,[37] but it was too weak; it was said it was made of the blood of a goat, the ashes of a heifer, and some of the juice of hyssop. Heb. 9:13, 19; 10: 1-4. When Mr. Skill had seen

34. The reader may recall the earlier scene in Part II where Matthew ate of the fruit in the garden of the evil one. At that time, nothing went wrong. But the suspense the reader was held in at that point is now resolved. Matthew falls sick because he ate this fruit. It was an unwise decision, but there is help and healing in the House Beautiful.

35. The "gripes" refers to indigestion.

36. "Chid" means to "chide" or "rebuke."

37. This "purge" is a medicine that allegorically refers to the blood animal sacrifices of the Old Testament. It is described as being "too weak" to help Matthew overcome the deadly fruit of the devil. Bunyan is reminding the reader that the sacrifices of the Old Testament could never take away sin. "But in those sacrifices there is a reminder of sins every year. For it is not possible that the blood of bulls and goats could take away sins." (Heb. 10:3-4)

38. The new medicine was made this time from the body and blood of Christ (this term is in Latin in the text). The pills containing the body and blood of Christ, are to be taken with fasting, along with tears of repentance and salt.

39. "He did not want to take it."

40. It is through the body and blood of Christ that we are healed. "By His stripes we are healed" (Isa. 53:5).

41. The word "physic" is an old English term for "medicine."

that that purge was too weak, he made one to the purpose. It was made ex carne et sanguine Christi,[38] John 6:54-57; Heb. 9:14; (you know physicians give strange medicines to their patients:) and it was made into pills, with a promise or two, and a proportionable quantity of salt. Mark 9:49. Now, he was to take them three at a time, fasting, in half a quarter of a pint of the tears of repentance. Zech. 12:10.

When this potion was prepared, and brought to the boy, he was loth to take it,[39] though torn with the gripes as if he should be pulled in pieces. Come, come, said the physician, you must take it. It goes against my stomach, said the boy. I must have you take it, said his mother. I shall vomit it up again, said the boy. Pray, sir, said Christiana to Mr. Skill, how does it taste? It has no ill taste, said the doctor; and with that she touched one of the pills with the tip of her tongue. Oh, Matthew, said she, this potion is sweeter than honey. If thou lovest thy mother, if thou lovest thy brothers, if thou lovest Mercy, if thou lovest thy life, take it. So, with much ado, after a short prayer for the blessing of God upon it, he took it, and it wrought kindly with him. It caused him to purge; it caused him to sleep, and to rest quietly; it put him into a fine heat and breathing sweat, and did quite rid him of his gripes. So in a little time he got up, and walked about with a staff, and would go from room to room, and talk with Prudence, Piety, and Charity, of his distemper, and how he was healed.[40]

So when the boy was healed, Christiana asked Mr. Skill, saying, Sir, what will content you for your pains and care to and of my child? And he said, You must pay the master of the College of Physicians, Heb. 13:11-15, according to rules made in that case and provided.

Christiana: But, sir, said she, what is this pill good for else?

Mr. Skill: It is a universal pill; it is good against all the diseases that pilgrims are incident to; and when it is well prepared, it will keep good, time out of mind.

Christiana: Pray, sir, make me up twelve boxes of them; for if I can get these, I will never take other physic.[41]

Mr. Skill: These pills are good to prevent diseases, as well as to cure when one is sick. Yea, I dare say it, and stand to it, that if a man will but use this physic as he should, it will make him live for ever. John 6:51. But, good Christiana, thou must give these pills no other way but as I have prescribed; for if you do, they will do no good.[42] So he gave unto Christiana physic for herself, and her boys, and for Mercy; and bid Matthew take heed how he ate any more green plums; and kissed them, and went his way.

It was told you before, that Prudence bid the boys, that if at any time they would, they should ask her some questions that might be profitable and she would say something to them.

Matthew: Then Matthew, who had been sick, asked her, why for the most part physic should be bitter to our palates.[43]

Prudence: To show how unwelcome the word of God and the effects thereof are to a carnal heart.

Matthew: Why does physic, if it does good, purge, and cause to vomit?[44]

Prudence: To show that the word, when it works effectually, cleanseth the heart and mind. For look, what the one doth to the body, the other doth to the soul.

Matthew: What should we learn by seeing the flame of our fire go upwards, and by seeing the beams and sweet influences of the sun strike downwards?

Prudence: By the going up of the fire, we are taught to ascend to heaven by fervent and hot desires. And by the sun sending his heat, beams, and sweet influences downwards, we are taught the Saviour of the world, though high, reaches down with his grace and love to us below.

Matthew: Whence have the clouds their water?

Prudence: Out of the sea.

Matthew: What may we learn from that?

Prudence: That ministers should fetch their doctrine from God.

Matthew: Why do they empty themselves upon the earth?

42. The "pills" containing the body and blood of Christ must be received with both faith and repentance. Apart from faith and repentance, the pills will do no good.

43. The Word of God acts as a medicine upon our souls. But it does rebuke sin in us, and it can "go down hard."

44. The Word has a cleansing effect. When it is received it purges sin, and cleanses the heart and mind.

Prudence: To show that ministers should give out what they know of God to the world.

Matthew: Why is the rainbow caused by the sun?

Prudence: To show that the covenant of God's grace is confirmed to us in Christ.

Matthew: Why do the springs come from the sea to us through the earth?

Prudence: To show that the grace of God comes to us through the body of Christ.

Matthew: Why do some of the springs rise out of the tops of high hills?

Prudence: To show that the Spirit of grace shall spring up in some that are great and mighty, as well as in many that are poor and low.

Matthew: Why doth the fire fasten upon the candle-wick?

Prudence: To show that unless grace doth kindle upon the heart, there will be no true light of life in us.

Matthew: Why are the wick, and tallow and all, spent to maintain the light of the candle?

Prudence: To show that body and soul, and all, should be at the service of, and spend themselves to maintain in good condition that grace of God that is in us.

Matthew: Why doth the pelican pierce her own breast with her bill?

Prudence: To nourish her young ones with her blood, and thereby to show that Christ the blessed so loved his young, (his people,) as to save them from death by his blood.

Matthew: What may one learn by hearing the cock to crow?

Prudence: Learn to remember Peter's sin, and Peter's repentance. The cock's crowing shows also, that day is coming on: let, then, the crowing of the cock put thee in mind of that last and terrible day of judgment.[45]

Now about this time their month was out; wherefore they signified to those of the house, that it was convenient for them to up and be going. Then said Joseph to his mother, It is proper that you forget not to send to the house of Mr. Interpreter, to

45. This line of questioning by Matthew draws out illustrations of God's creation. Matthew asks, "What is the meaning of these common scenes of creation?" In each case, Prudence provides a theological interpretation of these natural occurrences. This teaches us to look for illustrations of God's Word in creation.

pray him to grant that Mr. Great-Heart should be sent unto us, that he may be our conductor for the rest of the way. Good boy, said she, I had almost forgot. So she drew up a petition, and prayed Mr. Watchful the porter to send it by some fit man to her good friend Mr. Interpreter; who, when it was come, and he had seen the contents of the petition, said to the messenger, Go, tell them that I will send him.

When the family where Christiana was, saw that they had a purpose to go forward, they called the whole house together, to give thanks to their King for sending of them such profitable guests as these. Which done, they said unto Christiana, And shall we not show thee something, as our custom is to do to pilgrims, on which thou mayest meditate when thou art upon the way? So they took Christiana, her children, and Mercy, into the closet, and showed them one of the apples that Eve ate of, and that she also did give to her husband, and that for the eating of which they were both turned out of paradise, and asked her what she thought that was. Then Christiana said, It is food or poison, I know not which. So they opened the matter to her, and she held up her hands and wondered. Gen. 3:6; Rom. 7:24.

Then they had her to a place, and showed her Jacob's ladder. Gen. 28:12. Now at that time there were some angels ascending upon it. So Christiana looked and looked to see the angels go up: so did the rest of the company. Then they were going into another place, to show them something else; but James said to his mother, Pray, bid them stay here a little longer, for this is a curious sight. So they turned again, and stood feeding their eyes with this so pleasant a prospect.

After this, they had them into a place where did hang up a golden anchor. So they bid Christiana take it down; for said they, You shall have it with you, for it is of absolute necessity that you should, that you may lay hold of that within the veil, Heb. 6:19, and stand stedfast in case you should meet with turbulent weather, Joel 3:16: so they were glad thereof.[46]

46. This golden anchor is the hope of the gospel that will hold the pilgrims steadfastly through the storms they will meet. "This hope we have as an anchor of the soul, both sure and steadfast, and which enters the Presence behind the veil, where the forerunner has entered for us, even Jesus, having become High Priest forever according to the order of Melchizedek." (Heb. 6:19-20)

Then they took them, and had them to the mount upon which Abraham our father offered up Isaac his son, and showed them the altar, the wood, the fire, and the knife, for they remain to be seen to this very day. Gen. 22:9. When they had seen it, they held up their hands, and blessed themselves, and said, Oh, what a man for love to his Master, and for denial to himself, was Abraham!

After they had showed them all these things, Prudence took them into a dining room, where stood a pair of excellent virginals;[47] so she played upon them, and turned what she had showed them into this excellent song, saying,

> "Eve's apple we have showed you;
>   Of that be you aware:
> You have seen Jacob's ladder too,
>   Upon which angels are.
> An anchor you received have;
>   But let not these suffice,
> Until with Abra'm you have gave
>   Your best, a sacrifice."

Now, about this time, one knocked at the door; so the Porter opened, and behold, Mr. Great-Heart was there. But when he was come in, what joy was there! for it came now afresh again into their minds, how but a while ago he had slain old Grim Bloody-man the giant, and had delivered them from the lions.

Then said Mr. Great-Heart to Christiana and to Mercy, My Lord has sent each of you a bottle of wine, and also some parched corn, together with a couple of pomegranates; he has also sent the boys some figs and raisins; to refresh you in your way.[48]

Then they addressed themselves to their journey, and Prudence and Piety went along with them. When they came to the gate, Christiana asked the Porter if any of late went by. He said, No; only one, some time since, who also told me, that of late there had been a great robbery committed on the King's highway as you go. But, said he, the thieves are taken, and

47. "Virginals" refers to the harpsichord.

48. At this point, there is a contrast that is worth noting between Part I and Part II. In Part II, the band of pilgrims are abundantly provided for along the way. They are conducted by Great-Heart for the duration of their journey. Here, they are provided with food and drink for their journey. While it is true that Christian is sustained and provided for throughout Part I, in Part II Bunyan seems to emphasize this divine provision and protection even more with such examples.

will shortly be tried for their lives. Then Christiana and Mercy were afraid; but Matthew said, Mother, fear nothing, as long as Mr. Great-Heart is to go with us, and to be our conductor.

Then said Christiana to the Porter, Sir, I am much obliged to you for all the kindnesses that you have showed to me since I came hither; and also for that you have been so loving and kind to my children. I know not how to gratify your kindness; wherefore, pray, as a token of my respect to you, accept of this small mite. So she put a gold angel in his hand; and he made her a low obeisance,[49] and said, "Let thy garments be always white; and let thy head want no ointment." Eccles. 9:8. Let Mercy live and not die, and let not her works be few. Deut. 33:6. And to the boys he said, Do you fly youthful lusts, and follow after godliness with them that are grave and wise,[50] 2 Tim. 2:22: so shall you put gladness into your mother's heart, and obtain praise of all that are sober-minded. So they thanked the Porter, and departed.

49. The Porter bows low before Christiana.

50. This is always a timely exhortation for young men. When Paul instructed Titus to exhort the young men and old men, the older men were instructed to teach the young men sobriety above all (Tit. 2:6). When a young man flees youthful lusts and pursues godliness, it brings joy to a mother's soul and to all that are sober-minded.

Book 2

Chapter 5

Now I saw in my dream, that they went forward until they were come to the brow of the Hill; where Piety, bethinking herself, cried out, Alas, I have forgot what I intended to bestow upon Christiana and her companions: I will go back and fetch it. So she ran and fetched it. While she was gone, Christiana thought she heard, in a grove a little way off on the right hand, a most curious melodious note, with words much like these:

"Through all my life thy favor is
So frankly showed to me,
That in thy House for evermore
My dwelling-place shall be."

And listening still, she thought she heard another answer it, saying,

"For why? The Lord our God is good;
His mercy is forever sure;
His truth at all times firmly stood,
And shall from age to age endure."[1]

So Christiana asked Prudence who it was that made those curious notes. Song 2:11,12. They are, answered she, our country birds: they sing these notes but seldom, except it be at the spring, when the flowers appear, and the sun shines warm, and then you may hear them all day long. I often, said she, go out

1. This song sung by the country birds is a mixture of Psalm 23 and Psalm 100.

to hear them; we also oft-times keep them tame in our house. They are very fine company for us when we are melancholy:[2] also they make the woods, and groves, and solitary places, places desirable to be in.

By this time Piety was come again. So she said to Christiana, Look here, I have brought thee a scheme[3] of all those things that thou hast seen at our house, upon which thou mayest look when thou findest thyself forgetful, and call those things again to remembrance for thy edification and comfort.

Now they began to go down the hill into the Valley of Humiliation. It was a steep hill, and the way was slippery; but they were very careful; so they got down pretty well. When they were down in the valley, Piety said to Christiana, This is the place where Christian your husband met with the foul fiend Apollyon, and where they had that dreadful fight that they had: I know you cannot but have heard thereof. But be of good courage; as long as you have here Mr. Great-Heart to be your guide and conductor, we hope you will fare the better. So when these two had committed the pilgrims unto the conduct of their guide, he went forward, and they went after.

Mr. Great-Heart: Then said Mr. Great-Heart, We need not be so afraid of this valley, for here is nothing to hurt us, unless we procure it to ourselves. It is true, Christian did here meet with Apollyon, with whom he had also a sore combat: but that fray was the fruit of those slips that he got in his going down the hill: for they that get slips there, must look for combats here.[4] And hence it is, that this valley has got so hard a name. For the common people, when they hear that some frightful thing has befallen such an one in such a place, are of opinion that that place is haunted with some foul fiend, or evil spirit; when, alas! it is for the fruit of their doing, that such things befal them there. This Valley of Humiliation is of itself as fruitful a place as any the crow flies over; and I am persuaded, if we could hit upon it, we might find somewhere hereabouts something that might give us an account why Christian was so hardly beset in this place.

2. Singing the truth of God either through Psalms and Hymns is a healing balm for a sad soul. There is great value in singing to the Lord. It brings glory to God, it repels the devils, and it comforts our souls.

3. Piety provides an outline of all that was learned in the House Beautiful so that the group of pilgrims can remember the vital lessons they received.

4. The reader of Part I may be surprised with how the Valley of Humiliation is now presented in Part II. In Part I, Christian had a strenuous battle with Apollyon. But Mr. Great-Heart now explains in Part II, the reason for this battle was because Christian "fell hard" into the valley. That is, Christian's spiritual condition was such that he "fell" into the Valley of Humiliation and he therefore encountered difficulty. But if one enters the valley already "humbled," there is no such danger. For the Christian, to be in a humble position is a safe position. "He that is down already need fear no fall." But as Proverbs 16:18 says, a haughty (proud) spirit goes before a fall.

Then said James to his mother, Lo, yonder stands a pillar, and it looks as if something was written thereon; let us go and see what it is. So they went and found there written, "Let Christian's slips, before he came hither, and the battles that he met with in this place, be a warning to those that come after." Lo, said their guide, did not I tell you that there was something hereabouts that would give intimation of the reason why Christian was so hard beset in this place?[5] Then turning to Christiana, he said, No disparagement to Christian more than to any others whose hap and lot it was. For it is easier going up than down this hill, and that can be said but of few hills in all these parts of the world. But we will leave the good man; he is at rest: he also had a brave victory over his enemy. Let Him grant, that dwelleth above, that we fare no worse, when we come be tried, than he.

But we will come again to this Valley of Humiliation. It is the best and most fruitful piece of ground in all those parts. It is fat ground, and as you see, consisteth much in meadows; and if a man was to come here in the summer-time, as we do now, if he knew not any thing before thereof, and if he also delighted himself in the sight of his eyes, he might see that which would be delightful to him. Behold how green this valley is; also how beautified with lillies. Song 2:1. I have known many laboring men that have got good estates in this Valley of Humiliation; for God resisteth the proud, but giveth grace to the humble. James 4:6; 1 Pet. 5:5. Indeed it is a very fruitful soil, and doth bring forth by handfuls.[6] Some also have wished that the next way to their Father's house were here, that they might be troubled no more with either hills or mountains to go over; but the way is the way, and there is an end.

Now, as they were going along, and talking, they espied a boy feeding his father's sheep. The boy was in very mean clothes, but of a very fresh and well-favored countenance; and as he sat by himself, he sung. Hark, said Mr. Great-Heart,[7] to what the shepherd's boy saith. So they hearkened and he said,

"He that is down, needs fear no fall;

5. The pillar stands as a monument to warn other pilgrims of "slipping" into the valley and thus being beset by the same struggles that Christian encountered.

6. Humility is an essential grace granted by the Holy Spirit. Where there is humility, it is attended by many other fruits of grace.

7. Mr. Great Heart directs the pilgrims to listen to the song of the shepherd boy.

He that is low, no pride:
He that is humble, ever shall
  Have God to be his guide.[8]
I am content with what I have,
  Little be it or much;
And, Lord, contentment still I crave,
  Because thou savest such.
Fulness to such, a burden is,
  That go on pilgrimage;
Here little, and hereafter bliss,
  Is best from Age to Age."

Then said the guide, Do you hear him? I will dare to say, that this boy lives a merrier life, and wears more of that herb called heart's-ease in his bosom, than he that is clad in silk and velvet.[9] But we will proceed in our discourse.

In this valley our Lord formerly had his country-house:[10] he loved much to be here. He loved also to walk these meadows, for he found the air was pleasant. Besides, here a man shall be free from the noise, and from the hurryings of this life: all states are full of noise and confusion; only the Valley of Humiliation is that empty and solitary place. Here a man shall not be so let and hindered in his contemplation as in other places he is apt to be. This is a valley that nobody walks in but those that love a pilgrim's life. And though Christian had the hard hap to meet here with Apollyon, and to enter with him in a brisk encounter, yet I must tell you, that in former times men have met with angels here, Hos. 12:4,5, have found pearls here, Matt. 13:46, and have in this place found the words of life. Prov. 8:36.

Did I say our Lord had here in former days his country-house, and that he loved here to walk? I will add-in this place, and to the people that love and trace these grounds, he has left a yearly revenue, to be faithfully paid them at certain seasons, for their maintenance by the way, and for their further encouragement to go on in their pilgrimage.

8. Those who are humble can expect the Lord to teach them and guide them (Ps. 25:8-9). The Lord resists, but He gives grace to the humble (1 Pet. 5:5).

9. The humble and content man lives a happier life than a rich man who has an abundance of riches.

10. That is, our Lord Jesus once went through the Valley of Humiliation himself. This state of humiliation the Apostle Paul describes in Philippians 2. "Let this mind be in you which was also in Christ Jesus, who, being in the form of God, did not consider it robbery to be equal with God, but made Himself of no reputation, taking the form of a bondservant, and coming in the likeness of men. And being found in appearance as a man, He humbled Himself and became obedient to the point of death, even the death of the cross." (Phil. 2:5-8)

Samuel: Now, as they went on, Samuel said to Mr. Great-Heart, Sir, I perceive that in this valley my father and Apollyon had their battle; but whereabout was the fight? for I perceive this valley is large.

Mr. Great-Heart: Your father had the battle with Apollyon at a place yonder before us, in a narrow passage, just beyond Forgetful Green. And indeed that place is the most dangerous place in all these parts. For if at any time pilgrims meet with any brunt,[11] it is when they forget what favours they have received, and how unworthy they are of them. This is the place also where others have been hard put to it. But more of the place when we are come to it; for I persuade myself that to this day there remains either some sign of the battle, or some monument to testify that such a battle there was fought.

Mercy: Then said Mercy, I think I am as well in this valley as I have been anywhere else in all our journey: the place, methinks, suits with my spirit. I love to be in such places, where there is no rattling with coaches, nor rumbling with wheels. Methinks, here one may, without much molestation, be thinking what he is, whence he came, what he has done, and to what the King has called him. Here one may think, and break at heart, and melt in one's spirit, until one's eyes become as the fish-pools in Heshbon.[12] Song 7:4. They that go rightly through this valley of Baca, make it a well; the rain that God sends down from heaven upon them that are here, also filleth the pools. This valley is that from whence also the King will give to his their vineyards; and they that go through it shall sing, as Christian did, for all he met with Apollyon. Psa. 84:5-7; Hos. 2:15.

Mr. Great-Heart: 'Tis true, said their guide; I have gone through this valley many a time, and never was better than when here. I have also been a conduct to several pilgrims, and they have confessed the same. "To this man will I look," saith the King, "even to him that is poor, and of a contrite spirit, and trembleth at my word." Isa. 66:2.

11. A "brunt" refers to a "blow" or "attack."

12. In the Valley of Humiliation, it is appropriate that pilgrims traveling through this land have tears of humility and repentance.

Now they were come to the place where the aforementioned battle was fought: Then said the guide to Christiana, her children, and Mercy, This is the place; on this ground Christian stood, and up there came Apollyon against him; and look. And, look, did I not tell you? here is some of your husband's blood upon these stones to this day: Behold, also, how here and there are yet to be seen upon the place, some of the shivers of Apollyon's broken darts. See, also, how they did beat the ground with their feet as they fought, to make good their places against each other; how also with their by-blows they did split the very stones in pieces. Verily, Christian did here play the man, and showed himself as stout as Hercules could, had he been there, even he himself. When Apollyon was beat, he made his retreat to the next valley, that is called, the Valley of the Shadow of Death, unto which we shall come anon. Lo, yonder also stands a monument, on which is engraven this battle, and Christian's victory, to his fame, throughout all ages: So because it stood just on the way-side before them, they stepped to it, and read the writing, which word for word was this:

"Hard by here was a battle fought,
    Most strange, and yet most true;
Christian and Apollyon fought
    Each other to subdue.
The man so bravely play'd the man,
    He made the fiend to fly;
Of which a monument I stand,
    The same to testify."

When they had passed by this place, they came upon the borders of the Shadow of Death. This Valley was longer than the other; a place also most strangely haunted with evil things, as many are able to testify: but these women and children went the better through it, because they had daylight, and because Mr. Great-Heart was their conductor.[13]

When they were entering upon this valley, they thought they heard a groaning, as of dying men; a very great groaning.

13. The journey through the Valley of the Shadow of Death is also easier in Part II. There are two reasons for this. They travel in daylight, and they have Mr. Great-Heart as their guide and defender.

14. "Wan" is a synonym for "pale."

15. "Haply" does not mean "happily" but means "lest by chance."

16. We are to ponder the path of our feet lest we fall into temptation and then transgression. The Book of Proverbs gives this very exhortation. "Ponder the path of your feet, And let all your ways be established.
Do not turn to the right or the left;
Remove your foot from evil." (Prov. 4:26-27)

17. Though the sight of the devil approaching was a fearful one, the pilgrims resist the devil and he immediately flees.

They thought also that they did hear words of lamentation, spoken as of some in extreme torment. These things made the boys to quake; the women also looked pale and wan;[14] but their guide bid them be of good comfort.

So they went on a little further, and they thought that they felt the ground begin to shake under them, as if some hollow place was there: they heard also a kind of hissing, as of serpents, but nothing as yet appeared. Then said the boys, Are we not yet at the end of this doleful place? But the guide also bid them be of good courage, and look well to their feet; lest haply[15], said he, you be taken in some snare.[16]

Now James began to be sick; but I think the cause thereof was fear: so his mother gave him some of that glass of spirits that had been given her at the Interpreter's house, and three of the pills that Mr. Skill had prepared, and the boy began to revive. Thus they went on till they came to about the middle of the valley; and then Christiana said, Methinks I see something yonder upon the road before us, a thing of a shape such as I have not seen. Then said Joseph, Mother, what is it? An ugly thing, child; an ugly thing, said she. But, mother, what is it like? said he. 'Tis like I cannot tell what, said she; and now it is but a little way off. Then said she, It is nigh.

Well, said Mr. Great-Heart, let them that are most afraid keep close to me. So the fiend came on, and the conductor met it; but when it was come to him, it vanished to all their sights.[17] Then remembered they what had been said some time ago: "Resist the devil, and he will flee from you." James 4:7.

They went therefore on, as being a little refreshed. But they had not gone far, before Mercy, looking behind her, saw, as she thought, something most like a lion, and it came at a great padding pace after: and it had a hollow voice of roaring; and at every roar it gave, it made the valley echo, and all their hearts to ache, save the heart of him that was their guide. So it came up and Mr. Great-Heart went behind, and put the pilgrims all before him. The lion also came on apace, and Mr. Great-Heart addressed himself to give him battle. 1 Pet. 5:8,9.

But when he saw that it was determined that resistance should be made, he also drew back, and came no further.[18]

Then they went on again, and their conductor went before them, till they came to a place where was cast up a pit the whole breadth of the way; and before they could be prepared to go over that, a great mist and a darkness fell upon them, so that they could not see. Then said the pilgrims, Alas! what now shall we do? But their guide made answer, Fear not; stand still, and see what an end will be put to this also; so they stayed there, because their path was marred. They then also thought that they did hear more apparently the noise and rushing of the enemies; the fire also and the smoke of the pit were much easier to be discerned. Then said Christiana to Mercy, Now I see what my poor husband went through. I have heard much of this place, but I never was here before now. Poor man! he went here all alone in the night; he had night almost quite through the way: also these fiends were busy about him, as if they would have torn him in pieces. Many have spoken of it; but none can tell what the Valley of the Shadow of Death should mean until they come in themselves. The heart knoweth its own bitterness; and a stranger intermeddleth not with its joy. Prov. 14:10. To be here is a fearful thing.

Mr. Great-Heart: This is like doing business in great waters, or like going down into the deep. This is like being in the heart of the sea, and like going down to the bottoms of the mountains. Now it seems as if the earth, with its bars, were about us for ever. But let them that walk in darkness, and have no light, trust in the name of the Lord, and stay upon their God. Isa. 50:10. For my part, as I have told you already, I have gone often through this valley, and have been much harder put to it than now I am: and yet you see I am alive. I would not boast, for that I am not mine own saviour; but I trust we shall have a good deliverance. Come, let us pray for light to Him that can lighten our darkness,[19] and that can rebuke not only these, but all the Satans in hell.

18. Satan is a roaring lion looking for someone to devour. But just as in the previous paragraph, the devil is resisted, and he flees.

19. Great-Heart reminds the pilgrims to trust in the Lord for protection in the Valley of the Shadow of Death. "Yea, though I walk through the valley of the shadow of death, I will fear no evil; For You are with me; Your rod and Your staff, they comfort me." (Ps. 23:4)

So they cried and prayed, and God sent light and deliverance, for there was now no let in their way; no, not there where but now they were stopped with a pit. Yet they were not got through the valley. So they went on still, and met with great stinks and loathsome smells, to the great annoyance of them. Then said Mercy to Christiana, It is not so pleasant being here as at the gate, or at the Interpreter's, or at the house where we lay last.

O but, said one of the boys, it is not so bad to go through here, as it is to abide here, always; and for aught I know, one reason why we must go this way to the house prepared for us is, that our home might be the sweeter to us.

20. "Well said, Samuel, said Mr. Great-Heart."

Well said, Samuel, quoth the guide;[20] thou hast now spoke like a man. Why, if ever I get out here again, said the boy, I think I shall prize light and good way better than I ever did in all my life. Then said the guide, We shall be out by and by.

So on they went, and Joseph said, Cannot we see to the end of this valley as yet? Then said the guide, Look to your feet, for we shall presently be among the snares: so they looked to their feet, and went on; but they were troubled much with the snares. Now, when they were come among the snares, they espied a man cast into the ditch on the left hand, with his flesh all rent and torn. Then said the guide, That is one Heedless, that was going this way: he has lain there a great while. There was one Take-Heed with him when he was taken and slain, but he escaped their hands. You cannot imagine how many are killed hereabouts, and yet men are so foolishly venturous as to set out lightly on pilgrimage, and to come without a guide.[21] Poor Christian! it was a wonder that he here escaped; but he was beloved of his God: also he had a good heart of his own, or else he could never have done it.

21. The two characters provide an obvious contrast: Heedless did not take heed to the path of his feet. But Take-Heed watched carefully the path of his feet as he passed among the snares. To take heed to the path of our feet is to examine where we are going in light of God's Word.

Now they drew towards the end of this way; and just there where Christian had seen the cave when he went by, out thence came forth Maul, a giant. This Maul did use to spoil young pilgrims with sophistry; and he called Great-Heart by his name, and said unto him, How many times have you been forbidden to do these things? Then said Mr. Great-Heart, What things? What things! quoth the giant; you know what things: but I will put an end to your trade.

But, pray, said Mr. Great-Heart, before we fall to it, let us understand wherefore we must fight. Now the women and children stood trembling, and knew not what to do. Quoth the giant, You rob the country, and rob it with the worst of thefts. These are but generals, said Mr. Great-Heart; come to particulars, man.

Then said the giant, Thou practisest the craft of a kidnapper; thou gatherest up women and children, and carriest them into a strange country, to the weakening of my master's kingdom. But now Great-Heart replied, I am a servant of the God of heaven; my business is to persuade sinners to repentance. I am commanded to do my endeavors to turn men, women, and children, from darkness to light, and from the power of Satan unto God; and if this be indeed the ground of thy quarrel, let us fall to it as soon as thou wilt.[22]

Then the giant came up, and Mr. Great-Heart went to meet him; and as he went he drew his sword, but the giant had a club. So without more ado they fell to it, and at the first blow the giant struck Mr. Great-Heart down upon one of his knees. With that the women and children cried out. So Mr. Great-Heart recovering himself, laid about him in full lusty manner,[23] and gave the giant a wound in his arm. Thus he fought for the space of an hour, to that height of heat that the breath came out of the giant's nostrils as the heat doth out of a boiling cauldron.

Then they sat down to rest them; but Mr. Great-Heart betook himself to prayer.[24] Also the women and children did nothing but sigh and cry all the time that the battle did last.

When they had rested them, and taken breath, they both fell to it again; and Mr. Great-Heart, with a blow, fetched the giant down to the ground. Nay, hold, let me recover, quoth he: so Mr. Great-Heart fairly let him get up. So to it they went

22. In this paragraph, we learn more about the background of Mr. Great-Heart and who Bunyan intends him to represent. He is the man of God (the pastor or minister) who is a servant of the Lord. His job is to persuade sinners to repent and turn to God. It is his job to labor to see men, women, and children turned from darkness to light.

23. That is, Great-Heart attacks Maul with full strength.

24. The minister of God is a man of Word and prayer. He overcomes the evil one and the world by means of these spiritual weapons.

again, and the giant missed but little of all to breaking Mr. Great-Heart's scull with his club.

Mr. Great-Heart seeing that, runs to him in the full heat of his spirit, and pierceth him under the fifth rib. With that the giant began to faint, and could hold up his club no longer. Then Mr. Great-Heart seconded his blow, and smit the head of the giant from his shoulders.[25] Then the women and children rejoiced, and Mr. Great-Heart also praised God for the deliverance he had wrought.

When this was done, they amongst them erected a pillar, and fastened the giant's head thereon, and wrote under in letters that passengers might read,

"He that did wear this head was one
  That pilgrims did misuse;
He stopped their way, he spared none,
  But did them all abuse;
Until that I Great-Heart arose,
  The pilgrims guide to be;
Until that I did him oppose
  That was their enemy."

25. Mr. Great-Heart cuts the head of the giant off his shoulders.

Book 2
Chapter 6

Now I saw that they went on to the ascent that was a little way off, cast up to be a prospect for pilgrims. That was the place from whence Christian had the first sight of Faithful his brother. Wherefore, here they sat down and rested. They also here did eat and drink, and make merry, for that they had gotten deliverance from this so dangerous an enemy. As they sat thus and did eat, Christiana asked the guide, if he had caught no hurt in the battle? Then said Mr. Great-Heart, No, save a little on my flesh; yet that also shall be so far from being to my detriment, that it is at present a proof of my love to my master and you, and shall be a means, by grace, to increase my reward at last.

Christiana: But were you not afraid, good sir, when you saw him come with his club?

Mr. Great-Heart: It is my duty, said he, to mistrust my own ability, that I may have reliance on Him who is stronger than all.

Christiana: But what did you think when he fetched you down to the ground at the first blow?

Mr. Great-Heart: Why, I thought, quoth he, that so my Master himself was served, and yet he it was that conquered at last. 2 Cor. 4:10,11; Rom. 8:37.

1. Matthew wisely remarks that God's demonstrations of faithfulness to us should fortify us for future times of difficulty. If God has shown Himself faithful to us in the past, we can be sure He will remain faithful (Ps. 77:10-15).

2. That is, "I ask for your mercy" or "I beg your pardon" in terms of a modern idiom.

3. A good fighter or honest man

Matthew: When you all have thought what you please, I think God has been wonderfully good unto us, both in bringing us out of this valley, and in delivering us out of the hand of this enemy. For my part, I see no reason why we should distrust our God any more, since he has now, and in such a place as this, given us such testimony of his love.[1] Then they got up, and went forward.

Now a little before them stood an oak; and under it, when they came to it, they found an old pilgrim fast asleep. They knew that he was a pilgrim by his clothes, and his staff, and his girdle.

So the guide, Mr. Great-Heart, awaked him; and the old gentleman, as he lifted up his eyes, cried out, What's the matter? Who are you; and what is your business here?

Mr. Great-Heart: Come, man, be not so hot; here are none but friends. Yet the old man gets up, and stands upon his guard, and will know of them what they are. Then said the guide, My name is Great-Heart: I am the guide of these pilgrims that are going to the Celestial country.

Mr. Honest: Then said Mr. Honest, I cry you mercy:[2] I feared that you had been of the company of those that some time ago did rob Little-Faith of his money; but, now I look better about me, I perceive you are honester people.

Mr. Great-Heart: Why, what would or could you have done to have helped yourself, if indeed we had been of that company?

Mr. Honest: Done! Why, I would have fought as long as breath had been in me: and had I so done, I am sure you could never have given me the worst on't; for a Christian can never be overcome, unless he shall yield of himself.

Mr. Great-Heart: Well said, father Honest, quoth the guide; for by this I know thou art a cock of the right kind,[3] for thou hast said the truth.

Mr. Honest: And by this also I know that thou knowest what true pilgrimage is; for all others do think that we are the soonest overcome of any.

Mr. Great-Heart: Well, now we are so happily met, pray let me crave your name,[4] and the name of the place you came from.

Mr. Honest: My name I cannot tell you, but I came from the town of Stupidity: it lieth about four degrees beyond the city of Destruction.

Mr. Great-Heart: Oh, Are you that countryman? Then I deem I have half a guess of you: your name is Old Honesty, is it not?

Mr. Honest: So the old gentleman blushed, and said, Not honesty in the abstract, but Honest is my name; and I wish that my nature may agree to what I am called. But, sir, said the old gentleman, how could you guess that I am such a man, since I came from such a place?

Mr. Great-Heart: I had heard of you before, by my Master; for he knows all things that are done on the earth. But I have often wondered that any should come from your place; for your town is worse than is the city of Destruction itself.

Mr. Honest: Yes, we lie more off from the sun, and so are more cold and senseless. But were a man in a mountain of ice, yet if the Sun of righteousness will arise upon him, his frozen heart shall feel a thaw; and thus it has been with me.[5]

Mr. Great-Heart: I believe it, father Honest, I believe it; for I know the thing is true.

Then the old gentleman saluted all the pilgrims with a holy kiss of charity,[6] and asked them their names, and how they had fared since they set out on their pilgrimage.

Christiana: Then said Christiana, My name I suppose you have heard of; good Christian was my husband, and these four are his children. But can you think how the old gentleman was taken, when she told him who she was? He skipped, he smiled, he blessed them with a thousand good wishes, saying,

Mr. Honest: I have heard much of your husband, and of his travels and wars which he underwent in his days. Be it spoken to your comfort, the name of your husband rings all over these parts of the world: his faith, his courage, his enduring, and his sincerity under all, had made his name famous. Then he

4. That is, "Let me ask what your name is."

5. Mr. Honest comes from the town of Stupidity. The modern use of the word "stupid" usually refers to someone with a lack of intelligence. But the way that Mr. Honest describes the town of Stupidity is more in terms of a senselessness, a coldness, and a deadness. The only way someone can come out of such spiritual stupor is by the light of God's righteousness shining upon them to revive their dead hearts.

6. "Greet all the brethren with a holy kiss." (1 Thess. 5:26)

7. Matthew's name reminds Mr. Honest of the Matthew who wrote the Gospel of Matthew. Matthew was a tax collector. But he repented of his former way of life and followed Jesus.

8. Likewise, Samuel's namesake is Samuel the prophet who was a man of faith and prayer. The names of each of the boys should remind them of a pattern or example from Scripture they should follow.

9. Now, Mr. Great-Heart and Mr. Honest speak at length about the pilgrim journey of Mr. Fearing. Bunyan uses this opportunity to illustrate the pilgrimage of another kind of man. Mr. Fearing was a true believer, but he suffered from fear throughout his journey. Yet, by God's grace, he made it to the Celestial City. The pages that follow are very instructive for the reader. Fear is indeed a great snare, but we can be thankful that though we are weak and may struggle with anxiety and fear, we are sustained by a strong God.

10. Mr. Fearing's fearfulness made him a very difficult companion. Those constantly racked with fear, anxiety, and worry can be difficult to help.

turned him to the boys, and asked them of their names, which they told him. Then said he unto them, Matthew, be thou like Matthew the publican, not in vice, but in virtue.[7] Matt. 10:3. Samuel, said he, be thou like Samuel the prophet, a man of faith and prayer.[8] Psa. 99:6. Joseph, said he, be thou like Joseph in Potiphar's house, chaste, and one that flees from temptation. Gen. 39. And James, be thou like James the just, and like James the brother of our Lord. Acts 1:13. Then they told him of Mercy, and how she had left her town and her kindred to come along with Christiana and with her sons. At that the old honest man said, Mercy is thy name: by mercy shalt thou be sustained and carried through all those difficulties that shall assault thee in thy way, till thou shalt come thither where thou shalt look the Fountain of mercy in the face with comfort. All this while the guide, Mr. Great-Heart, was very well pleased, and smiled upon his companions.

Now, as they walked along together, the guide asked the old gentleman if he did not know one Mr. Fearing, that came on pilgrimage out of his parts.[9]

Mr. Honest: Yes, very well, said he. He was a man that had the root of the matter in him; but he was one of the most troublesome pilgrims that ever I met with in all my days.[10]

Mr. Great-Heart: I perceive you knew him, for you have given a very right character of him.

Mr. Honest: Knew him! I was a great companion of his; I was with him most an end; when he first began to think upon what would come upon us hereafter, I was with him.

Mr. Great-Heart: I was his guide from my Master's house to the gates of the Celestial City.

Mr. Honest: Then you knew him to be a troublesome one.

Mr. Great-Heart: I did so; but I could very well bear it;[11] for men of my calling are oftentimes intrusted with the conduct of such as he was.

Mr. Honest: Well then, pray let us hear a little of him, and how he managed himself under your conduct.

Mr. Great-Heart: Why, he was always afraid that he should come short of whither he had a desire to go. Every thing frightened him that he heard any body speak of, if it had but the least appearance of opposition in it. I heard that he lay roaring at the Slough of Despond for above a month together;[12] nor durst he, for all he saw several go over before him, venture, though they many of them offered to lend him their hands. He would not go back again, neither. The Celestial City-he said he should die if he came not to it; and yet he was dejected at every difficulty, and stumbled at every straw that any body cast in his way. Well, after he had lain at the Slough of Despond a great while, as I have told you, one sunshiny morning, I do not know how, he ventured, and so got over; but when he was over, he would scarce believe it.[13] He had, I think, a Slough of Despond in his mind,[14] a slough that he carried every where with him, or else he could never have been as he was. So he came up to the gate, you know what I mean, that stands at the head of this way, and there also he stood a good while before he would venture to knock. When the gate was opened, he would give back, and give place to others, and say that he was not worthy. For, all he got before some to the gate, yet many of them went in before him. There the poor man would stand shaking and shrinking;[15] I dare say

11. Mr. Great-Heart conducted Mr. Fearing to the Celestial City. But it was a difficult journey because of Mr. Fearing's struggles. Yet, Mr. Great-Heart bore with him despite his weaknesses. We are likewise called to bear with one another in love (Eph. 4:1-2).

12. Fear has a paralyzing effect. Because Mr. Fearing feared everyone and everything, he made very slow progress on the pilgrim journey. He sat for a month at the Slough of Despond and was unable to cross because he was controlled by fear. Fear can paralyze us from our faithfulness to Christ. When we feel paralyzed by fear, let us run to the throne of grace, asking for God to deliver us from the snare of fear. We must use the weapon of prayer to overcome this all-too-common sin.

13. Mr. Fearing finally crossed the Slough and was amazed that he had made it across. Often, our fears make the difficulty seem far greater than the reality. Satan may deceive us by convincing us to believe our fears rather than the promises of God.

14. That is, Mr. Fearing was always in a state of despondency. He carried a spiritual mud pit of despondency everywhere he went.

15. The solution to Mr. Fearing's fears was faith. He needed to believe in God. "We are not of those who shrink back and are destroyed, but of those who have faith and preserve their souls." (Heb. 10:39 ESV)

16. Mr. Fearing's journey is one of fits and starts. He is paralyzed by fear and cannot go forward. Likewise, he is so paralyzed by fear that he can't go back either. He is caught in the snare of fear, unable to move forward in faith.

17. Mr. Fearing carried with him the promise of God. This was a sure and infallible promise. The promises of God are infallible whereas our fears are unfounded. The promises of God provide us a sure foundation, a solid anchor for hope. "This hope we have as an anchor of the soul, both sure and steadfast, and which enters the Presence behind the veil, where the forerunner has entered for us, even Jesus, having become High Priest forever according to the order of Melchizedek." (Heb. 6:19-20)

18. A "trencher" is a wooden plate for food.

it would have pitied one's heart to have seen him. Nor would he go back again. At last he took the hammer that hanged on the gate, in his hand, and gave a small rap or two; then one opened to him, but he shrunk back as before. He that opened stepped out after him, and said, Thou trembling one, what wantest thou? With that he fell down to the ground. He that spoke to him wondered to see him so faint, so he said to him, Peace be to thee; up, for I have set open the door to thee; come in, for thou art blessed. With that he got up, and went in trembling; and when he was in, he was ashamed to show his face. Well, after he had been entertained there a while, as you know how the manner is, he was bid go on his way, and also told the way he should take. So he went on till he came out to our house; but as he behaved himself at the gate, so he did at my Master the Interpreter's door. He lay there about in the cold a good while, before he would adventure to call; yet he would not go back:[16] and the nights were long and cold then. Nay, he had a note of necessity in his bosom to my master to receive him,[17] and grant him the comfort of his house, and also to allow him a stout and valiant conductor, because he was himself so chicken-hearted a man; and yet for all that he was afraid to call at the door. So he lay up and down thereabouts, till, poor man, he was almost starved; yea, so great was his dejection, that though he saw several others for knocking get in, yet he was afraid to venture. At last, I think I looked out of the window, and perceiving a man to be up and down about the door, I went out to him, and asked what he was: but, poor man, the water stood in his eyes; so I perceived what he wanted. I went therefore in, and told it in the house, and we showed the thing to our Lord: so he sent me out again, to entreat him to come in; but I dare say, I had hard work to do it. At last he came in; and I will say that for my Lord, he carried it wonderful lovingly to him. There were but a few good bits at the table, but some of it was laid upon his trencher.[18] Then he presented the note; and my Lord looked thereon, and said his desire should be granted. So when he had been there a good while, he seemed to get some heart, and to be a little more comfortable. For my Master, you must know, is one of very tender bowels,[19] especially to them that are afraid; wherefore he carried it so towards him as might tend most to his encouragement. Well, when he had had a sight of the things of the place, and was ready to take his journey to go to the city, my Lord, as he did to Christian before, gave him a bottle of spirits, and some comfortable things to eat. Thus we set forward, and I went before him; but the man was but of few words, only he would sigh aloud.

When we were come to where the three fellows were hanged, he said that he doubted that that would be his end also. Only he seemed glad when he saw the cross and the sepulchre. There I confess he desired to stay a little to look; and he seemed for a while after to be a little cheery. When he came to the Hill Difficulty, he made no stick at that, nor did he much fear the lions: for you must know, that his troubles were not about such things as these; his fear was about his acceptance at last.[20]

I got him in at the house Beautiful, I think, before he was willing. Also, when he was in, I brought him acquainted with the damsels of the place; but he was ashamed to make himself much in company. He desired much to be alone; yet he always loved good talk, and often would get behind the screen to hear it. He also loved much to see ancient things, and to be pondering them in his mind. He told me afterward, that he loved to be in those two houses from which he came last, to wit, at the gate, and that of the Interpreter, but that he durst not be so bold as to ask.

When we went also from the house Beautiful, down the hill, into the Valley of Humiliation, he went down as well as ever I saw a man in my life; for he cared not how mean he was, so he might be happy at last. Yea, I think there was a kind of sympathy betwixt that Valley and him; for I never saw him better in all his pilgrimage than he was in that Valley.

19. The Lord is merciful and compassionate to us in our weakness. The Lord knows our frame, and He understands our fears (Ps. 103:13-14).

20. Mr. Fearing especially dealt with a lack of assurance. He was unsure whether he would be accepted into the Celestial City. When we struggle with a lack of assurance, we should not look at the weakness of faith, but we should set our eyes upon our Savior Jesus Christ. It is not the strength or weakness of faith that matters. Instead, even the weakest faith, if it is true faith, can lay hold of a strong Savior. Let us remember our Lord's words: any who come to Him He will not cast out (John 6:37).

21. The reader is not surprised to read that Mr. Fearing had one of his greatest struggles when they came to the Valley of the Shadow of Death. Here was a very fearful place for a man controlled by fear. Even before entering the valley, Mr. Fearing falls prey to his temptations to fear.

Here he would lie down, embrace the ground, and kiss the very flowers that grew in this valley. Lam. 3:27-29. He would now be up every morning by break of day, tracing and walking to and fro in the valley.

But when he was come to the entrance of the Valley of the Shadow of Death, I thought I should have lost my man: not for that he had any inclination to go back; that he always abhorred; but he was ready to die for fear. Oh, the hobgoblins will have me! the hobgoblins will have me! cried he; and I could not beat him out of it. He made such a noise, and such an outcry here, that had they but heard him, it was enough to encourage them to come and fall upon us.[21]

But this I took very great notice of, that this valley was as quiet when we went through it, as ever I knew it before or since.[22] I suppose those enemies here had now a special check from our Lord, and a command not to meddle until Mr. Fearing had passed over it.

It would be too tedious to tell you of all; we will therefore only mention a passage or two more. When he was come to Vanity Fair, I thought he would have fought with all the men in the fair. I feared there we should have been both knocked on the head, so hot was he against their fooleries.[23] Upon the Enchanted Ground he was very wakeful. But when he was come at the river where was no bridge, there again he was in a heavy case. Now, now, he said, he should be drowned forever, and so never see that face with comfort that he had come so many miles to behold.

22. Behold God's tender compassion upon His weak children! Here, Mr. Fearing is provided one of the calmest and most peaceful journeys through the dark valley. All the monsters were kept at bay so that Mr. Fearing could make it through without losing faith. This reminds us that our Heavenly Father providentially guides our lives and will provide special providences for us so that we will be sustained and preserved on our journey. God's faithfulness in this way is described in 1 Corinthians 10. "No temptation has overtaken you except such as is common to man; but God is faithful, who will not allow you to be tempted beyond what you are able, but with the temptation will also make the way of escape, that you may be able to bear it." (1 Cor. 10:13)

23. Though Mr. Fearing is a very fearful man, he has a zeal for righteousness. He is not afraid of worldly opposition. He would gladly fight against the people of Vanity Fair.

And here also I took notice of what was very remarkable: the water of that river was lower at this time than ever I saw it in all my life;[24] so he went over at last, not much above wet-shod. When he was going up to the gate, I began to take leave of him, and to wish him a good reception above. So he said, I shall, I shall. Then parted we asunder, and I saw him no more.

Mr. Honest: Then it seems he was well at last?

Mr. Great-Heart: Yes, yes, I never had doubt about him.[25] He was a man of a choice spirit, only he was always kept very low, and that made his life so burdensome to himself,[26] and so troublesome to others. Psa. 88. He was, above many, tender of sin: he was so afraid of doing injuries to others, that he often would deny himself of that which was lawful, because he would not offend. Rom. 14:21; 1 Cor. 8:13.

Mr. Honest: But what should be the reason that such a good man should be all his days so much in the dark?

Mr. Great-Heart: There are two sorts of reasons for it. One is, the wise God will have it so:[27] some must pipe, and some must weep. Matt. 11:16. Now Mr. Fearing was one that played upon the bass. He and his fellows sound the sackbut,[28] whose notes are more doleful than the notes of other music are: though indeed, some say, the bass is the ground of music.[29] And for my part, I care not at all for that profession which begins not in heaviness of mind. The first string that the musician usually touches is the bass, when he intends to put all

24. Here again is God's merciful providence. Knowing the weakness of Mr. Fearing, the Lord graciously lowers the water levels so that Mr. Fearing can make it across without despairing.

25. Mr. Great-Heart never doubted that Mr. Fearing was going to make it the whole length of the journey. This may surprise the reader since it would seem likely that Mr. Fearing would have just turned back at some point. But it is the Lord who sustains His children on this pilgrim journey. As Paul writes, "Being confident of this very thing, that He who has begun a good work in you will complete it until the day of Jesus Christ;..." (Phil. 1:6)

26. Mr. Fearing serves as a case-study on the bad effects of anxiety and fear. We need not carry such burdens of worry and anxiety with us, when we have our great God to help us, and His promises to deliver us from fear.

27. Mr. Great-Heart explains why Mr. Fearing had, in God's providence, such a lifelong struggle with fear. The first reason is that God wisely chooses to allow His children to struggle with different challenges. This is ordained according to God's wisdom and for the good of His children. However, we as God's children may not always know the reasons why.

28. A "sackbut" is a trumpet.

29. Mr. Great-Heart provides a musical illustration to explain Mr. Fearing's condition. He points out that the "bass," which refers to the heaviness of spirit, is the ground of the music. That is, a tender heart, a fear of the Lord, is foundational to the Christian life. Though Mr. Fearing had a fear of the Lord and a tender heart, he was unable to play any "other music but this." That is, he was sinfully afraid as well.

in tune. God also plays upon this string first, when he sets the soul in tune for himself. Only there was the imperfection of Mr. Fearing; he could play upon no other music but this till towards his latter end.

[I make bold to talk thus metaphorically for the ripening of the wits of young readers, and because, in the book of Revelation, the saved are compared to a company of musicians, that play upon their trumpets and harps, and sing their songs before the throne.[30]Rev. 5:8; 14:2,3.]

30. Bunyan inserts an author's comments explaining his method. He is using a metaphor that is indeed biblical (from the Book of Revelation) in order to teach a spiritual lesson to the reader.

Mr. Honest: He was a very zealous man, as one may see by the relation you have given of him. Difficulties, lions, or Vanity Fair, he feared not at all; it was only sin, death, and hell, that were to him a terror, because he had some doubts about his interest in that celestial country.

Mr. Great-Heart: You say right; those were the things that were his troublers; and they, as you have well observed, arose from the weakness of his mind thereabout, not from weakness of spirit as to the practical part of a pilgrim's life. I dare believe that, as the proverb is, he could have bit a firebrand, had it stood in his way; but the things with which he was oppressed, no man ever yet could shake off with ease.

Christiana: Then said Christiana, This relation of Mr. Fearing has done me good; I thought nobody had been like me.[31] But I see there was some semblance betwixt this good man and me: only we differed in two things. His troubles were so great that they broke out; but mine I kept within. His also lay so hard upon him, they made him that he could not knock at the houses provided for entertainment; but my trouble was always such as made me knock the louder.

31. Christiana is thankful for the retelling of Mr. Fearing's story. The reader may feel the same. We can deal with the same kinds of fears on the pilgrim journey to heaven.

Mercy: If I might also speak my heart, I must say that something of him has also dwelt in me. For I have ever been more afraid of the lake, and the loss of a place in paradise, than I have been of the loss other things. O, thought I, may I have the happiness to have a habitation there! 'Tis enough, though I part with all the world to win it.

Matthew: Then said Matthew, Fear was one thing that made me think that I was far from having that within me which accompanies salvation. But if it was so with such a good man as he, why may it not also go well with me?[32]

James: No fears no grace, said James. Though there is not always grace where there is the fear of hell, yet, to be sure, there is no grace where there is no fear of God.[33]

Mr. Great-Heart: Well said, James; thou hast hit the mark. For the fear of God is the beginning of wisdom; and to be sure, they that want the beginning have neither middle nor end. But we will here conclude our discourse of Mr. Fearing, after we have sent after him this farewell.

"Well, Master Fearing, thou didst fear
    Thy God, and wast afraid
Of doing any thing, while here,
    That would have thee betrayed.
And didst thou fear the lake and pit?
    Would others do so too!
For, as for them that want thy wit,
    They do themselves undo."

Now I saw that they still went on in their talk. For after Mr. Great-Heart had made an end with Mr. Fearing, Mr. Honest began to tell them of another, but his name was Mr. Self-will.[34] He pretended himself to be a pilgrim, said Mr. Honest; but I persuade myself he never came in at the gate that stands at the head of the way.

Mr. Great-Heart: Had you ever any talk with him about it?

Mr. Honest: Yes, more than once or twice; but he would always be like himself, self-willed. He neither cared for man, nor argument, nor yet example; what his mind prompted him to, that he would do, and nothing else could he be got to do.

Mr. Great-Heart: Pray, what principles did he hold? for I suppose you can tell.

Mr. Honest: He held that a man might follow the vices as well as the virtues of pilgrims; and that if he did both, he should be certainly saved.

32. Matthew notes that Mr. Fearing's story serves as an encouragement to other pilgrims. When we hear of the grace of God upon other weak sinners like ourselves, it strengthens us to remember God's goodness to His children. Such testimonies give us confidence.

33. The fear of God is foundational to the Christian life. As Proverbs says, the fear of the Lord is the beginning of wisdom and knowledge (Prov. 1:7, 9:10).

34. Mr. Honest recounts the story of another man. Mr. Self-will is an "antinomian." He disregards God's law and justifies his sins. He even used the Scriptures to try to justify his vice by looking to the ungodly examples in Scripture.

Mr. Great-Heart: How? If he had said, it is possible for the best to be guilty of the vices, as well as to partake of the virtues of pilgrims, he could not much have been blamed; for indeed we are exempted from no vice absolutely, but on condition that we watch and strive. But this, I perceive, is not the thing; but if I understand you right, your meaning is, that he was of opinion that it was allowable so to be.

Mr. Honest: Aye, aye, so I mean, and so he believed and practised.

Mr. Great-Heart: But what grounds had he for his so saying?

Mr. Honest: Why, he said he had the Scripture for his warrant.

Mr. Great-Heart: Prithee, Mr. Honest, present us with a few particulars.

Mr. Honest: So I will. He said, to have to do with other men's wives had been practised by David, God's beloved; and therefore he could do it. He said, to have more women than one was a thing that Solomon practised, and therefore he could do it. He said, that Sarah and the godly midwives of Egypt lied, and so did save Rahab, and therefore he could do it. He said, that the disciples went at the bidding of their Master, and took away the owner's ass, and therefore he could do so too. He said, that Jacob got the inheritance of his father in a way of guile and dissimulation, and therefore he could do so too.[35]

Mr. Great-Heart: High base indeed! And are you sure he was of this opinion?

Mr. Honest: I heard him plead for it, bring Scripture for it, bring arguments for it, etc.

Mr. Great-Heart: An opinion that is not fit to be with any allowance in the world!

Mr. Honest: You must understand me rightly: he did not say that any man might do this; but that they who had the virtues of those that did such things, might also do the same.

Mr. Great-Heart: But what more false than such a conclusion? For this is as much as to say, that because good men

35. Mr. Self-will was a man who twisted the Scriptures to his own destruction (2 Pet. 3:16). He misapplied the ungodly examples as a means of justifying sin.

heretofore have sinned of infirmity, therefore he had allowance to do it of a presumptuous mind; or that if, because a child, by the blast of the wind, or for that it stumbled at a stone, fell down and defiled itself in the mire, therefore he might wilfully lie down and wallow like a boar therein. Who could have thought that any one could so far have been blinded by the power of lust? But what is written must be true: they "stumble at the word, being disobedient; whereunto also they were appointed." 1 Peter, 2:8. His supposing that such may have the godly men's virtues, who addict themselves to their vices, is also a delusion as strong as the other. To eat up the sin of God's people, Hos. 4:8, as a dog licks up filth, is no sign that one is possessed with their virtues. Nor can I believe that one who is of this opinion, can at present have faith or love in him. But I know you have made strong objections against him; prithee what can he say for himself?

Mr. Honest: Why, he says, to do this by way of opinion, seems abundantly more honest than to do it, and yet hold contrary to it in opinion.

Mr. Great-Heart: A very wicked answer. For though to let loose the bridle to lusts, while our opinions are against such things, is bad; yet, to sin, and plead a toleration so to do, is worse: the one stumbles beholders accidentally, the other leads them into the snare.

Mr. Honest: There are many of this man's mind, that have not this man's mouth; and that makes going on pilgrimage of so little esteem as it is.

Mr. Great-Heart: You have said the truth, and it is to be lamented: but he that feareth the King of paradise, shall come out of them all.

Christiana: There are strange opinions in the world. I know one that said, it was time enough to repent when we come to die.[36]

Mr. Great-Heart: Such are not overwise; that man would have been loth, might he have had a week to run twenty miles in his life, to defer his journey to the last hour of that week.

36. Some will foolishly say, "I will repent of my sins when I'm about to die and God will forgive me." Such a foolish perspective despises the grace of God and forgets that the Lord may bring us to judgment at any time.

37. The rumored bandits never even approach the pilgrims. It is perhaps because Great-Heart was with them. With such a strong companion, it would be foolish to make their attack. But when Little-Faith passed their way, the bandits knew that they could take advantage of his weakness.

38. Bunyan uses a name mentioned in the letter to the Romans (Rom. 16:23) who served as Paul's "host." The inn of Gaius, like the House of the Interpreter and the House Beautiful, is another resting place for the pilgrims on their journey. The extended stay at Gaius' inn follows the same literary pattern of the previous resting place. It is an extended time of hospitality wherein the characters engage in spiritual conversation.

Mr. Honest: You say right; and yet the generality of them who count themselves pilgrims, do indeed do thus. I am, as you see, an old man, and have been a traveller in this road many a day; and I have taken notice of many things.

I have seen some that have set out as if they would drive all the world before them, who yet have, in a few days, died as they in the wilderness, and so never got sight of the promised land. I have seen some that have promised nothing at first setting out to be pilgrims, and who one would have thought could not have lived a day, that have yet proved very good pilgrims. I have seen some who have run hastily forward, that again have, after a little time, run just as fast back again. I have seen some who have spoken very well of a pilgrim's life at first, that after a while have spoken as much against it. I have heard some, when they first set out for paradise, say positively, there is such a place, who, when they have been almost there, have come back again, and said there is none. I have heard some vaunt what they would do in case they should be opposed, that have, even at a false alarm, fled faith, the pilgrim's way, and all.

Now, as they were thus on their way, there came one running to meet them, and said, Gentlemen, and you of the weaker sort, if you love life, shift for yourselves, for the robbers are before you.

Mr. Great-Heart: Then said Mr. Great-Heart, They be the three that set upon Little-Faith heretofore. Well, said he, we are ready for them: so they went on their way. Now they looked at every turning when they should have met with the villains; but whether they heard of Mr. Great-Heart, or whether they had some other game, they came not up to the pilgrims.[37]

Christiana then wished for an inn to refresh herself and her children, because they were weary. Then said Mr. Honest, There is one a little before us, where a very honorable disciple, one Gaius, dwells.[38] Rom. 16:23. So they all concluded to turn in thither; and the rather, because the old gentleman gave him so good a report. When they came to the door they went in, not knocking, for folks use not to knock at the door of an inn.

Then they called for the master of the house, and he came to them. So they asked if they might lie there that night.

Gaius: Yes, gentlemen, if you be true men; for my house is for none but pilgrims. Then were Christiana, Mercy, and the boys the more glad, for that the innkeeper was a lover of pilgrims. So they called for rooms, and he showed them one for Christiana and her children and Mercy, and another for Mr. Great-Heart and the old gentleman.

Mr. Great-Heart: Then said Mr. Great-Heart, good Gaius, what hast thou for supper? for these pilgrims have come far to-day, and are weary.

Gaius: It is late, said Gaius, so we cannot conveniently go out to seek food; but such as we have you shall be welcome to, if that will content.

Mr. Great-Heart: We will be content with what thou hast in the house; for as much as I have proved thee, thou art never destitute of that which is convenient.

Then he went down and spake to the cook, whose name was, Taste-that-which-is-good,[39] to get ready supper for so many pilgrims. This done, he comes up again, saying, Come, my good friends, you are welcome to me, and I am glad that I have a house to entertain you in; and while supper is making ready, if you please, let us entertain one another with some good discourse: so they all said, Content.

Gaius: Then said Gaius, Whose wife is this aged matron? and whose daughter is this young damsel?

Mr. Great-Heart: This woman is the wife of one Christian, a pilgrim of former times; and these are his four children. The maid is one of her acquaintance, one that she hath persuaded to come with her on pilgrimage. The boys take all after their father, and covet to tread in his steps; yea, if they do but see any place where the old pilgrim hath lain, or any print of his foot, it ministereth joy to their hearts, and they covet to lie or tread in the same.

Gaius: Then said Gaius, Is this Christian's wife, and are these Christian's children? I knew your husband's father, yea,

39. Bunyan may have in mind the language of Psalm 34: "Oh, taste and see that the LORD is good; Blessed is the man who trusts in Him!" (Ps. 34:8)

40. Gaius recounts the ancestry of Christian. He refers to Antioch because it was there that the disciples of Jesus Christ were first called Christians (Acts 11:26).

41. Ignatius and Polycarp were two early church martyrs who died for their faith in Christ. The reader can learn more about them by reading the "Apostolic Fathers." These documents are the earliest Christian writings we have after the New Testament. These writings are provided with commentary in *Essential Writings on Church History*, published by Generations. *Foxe's Book of Martyrs* (originally titled *Acts and Monuments*) also records these stories. Foxe's book was likely familiar to John Bunyan.

42. "Blessed is the man who fears the LORD, Who delights greatly in His commandments. His descendants will be mighty on earth; The generation of the upright will be blessed." (Ps. 112:1-2)

also his father's father. Many have been good of this stock; their ancestors dwelt first at Antioch.[40] Acts 11:26. Christian's progenitors (I suppose you have heard your husband talk of them) were very worthy men. They have, above any that I know, showed themselves men of great virtue and courage for the Lord of the pilgrims, his ways, and them that loved him. I have heard of many of your husband's relations that have stood all trials for the sake of the truth. Stephen, that was one of the first of the family from whence your husband sprang, was knocked on the head with stones. Acts 7:59, 60. James, another of this generation, was slain with the edge of the sword. Acts 12:2. To say nothing of Paul and Peter, men anciently of the family from whence your husband came, there was Ignatius, who was cast to the lions; Romanus, whose flesh was cut by pieces from his bones; and Polycarp, that played the man in the fire.[41] There was he that was hanged up in a basket in the sun for the wasps to eat; and he whom they put into a sack, and cast him into the sea to be drowned. It would be impossible utterly to count up all of that family who have suffered injuries and death for the love of a pilgrim's life. Nor can I but be glad to see that thy husband has left behind him four such boys as these. I hope they will bear up their father's name, and tread in their father's steps, and come to their father's end.

Mr. Great-Heart: Indeed, sir, they are likely lads: they seem to choose heartily their father's ways.

Gaius: That is it that I said. Wherefore Christian's family is like still to spread abroad upon the face of the ground, and yet to be numerous upon the face of the earth;[42] let Christiana look out some damsels for her sons,[43] to whom they may be betrothed, etc., that the name of their father, and the house of his progenitors, may never be forgotten in the world.

Mr. Honest: 'Tis pity his family should fall and be extinct.

Gaius: Fall it cannot, but be diminished it may; but let Christiana take my advice, and that is the way to uphold it. And, Christiana, said this innkeeper, I am glad to see thee and thy friend Mercy together here, a lovely couple. And if I may advise, take Mercy into a nearer relation to thee: if she will, let her be given to Matthew thy eldest son. It is the way to preserve a posterity in the earth. So this match was concluded, and in process of time they were married:[44] but more of that hereafter.

Gaius also proceeded, and said, I will now speak on the behalf of women, to take away their reproach. For as death and the curse came into the world by a woman, Gen. 3, so also did life and health: God sent forth his Son, made of a woman. Gal. 4:4. Yea, to show how much they that came after did abhor the act of the mother, this sex in the Old Testament coveted children, if happily this or that woman might be the mother of the Saviour of the world. I will say again, that when the Saviour was come, women rejoiced in him, before either man or angel. Luke 1:42-46. I read not that ever any man did give unto Christ so much as one groat;[45] but the women followed him, and ministered to him of their substance. Luke 8:2,3. 'Twas a woman that washed his feet with tears, Luke 7:37-50, and a woman that anointed his body at the burial. John 11:2; 12:3. They were women who wept when he was going to the cross, Luke 23:27, and women that followed him from the cross, Matt. 27:55,56; Luke 23:55, and sat over against his sepulchre when he was buried. Matt. 27:61. They were women that were first with him at his resurrection-morn, Luke 24:1, and women that brought tidings first to his disciples that he was risen from the dead. Luke 24:22,23. Women therefore are highly favored, and show by these things that they are sharers with us in the grace of life.[46]

43. Gaius counsels Christiana to find some young women that her boys may marry. The Puritans greatly valued the institution of marriage and saw it as a vehicle for God's saving purpose through the discipleship of the next generation.

44. Bunyan does not spend much time detailing the relationship between Matthew and Mercy. He only tells us that they were eventually married.

45. A term used for a variety of currency. In particular, the word was used for an English coin worth four pence. It is used by Bunyan to refer to a very small amount (something like "a single penny").

46. "Husbands, likewise, dwell with them [wives] with understanding, giving honor to the wife, as to the weaker vessel, and as being heirs together of the grace of life, that your prayers may not be hindered." (1 Pet. 3:7)

47. The Lord gives us an abundance of spiritual blessings in this life. He feeds us through preaching, through the reading of the Scriptures, and through the sacraments. But these are just a foretaste of the glorious riches that await us.

48. These portions were part of the sacrificial animal as described in the ritual offerings of Leviticus. "The breast of the wave offering and the thigh of the heave offering you shall eat in a clean place, you, your sons, and your daughters with you; for they are your due and your sons' due, which are given from the sacrifices of peace offerings of the children of Israel" (Lev. 10:14). Bunyan does not use this picture in the literal sense of a burnt offering. Rather, Bunyan is speaking about the spiritual significance of the Old Testament sacrifices. They were to teach God's people to "begin their meal with prayer and praise to God."

49. The background of this image is Peter's description of how the Word of God is like milk for newborn babes (1 Pet. 2:1-2).

Now the cook sent up to signify that supper was almost ready, and sent one to lay the cloth, and the trenchers, and to set the salt and bread in order.

Then said Matthew, The sight of this cloth, and of this forerunner of the supper, begetteth in me a greater appetite for my food than I had before.

Gaius: So let all ministering doctrines to thee in this life beget in thee a greater desire to sit at the supper of the great King in his kingdom; for all preaching, books, and ordinances here, are but as the laying of the trenchers, and the setting of salt upon the board, when compared with the feast which our Lord will make for us when we come to his house.[47]

So supper came up. And first a heave-shoulder and a wave-breast[48] were set on the table before them; to show that they must begin their meal with prayer and praise to God. The heave-shoulder David lifted up his heart to God with; and with the wave-breast, where his heart lay, he used to lean upon his harp when he played. Lev. 7: 32-34; 10:14,15; Psalm 25:1; Heb. 13:15. These two dishes were very fresh and good, and they all ate heartily thereof.

The next they brought up was a bottle of wine, as red as blood. Deut. 32:14; Judges 9:13; John 15:5. So Gaius said to them, Drink freely; this is the true juice of the vine, that makes glad the heart of God and man. So they drank and were merry.

The next was a dish of milk well crumbed; Gaius said, Let the boys have that, that they may grow thereby.[49] 1 Pet. 2:1,2.

Then they brought up in course a dish of butter and honey. Then said Gaius, Eat freely of this, for this is good to cheer up and strengthen your judgments and understandings. This was our Lord's dish when he was a child: "Butter and honey shall he eat, that he may know to refuse the evil, and choose the good." Isa. 7:15.

Then they brought them up a dish of apples, and they were very good-tasted fruit. Then said Matthew, May we eat apples, since it was such by and with which the serpent beguiled our first mother?[50]

Then said Gaius,

"Apples were they with which we were beguil'd,

Yet sin, not apples, hath our souls defil'd:

Apples forbid, if ate, corrupt the blood;

To eat such, when commanded, does us good:

Drink of his flagons then, thou church, his dove,

And eat his apples, who art sick of love."

Then said Matthew, I made the scruple,[51] because I a while since was sick with the eating of fruit.

Gaius: Forbidden fruit will make you sick; but not what our Lord has tolerated.

While they were thus talking, they were presented with another dish, and it was a dish of nuts. Song 6:11. Then said some at the table, Nuts spoil tender teeth, especially the teeth of children: which when Gaius heard, he said,

"Hard texts are nuts, (I will not call them cheaters,)

Whose shells do keep the kernel from the eaters:

Open the shells, and you shall have the meat;

They here are brought for you to crack and eat."

Then were they very merry, and sat at the table a long time, talking of many things. Then said the old gentleman, My good landlord, while we are cracking your nuts, if you please, do you open this riddle:

"A man there was, though some did count him mad,

The more he cast away, the more he had."

Then they all gave good heed, wondering what good Gaius would say; so he sat still a while, and then thus replied:

"He who bestows his goods upon the poor,

Shall have as much again, and ten times more."

Then said Joseph, I dare say, sir, I did not think you could have found it out.

50. Technically, of course, the Scriptures do not describe what kind of fruit the forbidden fruit was. It has popularly been pictured as an apple. However, part of the reason it is mentioned here is because Matthew had eaten an apple from the devil's garden earlier in Part II.

51. That is, Matthew mentioned this caveat because of his prior experience with the devil's poisonous fruit.

Oh, said Gaius, I have been trained up in this way a great while: nothing teaches like experience. I have learned of my Lord to be kind, and have found by experience that I have gained thereby. There is that scattereth, and yet increaseth; and there is that withholdeth more than is meet, but it tendeth to poverty: There is that maketh himself rich, yet hath nothing; there is that maketh himself poor, yet hath great riches. Prov. 11:24; 13:7.

Then Samuel whispered to Christiana, his mother, and said, Mother, this is a very good man's house: let us stay here a good while, and let my brother Matthew be married here to Mercy, before we go any further. The which Gaius the host overhearing, said, With a very good will, my child.

So they stayed there more than a month, and Mercy was given to Matthew to wife.

While they stayed here, Mercy, as her custom was, would be making coats and garments to give to the poor, by which she brought a very good report upon the pilgrims.[52]

52. Mercy is true to her name. She shows mercy to the poor. As our Lord Jesus said, "Blessed are the merciful, for they shall obtain mercy." (Matt. 5:7)

But to return again to our story: After supper the lads desired a bed, for they were weary with travelling: Then Gaius called to show them their chamber; but said Mercy, I will have them to bed. So she had them to bed, and they slept well: but the rest sat up all night; for Gaius and they were such suitable company, that they could not tell how to part. After much talk of their Lord, themselves, and their journey, old Mr. Honest, he that put forth the riddle to Gaius, began to nod. Then said Great-Heart, What, sir, you begin to be drowsy; come, rub up, now here is a riddle for you.[53] Then said Mr. Honest, Let us hear it. Then replied Mr. Great-Heart,

53. Mr. Great-Heart tries to rouse Mr. Honest with a riddle.

"He that would kill, must first be overcome:
Who live abroad would, first must die at home."

Ha, said Mr. Honest, it is a hard one; hard to expound, and harder to practise. But come, landlord, said he, I will, if you please, leave my part to you: do you expound it, and I will hear what you say.

No, said Gaius, it was put to you, and it is expected you should answer it. Then said the old gentleman,

"He first by grace must conquered be,
  That sin would mortify;[54]
Who that he lives would convince me,
  Unto himself must die."

It is right, said Gaius; good doctrine and experience teach this. For, first, until grace displays itself, and overcomes the soul with its glory, it is altogether without heart to oppose sin. Besides, if sin is Satan's cords, by which the soul lies bound, how should it make resistance before it is loosed from that infirmity?[55] Secondly, Nor will any one that knows either reason or grace, believe that such a man can be a living monument of grace that is a slave to his own corruptions. And now it comes into my mind, I will tell you a story worth the hearing. There were two men that went on pilgrimage; the one began when he was young, the other when he was old. The young man had strong corruptions to grapple with; the old man's were weak with the decays of nature. The young man trod his steps as even as did the old one, and was every way as light as he. Who now, or which of them, had their graces shining clearest, since both seemed to be alike?

Mr. Honest: The young man's, doubtless. For that which makes head against the greatest opposition, gives best demonstration that it is strongest;[56] especially when it also holdeth pace with that which meets not with half so much, as to be sure old age does not. Besides, I have observed that old men have blessed themselves with this mistake; namely, taking the decays of nature for a gracious conquest over corruptions, and so have been apt to beguile themselves.[57] Indeed, old men that are gracious are best able to give advice to them that are young, because they have seen most of the emptiness of things: but yet, for an old and a young man to set out both together, the young one has the advantage of the fairest discovery of a work of grace within him, though the old man's corruptions are naturally the weakest. Thus they sat talking till break of day.

54. That is, a man must be "conquered by grace" if he will have the power to mortify [kill] sin.

55. The natural condition of fallen mankind is bondage to sin and Satan. But the Lord Jesus Christ sets men free (John 8:36).

56. A comparison is drawn between a young man with strong sexual desire and an older man who has declining sexual desire ("decays of nature"). Which of the two show grace at its strongest? The answer is the young man because grace powerfully overcomes stronger lustful desire. Whereas in the case of the old man, that desire has already declined naturally.

57. "They have been prone to deceiving themselves."

Now, when the family were up, Christiana bid her son James that he should read a chapter; so he read 53d of Isaiah. When he had done, Mr. Honest asked why it was said that the Saviour was to come "out of a dry ground;" and also, that "he had no form nor comeliness in him."

Mr. Great-Heart: Then said Mr. Great-Heart, To the first I answer, because the church of the Jews, of which Christ came, had then lost almost all the sap and spirit of religion. To the second I say, the words are spoken in the person of unbelievers, who, because they want the eye that can see into our Prince's heart, therefore they judge of him by the meanness of his outside;[58] just like those who, not knowing that precious stones are covered over with a homely crust, when they have found one, because they know not what they have found, cast it away again, as men do a common stone.[59]

Well, said Gaius, now you are here, and since, as I know, Mr. Great-Heart is good at his weapons, if you please, after we have refreshed ourselves, we will walk into the fields, to see if we can do any good.[60] About a mile from hence there is one Slay-good, a giant, that doth much annoy the King's highway in these parts; and I know whereabout his haunt is. He is master of a number of thieves: 't would be well if we could clear these parts of him. So they consented and went: Mr. Great-Heart with his sword, helmet, and shield; and the rest with spears and staves.

When they came to the place where he was, they found him with one Feeble-Mind in his hand, whom his servants had brought unto him, having taken him in the way. Now the giant was rifling him,[61] with a purpose after that to pick his bones; for he was of the nature of flesheaters.[62]

Well, so soon as he saw Mr. Great-Heart and his friends at the mouth of his cave, with their weapons, he demanded what they wanted.

Mr. Great-Heart: We want thee; for we are come to revenge the quarrels of the many that thou hast slain of the pilgrims, when thou hast dragged them out of the King's high-

58. People who lacked spiritual eyes judged Jesus Christ by the outside (exterior) which was not impressive to the world.

59. Though Jesus did not appear "impressive" by the world's standards, yet He is to be considered the pearl of great price and worth more than all the riches of this world.

60. As Mr. Great-Heart is a warrior, Gaius counsels him to go on a hunt and defeat one of the Lord's enemies: Slay-good.

61. "Going through his pockets"

62. That is, he was a cannibal.

way: wherefore come out of thy cave. So he armed himself and came out, and to battle they went, and fought for above an hour, and then stood still to take wind.

Slay-Good: Then said the giant, Why are you here on my ground?

Mr. Great-Heart: To revenge the blood of pilgrims, as I told thee before. So they went to it again, and the giant made Mr. Great-Heart give back; but he came up again, and in the greatness of his mind he let fly with such stoutness at the giant's head and sides, that he made him let his weapon fall out of his hand. So he smote him, and slew him, and cut off his head, and brought it away to the inn. He also took Feeble-Mind the pilgrim,[63] and brought him with him to his lodgings. When they were come home, they showed his head to the family, and set it up, as they had done others before, for a terror to those that should attempt to do as he hereafter.

Then they asked Mr. Feeble-Mind how he fell into his hands.

Mr. Feeble-Mind: Then said the poor man,[64] I am a sickly man, as you see: and because death did usually once a day knock at my door, I thought I should never be well at home; so I betook myself to a pilgrim's life, and have traveled hither from the town of Uncertain, where I and my father were born. I am a man of no strength at all of body, nor yet of mind, but would, if I could, though I can but crawl, spend my life in the pilgrim's way.[65] When I came at the gate that is at the head of the way, the Lord of that place did entertain me freely; neither objected he against my weakly looks,[66] nor against my feeble mind; but gave me such things as were necessary for my journey, and bid me hope to the end. When I came to

63. While slaying the giant Slay-good, Mr. Great-Heart also rescues this man who was captive to the giant.

64. Mr. Feeble-Mind's story serves as another pilgrimage narrative in Part II. Bunyan provides a number of pilgrim narratives in the second part in order to show that the way to eternal life can look very different for different pilgrims. There are certain experiences common to all Christians. But there are also differences in each person's journey due to individual temperaments and God's providential dealings.

65. Though Mr. Feeble-Mind is a weak man both in body and mind, he is a committed disciple of the Lord. He will go on the journey even if it means he crawls the whole way.

66. The Christian faith isn't for the strong and proud. It is for weak beggars who simply need the grace of God and cleansing blood of Jesus Christ. The fact is, we are all weak. Blessed are the poor in spirit (Matt. 5:3).

the house of the Interpreter, I received much kindness there: and because the hill of Difficulty was judged too hard for me, I was carried up that by one of his servants.[67] Indeed, I have found much relief from pilgrims, though none were willing to go so softly as I am forced to do: yet still as they came on, they bid me be of good cheer, and said, that it was the will of their Lord that comfort should be given to the feeble-minded, 1 Thess. 5:14; and so went on their own pace. When I was come to Assault-lane, then this giant met with me, and bid me prepare for an encounter. But, alas, feeble one that I was, I had more need of a cordial;[68] so he came up and took me. I conceited he would not kill me. Also when he had got me into his den, since I went not with him willingly, I believed I should come out alive again; for I have heard, that not any pilgrim that is taken captive by violent hands, if he keeps heart whole towards his Master, is, by the laws of providence, to die by the hand of the enemy. Robbed I looked to be, and robbed to be sure I am; but I have, as you see, escaped with life, for the which I thank my King as the author, and you as the means. Other brunts I also look for; but this I have resolved on, to wit, to run when I can, to go when I cannot run, and to creep when I cannot go.[69] As to the main, I thank him that loved me, I am fixed; my way is before me, my mind is beyond the river that has no bridge, though I am, as you see, but of a feeble mind.

Mr. Honest: Then said old Mr. Honest, Have not you, sometime ago, been acquainted with one Mr. Fearing, a pilgrim?

Mr. Feeble-Mind: Acquainted with him! Yes, he came from the town of Stupidity, which lieth four degrees to the northward of the city of Destruction, and as many off of where I was born: yet we were well acquainted, for indeed he was my uncle, my father's brother. He and I have been much of a temper:[70] he was a little shorter than I, but yet we were much of a complexion.

Mr. Honest: I perceive you knew him, and I am apt to believe also that you were related one to another; for you have his

67. As with Mr. Fearing, the Lord is full of kind compassion. He does not break the "bruised reed" (Matt. 12:20). Even though some of Christ's servants may be weaker, the Lord mercifully provides help to sustain even His weakest children. In this case, Mr. Feeble-Mind was carried up the Hill of Difficulty by one of the Lord's servants. Christians are to help one another and be there for those who are weaker in our midst. "Now we exhort you, brethren, warn those who are unruly, comfort the fainthearted, uphold the weak, be patient with all." (1 Thess. 5:14)

68. A "cordial" is a medicine.

69. That is, "to crawl" when he cannot run.

70. Mr. Feeble-Mind and Mr. Fearing were of a very similar personality.

whitely look,[71] a cast like his with your eye, and your speech is much alike.

Mr. Feeble-Mind: Most have said so that have known us both: and, besides, what I have read in him I have for the most part found in myself.

Gaius: Come, sir, said good Gaius, be of good cheer; you are welcome to me, and to my house. What thou hast a mind to, call for freely; and what thou wouldst have my servants do for thee, they will do it with a ready mind.

Then said Mr. Feeble-Mind, This is an unexpected favor, and as the sun shining out of a very dark cloud. Did giant Slay-good intend me this favor when he stopped me, and resolved to let me go no further? Did he intend, that after he had rifled my pockets I should go to Gaius mine host? Yet so it is.

Now, just as Mr. Feeble-Mind and Gaius were thus in talk, there came one running, and called at the door, and said, that about a mile and a half off there was one Mr. Not-right, a pilgrim, struck dead upon the place where he was, with a thunderbolt.

Mr. Feeble-Mind: Alas! said Mr. Feeble-Mind, is he slain? He overtook me some days before I came so far as hither, and would be my company-keeper. He was also with me when Slay-good the giant took me, but he was nimble of his heels, and escaped; but it seems he escaped to die, and I was taken to live.

"What one would think doth seek to slay outright,
Ofttimes delivers from the saddest plight.
That very Providence whose face is death,
Doth ofttimes to the lowly life bequeath.
I taken was, he did escape and flee;
Hands cross'd gave death to him and life to me."

Now, about this time Matthew and Mercy were married; also Gaius gave his daughter Phebe to James, Matthew's brother, to wife; after which time they yet stayed about ten days at Gaius' house, spending their time and the seasons like as pilgrims use to do.

71. This is a somewhat humorous and very appropriate description of those who are fearful and weak.

When they were to depart, Gaius made them a feast, and they did eat and drink, and were merry. Now the hour was come that they must be gone; wherefore Mr. Great-Heart called for a reckoning. But Gaius told him, that at his house it was not the custom for pilgrims to pay for their entertainment.[72] He boarded them by the year, but looked for his pay from the good Samaritan, who had promised him, at his return, whatsoever charge he was at with them, faithfully to repay him. Luke 10:34,35. Then said Mr. Great-Heart to him,

Mr. Great-Heart: Beloved, thou doest faithfully whatsoever thou doest to the brethren, and to strangers, who have borne witness of thy charity before the church, whom if thou yet bring forward on their journey, after a godly sort, thou shalt do well. 3 John 5,6. Then Gaius took his leave of them all, and his children, and particularly of Mr. Feeble-Mind. He also gave him something to drink by the way.

Now Mr. Feeble-Mind, when they were going out of the door, made as if he intended to linger. The which, when Mr. Great-Heart espied, he said, Come, Mr. Feeble-Mind, pray do you go along with us: I will be your conductor, and you shall fare as the rest.[73]

Mr. Feeble-Mind: Alas! I want a suitable companion. You are all lusty and strong,[74] but I, as you see, am weak; I choose, therefore, rather to come behind, lest, by reason of my many infirmities, I should be both a burden to myself and to you. I am, as I said, a man of a weak and feeble mind, and shall be offended and made weak at that which others can bear. I shall like no laughing; I shall like no gay attire; I shall like no unprofitable questions. Nay, I am so weak a man as to be offended with that which others have a liberty to do. I do not yet know all the truth: I am a very ignorant Christian man. Sometimes, if I hear some rejoice in the Lord, it troubles me because I cannot do so too. It is with me as it is with a weak man among the strong, or as with a sick man among the healthy, or as a lamp despised; so that I know not what to do. "He that is

72. Gaius' hospitality is provided free of charge. "Be hospitable to one another without grumbling." (1 Pet. 4:9)

73. Mr. Feeble-Mind is invited to join the pilgrims on the journey. Though he is a weak man, yet with a strong conductor, he will be safe on the pilgrim path.

74. "Healthy, full of vigor, and strong"

ready to slip with his feet is as a lamp despised in the thought of him that is at ease." Job 12:5.

Mr. Great-Heart: But, brother, said Mr. Great-Heart, I have it in commission to comfort the feeble-minded, and to support the weak. You must needs go along with us; we will wait for you; we will lend you our help; we will deny ourselves of some things, both opinionative and practical, for your sake: we will not enter into doubtful disputations before you; we will be made all things to you, rather than you shall be left behind.[75] 1 Thess. 5:14; Rom. 14; 1 Cor. 8:9-13; 9:22.

Now, all this while they were at Gaius' door; and behold, as they were thus in the heat of their discourse, Mr. Ready-to-halt came by, with his crutches in his hand, and he also was going on pilgrimage.[76]

Mr. Feeble-Mind: Then said Mr. Feeble-Mind to him, Man, how camest thou hither? I was but now complaining that I had not a suitable companion, but thou art according to my wish. Welcome, welcome, good Mr. Ready-to-halt; I hope thou and I may be some help.

Mr. Ready-to-Halt: I shall be glad of thy company, said the other; and, good Mr. Feeble-Mind, rather than we will part, since we are thus happily met, I will lend thee one of my crutches.

Mr. Feeble-Mind: Nay, said he, though I thank thee for thy good-will, I am not inclined to halt before I am lame. How-beit, I think when occasion is, it may help me against a dog.

Mr. Ready-to-Halt: If either myself or my crutches can do thee a pleasure, we are both at thy command, good Mr. Feeble-Mind.

Thus, therefore, they went on. Mr. Great-Heart and Mr. Honest went before, Christiana and her children went next, and Mr. Feeble-Mind came behind, and Mr. Ready-to-halt with his crutches. Then said Mr. Honest,

Mr. Honest: Pray, sir, now we are upon the road, tell us some profitable things of some that have gone on pilgrimage before us.

75. Though Mr. Feeble-Mind is a weak Christian, often weak in conscience, weak in faith, and ignorant of certain truths, yet it is the obligation of all Christians to uphold the weak. Even if it means denying our own liberties for those weak in conscience, we should do so in order to love the weaker brother (Rom. 14).

76. Mr. Ready-to-halt is another picture of the weak disciple who makes the journey on crutches. As the group of pilgrims continues to expand, Bunyan's imagery seems more and more like the church, the body of Christ, journeying together to the Celestial City. While Part I did indeed contain companions for Christian, it did not have the same corporate and covenantal emphasis that we find in Part II. This large pilgrim band contains a diversity of people just as the Scriptures describe the body of Christ as a various and multi-colored tapestry of God's grace.

Mr. Great-Heart: With a good will. I suppose you have heard how Christian of old did meet with Apollyon in the Valley of Humiliation, and also what hard work he had to go through the Valley of the Shadow of Death. Also I think you cannot but have heard how Faithful was put to it by Madam Wanton, with Adam the First, with one Discontent, and Shame; four as deceitful villains as a man can meet with upon the road.

Mr. Honest: Yes, I have heard of all this; but indeed good Faithful was hardest put to it with Shame: he was an unwearied one.

Mr. Great-Heart: Aye; for, as the pilgrim well said, he of all men had the wrong name.

Mr. Honest: But pray, sir, where was it that Christian and Faithful met Talkative? That same was also a notable one.

Mr. Great-Heart: He was a confident fool; yet many follow his ways.

Mr. Honest: He had like to have beguiled Faithful.

Mr. Great-Heart: Aye, but Christian put him into a way quickly to find him out.

Thus they went on till they came to the place where Evangelist met with Christian and Faithful, and prophesied to them what should befall them at Vanity Fair. Then said their guide, Hereabouts did Christian and Faithful meet with Evangelist, who prophesied to them of what troubles they should meet with at Vanity Fair.

Mr. Honest: Say you so? I dare say it was a hard chapter that then he did read unto them.

Mr. Great-Heart: It was so, but he gave them encouragement withal. But what do we talk of them? They were a couple of lion-like men; they had set their faces like a flint. Do not you remember how undaunted they were when they stood before the judge?

Mr. Honest: Well: Faithful bravely suffered.

Mr. Great-Heart: So he did, and as brave things came on't; for Hopeful, and some others, as the story relates it, were converted by his death.

Mr. Honest: Well, but pray go on; for you are well acquainted with things.

Mr. Great-Heart: Above all that Christian met with after he had passed through Vanity Fair, one By-ends was the arch one.

Mr. Honest: By-ends! what was he?

Mr. Great-Heart: A very arch fellow, a downright hypocrite; one that would be religious, whichever way the world went; but so cunning, that he would be sure never to lose or suffer for it. He had his mode of religion for every fresh occasion, and his wife was as good at it as he. He would turn from opinion to opinion; yea, and plead for so doing, too. But, so far as I could learn, he came to an ill end with his by-ends; nor did I ever hear that any of his children were ever of any esteem with any that truly feared God.[77]

Now by this time they were come within sight of the town of Vanity, where Vanity Fair is kept. So, when they saw that they were so near the town, they consulted with one another how they should pass through the town; and some said one thing, and some another. At last Mr. Great-Heart said, I have, as you may understand, often been a conductor of pilgrims through this town. Now, I am acquainted with one Mr. Mnason,[78] Acts 21:16, a Cyprusian by nation, an old disciple, at whose house we may lodge. If you think good, we will turn in there.

Content, said old Honest; Content, said Christiana; Content, said Mr. Feeble-Mind; and so they said all.[79] Now you must think it was eventide by that they got to the outside of the town; but Mr. Great-Heart knew the way to the old man's house. So thither they came; and he called at the door, and the old man within knew his tongue as soon as ever he heard it; so he opened the door, and they all came in. Then said Mnason, their host, How far have ye come to-day? So they said, from

77. A character from Part I, By-ends, is mentioned here. By-ends was a picture of the man who goes with whatever the current public opinion is. He would change his convictions immediately when his previous convictions became unpopular.
78. This character, like Gaius, is another hospitable host who provides lodging for the pilgrims in Vanity Fair (Acts 21:16). Both Gaius and Mnason are mentioned in Scripture and adapted by Bunyan for his story.
79. The one-word reply "content" is a simple affirmation by each of the pilgrims agreeing to Mr. Great-Heart's suggestion.

80. "You have gone a good distance."

the house of Gaius our friend. I promise you, said he, you have gone a good stitch.[80] You may well be weary; sit down. So they sat down.

Mr. Great-Heart: Then said their guide, Come, what cheer, good sirs? I dare say you are welcome to my friend.

Mr. Mnason: I also, said Mr. Mnason, do bid you welcome; and whatever you want, do but say, and we will do what we can to get it for you.

Mr. Honest: Our great want, a while since, was harbor and good company, and now I hope we have both.

Mr. Mnason: For harbor, you see what it is; but for good company, that will appear in the trial.

Mr. Great-Heart: Well, said Mr. Great-Heart, will you have the pilgrims up into their lodging?

Mr. Mnason: I will, said Mr. Mnason So he had them to their respective places; and also showed them a very fair dining-room, where they might be, and sup together until the time should come to go to rest.

Now, when they were seated in their places, and were a little cheery after their journey, Mr. Honest asked his landlord if there was any store of good people in the town.

Mr. Mnason: We have a few: for indeed they are but a few when compared with them on the other side.

Mr. Honest: But how shall we do to see some of them? for the sight of good men to them that are going on pilgrimage, is like the appearing of the moon and stars to them that are sailing upon the seas.[81]

Mr. Mnason: Then Mr. Mnason stamped with his foot, and his daughter Grace came up. So he said unto her, Grace, go you, tell my friends, Mr. Contrite, Mr. Holy-man, Mr. Love-saints, Mr. Dare-not-lie, and Mr. Penitent, that I have a friend or two at my house who have a mind this evening to see them. So Grace went to call them, and they came; and after salutation made, they sat down together at the table.

Then said Mr. Mnason their landlord, My neighbors, I have, as you see, a company of strangers come to my house;

81. Mr. Honest wisely remarks that to see fellow Christians on pilgrimage refreshes the spirit of other pilgrims. Christian fellowship is a rich blessing in this fallen world. We are harassed by the devil, by the world, and by our own flesh. The refreshment of fellow pilgrims is much needed on the difficult journey we each walk.

they are pilgrims: they come from afar, and are going to Mount Zion. But who, quoth he, do you think this is? pointing his finger to Christiana. It is Christiana, the wife of Christian, the famous pilgrim, who, with Faithful his brother, was so shamefully handled in our town. At that they stood amazed, saying, We little thought to see Christiana when Grace came to call us; wherefore this is a very comfortable surprise. They then asked her of her welfare, and if these young men were her husband's sons. And when she had told them they were, they said, The King whom you love and serve make you as your father, and bring you where he is in peace.

Mr. Honest: Then Mr. Honest (when they were all sat down) asked Mr. Contrite and the rest, in what posture their town was at present.

Mr. Contrite: You may be sure we are full of hurry in fairtime. 'T is hard keeping our hearts and spirits in good order when we are in a cumbered condition. He that lives in such a place as this is, and has to do with such as we have, has need of an item to caution him to take heed every moment of the day.[82]

Mr. Honest: But how are your neighbors now for quietness?

Mr. Contrite: They are much more moderate now than formerly. You know how Christian and Faithful were used at our town; but of late, I say, they have been far more moderate. I think the blood of Faithful lieth as a load upon them till now; for since they burned him, they have been ashamed to burn any more. In those days we were afraid to walk the street; but now we can show our heads. Then the name of a professor was odious; now, especially in some parts of our town, (for you know our town is large,) religion is counted honorable.[83] Then said Mr. Contrite to them, Pray how fareth it with you in your pilgrimage? how stands the country affected towards you?

Mr. Honest: It happens to us as it happeneth to wayfaring men: sometimes our way is clean, sometimes foul; sometimes up hill, sometimes down hill; we are seldom at a certainty.[84] The wind is not always on our backs, nor is every one a friend

82. Living in this world requires us to be watchful. There are temptations and deceits all around us.

83. The death of Faithful at the hands of the people of Vanity Fair had a profound effect on the town. Some were loaded with guilt at killing an innocent man. Others came to the faith. As Tertullian once remarked, "The blood of the martyrs is the seed of the church."

84. Mr. Honest describes in appropriate terms the way the Christian life works. It is the way things go with "wayfaring men." Those on the pilgrim pathway can expect toils, dangers, and snares. "We are hard-pressed on every side, yet not crushed; we are perplexed, but not in despair; persecuted, but not forsaken; struck down, but not destroyed—always carrying about in the body the dying of the Lord Jesus, that the life of Jesus also may be manifested in our body." (2 Cor. 4:8-10)

85. "Rubs" refers to "blows" or "trials."

86. Bunyan explicitly refers to the house of Gaius here as a reference to the whole church (3 John).

that we meet with in the way. We have met with some notable rubs already,[85] and what are yet behind we know not; but for the most part, we find it true that has been talked of old, A good man must suffer trouble.

Mr. Contrite: You talk of rubs; what rubs have you met withal?

Mr. Honest: Nay, ask Mr. Great-Heart, our guide; for he can give the best account of that.

Mr. Great-Heart: We have been beset three or four times already. First, Christiana and her children were beset by two ruffians, who they feared would take away their lives. We were beset by Giant Bloody-man, Giant Maul, and Giant Slay-good. Indeed, we did rather beset the last than were beset by him. And thus it was: after we had been some time at the house of Gaius mine host, and of the whole church,[86] we were minded upon a time to take our weapons with us, and go see if we could light upon any of those that are enemies to pilgrims; for we heard that there was a notable one thereabouts. Now Gaius knew his haunt better than I, because he dwelt thereabout. So we looked, and looked, till at last we discerned the mouth of his cave: then we were glad, and plucked up our spirits. So we approached up to his den; and lo, when we came there, he had dragged, by mere force, into his net, this poor man, Mr. Feeble-Mind, and was about to bring him to his end. But when he saw us, supposing, as we thought, he had another prey, he left the poor man in his hole, and came out. So we fell to it full sore, and he lustily laid about him; but, in conclusion, he was brought down to the ground, and his head cut off, and set up by the way-side for a terror to such as should after practise such ungodliness. That I tell you the truth, here is the man himself to affirm it, who was as a lamb taken out of the mouth of the lion.

Mr. Feeble-Mind: Then said Mr. Feeble-Mind, I found this true, to my cost and comfort: to my cost, when he threatened to pick my bones every moment; and to my comfort, when

I saw Mr. Great-Heart and his friends, with their weapons, approach so near for my deliverance.

Mr. Holy-Man: Then said Mr. Holy-man, There are two things that they have need to possess who go on pilgrimage; courage, and an unspotted life.[87] If they have not courage, they can never hold on their way; and if their lives be loose, they will make the very name of a pilgrim stink.

Mr. Love-Saints: Then said Mr. Love-saints, I hope this caution is not needful among you: but truly there are many that go upon the road, who rather declare themselves strangers to pilgrimage, than strangers and pilgrims on the earth.

Mr. Dare-Not-Lie: Then said Mr. Dare-not-lie, 'Tis true. They have neither the pilgrim's weed, nor the pilgrim's courage; they go not uprightly, but all awry with their feet; one shoe goeth inward, another outward; and their hosen are out behind: here a rag, and there a rent, to the disparagement of their Lord.

Mr. Penitent: These things, said Mr. Penitent, they ought to be troubled for; nor are the pilgrims like to have that grace put upon them and their Pilgrim's Progress[88] as they desire, until the way is cleared of such spots and blemishes. Thus they sat talking and spending the time until supper was set upon the table, unto which they went, and refreshed their weary bodies: so they went to rest.

Now they staid in the fair a great while, at the house of Mr. Mnason, who in process of time gave his daughter Grace unto Samuel, Christian's son, to wife, and his daughter Martha to Joseph.[89]

The time, as I said, that they staid here, was long, for it was not now as in former times. Wherefore the pilgrims grew acquainted with many of the good people of the town, and did them what service they could. Mercy, as she was wont, labored much for the poor: wherefore their bellies and backs blessed her, and she was there an ornament to her profession. And, to say the truth for Grace, Phebe, and Martha, they were all of a very good nature, and did much good in their places. They

87. "Pure and undefiled religion before God and the Father is this: to visit orphans and widows in their trouble, and to keep oneself unspotted from the world." (Jas. 1:27)

88. Bunyan directly references the title of his book here.

89. The two remaining sons of Christiana are now married.

90. A reference to the women bearing children. Children are described as the "fruit of the womb." (Ps. 127:3)

91. "To nurture its offspring"

92. This monster is a reference to the ugly and evil beast of Revelation 17. Fallen mankind (the people of Vanity Fair) are subject to the enslavement of the beast.

93. Mr. Great-Heart and his companions go out to fight against the hideous beast. Bunyan wants us to see the power of God's army in this picture. By the spiritual weapons we have been supplied, we do battle against the principalities and powers (Eph. 6:10-20). Let us give thanks that our Lord Jesus is greater than "he who is in the world" (1 John 4:4).

were also all of them very fruitful;[90] so that Christian's name, as was said before, was like to live in the world.

While they lay here, there came a monster out of the woods, and slew many of the people of the town. It would also carry away their children, and teach them to suck its whelps.[91] Now, no man in the town durst so much as face this monster; but all fled when they heard the noise of his coming.

The monster was like unto no one beast on the earth. Its body was like a dragon, and it had seven heads and ten horns. It made great havoc of children, and yet it was governed by a woman. Rev. 17:3. This monster propounded conditions to men; and such men as loved their lives more than their souls, accepted of those conditions. So they came under.[92]

Now Mr. Great-Heart, together with those who came to visit the pilgrims at Mr. Mnason's house, entered into a covenant to go and engage this beast, if perhaps they might deliver the people of this town from the paws and mouth of this so devouring a serpent.

Then did Mr. Great-Heart, Mr. Contrite, Mr. Holy-man, Mr. Dare-not-lie, and Mr. Penitent, with their weapons, go forth to meet him. Now the monster at first was very rampant, and looked upon these enemies with great disdain; but they so belabored him, being sturdy men at arms, that they made him make a retreat: so they came home to Mr. Mnason's house again.

The monster, you must know, had his certain seasons to come out in, and to make his attempts upon the children of the people of the town. At these seasons did these valiant worthies watch him, and did still continually assault him; insomuch that in process of time he became not only wounded, but lame. Also he has not made that havoc of the townsmen's children as formerly he had done; and it is verily believed by some that this beast will die of his wounds.[93]

This, therefore, made Mr. Great-Heart and his fellows of great fame in this town; so that many of the people that wanted their taste of things, yet had a reverent esteem and respect for them. Upon this account, therefore, it was, that these pilgrims got not much hurt here.[94] True, there were some of the baser sort, that could see no more than a mole, nor understand any more than a beast; these had no reverence for these men, and took no notice of their valor and adventures.

94. The account of Vanity Fair is very different from Part I. They encounter little struggle against the people of the town. This is due, in part, to the influence men and women of faith have had upon the town. Christ's reign has been further established over Vanity Fair.

Book 2
Chapter 7

Well, the time grew on that the pilgrims must go on their way; wherefore they prepared for their journey. They sent for their friends; they conferred with them; they had some time set apart therein to commit each other to the protection of their Prince. There were again that brought them of such things as they had, that were fit for the weak and the strong, for the women and the men, and so laded them with such things as were necessary. Acts 28:10. Then they set forward on their way; and their friends accompanying them so far as was convenient, they again committed each other to the protection of their King, and parted.

They therefore that were of the pilgrims' company went on, and Mr. Great-Heart went before them. Now, the women and children being weakly, they were forced to go as they could bear; by which means Mr. Ready-to-halt and Mr. Feeble-Mind, had more to sympathize with their condition.

When they were gone from the townsmen, and when their friends had bid them farewell, they quickly came to the place where Faithful was put to death. Therefore they made a stand, and thanked him that had enabled him to bear his cross so well; and the rather, because they now found that they had a benefit by such a manly suffering as his was.

They went on therefore after this a good way further, talking of Christian and Faithful, and how Hopeful joined himself to Christian after that Faithful was dead.

Now they were come up with the hill Lucre,[1] where the silver mine was which took Demas off from his pilgrimage, and into which, as some think, By-ends fell and perished; wherefore they considered that. But when they were come to the old monument that stood over against the hill Lucre, to wit, to the pillar of salt, that stood also within view of Sodom and its stinking lake, they marvelled, as did Christian before, that men of such knowledge and ripeness of wit as they were, should be so blinded as to turn aside here. Only they considered again, that nature is not affected with the harms that others have met with, especially if that thing upon which they look has an attracting virtue upon the foolish eye.

I saw now, that they went on till they came to the river that was on this side of the Delectable Mountains; to the river where the fine trees grow on both sides, and whose leaves, if taken inwardly, are good against surfeits;[2] where the meadows are green all the year long, and where they might lie down safely. Psa. 23:2.

By this river-side, in the meadows, there were cotes and folds for sheep,[3] a house built for the nourishing and bringing up of those lambs, the babes of those women that go on pilgrimage. Also there was here one that was intrusted with them, who could have compassion; and that could gather these lambs with his arm, and carry them in his bosom, and gently lead those that were with young. Heb. 5:2; Isa. 40:11. Now, to the care of this man Christiana admonished her four daughters to commit their little ones,[4] that by these waters they might be housed, harbored, succored, and nourished, and that none of them might be lacking in time to come. This man, if any of them go astray, or be lost, will bring them again; he will also bind up that which was broken, and will strengthen them that are sick. Jer. 23:4; Ezek. 34:11-16. Here they will never want meat, drink, and clothing; here they will be kept

1. "Lucre" is a term for money, especially regarded as something that is gained in a dishonest way.

2. "Surfeits" is an old term for an illness caused by excessive eating or drinking.

3. A "cote" is a shelter for animals.

4. The grandchildren of Christiana are to be entrusted to this man who is the picture of the good shepherd. In this meadow near the Delectable Mountains, a beautiful picture is sketched by Bunyan of the Lord's tender mercy and loving shepherding of his lambs. He feeds them, and He protects them, He guides them.

from thieves and robbers; for this man will die before one of those committed to his trust shall be lost. Besides, here they shall be sure to have good nurture and admonition, and shall be taught to walk in right paths, and that you know is a favor of no small account. Also here, as you see, are delicate waters, pleasant meadows, dainty flowers, variety of trees, and such as bear wholesome fruit: fruit, not like that which Matthew ate of, that fell over the wall out of Beelzebub's garden; but fruit that procureth health where there is none, and that continueth and increaseth it where it is. So they were content to commit their little ones to him; and that which was also an encouragement to them so to do, was, for that all this was to be at the charge of the King, and so was as an hospital to young children and orphans.

Now they went on. And when they were come to By-path Meadow, to the stile over which Christian went with his fellow Hopeful, when they were taken by Giant Despair and put into Doubting Castle, they sat down, and consulted what was best to be done: to wit, now they were so strong, and had got such a man as Mr. Great-Heart for their conductor, whether they had not best to make an attempt upon the giant, demolish his castle, and if there were any pilgrims in it, to set them at liberty before they went any further. So one said one thing, and another said the contrary. One questioned if it was lawful to go upon unconsecrated ground; another said they might, provided their end was good; but Mr. Great-Heart said, Though that assertion offered last cannot be universally true, yet I have a commandment to resist sin, to overcome evil, to fight the good fight of faith:[5] and I pray, with whom should I fight this good fight, if not with Giant Despair? I will therefore attempt the taking away of his life, and the demolishing of Doubting Castle. Then said he, Who will go with me? Then said old Honest, I will. And so will we too, said Christiana's four sons, Matthew, Samuel, Joseph, and James; for they were young men and strong.[6] 1 John 2:13,14. So they left the women in the road, and with them Mr. Feeble-Mind, and Mr. Ready-to-

5. Mr. Great-Heart is a strong warrior called to fight against the world, the flesh, and the devil. Giant Despair is an enemy of God and His people. Therefore, he determines to go and engage combat with the giant.

6. "I have written to you, young men, because you are strong, and the word of God abides in you, and you have overcome the wicked one." (1 John 2:14)

halt with his crutches, to be their guard until they came back; for in that place the Giant Despair dwelt so near, they keeping in the road, a little child might lead them. Isa. 11:6.

So Mr. Great-Heart, old Honest, and the four young men, went to go up to Doubting Castle, to look for Giant Despair. When they came at the castle gate, they knocked for entrance with an unusual noise. At that the old Giant comes to the gate, and Diffidence his wife follows. Then said he, Who and what is he that is so hardy, as after this manner to molest the Giant Despair? Mr. Great-Heart replied, It is I, Great-Heart, one of the King of the Celestial country's conductors of pilgrims to their place; and I demand of thee that thou open thy gates for my entrance: prepare thyself also to fight, for I am come to take away thy head; and to demolish Doubting Castle.

Now Giant Despair, because he was a giant, thought no man could overcome him: and again thought he, Since heretofore I have made a conquest of angels, shall Great-Heart make me afraid? So he harnessed himself, and went out. He had a cap of steel upon his head, a breast-plate of fire girded to him, and he came out in iron shoes, with a great club in his hand. Then these six men made up to him, and beset him behind and before: also, when Diffidence the giantess came up to help him, old Mr. Honest cut her down at one blow. Then they fought for their lives, and Giant Despair was brought down to the ground, but was very loth die.[7] He struggled hard, and had, as they say, as many lives as a cat; but Great-Heart was his death, for he left him not till he had severed his head from his shoulders.[8]

Then they fell to demolishing Doubting Castle, and that you know might with ease be done, since Giant Despair was dead. They were seven days in destroying of that; and in it of pilgrims they found one Mr. Despondency, almost starved to death, and one Much-afraid, his daughter: these two they saved alive.[9] But it would have made you wonder to have seen the dead bodies that lay here and there in the castle yard, and how full of dead men's bones the dungeon was.

7. It was difficult to kill Giant Despair.

8. In almost all of the combats described in Part II, Great-Heart has severed the head of many an enemy. Like David who severed Goliath's head, so Great-Heart makes a complete end of these enemies of God. Let us take courage from these allegorical examples. The enemies of the Lord will fall under the power of Jesus Christ. We are well equipped for the battle when we are "strong in the Lord" (Eph. 6:10). "And the God of peace will crush Satan under your feet shortly." (Rom. 16:20)

9. Two people are rescued from the clutches of Giant Despair: Mr. Despondency and Much-Afraid. These two are now added to the large group of pilgrims.

10. "Jocund" means "cheerful" or "light-hearted."

When Mr. Great-Heart and his companions had performed this exploit, they took Mr. Despondency, and his daughter Much-afraid, into their protection; for they were honest people, though they were prisoners in Doubting Castle to that tyrant Giant Despair. They, therefore, I say, took with them the head of the giant, (for his body they had buried under a heap of stones,) and down to the road and to their companions they came, and showed them what they had done. Now, when Feeble-Mind and Ready-to-halt saw that it was the head of Giant Despair indeed, they were very jocund and merry.[10] Now Christiana, if need was, could play upon the viol, and her daughter Mercy upon the lute: so, since they were so merry disposed, she played them a lesson, and Ready-to-halt would dance. So he took Despondency's daughter, Much-afraid, by the hand, and to dancing they went in the road. True, he could not dance without one crutch in his hand, but I promise you he footed it well: also the girl was to be commended, for she answered the music handsomely.

As for Mr. Despondency, the music was not so much to him; he was for feeding rather than dancing, for that he was almost starved. So Christiana gave him some of her bottle of spirits for present relief, and then prepared him something to eat; and in a little time the old gentleman came to himself, and began to be finely revived.

Now I saw in my dream, when all these things were finished, Mr. Great-Heart took the head of Giant Despair, and set it upon a pole by the highway-side, right over against the pillar that Christian erected for a caution to pilgrims that came after, to take heed of entering into his grounds.

Then he writ under it upon a marble stone these verses following:

"This is the head of him whose name only
In former times did pilgrims terrify.
His castle's down, and Diffidence his wife
Brave Mr. Great-Heart has bereft of life.
Despondency, his daughter Much-afraid,

Great-Heart for them also the man has play'd.
Who hereof doubts, if he'll but cast his eye
Up hither, may his scruples satisfy.
This head also, when doubting cripples dance,
Doth show from fears they have deliverance."

When these men had thus bravely showed themselves against Doubting Castle, and had slain Giant Despair, they went forward, and went on till they came to the Delectable Mountains, where Christian and Hopeful refreshed themselves with the varieties of the place. They also acquainted themselves with the shepherds there, who welcomed them, as they had done Christian before, unto the Delectable Mountains.

Now the shepherds seeing so great a train follow Mr. Great-Heart, (for with him they were well acquainted,) they said unto him, Good sir, you have got a goodly company here; pray where did you find all these?

Then Mr. Great-Heart replied,[11]
"First, here is Christiana and her train,
Her sons, and her sons' wives, who, like the wain,[12]
Keep by the pole, and do by compass steer
From sin to grace, else they had not been here.
Next here's old Honest come on pilgrimage,
Ready-to-halt too, who I dare engage
True-hearted is, and so is Feeble-Mind,
Who willing was not to be left behind.
Despondency, good man, is coming after,
And so also is Much-afraid, his daughter.
May we have entertainment here, or must
We further go? Let's knew whereon to trust."

Then said the shepherds, This is a comfortable company. You are welcome to us; for we have for the feeble, as well as for the strong. Our Prince has an eye to what is done to the least of these; therefore Infirmity must not be a block to our entertainment. Matt. 25:40. So they had them to the palace door, and then said unto them, Come in, Mr. Feeble-Mind;

11. In the brief poem that follows, Mr. Great-Heart provides a list of all the pilgrims being conducted by this point in the story.

12. A "wain" is a "wagon" or "cart."

come in Mr. Ready-to-halt; Come in, Mr. Despondency, and Mrs. Much-afraid his daughter. These, Mr. Great-Heart, said the shepherds to the guide, we call in by name, for that they are most subject to draw back; but as for you, and the rest that are strong, we leave you to your wonted liberty. Then said Mr. Great-Heart, This day I see that grace doth shine in your faces, and that you are my Lord's shepherds indeed; for that you have not pushed these diseased neither with side nor shoulder, but have rather strewed their way into the palace with flowers, as you should. Ezek. 34:21.

So the feeble and weak went in, and Mr. Great-Heart and the rest did follow. When they were also set down, the shepherds said to those of the weaker sort, What is it that you would have? for, said they, all things must be managed here to the supporting of the weak, as well as to the warning of the unruly. So they made them a feast of things easy of digestion, and that were pleasant to the palate and nourishing; the which when they had received, they went to their rest, each one respectively unto his proper place.

When morning was come, because the mountains were high and the day clear, and because it was the custom of the shepherds to show the pilgrims before their departure some rarities, therefore, after they were ready, and had refreshed themselves, the shepherds took them out into the fields, and showed them first what they had shown to Christian before.

Then they had them to some new places. The first was Mount Marvel, where they looked, and beheld a man at a distance that tumbled the hills about with words.[13] Then they asked the shepherds what that should mean. So they told them, that that man was the son of one Mr. Great-grace, of whom you read in the first part of the records of the Pilgrim's Progress; and he is set there to teach pilgrims how to believe down, or to tumble out of their ways, what difficulties they should meet with, by faith. Mark 11:23,24. Then said Mr. Great-Heart, I know him; he is a man above many.

13. This man is the son of Mr. Great-grace who himself has great faith. By that faith, he is able to move mountains. This is a literal picture of what Jesus describes in Mark 11: "For assuredly, I say to you, whoever says to this mountain, 'Be removed and be cast into the sea,' and does not doubt in his heart, but believes that those things he says will be done, he will have whatever he says. Therefore I say to you, whatever things you ask when you pray, believe that you receive them, and you will have them." (Mark 11:23-24)

Then they had them to another place, called Mount Innocence. And there they saw a man clothed all in white; and two men, Prejudice and Ill-will, continually casting dirt upon him. Now behold, the dirt, whatsoever they cast at him, would in a little time fall off again, and his garment would look as clear as if no dirt had been cast thereat.[14] Then said the pilgrims, What means this? The shepherds answered, This man is named Godlyman, and this garment is to show the innocency of his life. Now, those that throw dirt at him are such as hate his well-doing; but, as you see the dirt will not stick upon his clothes, so it shall be with him that liveth innocently in the world. Whoever they be that would make such men dirty, they labor all in vain; for God, by that a little time is spent, will cause that their innocence shall break forth as the light, and their righteousness as the noonday.

Then they took them, and had them to Mount Charity, where they showed them a man that had a bundle of cloth lying before him, out of which he cut coats and garments for the poor that stood about him; yet his bundle or roll of cloth was never the less. Then said they, What should this be? This is, said the shepherds, to show you, that he who has a heart to give of his labor to the poor, shall never want wherewithal.[15] He that watereth shall be watered himself. And the cake that the widow gave to the prophet did not cause that she had the less in her barrel.[16]

They had them also to the place where they saw one Fool and one Want-wit washing an Ethiopian, with intention to make him white; but the more they washed him, the black-

14. A man who lives in a godly way enjoys the peace of a good conscience. For this reason, when people slander him, he can be sure that his conscience is clear before God. The mud cannot really stick. Peter describes this situation: "Having a good conscience, that when they defame you as evildoers, those who revile your good conduct in Christ may be ashamed." (1 Pet. 3:16)

15. We never need to worry about running out of resources to do good to others. When it comes to giving to others, let's remember that God owns the cattle on a thousand hills. He can provide all that we need to serve Him and to love others. "And God is able to make all grace abound toward you, that you, always having all sufficiency in all things, may have an abundance for every good work." (2 Cor. 9:8)

16. This is a reference to the widow of Zarephath who was miraculously provided food to feed her starving family as well as the prophet Elijah (1 Kings 17).

17. Bunyan is referring to the language of Jeremiah. "Can the Ethiopian change his skin or the leopard its spots? Then may you also do good who are accustomed to do evil." (Jer. 13:23) Just like an Ethiopian cannot change his skin color, so also a person who is wicked cannot be changed by external means. It is the grace of God that must transform such a person.

18. That is, Christiana informed the shepherds of Mercy's request.

19. The looking glass is likely a reference to the Word of God. James describes the Word of God as a mirror (Jas. 1:23-24).

er he was.[17] Then they asked the shepherds what that should mean. So they told them, saying, Thus it is with the vile person; all means used to get such a one a good name, shall in conclusion tend but to make him more abominable. Thus it was with the pharisees; and so it shall be with all hypocrites.

Then said Mercy, the wife of Matthew, to Christiana her mother, Mother, I would, if it might be, see the hole in the hill, or that commonly called the By-way to hell. So her mother brake her mind to the shepherds.[18] Then they went to the door; it was on the side of an hill; and they opened it, and bid Mercy hearken a while. So she hearkened, and heard one saying, Cursed be my father for holding of my feet back from the way of peace and life. Another said, Oh that I had been torn in pieces before I had, to save my life, lost my soul! And another said, If I were to live again, how would I deny myself, rather than to come to this place! Then there was as if the very earth groaned and quaked under the feet of this young woman for fear; so she looked white, and came trembling away, saying, Blessed be he and she that is delivered from this place!

Now, when the shepherds had shown them all these things, then they had them back to the palace, and entertained them with what the house would afford. But Mercy, being a young and married woman, longed for something that she saw there, but was ashamed to ask. Her mother-in-law then asked her what she ailed, for she looked as one not well. Then said Mercy, There is a looking-glass hangs up in the dining-room,[19] off which I cannot take my mind; if, therefore, I have it not, I think I shall miscarry. Then said her mother, I will mention thy wants to the shepherds, and they will not deny thee. But she said, I am ashamed that these men should know that I longed. Nay, my daughter, said she, it is no shame, but a virtue, to long for such a thing as that. So Mercy said, Then mother, if you please, ask the shepherds if they are willing to sell it.

Now the glass was one of a thousand. It would present a man, one way, with his own features exactly; and turn it but another way, and it would show one the very face and similitude of the Prince of pilgrims himself. Yes, I have talked with them that can tell, and they have said that they have seen the very crown of thorns upon his head by looking in that glass; they have therein also seen the holes in his hands, his feet, and his side. Yea, such an excellency is there in this glass, that it will show him to one where they have a mind to see him, whether living or dead; whether in earth, or in heaven; whether in a state of humiliation, or in his exaltation; whether coming to suffer, or coming to reign. James 1:23; 1 Cor. 13:12; 2 Cor. 3:18.

Christiana therefore went to the shepherds apart, (now the names of the shepherds were Knowledge, Experience, Watchful, and Sincere,) and said unto them, There is one of my daughters, a breeding woman,[20] that I think doth long for something that she hath seen in this house; and she thinks that she shall miscarry if she should by you be denied.

20. This simply means "a pregnant woman."

Experience: Call her, call her, she shall assuredly have what we can help her to. So they called her, and said to her, Mercy, what is that thing thou wouldst have? Then she blushed, and said, The great glass that hangs up in the dining-room. So Sincere ran and fetched it, and with a joyful consent it was given her. Then she bowed her head, and gave thanks, and said, By this I know that I have obtained favor in your eyes.

They also gave to the other young women such things as they desired, and to their husbands great commendations, for that they had joined with Mr. Great-Heart in the slaying of Giant Despair, and the demolishing of Doubting Castle.

About Christiana's neck the shepherds put a bracelet, and so did they about the necks of her four daughters; also they put ear-rings in their ears, and jewels on their foreheads.

When they were minded to go hence, they let them go in peace, but gave not to them those certain cautions which before were given to Christian and his companion. The reason was, for that these had Great-Heart to be their guide, who was one that was well acquainted with things, and so could give them their cautions more seasonably, to wit, even when the danger was nigh the approaching. What cautions Christian and his companion had received of the shepherds, they had also lost by that the time was come that they had need to put them in practice. Wherefore, here was the advantage that this company had over the other.

From thence they went on singing, and they said,
"Behold how fitly are the stages set
  For their relief that pilgrims are become,
And how they us receive without one let,
  That make the other life our mark and home!
What novelties they have to us they give,
  That we, though pilgrims, joyful lives may live;
They do upon us, too, such things bestow,
  That show we pilgrims are, where'er we go."

Book 2
Chapter 8

When they were gone from the shepherds, they quickly came to the place where Christian met with one Turn-away that dwelt in the town of Apostasy. Wherefore of him Mr. Great-Heart their guide now put them in mind, saying, This is the place where Christian met with one Turn-away, who carried with him the character of his rebellion at his back. And this I have to say concerning this man; he would hearken to no counsel, but once a falling, persuasion could not stop him. When he came to the place where the cross and sepulchre were, he did meet with one that did bid him look there; but he gnashed with his teeth, and stamped, and said he was resolved to go back to his own town. Before he came to the gate, he met with Evangelist, who offered to lay hands on him, to turn him into the way again; but this Turn-away resisted him, and having done much despite unto him, he got away over the wall, and so escaped his hand.

Then they went on; and just at the place where Little-Faith formerly was robbed, there stood a man with his sword drawn, and his face all over with blood. Then said Mr. Great-Heart, Who art thou? The man made answer, saying, I am one whose name is Valiant-for-truth.[1] I am a pilgrim, and am going to the Celestial City. Now, as I was in my way, there were three men that did beset me, and propounded unto me

1. The introduction of this new character, Valiant-for-truth, provides another opportunity to present a pilgrimage narrative. Many of the previous narratives of pilgrimage have been about those who are weak and yet sustained on the journey. Valiant-for-truth is presented as a picture of spiritual strength and maturity.

these three things: 1. Whether I would become one of them. 2. Or go back from whence I came. 3. Or die upon the place. Prov. 1:11-14. To the first I answered, I had been a true man for a long season, and therefore it could not be expected that I should now cast in my lot with thieves. Then they demanded what I would say to the second. So I told them that the place from whence I came, had I not found incommodity there, I had not forsaken it at all; but finding it altogether unsuitable to me, and very unprofitable for me, I forsook it for this way. Then they asked me what I said to the third. And I told them my life cost far more dear than that I should lightly give it away. Besides, you have nothing to do thus to put things to my choice; wherefore at your peril be it if you meddle. Then these three, to wit, Wild-head, Inconsiderate, and Pragmatic, drew upon me, and I also drew upon them. So we fell to it, one against three, for the space of above three hours. They have left upon me, as you see, some of the marks of their valor, and have also carried away with them some of mine. They are but just now gone; I suppose they might, as the saying is, hear your horse dash, and so they betook themselves to flight.

Mr. Great-Heart: But here was great odds, three against one.

Valiant-for-Truth: 'Tis true; but little and more are nothing to him that has the truth on his side: "Though an host should encamp against me," said one, Psa. 27:3, "my heart shall not fear: though war should rise against me, in this will I be confident," etc. Besides, said he, I have read in some records, that one man has fought an army: and how many did Samson slay with the jawbone of an ass![2]

Mr. Great-Heart: Then said the guide, Why did you not cry out, that some might have come in for your succor?

Valiant-for-Truth: So I did to my King, who I knew could hear me, and afford invisible help, and that was sufficient for me.[3]

2. Samson slayed one thousand men (Judg. 15:15-16).

3. Valiant-for-Truth took up the weapon of prayer and the Lord sent help. "Arise, O LORD; Save me, O my God! For You have struck all my enemies on the cheekbone; You have broken the teeth of the ungodly." (Ps. 3:7)

Mr. Great-Heart: Then said Great-Heart to Mr. Valiant-for-truth, Thou hast worthily behaved thyself; let me see thy sword. So he showed it him.

When he had taken it in his hand, and looked thereon awhile, he said, Ha, it is a right Jerusalem blade.[4]

Valiant-for-Truth: It is so. Let a man have one of these blades, with a hand to wield it, and skill to use it, and he may venture upon an angel with it. He need not fear its holding, if he can but tell how to lay on. Its edge will never blunt. It will cut flesh and bones, and soul, and spirit, and all. Heb. 4:12.

Mr. Great-Heart: But you fought a great while; I wonder you were not weary.

Valiant-for-Truth: I fought till my sword did cleave to my hand; and then they were joined together as if a sword grew out of my arm; and when the blood ran through my fingers, then I fought with most courage.

Mr. Great-Heart: Thou hast done well; thou hast resisted unto blood, striving against sin. Thou shalt abide by us, come in and go out with us; for we are thy companions. Then they took him and washed his wounds, and gave him of what they had, to refresh him: and so they went together.

Now, as they went on, because Mr. Great-Heart was delighted in him,[5] (for he loved one greatly that he found to be a man of his hands,) and because there were in company those that were feeble and weak, therefore he questioned with him about many things; as first, what countryman he was.

Valiant-for-Truth: I am of Dark-land; for there was I born, and there my father and mother are still.

Mr. Great-Heart: Dark-land! said the guide; doth not that lie on the same coast with the City of Destruction?

Valiant-for-Truth: Yes, it doth. Now that which caused me to come on pilgrimage was this. We had one Mr. Tell-true come into our parts, and he told it about what Christian had done, that went from the City of Destruction; namely, how he had forsaken his wife and children, and had betaken himself to a pilgrim's life. It was also confidently reported, how he had

4. The sword of believers is the Word of God (Eph. 6:17).

5. Men and women of faith are naturally drawn to others who are full of faith in the living God. Such was the case with Jonathan who made a covenant with David after the defeat of Goliath (1 Sam. 18:1-4).

killed a serpent that did come out to resist him in his journey; and how he got through to whither he intended. It was also told what welcome he had at all his Lord's lodgings, especially when he came to the gates of the Celestial City; for there, said the man, he was received with sound of trumpet by a company of shining ones. He told also how all the bells in the city did ring for joy at his reception, and what golden garments he was clothed with; with many other things that now I shall forbear to relate. In a word, that man so told the story of Christian and his travels that my heart fell into a burning haste to be gone after him; nor could father or mother stay me. So I got from them, and am come thus far on my way.

Mr. Great-Heart: You came in at the gate, did you not?

Valiant-for-Truth: Yes, yes; for the same man also told us, that all would be nothing if we did not begin to enter this way at the gate.

Mr. Great-Heart: Look you, said the guide to Christiana, the pilgrimage of your husband, and what he has gotten thereby, is spread abroad far and near.

Valiant-for-Truth: Why, is this Christian's wife?

Mr. Great-Heart: Yes, that it is; and these also are his four sons.

Valiant-for-Truth: What, and going on pilgrimage too?

Mr. Great-Heart: Yes, verily, they are following after.

Valiant-for-Truth: It glads me at the heart.[6] Good man, how joyful will he be when he shall see them that would not go with him, yet to enter after him in at the gates into the Celestial City.

Mr. Great-Heart: Without doubt it will be a comfort to him; for, next to the joy of seeing himself there, it will be a joy to meet there his wife and children.

Valiant-for-Truth: But now you are upon that, pray let me hear your opinion about it. Some make a question whether we shall know one another when we are there.

Mr. Great-Heart: Do you think they shall know themselves then, or that they shall rejoice to see themselves in that

6. "It makes my heart glad."

bliss? And if they think they shall know and do this, why not know others, and rejoice in their welfare also? Again, since relations are our second self, though that state will be dissolved there, yet why may it not be rationally concluded that we shall be more glad to see them there than to see they are wanting?

Valiant-for-Truth: Well, I perceive whereabouts you are as to this. Have you any more things to ask me about my beginning to come on pilgrimage?

Mr. Great-Heart: Yes; were your father and mother willing that you should become a pilgrim?

Valiant-for-Truth: O no; they used all means imaginable to persuade me to stay at home.

Mr. Great-Heart: Why, what could they say against it?

Valiant-for-Truth: They said it was an idle life; and if I myself were not inclined to sloth and laziness, I would never countenance a pilgrim's condition.

Mr. Great-Heart: And what did they say else?

Valiant-for-Truth: Why, they told me that it was a dangerous way; yea, the most dangerous way in the world, said they, is that which the pilgrims go.

Mr. Great-Heart: Did they show you wherein this way is so dangerous?

Valiant-for-Truth: Yes; and that in many particulars.

Mr. Great-Heart: Name some of them.

Valiant-for-Truth: They told me of the Slough of Despond, where Christian was well-nigh smothered. They told me, that there were archers standing ready in Beelzebub-castle to shoot them who should knock at the Wicket-gate for entrance. They told me also of the wood and dark mountains; of the hill Difficulty; of the lions; and also of the three giants, Bloody-man, Maul, and Slay-good. They said, moreover, that there was a foul fiend haunted the Valley of Humiliation; and that Christian was by him almost bereft of life. Besides, said they, you must go over the Valley of the Shadow of Death, where the hobgoblins are, where the light is darkness, where the way is full of snares, pits, traps, and gins. They told me also of Giant Despair, of Doubting Castle, and of the ruin that the pilgrims met with here. Further they said I must go over the Enchanted Ground, which was dangerous; And that after all this I should find a river, over which there was no bridge; and that that river did lie betwixt me and the Celestial country.

Mr. Great-Heart: And was this all?

Valiant-for-Truth: No. They also told me that this way was full of deceivers, and of persons that lay in wait there to turn good men out of the path.

Mr. Great-Heart: But how did they make that out?

Valiant-for-Truth: They told me that Mr. Worldly Wise-man did lie there in wait to deceive. They said also, that there were Formality and Hypocrisy continually on the road. They said also, that By-ends, Talkative, or Demas, would go near to gather me up; that the Flatterer would catch me in his net; or that, with green-headed Ignorance,[7] I would presume to go on to the gate, from whence he was sent back to the hole that was in the side of the hill, and made to go the by-way to hell.

Mr. Great-Heart: I promise you this was enough to discourage you; but did they make an end here?

Valiant-for-Truth: No, stay.[8] They told me also of many that had tried that way of old, and that had gone a great way therein, to see if they could find something of the glory there that so many had so much talked of from time to time, and how they came back again, and befooled themselves for setting a foot out of doors in that path, to the satisfaction of all the country. And they named several that did so, as Obstinate and Pliable, Mistrust and Timorous, Turn-away and old Atheist, with several more; who, they said, had some of them gone far to see what they could find, but not one of them had found so much advantage by going as amounted to the weight of a feather.

Mr. Great-Heart: Said they any thing more to discourage you?

Valiant-for-Truth: Yes. They told me of one Mr. Fearing, who was a pilgrim, and how he found his way so solitary that

7. "Green headed" means "naïve."

8. "Stay" means "no, wait" or "no, hold on."

he never had a comfortable hour therein; also, that Mr. De-spondency had like to have been starved therein: yea, and also (which I had almost forgot) that Christian himself, about whom there has been such a noise, after all his adventures for a celestial crown, was certainly drowned in the Black River, and never went a foot further; however it was smothered up.[9]

Mr. Great-Heart: And did none of these things discourage you?

Valiant-for-Truth: No; they seemed but as so many nothings to me.

Mr. Great-Heart: How came that about?

Valiant-for-Truth: Why, I still believed what Mr. Tell-true had said; and that carried me beyond them all.[10]

Mr. Great-Heart: Then this was your victory, even your faith.[11]

Valiant-for-Truth: It was so. I believed, and therefore came out, got into the way, fought all that set themselves against me, and, by believing, am come to this place.

"Who would true valor see,
  Let him come hither;
One here will constant be,
  Come wind, come weather
There's no discouragement
Shall make him once relent
His first avow'd intent
To be a pilgrim.
Whoso beset him round
  With dismal stories,
Do but themselves confound;
  His strength the more is.
No lion can him fright,
He'll with a giant fight,
But he will have a right
To be a pilgrim.
Hobgoblin nor foul fiend
  Can daunt his spirit;

9. That is, the towns-people believed that the news of Christian's death had been covered up.

10. The Word of God spoken by Mr. Tell-true helped Valiant-for-Truth to overcome all the objections and warnings of his family.

11. "For whatever is born of God overcomes the world. And this is the victory that has overcome the world—our faith." (1 John 5:4)

12. The Enchanted Ground is a very dangerous place for the Christian. It is a place of spiritual stupor, listlessness, and sleep. There are many things in this present life that can be like this "enchanted ground." Distractions abound. We can become spiritually asleep when we become preoccupied with these distractions. This is a treacherous condition for any Christian to fall into since we are called to be watchful and sober. We cannot sleep as those in the world sleep, numb to the spiritual realities all around them. Paul writes, "And do this, knowing the time, that now it is high time to awake out of sleep; for now our salvation is nearer than when we first believed. The night is far spent, the day is at hand. Therefore let us cast off the works of darkness, and let us put on the armor of light." (Rom. 13:11-12)

13. "We walk by faith, not by sight." (2 Cor. 5:7)

14. "An effort to trot along"

15. A "victualling-house" would be a pub selling food.

> He knows he at the end
>   Shall life inherit.
> Then fancies fly away,
> He'll not fear what men say;
> He'll labor night and day
> To be a pilgrim.

By this time they were got to the Enchanted Ground, where the air naturally tended to make one drowsy.[12] And that place was all grown over with briars and thorns, excepting here and there, where was an enchanted arbor, upon which if a man sits, or in which if a man sleeps, it is a question, some say, whether ever he shall rise or wake again in this world. Over this forest, therefore, they went, both one and another, and Mr. Great-Heart went before, for that he was the guide; and Mr. Valiant-for-truth came behind, being rear-guard, for fear lest peradventure some fiend, or dragon, or giant, or thief, should fall upon their rear, and so do mischief. They went on here, each man with his sword drawn in his hand; for they knew it was a dangerous place. Also they cheered up one another as well as they could. Feeble-Mind, Mr. Great-Heart commanded should come up after him; and Mr. Despondency was under the eye of Mr. Valiant.

Now they had not gone far, but a great mist and darkness fell upon them all; so that they could scarce, for a great while, the one see the other. Wherefore they were forced, for some time, to feel one for another by words; for they walked not by sight.[13] But any one must think, that here was but sorry going for the best of them all; but how much worse for the women and children, who both of feet and heart were but tender! Yet so it was, that through the encouraging words of him that led in the front, and of him that brought them up behind, they made a pretty good shift to wag along.[14]

The way also here was very wearisome, through dirt and slabbiness. Nor was there, on all this ground, so much as one inn or victualling-house[15] wherein to refresh the feebler sort. Here, therefore, was grunting, and puffing, and sighing, while one tumbleth over a bush, another sticks fast in the dirt, and the children, some of them, lost their shoes in the mire; while one cries out, I am down; and another, Ho, where are you? and a third, The bushes have got such fast hold on me, I think I cannot get away from them.

Then they came at an arbor, warm, and promising much refreshing to the pilgrims; for it was finely wrought above-head, beautified with greens, furnished with benches and settles. It also had in it a soft couch, whereon the weary might lean. This, you must think, all things considered, was tempting; for the pilgrims already began to be foiled with the badness of the way: but there was not one of them that made so much as a motion to stop there. Yea, for aught I could perceive, they continually gave so good heed to the advice of their guide, and he did so faithfully tell them of dangers, and of the nature of the dangers when they were at them, that usually, when they were nearest to them, they did most pluck up their spirits, and hearten one another to deny the flesh. This arbor was called The Slothful's Friend, and was made on purpose to allure, if it might be, some of the pilgrims there to take up their rest when weary.[16]

I saw them in my dream, that they went on in this their solitary ground, till they came to a place at which a man is apt to lose his way. Now, though when it was light their guide could well enough tell how to miss those ways that led wrong, yet in the dark he was put to a stand. But he had in his pocket a map[17] of all ways leading to or from the Celestial City; wherefore he struck a light (for he never goes without his tinder-box also), and takes a view of his book or map, which bids him to be careful in that place to turn to the right hand. And had he not been careful here to look in his map, they had all, in probability, been smothered in the mud; for just a little before them, and that at the end of the cleanest way too, was a pit, none knows how deep, full of nothing but mud, there made on purpose to destroy the pilgrims in.[18]

16. This arbor was a very tempting place to stop and rest. But the Enchanted Ground was a dangerous place. To stop and rest would lead to drowsiness and then eventually the traveler would fall asleep completely, opening them up to attack. The arbor was intentionally designed to tempt pilgrims to become slothful. Likewise, when we become slothful in the daily spiritual battles of the Christian life, we become open to spiritual attack. Let us be watchful and sober. Let us be awake and pray as our Lord instructed His disciples (Matt. 26:41).

17. The Bible is that guide to the Celestial City. "Your word is a lamp to my feet
And a light to my path." (Ps. 119:105)

18. "How can a young man cleanse his way? By taking heed according to Your word." (Ps. 119:9)

19. Too-bold is the picture of the self-confident man who doesn't have a sufficient sobriety about his own weaknesses. Heedless is the man who did not take heed to the path of his feet and soon fell asleep in this dangerous place.

20. "Brethren, if a man is overtaken in any trespass, you who are spiritual restore such a one in a spirit of gentleness, considering yourself lest you also be tempted." (Gal. 6:1)

21. These two men are dreaming of money and violence.

22. That is, when heedless and self-confident men go on pilgrimage, it is quite likely that they will fall into such traps.

Then thought I with myself, Who that goeth on pilgrimage but would have one of these maps about him, that he may look, when he is at a stand, which is the way he must take?

Then they went on in this Enchanted Ground till they came to where there was another arbor, and it was built by the highway-side. And in that arbor there lay two men, whose names were Heedless and Too-bold.[19] These two went thus far on pilgrimage; but here, being wearied with their journey, they sat down to rest themselves, and so fell fast asleep. When the pilgrims saw them, they stood still, and shook their heads; for they knew that the sleepers were in a pitiful case. Then they consulted what to do, whether to go on and leave them in their sleep, or to step to them and try to awake them; so they concluded to go to them and awake them, that is, if they could; but with this caution, namely, to take heed that they themselves did not sit down nor embrace the offered benefit of that arbor.[20]

So they went in, and spake to the men, and called each by his name, for the guide, it seems, did know them; but there was no voice nor answer. Then the guide did shake them, and do what he could to disturb them. Then said one of them, I will pay you when I take my money. At which the guide shook his head. I will fight so long as I can hold my sword in my hand, said the other.[21] At that, one of the children laughed.

Then said Christiana, What is the meaning of this? The guide said, They talk in their sleep. If you strike them, beat them, or whatever else you do to them, they will answer you after this fashion; or, as one of them said in old time, when the waves of the sea did beat upon him, and he slept as one upon the mast of a ship, Prov. 23:34,35, When I awake, I will seek it yet again. You know, when men talk in their sleep, they say any thing; but their words are not governed either by faith or reason. There is an incoherency in their words now, as there was before betwixt their going on pilgrimage and sitting down here. This, then, is the mischief of it: when heedless ones go on pilgrimage, 'tis twenty to one but they are served thus.[22] For this Enchanted Ground is one of the last refuges that the enemy to pilgrims has;[23] wherefore it is, as you see, placed almost at the end of the way, and so it standeth against us with the more advantage. For when, thinks the enemy, will these fools be so desirous to sit down as when they are weary? and when so like to be weary as when almost at their journey's end? Therefore it is, I say, that the Enchanted Ground is placed so nigh to the land Beulah, and so near the end of their race. Wherefore let pilgrims look to themselves, lest it happen to them as it has done to these that, as you see, are fallen asleep, and none can awake them.

Then the pilgrims desired with trembling to go forward; only they prayed their guide to strike a light, that they might go the rest of their way by the help of the light of a lantern. So he struck a light, and they went by the help of that through the rest of this way, though the darkness was very great.[24] 2 Pet. 1:19. But the children began to be sorely weary, and they cried out unto him that loveth pilgrims, to make their way more comfortable. So by that they had gone a little further, a wind arose that drove away the fog, so the air became more clear.[25] Yet they were not off (by much) of the Enchanted Ground; only now they could see one another better, and the way wherein they should walk.

Now when they were almost at the end of this ground, they perceived that a little before them was a solemn noise, as of one that was much concerned. So they went on and looked before them: and behold they saw, as they thought, a man upon his knees, with hands and eyes lifted up, and speaking, as they thought, earnestly to one that was above. They drew nigh, but could not tell what he said; so they went softly till he had done. When he had done, he got up, and began to run towards the Celestial City. Then Mr. Great-Heart called after him, saying, Soho, friend,[26] let us have your company, if you go, as I suppose you do, to the Celestial City. So the man stopped, and they came up to him. But as soon as Mr. Honest saw him, he said, I know this man. Then said Mr. Valiant-for-

23. The evil one loves to use distractions in order to lull us into a spiritual stupor that will ultimately end in eternal perdition. The "thorny ground" hearer is the man who hears the Word but the cares of the world and deceitfulness of riches (two dangerous distractions) choke the Word (Matt. 13:22).

24. The Word of God continues to light the path forward. "And so we have the prophetic word confirmed, which you do well to heed as a light that shines in a dark place, until the day dawns and the morning star rises in your hearts;..."
(2 Pet. 1:19)

25. The pilgrims pray as the Psalmist does in Psalm 43: "Oh, send out Your light and Your truth! Let them lead me; Let them bring me to Your holy hill And to Your tabernacle." (Ps. 43:3)

26. "Soho" was a hunting call, but is here used as a form of greeting.

27. "Please tell me, who is it?"

truth, Prithee, who is it?[27] It is one, said he, that comes from whereabout I dwelt. His name is Standfast; he is certainly a right good pilgrim.

So they came up to one another; and presently Standfast said to old Honest, Ho, father Honest, are you there? Aye, said he, that I am, as sure as you are there. Right glad am I, said Mr. Standfast, that I have found you on this road. And as glad am I, said the other, that I espied you on your knees. Then Mr. Standfast blushed, and said, But why, did you see me? Yes, that I did, quoth the other, and with my heart was glad at the sight. Why, what did you think? said Standfast. Think! said old Honest; what could I think? I thought we had an honest man upon the road, and therefore should have his company by and by. If you thought not amiss, said Standfast, how happy am I! But if I be not as I should, 't is I alone must bear it. That is true, said the other; but your fear doth further confirm me that things are right betwixt the Prince of pilgrims and your soul. For he saith, "Blessed is the man that feareth always." Prov. 28:14.

Valiant-for-Truth: Well but, brother, I pray thee tell us what was it that was the cause of thy being upon thy knees even now: was it for that some special mercy laid obligations upon thee, or how?

Standfast: Why, we are, as you see, upon the Enchanted Ground; and as I was coming along, I was musing with myself of what a dangerous nature the road in this place was, and how many that had come even thus far on pilgrimage, had here been stopped and been destroyed. I thought also of the manner of the death with which this place destroyeth men. Those that die here, die of no violent distemper:[28] the death which such die is not grievous to them. For he that goeth away in a sleep, begins that journey with desire and pleasure. Yea, such acquiesce in the will of that disease.

Mr. Honest: Then Mr. Honest interrupting him, said, Did you see the two men asleep in the arbor?

28. "Distemper" refers to a disease.

Standfast: Aye, aye, I saw Heedless and Too-bold there; and for ought I know, there they will lie till they rot. Prov. 10:7. But let me go on with my tale. As I was thus musing, as I said, there was one in very pleasant attire, but old, who presented herself to me, and offered me three things, to wit, her body, her purse, and her bed.[29] Now the truth is, I was both weary and sleepy. I am also as poor as an owlet, and that perhaps the witch knew. Well, I repulsed her once and again, but she put by my repulses, and smiled. Then I began to be angry; but she mattered that nothing at all. Then she made offers again, and said, if I would be ruled by her,[30] she would make me great and happy; for, said she, I am the mistress of the world, and men are made happy by me. Then I asked her name, and she told me it was Madam Bubble.[31] This set me further from her; but she still followed me with enticements. Then I betook me, as you saw, to my knees, and with hands lifted up, and cries, I prayed to Him that had said he would help.[32] So, just as you came up, the gentlewoman went her way. Then I continued to give thanks for this my great deliverance; for I verily believe she intended no good, but rather sought to make stop of me in my journey.

Mr. Honest: Without doubt her designs were bad. But stay, now you talk of her, methinks I either have seen her, or have read some story of her.

Standfast: Perhaps you have done both.

Mr. Honest: Madam Bubble! Is she not a tall, comely dame, something of a swarthy complexion?[33]

29. Madam Bubble is described here by Standfast. He was tempted by this woman to commit sexual sin with her and also partake of her wealth. Madam Bubble offered sensual pleasures and financial gain.

30. The temptress may present the sexual temptation as something that we gain, but in reality, she is offering chains to those who commit sexual immorality with her. "His own iniquities entrap the wicked man, And he is caught in the cords of his sin." (Prov. 5:22)

31. The name given to this character by Bunyan is very fitting. She is called "Bubble" because she promises delights and riches, but ultimately her promises are empty.

32. Men and women will not escape the temptations of sexual sin unless they cry to the Lord for help. Watchfulness and prayer are essential to resisting temptation.

33. This description of Madam Bubble could be modernized in the following way: "Is she not a tall, attractive woman with a dark-skinned complexion?"

34. The temptress is described this way in Proverbs 5: "For the lips of an immoral woman drip honey, And her mouth is smoother than oil;..." (Prov. 5:3)

35. Madam Bubble's temptations are doubly powerful because she promises not only sensual pleasure but also money. These two temptations are designed to ensnare the man who is driven by lust and covetousness.

36. A "limner" is a painter or one who sketches. Mr. Honest is referring to the descriptions found in the Bible of the forbidden woman. The pictures given in Proverbs 5-7 are accurate.

37. Madam Bubble is a witch who casts spells upon men who pass by, ensnaring them in her temptations.

38. This is a powerful warning. Whoever wants to say yes to the enticements of the temptress might as well just put his head under the axe block and be decapitated. Such is the danger of sexual sin (Prov. 7:21-23).

39. A "slut" is a woman who is habitually sexually immoral.

Standfast: Right, you hit it: she is just such a one.

Mr. Honest: Doth she not speak very smoothly, and give you a smile at the end of a sentence?[34]

Standfast: You fall right upon it again, for these are her very actions.

Mr. Honest: Doth she not wear a great purse by her side, and is not her hand often in it, fingering her money, as if that was her heart's delight.[35]

Standfast: 'Tis just so; had she stood by all this while, you could not more amply have set her forth before me, nor have better described her features.

Mr. Honest: Then he that drew her picture was a good limner,[36] and he that wrote of her said true.

Mr. Great-Heart: This woman is a witch, and it is by virtue of her sorceries that this ground is enchanted.[37] Whoever doth lay his head down in her lap, had as good lay it down on that block over which the axe doth hang;[38] and whoever lay their eyes upon her beauty are counted the enemies of God. This is she that maintaineth in their splendor all those that are the enemies of pilgrims. James 4:4. Yea, this is she that has bought off many a man from a pilgrim's life. She is a great gossiper; she is always, both she and her daughters, at one pilgrim's heels or another, now commending, and then preferring the excellences of this life. She is a bold and impudent slut:[39] she will talk with any man. She always laugheth poor pilgrims to scorn, but highly commends the rich. If there be one cunning to get money in a place, she will speak well of him from house to house. She loveth banqueting and feasting mainly well; she is always at one full table or another. She has given it out in some places that she is a goddess, and therefore some do worship her.[40] She has her time, and open places of cheating; and she will say and avow it, that none can show a good comparable to hers. She promiseth to dwell with children's children, if they will but love her and make much of her. She will cast out of her purse gold like dust in some places and to some persons. She loves to be sought after, spoken well of, and to lie in the bosoms of men. She is never weary of commending her commodities, and she loves them most that think best of her. She will promise to some crowns and kingdoms, if they will but take her advice; yet many has she brought to the halter, and ten thousand times more to hell.[41]

Standfast: Oh, said Standfast, what a mercy is it that I did resist her; for whither might she have drawn me!

Mr. Great-Heart: Whither? nay, none but God knows whither. But in general, to be sure, she would have drawn thee into many foolish and hurtful lusts, which drown men in destruction and perdition. 1 Tim. 6:9. 'T was she that set Absalom against his father, and Jeroboam against his master. 'T was she that persuaded Judas to sell his Lord; and that prevailed with Demas to forsake the godly pilgrim's life.[42] None can tell of the mischief that she doth. She makes variance betwixt rulers and subjects,[43] betwixt parents and children, betwixt neighbor and neighbor, betwixt a man and his wife, betwixt a man and himself, betwixt the flesh and the spirit. Wherefore, good Mr. Standfast, be as your name is, and when you have done all, stand.[44]

At this discourse there was among the pilgrims a mixture of joy and trembling; but at length they broke out and sang,

"What danger is the Pilgrim in!
How many are his foes!
How many ways there are to sin
No living mortal knows.
Some in the ditch are spoiled, yea, can
Lie tumbling in the mire:
Some, though they shun the frying-pan
Do leap into the fire."

40. For many men caught in the snare of sexual sin, sexual immorality becomes an idol, a god they worship.

41. Madam Bubble promises the greatest treasures to the men she ensnares, but in reality she puts them in the noose (the "halter") and then sends them off to hell. Let the reader soberly consider the warnings Bunyan provides about sexual sin. Take some time to read Proverbs 5-7 and pray that the Lord would deliver you from the evil one and his temptations.

42. From these other examples given (Judas and Demas), we learn that Madam Bubble doesn't just represent sexual sin but also the deadly temptation of seeking after riches which drown men in destruction (1 Tim. 6:9).

43. "Variance" refers to conflicts between these different parties.

44. "Therefore take up the whole armor of God, that you may be able to withstand in the evil day, and having done all, to stand." (Eph. 6:13)

45. The land of Beulah is very close to the Celestial City. The pilgrims are nearing the end of their journey.

After this, I beheld until they were come into the land of Beulah, where the sun shineth night and day.[45] Here, because they were weary, they betook themselves a while to rest. And because this country was common for pilgrims, and because the orchards and vineyards that were here belonged to the King of the Celestial country, therefore they were licensed to make bold with any of his things. But a little while soon refreshed them here; for the bells did so ring, and the trumpets continually sound so melodiously, that they could not sleep, and yet they received as much refreshing as if they had slept their sleep ever so soundly. Here also all the noise of them that walked the streets was, More pilgrims are come to town! And another would answer, saying, And so many went over the water, and were let in at the golden gates to-day! They would cry again, There is now a legion of shining ones just come to town, by which we know that there are more pilgrims upon the road; for here they come to wait for them, and to comfort them after all their sorrow. Then the pilgrims got up, and walked to and fro. But how were their ears now filled with heavenly noises, and their eyes delighted with celestial visions! In this land they heard nothing, saw nothing, felt nothing, smelt nothing, tasted nothing that was offensive to their stomach or mind; only when they tasted of the water of the river over which they were to go, they thought that it tasted a little bitterish to the palate;[46] but it proved sweeter when it was down.

46. This refers to the river of death which all pilgrims must cross in the present age before Christ's return. It seemed "bitter" of course, but after they would cross, death would have no sting.

In this place there was a record kept of the names of them that had been pilgrims of old, and a history of all the famous acts that they had done. It was here also much discoursed, how the river to some had had its flowings, and what ebbings it has had while others have gone over. It has been in a manner dry for some, while it has overflowed its banks for others.

In this place the children of the town would go into the King's gardens, and gather nosegays for the pilgrims, and bring them to them with much affection. Here also grew camphire, with spikenard and saffron, calamus and cinnamon, with all the trees of frankincense, myrrh, and aloes, with all chief spices.[47] With these the pilgrims' chambers were perfumed while they stayed here; and with these were their bodies anointed, to prepare them to go over the river, when the time appointed was come.

Now, while they lay here, and waited for the good hour, there was a noise in the town that there was a post come from the Celestial City,[48] with matter of great importance to one Christiana, the wife of Christian the pilgrim. So inquiry was made for her, and the house was found out where she was. So the post presented her with a letter. The contents were, Hail, good woman; I bring thee tidings that the Master calleth for thee, and expecteth that thou shouldst stand in his presence in clothes of immortality within these ten days.

When he had read this letter to her, he gave her therewith a sure token that he was a true messenger, and was come to bid her make haste to be gone. The token was, an arrow with a point sharpened with love, let easily into her heart, which by degrees wrought so effectually with her, that at the time appointed she must be gone.

When Christiana saw that her time was come, and that she was the first of this company that was to go over, she called for Mr. Great-Heart her guide, and told him how matters were. So he told her he was heartily glad of the news, and could have been glad had the post come for him. Then she bid him that he should give advice how all things should be prepared for her journey. So he told her, saying, Thus and thus it must be, and we that survive will accompany you to the river-side.

Then she called for her children, and gave them her blessing, and told them that she had read with comfort the mark that was set in their foreheads, and was glad to see them with her there, and that they had kept their garments so white. Lastly, she bequeathed to the poor that little she had, and commanded her sons and daughters to be ready against the messenger should come for them.[49]

When she had spoken these words to her guide, and to her children, she called for Mr. Valiant-for-truth, and said unto

47. These different spices are mentioned in the Song of Solomon, again reflecting the constant biblical imagery throughout Bunyan's masterpiece.

48. Christiana receives a letter from a mail courier (a "post") before going through the river. What follows in the last page of *Pilgrim's Progress* is a series of pilgrims crossing the river of death and saying their farewells.

49. "Until [or when] the messenger should come for them"

him, Sir, you have in all places showed yourself true-hearted; be faithful unto death, and my King will give you a crown of life. Rev. 2:10. I would also entreat you to have an eye to my children; and if at any time you see them faint, speak comfortably to them. For my daughters, my sons' wives, they have been faithful, and a fulfilling of the promise upon them will be their end. But she gave Mr. Standfast a ring.

Then she called for old Mr. Honest, and said of him, "Behold an Israelite indeed, in whom is no guile!" John 1:47. Then said he, I wish you a fair day when you set out for Mount Sion, and shall be glad to see that you go over the river dry-shod. But she answered, Come wet, come dry, I long to be gone; for however the weather is in my journey, I shall have time enough when I come there to sit down and rest me and dry me.

Then came in that good man Mr. Ready-to-halt, to see her. So she said to him, Thy travel hitherto has been with difficulty; but that will make thy rest the sweeter. Watch, and be ready; for at an hour when you think not, the messenger may come.

After him came Mr. Despondency and his daughter Much-afraid, to whom she said, You ought, with thankfulness, forever to remember your deliverance from the hands of Giant Despair, and out of Doubting Castle. The effect of that mercy is, that you are brought with safety hither. Be ye watchful, and cast away fear; be sober, and hope to the end.

Then she said to Mr. Feeble-Mind, Thou wast delivered from the mouth of Giant Slay-good, that thou mightest live in the light of the living, and see thy King with comfort. Only I advise thee to repent of thine aptness to fear and doubt of his goodness,[50] before he sends for thee; lest thou shouldst, when he comes, be forced to stand before him for that fault with blushing.

Now the day drew on that Christiana must be gone. So the road was full of people to see her take her journey. But behold, all the banks beyond the river were full of horses and chariots, which were come down from above to accompany

50. Fear is not just weakness. It is also a sin because it is a lack of faith in God and His goodness.

her to the city gate. So she came forth, and entered the river, with a beckon of farewell to those that followed her. The last words that she was heard to say were, I come, Lord, to be with thee and bless thee! So her children and friends returned to their place, for those that waited for Christiana had carried her out of their sight. So she went and called, and entered in at the gate with all the ceremonies of joy that her husband Christian had entered with before her. At her departure, the children wept. But Mr. Great-Heart and Mr. Valiant played upon the welltuned cymbal and harp for joy. So all departed to their respective places.[51]

In process of time there came a post to the town again, and his business was with Mr. Ready-to-halt. So he inquired him out, and said, I am come from Him whom thou hast loved and followed, though upon crutches; and my message is to tell thee, that he expects thee at his table to sup with him in his kingdom, the next day after Easter; wherefore prepare thyself for this journey. Then he also gave him a token that he was a true messenger, saying, "I have broken thy golden bowl, and loosed thy silver cord." Eccles. 12:6.

After this, Mr. Ready-to-halt called for his fellow-pilgrims, and told them, saying, I am sent for, and God shall surely visit you also. So he desired Mr. Valiant to make his will. And because he had nothing to bequeath to them that should survive him but his crutches, and his good wishes, therefore thus he said, These crutches I bequeath to my son that shall tread in my steps, with a hundred warm wishes that he may prove better than I have been.

Then he thanked Mr. Great-Heart for his conduct and kindness, and so addressed himself to his journey. When he came to the brink of the river, he said, Now I shall have no more need of these crutches,[52] since yonder are chariots and horses for me to ride on. The last words he was heard to say were, Welcome life! So he went his way.

After this, Mr. Feeble-Mind had tidings brought him that the post sounded his horn at his chamber door. Then he came

51. Part II ends differently than Part I. At the end of Part I, Bunyan focuses on the glories of heaven after Christian enters into the Celestial City. In Part II, Bunyan wants to focus on the words of farewell spoken by the pilgrims to those they leave behind.

52. Once we enter glory, all of our human frailties and sinful tendencies will be done away with.

in, and told him, saying, I am come to tell thee that thy Master hath need of thee, and that in a very little time thou must behold his face in brightness. And take this as a token of the truth of my message: "Those that look out at the windows shall be darkened." Eccles. 12:3. Then Mr. Feeble-Mind called for his friends, and told them what errand had been brought unto him, and what token he had received of the truth of the message. Then he said, since I have nothing to bequeath to any, to what purpose should I make a will? As for my feeble mind, that I will leave behind me, for that I shall have no need of it in the place whither I go, nor is it worth bestowing upon the poorest pilgrims: wherefore, when I am gone, I desire that you, Mr. Valiant, would bury it in a dunghill. This done, and the day being come on which he was to depart, he entered the river as the rest. His last words were, Hold out, faith and patience! So he went over to the other side.

When days had many of them passed away, Mr. Despondency was sent for; for a post was come, and brought this message to him: Trembling man! these are to summon thee to be ready with the King by the next Lord's day, to shout for joy for thy deliverance from all thy doubtings. And, said the messenger, that my message is true, take this for a proof: so he gave him a grasshopper to be a burden unto him. Ecclesiastes 12:5.

Now Mr. Despondency's daughter, whose name was Much-afraid, said, when she heard what was done, that she would go with her father. Then Mr. Despondency said to his friends, Myself and my daughter, you know what we have been, and how troublesomely we have behaved ourselves in every company. My will and my daughter's is, that our desponds and slavish fears be by no man ever received, from the day of our departure, forever; for I know that after my death they will offer themselves to others.[53] For, to be plain with you, they are ghosts which we entertained when we first began to be pilgrims,[54] and could never shake them off after; and they will walk about, and seek entertainment of the pilgrims: but for our sakes, shut the doors upon them. When the time was

53. Each character makes their "will" before departing to die and go to glory. Those characters with certain habitual sins and weaknesses do not wish to leave behind these things to other pilgrims. No one should have to inherit their slavish despondency and fear. These should rather be done away with entirely.

54. This is a wise insight by Bunyan. Fears and despondency are mere "ghosts." They really are nothing, but they can seem quite real to our fearful hearts.

come for them to depart, they went up to the brink of the river. The last words of Mr. Despondency were, Farewell, night; welcome, day! His daughter went through the river singing, but none could understand what she said.

Then it came to pass a while after, that there was a post in the town that inquired for Mr. Honest. So he came to the house where he was, and delivered to his hand these lines: Thou art commanded to be ready against this day seven-night, to present thyself before thy Lord at his Father's house. And for a token that my message is true, "All the daughters of music shall be brought low." Eccles. 12:4. Then Mr. Honest called for his friends, and said unto them, I die, but shall make no will. As for my honesty, it shall go with me;[55] let him that comes after be told of this. When the day that he was to be gone was come, he addressed himself to go over the river. Now the river at that time over-flowed its banks in some places; but Mr. Honest, in his lifetime, had spoken to one Good-conscience to meet him there, the which he also did, and lent him his hand, and so helped him over.[56] The last words of Mr. Honest were, Grace reigns! So he left the world.

After this it was noised abroad that Mr. Valiant-for-truth was taken with a summons by the same post as the other, and had this for a token that the summons was true, "That his pitcher was broken at the fountain."[57] Eccl. 12:6. When he understood it, he called for his friends, and told them of it. Then said he, I am going to my Father's; and though with great difficulty I have got hither, yet now I do not repent me of all the trouble I have been at to arrive where I am. My sword I give to him that shall succeed me in my pilgrimage, and my courage and skill to him that can get it. My marks and scars I carry with me, to be a witness for me that I have fought His battles who will now be my rewarder. When the day that he must go hence was come, many accompanied him to the river-side, into which as he went, he said, "Death, where is thy sting?" And as he went down deeper, he said, "Grave, where is

55. Any remnants of sin and frailty are not taken to glory. However, honesty, reflecting the righteousness of God, will go with Mr. Honest.

56. Mr. Honest, because of his honest life, can cross the river with a good conscience.

57. The various images here are drawn from Ecclesiastes. In Ecclesiastes 12, verses 2-7, Solomon draws a variety of pictures for the end of life. Bunyan adapts these for his different characters as they are summoned to be with the Lord.

thy victory?" 1 Cor. 15:55. So he passed over, and all the trumpets sounded for him on the other side.

Then there came forth a summons for Mr. Standfast. This Mr. Standfast was he whom the rest of the pilgrims found upon his knees in the Enchanted Ground. And the post brought it him open in his hands: the contents thereof were, that he must prepare for a change of life, for his Master was not willing that he should be so far from him any longer.[58] At this Mr. Standfast was put into a muse. Nay, said the messenger, you need not doubt of the truth of my message; for here is a token of the truth thereof, "Thy wheel is broken at the cistern." Eccles. 12:6. Then he called to him Mr. Great-Heart, who was their guide, and said unto him, Sir, although it was not my hap[59] to be much in your good company during the days of my pilgrimage, yet, since the time I knew you, you have been profitable to me. When I came from home, I left behind me a wife and five small children; let me entreat you, at your return, (for I know that you go and return to your Master's house, in hopes that you may yet be a conductor to more of the holy pilgrims,) that you send to my family, and let them be acquainted with all that hath and shall happen unto me. Tell them moreover of my happy arrival at this place, and of the present and late blessed condition I am in. Tell them also of Christian and Christiana his wife, and how she and her children came after her husband. Tell them also of what a happy end she made, and whither she is gone. I have little or nothing to send to my family, unless it be prayers and tears for them; of which it will suffice that you acquaint them, if peradventure they may prevail.[60] When Mr. Standfast had thus set things in order, and the time being come for him to haste him away, he also went down to the river. Now there was a great calm at that time in the river; wherefore Mr. Standfast, when he was about half-way in, stood a while, and talked with his companions that had waited upon him thither. And he said, This river has been a terror to many; yea, the thoughts of it also have often frightened me; but now methinks I stand easy;

58. When our Lord calls us to himself through the river of death, it is so that we might be "with the Lord" which is far better (Phil. 1:23).

59. That is, "It was not my opportunity." Sometimes, "hap" refers to fortune or chance. Of course, such language must be understood in light of Bunyan's commitment to God's providence over all things.

60. Mr. Standfast, like Christian in Part I, left behind his family. He asks Mr. Great-Heart to go and take news of his prayers and tears for their salvation. He hopes that this will prevail with them and convince them to join him on the pilgrimage.

my foot is fixed upon that on which the feet of the priests that bare the ark of the covenant stood while Israel went over Jordan. Josh. 3:17. The waters indeed are to the palate bitter, and to the stomach cold; yet the thoughts of what I am going to, and of the convoy that waits for me on the other side, do lie as a glowing coal at my heart. I see myself now at the end of my journey; my toilsome days are ended. I am going to see that head which was crowned with thorns, and that face which was spit upon for me. I have formerly lived by hearsay and faith; but now I go where I shall live by sight, and shall be with him in whose company I delight myself. I have loved to hear my Lord spoken of; and wherever I have seen the print of his shoe in the earth, there I have coveted to set my foot too. His name has been to me as a civet-box;[61] yea, sweeter than all perfumes. His voice to me has been most sweet, and his countenance I have more desired than they that have most desired the light of the sun. His words I did use to gather for my food, and for antidotes against my faintings. He hath held me, and hath kept me from mine iniquities; yea, my steps hath he strengthened in his way.[62]

Now, while he was thus in discourse, his countenance changed; his strong man bowed under him:[63] and after he had said, Take me, for I come unto thee, he ceased to be seen of them.

But glorious it was to see how the open region was filled with horses and chariots, with trumpeters and pipers, with singers and players upon stringed instruments, to welcome the pilgrims as they went up, and followed one another in at the beautiful gate of the city.

As for Christiana's children, the four boys that Christiana brought, with their wives and children, I did not stay where I was till they were gone over. Also, since I came away, I heard one say that they were yet alive, and so would be for the increase of the church, in that place where they were, for a time.[64]

61. A "civet-box" is a package containing fragrances.

62. Standfast knows it is the Lord who has upheld him. Jesus will lose none of his sheep. No one is able to snatch them out of Christ's hand (John 10:28).

63. That is, "His physical strength diminished."

64. Bunyan ends his narrative with the four sons of Christiana dwelling in Beulah Land near the Celestial City. They remained alive some time "for the increase of the church."

Should it be my lot to go that way again, I may give those that desire it an account of what I here am silent about: meantime I bid my reader farewell. The End.